Lecture Notes in Computer Sc

Edited by G. Goos, J. Hartmanis, and J. van Leeuwen

Springer
Berlin
Heidelberg
New York
Barcelona
Hong Kong
London
Milan
Paris
Tokyo

Paul F. Syverson (Ed.)

Financial Cryptography

5th International Conference, FC 2001
Grand Cayman, British West Indies, February 19-22, 2001
Proceedings

 Springer

Series Editors

Gerhard Goos, Karlsruhe University, Germany
Juris Hartmanis, Cornell University, NY, USA
Jan van Leeuwen, Utrecht University, The Netherlands

Volume Editor

Paul Syverson
Naval Research Laboratory
Washington, DC 20375, USA

Cataloging-in-Publication Data applied for

Die Deutsche Bibliothek - CIP-Einheitsaufnahme

Financial cryptography : 5th international conference ; proceedings /
FC 2001, Grand Cayman, British West Indies, February 19 - 22, 2001.
Paul Syverson (ed.). - Berlin ; Heidelberg ; New York ; Barcelona ;
Hong Kong ; London ; Milan ; Paris ; Tokyo : Springer, 2002
  (Lecture notes in computer science ; Vol. 2339)
  ISBN 3-540-44079-8

CR Subject Classification (1998): E.3, D.4.6, K.6.5, C.2, J.1, F.2.1-2, K.4.4

ISSN 0302-9743
ISBN 3-540-44079-8 Springer-Verlag Berlin Heidelberg New York

Springer-Verlag Berlin Heidelberg New York
a member of BertelsmannSpringer Science+Business Media GmbH

http://www.springer.de

© Springer-Verlag Berlin Heidelberg 2002
Printed in Germany

Typesetting: Camera-ready by author, data conversion by Christian Grosche, Hamburg
Printed on acid-free paper   SPIN 10869919   06/3142   5 4 3 2 1 0

Preface

The fifth Financial Cryptography conference was held February 19–22, 2001. After half a decade, we moved beyond our Anguillan origins to Grand Cayman, BWI. The venue changed but the focus of the program remained to present the best research in securing electronic financial transactions and electronic commerce. As in the past few years, most of the contributed papers focused on the technical cryptographic and security aspects of financial cryptography, while the financial aspects are reflected primarily in invited talks and panels. (And in the informal discussion.) This year, in addition to the submitted papers, we had a provocative invited talk by Richard Rahn on money laundering as well as panels on digital rights management and the business of electronic voting. There was also a rump session, chaired by Rebecca Wright.

There were many interesting and many technically strong submissions. I thank the program committee (listed on the next page) for their help in the difficult task of choosing those papers that made the strongest contribution to the conference. We had additional reviewing help from Olivier Baudron, Paul Fahn, Juan Garay, Markus Jakobsson, Guenter Karjoth, Phong Nguyen, David Pointcheval, Thomas Pornin, Sholom Rosen, Dawn Song, Susanne Wetzel, and Rebecca Wright. (My apologies if I have overlooked anyone.) I would also like to thank George Davida, the electronic submissions chair, and his student, Dawn Marie Gibson, for setting up and running the submissions process at the University of Wisconsin. An extra big thank you to Yair Frankel, who was always there with his experience and advice that greatly improved the job I did as program chair, as well as making it more enjoyable. Matt Franklin also provided valuable advice. Thanks to all the people who submitted papers, without which there would be no program. Authors were given the opportunity to revise their papers following the conference. These were collected without further review and are included in this volume.

Thanks to general chair Stuart Haber for doing many things that none of the attendees noticed because he did them so nicely. He was ably assisted by Hinde ten Berge. Thanks to Harris McCoy for handling local arrangements and Jason Cronk for maintaining the Web site. Thanks to the IFCA directors for keeping FC thriving, to Adam Shostack for venue arrangements, and to Barb Fox, the sponsorship chair. Thanks to our financial sponsors, who are listed on the next page.

Special thanks to Ray Hirschfeld whose advice to me and to the others mentioned here has been invaluable. Thanks finally to attendees without whom there would be no conference.

March 2001   Paul Syverson

Program Committee

Matt Blaze, AT&T Labs - Research
Yair Frankel, Ecash
Matt Franklin, UC Davis
David Kravitz, Wave Systems Corp.
Arjen Lenstra, Citicorp
Philip MacKenzie, Lucent Bell Labs
Avi Rubin, AT&T Labs - Research
Jacques Stern, Ecole Normale Supérieure
Kazue Sako, NEC
Stuart Stubblebine, CertCo
Paul Syverson (Chair), Naval Research Lab
Win Treese, Open Market, Inc.
Doug Tygar, UC Berkeley
Michael Waidner, IBM Zurich Research Lab
Moti Yung, CertCo

General Chair

Stuart Haber, Intertrust

Sponsorship Chair

Barb Fox, Microsoft

Financial Cryptography 2001 was organized by the International Financial Cryptography Association (IFCA), and was sponsored by Bibit Internet Payments, CertCo, Certicom, Hush Communications, IBM, InterTrust STAR Lab, Microsoft, nCipher, RSA Security, and Zero-Knowledge Systems.

Table of Contents

Invited Talk

Certificates and Authentication

Credit Card Security

Panel (II)

Markets and Multiparty Computation

Signatures in Financial Cryptography

Auctions

Amortized E-Cash

Moses Liskov[1] and Silvio Micali[2]

[1] MIT Laboratory for Computer Science
mliskov@theory.lcs.mit.edu
[2] MIT Laboratory for Computer Science
silvio@lcs.mit.edu

Abstract. We present an e-cash scheme which provides a trade-off between anonymity and efficiency, by amortizing the cost of zero-knowledge and signature computation in the cash generation phase.

Our work solves an open problem of Okamoto in divisible e-cash. Namely, we achieve results similar to those of Okamoto, but (1) based on traditional complexity assumptions (rather than ad hoc ones), and (2) within a much crisper definitional framework that highlights the anonymity properties, and (3) in a simple fashion.

1 Introduction

Ever since the work of Chaum [5], there has been an interest in e-cash systems that are not only unforgeable and anonymous but also *off-line*. That is, the merchant can recognize the value of the e-cash without having to check with the bank (unlike, for example, in a credit-card transaction). While very desirable, however, off-line e-cash comes at a price: it cannot totally prevent *double spending*; that is, the ability of a malicious user to spend an "e-coin" more than once. Indeed, an e-coin is a self-verifiable string of bits that is easily reproducible, and therefore could be spent multiple times given the absence of any checking with a central database. Thus, the typical defense envisaged against double spending in off-line e-cash is less than ideal: if double spending occurs, then anonymity is removed and the malicious customer's identity is revealed.[1]

Most e-cash schemes use zero knowledge computation during e-coin generation to guarantee these complex properties and security requirements.

ZERO-KNOWLEDGE AND SIGNATURES IN E-CASH. To exemplify a common use of zero-knowledge and signatures in off-line e-cash, let us use the proposal of [19]. In their work, an e-coin is authenticated by a blind signature from the bank, so that the bank is unaware of the actual coin it is issuing. As a protection against double spending, the e-coin has the customer's identity secretly embedded, in a way that enables this identity to be revealed if double spending occurs. Of course, before the bank signs such an e-coin, it must be assured that this secret embedding has been properly done. It is here that zero knowledge plays its role: it enables the bank to check the correctness of the coin structure without learning its specifics, which otherwise would violate the anonymity requirement.

---

[1] Of course, the possibility of revealing a malicious customer's identity necessitates the assurance that an honest customer cannot be framed for double spending.

P. Syverson (Ed.): FC 2001, LNCS 2339, pp. 1–20, 2002.

1.1   Amortized E-Cash

Signatures and zero-knowledge protocols are the most expensive steps of e-coin generation, and thus make it impractical for coins to have small denominations: such coins would not be worth the computation it takes to generate them. In this paper, therefore, we put forward a method to amortize these expensive steps across *many* coins.

Notice that having the bank validate a list of coins with a single signature, after verifying with zero-knowledge computation that each coin in the list is well-formed, does not provide sufficient amortization: the zero-knowledge computation is simply n times as large as it was before. For amortization to be at all useful, the efficiency of generating n new coins should be significantly less than n times that required for generating a single old coin. Ideally, we should be able to generate n new coins with essentially the same effort required for a single coin.

Let us give an overview of how our solution achieves amortization and double spending protection.

AMORTIZATION. Our solution is based on the notion of a *wallet*. A wallet is a collection of n coins (strings), each composed of two *logically indivisible* subcoins (substrings). The first subcoin of each coin is *common* to the wallet: it specifies the wallet name and the number of coins in it, secretly embeds the customer's ID, and contains a compact description of all allowable second subcoins. The second subcoin of each coin is *individual*: it contains information essential for spending that coin.

The common subcoin contains all the information the bank verifies by means of a zero-knowledge protocol. Therefore, a single zero-knowledge computation is amortized across many coins. Moreover, the common subcoin is the only data that the bank needs to sign. Therefore, a single signature computation is amortized across many coins.

We shall show that double spending any coin in the wallet causes the customer's identity, secretly embedded in the common subcoin, to be revealed. Moreover, we shall also prove that the common subcoin specifies all the individual subcoins that can be used with it, so that it is impossible for a malicious user to generate unpaid-for coins by using the already bank-signed common subcoin, and then manufacturing additional individual subcoins.

DOUBLE SPENDING. Our scheme includes choosing a secret key SK that is *both* the encryption key of a symmetric-key encryption scheme (E, D) and the secret signing key of a digital signature scheme with public key PK.[2]

The way in which we use such a step to protect against double spending is best explained in the simple case in which a wallet contains a single coin.

---

[2] Such "secret key overloading" is potentially dangerous: many security flaws are known to arise when this is done. Thus, we will have to argue that these flaws to not arise in our scheme. We discuss this issue in section 4.4, under "wallet anonymity."

In this case, a customer C randomly generates a signature key pair (PK, SK). Then, the common subcoin of the wallet contains PK and the customer's identity encrypted with SK: $E_{SK}(ID_C)$. Spending the coin consists of providing a signature (on a challenge) relative to the signature public key PK. The signature scheme used will be *one-time*, meaning that signing a single message is secure, while signing any two different messages is guaranteed to reveal the secret signing key SK. Because the secret signing key is also the encryption key (and thus the decryption key), double spending (i.e. signing two different challenges) reveals the customer's identity.

This approach becomes more complex when there are more coins in the same wallet. Having a single, one-time signature public key PK for all coins in the wallet does not work: legitimately spending two different coins in the wallet would correspond to signing two different challenges relative to the same one-time PK, thus revealing SK and therefore, the customer's identity. On the other hand, if each key in the wallet were to have its own key pair (PK_i, SK_i), then the common coin would have to include $E_{SK_i}(ID_C)$ for every i. Regardless that the common subcoin is growing rapidly in size, this does not provide adequate amortization because each $E_{SK_i}(ID_C)$ must be verified as correct through a zero-knowledge protocol.

As we shall see, our solution uses n ephemeral signing keys (one per coin in the wallet) so that any two signatures computed using the same *ephemeral* signing key reveal a master signing key SK, which is the same as the encryption key used to embed the customer's identity.

ANONYMITY. Our scheme satisfies a new type of anonymity requirement: *wallet anonymity*. Informally,

– Coins (from *any* wallet) cannot be linked to a user's identity.
– Coins from *different* wallets (of course, if spent in different transactions) cannot be linked to one another.

However, coins from the *same* wallet can be linked to one another, since they have the same common subcoin. This linkage could be utilized to infer something about the customer from his coin transactions. For example, two merchants, one selling tobacco products and the other gambling products, could compare notes, discover that coins have been spent with each of them that possess the same common subcoin, and thus deduce that they share an anonymous customer (who smokes *and* gambles). In the extreme, imagine that all the coins a customer spends are from the same wallet. Then, if all the merchants he visits compare notes, they might be able to pinpoint the customer not by mathematically breaking the scheme, but with the sheer amount of information about his spending habits.[3]

Though less than perfect, wallet anonymity is useful. Zero-knowledge computation is the true bottleneck of e-cash generation, and our scheme allows e-coins to be generated efficiently, while still providing a good deal of anonymity.

---

[3] It is worth noting that in practice our scheme will not be that vulnerable to this kind of linking. Small wallets, the certainty of there being some honest merchants, and the low value of most associates make this kind of linking not a great concern.

Furthermore, our anonymity level can be increased by either (1) having wallets consist of few coins, or (2) having a customer devote different wallets to different type of purchases.

For example, Alice may have one wallet to purchase a given magazine, and a different wallet to purchase electronics. Then, the fact that the same customer keeps on buying the same (or similar) magazines is not much information. Furthermore, because the two wallets are distinct, the producers of the electronics cannot discover that they have a client who reads those magazines, and thus have no incentive to increase their advertising in those magazines.

1.2   Amortized E-Cash vs. Divisible E-Cash and Multi-spendable Coins

The concept of amortized e-cash has been studied previously under the name of "divisible e-cash" ([26,27,8,10,28]) and "multi-spendable coins" [1]. Divisible e-cash is based on the idea of having a coin which can be divided, at spending, into smaller coins. What we call a wallet is what was previously called a (divisible or multi-spendable) coin, and what we call a coin is merely the atomic part of a coin. However,

1. It is fair to say that most of the research in this area has privileged the algorithmic aspects at the expense of defining what this different concept should mean. No formal treatment of the subtle anonymity properties satisfied by a divisible e-cash scheme has been presented. After been pointed to some "linkability problems," the reader was largely left alone in figuring out precisely what they were. Indeed, in his 95 paper [26], Okamoto recognizes that the security requirements discussed in his paper are quite ad hoc, and poses as a remaining problem to
   "Find requirements which are formally shown to be sufficient for the security of electronic cash schemes."
2. Prior e-cash schemes such as that of Okamoto [26], were based on *ad hoc* complexity assumptions, that leave in doubt the security of these fast schemes. Indeed, Okamoto poses as an open problem in his paper to
   "Prove the security under more primitive assumptions such as the hardness of factoring and discrete logarithm."

In our paper, we fill the mentioned definitional gap, and use the term "amortized" to evoke that the traditional anonymity requirements have purposely been weakened.

Further, we prove the security of our scheme based on the simple assumption that a zero-knowledge based signature scheme (e.g., any of [12,21,17,30]) is secure. (For concreteness, we present our scheme based on the Schnorr signature scheme [30], whose security provably equals that of the discrete logarithm problem in the random-oracle model. Thus this security assumption alone suffices for amortized e-cash.)

We also attain efficiency in our scheme that is approximately as good as that in [26]. The actual efficiency issues will be discussed later, but for now we should mention that for simplicity we present a scheme in which only one coin can be spent at a time. This simplified scheme is not as efficient in terms of the computation needed to make and verify payments, but we present an improvement over the simplified scheme that makes our scheme comparable to divisible e-cash schemes in these aspects.

Finally, our algorithmic structure is conceptually simpler. For instance, rather than using complex tree-structures of special type of commitments, we can get by with conventional Merkle trees.

2 Definition of Wallet-Based E-Cash

2.1 Notation

PROTOCOLS. [4] A two-party protocol, P, to be run by parties A and B, is a pair of Interactive Turing Machines (ITMs): $P = (P_A, P_B)$. Following [14], on *input* (x, y), where x is a private input for A and y a private input for B, and *random input* (r_A, r_B), where r_A is a private random tape for A and r_B a private random tape for B, protocol (P_A, P_B) computes in a sequence of rounds, alternating between A-rounds and B-rounds. In an A-round (B-round) only A (only B) is active and sends a message (i.e., a string) that will become an available input to B (to A) in the next B-round (A-round). A computation of (P_A, P_B) ends in a B-round in which P_B sends the empty message and computes a private *output*.[5]

An ITM A is called a *polynomial-time* ITM (ptITM) if there exists a fixed polynomial p such that, for any ITM B and for any execution of (A, B) or (B, A) in which the length of A's private input is $\leq k$, the number of steps taken by A in that execution is $\leq p(k)$. A *polynomial time protocol* is a protocol in which both ITMs are polynomial-time.

TRANSCRIPTS, VIEWS, AND OUTPUTS. Letting E be an execution of protocol (P_A, P_B) on input (x, y) and random input (r_A, r_B), we make the following definitions:

- The *transcript* of E consists of the sequence of messages exchanged by A and B, and is denoted by $\text{TRANS}^{P_A, P_B}(x, y, r_A, r_B)$;
- The *view of A* consists of the triplet (x, r_A, t), where t is E's transcript, and is denoted by $\text{VIEW}_A^{P_A, P_B}(x, y, r_A, r_B)$;
- The *view of B* consists of the triplet (y, r_B, t), where t is E's transcript, and is denoted by $\text{VIEW}_B^{P_A, P_B}(x, y, r_A, r_B)$;
- The *output of E* consists of the string z output by P_B in the last round of E, and is denoted by $\text{OUT}^{P_A, P_B}(x, y, r_A, r_B)$.

We consider the three random variables $\text{TRANS}(x, y, \cdot, r_B)$, $\text{TRANS}(x, y, r_A, \cdot)$, and $\text{TRANS}(x, y, \cdot, \cdot)$, respectively obtained by randomly selecting r_A, r_B, or both, and then outputting $\text{TRANS}(x, y, r_A, r_B)$.

---

[4] We shall use almost verbatim the protocol notation of [4].

[5] Due to the one-sidedness of secure computation, only machine P_B produces an output.

We also consider the similarly defined random variables $\text{VIEW}_A(x, y, \cdot, r_B)$, $\text{VIEW}_A(x, y, r_A, \cdot)$, $\text{VIEW}_A(x, y, \cdot, \cdot)$, $\text{VIEW}_B(x, y, \cdot, r_B)$, $\text{VIEW}_B(x, y, r_A, \cdot)$, $\text{VIEW}_B(x, y, \cdot, \cdot)$, $\text{OUT}_B(x, y, \cdot, r_B)$, $\text{OUT}_B(x, y, r_A, \cdot)$, and $\text{OUT}_B(x, y, \cdot, \cdot)$.

PROBABILISTIC EXPERIMENTS. [6] If $A(\cdot)$ is an algorithm, then for any input x, the notation "$A(x)$" refers to the probability space that assigns to the string σ the probability that A, on input x, outputs σ. The set of strings having a positive probability in $A(x)$ will be denoted by "$\{A(x)\}$".

If S is a probability space, then "$x \leftarrow S$" denotes the algorithm which assigns to x an element randomly selected according to S, and "$x_1, \ldots, x_n \leftarrow S$" denotes the algorithm that respectively assigns to, $x_1, \ldots, x_n$, n elements randomly and independently selected according to S. If F is a finite set, then the notation "$x \leftarrow F$" denotes the algorithm that chooses x uniformly from F.

If p is a predicate, the notation $Pr[x \leftarrow S; y \leftarrow T; \cdots : p(x, y, \cdots)]$ denotes the probability that $p(x, y, \cdots)$ will be true after the ordered execution of the algorithms $x \leftarrow S; y \leftarrow T; \cdots$.

The notation $[x \leftarrow S; y \leftarrow T; \cdots : (x, y, \cdots)]$ denotes the probability space over $\{(x, y, \cdots)\}$ generated by the ordered execution of the algorithms $x \leftarrow S$, $y \leftarrow T, \cdots$.

ADVERSARIAL TMs. An *adversarial TM* (ATM) is a probabilistic, polynomial-time Turing machine that is capable of retaining its internal state from one execution to the next. If the same ATM A occurs twice or more in a probabilistic experiment, it is understood that the first time A starts executing on its initial state, the second time starts with the state reached at the end of its first execution, and so on.

2.2   Wallet-Based E-Cash

To be as general as possible, a wallet-based e-cash scheme involves

- three players: the bank, the customer, and the merchant;
- three protocols: *withdrawal* (to be run between the bank and the customer to generate wallets and e-coins); *spending* (to be run between the customer and the merchant in which an e-coin is spent on a transaction); and *depositing* (to be run between the merchant and the bank, in which a merchant convinces the bank that an e-coin was spent with him); and
- a procedure *reveal* (in principle a protocol too), that reveals the customer's identity in case of double spending.

However, our scheme is simpler and more efficient: spending an e-coin consists of running an algorithm *pay* producing a signature-like string, which is universally verifiable by running an algorithm *ver*. Thus, assuming that a transaction specifies the merchant involved, depositing an e-coin simply consists of the merchant sending such a string to the bank (who can then run *ver* on its own). Further *rev* also is an algorithm, which reveals the identity of a double-spending customer

---

[6]   Verbatim from [2] and [15].

when run on two payments relative to the same coin. It is therefore this better (because less interactive) type of wallet-based e-cash that we formalize below.

Because wallet-based e-cash is a special case of e-cash, our formalization will necessarily need to include basic properties common to other e-cash schemes. Because these are not particularly novel, however, we shall deal with them rather informally, so as to focus the reader's attention to the anonymity properties unique to wallet-based e-cash.

Fundamental Components. A *wallet-based e-cash scheme* consists of

- A security parameter, 1^k (i.e., an integer k in unary notation).
- A GMR-secure digital signature scheme, DSS = (GEN, SIG, VERIFY). [15] (It is assumed that each DSS public key has been authenticated by a certifying authority.)
- A polynomial-time protocol $W = (W_B, W_C)$, for e-coin withdrawal.
- A probabilistic polynomial-time algorithm *pay*.
- A probabilistic polynomial-time algorithm *ver*.
- A probabilistic polynomial-time algorithm *rev*.

Basic Properties

Honest Inputs and Honest Outputs. Protocol W is performed between the bank and the customer. In an execution of W, both parties must be aware of n, the size of the wallet to be produced, and the security parameter 1^k. The bank takes as additional inputs its DSS secret key, SK_B, and the DSS public key of the customer, PK_C. The customer takes as an additional input his DSS secret key, SK_C.

Because W_C is the second ITM in protocol W, it is the customer who sees the output of W. Each such output is called a *wallet* and consists of a pair (x, x_s). Component x is referred to as the *public wallet* (since it is shown with payment) and specifies its own size, n, and the public key, PK_B, of the bank that issued it. Component x_s is referred to as the *secret wallet*, since it must be kept secret as it allows the customer to spend the coins in the wallet. Conceptually, x and x_s can be considered as a public-secret key pair of a special kind of digital signature scheme.[7] It is worth remarking that x and x_s *together* make up the common subcoin for any coin in the wallet, while the individual subcoin is just an integer i in the range $[1, n]$.

Algorithm *pay* receives 4 inputs: x, x_s, a wallet of size n, an integer $i \in [1, n]$ (the coin number), and t, the transaction on which to spend the coin (conceptually, a string to be signed). The output of *pay* on such inputs is a 4-tuple y, x, i, t. Conceptually, y is the signature of t with public key x and coin i.

Algorithm *ver* receives 4 inputs: y, x, i, and t, and outputs a bit: 1 indicates that the payment was valid, while 0 indicates otherwise.

---

[7] It is not quite a signature key pair, because it has not been generated by an independent key generation algorithm, but has similar properties.

If the customer and the bank behave honestly in withdrawal and payment, the customer should be able to spend any coin in the wallet produced. That is, if *ver* is run on the output of an honest execution of *pay*, based on a wallet of size n which was the output from an honest execution of W, and a value $i \in [1, n]$, *ver* should always output 1.

E-Coins Cannot Be Forged. Informally, this is the old e-cash property that a malicious customer cannot ever spend more different coins than he withdrew from the bank. In our setting, this means two things. First, he cannot interact with an honest bank and end up with a wallet with more than n coins if the common input was n. Second, he cannot use a wallet of size n to produce a valid payment on a coin $i > n$. This basic property remains true even if the customer is allowed to be adaptive, in that he may interact with the bank to withdraw wallets many times, each time based on information he learned before.

Double-Spending and No Framing. On any input, algorithm *rev* outputs either the empty string ε or a customer identity with the following constraints:

1. On input two quadruples (y_1, x, i, t_1) and (y_2, x, i, t_2) such that $ver(y_1, x, i, t_1) = ver(y_2, x, i, t_2) = 1$, but $t_1 \neq t_2$, algorithm *rev* outputs the identity of some customer with probability essentially equal to 1.
2. If a customer C never double spends any coins, then it is computationally hard to find an input to *rev* (even given all the payments C legitimately makes) on which *rev* outputs C's identity.

This, we can consider inputs to *rev* that produce a customer's identity to be irrefutable proof that the customer has double-spent, since if they have not, it would be computationally intractable to generate such proof. (It should be noted that while this requirement is so formulated not to lose generality, in our scheme a "more convincing" requirement is actually met: namely, *rev* outputs a customer's DSS signature of the sentence "I have double spent.")

No Spending on Behalf of Others. If (x, x_s) is a wallet of an honest customer C, then it is computationally hard to generate a 4-tuple (y, x, i, t) such that $ver(y, x, i, t) = 1$ with only x, i, and t as inputs. This continues to hold even if the adversary can impersonate any player except C and force C to withdraw arbitrarily many wallets of arbitrary size in an adaptive manner, as well as produce payment for arbitrarily many transactions $t' \neq t$ in an adaptive manner.

Anonymity. We now wish to express more formally the two crucial anonymity properties, that characterize wallet-based e-cash, that we discussed informally in the introduction.

Wallet Anonymity. At a minimum, this requirement should ensure that given a *single* coin i, from some wallet x, it is impossible to determine to which customer the coin belongs. Notice that the customer necessarily is one having withdrawn money. Moreover, because each coin reveals the size of the wallet, the customer must be one who has retrieved a wallet of that size. Thus, wallet anonymity guarantees that, if m customers have withdrawn wallets of size n, the bank cannot determine which of the customers is spending a given coin better than random guessing. This should remain true even if the bank is dishonest both during its own key generation (it may help to have a special key rather than a random one!) and during the withdrawal protocol.

But we wish to guarantee a stronger property, namely, that the customer behind *any* spent coin cannot be guessed better than at random, even if the bank has available how all other $mn-1$ coins have been spent. This should be true even if the bank chooses all the transactions on which each coin is to be spent (which might arise via collaboration with the merchants). We allow these transactions to be chosen adaptively as follows. Initially, the m customers' original names are renamed according to a random permutation σ: $i \to \sigma(i)$. After that, the bank chooses a transaction t_1, a customer name j_1 (which under the permutation corresponds to customer $\sigma(j_1)$), and a coin i_1 from that customer's wallet. Then, the bank receives a payment of that transaction with that coin. Based on this result, the bank chooses a second transaction, a second identity, and a second coin, and receives the corresponding payment. And so on, for mn times. At the end, we let the bank choose a single coin and guess the *original* identity of its customer. Of course, if the bank asks for any coin to be spent twice, it will (by double-spending) learn the identity of the corresponding customer, but if all spending requests relate to different coins, then the bank should not be able to do better than random guessing.

Formally, denoting by S_m, the set of all permutations over m elements, wallet anonymity is so expressed:

$$\forall c > 0,\ \forall m, n > 0,\ \forall \text{ ATM } A,\ \exists k_0 : \forall k > k_0$$
$$Pr[(SK_{C_1}, PK_{C_1}), \ldots, (SK_{C_m}, PK_{C_m}) \leftarrow \text{GEN}(1^k);$$
$$(SK_B, PK_B) \leftarrow A(PK_{C_1}, \ldots, PK_{C_m});$$
$$(x_1, x_{s_1}) \leftarrow \text{OUT}^{A, W_C}(\varepsilon, (SK_{C_1}, PK_B, n), \cdot, \cdot);$$
$$\ldots$$
$$(x_m, x_{s_m}) \leftarrow \text{OUT}^{A, W_C}(\varepsilon, (SK_{C_m}, PK_B, n), \cdot, \cdot);$$
$$\sigma \leftarrow S_m;$$
$$(t_1, j_1, i_1) \leftarrow A(\varepsilon);$$
$$(y_1, x_{\sigma(j_1)}, i_1, t_1) \leftarrow pay(x_{\sigma(j_1)}, x_{s_{\sigma(j_1)}}, i_1, t_1);$$
$$(t_2, j_2, i_2) \leftarrow A(y_1, x_{\sigma(j_1)});$$
$$\ldots$$
$$(y_{mn}, x_{\sigma(j_{mn})}, i_{mn}, t_{mn}) \leftarrow pay(x_{\sigma(j_{mn})}, x_{s_{\sigma(j_{mn})}}, i_{mn}, t_{mn});$$
$$(a, b) \leftarrow A(y_{mn}, x_{\sigma(j_{mn})}) :$$
$$\sigma(a) = b \text{ and } ((j_u, i_u) = (j_v, i_v) \Rightarrow u = v)] < 1/m + k^c.$$

Wallet Unlinkability. At a minimum, this requirement should ensure that given a pair of wallets each of the same size, it is impossible for the dishonest bank to determine whether the wallets belong to the same customer or not. This is extended and formalized by means of the following game.

First, each of the two customers withdraws two wallets (each consisting of n coins).

Second, the bank determines adaptively the transactions on which all the $4n$ coins will be spent. Initially, the 4 original wallets are renamed according to a random permutation $\sigma: i \to \sigma(i)$. Then, the bank selects a transaction t_1, and a wallet name j_1 (which under the permutation corresponds to wallet $\sigma(j_1)$) as well as a coin i_1 in that wallet. The bank then receives a payment of that transaction with that coin from customer who owns wallet $\sigma(j_1)$. (Notice that such a customer is $\lfloor \sigma(j_1)/2 \rfloor$, if we assume that customer 0 owns wallets 0 and 1, and customer 1 owns wallets 2 and 3.) Based on this result, the bank chooses a second transaction, a second (possibly different) wallet, and a second coin, and receives the corresponding payment, and so on, for $4n$ times.

Finally, we let the bank choose two different wallets: the bank tries to choose two wallets that belong to the same customer. Of course, if the bank requests double spending, it will be able to correctly choose two such wallets, but if all spending requests relate to different coins, then the bank should not be able to do better than randomly guessing a pair of wallets (which has a probability of success of $1/3$, since there are two correct answers out of six choices). Formally, wallet unlinkability is so expressed:

$\forall c > 0, \forall n > 0, \forall$ ATM $A, \exists k_0 : \forall k > k_0$
$Pr[(SK_{C_0}, PK_{C_0}), (SK_{C_1}, PK_{C_1}) \leftarrow \text{GEN}(1^k);$
$\quad (PK_B, SK_B) \leftarrow A(PK_{C_0}, PK_{C_1});$
$\quad (x_0, x_{s_0}) \leftarrow \text{OUT}^{A, W_C}(\varepsilon, (PK_B, SK_{C_0}, n), \cdot, \cdot);$
$\quad (x_1, x_{s_1}) \leftarrow \text{OUT}^{A, W_C}(\varepsilon, (PK_B, SK_{C_0}, n), \cdot, \cdot);$
$\quad (x_2, x_{s_2}) \leftarrow \text{OUT}^{A, W_C}(\varepsilon, (PK_B, SK_{C_1}, n), \cdot, \cdot);$
$\quad (x_3, x_{s_3}) \leftarrow \text{OUT}^{A, W_C}(\varepsilon, (PK_B, SK_{C_1}, n), \cdot, \cdot);$
$\quad \sigma \leftarrow S_4;$
$\quad (t_1, j_1, i_1) \leftarrow A(\varepsilon);$
$\quad (y_1, x_{\sigma(j_1)}, i_1, t_1) \leftarrow pay(x_{\sigma(j_1)}, x_{s_{\sigma(j_1)}}, i_1, t_1);$
$\quad (t_2, j_2, i_2) \leftarrow A(y_1, x_{\sigma(j_1)});$
$\quad \ldots$

$\quad (y_{4n}, x_{\sigma(j_{4n})}, i_{4n}, t_{4n}) \leftarrow pay(x_{\sigma(j_{4n})}, x_{s_{\sigma(j_{4n})}}, i_{4n}, t_{4n});$
$\quad (a, b) \leftarrow A(y_{4n}, x_{\sigma(j_{4n})}) :$
$a \neq b$ and $\lfloor \sigma(a)/2 \rfloor = \lfloor \sigma(b)/2 \rfloor$ and $((j_u, i_u) = (j_v, i_v) \Rightarrow u = v)] < 1/3 + k^c.$

3   Our Scheme

Our solution relies on zero-knowledge based signature schemes such as those presented in [12,17,21,30]. Such schemes sign a message M in three steps: a *commitment step*, which is independent of the message, a *challenge step*, which is message dependent, and a *response step*, in which the secret key is used. Our e-cash scheme can work with *any* such a signature scheme. But, for concreteness (and to avoid an ad hoc, general notation), in this extended abstract we shall present our scheme based on the Schnorr signature scheme. Our solution, like most other e-cash schemes, relies on blind signatures [5] for security.

3.1 Blind Signatures

We present an ad hoc summary of blind signatures, using blind RSA signatures as our example [5].

In a blind signature scheme, there is a finite message space, and if Alice wants Bob to sign a message M without revealing it to him, she first generates a random value ρ and then uses the "blinding" function F to compute a random $M' = F(M, \rho)$ and asks Bob to generate the signature $\text{SIG}_{SK_B}(M')$ on M'. (Function F is such that, for every M, for a random choice of ρ $F(M, \rho)$ is uniformly distributed in the message space.) Then, Alice uses the "unblinding" function G to compute $\text{SIG}_{SK_B}(M) = G(\text{SIG}_{SK_B}(M'), \rho)$. For example, suppose $N = PQ$ is an RSA public modulus and that d and e are the private and public exponents, respectively, for Bob's RSA key. In order to compute a blind signature, Alice generates ρ, a random value modulo N, and computes $M' = F(M, \rho) = \rho^e M$ Then, Bob computes the signature $(\rho^e M)^d = \rho M^d$ and Alice computes M^d by dividing ρM^d by ρ modulo N. Conceptually, Bob will have no idea what he signed since the distribution of M' is independent of M. To highlight that any secure blind signature scheme can be used with our protocol, we will use the abstract notation. However, it should be mentioned that it is important if the overall scheme is to have security based on only one cryptographic assumption that a blind signature scheme be chosen whose security depends on the same assumption. For example, the protocol of [20] depends on the discrete logarithm assumption, which is in line with the other assumptions we will need (since we use the Schnorr signature scheme).

3.2 Schnorr's Signature Scheme

We present a summary of the Schnorr signature scheme [30]:

- **Common public parameters:** p and q (two large primes such that q divides $p-1$), g (a generator of the subgroup of Z_p^* of size q), and H (a collision resistant hash function producing outputs in Z_q).
- **Secret-public key pairs:** (x, g^x), where x is generated at random in the interval $[1, q-1]$.
- **Signing a message M:**
  STEP 1: Randomly select $r \in [1, q-1]$ and compute $g^r \bmod p$ (the commitment)
  STEP 2: Compute $e = H(M, g^r)$ (the challenge)
  STEP 3: Output $(g^r \bmod p, r + ex \bmod q)$ (the signature of M)
- **Verifying a signature of a message M:** To verify a signature (a, b), compute $e = H(M, a)$ and check that $g^b = a(g^x)^e \bmod p$.

3.3 Crucial Properties of the Schnorr Scheme

The quantity $g^r \bmod p$ computed in Step 1 is called an *ephemeral key*, because it is generated just as a public key and because it is used only once: signing a new message entails generating a new ephemeral key.

Let us now highlight two properties of the Schnorr scheme that we use heavily in our scheme:

1. *The ephemeral key can be generated off line.* That is, it can be generated before the message to be signed is chosen or known: g^r is a random public key!

2. *If the ephemeral key is fixed, then the Schnorr scheme is strictly one-time.* That is, if one insists in using the Schnorr scheme only with a particular ephemeral key, then the scheme is secure (i.e., not existentially forgeable against a chosen ciphertext attack) as long as one signs no more than one message. However, as soon as one signs any two different messages M_1 and M_2 with the same ephemeral key, then the scheme becomes totally insecure, meaning that the very secret signing key x is revealed. Indeed, because H is collision resistant and because $M_1 \neq M_2$, we are essentially guaranteed that $e_1 = H(M_1, g^r) \neq e_2 = H(M_2, g^r)$, and the two signatures will consist of g^r mod p and, respectively, $r + e_1 x$ and $r + e_2 x$ mod q. Because $e_1 - e_2 \neq 0$ mod q, we can solve:

$$x = [(r + e_1 x) - (r + e_2 x)](e_1 - e_2)^{-1} \bmod q.$$

3. *The Schnorr scheme's security is based on simple assumptions.*
   The security of the Schnorr scheme depends on the difficulty of the discrete logarithm problem. The proof of this is done under the random oracle model in the paper by Schnorr [30].

3.4   Our Use of the Crucial Properties

To embed the customer's identity we use a secure symmetric scheme (E', D'). (Our scheme actually construct (E', D') from an underlying secure symmetric encryption scheme (E, D). The precise description of how (E', D') are derived from (E, D) and why this auxiliary step is needed will be explained in the security sketch, section 3.5.)

Our scheme also uses Schnorr's signature scheme with public parameters p, q, g, and H, but only to compute and verify payments. (If the security parameter is 1^k, then we assume q is of length k and thus so are the outputs produced by H.)

For all other purposes, as demanded by our definition, our scheme uses a second signature scheme. To avoid confusion between the two schemes, the Schnorr keys and signatures are explicitly spelled out, while keys and signatures under the second scheme are denoted "abstractly." Thus, the permanent key pair (i.e., that relative to the second scheme) of a customer C is denoted (PK_C, SK_C), and that of a bank B is denoted (PK_B, SK_B). Customer C's signature of a message M in this second scheme will be denoted by $\mathrm{SIG}_{SK_C}(M)$; B's signature of M will be denoted by $\mathrm{SIG}_{SK_B}(M)$.

NOTE: For simplicity, we assume that in the second scheme the signature of a message M always includes M (in the clear).

The second signature scheme is chosen so as to allow blind signatures [5]. To highlight that any such a secure scheme can be used, we use the following abstract notation. There are two efficient algorithms, F and G. The bank's blind signature of M is obtained by (1) computing $F(M) = (M', \rho)$; (2) asking the bank to sign M', and (3) computing $\mathrm{SIG}_{SK_B}(M)$ by running $G(\mathrm{SIG}_{SK_B}(M'), \rho)$.

The Withdrawal Protocol W. For simplicity, we assume that each wallet size is a fixed power of 2, 2^d.

Here is how a customer withdraws a wallet of size 2^d.

1. The customer generates a random public/private key pair (g^x, x) in the Schnorr scheme.

2. The customer uses his permanent secret key to sign the sentence "C has double spent"; that is, he computes $s = \text{SIG}_{SK_C}(C$ has double spent $)$. Then, he uses the symmetric encryption scheme to encrypt signature s using as encryption key the just generated Schnorr secret signing key; that is, he computes $z = E'_x(s)$.

3. The customer then generates 2^d ephemeral key pairs $(g^{r_1}, r_1) \ldots (g^{r_{2^d}}, r_{2^d})$.

4. The customer creates a Merkle hash tree [23], T, of depth d which stores the public parts of the ephemeral keys $(g^{r_1}, \ldots, g^{r_{2^d}})$ in its leaves (where g^{r_i} is stored in leaf i). Denote by R the root value of T.

5. The customer generates a random value ρ, computes $M' = F(M, \rho)$, and sends M' to the bank, where $M = (R, d, z, g^x)$.

6. The customer proves interactively with the bank that M' has properly formed. Specifically, the customer proves that $M' = F(M, \rho)$ where M is a quadruple of values (a_1, a_2, a_3, a_4) such that (1) $a_2 = d$ and (2) a_3 is the encryption under E', using the discrete log of a_4 as a secret key, of C's permanent signature of the value "C has double spent". These proofs are accomplished via general zero-knowledge proof methods, such as those in [16].[8]

(*Comment:* the complexity of such a zero-knowledge proof is essentially independent of d: it grows in $poly(\log(d))$, and thus is polynomial in $\log \log(n)$, where $n = 2^d$ is the size of the wallet.)

7. The bank provides a signature $\text{SIG}_{SK_B}(M')$ and sends it to the customer.

8. The customer unblinds the signature, that is, he computes $w = G(\text{SIG}_{SK_B}(M'), \rho)$. The public part of the wallet consists of (w, R, d, z, g^x), while the secret part of the wallet consists of the secret parts of the ephemeral keys $(r_1, \ldots, r_{2^d})$ along with the secret key x.

(*Comment:* the public wallet is compact as its size does not depend on d, but on $\log d$. As described above, the secret wallet grows linearly in n, the size of the wallet. However, $r_1, \ldots, r_{2^d}$ could be outputs from a pseudorandom generator on input a short seed of length k, the security parameter: then, the secret wallet could consist of just $2k$ bits: the seed and x.)

The Payment Algorithm *pay*. On input $((w, R, d, z, g^x), (r_1, \ldots, r_{2^d}), x, i, t)$, *pay* runs as follows:

1. The customer (re)generates the ephemeral public key g^{r_i} from r_i and the public parameters. Then he computes $(g^{r_i} \bmod p, r_i + ex \bmod q)$, the Schnorr signature on message t using secret key x and ephemeral key pair (g^{r_i}, r_i).

---

[8] The [16] result shows how to solve any NP problem in zero-knowledge. The problem of whether M' was generated from appropriate inputs can obviously be solved in NP (we just "guess" the a_1, a_2, a_3, a_4 values that were used).

2. The customer generates the authentication path, *path*, in Merkle tree T for leaf i. (*Comment:* This list of d values of length k authenticates g^{r_i} as the ith public ephemeral key.)

3. The customer outputs $((g^{r_i} \bmod p, r_i + ex \bmod q, path), (w, R, d, z, g^x), i, t)$.

The Payment Verification Algorithm *ver*. On input $((a, b, path)$, (w, R, d, z, g^x), $i, t)$, *ver* runs as follows:

1. Check that (a, b) is a valid Schnorr signature relative to public key g^x on message t. If not, halt and output 0.

2. Check that w is a signature on (R, d, z, g^x) relative to the bank's public key PK_B. If not, halt and output 0.

3. Check that *path* is of size d and correctly authenticates that a is stored in the ith leaf of a Merkle tree with root value R. If not, output 0.

4. (Else) output 1.

The Identity Revealing Algorithm *rev*. The *rev* algorithm, on input $y_1 = ((a_1, b_1, path_1), (w_1, R_1, d_1, z_1, g^{x_1}), i_1, t_1)$ and
$y_2 = ((a_2, b_2, path_2), (w_2, R_2, d_2, z_2, g^{x_2}), i_2, t_2)$ runs as follows:

1. Check that (1) $ver(y_1) = 1$, (2) $ver(y_2) = 1$, (3) $w_1 = w_2$, (4) $i_1 = i_2$, and (5) $t_1 \neq t_2$. If any of these checks fail, halt and output ε.

2. Let $e_1 = H(t_1, a_1)$ and $e_2 = H(t_2, a_2)$, and compute $(e_1 - e_2)^{-1} \bmod q$.

3. Compute $x = (b_1 - b_2)(e_1 - e_2)^{-1} \bmod q$.

4. Compute $s = D'_x(z_1)$. Output s, which should be customer C's signature of "C has double spent."

3.5   Security Sketch

In this extended abstract, we only informally give arguments that our scheme satisfies our definitions of a wallet-based e-cash scheme. In particular,

Honest Inputs and Honest Outputs. All the algorithms fit the format specified for a wallet-based e-cash scheme. All that must be shown is that when the withdrawal protocol is run honestly, the customer can successfully spend any coin in the wallet she generates.

Since the customer has access to x, r_i, and t, she can generate the signature $(g^{r_1} \bmod p, r_i + ex \bmod q)$ correctly. Furthermore, since she knows all the leaves of the Merkle tree, she can easily compute *path*. Thus, she can compute *pay* correctly.

Since the signature generated in *pay* was valid, and the wallet involved was signed by the bank in the withdrawal protocol, and *path* was correct, the algorithm *ver* will approve the output the customer generates.

E-Coins Cannot Be Forged. Since we assume that the blind signature scheme is immune to forgery, and the zero-knowledge proofs are correctly implemented, there is no way the customer can create any wallets other than those she generates with the bank, and the wallets so generated all have the same size as the bank was aware of. Thus, the only possible way the customer could forge coins is if the customer were able to spend more than 2^d different coins out of a wallet. However, if this were possible, the customer would have been able to produce $2^d + 1$ different authentication paths of length d, which can be used to produce a hash collision. Since we assume it is computationally hard to find hash collisions, it is computationally hard for the customer to forge coins.

Double-Spending and No Framing. Clearly, if the customer spends the same coin on two different transactions, then unless those two transactions represent a collision for the hash function H, then the *rev* algorithm "extracts" x and decrypts z to get the user's identity. On the other hand, since the Schnorr signature scheme is secure when we never use an ephemeral key more than once, it is computationally hard for the bank to come up with inputs to *rev* which reveal a customer's identity if that customer did not double spend any coins.

No Spending on Behalf of Others. If one has a wallet but is not aware of x, one cannot produce signatures where x is the secret signing key, because the Schnorr signature scheme is secure. Thus, one cannot sign without access to the secret wallet.

Wallet Anonymity. Informally, in the withdrawal protocol the bank only sees M' (which it receives in Step 5 and digitally signs by w), and the values PK_C and d (which it receives in order to carry out the zero knowledge proof that M' is the "blinded version" of a wallet being issued to customer C of size 2^d).

The bank never sees $M = (R, d, z, g^x)$. Moreover, by the security of a blind signature, the bank cannot infer anything about M from M'. It is true that the customer proves to the bank that M' corresponds to an M which embeds an encryption of the customer's identity. But because this proof is a zero-knowledge one, the bank cannot learn any more about M than claimed.

During payment verification, the bank only sees the values $((a, b, path),$ $(w, R, d, z, g^x), i, t)$, the value $M = (R, d, z, g^x)$, its own signature w of M, the coin number i, the transaction t, the Schnorr's signature (a, b) of t relative to public key g^x, and the authentication path that coin i equals a in the Merkle tree rooted at R. Thus the only thing the bank learns which depends on the customer's identity in any way is M, because M contains the value $z = E'_x(\text{SIG}_{SK_C}(C \text{ has double spent}))$. Due to the security of the blind signature, the bank cannot link M to the M' it saw during withdrawal. Thus, the only way the bank can associate the customer's identity to his payments is through z, and all that remains to prove is that this is impossible.

Being the encryption scheme E' secure, if $\text{SIG}_{SK_C}(C \text{ has double spent})$ were encrypted with a *totally secret* random key, z would provably not betray C. Notice, however, that, in order to guarantee that double spending reveals C, we must encrypt $\text{SIG}_{SK_C}(C \text{ has double spent})$ with key x, that is with the same secret key corresponding to the Schnorr's public key g^x that is known to the bank. While in practice this step may very well be secure, the same cannot be claimed from a theoretical point of view: x is essentially random (because the secret key in the Schnorr scheme is a random element of Z_q and therefore is essentially a random string), but it is not totally secret (because g^x is information about x). The best way to prove that g^x does not interfere with the security of encryption would be a "simulation argument," but no such an argument appears to be possible here. Therefore, we resort to design the encryption scheme E' *so that* we can prove that the information provided by g^x is computationally irrelevant.

The idea is to use the Goldreich-Levin bit construction [13].

Let us assume that the discrete logarithm problem is at least as hard as 2^{k^α}. More formally,

$\forall A$ probabilistic TM $\exists n : \forall k \geq n$

$Pr[(q, g) \leftarrow DLGEN(1^k); x \leftarrow \{2, \dots, q - 2\};$

$y \leftarrow A_{2^{k^\alpha}}(q, g, g^x) : y = x] < \frac{1}{2^k},$

where $A_{2^{k^\alpha}}(q, g, g^x)$ denotes that A is allowed to run on input q, g, g^x for only 2^{k^α} steps before its execution is cut off and an empty result returned.

This is not the traditional discrete logarithm assumption. The difference is that in the traditional discrete logarithm assumption, we assume the above is true for *some* $\alpha > 0$, but in our case we need to use α in the protocol, so we need to assume the truth of the above statement using our given α.

Let $f : \{0,1\}^\ell \to \{0,1\}^\ell$ be a one-way function with complexity greater than 2^k, let x be a random ℓ-bit string, and let $\rho_1, \dots, \rho_k$ be ℓ-bit random strings. Then informally, on auxiliary inputs f, $f(x)$ and $\rho_1, \dots, \rho_k$, the k bits $b_i = x \cdot \rho_i$ are indistinguishable from k random bits by any polynomial-time algorithm.

This suggests to construct (E', D') from a secure symmetric cipher (E, D) and Schnorr public parameters p, q and g as follows. Select $\rho_1, \dots, \rho_k$, x at random in Z_q, compute $g^x \mod p$, compute $b_1, \dots, b_k$ such that $b_i = x \cdot \rho_i$, and define the encryption of a string σ with key x to be $E'_x(\sigma) = (g^x \bmod p, \rho_1, \dots, \rho_k, E_{b_1 \dots b_k}(\sigma))$. Because $b_1 \dots b_k$ is polynomially random even given knowledge of $g^x \bmod p, \rho_1, \dots, \rho_k$, this encryption is secure.

In terms of how to apply these techniques to our protocol, if k is the security parameter desired for the scheme, it should represent the length of the encryption key. Thus, the security parameter needed for the Schnorr scheme is in fact not k but $k^{1/\alpha}$. (It is presumed that $0 < \alpha < 1$). The encryption of a message M is computed by first generating k random bit strings $t_1, \dots, t_k$ of length equal to that of x. (The discrete log function $x \mapsto g^x$ is the one-way function we will use.) Then, the bits $b_1, \dots b_k$ are calculated by computing $b_i = x \cdot t_i$. Finally, the underlying secure symmetric encryption scheme is used to compute $E_b(M)$ where $b = b_1 b_2 \dots b_k$. The ciphertext consists of the list of strings $t_1, \dots, t_k$ and the encryption $E_b(M)$. Decryption using x as the key involves recalculating b and then decrypting $C = E_b(M)$ to get M.

For our scheme to be secure, we depend on the strong discrete log assumption described above. It is worth mentioning, however, that in practice the difference between this assumption and the discrete log assumption is insignificant. Whenever we use a scheme the security of which is based on some problem, we must make a concrete guess as to the difficulty of that problem. Without doing this, we could not adequately choose security parameters to use in such schemes. Thus, ultimately, our scheme differs from these other schemes only in that we use this guess about the difficulty of the discrete logarithm problem not just to pick our security parameter but also in the details of our scheme.

Wallet Unlinkability. Since the scheme satisfies wallet anonymity, the only way an adversary can correlate two wallets of the same customer is for payments from those two wallets to be correlated to one another.

Informally, the only way in which two different wallets belonging to the same customer are related is that the same customer's identity is embedded in both wallets. Other than these two encryptions, z_1 and z_2, all other information in the two wallets is generated independently.

Thus, if the symmetric encryption algorithm satisfies polynomial indistinguishability, to determine whether z_1 and z_2 relate to the same customer is computationally hard.

4   Efficiency

We are concerned with the time complexity of the withdrawal protocol, the storage requirement of the wallet, the time complexity of the *pay* algorithm, and the time complexity of the *ver* algorithm. In the following, we will assume 1^k is the security parameter, and n is the number of coins in a wallet. *poly* will represent some unnamed polynomial.

The withdrawal protocol requires $O(n)$ modular exponentiations (modulo a prime the size of which depends on 1^k) which the customer computes before interacting with the bank, a zero-knowledge proof protocol between the bank and the customer, which takes $O(poly(\log \log n + 1^k))$ time, and a signature by the bank on a message of length $O(\log \log n + 1^k)$. Thus, the entire protocol takes time $O(poly(\log \log n + 1^k))$.

There is a simple trade-off between the time complexity of the *pay* algorithm and the storage size of a wallet. On one side, the customer keeps stored the entire tree and all its leaves (which takes $O(1^k n)$ space), in addition to x and d, but needs only compute one modular exponentiation in *pay*. On the other side, the customer keeps only x, d and a pseudo-random seed stored in the wallet, which takes only $O(1^k + \log \log n)$ space, but must compute all the leaves each time, which takes $O(n)$ modular exponentiations.

However, there is a middle ground. The customer can choose a parameter ϵ (presumably as large as possible so that his available storage space is not exceeded), and store the top $h = \epsilon \log n$ levels of the tree in addition to x and d. This takes $O(1^k n^\epsilon)$ storage. The customer will still have to recompute part of the tree each time they execute the *pay* protocol, but the portion they must compute is smaller, and thus requires only $O(n^{1-\epsilon})$ modular exponentiations.

The time complexity of the *ver* algorithm is simply the time required to do two signature verifications.

4.1   Multi-coin Spending

It is also worth discussing a solution to the problem that the scheme described above is only capable of spending one coin at a time. However, it can be easily modified to spend multiple coins at once as follows.

Instead of having a typical hash tree where the parent is computed from left and right children by computing $H(LR)$ where LR denotes the concatenation of the two child node values, we each internal node of the tree have its own ephemeral key g^r. Then, the parent node is computed as $H(Lg^rR)$. In order to spend a node (and any node may be spent, not just leaf nodes) the customer must provide a signature on the transaction t using the ephemeral key of that node, and must provide a signature on a standard phrase (for example, "PATH") on all ancestors of that node. The customer must also provide the ephemeral keys for all internal nodes on the path from the node being spent to the root.

Now, in order to prevent double-spending we must ensure that (1) no node can be spent twice without revealing the customer's identity and that (2) if a node is spent, no ancestor or descendent of that node can be spent without revealing the customer's identity.

If the customer violates (1), then some node will be used to sign two different transactions t and t' and these signatures can be used to reveal x.

If the customer violates (2), then the node of the two which was closer to the root would be used to sign both the standard phrase and a transaction t, and these signatures can be used to reveal x.

Note that two different descendents of the same node can be spent without revealing the customer's identity. Those keys on both paths will only be used to sign the standard phrase, and thus the bank cannot recover the customer's secret key. Also note that the customer does not actually have to take the time to generate all the signatures on the standard phrase when running the spending protocol; these can be precomputed and stored with the secret information of the wallet.

With this technique, transactions of size m can be completed by spending $O(\log m)$ nodes in this manner. This requires $O(d \log m)$ signature verifications for the total transaction, which may be more than m (for example, if m is small relative to d). The size of the wallet also grows by a factor of 2.

Acknowledgments

The authors would like to acknowledge valuable discussions with Madhu Sudan which led to the development of the multi-coin spending technique described in section 4.1

References

1. S. Brands. Untraceable off-line cash in wallet with observers. In *Advances in Cryptology – CRYPTO'93*, 1993.
2. M. Blum, A. De Santis, S. Micali, and G. Persiano. Noninteractive Zero-Knowledge. In *SIAM Journal on Computing* 20(6): pp. 1084-1118, 1991.
3. E. Brickell, P. Gemmell, and D. Kravitz. Trustee-Based Tracing Extensions to Anonymous Cash and the Making of Anonymous Change. In *Proceedings of SODA'95*, 1995.
4. A. Beimel, T. Malkin, and S. Micali. The All-or-Nothing Nature of Two-Party Secure Computation. In *Advances in Cryptology: Crypto'99*, 1999.

5. D. Chaum. Blind Signatures for Untraceable Payments. In *Advances in Cryptology: Crypto'82*, 1983.

6. J. Camenisch, U. Maurer, and M. Stadler. Digital Payment Systems with Passive Anonymity-Revoking Trustees. In *Lecture Notes in Computer Science vol. 1146*, 1996.

7. J. Camenisch, J. Piveteau, and M. Stadler. Fair Blind Signatures. In *Proceedings of EuroCrypt'95*, 1995.

8. S. D'amingo and G. Di Crescenzo. Methodology for Digital Money based on General Cryptographic Tools. In *Advances in Cryptology: Eurocrypt'94*, 1994.

9. G. Davida, Y. Frankel, Y. Tsionnis, and M. Yung. Anonymity Control in Electronic Cash Systems. In *Proceedings of 1st Financial Crypto*, 1997.

10. T. Eng and T. Okamoto. Single-Term Divisible Coins In *Advances in Cryptology: Eurocrypt'94*, 1994.

11. E. Fujisaki and T. Okamoto. Practical Escrow Cash System. In *Lecture Notes in Computer Science vol. 1189*, 1997.

12. A. Fiat and A. Shamir. How to prove yourself: Practical solutions to identification and signature problems. In *Advances in Cryptology: Crypto'86*, 1986.

13. O. Goldreich, L. Levin. A hard-core predicate for all one-way functions. In *Proceedings of the Twenty-First Annual ACM Symposium on Theory of Computing*, 1989.

14. S. Goldwasser, M. Micali, and C. Rackoff. The knowledge complexity of interactive proof systems. In *SIAM Journal on Computing* 18, pp. 186-208, 1989. Preliminary version in *Proceedings of STOC'85*, 1985.

15. S. Goldwasser, S. Micali, and R. Rivest. A digital signature scheme secure against adaptive chosen-message addatcks. In *SIAM Journal on Computing* 17(2), pp. 21-25, 1988.

16. O. Goldreich, S. Micalia, and A. Wigderson. Proofs that yield nothing but their validity, or all languages in NP have zero-knowledge proof systems. In *Journal of the ACM*, 38(3), pp. 691-729, 1991.

17. Louis Claude Guillou and Jean-Jacques Quisquater. A "paradoxical" indentity-based signature scheme resulting from zero-knowledge. In *Advances in Cryptology: Cyrpto'88*, 1988.

18. M. Jakobsson and J. Muller. Improved Magic Ink Signatures Using Hints. In *Proceedings of Financial Crypto'99*, 1999.

19. M. Jakobsson and M. Yung. Revokable and Versatile Electronic Money. In *3rd ACM Conference on Computer and Communications Security*, 1996.

20. E. Mohammed, A.-E. Emarah, and K. El-Shennaway. A Blind Signature Scheme Based on ElGamal Signature. In *Proceedings of the Seventeenth National Radio Science Conference, 17th NRSC 2000*, 2000.

21. Silvio Micali. A secure and efficient digital signature algorithm. Technical Report MIT/LCS/TM-501, Massachusetts Institute of Technology, Cambridge, MA, March 1994.

22. R. Molender, D. Mussington, and P. Wilson. Cyberpayments and Money Laundering: Problems and Promise. Document MR-965-OSTP/FinCEN, 1998. Available at http://www.rand.org/publications/MR/MR965/MR965.pdf

23. R. Merkle. Protocls for Public Key Cryptosystems. In *Proceedings of the 1980 Symposium on Security and Privacy*, 1980.

24. D. M'Raihi. Cost-Effective Payment Schemes with Privacy Regulation. In *Proceedings of ASIACRYPT'96*, 1996.

25. D. Naccache and S. von Solms. On Blind Signatures and Perfect Crimes. In *Computation and Security*, 1992.

26. T. Okamoto. An Efficient Divisible Electronic Cash Scheme. In *Advances in Cryptology: Crypto'95*, 1995.
27. K. Ohta and T. Okamoto. Universal Electronic Cash. In *Advances in Cryptology: Crypto'91*, 1992.
28. J.C. Pailles. New Protocols for Electronic Money In *Proceedings of Auscrypt'92*, 1993.
29. H. Peterson and G. Poupad. Efficient Scalable Fair Cash with Offline Extortion Protection. In *Lecture Notes in Computer Science vol. 1334*, 1997.
30. C.P. Schnorr. Efficient Identification and Signatures for Smart Cards. In *Advances in Cryptology: EUROCRYPT'89*, 1989.
31. T. Sander and A. Ta-Shma. Auditable, Anonymous Electronic Cash Extended Abstract In *Advances in Cryptology: Crypto'99*, 1999.

Offline Micropayments
without Trusted Hardware

Matt Blaze[1], John Ioannidis[1], and Angelos D. Keromytis[2]

[1] AT&T Labs - Research
180 Park Avenue, Florham Park, NJ 07932 USA
{mab,ji}@research.att.com
[2] Computer Science Department, Columbia University
1214 Amsterdam Avenue, M.C. 0401, New York, NY 10027 USA
angelos@cs.columbia.edu

Abstract. We introduce a new micropayment scheme, suitable for certain kinds of transactions, that requires neither online transactions nor trusted hardware for either the payer or payee. Each payer is periodically issued certified credentials that encode the type of transactions and circumstances under which payment can be guaranteed. A risk management strategy, taking into account the payers' history, and other factors, can be used to generate these credentials in a way that limits the aggregated risk of uncollectable or fraudulent transactions to an acceptable level. These credentials can also permit or restrict types of purchases. We show a practical architecture for such a system that uses a Trust Management System to encode the credentials and policies. We describe a prototype implementation of the system in which vending machine purchases are made using consumer PDAs.

Keywords: Trust Management; Risk Management; Microbilling; Payments; Digital Cash.

1 Introduction

Current electronic payment systems are not well matched to occasional, low-valued transactions. (For the purposes of this discussion, we use the term "electronic payment system" broadly, to encompass conventional credit cards, stored-value cards, online and offline digital cash, *etc.*)

A central requirement for any electronic payment system is that a single compromise or failure should not have catastrophic consequences. For example, it should not be possible to double spend in a digital cash system, nor should the compromise of a client's authorization secret entail unlimited client liability or uncollectible transactions. Traditional payment systems are designed to *prevent* such failures. Unfortunately, the prevention mechanisms are generally too expensive to support occasional, low-valued transactions. Typically, such systems require online transactions, trusted client hardware such as smartcards, or must assume conditions that are not always true, such as that payers can be held responsible for any and all fraud or misuse of their authorization secrets.

In this paper, however, we present a new approach that focuses instead on *risk management.* Our central observation is that in some applications we can relax

P. Syverson (Ed.): FC 2001, LNCS 2339, pp. 21–40, 2002.

many of the expensive requirements associated with electronic payment systems while still keeping fraud or uncollectible transactions within acceptable levels. We shift the security functions performed by online authorization of transactions to certified code that can authorize offline transactions under certain conditions. These conditions are customized to each client according to a risk management strategy customized to the application.

There are three main contributions in this paper. First, we describe a framework in which certified offline authorizations created by a risk management strategy replace online authorizations for occasional, low-valued transactions. We then describe an architecture for a practical payment system in which a trust management system [BFL96] is used to encode the client risk management strategy. Finally, we describe a prototype implementation based on the KeyNote trust management toolkit [BFIK99], in which users can purchase vending machine items using credentials stored on conventional palmtop computers.

1.1   Related Work

Most currently-used protocols for Internet e-commerce are based on credit card charging over SSL [Hic95]. Such schemes require the merchant to perform a "hidden" (from the user's point of view) online credit check. The cost of such checks can be on the order of 10 (US) cents, making them expensive for low-value transactions. The more recently developed SET [SET] and CyberCash protocols [EBCY96] do not address this issue.

NetBill [CTS95] is a transactional payment protocol with many advanced features (atomicity, group membership, pseudonyms, *etc.*) that requires communication with the NetBill server for each transaction, thus exhibiting the same drawback with respect to micropayments as the simpler online protocols already mentioned. Other general-purpose payment protocols [NM95, BGH+95, FB98] are unattractive for micropayments for these same reasons.

Digital cash-based systems [Cha82, Cha92, MN94, BGJY98, dST98] provide many desirable features (potentially total anonymity, inherent off-line operation), but do not directly address the issue of double-spending (fraud). Some e-cash systems use online checking (thus negating the off-line operation capability). Others rely on detection after the fact, which introduces the potential for large-scale simultaneous multiple-spending. The same drawback is manifest in several micropayment protocols, such as PayWord [RS], PayTree [JY96], micro-iKP [HSW96], and others [Tan95]. While the double-spending possibility is an inherent property of all such systems, none of the above protocols employ any kind of risk management scheme to address it.

NetCents [PHS98] and Millicent [Man95] are scrip-based off-line-friendly micropayment protocols. As the monetary unit used in these protocols is vendor-specific, double-spending is made very difficult (if not impossible). The assumption behind both protocols is that people tend to re-use the same merchants repeatedly. If this assumption holds, the interactions between the customer and the bank are kept at a minimum. A hidden assumption is that merchants have "total information" over their sales, so double-spending with the same merchant is detectable. If the merchant has many distinct points of sale, the potential for double-spending is re-introduced, unless continuous communication and database synchronization is maintained between the different points. This would consequently negate the benefits of off-line operation.

IBM's MiniPay [HY96, Her98] uses a protocol that is somewhat similar to that described in this paper. MiniPay was developed primarily for use within a web browser, and a lot of effort has gone into the user interface aspect. Risk management is implemented as a decision to perform an online check with the billing server based on the total spending by the customer that day, and some parameter set by the merchant. The billing provider cannot customize risk-management parameters on a per-customer and/or per-merchant basis.

Person-to-person (P2P) payment systems, such as PayPal or X.com (now merged), allow users to exchange money online. Typically, the provider's web server needs to be contacted and an instruction issued for a money transfer. In that respect, the transaction is very similar to a bank wire transfer. There also exist modules that allow users to directly exchange money through palmtop computers. Such systems typically have no built-in security mechanisms; in the best of circumstances, they are a straight variant of offline digital cash.

While our system can operate on its own, it could also be integrated in some type of electronic wallet, such as SWAPEROO [DBGM+98].

Finally, the use of a PDA as an electronic wallet is not new. [DB99] describes an implementation of the PayWord system for the PalmPilot.

1.2   Offline Transactions and Risk Management

Consider a simplified view of how transactions are processed in traditional credit- or debit- card systems. Each payer has an account with a card issuer, against which charges can be made up to some limit. When a user wants to charge a transaction, she provides her account number to the merchant, who calls the card issuer for authorization. The card issuer checks that the transaction is less than the available balance, and if so, subtracts the transaction amount from the balance and authorizes the transaction. The user also signs an authorization to charge her account for the transaction amount. At periodic intervals, each merchant sends the signed authorizations they have collected to the card issuer, which transfers appropriate funds to the back to the merchants and bills the cardholders' accounts accordingly. (Real credit and check card authorization and clearing mechanisms are more complicated than this in practice, but still follow approximately this basic procedure).

Observe that even though settlement and clearing can be (and are) done offline and in batches, each transaction still requires an online authorization. This step is needed for two reasons, both related to the general-purpose design of the credit / check card model. First, losses from uncollectible transactions are limited by imposing an account limit on each user, which must be checked and debited with each transaction to prevent credit overruns or negative balances. Secondly, the account number must be checked to be sure that it is actually associated with an account in good standing, to prevent fraud from stolen or forged account numbers. (Observe that the online transaction could, in principle, be eliminated if the card holder can be given trusted hardware, such as a smartcard, that maintains its own state about the status of the account and produces signed transaction authorizations).

Such systems become extremely vulnerable to fraud and abuse if the online transaction authorization (or the trusted hardware) is eliminated. (For example, consider why few retailers will accept checks from random customers without verifying their validity with the bank). There would be no limit to what the account holder could spend during the validity period of the card, and no mechanism to detect invalid or forged account numbers. Clearly, such a vulnerability is unacceptable in a general-purpose payment system.

We observe that in some applications, however, it is acceptable to risk the occasional uncollectible or fraudulent transaction if, in the aggregate, tolerating the losses costs less than preventing them through online transactions or deploying secure hardware. In fact, assuming risk and tolerating loss is the basis upon which credit systems work.

The basic idea behind our scheme is that we include with the user's account identifier certified information that describes the circumstances under which transactions can be authorized offline. These circumstances would differ from application to application, and indeed, from user to user, but are selected in a way that makes it difficult to profitably exploit or abuse a compromised account. The rules are designed to allow offline authorization for those transactions where fraud is unlikely and in which the cost of an online authorization is greater than the value of the transaction itself.

We assume that each user's authorization data is managed by a small, portable device of modest computational ability and with some capacity for communication, such as infrared or low-power radio. Ideally, the device is something the user already owns for some other purpose; PDAs and cellular telephones are especially good examples.

In this scheme, the users' credentials manage and limit risk in several ways. First, credentials would have a limited lifetime, perhaps a day or two, and would have to be refreshed by communicating with the issuer at regular intervals. The validity period would be determined by the length of time the issuer is willing to tolerate loss from stolen client devices, and also by the natural interval that the user is likely to be able to communicate back with the issuer.

Because each transaction is authorized by trust management credentials, the system can also be used in applications where the ability to conduct certain kinds of transactions must be restricted in various ways and where different treatment is given to different classes of customers. For example, some transactions (alcohol, tobacco, pornography, binding contracts, *etc.*) might be restricted to adults; it is a simple matter to encode a requirement for an "adulthood" credential in the vendor's policy. Similarly, certain transactions might require licenses or special permission (dangerous goods, car rental, medical supplies), which are also easy to encode as credentials and check for in a policy. Conversely, the credential-based mechanism also makes it easy to create restricted forms of money that can only be used for certain things, such as social welfare food stamps or spending money given by parents to their children.

The most important mechanism for limiting fraud and abuse is the transaction limit encoded in the credentials. The kinds of transactions permitted are determined according to the risk management strategy of the account issuer, and are designed to limit the usefulness to a thief of a compromised user's credentials and secrets. For example, an encoded strategy might permit the offline purchase of newspapers, but only a few copies from any given vendor. If a user's device is stolen, the thief would be able to buy only newspapers, and only as many as she can find vendors.

Although not suitable as a general replacement for credit cards or cash, such a scheme has a number of important properties that make it especially well suited to the kinds of occasional transactions for which credit cards and specialized digital cash systems are too expensive.

2   Architecture

First, some terminology. The main players in our scheme are *Merchants*, who sell things and collect payments, and *Payers*, who buy things and pay for them. Merchants and Payers sign up for service with a *Provisioning Agent* (PA). Merchants interact with Payers through the *Merchant Payment Processor* (MPP). Payers are assumed to hold portable lightweight devices capable of some processing (cellphones, PDAs, *etc.*) A *Clearing and Settlement Center* (CSC) for reconciling transactions may be a separate entity, or may be part of the PA.

Our microbilling architecture is designed to operate efficiently under a number of constraints.

Foremost is that communication between the PA and the Payers and Merchants is relatively expensive. This implies that transactions must be able to be consummated between Payers and Merchants directly, with the CSC verifying them at a later time[1]. Thus, the Payer will have to provide proof that she is allowed to perform a transaction. Likewise, the Merchant will have to convince the Payer that she really is an authorized Merchant. Assuming a large number of Payers and Merchants, with a potentially high turnover rate, massive periodic reconfiguration of all devices involved is impractical.

A public-key credential-based architecture fits nicely here. The PA would act as a trusted third party to Payers and Merchants, who would be able to authenticate each other offline using the appropriate credentials. Although computationally intensive, public key operations are not prohibitively expensive on the latest generation of lightweight computing devices (see Section 3 for some performance figures for the Palm PDA). Some devices also provide hardware cryptographic acceleration in the form of ASIC modules. Modern cellphones, for example, already have significant cryptographic support in hardware. These trends should mitigate, if not altogether eliminate, performance concerns.

Loss of the Payer's (or Merchant's) device/credentials should not be catastrophic. While the Merchant, Payer, or PA (depending on agreements) may have to incur some costs as a result of the loss (similar to credit card loss or theft), it should be possible to limit the potential damage. Payer and Merchant credentials

---

[1] There exist established and efficient infrastructures that can process large volumes of micro-transactions and reconcile these against the associated accounts. Obvious examples are telephone and utility companies, banks, *etc.*

utilized should therefore be short-lived (and thus frequently-refreshed) and fairly restrictive with regard to the Payer's or Merchant's capabilities (what items can be bought/sold, in what quantities/prices, *etc.*) Thus, we must be able to encode risk-management strategies in the credentials we use. The refresh rate of the credentials and the capabilities expressed therein depend on the risk-management strategy of the PA and thus have to be flexible[2].

An added benefit of such an approach is that the different levels of physical security and tamper-resistance (ranging from none to very secure) can be taken into consideration on an individual-user basis as part of the PA's risk-management strategy. Other parameters that may influence risk-management can also be adjusted on a per-user basis as well.

The user devices used for the transactions can be very versatile (*e.g.*, cellphones, PDAs, even laptop or desktop computers), and the architecture does not depend on any particular communication technology for the transactions, only that the user device has some ability to communicate back to the PA from time-to-time, whether by telephone, cellular text message, Internet, *etc.*

Since the PA has no physical control over the user device, it is necessary to verify any information received by it. Thus the Payer device must provide prove to the Merchant that it is authorized to perform a transaction, and must able to provide signed messages that the Merchant can use to clear payment for a transaction.

A central principle behind our system is the use of a trust-management system as the core component to express and encode the risk-management strategies. The following subsections give an overview of trust management, describe the mapping between risk and trust management, present our architecture, and discuss how it meets the requirements for an offline micropayment system.

2.1   Trust Management

Trust management, introduced in the PolicyMaker system [BFL96], is a unified approach to specifying and interpreting security policies, credentials, and relationships between users of the system (principals); it allows direct authorization of security-critical actions. A trust-management system provides standard, general-purpose mechanisms for specifying application security policies and credentials. Trust-management credentials describe a specific delegation of trust and subsume the role of public key certificates; unlike traditional certificates, which bind keys to names, credentials can bind keys directly to the authorization to perform specific tasks.

A trust-management system has five basic components:

- A language for describing 'actions', which are operations with security consequences that are to be controlled by the system.
- A mechanism for identifying 'principals', which are entities that can be authorized to perform actions.

---

[2] The refresh rate also depends on the frequency of communication between the user's device and the PA. We discuss this later in this section.

- A language for specifying application 'policies', which govern the actions that principals are authorized to perform.
- A language for specifying 'credentials', which allow principals to delegate authorization to other principals.
- A 'compliance checker', which provides a service to applications for determining how an action requested by principals should be handled, given a policy and a set of credentials.

Trust management unifies the notions of security policy, credentials, access control, and authorization. An application that uses a trust-management system can simply ask the compliance checker whether a requested action should be allowed. Furthermore, policies and credentials are written in standard languages that are shared by all trust-managed applications; the security configuration mechanism for one application carries exactly the same syntactic and semantic structure as that of another, even when the semantics of the applications themselves are quite different.

2.2   Mapping Risk Management to Trust Management

Given a trust-management system, it is possible to describe risk-management strategies in the language used for specifying credentials. The details of the transaction (such as item purchased, price, quantity, *etc.*), potential history information (prior transactions between the Payer and Merchant), and other information (time of day, device status, *etc.*), are encoded in the trust management action language. The credential language then determines whether the transaction should be permitted based on that information. The principals in the system (Merchants, Payers, PAs, and CSCs) are identified by their public keys.

User policies identify the PAs that are trusted to introduce other users. For a Payer and a Merchant to be able to perform a transaction, they must share at least one common PA. Note that it is not necessary to restrict the architecture to a two-layer scheme (PAs and Payers/Merchants); multiple layers of PAs can be used.

All user devices and CSCs utilize compliance checkers; these are used by the users to verify transactions as they are performed, and by the CSCs during reconciliation. This allows for a decentralized decision-making process with regards to risk-management, relieving CSCs or PAs from the burden of maintaining a large, online, highly-available infrastructure for transaction verification.

2.3   Microbilling through Risk Management

We can now describe our microbilling architecture in some detail.

The users (Payers and Merchants) are assumed to possess some device that can perform transactions on their behalf. Each user has a public/private key pair, and signs up for service with one or more PAs who issue the necessary credentials. While the details of the business arrangements that might arise are outside the scope of our architecture, it is important to note that these do affect the risk decisions made by the agents and thus the strategies encoded in the credentials. For example, an account with a higher monthly premium may be allowed to make more purchases every day than one with no premium. We give some example credentials in Section 3.

As we have already mentioned, credentials are short-lived to restrict potential damage from loss of the device or compromise of the cryptographic key, and to avoid maintaining and distributing revocation lists at update time[3]. Thus, relatively frequent updates of the credentials have to be performed, depending on the specific implementation. When and how the updates are performed (and their frequency) is device-specific: cellphones might receive their credentials every night in the form of an SMS (or similar) message, or they might place a call to a voicemail or other service number; PDAs might download new credentials every few days during backup. To avoid disruption of service, a device could be issued several credentials representing different tradeoffs between purchasing power and validity duration; the higher-value credential would expire first, but the longer-lived lower value credential would still allow some purchases to be made in the event a credential update is missed. Also note that credentials issued to some Merchants can be made longer-lived, to avoid frequent updates to unattended selling points.

A pair of Payers and Merchants thus equipped with their respective credentials can perform a transaction through a simple authentication/authorization protocol, an example of which is given in Section 3. In simple terms, the two users authenticate each other and then verify each other's capabilities: the Payer verifies that the Merchant is known to the PA and is authorized to charge the Payer's account for the particular type of transaction; the Merchant verifies that the Payer is authorized by a recognized and accepted PA to proceed with the specific transaction.

When a transaction completes, the Payer receives the goods or services purchased; in return, the Merchant receives from the Payer a *Microcheck*, which is a specially encoded signed message that authorizes a one-time charge to the Payer's account and a credit to the Merchant's account; for simplicity, the Microcheck can also be encoded as a trust-management credential.

Periodically, the Merchant provides its collected Microchecks (along with the related transaction records) to the CSC, which uses this information to verify the transaction and charge/credit the relevant accounts. The Payer's device (the "Microcheck Writer") may also keep a record of all transactions, which can be used to reconcile posted and billed charges against the payer's records. CSCs communicate with PAs to indicate the status of Payers' and Merchants' accounts.

Note that it is not strictly necessary for the Payer to authenticate the Merchant during the transaction. Surprisingly, this carries no loss in security: regardless of whether the transaction protocol was completed or not, the Merchant can always not dispense the goods, or the Payer can always claim that she never received them. Mutual authentication does not help in either case, and the dis-

---

[3] Since we cannot do online revocation check at the time a transaction is underway, the only other approach involving revocation lists involves updating all the users of a PA with the revoked credentials at update time.

pute would have to be settled through other means[4]. Given the low value of the transactions, and the fact that a dispute history of the Merchant and the Payer can be maintained and referenced by the PA and/or CSC, fraudulent transaction disputes need not be a major concern. For the remainder of this paper, we will assume Payers do not authenticate the Merchants.

Figure 1 gives a schematic description of the architecture.

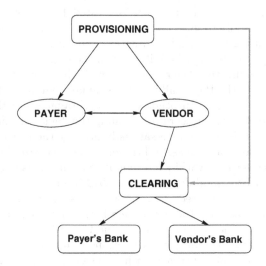

Fig. 1. Microbilling architecture diagram. The arrows represent communication between the two parties: Provisioning issues credentials to Payers and Merchants; these communicate to complete transactions; Merchants send transaction information to Clearing which verifies the transaction and posts the necessary credits/charges or arranges money transfers. Provisioning and Clearing exchange information on the status of Payer and Merchant accounts

2.4 Security Analysis

We need to examine a number of issues associated with our system. Minimally, we have three types of communication: provisioning, reconciliation, and transaction. We shall not worry about the value transfers to banks, as there already exist well-established systems for handling those. The inter-PA and PA-CSC communication is also relatively simple to secure, and can use well-established cryptographic protocols such as IPsec or SSL.

The Payer must be provisioned over a secure link; security can be physical, as in our prototype where the Palm PDA is connected to the provisioning computer

---

[4] The Payer can simply verify the signature on the Merchant credential, to avoid beginning a transaction with an unauthorized Merchant. A fraudulent Merchant cannot use another's credentials, as those will not be accepted by the CSC (and since no charges will be posted to the Payer's account, no dispute needs to be resolved.)

over a direct serial link in the user's presence. More commonly, security would be provided over a cryptographically protected network link. For that purpose, the Payer and the PA must share some long-term security parameters, so that short-term credentials can be generated with fresh public keys every refreshing period. An IPsec or SSL link between the PA and the Payer, or the encrypted channel already being used by a cellphone to exchange signaling information with its provider, is sufficient – there is no need to invent another protocol.

The length of the asymmetric keys generated for the short-term credentials needs some examination. The public key of the Payer may be exposed to third parties during the actual transaction and during the deposit of all the Microchecks by the Merchant. In addition, if the adversary is the Merchant himself, then he already has the Payer's public key. Either way, if an adversary can factor the RSA key of the Payer, all it can do is make purchases for the duration of the short-lived credential. In other words, cryptanalysis of the Payer key is no worse than discovering the secret by stealing the device or hardware compromise. The utility of this to the adversary is limited by the fact that the possible transactions are all low-value ones, and therefore the amortized cost of a machine big enough to discover keys within the time-frame allowed is uneconomical even for relatively small RSA modulus sizes (e.g., 512 bits).

If the Merchant is considered an adversary, the situation is slightly different; the Merchant really also has the extra time between the expiration of the credential and the next time he has to call up the CSC to deposit the Microchecks (since he can "pre-date" fraudulent transactions). Since this might happen only infrequently (perhaps only once a month), the vulnerability interval could be larger. Therefore, it may be advisable to encode a maximum number of purchases per day per vendor ID in the payer's short-term credential. This is where fraud-detection techniques also come into play. The CSC can verify, e.g., that only a reasonable number of purchases have been made per vending machine; it can also verify that the purchases have not been made at unreasonably disparate geographical locations, and so on. This is one of the ways where using a trust-management system with programmable policies (such as KeyNote) is especially advantageous. If better policies for fraud detection have to be deployed, or different policies need to apply to different people, they can all be encoded in the credentials.

Provisioning the Merchant's Payment Processor (MPP) is in many ways easier than provisioning the Payer. The MPP need never sign anything – it only verifies the signatures of the credentials that the Payer sends it. The MPP does need to have long-term secrets so that its communication with the CSC can be secure, but this is just part of the communication protocol, so all the well-known IPsec considerations apply. Provisioning the MPP can be as simple as inserting a floppy disk or a read-only memory chipcard with the necessary IPsec key material. The MPP should also have some concept of real time, but that does not need to be very accurate. In the case of the Merchant, the adversary is the Payer.

Since value is not stored in either the Payer or the Merchant, there is no need for tamper resistance against the owner of the Payer or Merchant hardware. The security of the payment system really only depends on the signing key of the PA; the PA secret must be well protected, and in many applications it will be appropriate to use techniques such as hardware security and shared secrets to protect it.

3 KeyNote Microchecks

It was straightforward to design a practical payment system based on the architecture of the previous section, using the *KeyNote Trust Management System* [BFIK99] as the basis for specifying credentials and risk-management policies.

KeyNote is a simple trust management system and language developed to support a variety of applications. Although it is beyond the scope of this paper to give a complete tutorial or reference on KeyNote syntax and semantics (for which the reader is referred to [BFIK99]), we review a few basic concepts to give the reader a taste of what is going on.

The basic service provided by the KeyNote system is *compliance checking;* that is, checking whether a proposed *action* conforms to local *policy*. Actions in KeyNote are specified as a set of name-value pairs, called an *Action Attribute Set*. Policies are written in the KeyNote *assertion language* and either accept or reject action attribute sets presented to it. Policies can be broken up and distributed via *credentials*, which are signed assertions that can be set over a network and to which a local policy can defer in making its decisions. The credential mechanism allows for complex graphs of trust, in which credentials signed by several entities are considered when authorizing actions.

In our micropayment system, various players issue KeyNote credentials to encode the short-lived risk management strategies and use KeyNote compliance checkers to make risk management decisions. We also use KeyNote credentials to encode the payment messages, which we call *KeyNote Microchecks*.

Let us now examine how we encode various aspects of our system with KeyNote.

3.1 Merchant Policy

Each merchant must have a policy that identifies the public keys of the Provisioning Agents (PAs) that are trusted to issue Payer credentials.

For the purpose of simplicity, we assume that there is only one PA (and only one PA key). Each merchant would then have a KeyNote policy as follows:

```
Local-Constants: PA_KEY = "rsa-base64:MIGJAoGBAM8ibp27102IIZA+\
    5xANbFmgRtV3YhOpSic2wk8YB/dGpHQDysmQ9buUtf7pJ/xhW5s+GV\
    4K5HwXsPo1MSimOw4z5fjvCDEfSwzBOfsp7pO1u+NWwJyd8hrb/iLYq\
    6tGmhha7RO+KG+fUEvLhArtyVOpQOoWfVBji4oOtIa9GrGzAgMBAAE="
Authorizer: "POLICY"
Licensees: PA_KEY
Conditions: app_domain == "deli" -> "true";
```

This KeyNote policy essentially says that any actions in the "deli" application should be authorized if they are signed with (or authorized by a credential issued by) the RSA key identified as "PA_KEY".

This policy is stored in each Merchant's computer and is consulted whenever an offline purchase is to be made.

As another example from a different application area, the following policy could be used by a car rental agency. This policy not only requires proof of payment, but also a driver's certificate from the Department of Motor Vehicles.

```
Local-Constants: PA_KEY = "rsa-base64:MIGJAoGBAM8ibp27102IIZA+\
    5xANbFmgRtV3YhOpSic2wk8YB/dGpHQDysmQ9buUtf7pJ/xhW5s+GV\
    4K5HwXsPo1MSimOw4z5fjvCDEfSwzBOfsp7pO1u+NWwJyd8hrb/iLYq\
    6tGmhha7RO+KG+fUEvLhArtyVOpQOoWfVBji4oOtIa9GrGzAgMBAAE="
    DMV_KEY = "rsa-base64:MCgCIQGBOf81SVZfHDwdck\
    ESR/Dh+ONPMrYvdOQlU9QdKbKbRQIDAQAB"
Authorizer: "POLICY"
Licensees: PA_KEY && DMV_KEY
Conditions: app_domain == "car rental" -> "true";
```

3.2 Payer Credentials

The Payer credentials are where most of the risk management strategy is encoded. These credentials are issued to each payer by the PA at relatively frequent intervals and specify the exact conditions under which an offline payment can be authorized. Recall that the Merchant policies will authorize anything authorized by the PA public key; the Payer credentials, therefore, are signed by the PA key and encode the exact restrictions for a given payer.

Different payers can be allowed to do different things, and this will be reflected in the details of their credentials. Each Payer has her own public key, which is encoded in the credential along with the restrictions. For example:

```
Local-Constants: PA_KEY = "rsa-base64:MIGJAoGBAM8ibp27102IIZA+\
    K5Hw5xANbFmgRtV3YhOpSic2wk8YB/dGpHQDysmQ9buUtf7pJ/xhW5s+\
    GV4XsPo1MSimOw4z5fjvCDEfSwzBOfsp7pO1u+NWwJyd8hrb/iLYq6tG\
    mhha7RO+KG+fUEvLhArtyVOpQOoWfVBji4oOtIa9GrGzAgMBAAE="
    PAYER_KEY = "rsa-base64:MCgCIQGBOf81SVZfHDwdck\
    ESR/Dh+ONPMrYvdOQlU9QdKbKbRQIDAQAB"
Authorizer: PA_KEY
Licensees: PAYER_KEY
Conditions: app_domain == "deli" && currency == "USD"
    && &amount < 1.51 && date < "20001024" -> "true";
Signature: "sig-rsa-sha1-base64:QU6SZtG9R3IXXAU9vRDBguUp\
    PpFgh8s5OOpbOOKOYMRxbzLfVpLvyyzV16fw9uT4Gkq1ToZAdhZVkF5z\
    uhumHXi2wmgZqzFexpoiitvpXRCuERkZPPK6OSikMpziOIfNkPYLiqSp\
    p7mHrdEAChZpPnBT12tUGxQBK/17fKVSRPaO="
```

This very simple credential allows the Payer holding the PAYER_KEY to make any offline purchases in the "deli" application for up to 1.51 each (in USD) until the date is "20001024". Presumably, this credential would have been issued to the payer a day or two before that.

The conditions in the Payer credential can be more complex, of course, if the risk management strategy demands it and if the merchant is able to store and refer to state about recent transactions. For example, we might provide a maximum number of transactions or maximum total value than can be purchased from any one Merchant, or it might require that the time between two transactions at the same merchant be at least some interval.

The payer credential is stored on the Payer's portable computing device and is transmitted to the Merchant whenever she wants to make a purchase.

3.3   Making a Purchase

When a Payer wants to buy something from a Merchant, the Merchant first encodes the details of the proposed transaction into an *offer* which is transmitted to the Payers computer. (We assume that the parties have some mechanism for negotiating the details of the offer, such as entering keys on a cash register or pushing buttons on a vending machine, and that there is some communication mechanism, such as infrared, between the Merchant's and Payer's devices).

The offer is a set of attributes and values that describes the transaction, *e.g.*:

```
merchant = "LEE'S DELI"
currency = USD
product = "CelRay Soda"
date = 20001023
amount = 0.55
app_domain = "deli"
nonce = eb2c3dfc860dde9a
```

This offer is from "Lee's deli" and is for a product called "CelRay Soda" that costs 0.55 in USD.

Observe that the name of the Merchant and the product description are just text strings. These, along with the price of the product, will be displayed on the Payer's device to prompt the user for approval.

If the Payer wishes to proceed, she must issue to the Merchant a KeyNote Microcheck for this offer. The Microchecks are also encoded as KeyNote credentials, that authorize payment for a specific transaction. The Payer creates the following KeyNote credential signed with her RSA key, and sends it, along with her Payer credential, from the PA to the Merchant:

```
Local-Constants: PAYER_KEY = "rsa-base64:Mcg..."
Authorizer: PAYER_KEY
Licensees: "LEE'S DELI"
Conditions: app_domain == "deli" &&
       currency == "USD" && amount == "0.55" &&
       nonce == "eb2c3dfc860dde9a" &&
       date == "20001023" -> "true";
Signature: "sig-rsa-sha1-base64:Qpf..."
```

(Key and signature encodings have been truncated for readability.)

This credential is effectively a check signed by the Payer (the Authorizer), and payable to Lee's Deli (the Licensee). The conditions under which this check is valid are that the payment is for something costing 55 cents, purchased on the 23rd of October 2000, and for the particular nonce given in the Merchant's offer. The nonce maps payments to specific transactions, and prevents double-depositing of Microchecks by the Merchant.

To determine whether he can expect to be paid (and therefore whether to accept the payment), the Merchant sends the action description (the attributes and values in the offer) and the Payer's key along with his policy (that identifies the PA key), the Payer credential (signed by the PA) and the Microchecks credential (signed by the Payer) to his local KeyNote compliance checker. If the compliance checker authorizes the transaction, the Merchant is guaranteed that the PA will allow payment. In the case of the policies, credentials, and transaction details given in the examples, the compliance checker would approve the transaction. The correct linkage among the Merchant's policy, the PA key, the Payer key, and the transaction details follow from KeyNote's semantics.

If the transaction is approved, the Merchant should give the item to the Payer and should store a copy of the Microcheck along with the payer credential and associated offer details for later settlement and payment.

If the transaction is not approved because the limits in the payer credentials have been exceeded, then, depending on their network connectivity, either the Payer or the Merchant can request a transaction-specific credential that can be used to authorize the transaction. Observe that if this is implemented transparently and automatically it provides a continuum between online and offline transactions tuned to the risk and operational conditions.

3.4   Clearing and Settlement

Periodically, the Merchant will 'deposit' the Microchecks (and associated transaction details) he has collected with the Clearing and Settlement Center (CSC). The CSC may or may not be run by the same company as the PA, but it must have the proper authorization to transmit billing and payment records to the PA for the PA's customers. The CSC receives payment records from the various Merchants; these records consist of the Offer, and the KeyNote Microcheck and credential from the payer sent in response to the offer.

In order to verify that a Microcheck is good, the CSC goes through the same procedure as the Merchant did when accepting the Microcheck. If the KeyNote compliance checker approves, the check is accepted. Using her public key as an index the payer's account is debited for the amount of the transaction. Similarly, the Merchant's account is credited for the same amount.

3.5 Prototype Implementation

We built a prototype KeyNote Microcheck system based on soda vending machines and Palm PDA computers. It is described in detail in the Appendix.

4 Discussion and Conclusions

We have demonstrated a simple and, for some applications, practical scheme for offline micropayments without the overhead of either secure hardware or online transaction authorization. Our scheme represents a departure from the usual approach to designing such systems. In particular, we chose to tolerate manageable losses, rather than preventing them, and we made no attempt to provide anonymity.

Risk management has long been a central part of the financial world - it is the basic value-service provided by credit card issuers, loan underwriters, insurers, the financial markets, *etc.* In this respect, it is rather surprising that platforms to support risk management techniques for avoiding online authorization have not previously been applied to electronic micropayment systems. (Indeed, older manual credit card processing protocols often included a "floor limit" on transactions below which it a telephone authorization was not required, although the limit was not specific to the individual cardholder.) Instead, previous electronic systems have focused on preventing fraud and failure, rather than on managing it. Unfortunately, the prevention mechanisms can be too expensive for micropayments, making a risk management approach especially attractive.

We have described a platform that makes it possible to encode risk management rules for offline micropayments. An obvious future direction for research is in the area of systems that generate and adapt these rules to actual operational conditions. We hope to stimulate work in this direction.

References

[BFIK99]   M. Blaze, J. Feigenbaum, J. Ioannidis, and A.D. Keromytis. The KeyNote Trust Management System Version 2. Internet RFC 2704, September 1999.

[BFL96]   M. Blaze, J. Feigenbaum, and J. Lacy. Decentralized Trust Management. In *Proc. of the 17th Symposium on Security and Privacy*, pages 164–173. IEEE Computer Society Press, Los Alamitos, 1996.

[BGH+95]   M. Bellare, J. Garay, A. Herzberg, H. Krawczyk, M. Steiner, G. Tsudik, and M. Waidner. iKP – A Family of Secure Electronic Payment Protocols. In *Proceedings of the First USENIX Workshop on Electronic Commerce*. USENIX, July 1995.

[BGJY98]   M. Bellare, J. Garay, C. Jutla, and M. Yung. VarietyCash: a Multi-Purpose Electronic Payment System. In *Proceedings of the Third USENIX Workshop on Electronic Commerce*. USENIX, September 1998.

[Cha82]   D. Chaum. Blind signatures for untraceable payments. In *Advances in Cryptology: Crypto'82 Proceedings*. Plenum Press, 1982.

[Cha92]   D. Chaum. Achieving Electronic Privacy. *Scientific American*, pages 96–101, August 1992.

[CTS95]   B. Cox, D. Tygar, and M. Sirbu. NetBill security and transaction protocol. In *Proceedings of the First USENIX Workshop on Electronic commerce*. USENIX, July 1995.

[DB99]   N. Daswani and D. Boneh. Experimenting with Electronic Commerce on the PalmPilot. In *Proceedings of the Third International Conference on Financial Cryptography*, Volume 1648 in Lecture Notes in Computer Science, pages 1–16. Springer-Verlag, 1999.

[DBGM+98]   N. Daswani, D. Boneh, H. Garcia-Molina, S. Ketchpel, and A. Paepcke. SWAPEROO: A Simple Wallet Architecture for Payments, Exchanges, Refunds, and Other Operations. In *Proceedings of the Third USENIX Workshop on Electronic Commerce*. USENIX, September 1998.

[dST98]   A. de Solages and J. Traore. An Efficient Fair Off-Line Electronic Cash System with Extensions to Checks and Wallets with Observers. In *Proceedings of the Second International Conference on Financial Cryptography*, Volume 1465 in Lecture Notes in Computer Science, pages 275–295. Springer-Verlag, 1998.

[EBCY96]   D. Eastlake, B. Boesch, S. Crocker, and M. Yesil. CyberCash Credit Card Protocol Version 0.8. Internet RFC 1898, February 1996.

[FB98]   E. Foo and C. Boyd. A Payment Scheme Using Vouchers. In *Proceedings of the Second International Conference on Financial Cryptography*, Volume 1465 in Lecture Notes in Computer Science, pages 103–121. Springer-Verlag, 1998.

[Her98]   A. Herzberg. Safeguarding Digital Library Contents. *D-Lib Magazine*, January 1998.

[Hic95]   K. Hickman. Secure Socket Library, February 1995. http://home.netscape.com/security/techbriefs/ssl.html.

[HSW96]   R. Hauser, M. Steiner, and M. Waidner. Micro-payments based on ikp. In *Proceedings of the 14th Worldwide Congress on Computer and Communication Security Protection*, June 1996.

[HY96]   A. Herzberg and H. Yochai. Mini-Pay: Charging per Click on the Web. http://www.hrl.il.ibm.com/mpay/, 1996.

[JY96]   C. Jutla and M Yung. Paytree: amortized signature for flexible micropayments. In *Proceedings of the Second USENIX Workshop on Electronic Commerce*. USENIX, 1996.

[Man95]   M. S. Manasse. The Millicent protocols for electronic commerce. In *Proceedings of the First USENIX Workshop on Electronic Commerce*. USENIX, July 1995.

[MN94]   G. Medvinsky and C. Neuman. NetCash: A design for practical electronic currency on the internet. In *Proceedings of the Second ACM Conference on Computer and Communication Security*, November 1994.

[NM95]   C. Neuman and G. Medvinsky. Requirements for network payment: The Netcheque prospective. In *Proceedings of IEEE COMCON*, March 1995.

[PHS98]   T. Poutanen, H. Hinton, and M. Stumm. NetCents: A Lightweight Protocol for Secure Micropayments. In *Proceedings of the Third USENIX Workshop on Electronic Commerce*. USENIX, September 1998.

[RS]   R. Rivest and A. Shamir. PayWord and MicroMint. *CryptoBytes*, 2(1):7–
            11.
[SET]   Secure Electronic Transactions (SET). http://www.setco.org/.
[Tan95]   Lei Tang. A Set of Protocols for MicroPayments in Distributed Systems.
            In *Proceedings of the First USENIX Workshop on Electronic Commerce*.
            USENIX, July 1995.

A   Prototype Implementation

We built a prototype microbilling system in order to test the feasibility of a such
a system, and also study users' reactions. We chose to implement our prototype
Payer system, the "Electronic Check Writer (ECW)" on a 3Com Palm-III PDA.
A large number of people in our location already have Palm PDAs, which makes
it easy to get volunteers to test our system without having to buy or carry
additional hardware. (Many modern mobile phones have infrared ports, and
would also have been suitable as an ECW platform).

We developed the ECW software for the Palm Computing Platform using the
ssl port, gnu utilities under Linux. The Palm-III (as well as all newer models) has
an infrared interface, and sufficient processing power to compute an RSA signature with a 257-bit modulus in approximately five seconds, which makes for an
acceptable user delay. While a 257-bit modulus can hardly be considered secure,
it makes for acceptable user delay while still providing proper authentication.

In order to make this an attractive and realistic demonstration, we used an
actual soda vending machine. We purchased and modified a generic vending
machine from a mail-order distributor. Figure 2 is a sketch of the machine with
the associated hardware. It can dispense eight kinds of 12oz cans of soda. It has
eight selection buttons in the front, and eight 24V motors to operate the dispense
mechanisms. To use it, we removed and discarded the original controller, the bill
collector, and the coin collector, and brought the wires that sense the pushbuttons and drive the dispensing motors out to a Z-World PK2275 industrial
controller (Figure 3), which is programmed in a variant of C called Dynamic C.
The controller is connected via a serial port to a Linux PC.

A Vacuum Fluorescent Display (VFD) is mounted on vending machine, and
is used to give prompts and status information to the user (Figure 4). It is
connected to the PC using a serial port.

Also connected to the Linux PC is a JetEye IrDA adaptor, which is used to
communicate with the Palm unit with the IrDA protocol suite.

The "Provisioning Agent" in our system is a BSD Unix workstation with a
palm cradle; users get their initial credentials (and the ECW software) in person
but receive their ongoing short-term credentials via electronic mail.

Before the system can be put to work, the Provisioning Agent station must
set up keys for itself. This one-time operation is done with a key generation
command to the KeyNote toolkit. Specifically, we generate an RSA key pair
with a modulus size of 1024 bits. The public and private components are stored
in regular text files.

The provisioning agent must make its public key known to all Merchants and
clearing agents. In our case, the provisioning agent also serves as the clearing

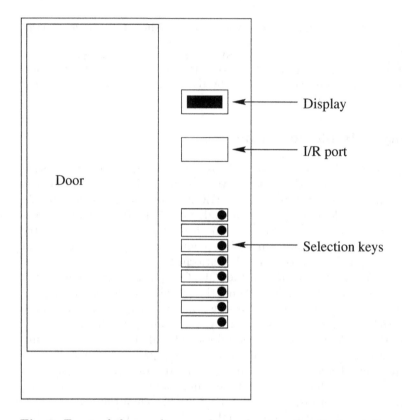

Fig. 2. Front of the vending machine, showing the display, infrared port, and some of the pushbuttons.

agent; sending the key to the Merchants is simply done by copying the public key to the vending machine's permanent storage.

Provisioning each user PDA consists of generating a short-term certificate, in the form of a signed KeyNote assertion, specifying that its public key can sign electronic checks meeting the conditions expressed in the assertion. As an implementation shortcut, the provisioning agent also generates the PDA's RSA key pair, and uses the public key in the assertion it generates. The key pair, along with the short-live certificate, are then compiled into an executable, called "SodaPop", which is loaded in the PDA.

The PDA is provisioned by going to a provisioning station, which is a PC running Linux, and has a copy of the source code of the ECW application. A simple command line interface is used to invoke a script that builds the new set of keys and the certificate, compiles them into the ECW application, and uploads it to the PDA which has been placed on the synchronization cradle.

Our vending machine looks superficially like a standard vending machine, but the coin mechanism has been replaced with a small display and infrared port. There are eight buttons to select drinks. Upon approaching, the user is prompted

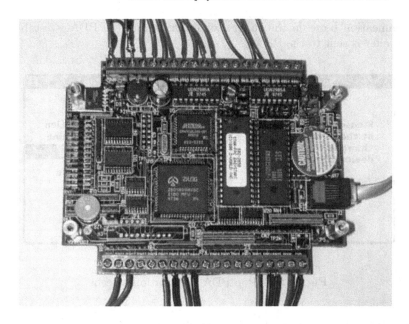

Fig. 3. Z-World PK-2275 Industrial Controller

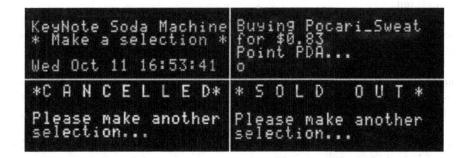

Fig. 4. Various prompts and status messages.

to make a selection (see Figure 4, first panel). Hidden inside the machine are the Merchant Linux PC and controller.

When a button is pressed on the soda machine, the supervisor program running on the Merchant Linux PC, which is polling the controller several times a second, registers that a button has been pressed. It then asks the controller whether the drink is available or sold out (there is circuitry in the vending machine to detect that). If the drink is sold out, the user is told so; if not, the user is told to aim their PDA at the IrDA interface of the vending machine. The PDA is running the "SodaPop" application; figure 5-left shows the opening screen.

Communication between the supervisor program and the PDA is established, and an offer is sent to the PDA.

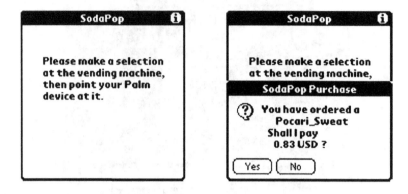

Fig. 5. SodaPop PDA Application screens

The PDA then prompts the user with the screen shown in Figure 5-right. If the user clicks on "no", no purchase is made (and, as a courtesy to a subsequent user, the PDA sends a "no" to the vending machine so that it will not wait until it times out).

If the purchase is accepted by the user, the PDA will build a KeyNote Microcheck and will send it, along with its credential, to the vending machine via infrared.

Upon receipt, the vending machine will query its local KeyNote compliance checker with the credential and Microchecks it got, along with the provisioning agent's public key, using the fields from the offer as the Keynote Action Attribute Set.

If everything is approved, the PC sends a command to the micro-controller to turn the corresponding dispensing motor on, and, in this example, a nice cold can of Pocari Sweat will be dispensed.

The Practical Problems
of Implementing MicroMint

Nicko van Someren

nCipher Plc.
nicko@ncipher.com

Abstract. Rivest and Shamir[2] proposed a system for generating micro-payment 'coins' using an engine that finds collisions in the output of a hash function. Such coins, they argued, would be quick to verify. Furthermore, by virtue of the birthday paradox, the cost of generation a large number of coins could be kept to an acceptable level through economies of scale while the cost of generating a small number of forgeries would be high compared to the return.

In this paper we examine the practicalities of building a MicroMint and we question some of the security statements made in the original paper.

Keywords: Micro-payments, electronic cash, system engineering.

1 Introduction

The MicroMint payment scheme was first proposed by Rivest and Shamir in 1995[2]. In this scheme 'coins' are created by a bank or broker and are distributed to users. The users can pass these coins to merchants who can quickly verify that they are valid coins and then provide services or goods in return for the payment. As with most micro-payment schemes the goal is to make the cost of validating the coins sufficiently low that it does not outweigh the value of the coins themselves. The MicroMint system attempts to do this by avoiding the use of all public key cryptography.

MicroMint coins consist of a tuple of values that, when passed through a publicly known hash function, all hash to the same value. Creating an individual coin of this form is costly since the hash function is chosen to be one-way. The MicroMint scheme relies on the fact that the bank expects to make a great many coins and can therefore devote a great deal of resources to the exercise.

A MicroMint system can be parameterized by the number of ways for the necessary collision k and hash function $\mathcal{H}$ along with its input size w and its output size n. (Note that in practice we may have some larger hash function $\mathcal{H}'$ and we construct $\mathcal{H} = \mathcal{H}' \bmod 2^n$). We may also choose to limit the valid coins to have some specific form in their hash output. We do this so as to increase the work required to mint coins (by having a large n) while keeping relatively low the cost of finding hash collisions through sorting. In this case we may divide the n bits of hash output into a prefix z of length t and a variable part of length $u = n - t$. If the hash of all the inputs must start with the prefix z then only one in every 2^t inputs will yield a useful output and we can increase the work involved to a level that will deter would-be attackers.

P. Syverson (Ed.): FC 2001, LNCS 2339, pp. 41–50, 2002.

1.1 Economies of Scale

The proposed design for a MicroMint relies on the Birthday Paradox: if we take random values independently taken from a set of size n (for example the birthdays of a bunch of people from the set of 366 birthdays) then when we have more than about $\sqrt{n}$ values we expect to see two values that are the same.

Given a hash function $\mathcal{H}(x)$ with an output of n bits, we can input either random or sequential values of x and collect the values in buckets labeled with the value $\mathcal{H}(x)$. With 2^n buckets the first 2-way collision will probably occur after $2^{n/2}$ inputs have been hashed. We can also expect the first k-way collision occurs after $N_k = 2^{n(k-1)/k}$ inputs and furthermore after time cN_k one can expect c^k different k-way collisions.

A MicroMint coin consists of a tuple $x_1, x_2, ..., x_k$ such that $\mathcal{H}(x_1) = \mathcal{H}(x_2) = ... = \mathcal{H}(x_k)$, which is to say that all the values in the tuple sorted into the same bucket. We can see from this that once we have the time to hash a few times more inputs than are needed to make one coin we will be able to make a great many coins. Thus we can achieve the economies of scale that we would like for our mint.

1.2 The Security Assumption of MicroMint

It is proposed that in a MicroMint system coins would have a limited lifetime (maybe a month). Coins would be released at the beginning of the month and would have to be redeemed with the bank at the end of the month. The mint itself would be equipped with a keyed hash function of some sort and the key would be kept secret until the start of the validity period for the coins. Thus an adversary trying to forge coins would not be able to start before the start of the validity period. If any reasonably funded adversary can not carry out significantly more than $2^{n(k-1)/k}$ hash operation during the validity period then they will not be able to forge a significant number of coins.

The authors of MicroMint go on to suggest that additional criteria above and beyond the nature of the prefix z might be chosen by the mint while creating the coins but that they would keep these criteria secret initially. If they suspect that there is some forgery taking place then they would release information about an extra test so that coins could be checked more thoroughly.

1.3 An Oligopoly of Banks

It is worth noting that given the high cost of entry into the MicroMint business, due to what economists call the high 'minimum efficient scale' for the mint, it is unlikely that any MicroMint protocol will be supported by a large number of banks. While an open MicroMint protocol would in theory be open to any player willing to underwrite a currency the practical costs of getting into the business will mean that in fact we would only expect a few players. In many ways this is akin to the practicalities of operating a physical currency.

2   Assumptions

In the following sections we will consider the practical implications of building a MicroMint system. Before we can do this we need to decide a few parameters. These include the number and value of the coins, the length of the validity period, what is a reasonable cost to the bank and what is a reasonable level of resources for an adversary.

For the purpose of this paper we will assume that the total value of coins minted in a period needs to be up to one billion dollars. While this may sound high it is necessary to consider it in the context of a successful micro-payment scheme in an Internet based economy. After all, if this scheme takes off we might hope that as much as some tens of percent of the value carried by todays web credit card transactions will move to micro-payments so a billion dollars is not at all excessive. In order for the system to be usable for very small value transactions we will need a very small denomination. For our analysis we will take each coin to be worth $1/10$ cent. This gives a total of 2^{40} coins.

The original paper suggests a validity period of 1 month and we will use this figure in our discussion. This equates to $60 \times 60 \times 24 \times 30 \approx 2^{21.3}$ seconds and we will round this to 2^{21} seconds for ease of calculation.

It is hard to say what is a reasonable cost for building a MicroMint. The theoretical upper bound is the interest earned on the value of the MicroMint cash in circulation over the lifetime of the machine. Clearly the bank will never be willing to commit this much to the construction since this would not take into account the risk involved and would leave no room for making a profit. A more reasonable figure might be obtained by looking at how much existing banks spend on computer systems for processing payments. Since the whole idea is that this system must be cheaper to operate than existing payment systems we can safely assume that the capital cost is no greater than that for existing systems. To this end we will assume that the mint itself must cost no more than $10,000,000.

The amount of money an attacker is willing to throw at attacking the system is bounded by the amount of value that they can obtain by defrauding the system multiplied by the probability of getting caught. This is the expected return of the attack and it makes no economic sense to attack the system unless the expected return is more than the cost. If we assume that the attacker has the channels available to organized crime for the distribution of the forgeries, and that they feel they can introduce an extra one hundredth of one percent of value into the system with a good change of getting away with it, then they may be able to extract $100,000 in value each month. If we assume that crooks have a rather short term view of investment and expect a good rate of return then it is unlikely that the crooks will be willing to spend more than $1,000,000 to set up their on-line bank robbery.

3   The Arms Race

Given the assumptions above, the initial prognosis for MicroMint looks just about OK. The design is based on the idea that honest people can out-gun the crooks by spending more on hardware than the attacker. We saw from section 1.1 that the number of coins produces is a kth power of the effort spent, where the coins are made of k-way collisions. It has been suggested by Rivest and others that a value of $k = 4$ be used. If the bank is only willing to spend ten times as much as the crooks on the construction of the hardware then they can make coins at a rate 10^4 times faster. If we consider that a party with \$10,000,000 can make \$1,000,000,000 worth of coins in a month then the attacker with only \$1,000,000 can make 10^{-4} as many, or \$100,000 in the same amount of time. Although this is enough to break even the key used to generate these coins is not revealed until the beginning of the month. So the attacker will not have made the requisite forgeries until the end of the validity period and thus they will not have time to spend them.

The problem, however, is that technology moves on. Moore's Law states that computer hardware gets faster by a factor of 2 every eighteen months. By the same observation from section 1.1 that gave us the economies of scale, Moore's Law is amplified for the production of forged coins and in 18 months time the forger will be able to make $2^4 = 16$ times as many coins for the same cost. This means that if the crooks funding the attack think that they can move their \$100,000 worth of forged coins in only half a month then they simply need to wait five months before they start their design and technology will have moved on enough to double the speed of production.

The amplification of Moore's law is a big problem for MicroMint. The bank must have a value of k that is large enough to ensure that at the start of the exercise the bank has a reasonable lead of the less well funded attacker. On the other hand, a large value of k means that the attackers ability to compete increases at a rate with a much higher exponent that Moore supposed. The only way for the bank to deal with this threat is to engage in an arms race. The bank must ensure that their hardware is always a suitable margin faster than any hardware that the attacker might have. As each year goes by they need to build a bigger machine because they know that the attacker can also build a bigger machine. A careful balance needs to be struck to ensure that the bank can make coins in a realistic time scale, at a reasonable price, but still expect that the attacker can not do the same. With $k = 4$ the bank may need to consider replacing their hardware every 15 month since in that time the attacker will get ten times faster. Worse, the cost of the hardware is now starting to look like a running cost rather than capital equipment.

The additional selection criteria for coins can indeed help somewhat in combating the forgery of coins. That said, they only help for as long as the predicate is kept secret. As we will see in the next section adding extra checks in the coin production process greatly increases the cost of the coin generation for the mint so it is unlikely that very many extra criteria can be used in a practical system.

4 System Complexity

In most computer systems the cost of the system is determined by the complexity of the problem. With the MicroMint it is, to a large extent, the the other way around; the complexity of the system is driven by the cost. Our goal is to make the system as complex as we can afford, so as to make it as hard as possible to forge. Thus in order to work out the complexity of the system we need to cost the parts of the system and then divide the total budget by the component cost.

For the time being we will allocate 80% of the budget to the hash engine, which will be split 50-50 between the cost of the chips and the cost of the supporting infrastructure (circuit boards, power supplies, racks, cases and construction). The rest will be spent on the coin storage and sorting.

4.1 Cost of Hashing

Current high speed ASIC[1] parts can hold a few hundred thousand gates, can run at upwards of 60MHz and cost a few tens of dollars (plus the design and NRE costs). Such a part could probably hold a small handful of pipelined hash engines that could each be made to produce a new hash output on each clock tick. Thus a chip might be able to mint about 2^{28} or 256 million hashes a second for an average cost (including amortized NREs) of $32, or 2^{23} hashes per second per dollar. If we assume that 40% of our budget goes to the cost of the chips then we have about $4,000,000 or 2^{22} to spend. This means that our engine will compute $2^{23} \times 2^{22} \times 2^{21} = 2^{66}$ hashes each month and we need about 2^{17} chips to do this.

In order to end up with 2^{40} coins made from four hashes that collide in a 44 bit output space we can expect to need to compute at least 2^{44} hashes that pass all of the coin criteria. This means that the tests will need to discard all but one in 2^{22} hashes. This would suggest a prefix z of 22 bits if this were the only test, or a much shorter prefix other hidden criteria were used as well.

Note that valid hashes are generated at a rate of $2^{(44-21)} = 2^{23}$ a second. This is 'slow' enough that we should not have too much of a problem designing a bus that can handle the rate, although it should be noted that this bus will ultimately have 256,000 devices connected to it.

¿From the point of view of physical construction, we might look at the building of "Deep Crack"[1], the machine built to crack DES. We should be able to place 32 chips onto each side of large circuit boards, thus needing about 2^{11} cards. With chips on both side and space for a decent cooling air flow the cards would be able to sit about an inch apart so we might be able to fit two cards into a single "U" of 19 inch rack cabinate. So we need about 1024U of rack space. A floor to ceiling (8 foot) rack holds 44 U so we will need about 25 racks.

---

[1] Application Specific Integrated Circuit.

4.2 Cost of Storage

If we compute 2^{44} hashes that pass the initial tests we will then need to store their values and the preimage value so that they can be sorted. If we allocate 16 bytes for the combination of preimage and hash value (this may be generous but we can be sure we need more than eight bytes) then we need 2^{48} bytes or one quarter of a petabyte or storage. In volume dynamic RAM costs a about one dollar a megabyte so we clearly can not afford to store these values in RAM; it would cost a quarter of a billion dollars to do so. Modern hard discs cost in the region of $10 per gigabyte so if we put all our data onto disc we can get the cost down to about $2.5 million. This is over budget for the storage and sorting but with the sort of bulk discount we might expect from buying 8,000 hard discs we might be able to get the price down to an acceptable level. A third option is to put the data onto tape. Unfortunately these days tape media are not much cheaper than hard discs. A quick search of online catalogues show digital linear tapes, the only media with acceptably large capacity, to be about $2.5 a gigabyte, putting our storage costs at about $900,000 once the cost of the tape drives and loading robots are considered. Of course, switching to a linear medium means that we can not make random accesses to the data.

4.3 Cost of Sorting

As we all know, sorting is an $\mathcal{O}(n \log(n))$ process. In our case n is very big indeed, about 2^{44}, so we're looking are between 2^{59} and 2^{60} comparisons to be made in order to sort our data hashes so that we can find the collisions.

Rivest suggests that the data could be sorted using tape sort methods. In such a scheme the 2^{48} bytes of data, representing the 2^{44} items to be sorted, would be written to 2^{14} tapes each holding about 16 gigabytes. A set of machines, each with 32 tape drives (16 for input and 16 for output) would stream data in in parallel from all the drives and send each datum to one of the output drives on the basis of four bits of the entry. After each pass all the data on any given output tape have the same value in the chosen bits and once all the tapes have been processed in such batchs the tapes are swaped around and the process is repeated. Since 4 bits of value are sorted for in each pass each tape will need to undergo 11 passes, and we have about 175,000 tape passes to carry out the sort. Tape drives can read a tape in about an hour.

Our budget for sorting is about $2,000,000. A powerful PC with 32 high capacity tape drives will cost about $20,000 one off but might go as low as $10,000 in the quantity we need, so ignoring the cost of the tapes themselves we can afford about 200 machines. With 200 such machines we will be spinning the tapes for about 875 hours, or 5.2 weeks. In practice it will take longer since we have have to move the tapes around but if we can get a bigger discount on our tape drives we might be able to get the sorting time within a month.

4.4   Heat and Power

We have 256,000 custom chips runing at high speed, 6400 high capacity tape drives rolling flat out, another 200 processors working on the sort, and a set of tape moving robots moving a tape ever 0.5 seconds. Not only is this a monstrous construction, it is going to use a huge amount of power.

A 100,000 gate custom CMOS chip, running at 64MHz, using a $0.18\mu m$ process, will consume about 2 watts. 2^{17} of them will consume a little over half a megawatt. A high performance tape drive, in the worst case (and this is, indeed, the worst case), consume about 30 watts. 6,400 of them will consume 192,000 watts. Add to this the necessary bus drivers, the sort processors and all the "glue" circuitry and it looks likely that the whole edifice will consume in the region of a megawatt while running.

Of course the mint does not really *consume* a megawatt as it transforms it from one form to another. To be precise it converts the electrical energy coming, mosting into heat but with a not insignificant amount of sound. Removing the megawatt of heat from the room housing the mint will require the further consumption of another megawatt of electricity or, EPA permitting, the dumping of the heat into a nearby river.

Assuming for the moment that we use air conditioning, and thus can expect to use upward of 1.5 megawatts of electricity, the cost of around $1.25 million a year.

4.5   Cost of Distribution

There is one final cost to consider in minting coins with a value of only $0.001 and this is the cost of distribution. These coins take up about 320 bits (for a four way collision on an 80 bit pre-image). This means that a 1.5MB/s T1 line can only move $4.80 a second. Using a protocol with only small overheads we need a couple of 155MB/s OC3 lines simply to send our 2^{40} coins out during the course of the month. In practice the overheads of the payment protocol will at least double this and various issues to do with the Internet Protocols will probably double this again.

5   All Your Eggs in One Basket

It is rare for a large quantity of cash to be kept in one place. Indeed, it is exceedingly rare to keep more than a few million dollars in one place, all protected by the same security system, since it is often said that "every man has his price" and entrusting a vast value to one system makes a very enticing target. In fact the only places that the authors know of in which one billion dollars in barer devices ever reside under one security system are in national precious metal reserves.

Given this fact, it is a very unfortunate feature of MicroMint that, in order for the system to be practical, all the value must reside in the same place at some point in the production process. The problem is that in order to sort the hash values they all need to be brought together in the same place. While the sorting process can be carried out in on encrypted copies of the data (we are only testing for equality) they would all need to be encrypted under the same key and that key would need to be known to all the distribution devices.

MicroMint can be split into a number of mints, each minting a fraction of the coins, but by the nature of the one-way functions being used in the minting process the only reduction in size at each mint is in the storage. Each mint will still need to carry out the full set of hash computations even if it one stores and sorts a subset.

Given these limitations it would seem that a practical MicroMint would have to be build in, for instance, a Marines base outside Knoxville, TN, rather like the US government's gold repository.

6   A More Practical Alternative?

Given the problems with MicroMint, are there alternatives that would do the job better? We think yes.

MicroMint was designed a number of years ago from the viewpoint that public key based cash systems were too computationally intensive to be useful for small value transactions. Times have changed and the cost of processing has gone down a great deal since 1995. It should also be noted that MicroMint does not even try to offer some of the benefits of the most costly digital cash schemes and public key based systems can be designed to offer better speed than Chaum's blind cash.

6.1   Rabin Signatures

The main benefit of MicroMint is the speed with which coins can be verified as authentic, at the cost of taking a great deal of effort to generate in the first place. To verify a MicroMint coin we need to compute four hashes and carry out a few comparisons. Depending on the type of hash function we can expect this to take between several hundred and a few thousand processor cycles on a modern PC.

If we look at designing a public key based coin system from the same viewpoint, that verification cost is paramount, then the Rabin signature scheme stands out as an obvious choice. Rabin signatures are based on the fact that taking the square root of a number modulo a composite number is very hard if you do not know the factorization of the modulus and relatively easy if you do. It also relies on the fact that checking if a value is indeed the square root of another value is very simple. In fact to test if $a^2 = b \pmod{n}$ takes just one modulo multiplication, or given suitable precomputation using a known modulus, just three standard multiplications and a handful of additions and subtractions.

¿From the point of view of "minting" Rabin signatures, if the factorization of n is known then taking a signature is only factionally more expensive than a standard RSA signature.[2] Given that off the shelf hardware can be bought

---

[2] The extra cost comes from having to check on average three different forms of the signature padding before a quadratic root is found.

for a few thousands of dollars that will not only produce 700 RSA signatures a second (or 1.8 billion a month) with a 768 bit modulus but also keep the key with a level of security suitable for banking applications, it seems that minting a requisite number of coins at a reasonable cost will not be hard.

6.2   Signatures verses MicroMint

While we feel that the idea of using Rabin signatures in place of MicroMint needs more analysis it is useful to take a quick look at the the two schemes side by side to see how the implementations compare.

Cost of Computation. One square root needs to be taken per coin. This costs the same as an RSA signature plus a tiny overhead to check (on average three times) to find a padding which gives a quadratic residue. If we pick $p, q = 3 \mod 4$ then we can use off the shelf RSA hardware trivially and not have to build a custom chip. At the time of writing Broadcom have chips that will deliver just under 2000 768 bit square roots per second and this will be up to 10,000 by the 3rd quarter of 2001. Cost is totally linear with the number of coins minted. For 10^{12} coins a month we need 193 chips and about 7 PC and the component cost will be able $30,000 plus some storage.

Cost of Storage. Micromint usually uses about half the valid hashes in the final valid coins. If the signatures are 96 bytes as opposed to about 64 for MicroMint then the signature based system uses about 75% as much storage in total. Note that since the signature scheme supports message recovery there is no need to store any ancillary information with the coins whereas their might be with MicroMint. In fact we may be able to generate the coins on the fly since we don't have to have them all together to sort. Also note that there are no specific access requirements at all and that the storage can be distributed with ease.

Power. Given the ability to compute 2000 768 bit modulo square roots per second, and a need for 10^{12} of these to be computed each month, we need 193 Broadcom chips (or about 40 of the version out in the Q3 2001) The existing chip uses about 3 watts; we can fit eight on a full length PCI card and fit 4 PCI cards in a PC, adding about 100 watts to the 300 watts of a standard PC. We need 6.03 PCs so we can use seven and as long as we don't get a failure on the first day of the month we have a useful standby. The total power consumption is less than three kilowatts. Note that the seven machines can be on seven different sites so the cooling is unlikely to be a major issue.

Distribution. This is basically the same as for MicroMint and the signature based coins. If we use 768 bit coins it is a little worse for signatures but not by as much as a factor of two. Of course, it can be distributed.

Double Spend Detection. It should be noted that the double spend detection is also much easier with the signature based scheme since we have message recovery so we can keep a unique, sequential serial number inside the coin and just use a bit field somewhere to tell is a coin a has been spent. For MicroMint we actually need to know at very least the hash output value of each spent tuple. This means that MicroMint's double spend detection will use several tens of times as much storage and will almost certainly be several orders of magnitude more expensive to operate.

7   Conclusions

Building a large scale MicroMint, or perhaps we should call it a MegaMint, is on the verge of practicality. If a bank was willing to devote a huge amount of resources up front to building a mint then it would not be beyond the limits of todays technology. That said, it is not clear that it will ever be economical to do so. The cost of the initial mint construction is only the beginning of the story. The mint will cost a fortune to run and it will need to be replaced with larger, more complex mints as technology improves the abilities of the attackers. The MicroMint is one rare case where Moore's Law works against the users of technology rather than for them. Basing the security of the system on winning an arms race leads inevitably to spiraling costs.

Having considered the practical issues surrounding building MicroMint we belive that it is not the right way to make micropayments. A coin system based on cryptographically hard problems, rather than big iron, seems to have many advantages over MicroMint both in terms of the complexity of the system and of its long term security. In particular, we feel that public key cryptography can now be used to mint micropayment coins efficiently, something that perhaps was not the case when the MicroMint scheme was originally proposed.

Acknowledgments

I would like to thank Zully Ramzan for his initial design specification for a production MicroMint since to a large extent this paper started life as a critique of that design. I would also like to thank Bob Hettinga for offering me the opportunity to examine that design with a view to building it, and for accepting my opinion when I declined to build that mint. Finally I would like to thank both Ron Rivest and Adi Shamir for putting up with my criticizing their work and for the constructive comments that they have fed back to me.

References

1. J. Gillmore, editor. *Cracking DES: Secrets of Encryption Research, Wiretap Politics & Chip Design.* O'Reilly & Associates, 1998.
2. Ronald L. Rivest and Adi Shamir. Payword and micromint: Two simple micropayment schemes. (A preliminary version has appeared in CryptoBytes 3,1 (Spring 1996), pages 7–11. The full version is posted by Rivest on the Web.), 1995.

Protecting Digital Rights

Yair Frankel

TechTegrity L.L.C
P.O. Box 2125, Westfield, NJ 07091
yfrankel@techtegrity.com, yfrankel@cryptographers.com

Abstract. The Internet has made it possible to distribute and exchange various forms of digital media (e.g., music, video, etc.) cheaply. End-users now have an effective, low cost means to distribute, search and obtain digital content. Some end-users now even expect the content to be free, causing the intellectual property to holders find new approaches to obtain revenues from the use of the content. As new technology is being developed to make it easier to obtain digital content, a fast growing industry is forming to control the use of digital content. Here we discuss the Financial Cryptography 2001 panel on protecting digital rights.

1 Introduction

As the transmission of copyrighted material through the Internet proliferates, controlling the distribution of digital content has become a difficult balancing act of protecting the rights of the copyright holders, distributors and end-users. Companies in the digital rights management industry are now proposing various digital rights protection technologies to control and monitor the trusted exchanges of digital content over digital networks. To date there are numerous technology solutions on the market and many more are expected to be available soon. Many solutions take very different approach. Some of these technologies take a proactive approach by granting the recipient rights to access content yet safeguard the content from individuals without the necessary permissions. Other technologies enable the monitoring of the content's usage and transfers. Many times solution providers mix technologies to obtain a comprehensive solution.

Most digital rights protection solutions attempt to resolve to some extent *content providers*, *end-users* and *legal* concerns. For the *end-user*, whether a consumer or corporation, a solution must produce minimal markup to the end product's price and it should not require costly equipment or software to use. The end-user further desires a solution that is easy to learn and use. The solution must work well with a multitude of media technologies. The *content provider* requires an enabling solution that is robust, scalable, extensible and secure solution. It must be a solution that works well within the business's existing infrastructure and the infrastructures of its corporate partners. The solution must justify its cost. Finally, the technology must satisfy *legal and regulatory requirements*. In the United States, it is essential that it must meet fair use provisions. It must protect the rights of copyright holders. It may require some form of privacy

P. Syverson (Ed.): FC 2001, LNCS 2339, pp. 51–53, 2002.

preservation since some solutions transmit user demographic information as part of their process.

The panel consisted of representatives from several technology providers each with its own unique approach to digital rights protection. Four of the panelists have provided additional papers which have been included in these proceedings[1].

- Barbara Fox, Microsoft Inc.
- David W. Kravitz, Wave Systems Corp.
  Aspects of digital rights management and the use of hardware security devices
- Scott Moskowitz, Blue Spike Inc.
  A Solution to the Napster(tm) phenomenon: Why value cannot be created absent the transfer of subjective data
- Tomas Sander, Intertrust Technologies STAR Lab
  Golden times for digital rights management
- Jeremy Wyant, NTRU Cryptosystems
  Applicability of public key cryptosystems to digital rights management applications

The panelists were provided with several questions to discuss from a technical as well as a business perspective. They were asked: What are the different approaches to protect digital rights? What is the efficacy of various technologies under different medias? What is acceptable from a consumer perspective? What is required of a technical solution which is cost effective yet sufficiently strong to prevent theft of media? What is needed for the wide acceptance of any technology? What is currently being piloted or in production to demonstrate success or deficiencies of various approaches (i.e., what are the lessons learned to date)?

The panelists discussed the various technical solution that their companies offered. As we noted, there are diverse approaches which present many opportunities for technology companies. It was particularly interesting the implications of the various technology solutions to user adoption, scalability for market penetration, cost effectiveness, etc.

The interplay of technology with model is very interesting. For instance, there exists efforts that require a secure hardware solution. With these solutions the hardware provides "safety" for a third parties content rather than providing efficient processing. Similar ideas have been seen for electronic payments. We have yet to see if consumers will accept such an approach as well as whether the distribution of any popular content will be limited to this form of protection.

An important issue to still be resolved is the fair use provisions. The balance between the end-users rights and those of the intellectual property rights holders will be interesting.

While we did not have the opportunity to see all of the existing approaches, we were able to see a small portion of the diversity of the solutions. As has happened with many other industries there are many proprietary technologies

---

[1] The panelist's papers have not been reviewed by the organizers or the program committee.

at the start of the industries acceptance and growth. Standardization has yet to occur for digital content protection though we should expect to witness some convergence in the future. The future looks very promising for digital rights protection technology from a business and scientific perspective.

Acknowledgments

I would like to thank the panelists for their participation in this panel. I would also like to thank the audience members for their questions and interest.

Aspects of Digital Rights Management and the Use of Hardware Security Devices

David W. Kravitz

Wave Systems Corp.
P.O. Box 3543, Princeton, NJ 08543
+1 609-750-6880 (voice), +1 609-750-1480 (fax)
dkravitz@wavesys.com

1 Conditional Access: Controlling Content while Attracting Customers and Earning Revenue

Consider a conditional access module, or CAM, which decrypts (or descrambles) content using its knowledge of conditional access (CA) keys [6]. The CA-descrambled content is communicated to a set-top box (STB) to enable display. The alternative model in which the CAM or smart card acts as a permissioning device only, which transfers content-descrambling keys to the STB, may have lesser processing and data-rate requirements. However, successful attack under this latter model may not necessitate compromise of the CAM itself. The definition of successful attack varies depending on several factors. Localized forms of piracy may be harder to monitor, and thus control, but also should be of less concern to the providers of the legitimate infrastructure. In particular, unauthorized replay of rented content which does not result in additional revenue to the legitimate provider is qualitatively different than, say, taking delivery on two washing machines when only one was paid for. There is a fundamental distinction, however, between a consumer who pays the legitimate rental price once and reaps further play without further payment, and a large-scale pirate who compromises content and provides the ability for consumers to play content which does not result in payment to the legitimate provider proportional to the number of effective consumers of that content. In the case that there is a considerable difference between the rental price and outright purchase price of content, that is not to say that every consumer who is willing to pay the initial rental price and cheat the provider out of further revenue for any additional play would be willing to pay the full purchase price if cheating were not a reasonable alternative. Consequently, it is difficult to measure revenue lost to piracy. The more options that the legitimate provider offers to consumers, such as rent-to-own content of enduring value and live broadcast of highly-perishable content such as sporting events, the harder it may be for large-scale pirates to compete effectively as surrogate providers, although this may come at the expense of additional complexity in implementation or user interface. If high-valued content is (legitimately) offered to consumers only through DRM-controlled systems, consumers may be willing to tolerate a certain level of inconvenience if justified by

P. Syverson (Ed.): FC 2001, LNCS 2339, pp. 54–58, 2002.

the perceived value. The computation of expected profit accruing to large-scale pirates should take into account the risk of capture and prosecution.

The large-scale pirate may be willing to undergo very considerable expense in order to compromise a CAM, if this can be parlayed into a business venture which does not entail the compromise of each individual consumer's CAM. While using distinct keys for each short burst of content can affect the difficulty of cryptanalysis, compromise of a working CAM will yield all keys until revocation of the CAM. Furthermore, non-invasive measures such as differential power analysis [4] may recover a long-term key used by the CAM to recover the short-term content keys. Security measures which rely on collusion-resistance [1] may be circumnavigated by the theft or anonymous purchase of multiple "copies" of security components such as CAMs and STBs. Probing [5] or other invasive techniques, which may result in the destruction of many CAMs before successful reverse engineering or key compromise, can also benefit from the availability of multiple units. A service-provider administered distribution and registration operation, such as employed in home-installed cable, is less convenient but offers a margin of security.

If a particular STB unit is compliant, it can be used to reject a cloned (or counterfeit) copy of a CAM by having the infrastructure limit the number of STB units with which a particular CAM unit is allowed to interact. If each legitimate CAM is uniquely keyed for this purpose in the factory, when a compliant STB is registering with the service provider, the service provider can make a decision whether the association or "pairing" of that STB with a particular CAM ID is permissible. The CAM ID may correspond to a certified public key, where the associated private key is held by that CAM. This CAM public key can be used in a challenge-response protocol with the STB to detect and reject the substitution of the CAM by one with which the STB was not paired. The large-scale pirate may instruct customers to plug their legitimately paired CAM into the pirate-provided cloned CAM. The intent here would be for the legitimately paired CAM to handle the challenge-responses, and the pirate-provided CAM to use its knowledge of the conditional access keys to descramble the content. This is particularly applicable in the case of content legitimately distributed on hard media, where all copies of a given title are encrypted the same way to minimize pressing costs. The challenge-responses should be interwoven into the content in such a way that the pirate's customers "pay" enough so that use of the pirate's services is not considered worthwhile [2]. One form of "payment" may be to induce shutdowns to avoid accumulation of penalty points, in the case where the STB does not use non-volatile memory to run the protocol. Payment may also take the form of a significant portion of content being delivered garbled to the display device in order to reduce the chance of getting caught by the legitimate service provider. A couple of cautionary notes apply here: Use of a paid-up subscription key to descramble pay-per-view content, thus resulting in garbled plaintext, may not be a penalty if the pirate-provided CAM feeds the properly descrambled content into another port, such as one intended for input of a digital camcorder signal which is not under conditional access control since it is intended to handle user-generated content. Secondly, penalties which are too severe (such as the legitimate CAM or service provider mandating an extensive period of suspension of service by refusing to process signals as required by the compliant STB, if the legitimate CAM suspects cheating), thus turning away potential subscribers of the legitimate service rather than bringing them back into the fold, or which have a non-negligible probability of false-alarms, can render the system untenable.

In an attempt to restrict the proliferation of non-compliant units of STBs, the service provider can aggressively enforce licensing of STB technology, such as proprietary tuners or disc readers.

Mandating periodic communications between the service provider backend system and the CAM in order to keep compliant CAMs alive provides an audit capability. Another way to tie the CAMs to the backend is to have the CAMs learn new keys through communication with the backend. Such point-to-point acquisition of keys, unlike tuning in to satellite broadcast, can be monitored and limited by the backend. This means that devices, such as modified CAM clones sold to customers by a pirate, cannot be loaded with all the content keys initially because they are not known by the pirate, and cannot call in to the backend without being detected because of the high multiplicity of calls associated with the same CAM ID. The implication is that customers who use pirate devices will have to maintain a long-term relationship with the pirate in order to avail themselves of content encrypted under newer keys. This increases the complexity, cost, and risk of the pirate's service offering.

2   Piracy for Profit

Measures such as pairing STBs to CAM IDs, enforced licensing of proprietary STB technology, auditability of CAMs by the service provider backend, and a capability for CAM renewal by distributing upgraded units which can be installed by consumers via an accessible slot in the STB, can make it substantially more difficult for pirates to leverage off the legitimate infrastructure in establishing their own customer base. Distribution of plaintext content by the pirate can be unwieldy or infeasible, and may run counter to profitability in that this can easily spawn second-hand piracy. A pirate who is interested in operating for profit would like to protect his investment in successfully attacking CAMs or otherwise gaining access to content keys. He would like to protect this investment through tamper-resistant hardware analogously to the perspective held by the legitimate service provider. Other issues which a pirate may face include the difficulty in anticipating the legitimate next-generation security architecture which may force the pirate to periodically re-distribute hardware to customers, and the degree of confidence the pirate has in his ability to reverse-engineer the legitimate CAMs (potentially missing latent design features) so that this knowledge can be used to modify legitimate CAMs or produce clones which behave appropriately except to have certain features turned off, such as logging of content play, calling in to the legitimate backend, and automatic shutdown. Latent design features may be activated to disable pirate devices while maintaining the efficacy of compliant devices [7]. In some instances, the pirate may also have to support legacy content in order to remain competitive with the legitimate service provider.

3   Interface Protection: Combating Local Piracy

As a detection mechanism for cloned or counterfeit STBs, a pairing between the STB and CAM can be initiated through communication with the service provider and used to lend assurance to a compliant CAM that it is communicating (valuable usable-form content) to only an approved STB unit or used to revoke an STB unit by notifying the CAM that it should suspend communication to that unit. This can be accomplished by pairing the CAM ID with an STB ID, where the STB ID corresponds to a certified public key (with the associated private key being held by that STB). The STB public key is used by the CAM in such a way that leads to either explicit detection by the CAM of lack of knowledge of the private key by the STB, or implicit failure of the STB to receive usable-form content because it is encrypted under a locally derived interface protection key protected under the (long-term) STB key. Furthermore, compliant STBs can be configured so as to require periodic refreshes of local interface protection keys in order to thwart free replay of content, where transmission of the content under the refreshed interface protection key signifies a logged event.

4   Logging and Playback

One of the functions of a digital rights management (DRM) system, and of a CAM, in particular, is to handle the logging of content access. The CAM and STB may remain oblivious of the actual billing policy, and the challenge-response regime, if any, used between the CAM and STB to effect verification of CAM compliance may be designed to operate without requiring such knowledge. Example metrics of logging are time and footage (for static content), and bullets (for games). The client-side system (consisting of CAM and STB, for example) may upload logs for out-of-band payment processing, or may decrement locally held funds. The services of a payment clearinghouse may be utilized. Locally held (client-side) payment records may indicate current access privileges status and may affect pricing of future purchases or rentals. A possible tool to use in an attempt to handle the wide-scale distribution of illicit plaintext, is to make the display of content dependent on the CAM's authorization to a compliant monitor (with which it is paired) that watermarked content bears a local license [3]. Note that there is an analogy between securing a (static-) content player (such as an STB, or application running on a PC) via a tamper-resistant transaction checker (such as a CAM) and securing a game executable via a peripheral device, or dongle. Although an application running in a PC or one running in a STB can each be "personalized" with unique keying material, adversarial extraction of this data from a STB may require an action such as reading out flash (by the customer), while exploitation of this data within a PC application may be able to be accomplished through the loading of rogue software distributed by a pirate.

5   Consolidated Hardware Deployment

There is a viable alternative to each DRM application provider distributing devices initialized with unique secrets (keys) and containing adequate non-volatile memory for state data:

"Point" solutions can be replaced by "shared" secure hardware devices serviced by a backend infrastructure which permissions and tracks the installation of multiple applications, thus simulating the multiple dongle scenario. This can be done in such a way as to preserve user privacy and handle revocation, while ensuring that the critical code of individualized copies of applications executes within compliant devices. This backend infrastructure is distinct from that set up and used by each individual service provider to allow communication with users of the applications. The goal is for each application to inherit the security of hardware while maintaining the simplicity in distribution and ease of use of software.

Wave Systems (http://www.wave.com) has been extensively involved in this area.

References

1. B. Chor, A. Fiat, and M. Naor, "Tracing Traitors," *Advances in Cryptology: Proceedings of Crypto'94*, Springer-Verlag, pp. 257-270, August 1994.
2. D. Goldschlag and D. Kravitz, "Pirate Card Rejection," *PreProceedings of Cardis 98 - Third Smart Card Research and Advanced Application Conference*, Louvain-la-Nueve, Belgium, September 14-16, 1998.
3. D. Goldschlag and D. Kravitz, "Beyond Cryptographic Conditional Access," *Proceedings of the USENIX Workshop on Smartcard Technology*, Chicago, Illinois, pp. 87–91, USENIX Association, May 10-11, 1999.
4. P. Kocher, J. Jaffe, and B. Jun, "Differential Power Analysis," *Advances in Cryptology: Proceedings of Crypto'99*, Springer-Verlag, August 1999.
5. O. Kommerling and M. Kuhn, "Design Principles for Tamper-Resistant Smartcard Processors," *Proceedings of the USENIX Workshop on Smartcard Technology*, Chicago, Illinois, pp. 9–20, USENIX Association, May 10-11, 1999.
6. D. Kravitz and D. Goldschlag, "Conditional Access Concepts and Principles," *Proceedings of the Third International Conference on Financial Cryptography*, Lecture Notes in Computer Science 1648, pp. 158–172, Springer-Verlag, 1999.
7. D. Sims, "DirecTV Hacks Back," *The Industry Standard, TheStandard.com*, http://biz.yahoo.com/st/010129/21749.html, January 29, 2001.

A Solution to the Napster Phenomenon: Why Value Cannot Be Created Absent the Transfer of Subjective Data

Scott Moskowitz

Blue Spike, Inc.
16711 Collins Avenue No. 2505, Miami Beach, Florida 33160
scott@bluespike.com

1 Introduction

The efficacy of various copyright management systems will depend largely on keeping the "security" out of view from consumers while enabling clear responsibility to be attributed to the content being traded. Consumers have clearly rejected access restriction and registration protocols as currently deployed. The general failure of such systems is best represented by the widespread acceptance of Napster and the difficulty with implementations of digital rights management ("DRM") systems on consumer PCs. Further, ignoring the historical notion of "fair use" and the "first sale doctrine" serves to obscure the value attributed to content. Success in commercializing the exchange of media content must focus on value in the media; the file format must be relegated to convenience.

The presence of a content identification watermark is the hook to facilitate a number of potential markets surrounding the use of music, and other media, by consumers. Some of these uses include: monitoring of broadcast playback by performing rights organizations ("PROs"), premium services for peer-to-peer music distribution networks (a commercial Napster), and consumer content identification services (like Gracenote/CDDB for individual tracks). The cost on a computational and resource basis is lower than competing identification systems using so-called signal fingerprinting. Furthermore, the cost is borne by each client in a distributed manner, avoiding processing and bandwidth bottlenecks, similar to the way that Napster distributes storage.

In this document, we will lay out how several of the decoding systems work, and why watermarks are a necessary feature of any workable market for the commercial exchange of content.

2 Broadcast Monitoring

At present, a variety of technologies are used to monitor the playback of sound recordings on broadcast outlets. Digital watermarking is a better alternative to all of the deployed technologies because it couples automated detection with extremely high reliability. A single PC-based monitoring station can continuously

P. Syverson (Ed.): FC 2001, LNCS 2339, pp. 59–63, 2002.

monitor up to 16 channels of audio broadcasts 24 hours a day with no human interaction. The results of the monitoring are assembled at a central server and made available to interested licensees, such as the PROs, for a fee equivalent to the price they currently pay for monitoring data. Unlike currently deployed systems, there is an extremely low statistical chance of misdetection. Additionally, the system can distinguish between otherwise identical versions of a song which are watermarked for different distribution channels, further improving the quality of the reported data.

Deployment of such a system requires two things: a monitoring infrastructure and the watermarks to be present in the content. Leading monitoring companies have developed and deployed extensive infrastructures that have been designed to identify certain encoded audio and video signals as they are distributed. Encoding the music or video is planned by all major entertainment companies.

3   Peer-to-Peer File Sharing

The immense popularity of Napster, in combination with recent legal rulings, presents a challenge: how to commercialize a file-sharing network. Watermark-based content identification is the solution. Each track is identified by the client's computer using a watermark detector. The identity of the track is then used to filter the server search engine, so that each subscription level only provides access to the allowed content. Here is how it works in action:

3.1   Encoding

Encoding happens at the mastering level of each sound recording, as currently contemplated by the major label music companies. Each song is assigned a unique ID from the identifier database, and that ID is encoded in the sound recording after all other mastering processes are completed, but prior to the song being prepared for a specific distribution channel. To enhance imperceptible encoding of those few audio recordings that require special processing, human-assisted watermark key generation is readily available.

3.2   Decoding

Decoding happens each time a new song is made available on a Napster user's computer. A highly efficient background process decodes each sound recording, and queries Napster's main server as to the status of the selected track. The server would respond that the sound recording falls into one of the following categories:

Uncontrolled: The sound recording either does not contain a watermark, or the copyright owner has chosen to make the song freely available to all users. In this example, the sound recording will be freely available to pass through the Napster server.

Premium: The sound recording is part of a subscription package and is made available only to the premium subscriber of that subscription package.

Restricted: The sound recording is not authorized to be shared on the main server and will not be available for file sharing purposes.

4   A Real World Example

Alice is a Napster user. She has a hard drive directory of audio files which her Napster application monitors. She rips a new CD into that folder and starts the Napster application. The application reads the watermark on each track to identify those tracks. The new tracks, like all on her computer, are available for her own, unlimited, use.

When Alice connects to the Napster server, her computer broadcasts the identity of all of the sound recordings in her shared folder. These are a mix of uncontrolled, premium, and restricted content, as determined by the server at that time. For the new tracks that were recently added to her folder, the server identifies that one song is premium, and the others are uncontrolled.

Bob is a Napster user, and is looking for music. He is a premium subscriber. The Napster server makes the uncontrolled and premium music on Alice's computer available to Bob.

Carl is another Napster user, but not yet a subscriber. He sees only the uncontrolled music when he logs on to the Napster server.

This system provides the minimum impact on Napster users, while maintaining the safeguards necessary for the sharing of copyrighted material. Each user is not prevented from using restricted songs on their own computer, since in most cases they will have purchased them legally, for instance on CD. Those songs are simply not available to others against the wishes of the copyright owner. No other approach to this rampant problem of unfettered file sharing is technically reasonable. When combined with technologies such as a Blue Spike Scrambler, which encrypts data in such a manner as to retain perceptibility but distort the audio track in a tiered fashion (a predetermined key combined with a transfer function), copyright owners can estimate the highest optimized mix of quality thresholds demanded by consumers. Users can purchase individualized keys (essentially tied to their public key for purchase options) based on observable music and reasonably open access which improve the quality of the music. A reduction in server overhead and cost, as well as maintenance of recognizable but secure audio files, combined with digital watermarking, represent the state of the art in addressing file sharing. This also allows for multiple subscription levels based on content types and quality settings. The need to store multiple versions, both compressed and uncompressed, in an encrypted state is likewise reduced. Commercially, owners or aggregators of content will be able to estimate payment and bandwidth resources in real time.

In the event that the sound recordings are not available with watermarking, application of signal recognition (fingerprinting) offers additional coverage. A unique abstract of the selected sound recording is taken and its signal characteristics are compared to an associated database. This comparison will identify the name of the performance if the sound recording is included in the database. Simple hashes or checksums of the audio file are ineffective given the range of reasonable alterations conceivable. Predetermination of the types or amount of signal manipulations expected on the audio file can be used to create a better "signal abstract" (which may be stored publicly or at a certification authority to point out authorized versions of the recording) than currently available signal fingerprinting applications.

The signal recognition application is primarily useful for legacy, unwatermarked, material. This specifically limits the scope of the fingerprint database, which is crucial to maintaining the feasibility of fingerprinting. At present, no company has demonstrated fingerprint technology which can scale to cover the daily increase in available musical content.

5 Consumer Song Identification

Gracenote (formerly CDDB) offers a hugely successful system to identify physical CD's based on their Table of Contents. The hole in the system is that it is useless for content that arrives as an individual digital track. An MP3 found on a peer-to-peer system can arrive without any linkage to the distributor or artist. Watermarking can fix this, allowing an anonymous track to be reassociated with its creator, and facilitating sales by all of the members of the value chain.

An inexpensive watermark detector would be added as a feature or plug-in to all popular music players, just as the present Gracenote software is included. Any incoming track could be decoded, and a resulting query could be made to a server which not only identifies the track, but places it in a sales context for the up-sell of all manner of associated items, from other tracks by the same artist, to concert tickets and merchandise.

Best of all, the consumer's identification act also provides critical data on the use and popularity of each track. Here the watermark is crucial, because it can distinguish between identical tracks obtained from different sources, thus informing the viability and market potential of different modes of distribution. Finally, if the distribution channel is correctly identified, the consumer can be up-sold the appropriate items. For example, if they recorded the song from an Internet broadcast, sell them the CD. If they already have the CD, sell them a different CD, concert tickets, or a t-shirt. And in all cases, create a two-way relationship which benefits both parties.

6 Conclusion

Consumers have created and embraced particular usage models for music, which include CD copying, file-swapping, and format indifference. They expect to be able to play music on any of a number of device platforms, from stereos to computers to cell phones. Any system of music distribution which ignores or significantly impedes these models will meet with limited success.

More pointedly, the economics of traditional notions of DRM are questionable at best. The cost of recognition, promoting or otherwise creating demand for information content is separate from responsibility once that information content has been transacted. Access restriction threatens the viability of the historic reality that a few copyrights account for a lion's share of revenues. In 1999, for instance, only 0.03% of compact discs accounted for over a quarter of all revenues ("The Heavenly Jukebox", *Atlantic Monthly*, September 2000). Similar market realities apply to all forms of entertainment, limiting any supposition that we can predetermine the success of any given content release.

Arguments that "superdistribution" can be supported also lack any real world examples; in fact, financial success generally demonstrates models seeking monopolistic or oligopolistic control of profitable intellectual property. As with physical media distribution emphasis is better placed on enabling differentiations between authorized and pirated versions of a given media file copy. Concatenating a digital signature to a media file, a key-based digital watermark, is the most appropriate means to enable markets for the open, accessible exchange of media content. Ultimately, key-based digital watermarks enable a balance to be struck between privacy and piracy.

The key to successful commerce using these usage models is appropriate identification and incentivization. Watermarking is the most appropriate tool to enable seamless identification. Essentially enabling receipts for information commerce. It is the conduit through which the business of music will be conducted, now and in the future.

Acknowledgments

Special thanks to both Mike Berry and Peter Cassidy for their contributions to this work.

Golden Times for Digital Rights Management?

Tomas Sander

InterTrust Technologies
STAR Lab, 4750 Patrick Henry Drive
Santa Clara, CA 95054, USA
sander@intertrust.com

Abstract. Music, books and video can be distributed very cost effectively over the Internet to end consumers. As bandwidth capacity is
growing and getting cheaper, the economics is so clearly on the side of
digital distribution that distribution of digital goods on the Internet will
surely happen. Digital Rights Management (DRM) technology makes
it possible to manage all the intellectual property aspects of electronic
distribution and also the exchange of value for receiving digital goods.
Thus it is a key component of any electronic marketplace for information
goods. In this paper I will point to some of the reasons that digital distribution (and thereby DRM) will be successful in a mass market; point
to some common misconceptions about DRM; argue that we have most
of the core technology for an attractive, yet still reasonably secure, DRM
system in place; and discuss how security and privacy features can and
should be implemented.

1 Business Factors for the Success of DRM

1.1 Attractive Business Models

One of the most appealing features of digital distribution is that it enables
business models for the world of information goods that are potentially very
attractive to consumers. The best example is subscription-based access to music
catalogs. Experience shows that consumers embrace flat rate services and often
prefer them to metered services (cf.[2]). Realizing flat-fee access to a complete
music catalog in the physical world would be rather difficult. Mailing physical
CDs (or having consumers pick them up in stores) seems to be cumbersome and
not cost-effective. Record companies have partnered with technology companies
to offer these novel services very soon. When these subscription-based services
are in place and widely promoted by the record industry, this will probably be
the first mass deployment of legitimate distribution of digital goods - and thereby
also of DRM technology that provides the infrastructure to make it all work.

1.2 Commitment of the Content Industry

The commitment of the major players in the content industry to make their
premium content available on the Internet is one of the most important success

P. Syverson (Ed.): FC 2001, LNCS 2339, pp. 64–74, 2002.

factors for digital distribution. Independently produced music or books are alone unlikely to lead by themselves to a mass market. We have this commitment right now at least in the music industry whereas publishing and video are still in the early stages.

Economic issues caused the commitment of the music industry to take longer than required by the technology. No wonder. Although subscription-based business models promise high revenues, they are radically different from the highly profitable ones the labels engaged in for decades, such as selling individual CDs (and previously LPs) - and it utilizes the unknown territory of the Internet with its piracy worries. Ironically the success of "piracy based" technology companies such as Napster helped to force a rapid reappraisal. Firstly, Napster demonstrated that there is a consumer demand for digital goods, once it is offered to them in the form they liked. Secondly, Napster provided a black-market model for digital goods, which threatens to eat into the content companies' revenues. Although Napster and MP3.com and their likes were tamed in court (and eventually bought out by the content industry), it became clear that the best strategy to preempt future black markets is to offer simply a better product. We will argue later in this article that legitimate services will actually be able to offer much better services to consumers than pirate services. Thirdly, there is a danger that content companies that jointly refuse to do business on the Internet could be subject to antitrust accusations. For all these reasons the music industry has started to embrace the new medium and other content industries are likely to follow them soon.

1.3 The Right Price Point

To attract many consumers it is additionally crucial to find the right price point that ensures enough revenue for the content industry while simultaneously being compelling for consumers. To date, online music products, that were offered, have been relatively high priced (e.g., $2 per song) and have not been overly successful. That these prices have been perceived to be too high is at least partially due to the fact that buying bits has not been perceived to be as valuable as buying disks. Once digital purchases are perceived to be as "real" and useful as physical ones, the ability to buy individual tracks online could actually serve the needs of consumers and may be a valuable addition to all-you-can-eat subscription models. Consumers had for example complained that they needed to buy a whole CD with 12 songs although they were only interested in 2 of them. Bundling more and less attractive songs on a CD has been a classical strategy of music marketing and pricing. Offering unbundled content is another indicator that the record industry is seriously considering radical changes to their business models. Many industry observers believe that prices will come down as the music industry gains experience, trust and revenues from the new distribution medium. The added efficiencies of a digital market leave room for that. In another market, announcements by book publishers offering electronic versions of books cheaper than physical copies should promote the adoption of digital books. Prices between $5 - $15 per month for subscription services that have been discussed in the music space promise a successful pricing strategy.

2 Technological Factors for the Success of DRM

2.1 Dependable Digital Rights and Portability

One important requirement for consumer acceptance is to make digital rights dependable and rock-solid. The term "digital rights" denotes the rights a consumer has to use and access specific content. This includes subscription rights, rights to play or view individual pieces of content, rights to access content from various devices, rights to redistribute content, etc. Why should a person pay a few dollars for a bunch of bits, instead of a physical CD? The key is that buying digital goods and the associated rights can be implemented so that consumers enjoy access to the content at least as reliable and convenient as, what they have in the physical world. We don't really want a clunky CD, we really want what a CD allows us to do, - and more. This includes being able to play our digital music on the various devices we own. Thus portability of digital rights among various platforms is important, such as PCs and consumer electronic devices, and in the near future also wireless phones. Equally important are reliable backup mechanisms for digital rights, as this addresses consumer fears about losing their rights due to hardware failures or by buying a new computer.

A key technical tool for these goals of portability and recoverability of digital rights is a "rights locker" architecture. Lockers serve as a central depository for the digital rights a consumer has purchased. Rights, such as individual content rights as well as subscription rights, are uploaded when a consumer purchases them via any of multiple channels, such as web retailers and music stores. Those centrally stored rights can be accessed and used by multiple devices. Lockers are likely to be one of the key enablers for a seamless, interoperable world for the consumption of content, possibly even across the platforms of various technology providers. The ultimate challenge is to bind digital rights to a person, and not to a (set of) device(s). Locker architectures are likely to facilitate desirable goals for end users such as anytime, anywhere access to their content, via car, mobile devices, cell phones, PCs or from a hotel room on another continent. Anytime, anywhere access to all "my" content is impossible to realize in the physical world and might well be another killer app of digital distribution. To implement this vision the DRM client should be portable to multiple devices.

2.2 Ease of Use

Ease of use is another crucial success factor for any mass market product. Unfortunately usability has always been one of the major challenges in computer security. DRM is no exception. Users typically turn off security features because they are too cumbersome or restrictive. In a DRM environment security measures may be perceived to be even more annoying by honest users as they do not add any benefits for them.

Ease of use has been a problem of various first-generation DRM products. Second-generation products have user interfaces on a drag-and-drop level and intuitive mechanisms for presenting offers of digital goods, in short mechanisms without a steep learning curve. Further user authentication mechanisms are required, e.g. to control access to rights stored in a locker. These authentication mechanisms need to be simple and cheap, but still reasonably secure. This is in fact doable. As an example, conventional password identification mechanisms may be enough in practice to control access to rights stored in a digital rights locker. The most significant threat to the overall system security is that users freely share their password with many others. A simple countermeasure is to link access to digital rights to the ability to spend money, e.g. by enabling "one-click shopping" for more digital rights (the locker service will likely have the consumer's credit data anyway for natural business reasons). This will make users think twice before they share their password, but doesn't inconvenience honest users.

For example, a key component of InterTrust's strategy to address usability issues is to move security measures out of the (honest) user's face into the underlying infrastructure. Instead of having complicated and burdensome procedures that need to be followed to OK the transfer of content to other devices, the underlying infrastructure utilizes public-key certificates to determine automatically and transparently whether a device is "good" for this operation. Sound risk management is still possible at this layer by observing and monitoring whether certain suspicious activities occur.

Furthermore users do not like to be unreasonably restricted in what they can do. For example, it may be useful to allow users to burn CDs from their digital music, possibly for an additional charge. This might allow average users (possibly illegally) to redistribute physical CDs on a small scale. However this threat needs to be balanced against the added benefit honest users enjoy by being able to listen to their music in a car CD player and other legacy devices that they already own, and which are not yet electronically and DRM-enabled.

Building an interoperable platform is the key to accomplish ease of use and convenience.

3 DRM and Security

DRM has been traditionally seen as a technology to prevent consumers from unlicensed copying and to enable metered consumption business models, such as pay-per-play. This is far too narrow a view. The goal of DRM technology is to enable an electronic marketplace and to maximize the utility to the total community. This requires that many consumers join such a system, i.e. that they get something they are willing to pay for. DRM is not a restrictive but an enabling technology. Reducing piracy is neither valuable in itself nor commercially an ultimate goal. It is only one of the many measures needed to enable an effective electronic marketplace. Of course, if everything is out there for a free grab there is no point in trying to sell anything. On the other hand, tolerating a certain degree of piracy in a mass market is likely to be much more lucrative than a "piracy free" market that is so secure that it is unattractive or too expensive to join. Requiring consumers to purchase extra hardware may not be acceptable at this time. But security will remain an important feature of DRM technology.

From a risk-management perspective security measures should help to keep a product commercially viable, so losses are manageable and each participant makes a profit. What this means might differ from business model to business model. To support a pay-per-play model, for example, it seems important to prevent a consumer from easily capturing music from one play for "eternal" use. To support a download-and-purchase model this threat could be much less important, but illegal redistribution might be more of a problem. The role of security in the success of a DRM system is often misunderstood, in particular by experts in security and cryptography and by the content industry. This is understandable as (many) security experts tend to focus on the technical aspects alone. Content companies have traditionally fought mightily against piracy; it's their mindset. However, the goal of the share holders of a content company is not to fight piracy, but to make money from the company's creative assets. There is an attitude change in the industry, shifting from requiring 100 % secure solutions for serious deployment to looking for workable solutions. They are recognizing that the DRM system with the greatest consumer acceptance will eventually get the lion share of the market.

A historical analogue is that while piracy in the software market has been publicly fought by the software industry, on the other hand it has often been considered a valuable tool to build market share. The content distribution world seems different. However, one could argue that the pirate service Napster made a splash by creating a sudden demand for digitally delivered music. They hooked millions of new users introducing them to this new technology and benefitting the overall market. Note that typically the adoption of new technologies into the consumer market takes about 10 years (e.g., ATM machines, fax machines, cf. [2])

3.1   Security = Unbreakability ?

Soundness of the security model of a system certainly does not mean unbreakability. A good example is the pay TV industry, which has been constantly under attack. Most of its protection schemes were (quickly) broken. Still pay TV is a big, profitable business. Another example is the DeCSS case. DVD encryption was weak and broken. So how do we evaluate the security of DVDs? A cryptographer might say that it was "broken" and didn't work. However no major cases of piracy via DeCSS have been reported for DVDs, and major studios continue to release new DVDs. Thus a business person might well say that DVD protection worked "sufficiently well". The conclusion is that the soundness of a security model from a business perspective relies on many more factors than just its technical unbreakability.

3.2   Incentives + Security Measures = Commercially Viable System

What we are really interested in is the users' willingness to play by the rules. Security measures help to raise the bar preventing users from circumventing the system. They make it more difficult and time-consuming to get around the system rules. But the function determining users' willingness to play by the rules depends on many more variables than security alone. Attractive pricing, business models, services and ease of use are decisive factors to keep users voluntarily within the system, i.e. they also raise the bar for any intent to circumvent the system. Furthermore, a legitimate service can deliver incentives that a pirate service is unlikely ever to be able to deliver. To give an example: a music distribution service may strike a deal with a wireless provider allowing subscribers to download music to their mobile phone under very favorable terms. A pirate service is unlikely to be able to strike such a deal. Access to music with high quality-of-service guarantees requires a sophisticated infrastructure that pirates can not match.

Encouraging ongoing usage (and thereby payment) of a legitimate service like a subscription service by creating user incentives seems one of the best "security measures" possible. A. Odlyzko weights social and business factors and encouragement of usage as even more important than security measures and legal protection for the successful development of an ecommerce market for digital goods [3].

3.3 Strong Legal Protection Is Likely to Deter Large-Scale Illegitimate Distribution

The early court rulings around Napster and MP3.com seem to show that there is no way to run a large-scale legitimate business using copyrighted content on the Internet without the consent of copyright holders. Large-scale commercial pirate services (that do not claim legitimacy but try to make money from their services) will have no smooth sailing either, as it is usually easy for law enforcement to follow and shut down the money flow on the Internet. (This is certainly true for credit-card payments, the preferred payment method on the Internet, but even anonymous electronic cash wouldn't solve the problems for the pirates as only the payer remains anonymous, while the payee remains known to the bank.) This leaves us in essence with non-commercial entities practicing unlicensed copying and redistribution. Decentralized peer-to-peer systems such as Gnutella or Freenet have technical problems with scalability, search capabilities, true decentralization, bandwidth eaten up by the communication for searching (cf., e.g., [4]) and more generally with quality of service. It is currently an open problem whether a fully distributed P2P service can be built - although the answer is probably yes. However even then it is hard to hide the identity of illegitimate music servers: the same search technology that allows P2P network participants to find content can be and has been converted into tracking technology that can be used by copyright holders to identify (the IP addresses of) users serving unlicensed content. In the end the content industry would need to threaten and sue end consumers or ISPs hosting illegitimate material, instead of suing companies running central servers. One may expect this to happen, if illegitimate distribution in such systems is an economically significant problem for the industry. Although these legal actions alone are unlikely to give a complete solution, they will be another factor driving consumers towards legitimate services.

It should further be noted that "piracy", the unlicensed distribution of content à la early Napster and Gnutella is completely independent of the question of whether or not DRM systems are secure. The CD music master is cheaply available in an unsecure format anyway and can be uploaded to the Internet by anybody. Although secure CD formats have been considered by the industry, the CD is not going to go away any time soon. But even if it did, and even if DRM systems were fully secure, still the analog music output can be captured and be redigitized at a decent quality. Thus the problem of illegal distribution of captured content is here to stay. However, there is currently no reason to assume that a combination of technical, legal and business measures will not suffice to make the majority of consumers choose a good legitimate service over black-market services. The majority of (honest) consumers will benefit from the threat of black markets in an indirect way. To compete with black-market models legitimate services will have to deliver the best possible quality of service at reasonably low prices.

Protection purists might not be satisfied with this and argue for encrypted CDs, secure speakers and watermarking, to deal with the redistribution problem. But they may be losing sight of the market and technical realities. Firstly, secure speakers may be a tough sell, and consumer electronics manufacturers will have little incentive to build and promote these devices. Secondly, watermarking technology is currently insecure and many researchers are pessimistic about the prospect that this will change. But even if watermarking and fingerprinting were safe, would audiophile consumers pay for high quality codecs of, say, Wagnerian operas, where Isolde's arias were depurified by a watermark? We currently don't know. This points again to the potential danger of introducing possibly unpopular security measures. "The surgery was successful, but the patient is dead." The DRM system might be secured, but its market could be killed. Security measures always need to be carefully balanced against their potentially negative effects. Much more real-world experience is needed before the strength of, the need for, and consumer acceptance of these technologies can be reliably predicted.

3.4   On the Security of InterTrust's System

In light of this discussion InterTrust makes it a top priority to provide the best possible security measures for its DRM system, while simultaneously avoiding inconvenience to the user. (InterTrust's DRM system is called Rights/System.)

For this reason InterTrust favors solutions that involve end-to-end encryption wherever possible. The content is essentially encrypted under the public key of the receiver. In the case of leakage of an individual key only content encrypted under this single key is compromised, a relatively small risk. InterTrust provides an infrastructure that manages these public keys. Content (and rights) downloads that have been individualized to the receiver's public keys are further very helpful in building a sound risk management infrastructure at the back end, as it allows monitoring for suspicious activities. For example, if one of the public keys receives too much content without ever initiating a payment, this may raise a red flag. Locker architectures allow for a centralized management of digital rights. Besides adding interesting functionality to a DRM system they are also a valuable addition from a security perspective. They complement the security mechanisms taken at the client side, which is certainly harder to secure. Software tamper resistance measures help to further raise the bar for consumers trying to circumvent such a system.

A further key idea for sound risk management is the concept of renewability (in contrast to unbreakability) of security measures. Renewability allows system operators to frustrate the efforts of pirates greatly, by forcing them to constantly to break into updated systems. This forces not only an arms race on the hackers, but also on their consumers, who have a great interest in a seamless continuation of their (pirate) service. Well-calculated disruption of pirated service had turned out to be a very effective measure in the pay TV industry, making many end consumers turn their back on pirate services, and many commercial pay TV hackers eventually gave up. If distributing hacks of effective security measures is furthermore illegal under the DMCA, this adds a legal leg for any such system to stand on, in addition to its technical measures.

It is essential that a DRM system should not facilitate piracy. This alone is a good reason for the use of point-to-point encryption. Otherwise, consider the case of a global key system, in which the global key is compromised and distributed in hacker software. Then downloaded content, encrypted under this global key by users running the hacker software, could masquerade as legitimate P2P downloads of "protected" files. This makes it harder to identify piracy than in the case where no encryption was used at all. Cleartext MP3 files of pirated material that are posted on the Internet can at least be easily identified as such.

Security measures shouldn't be draconian and don't have to be unbreakable. To be effective they should not be designed so that they have single points of failures, allowing for complete, irreparable breaks, which would make it too easy and convenient for consumers to use pirated software or hardware. Instead they should limit the risks due to key compromises and equally important, they should be renewable. In summary, appropriate security for DRM systems seems to be achievable.

3.5   Cryptographic Techniques

Most of the research in the crypto community related to content protection has been focused on variants of the "global-key" model, such as traitor tracing and broadcast encryption. I call these "global-key" variants because every user possesses a key (included in a tamper-resistant environment) that allows the decryption of all content that has been encrypted until this time. Keys found in pirate devices can be traced back to the leaker (at least they could in an ideal world where we had good user authentication, which we don't) and disabled for decryption of future content. On the downside a compromised key in those systems decrypts all past content, and therefore has a huge risk potential. For distribution of content on physical media like DVDs, the broadcast model seems to be the only feasible one. However this is no longer true in an Internet distribution world, where one can support point-to-point encryption between content servers and consumers very much as done today with SSL. The content (key) is essentially encrypted under the public key of the receiver. End-user devices can also talk to each other using their public keys, enabling offline superdistribution. Disabling bad keys can be done quite efficiently, by employing short-lived certificates. Note that point-to-point encryption achieves the goals of tracing and revocation of keys even more easily than traitor tracing and broadcast encryption methods, without inheriting some of the risks of those global-key methods and their limitations due to practically limited collusion bounds. E.g., the attack mentioned above, in which content downloads in a "protected", but hacked, format masquerade as legitimate downloads or file sharing, is no longer easily to mount. The price to pay is that the infrastructure for these keys needs to be managed. However this seems feasible given the current state of technology, computing power in small devices, and connectivity. The certificate infrastructure that InterTrust provides is also very useful to solve the dual problem to providing security at the client side, namely making sure that a packaging application packages only content it is authorized to package. A garage band may package its own music but not the new Madonna CD. The certificates of misbehaving packagers can be revoked, limiting the damage they can cause.

Point-to-point encryption offers a much finer granularity for risk management purposes than global key methods.

4   Privacy and DRM

DRM systems have been denounced as the end of privacy for consumption of digital goods. Technically, a DRM client can be configured to collect usage data each time a consumer accesses content and send it off to a central server - a potential privacy nightmare for many. On the other hand, one could argue that DRM enables a "fair" exchange of monetary value for goods. This reduces the economic necessity to use targeted marketing and related business models for revenue generation. Those business models typically tend to involve immense data collection and potential privacy invasion.

DRM could also be a technology fundamentally important for maintaining privacy. There is no technological need for extensive data collection beyond the need to collect certain data to be used only for the purpose of risk management, by some party that is trusted for this task. The role of such a party is conceptually not much different from the risk management division of a credit card company, which most of us live with quite comfortably, assuming the information will not be shared with others.

DRM technology can be designed to be privacy-neutral. How privacy and DRM will play out in the end will be decided by market forces and potentially by applicable privacy-protecting laws, not by technology. The industry is likely to follow the "Know your customer" mantra and will wish to collect data that promise to be commercially valuable. Privacy activists and consumers may have other interests and will raise them. This tension is natural, and public debate plus competition in the market will likely lead to generally acceptable solutions.

How can privacy be built into a DRM system so that it works? Unfortunately the many beautiful cryptographic protocols that have been developed do not help much. That these protocols tend to be computationally inefficient is one, but not the most important, reason for their market failure. The true reason is that the parties running cryptographic protocols, which protect the privacy of the inputs, have to agree up front to be willing to give up on collecting the information that is hidden by these protocols. A powerful party Bob wanting to learn information about Alice will simply never agree in the first place to run a crypto protocol that protects Alice's information from Bob. Why should he? But once Bob agrees, not wanting to learn or misuse information about Alice, there are practically much better solutions available than implementing complicated cryptographic protocols. In particular, real-life privacy implications often require that Bob learns information for some legitimate purpose anyway, such as billing, risk management, statistics or customization. But Bob should not use it for other purposes such as targeted marketing or share it with other parties that do not have a need to know. In practice Bob will simply limit collection and usage of info and possibly even agree to anonymize, pseudonymize or erase personalized information after a certain time. That's why it's important for privacy protection to have business models in place that allow Bob to not collect, or not misuse, all this information.

A good guideline for a practically useful approach to privacy protection are the fair information principles [1]. The cornerstones of these principles are giving notice to consumers about data collection practices, giving consumers reasonable choices about which data are collected about them, giving consumers access to the information collected about them, and providing adequate security for collected data. These principles underlie most privacy-friendly proposals, legislation and privacy policies of web sites.

There is a big community demanding three things for digital distribution: information should be free; creators should be paid; privacy should be provided. In my view this is inconsistent. You can have any two of them, but not all three together.

Technologically simple solutions, with a combination of laws, self regulation and trusted third parties (that may have a business interest not to disappoint the trust placed in them), will be the cornerstone of real life privacy protecting solutions in DRM and many other ecommerce applications.

How can we get there? Although consumers tend to claim in research studies that they are concerned about privacy, I am not aware of any successful privacy-protecting solution on the Internet using sophisticated cryptographic techniques. By "successful" I mean commercially successful or at least successful in the sense that a lot of consumers use it (examples are electronic cash, email encryption, anonymous web browsing). I am not aware either of an example where consumers have been willing to pay for privacy on the Internet. On the other hand an example of a successful "privacy-protecting" solution on the Internet is a service such as Hotmail. Here again, privacy is based on simple pseudonymization plus a trusted third party, not on cryptography. Another example is Yahoo which learns a lot of information about its users from their many single-sign-on- services (stock portfolios, calendars, email, personal ads etc.) but uses it essentially only in depersonalized ways. Most consumers seem happy with that approach.

Those who feel privacy protection is important (like the author) should neither blame nor overestimate the role technology can play here. Both approaches will lead to an eventual failure of privacy. Rather we should make sure we influence the market and legislation in appropriate ways. InterTrust's privacy strategy focuses on providing practically useful technological means that flexibly accommodate whatever privacy practices the market chooses.

Another hot-button issue for DRM are the benefits that consumers have traditionally enjoyed under copyright law such as "fair use" and the "first-sale doctrine", access to library archives, etc. The technical difficulty here is that, at least in the US, (unlike in Europe) fair use is a very fuzzy notion that seems to defy a clear technical definition useful for implementations. A further complication comes from the fact that fair use depends on the business model deployed. What does fair use mean, e.g., for a 10 cent pay-per-play model? I expect that many goals can nevertheless be technologically achieved. For example public libraries may be automatically granted certain access and usage rights. This is another point where society, not technology, should decide how it wants to handle its intellectual property assets in an electronic world. Technology will follow accordingly.

5   Conclusion

Most of the technology needed for a functioning marketplace for digital goods is already there or will be available shortly. Some major content providers are ready to go ahead. The next step is to use the data from the upcoming large scale deployments to refine, adapt, and improve the way we distribute creative assets on the Internet so as to benefit creators, consumers and ultimately society as a whole.

Acknowledgments

I would like to thank Joan Feigenbaum, Matt Franklin, Nic Garnett, Stuart Haber, Bill Horne, Jim Horning, Dave Maher, and Greg Napiorkowski for helpful discussions and comments.

References

1. OECD, "Guidelines on the Protection of Privacy and Transborder Flows of Personal Data", 1980,
   http://www.oecd.org/dsti/sti/it/secur/prod/PRIV-EN.HTM.
2. A.M. Odlyzko, "The history of communications and its implications for the Internet", http://www.research.att.com/~amo/.
3. A.M. Odlyzko, "Stronger copyright protection for cyberspace: desirable, inevitable, and irrelevant", Presentation at DIMACS Workshop on Management of Digital Intellectual Property, 2000.
4. D. Weekly, "Gnutella and the State of P2P",
   http://david.weekly.org/writings/p2p.php3.

Applicability of Public Key Cryptosystems to Digital Rights Management Applications

Jeremy Wyant

NTRU Cryptosystems, Inc.
5 Burlington Woods, Burlington, MA 01803 USA
jwyant@ntru.com

Abstract. Applications that incorporate Digital Rights Management (DRM) capabilities are enabled to specify, implement and manage the rights and permissions associated with the use of intangible goods. Many different inter-related technologies can be incorporated into DRM enabled applications including technology that incorporates public key cryptography. The success of DRM enabled applications will depend on how well the solutions satisfy requirements of the different stakeholders involved with the production, distribution and use of intangible goods. A key success factor is the ability of an application to provide superior ease of use from the end user's perspective. The success also depends on how well the application can adapt to new technology and emerging distribution and business models. This paper describes DRM applications, the requirements of the different stakeholders in this environment and critical attributes of public key cryptosystems that must be considered to ensure effective solutions.

1 Introduction

It is important to understand the requirements of stakeholders in any system that proposes to use DRM technology to protect and manage intangible goods (referred to as content for the remainder of this paper). Selection of appropriate technology is critical if these applications are to be widely accepted and deployed. The success of these applications can be a catalyst to drive entirely new business models involving the distribution of a vast quantity of legacy content and a wide array of emerging digital content that includes books, music, video, games and any content that has some level of sensitivity whether due to copyrights on the content or the nature of the content.

Public key cryptosystems (PKCS) combined with other technology can provide a strong foundation for effective DRM applications. It is important to recognize that there are several other key technologies that typically play a part in complete DRM applications including rights languages, object identification schemes, watermarking, fingerprinting and symmetric cryptography. However PKCS based systems can provide essential security services including entity authentication, key exchange, encryption and digital signature. Digital signature can be used for a wide array of services including ensuring data integrity, binding of rules to content, receipts and proof of purchase. Selection of appropriate PKCS algorithms is critical to ensure solutions that are acceptable to both content users and providers.

P. Syverson (Ed.): FC 2001, LNCS 2339, pp. 75–78, 2002.

2   DRM Application Stakeholder Requirements

The following subsections are not an exhaustive list of stakeholder requirements but identify key requirements and especially those where PKCS components may provide an optimal solution.

2.1   Content Owner Requirements

Requirements for content owners are very dependent on the value and type of content. The solution must also in large part meet the requirements of all other stakeholders in order to be viable. Key requirements for content owners include:

- Content protection
- End user authentication
- End user device or application authentication
- Ability to bind content to rights and optionally to a user or a user's devices.
- End to end trusted services

   Ideally content should be protected end to end, from a secure storage point to the point at which it is rendered by the end user. In addition this protection should be persistent, i.e., when content is on storage media, in transit and on the rendering device. In many scenarios intermediate distribution agents or affiliates may be required to provide secure resources for the "last mile" protection to the end user. The content owner may require end user authentication for the purposes of payment authorization or identification of a user as a subscriber to a specific service. End user device or application authentication may be required to ensure that content is protected end to end. Customized encryption on a per user or per device basis may also be required. In order to achieve end-to-end trusted services it may be appropriate, depending on the specific architecture, to authenticate other control data and software and hardware components.

2.2   End User Requirements

Key requirements for end users include:

- Ease of installation, configuration and de-installation
- Overall system responsiveness (includes client, server and any intermediate elements)
- Simplicity of use
- Reliability
- Minimal use of resources (storage, CPU, battery)
- Portability of content across a full range of rendering applications and devices
- Access to a full range of content from all providers
- Preservation of content quality.
- Ease of content sharing within authorized domains.

   Ease of use is arguably the most critical requirement that a DRM application must meet. If an application is simple to install and use and can deliver content effectively it is a good candidate for market acceptance. If the application can meet the security requirements of content providers yet do so in a way that is transparent to the end user, then there is an improved likelihood that it will be accepted by a broad range of content providers.

2.3   Client Application and Device Providers

Key requirements for providers of client side applications and devices include:

- Ability to meet customer expectations
- Ability to meet content owner requirements
- Minimal consumption of resources, especially battery consumption, on constrained devices
- Total cost of goods, e.g. minimizes or eliminates requirements for special co-processors
- Provides a platform with flexibility for future applications
- Flexible infrastructure to support a wide range of devices and content

An increasing array of wired and wireless client side devices are becoming available that can render content. Ease of use and performance are critical features that must be incorporated into these products. It is critical that DRM solutions provide effective security that is transparent to the user, provides flexibility for future applications and minimizes resource consumption. In the device space the solutions must also be cost effective given the competitive nature of this business.

2.4   Infrastructure Providers

Key requirements for content distribution infrastructure providers include:

- Ability to meet content owner requirements
- Interoperability with the broadest range of current and anticipated client side applications and devices.
- Ability to cost effectively scale up to meet peak demands.
- Ability to provide support for client side digital signature and validation for receipting, proof of purchase and other applications.
- Flexibility to support multiple protocols and changing business models and relationships.
- Ability to offer customized encryption services on a per user or per device basis.

Few DRM applications have been truly tested under heavy loads. It is imperative that infrastructure providers characterize these loads and anticipate support for more robust security protocols and secure interoperability with a more demanding range of wired and wireless end user devices and other application servers. New services that include transaction and field level authentication and encryption operations will increase the load on infrastructure servers. The ability of infrastructure providers to be able to adapt to new security paradigms will, in part, determine their ability to offer new trusted services to their customers.

3   Applicability of Public Key Cryptosystems

Public key cryptosystems have ideal attributes to meet key requirements of stakeholders in DRM applications. However selection of appropriate algorithms should be made considering a range of factors including the ability to:

- meet server side scalability requirements supporting mutual authentication protocols, transaction level security and field level security.
- be ported to a full range of current and anticipated end user platforms and infrastructure components (e.g. identity tokens and constrained consumer electronic devices and appliances)
- be cost effectively implemented on a broad range of end user platforms
- support DRM applications and provide the flexibility to meet security requirements of other end user platform applications (current or planned)
- meet end user ease of use requirements yet provide the option for support of complete security protocols (e.g. client side authentication) and tailorable transaction and field level security.
- meet full security requirements under the constraints and limitations imposed by the device and communications infrastructure.

RSA, ECC, and NTRU PKCS based solutions each have differing performance and size characteristics depending on the specific server and client platforms, security protocols, other DRM complementary technology and infrastructure components. Selection of an appropriate algorithm depends on a critical evaluation of the complete system under peak loads while anticipating future growth and flexibility to support new applications and services. Bandwidth will continue to grow as will client side processing and resource availability. However, client side applications on low powered processors will continue to grow in size and resource consumption. It is critically important to provide fully secure implementations with minimal resource consumption thus maximizing resource availability for revenue generating applications.

4   Acceptance of DRM Applications

More and more content is being made available electronically via an increasingly diverse set of consuming end clients, distribution methods and business models. Some business models requiring minimal DRM, like fees on media or honor system type solutions, may gain acceptance but there will always be a significant and ever expanding volume of valuable and/or sensitive content that will require DRM. Public key cryptographic technology can play a critical role in ensuring that DRM applications meet the essential requirements of all stakeholders. If architected properly, DRM applications can provide content distribution mechanisms that are flexible, scalable and secure. Appropriate selection of public key algorithms will in large part determine the success of these applications and their ability to evolve to meet current and future business requirements.

On the Global Content PMI: Improved Copy-Protected Internet Content Distribution

Tadayoshi Kohno and Mark McGovern

Software Security Group, Cigital
{kohno,markmc}@cigital.com

Abstract. This article addresses a problem with copy-protecting a large collection of electronic content. The notion and severity of a *generic attack* are raised in the context of Adams and Zuccherato's Privilege Management Infrastructure. A solution is then proposed that reduces a content distributor's risk of piracy.

Keywords: Content distribution, copy-protection, PMI, risk management.

1 Introduction

The Internet is changing the way companies do business. News agencies such as the New York Times and CNN publish volumes of online articles daily. The ACM Digital Library sells online access to thousands of journal articles and conference proceedings; and the U.S. Patent Office sells copies of patents online. Sony and Seagram have recently announced that they will distribute music from their websites on a subscription basis. And software companies are beginning to rent and sell software over the Internet.

The Internet is clearly becoming one of the preferred methods for all forms of electronic content distribution: documents, music, images, videos, and software. Unfortunately, without some form of copy-protection, content distributed online could be bought once and then illegally redistributed *ad infinitum*. Under certain business models, such unrestricted redistribution could pose a threat to the financial stability of companies that depend on Internet content sales for their survival.

The protection against and prevention of illegal copying and redistribution of electronic content is called copy-protection. In general, copy-protection schemes are not perfect. That is, in general, no copy-protection mechanism will prevent a determined attacker with unlimited resources from making and distributing illegal copies of copy-protected data. A fundamental goal (and the goal we wish to discuss in this article) is to design copy-protection schemes that *minimize* the illegal copying and redistribution of copy-protected content.

The copy-protection problem is compounded when one tries to protect a large collection of titles using a single copy-protection technique. For example,

P. Syverson (Ed.): FC 2001, LNCS 2339, pp. 79–90, 2002.

the Privilege Management Infrastructure (PMI) described in [AZ00] is susceptible to a *generic attack* — an attack that, once found, could be used to un-
copy-protect *everything* distributed through that PMI. The presence of generic
attacks on copy-protection mechanisms can be devastating. Consider, for example, a company that rents ten thousand different software packages online. If a
cracker can figure out a generic attack against the copy-protection scheme used,
then the cracker could, with very little effort, automate the removal of the software protection mechanism from all ten thousand packages and distribute those
packages (or the automated tools that performs the generic attack) from his or
her pirate website.

This article considers a strategy one could use when copy-protecting a large
collection of electronic content. That is, this article considers techniques that are
resistant to the generic attack described above. The proposed solution is one of
risk management. It is a heuristic solution that involves increasing an attacker's
work-factor while maintaining an acceptable cost for the content distributor.

The remainder of this article is organized as follows. This article opens with
a discussion of terminology (Section 2) and a summary of the Adams and Zuccherato PMI proposal [AZ00] (Section 3). The notion of a *generic attack* is then
further developed in Section 4.

Section 5 introduces a PMI variant for protecting dynamic content (such as
software) and Section 6 shows how to modify the dynamic content PMI variant
so that it is less susceptible to a generic attack (with certain caveats that will
be discussed later). The discussion in Section 6 centers around the notion of risk
management. The article closes in Section 7 with a summary of results.

2   Terminology

The term *content* refers to any form of digital information that has *value* (to some
here unspecified entity). Typical forms of content include electronic documents,
music, images, videos, and executable code.

A set of digital information is *dynamic content* if that content executes and
if it is the execution of that content that has *value*. More generally, *dynamic
content* is content whose output or appearance varies depending on input. A
CAD program or a computer game are examples of *dynamic content*. A set of
digital information is *static content* if that information has *value* when some
(typically external) application executes on it and if each execution produces
the same output. Examples of *static content* include images, music, and videos.
For dynamic content, one tries to copy-protect the functionality of that content;
for static content, one tries to copy-protect the data itself.

The term *title* refers to a specific piece of electronic content. The game
"`game.exe`" (and associated data files), the image "`picture.jpg`," and the song
"`music.mp3`" are all *titles*. Note that any given title may contain both *static* and
dynamic portions.

The term *copy-protection* refers to any technique, protocol, or scheme designed to protect electronic content from illegal copying and redistribution. Any

digital content that has had a copy-protection technique applied to it is considered *copy-protected*.

Copy-protection techniques may be technical in nature (e.g., use proprietary hardware or cryptography to prevent unauthorized copying), non-technical in nature (e.g., penalize violators with heavy fines and jail time), or both.

3 Privilege Management Infrastructure (PMI)

In [AZ00] Adams and Zuccherato propose a *Privilege Management Infrastructure* (PMI) designed to prevent attackers from illegally copying and redistributing protected electronic content. The technique proposed in [AZ00] is similar to an approach mentioned (though later discounted) in [DLN96, 491].

The PMI for Internet content distribution works as follows. Suppose a company wishes to sell PDF documents online. That company wants users that purchase those documents to be able to view them but also wants users that do not purchase those documents to not be able to view them. That is, if a user purchases a document and then gives that document to a friend, that friend should not be able to view that document.

PMIs are structured after Public Key Infrastructures (PKIs) and consist of a root *attribute authority*. See Figures 1 and 2. The attribute authority signs *attribute certificates*. Attribute certificates bind customer identities with certain content access rights or privileges. In the tradition of [WC87], a user's access privilege list for a given title is called his or her *right-to-execute* (RTE). The RTE may specify unlimited usage (such as in the purchase of a title) or limited-time usage (such as in the rental of a title). The attribute certificate may also contain additional information about the purchased title.

The PMI also consists of a PMI-enabled PDF viewer. Embedded in the PDF viewer is the public key of the root attribute authority. The PDF viewer uses this public key to verify the authenticity of a user's attribute certificate. The PDF viewer also has a copy of a root certificate authority's public key (to verify the identity of the user) and an embedded master symmetric encryption key.

Attribute Authority	PDF Viewer	User
AA private key	AA public key	
Master symmetric key	Master symmetric key	
	Customer symmetric key	Customer symmetric key
Title symmetric key	*Title symmetric key*	

Fig. 1. PMI-related keys known to the Attribute Authority (content distributor), the PDF Viewer, and the user. A purchased title is encrypted under its title symmetric key. The italicized keys are not stored in the PDF Viewer but are known to the Viewer when it decrypts a title

Attribute Certificate Contents
User identity information (PKI certificate)
User right-to-execute (RTE)
Doubly-encrypted title symmetric key

Fig. 2. Attribute certificate contents. The title symmetric key is encrypted first under the master symmetric key and then under the user symmetric key

The protocol for purchasing a PDF document is as follows. The purchaser and the content provider first establish a private, authenticated communications channel. The purchaser then purchases a title (using some standard e-commerce system) and provides the content provider with a customer symmetric key. The content provider encrypts the title with the title symmetric key and then encrypts the title symmetric key first with the master symmetric key and then with the customer symmetric key.[1] The content provider (as an attribute authority) creates an attribute certificate for the customer containing the customer's identity, the doubly-encrypted title symmetric key, and the customer's RTE.

The content provider then sends the user the encrypted title and the attribute certificate. The user authenticates with the PDF viewer and presents the PDF viewer with the attribute certificate and customer symmetric key. After verifying the user's identity, the signature on the attribute certificate, and the privileges specified in the RTE, the PDF viewer decrypts and displays the purchased PDF document.

As with PKIs, PMIs are designed to allow delegation. That is, the root attribute authority can delegate certain rights to other companies or organizations. In the PDF example above, the creator of the PDF viewer would be the root attribute authority and could delegate attribute certificate creation rights to various online magazine publishers.

3.1 PMI Observations

Because later sections of this article build on the PMI, it is important to first consider some of the PMI's limitations and features:

PMIs VERSUS PKIs. Although PMIs are modeled after PKIs, it is important to note that the trust relationship in PMIs is fundamentally different than the trust relationship in PKIs. In a PKI, when a user or application fails to verify a certificate authorities signature on a certificate, it is usually the user that suffers. In the global content PMI, however, when the PDF viewer fails to verify an attribute authorities signature on a certificate, it is the content provider that suffers. This means that if the PMI PDF viewer is under a user's control and if

---

[1] The encryption of the title with the title symmetric key and the encryption of the title symmetric key with the master symmetric key could both be performed in a precomputation phase.

the user forces the PDF viewer to ignore the signature on attribute certificates, the user could trick the PDF viewer into displaying documents he or she should not be allowed to view.

EXECUTION ENVIRONMENT. A more general observation is that an attacker with control over the execution environment of a copy-protection scheme will, with enough effort, be able to circumvent that scheme. This observation serves as the basis for our discussions beginning in Section 4 as well as for several secure coprocessor-based copy-protection schemes.

MALICIOUS DISTRIBUTORS. The PMI is vulnerable to a protocol-level attack. In particular, allowing delegation opens the PMI to attacks from malicious distributors. Consider, for example, a malicious distributor of PDF documents. Because the PDF viewer has *one* embedded master symmetric key (i.e., the embedded key does not vary depending on the distributor), a malicious distributor could create valid attribute certificates for a competitor's documents. Although such a distributor might quickly be caught, the potential for "illegitimate" attribute certificates may be a problem in some scenarios.

IDENTITIES AND ANONYMITY. Attribute certificates bind user identities (typically PKI certificates) with access rights. A user must have knowledge of the associated private key in order to authenticate with the PMI-enabled PDF viewer. The PMI therefore enforces copy-protection through the "threat of discovery." In particular, one way for a user to illegally distribute protected PDF documents is to distribute his or her attribute certificates along with his or her PKI private key. However, in an ideal world (where certificate authorities validate users' identities before issuing certificates), users will be ill-advised to distribute their identities and private keys.

The use of identities to enforce copy-protection, however, makes anonymity difficult. The PMI may therefore be unsuitable for distributing fringe content or other forms of content with which users may not want their identities associated.

DOUBLY-ENCRYPTED CONTENT KEY. Encrypting the content symmetric keys first by the PDF viewer's master symmetric key and then by the customer-chosen symmetric key does not appear to significantly increase the security of the PMI against theft of content by legitimate users. In particular, the customer symmetric key is superficial; because a user (or attacker) chooses the customer symmetric key, that user could easily strip off the outer encryption of the content symmetric key. The double encryption does, however, appear to aid in the protection of titles against theft by third parties that have learned the master key but do not know any customer symmetric keys.

4   The Generic Attack

As pointed out in the introduction, *generic attacks* on copy-protection schemes can be devastating. A generic attack is an attack on a copy-protection mechanism that, once discovered, can circumvent the copy-protection of *any* title protected by that copy-protection scheme. Consider the PDF PMI described in Section 3. A potential *generic attack* on the PDF PMI might simply consist of an attacker reverse engineering the legitimate PMI-enabled PDF viewer in order to extract the master key. The attacker could then write a PDF PMI extraction program that, given a protected PDF document and a legitimate attribute certificate, decrypts and saves an unprotected version of the PDF document.

If the cracker posts this generic crack to some website (e.g., [Roo00]), then *anyone* (including normal, non-cracker users) could unprotect and redistribute *any* title purchased through the PDF PMI. Although [AZ00] observes that a sophisticated user could circumvent the PMI copy-protection scheme, the assumption in [AZ00] is that the sophisticated user would do so only for his or her own purposes; [AZ00] does not address the presence and significance of a *generic attack*.

5   A Dynamic Content PMI

We now focus on copy-protecting dynamic content and, in particular, software. In this section we describe a dynamic content PMI in which protected titles themselves authenticate users and check for appropriate attribute certificates (in contrast to the PMI-enabled PDF viewer of Section 3). As with the original PMI in Section 3, part of the security of the dynamic content PMI rests in an attacker's inability to reverse engineer and tamper with executable code.

In Section 6 we discuss how to convert the dynamic content PMI into an approach resistant to the generic attack.

PRELIMINARIES. Let P refer to a dynamic content publisher and attribute authority. Let A refer to a legitimate user that wishes to purchase a title and let T refer to the software title the user wishes to purchase. Let L refer to an executable module that wraps and decrypts T. Let K_T refer to the the title's symmetric key, let K_A refer to A's symmetric key, and let K_L refer to the key embedded in the loader L.

Let I_A represent A's identity with respect to some PKI and let $R_{A,T}$ represent A's access privileges (RTE) with respect to title T. In addition to decrypting and running the content T, the loader L is responsible for authenticating the user and checking the user's attribute certificate for the appropriate RTE.

THE PURCHASE PROTOCOL. The dynamic content PMI distribution algorithm proceeds as follows. In the precomputation stage, P selects a randomly distributed key K_T and then encrypts the content T using the title key K_T. The encrypted title is then bundled with a loader L to create an executable T'.

After performing the necessary e-commerce transactions to purchase a title T, A and P establish a private, mutually authenticated channel. A then sends P his or her identity information I_A and symmetric key K_A.

P doubly-encrypts the title key K_T first with the loader key K_L and then with the user key K_A. P then creates and signs an attribute certificate X composed of I_A, $R_{A,T}$, and the doubly-encrypted key K_T. P sends this attribute certificate to A.

PLAYING THE PURCHASED TITLE. To play the purchased title, the user runs T' with input X and K_A. After T' verifies P's signature on X, the user authenticates with T' using his or her private key. T' then decrypts and runs the original title T with the permissions specified in the RTE $R_{A,T}$.

INCORPORATING THE LOADER L WITH THE TITLE T. The above description assumes that the software distributor P retrofits titles T with loaders L in order to produce protected titles T'. Such retrofitting is primarily applicable when P is a third party distributor not involved with the development of T. A better solution, however, would be to intersperse access checks and other protection mechanisms throughout T.

ATTACKS ON SELF-DECRYPTING EXECUTABLES. As with any cryptographic system, one should not confuse privacy (and encryption) with authenticity. A user of the dynamic content PMI should therefore be cautioned that unless he or she receives a "protected" software title T' through a mutually authenticated channel (as described in *The Purchase Protocol* above), the executable T' may contain trojan, virus, or other malicious code and should not be trusted. This problem is common to all self-decrypting executables.

PLATFORM DEPENDENCE. One of the advantages of the original global content PMI [AZ00] is that it was designed to allow customers to access purchased content on any appropriate device. It is therefore prudent to note that, because both the dynamic content itself and the loader may be platform dependent, the dynamic content PMI may be platform dependent. This observations remains true even when the dynamic content PMI is used to protect static content (Section 5.1) unless the loader is written in a platform independent manner.

5.1 The Dynamic Content PMI with Static Content

This section shows how to adapt the dynamic content PMI for use with static content. There are several caveats to this approach. For example, this approach will increase the bandwidth requirements for static content distribution. Changing static content into executable content could also create another channel for the distribution of viral or malicious code. Additional caveats will be discussed in Section 6.3.

The general technique is to bundle the static content with a viewer V in much the same way that an executable T is bundled with a loader L in the above dynamic content protocol. For example, to copy-protect digital images, a content provider could wrap each image in a Java applet that checks for an appropriate attribute certificate before decrypting and rendering a picture. This technique is very similar to a technique proposed by Petitcolas, Anderson, and Kuhn to defeat web-crawling watermark detectors [PAK99, 1071]. Although there are obvious flaws with this approach, static content distributed this way is no more susceptible to illegal redistribution than unprotected static content.

Section 6.3 raises additional concerns with using the dynamic content PMI to protect static content (and presents additional motivation for distinguishing between the protection of static content and dynamic content).

6   Risk Management and Per-Title Copy-Protection

The copy-protection problem in an insecure environment exemplifies the fact that there are seldom absolutes in computer security: The question is not whether the dynamic content PMI in Section 5 is secure — the question is *how* secure the dynamic content PMI is and how much *work* must an attacker exert to break it.

While one could certainly modify the dynamic content PMI for use with secure coprocessors (such that only trusted coprocessors could decrypt and execute critical portions of the protected title), we shall restrict ourselves to software-only copy-protection.[2]

6.1   Risk Management

As with the standard PMI (Section 3), the dynamic content PMI in Section 5 is susceptible to a generic attack. To paraphrase Section 4, a generic attack against a copy-protection scheme is extremely devastating because an attacker could use the attack to break *any* title protected by the copy-protection scheme. For example, suppose an attacker creates a generic attack tool that, given a protected title T' and an attribute certificate X, creates an executable title T'' functionally equivalent to the original, un-protected title T. The attacker could then use the generic attack tool to un-protect any title distributed through the dynamic content PMI.

Obviously, the content distributor would prefer for *none* of the titles it distributes to be attacked. However, as noted above, the question is not whether an attacker could circumvent the copy-protection mechanism, but how much *work* an attacker would have to exert in order to do so. In order to justify that work, the attack must be highly profitable for the attacker. This leads to the

---

[2] As secure coprocessors become more prevalent, a secure coprocessor PMI may become a more viable solution (in addition to other secure coprocessor-based schemes; e.g., [PSS82,WC87,HP87,YT95,GO96]). However, if the coprocessors used in a copy protection scheme are vulnerable to tampering attacks or side-channel analysis, then the secure coprocessors become insecure processors and the strategy discussed in this section can be used to increase the security of the protection mechanism.

notion of a *work-factor*, or the ratio of the effort an attacker must exert in relation to the resulting profit or yield. The higher the work-factor, the better the copy-protection mechanism.

For example, a professional pirate might be justified in spending a solid month to create a generic attack that could be used to un-copy-protect a thousand titles valued at a hundred U.S. dollars each. The work-factor in this scenario is very low. The same pirate would be hard-pressed to justify spending the same amount of time to break a copy-protection mechanism that is only used with one (or perhaps even a few) similarly priced titles because the work-factor would be much greater.

To compliment the desire to maximize an attacker's work-factor, the proposed solution must be efficient for the content distributor. This means that the content distributor should not have to exert a large amount of extra work in order to increase an attacker's work-factor. The appropriate balance between the advantage gained by increasing an attacker's work-factor with the amount of extra work a content distributor must perform will depend on the content distributor's business model and the value of the protected content.

The solution proposed in this paper is one of *per-title copy-protection* — protecting each title in a slightly different way. This could have three results: (1) the attacker would have to exert much more time and effort to break all the titles distributed by the content provider, (2) the attacker would become discouraged during the process of breaking individual titles and give up, or (3) the attacker would realize the futility in attacking the system. Obviously (2) and (3) are the preferred results. But even if a protection mechanism only succeeds in (1), that protection mechanism is still useful — it successfully *increased* the copy-protection afforded each title.

6.2   Per-Title Copy-Protection

Before proposing a method for per-title copy-protection, let us consider the ways an attacker might break the copy-protection of a dynamic content PMI-protected title T'. The attacker could exhaustively search the symmetric key K_T or K_L, the attacker could find an attack against the algorithm used to encrypt the title, or the attacker could obtain the content distributor's attribute authority private key. Most likely, however, the attacker would break the copy-protection mechanism through reverse engineering T'. For example, the attacker could defeat the copy-protection mechanism by changing T' so that it no longer attempts to verify the attribute authority's signature on a user's attribute certificate. An attacker could also defeat the protection mechanism by reverse engineering T' in order to obtain K_L.

The point of the above paragraph is not to present a complete taxonomy of attacks against protected titles, but rather to illustrate that most practical attacks will involve the attacker stepping through, understanding, and/or modifying the execution of T'.

The solution proposed here consists of randomized, per-title obfuscation and software tamper resistance [CTL97,MMO97]. According to [CTL97], "code ob-

fuscation is currently the most viable method for preventing reverse engineering."
By applying potent and highly resilient obfuscation techniques (see [CTL97]) to
each title, the content provider would force an attacker to exert work when
breaking each title. This results in an increase in the attacker's work-factor and,
consequently, an increase in the security of the copy-protection scheme. A similar
approach can be found in [MC98].

In addition to obfuscation, a content distributor could employ other per-title
access checks or protection mechanisms. Randomized code obfuscation has an
advantage over these additional protection mechanism because code obfuscation
is automateable and therefore efficient for content distributors to apply. If the
value of the protected title is high, however, the content distributor may be justified in implementing additional, title-specific access checks throughout different
components of the title.

Unfortunately, the resulting per-title scheme may still be vulnerable to attacks on a per-title basis. Furthermore, because of potential commonality between protected titles (especially with respect to the transition between the
PMI access checks and the execution of the title itself), the per-title protection
mechanism above does not preclude the existence of more sophisticated generic
attacks. However, if the obfuscation techniques used are highly resilient, creating
such a generic attack may be exceedingly difficult and would be of independent
interest.

6.3   The Dynamic Content PMI with Static Content (Revisited)

Although the dynamic content PMI is, by definition, designed to protect dynamic
content (such as software), Section 5.1 showed that the dynamic content PMI
could also be used to protect static content (such as documents, images, and
videos). There are, however, some fundamental differences between static and
dynamic content that make the per-title dynamic content PMI more suitable for
dynamic content than static content.

The biggest problems with using the dynamic content PMI (and similar)
techniques to protect static content is that the PMI protection mechanism has
no control over what happens to static content after the content is displayed to
the end user. This leads to an exploitable disassociation between the protection
mechanism (the loader) and the protected content — an attacker might attack
the dynamic content PMI (for static content) by stealing the content after the
loader verifies the user's attribute certificate and presents the title (rather than
by attacking the loader itself). This disassociation remains even if the protection
mechanism checks for permission periodically *throughout* the play or rendering
of the static content.

To further develop this notion, first observe that because static content must
eventually be displayed to the end user in order to have value, an attacker able to
intercept that display channel will be able to copy that data (at a potential loss
in quality). Second and more importantly because static content does not vary
between views, an attacker able to steal a copy of *one view* of a static title will
have obtained all the value of that title. This is compared to stealing a "trace"

of a single execution of some dynamic content such as a game — after the game is played, the trace has very little value.

The proposed dynamic content solution attempts to "glue" together (on a per-title basis) the functionality (value) of dynamic content with the protection mechanism. Additional security (perhaps at additional developer expense) could be obtained by permeating a variety of protection mechanisms throughout each component (and hence the execution) of a title.

7 Conclusions

This article addresses a problem with copy-protecting a collection of electronic content. Software-based copy-protection of electronic content in an attacker-controlled environment is adequate at best. An attacker can capture static content (e.g., images, music, and videos) as the content passes between some decoding device and an end user. And an attacker can disassemble dynamic content (e.g., software) and remove the content's copy-protection mechanism. Assuming that all software-based copy-protection mechanism are breakable given enough effort, this article presents a strategy to reduce a content provider's risk of content piracy.

This article begins with a discussion of Adams and Zuccherato's Privilege Management Infrastructure (PMI) [AZ00] (Section 3). Several attacks against the PMI are discussed and, in particular, Section 4 presents a *generic attack* against the PMI. A *generic attack* is an attack against a copy-protection system that, once found, can be used to break the copy-protection of *all* content protected through that system.

Sections 5 and 6 show how to modify the PMI so that it is less vulnerable to a generic attack. Although developed in the context of Adams and Zuccherato's PMI, the general principle of *per-title copy-protection* presented in Section 6 can be used in conjunction with other copy-protection schemes.

Although the solution presented here may be disheartening to those who prefer provably secure protocols, this article argues that because content copy-protection in attacker-controlled environments (e.g., without secure hardware) may be an unsolvable problem, any cost-effective (e.g., efficient to apply; not inordinately complex) increase in security is advantageous. This is analogous to the state of the art in watermarking (as described in [CT98]) where the philosophy is to provide as many layers of protection as possible in order to prevent all but the most dedicated attacker.

Acknowledgments

The authors thank Tim Hollebeek, Gary McGraw, Win Treese, Robert Zuccherato, and the anonymous referees for invaluable comments and suggestions.

References

AZ00.   C. Adams and R. Zuccherato. A global PMI for electronic content distribution. In *Seventh Annual Workshop on Selected Areas in Cryptography.* Preproceedings, 2000. Springer-Verlag, to appear.

CT98.   C. Collberg and C. Thomborson. On the limits of software watermarking. Technical Report 164, Department of Computer Science, University of Auckland, Auckland, New Zealand, 1998.

CTL97.   C. Collberg, C. Thomborson, and D. Low. A taxonomy of obfuscating transformations. Technical Report 148, Department of Computer Science, University of Auckland, Auckland, New Zealand, 1997.

DLN96.   C. Dwork, J. Lotspiech, and M. Naor. Digital signets: Self-enforcing protection of digital information (preliminary version). In *Proceedings of the Twenty-Eighth Annual ACM Symposium on Theory of Computing,* 1996.

GO96.   O. Goldreich and R. Ostrovsky. Software protection and simulation on oblivious RAMs. *Journal of the ACM,* 43(3), 1996.

HP87.   A. Herzberg and S.S. Pinter. Public protection of software. *ACM Transactions on Computer Systems,* 5(4), 1987.

MC98.   S. A. Moskowitz and M. Cooperman. Method for stega-cipher protection of computer code. US Patent 5745569, April 1998.

MMO97.   M. Mambo, T. Murayama, and E. Okamoto. A tentative approach to constructing tamper-resistant software. In *Proceedings of the Workshop on New Security Paradigms Workshop,* 1997.

PAK99.   F.A.P. Petitcolas, R.J. Anderson, and M.G. Kuhn. Information hiding: A survey. *Proceedings of the IEEE, Special Issue on Protection of Multimedia Content,* 87(7), 1999.

PSS82.   G.B. Purdy, G.J. Simmons, and J.A. Studier. A software protection scheme. In *1982 Symposium on Security and Privacy,* 1982.

Roo00.   Rootshell. `http://rootshell.com/`, 2000.

WC87.   S.R. White and L. Comerford. ABYSS: A trusted architecture for software protection. In *1987 IEEE Symposium on Security and Privacy,* 1987.

YT95.   B. Yee and J.D. Tygar. Secure coprocessors in electronic commerce applications. In *First Usenix Workshop on Electronic Commerce,* 1995.

Trust: A Collision of Paradigms

L. Jean Camp[1], Helen Nissenbaum[2], and Cathleen McGrath[3]

[1] Kennedy School of Government
Harvard University, Cambridge, MA
jean_camp@harvard.edu
[2] University Center for Human Values
Princeton University, Princeton, NJ
helen@princeton.edu
[3] College of Business Administration
Loyola Marymount University, Los Angeles, CA
cmgrath@lmu.edu

Abstract. The technological challenges of securing networks are great, as recently witnessed in widespread denial of service and virus attacks. The human reaction to these attacks may be either a loss of trust or a willingness to tolerate increasing risk having weathered one assault. Examining human and computer interaction with a focus on evaluations, the human response to loss of trust is a key part of the search for more secure networks. The success of current efforts to design appropriate security mechanisms depends as much on an understanding of human extensions of trust to computers as it does on an understanding of underlying mathematics. However, the former has not been sufficiently examined.

In this work we survey the findings in social psychology and philosophy with respect to trust. We introduce three hypotheses that remain unanswered with respect to the manner in which humans react to computers. We discuss potential design revisions in light of findings from other disciplines. Then we conclude by noting that research which empowers users to be their own security manager may be based on a fundamentally flawed view of human- computer interaction. We close by encouraging designers of computer security systems to examine the humans, which these systems are intended to empower, and recommend that any security system be built on the basis of understanding of human trust provided by the social sciences.

1 Introduction

Although there has been progress in the quest to build more secure and trustworthy systems, regular news of intrusions, breaches, and rogue attacks serve as reminders that there is a great deal more to be done. Experts focus on the considerable technological challenges of securing networks, designing strategies, building mechanisms, and devising policies. Although these efforts are essential, the study of trust and security would be even better served if designs more systematically addressed the sometimes irrational people and institutions who are

P. Syverson (Ed.): FC 2001, LNCS 2339, pp. 91–105, 2002.

critical components of networked information systems. Accordingly, efforts at securing these systems should involve not only attention to machines, networks, protocols, and policies, but also a systematic understanding of how the social agents (individuals and institutions) participate in and contribute to the security and trust of networks.

This is not to imply that technical work in security ignores the role of people and institutions in networks and network security. Rather, good network security requires a more systematic account of the ways people feature into network security in addition to the technical perspectives previously incorporated. The goal of our paper is to offer a way in which to begin to address the ubiquity of human engineering by understanding how current security systems may be built on hypotheses of human action which are not sustainable. Certainly this has been recognized with respect to the fact that humans are unreliable sources of random information.

We examine the study of trust from social and philosophical perspectives. This leads to identification of implicit assumptions about the ways people behave, trust, and conceptualize security. We show that these assumptions conflict with results and arguments found in theoretical and empirical work in philosophy and social science.

The Variable of Trust

We develop three hypotheses where technology and social science seem to be on a collision course. However, each of these hypotheses at its core points to a common point of collision: technologists often assume that humans are attentive, discerning, and ever-learning. Philosophy argues that humans are simplifiers, and this implies that humans will use trust of machines to simplify an ever more complex world. Social science argues that humans may slowly lower barriers against trust, rather than refining them.

To be specific, theories relating social capital and trust predict that, if computers are perceived as elements of a single undifferentiated network, then trust in computers will increase as computing experience increases. If these theories of human behavior are applicable to computer/human interaction then computer security mechanisms must be built with the assumption that individuals will be too likely to trust untrustworthy machines, and that this risk-taking behavior will increase over time.

Conversely, in computer science there has been an implicit assumption that humans learn to manage their own network security as individuals. If humans do learn to differentiate between servers then increased experience on the network will correlate with a greater ability to distinguish trustworthy and untrustworthy machines. Mechanisms from content selection (e.g. PICS), and privacy calculations (e.g. P3P), to public key systems (e.g. PGP) require that humans learn to manage trust on a machine-by-machine or transaction-by-transaction basis.

If the view of the social sciences is correct then the autonomy provided to users in an end-to-end network may in fact undermine the autonomy of a naive user, rather than enhance it, through exposing the user to risk which the naive user cannot reasonably be expected to manage. A user who cannot secure his or her machine from malicious code and malevolent crackers cannot be said to be autonomous.

Research has found that interface design (e.g. Kiesler, Sproull, and Waters, 1996), group affiliation (e.g. Dawes, McTavish, and Shaklee, 1977) and communication (e.g. Kerr and Kaufman-Gilliland, 1994) influence the extension of trust. While these studies focus on the effect of computer mediation on the extension of trust, they do not address the issue of the trustworthiness of the underlying computer technology with which individuals interact. The rapid advance of computer performance and connectivity means that individuals are often interacting with and depending on more computer systems, with a greater diversity in computer hardware and computer software. In addition the owners of these machines are increasingly diverse as the Internet is adopted for business across the globe and across the demographic range of industrialized nations.

As computer systems become more integral to individual action, social interaction, and commerce, the study of trust must extend to explain how individuals extend trust to computers and computer systems. Since the early work on computer mediated trust, human/computer interaction has become extremely common. Bloom (1998) proposes that the human willingness to expose information to a computer will usher in a new age of social science, in which data accuracy is ever increasing, as computers become ubiquitous. As computer use becomes more widespread and computer users more sophisticated, human willingness to divulge information may suggest an overall increase in users' trusting behavior regarding computer mediated interaction. Such observed behavior may indicate a decreased ability to distinguish between various machines and thus suggests that computer security policies and mechanisms which require active learning on the part of users may prove to be inadequate.

In contrast, other research suggests people now have large and increasing concerns with privacy and security in information technology (e.g. Wacker, 1995; Walden, 1995; Hoffman and Clark 1991; Compaine, 1988; Computer Science and Telecommunications Board, 1994). Examinations of computer systems show that security protections are inadequate (Office of Technology Assessment, 1985; Office of Technology Assessment, 1986; National Research Council, 1996). Professionals in computer science, law and business (e.g. Wacker, 1995; Walden, 1995; Anderson, Johnson, Gotterbarn, and Perrolle, 1993; United States Council for International Business, 1993) point to privacy and security as the stumbling blocks of electronic commerce.

Privacy and security concerns reflect a growing unwillingness to expose information to computers, and suggest greater discernment on the part of users called on to trust the machines which increasingly dominate transactions in daily life. The emergence of electronic commerce and public key-based encryption systems increases the need for computer security and appropriate evaluation of computer trustworthiness. Public key cryptography uses certificates to link (usually) a person, an electronic key and some attributes. With public key infrastructures individual computer users are expected to become security managers. The design decision is based on the assumption that users are increasingly discerning of distinct machines. Yet this core assumption remains unexamined, as technologies that require users to select which individual public keys, key hierarchies and computer systems to trust proliferate. In designing public key infrastructures for the mass market, it is critical to understand the direction and nature of individual user's approach to computers with respect to trust. The implications of previous studies suggest that beliefs commonly implemented in computer security systems should perhaps be reversed – for example, the interface should be purposefully less attractive to avoid lulling users into potentially inappropriate high trust behavior. Understanding how the trust that computers engender will evolve over time is critical to the appropriate evolution of security mechanisms.

2   The Internet as Self-Organizing

In order to argue that social theory results should have a significant impact on the design of security systems we consider the definition of trust that social theory provides. Axelrod (1984) poses the question, "Under what conditions will cooperation emerge in a world of egoists without central authority?" (p.3). His results suggest that the willingness to extend trust initially and to display forgiveness at some point after a defection are important to the maintenance of a cooperative social group. We argue that the Internet illustrates trust as exhibited by the self-organization of egoists who choose to extend trust in order to connect. The Internet has central authority with respect to the assignment of domain names and Internet protocol addresses. However, there is no central authority to govern the daily interactions on the Internet.

We argue that the emergence of connectivity and ordered communication illustrates the applicability of the social theory studies to the Internet and in particular to the design of security systems. On at least three levels, trust is necessary and extant on the Internet. First, at the nuts and bolts level of the router system, users must explicitly and implicitly trust that each link of the underlying technology of the Internet will behave as expected. Second, users must trust that other people will behave in ways that uphold the community norms in the absence of central authority enforcing norms. Finally, users must trust that institutions - such as Internet businesses - will conduct themselves in ways that are conducive to productive ongoing transactions. Trusting the nuts and bolts level, means trusting the underlying infrastructure of the Internet, which in turn is made up of the collaborative effort of several computers connected together. A router that must be maintained by individuals at the site controls each top-level domain.

Any single router can seriously impede the functioning of the Internet. (For example, a router on the East Coast once decided it was in Berkeley and became a black hole for what would otherwise have been smoothly-flowing traffic.) Changing a single parameter in a single router table can cause significant damage to network traffic. At the level of infrastructure, the integrity of the Internet can be compromised through individual error or guile. That it is rarely so compromised underscores the high level of collaboration and mutual trust underlying the Internet's functioning. The TCP SYN flooding attack was an open secret on the Internet for many years. Anyone who knew TCP could have implemented the attack, but for more than a decade no one did.

The picture is similarly challenging in the case of trusting the people of the Internet. For example, every USENET newsgroup is self-governing and therefore vulnerable to the bad behavior of a small subset of users. Every group member must adhere to the rules of participating in the USENET newsgroup. Members may only post on topics relevant to the group, and they must treat others in the group with respect. Periodically, the ground rules of group participation are posted to the entire group, but no mechanism for enforcement of the rules is in place. Some USENET newsgroups have been disbanded, and others have descended into eternal flamewars or spam pits because users did not adhere to the rules. Yet many continue to flourish.

As necessary as trust is in Internet commerce as it is implemented today, trusting virtual institutions poses special challenges as well. The consumer has no way to validate the existence of a business, nor the comfort offered by the location and presentation of a storefront. Items can not be examined in a tactile manner before purchase. The existence of the item may be pure fiction, and transmitting one's credit card number to such a merchant is indeed an exercise in trust.

A question of particular interest to the design of secure systems is how people individuate the agents with which they interact. How users individuate networked machines is relevant to when and how they extend trust initially, and how various kinds of betrayals affect this trust. In other words, do people extend trust to computers as single agents, or do they individuate and distinguish among them? Alternatively do people consider all computers as elements of a single network with out distinguishing between what are, in fact, very distinct machines? Outside of the question of the way users experience their interactions with computers, system designers may reasonably think that users should distinguish among individual computers as they do among individual people, or individual institutions. This is because, despite attempts at quality control and reliability, computers differ from each other from the moment they are shipped from the factory floor. They differ in terms of operating systems, exposure to the environment, exposure to viruses, and history of use.

All of this makes it likely that individuals will have different experiences with different computers. By "surfing the net" users are choosing to interact with many different computers. Certainly, the trustworthiness of the people themselves behind the computers on the Internet covers the range of humanity. However, it may be the case that individuals do not differentiate among different computers or different human agents behind the computer with which they interface, knowingly or unknowingly. If users do not make distinctions among different computers that they use, then they may extend trust or refuse to extend trust using past information and experiences that are not entirely applicable to the new situation.

3   Defining Trust from the Social Science Perspective

The social sciences offer us a definition of trust which may be useful in computer security; and is certainly useful for this discussion. Coleman's (1990) definition of trust accounts for the rational action of individuals in social situations. Coleman's definition of trust has four components:

1. Placement of trust allows actions that otherwise are not possible.
2. If the person in whom trust is placed (trustee) is trustworthy, then the trustor will be better off than if he or she had not trusted. Conversely, if the trustee is not trustworthy, then the trustor will be worse off than if he or she had not trusted.
3. Trust is an action that involves the voluntary placement of resources (physical, financial, intellectual, or temporal) at the disposal of the trustee with no real commitment from the trustee.
4. A time lag exists between the extension of trust and the result of the trusting behavior.

Coleman's definition is consistent with a rational decision making model. His definition is behavioral rather than affective. In this framework, trust is an action, not a feeling. If a person would be no worse off after placing resources in the hand of the trustee and having the trustee cheat, then trust is not an issue. So, for example, trust would not be an issue if an individual delivers a message to a client and also asks a colleague to deliver the same message to the client. In this case, the individual does not have to trust his or her colleague because the message has already been delivered, and no bad consequence will occur if the colleague does not hold up his or her end of the agreement.

Notice that trusted in the social sciences has exactly the same meaning of trusted in computer science. Namely, that which is trusted is trusted exactly because if it fails there is a loss. Except in the case of computer security there is often an assumption that the trusted third party is trustworthy, and there is no such assumption in social theory.

Often the costs of safeguarding against untrustworthy behavior are so high that the only solution is to extend trust to others. This is currently the case in routing, USENET newsgroups, and commerce described above. Trustees must make judgments about whether or not the people with whom they enter agreements are likely to uphold them.

Trustees may not hold up their end of the agreement because they lack the ability to take the agreed-upon actions, committing error. Alternatively, trustees may not hold up their end of the agreement because they have made a decision to defect on the agreement, or cheat, to improve their own welfare at the cost of the trustee, acting with guile.

Error and guile are two possible causes of the breakdown of trust agreements. For example, in the case of Internet routers, an individual at a single site, may not be able to handle the volume of traffic going through the domain and make an error in routing. Alternatively, an individual at the site may decide to take down another site for self- interested reasons. The result is the same in both cases. However, the individual extending trust may react differently in response to error versus guile. We propose that reactions to computer betrayals as opposed to betrayals through obvious human action will result in different forgiveness behavior. People's decisions to trust computers may be affected by their perceptions of the difference between computers and humans in error making and acting with guile. It is a commonly held belief that computers only replicate human error and that computers can be easily monitored to find the source of error. Also, most individuals do not perceive computers are able to act with guile.

Previous research has supported the hypothesis that people are more trusting of computers than of other people. For example, people disclose more information and more accurate information during interviews with computers than during interviews with humans (Sproull and Kiesler, 1991). However, these studies do not consider people's willingness to distinguish between trustworthy and untrustworthy computers (or, reliable and unreliable computers) in the same way that people are willing to characterize different individuals as either trustworthy or untrustworthy. Thus there has been a disconnect between the critical trust questions in computer security and those questions as framed in other fields.

Besides the connections we wish to make between the proposed study and past empirical studies of trust in computer mediated environments, our work is informed by social-theoretic and philosophical work on trust. Social theorists, like Niklas Luhmann (1979) stress the trial-and-error nature of the development of trust, suggesting that starting with a baseline desire (indeed need to trust) people begin with a readiness to trust. This initial readiness to trust is then put to the test in transactions with others, where it is either confirmed or undermined by their experiences with the particular object of their trust. Another relevant thesis that emerges out of both philosophical and social scientific work on trust is that trust is not as vulnerable to incompetence as it is to bad intention. That is, people are ready to forgive harms they may have suffered due to incompetence far more quickly and readily than harms they perceive to have been caused by the bad intentions of others. (See for example, Becker 1996 and Slovic 1993.)

4 Conflicting Assumptions

Implicit and unexamined assumptions about trust are embodied in many widely prominent technical security techniques and mechanisms. Yet, work in philosophy and social science on trust offers reasons for thinking that at least some of these assumptions are wrong. In this section we discuss three hypotheses, showing how they have informed existing security mechanisms and policies and suggesting ways that the mechanisms and policies might be altered in light of this knowledge. The cases fit our paper's theme, namely that optimal security systems would draw on what is known about trust in non-technical literatures and paradigms.

Hypothesis I: In terms of trust and forgiveness in the context of computer-mediated activities, there is no significant systematic difference in people's reactions to betrayals that originate from human actions, on the one hand, and computer failure, on the other.

According to this hypothesis, in terms of effects on trust in computers and computer-mediated activity and readiness to forgive and move on, people do not discriminate on the basis of the origins of harms such as memory damage, denial of service, leakage of confidential information, etc. In particular, it does not matter whether users believe the harms are the result of technical failure, on the one hand, or human (or institutional) malevolence.

For example, key revokation policies and software patches all have an assumption of uniform technical failure. Consider key revokation. A key may be revoked because of a flawed initial presentation of the attribute, a change in the state of an attribute, or a technical failure. Currently key revokation lists are monolithic documents where the responsibility is upon the key recipient to check. Often, the key revokation lists only the date of revokation and the key. The social sciences would argue that the three cases listed above would be very different and would be treated differently. Consideration of that possibility leads to a key revokation system which may better fit human consideration of trust, and manage risk more effectively as well.

Consider the case of an incorrect initial attribute. In this case, the possibility of malevolent action is most likely. Consider identity theft, since identity is a favored attribute linked to public keys (and was in fact required by the first X.509 standard). Identity theft would call for more than revokation at the date of discovery. In a web of trust system; for example, the revokation should be able to be broadcast or narrowcast to anyone whose key or reputation is authentication by the stolen identity. Any extension of cumulative trust enabled by the use of the key should be removed, and this should occur recursively until the entire result of the stolen identity is removed. Alternatively any accounts set up or configured with this key should be terminated. The capacity to create additional accounts and thus implement a domino of trust extensions is exactly the feature which makes identity theft attractive. Thus, key revokation schemes should take into account this capacity when evaluating methods for addressing the revokation of a particular key.

Consider a change in the state of an attribute. For example, a particular employee may be unauthorized to charge a particular account after a sudden, unexpected, or particularly unpleasant termination. In this case, again, accounts that may have been created for the duration of the certification should be reconfigured. An example may be an account at B2B exchange that requires certification at account initiation and considers the key lifetime, as set by the employer, as the appropriate duration of a valid account. Noting that this is a sub-optimal policy by the exchange is not likely to prevent flawed policies from being adopted; in particular when the interest of the businesses and the exchange is to accept risk in order to prevent denial of service. Recall that the Electronic Funds Transfer Act was initiated by exactly this type of change in attribute and malevolence, although in that case the malevolence resulted from divorce and not employment termination. The card issuer had a policy that expected individuals to know in advance how long the attributes – in that case the marriage – would last. In contrast, given a technical failure of a lost key all that would be necessary is that future assertions by the holder of the subverted key. By having a single standard key revokation systems implement the assumption that there is no significant systematic difference in people's reactions to betrayals which originate from human actions, on the one hand, and computer failure, on the other.

With respect to software patches, the possibility of a purposefully malevolent alteration of the code is not considered. The social sciences would argue that such cases require a different level of active response and oversight than technical error made in the market equivalent of good faith. For example, a bug purposefully placed by hackers who had access to Microsoft's source code would presumably be meant for harm; while the other 63,000 bugs in Win2k (Foley, 2000) could be considered either minor or less likely to enable malevolent action. Thus the discovery of a malevolent bug should result in active contact with all customers who had installed the product and technical support to enable effective patching; while the standard policy of customer-driven seeking and downloading could be adequate for other cases.

The hypothesis makes sense from a purely technical standpoint. Certainly good computer security should protect users from harms no matter what their sources and failure to do so is bad in either case. Yet a closer examination, based on an understanding of social theory, yields a more complex problem space and more nuanced solution to the problem of key revokation or patch distribution.

Nevertheless, there are good reasons for questioning the hypothesis. One is related to a view that a number of researchers hold about trust: that it should be reserved for the case of people only, that people can only trust (or not trust) other people not inanimate objects.

These researchers suggest that we use a term like confidence or reliance to denote the analogous attitude people may hold toward things like computers and networks. To the extent that this is more than merely a dispute over word-usage, we are sympathetic to the proposal that there are important differences in the ways trust and confidence or reliance operate (See, for example, Seligman; Nissenbaum; and Friedman, Kahn and Howe.) One reason to reserve the concept of trust for a relation between people is the role motives and intentions seems to play in it. Various works on the subject of trust have discussed this. For example, the philosopher Lawrence Becker argued that the motives and intentions we perceive others to have are far more relevant to our readiness to trust than are actions and outcomes. So, if we believe that things have gone wrong as a result of incompetence, our trust will be far less affected than if we believe ill-will to be behind it. Psychologists Paul Slovic and Tom Tyler, in separate works, demonstrated similar themes, namely, that the way people see intentions mediating outcomes is significant for trust and forgiveness. What this means for our purposes is that people's trust would likely be affected differentially by conditions that differ in the following ways: cases where things are believed to have gone wrong (security breaches) as a result of purely technical glitches, as compared with cases where failures are attributed to human engineering, as compared with cases where evil intention is seen as the cause of harm. Even within these categories, there is quite a range of difference. A number of the cases involving identifiable human agents (i.e. including incompetence and malevolence) can, for example, be seen as points along a continuum rather than as instances of entirely non-overlapping categories. To briefly illustrate, a security breach which is attributed to an engineering error might be judged accidental and forgiven if things went wrong despite considerable precautions taken. Where, however, the breach is due to error that was preventable, we might react to it in a manner that is closer to our reaction to malevolence. Readers familiar with categories of legal liability will note the parallel distinctions that the law draws between, for example, negligence versus recklessness.

Efforts at designing security mechanisms and policies which reflect the varieties of human judgments and reactions and be sensitive to these distinct conditions will be more robust in real-world environments. This hypothesis also has implications for the design of intrusion detection systems. It implicitly suggests that up to a point the false negatives in intrusion detection are more dangerous than false positives. Currently there are risks in these systems which allow suspicious activity versus the risk of producing too many false positives. If humans perceive much malicious activity to be simple reliability failures, a higher level of suspicion generated through false positives would be preferable to a false sense of security, as undetected attacks will be unduly accepted and forgiven.

Hypothesis II: When people interact with networked computers, they sensibly discriminate among distinct computers (hosts, websites), treating them as distinct individuals particularly in their readiness to extend trust and secure themselves from possible harms.

In terms of best practices for security, it makes most sense for people to view distinct remote computers as distinct individuals, each one warranting independent evaluation. Yet, there are several reasons that converge on a quite different story suggesting that users tend to view networked computers as constituting a more homogeneous system. Social theory predicts that individuals' initial willingness to trust and therefore convey information in the context of a web form will depend more on the characteristics of the individual and interface than the perceived locality of or technology underlying the web page. An empirical study of computer science students also demonstrated that experience with computers increases a willingness to expose information across the board.

What this means is that users, even those with considerable knowledge and experience, tend to generalize broadly from their experiences. Thus, positive experiences with a computer generalize to the networked system (to computers) as a whole and presumably the same would be true of negative experiences. In other words, users draw inductive inferences to the whole system, across computers, and not simply to the particular system with which they experienced the positive transaction. Such a finding would have grave implications for the design of user-centered security. Security systems which empower the user, for example, ActiveX, to select between trustworthy and untrustworthy code may not, in fact, be empowering if humans do not differentiate between machines. Human centered security mechanisms may prove to offer no more autonomy to the naive user than the option to perform brain surgery at home would offer medical autonomy to the naive patient. In fact, the argument that alterable code is not empowering to the user has been presented in the case of applications (Clark and Blumenthal, 2000). This tendency to generalize across computers has other implications for security strategies. It suggests that we should be thinking of ways to impress users with the distinctiveness of different machines so that they realize that trustworthiness of one is independent of trustworthiness of another.

In particular the Secure Sockets Layer and the pop-up windows as implemented in all currently and previously predominant browsers encourage users to consider the network to consist of two elements: secure and trustworthy pages versus insecure and untrustworthy pages. This is done by providing a uniform graphic to display at every site with no customization for user or site. The combination of the "lock" in the lower right-hand side and the notice of "leaving a secure" page encourages users to view all sites which use SSL to be equivalent in terms of trustworthiness.

In a related issue, that of ensuring that the person at one end of a connection is indeed connected to the host as believed, a useful solution for this problem has been proposed. Tygar and Whitten (1996) propose window personalization to prevent proxy attacks or Java Trojan Horses from stealing passwords. A similar window personalization could require that the installation of SSL includes a selection of a JPEG image to be included as part of the 'lock' image. This would communicate to the user that no two SSL-using sites are, in fact, the same. Furthermore, the deletion of this image would identify any redirections, for example from a conference site to a secure payment mechanism site – a transition that now appears seamless to the SSL user. An examination of social theory suggests that the implementation of a program which has only increased security in the near term (SLL) could prove problematic in the long term by encouraging users to treat all machines with SLL as equally trustworthy.

Hypothesis III: Over time and with experience users will tend toward greater discernment among distinct remote computers.

According to this hypothesis, the tendency to draw narrow inferences based on experience with remote computers will increase with users' level of experience with computers and computer mediated interactions. Computer experience alone cannot increase the tendency toward greater discernment among remote computers until the design of those parts of security mechanisms that users experience clearly signal differences among distinct computers. Current design encourages users to continue to generalize broadly on the basis of experience with individual cases. They simply will have more experience. This reduction is reinforced by theories of social capital addressing a broader social context. This work suggests that when decisions to trust individual members of a community are vindicated, these positive experiences will generalize to the community as a whole and thus will contribute to social capital.

It is often noted that if telephone systems still required operator assistance, the services of every man, woman, and child in the United States as operators would be required to support today's traffic on the public switched telephone network (PSTN). Similarly, the evolution of computers into ubiquity requires a decrease in the level of human labor as system operators. In the case of the PSTN, there were no requirements for alterations in human trust, as the smart network addressed issues of trust and security in billing and dialing. In fact, almost every man, woman and child in America is a telephone operator. Instead of requesting a location or number, we enter seven or more digits to enable a connection to the end user whom we seek.

In the packet-switched world end users must evolve into network operators. The switch from human-to-human requests (as dominates system operation today) to human-to-machine requests is far more problematic when the machine is multi-purpose. This is compounded by the requirement that humans become security managers. The capacity of humans as security managers is assumed to be high when hypothesis three is assumed correct. However, social theory and philosophy argue that hypothesis three is incorrect. If humans monotonically increase trust then user-managed security systems which monotonically increase trust are problematic.

Consider an implementation of cumulative trust, as with PGP or Lilith. In both cases the user begins with a small set of trusted parties and expands this set of trusted parties as these trusted parties vouch for others. In no cases are the system implemented with a requirement for a reset. That is, at each moment as trust accumulates it becomes more likely that the trust is being extended to an untrustworthy participant. A requirement that the machine effectively reset its trust barriers; for example, by requiring that the user select a predefined size for a set of initial trusted parties before the set is defined anew, could mitigate against the tendency of humans to increase trust for all computers. Assuming long term use, and the human tendency to be increasingly trusting, the social argument for a reset function is strong; although the technical argument is weak at best.

Consider the case of the Platform for Privacy Preferences. P3P allows a user to do business with a site which has privacy practices which follow the user's preferences. A natural result would be for a user to be informed, "To use this site you must enable privacy preference n," just as today sites commonly recommend closed standards or lower security settings (e.g. accepting cookies) for interaction. Such a site may be one which has a particularly high draw. Eventually users may decrease their privacy thresholds so that P3P offers little or no protection. Again, a reset mechanism is called for. At the least, privacy settings should be lowered at a site-by-site basis when they are lowered, or lowered for a specific duration after initially being set. Conversely, if the hypothesis is correct then privacy protection increases should be implemented across all sites without a temporal limit.

5 Conclusions

In this work we have offered and supported three hypotheses with respect to the manner in which humans extend trust to computers. We have shown that the hypotheses are assumed to be correct in social theory and philosophy, and at least implicitly assumed correct in computer security implementations. For each hypothesis we have offered design suggestions which would align the computer science with the social science.

The first hypothesis was, "In terms of trust and forgiveness in the context of computer-mediated activities, there is no significant systematic difference in people's reactions to betrayals which originate from human actions, on the one hand, and computer failure, on the other." In this case the hypothesis lead to criticisms of common key revokation practices. The second hypothesis was, "When people interact with networked computers, they sensibly discriminate among distinct computers (hosts, websites), treating them as distinct individuals particularly in their readiness to extend trust and secure themselves from possible harms." This hypothesis lead to recommendations that visual identifiers which indicate that some particular mechanism is in use integrate signals which encourage users to differentiate between machines. The third hypothesis was, "Over time and with experience users will tend toward greater discernment among distinct remote computers." This hypothesis is the most radical in terms of the differences between computer and social sciences. In general this hypothesis calls for caution in the implementation of user-managed computer security mechanisms. Specifically, this hypothesis, if correct, would argue that any user-managed system that tends to monotonically increasing trust would, over time, be completely subverted by user tendencies to extend trust. In each case a social science and philosophical hypothesis had direct technical implications for the design of a purely technical system to implement trust. If it is not possible to design a computer security system without assumptions about human behavior then the design of computer security systems should be informed by philosophical and social science theories about trust.

References

1. Anderson, R.E., Johnson, D.G., Gotterbarn, D., and Perrolle, J., 1993, "Using the ACM Code of Ethics in Decision making", *Communications of the ACM*, Vol. 36, 98–107.
2. Abric and Kahanês, 1972, "The effects of representations and behavior in experimental games", *European Journal of Social Psychology*, Vol. 2, pp. 129–144.
3. Axelrod, R., 1994, *The Evolution of Cooperation*, HarperCollins, USA.
4. Becker, Lawrence C. "Trust in Non-cognitive Security about Motives", *Ethics* 107 (Oct. 1996): 43–61.

5. Blaze, M., Feigenbaum, J., and Lacy, J., 1996, "Decentralized Trust Management", *Proceedings of the IEEE Symposium on Security and Privacy*, pp. 164–173.

6. Bloom, 1998, "Technology Experimentation, and the Quality of Survey Data", *Science*, Vol. 280, pp. 847–848.

7. Boston Consulting Group, 1997, *Summary of Market Survey Results prepared for eTRUST*, The Boston Consulting Group San Francisco, CA, March.

8. Clark and Blumenthal, "Rethinking the design of the Internet: The end to end arguments vs. the brave new world", *Telecommunications Policy Research Conference*, Washington DC, September 2000.

9. Coleman, J., 1990, *Foundations of Social Theory*, Belknap Press, Cambridge, MA.

10. Compaine B.J., 1988, *Issues in New Information Technology*, Ablex Publishing; Norwood, NJ.

11. Computer Science and Telecommunications Board, 1994, *Rights and Responsibilities of Participants in Networked Communities*, National Academy Press, Washington, D.C.

12. Keisler, Sproull, and Waters, 1996, "A Prisoners Dilemma Experiments on Co-operation with People and Human-Like Computers", *Journal of Personality and Social Psychology*, Vol. 70, pp. 47–65.

13. Dawes, McTavish, and Shaklee, 1977, "Behavior, communication, and assumptions about other people's behavior in a commons dilemma situation", *Journal of Personality and Social Psychology*, Vol. 35, pp. 1–11.

14. B.Friedman, P.H. Kahn, Jr., and D.C. Howe, "Trust Online", *Communications of the ACM*, December 2000, Vol. 43, No. 12 pp. 34–40.

15. Foley, 2000, "Can Micrsoft Squash 63,000 Bugs in Win2k?", *ZDnet Eweek*, on-line edition, 11 February 2000, available at `http://www.zdnet.com/eweek/stories/general/0,11011,2436920,00.html`.

16. Fukuyama F., 1996, *Trust: The Social Virtues and the Creation of Prosperity*, Free Press, NY, NY.

17. Garfinkle, 1994, *PGP: Pretty Good Privacy*, O'Reilly and Associates, Inc., Sebastopol, CA, pp. 235–236.

18. Hoffman, L. and Clark P., 1991, "Imminent policy considerations in the design and management of national and international computer networks", *IEEE Communications Magazine*, February, pp. 68–74.

19. Kerr and Kaufman-Gilliland, 1994, "Communication, Commitment and cooperation in social dilemmas", Journal of Personality and Social Psychology, Vol. 66, pp. 513–529.

20. Luhmann, Niklas. "Trust: A Mechanism For the Reduction of Social Complexity", *Trust and Power: Two works by Niklas Luhmann*. New York: John Wiley & Sons, 1979. pp. 1–103.

21. National Research Council, 1996, *Cryptography's Role in Securing the Information Society*, National Academy Press, Washington, DC.

22. Nissenbaum, H. "Securing Trust Online: Wisdom or Oxymoron?" Forthcoming in *Boston University Law Review*.

23. Office of Technology Assessment, 1985, *Electronic Surveillance and Civil Liberties*, OTA-CIT-293, United States Government Printing Office; Gaithersburg, MD.

24. Office of Technology Assessment, 1986, *Management, Security and Congressional Oversight* , OTA-CIT-297, United States Government Printing Office; Gaithersburg, MD.

25. Seligman, Adam. *The Problem of Trust*. Princeton: Princeton University Press, 1997.

26. Slovic, Paul. "Perceived Risk, Trust, and Democracy", *Risk Analysis* 13.6 (1993): 675–681.

27. Sproull L. and Kiesler S., 1991, *Connections*, The MIT Press, Cambridge, MA.

28. Tygar and Whitten, 1996, "WWW Electronic Commerce and Java Trojan Horses", *Proceedings of the Second USENIX Workshop on Electronic Commerce*, Nov. 18–21 Oakland, CA 1996, pp. 243–249.

29. United States Council for International Business, 1993, *Statement of the United States Council for International Business on the Key Escrow Chip*, United States Council for International Business, NY, NY.

30. Wacker, J., 1995, "Drafting agreements for secure electronic commerce", *Proceedings of the World Wide Electronic Commerce: Law, Policy, Security, and Controls Conference*, October 18–20, Washington, DC, p. 6.

31. Walden, I., 1995, "Are privacy requirements inhibiting electronic commerce", *Proceedings of the World Wide Electronic Commerce: Law, Policy, Security, and Controls Conference*, October 18–20, Washington, DC, p. 10.

On the Security of *Homage* Group Authentication Protocol

Éliane Jaulmes and Guillaume Poupard

DCSSI Crypto Lab,18, rue du docteur Zamenhof
F-92131 Issy-Les-Moulineaux
eliane.jaulme@wanadoo.fr   Guillaume.Poupard@ens.fr

Abstract. This paper describes two attacks on an anonymous group identification scheme proposed by Handley at *Financial Crypto 2000*. The first attack enables to forge valid proofs of membership for any secret key. As a consequence, any user, registered or not, can be properly authenticated by the group manager. The second attack enables the authority to recover the identity of any user who authenticates. Those two attacks can be very easily conducted in practice, without any heavy computation. Those attacks can be fixed with simple modifications and additions to the protocol but we think that the technique used to issue certificates is conceptually flawed and we propose a way to repair this phase of the protocol using zero-knowledge proof techniques.
Keywords: Anonymity, group authentication, cryptanalysis.

1   Introduction

The problem of secure identification was first introduced by Feige, Fiat, Shamir in Stoc 86 [9]. Later the problem of anonymity in group identification was first posed and studied by A. De Santis, G. Di Crescenzo, G. Persiano, and M. Yung [18]. These protocols are immediately converted in perfectly anonymous group identification protocols.

Then, other perfectly anonymous group identification protocols were given by A. De Santis, G. Di Crescenzo, and G. Persiano [17] using only quadratic residuosity as the underlying assumption, and by D. Boneh and M. Franklin [3].

Informally speaking, an anonymous group identification protocol is a scheme that enables previously registered users to convince an authority they belong to a specified group without revealing any information about their identity. Such protocols can be designed using public key cryptography tools. During a first phase, users prove their identity to an authority who issues certificates. Then, when a user wants to be authenticated without revealing his identity, he proves that he knows a certificate and convinces the authority that he has been properly registered.

A group authentication protocol has to satisfy some security properties: legitimate users must always be correctly authenticated, non-authorized people must always be rejected; it should be impossible for the authority to uncover any information on the user who authenticates or link different authentications...

The notion of anonymous group identification is closely related to other notions such as group signature [6, 7, 4, 2, 1] and identity escrow [13], which provide

P. Syverson (Ed.): FC 2001, LNCS 2339, pp. 106–116, 2002.

a revocable anonymity, and to multisignatures [15] that enable people to sign messages for a group.

Our Results

This paper describes two attacks on an anonymous group identification scheme proposed by Handley [11] and that we recall in section 2. The first attack, described in section 3, enables any registered user to forge valid proofs of membership for any secret key. As a consequence, any user, registered or not, can be properly authenticated by the group manager. Notice that this specific attack is fixed in Hanley's final paper [12].

The second attack, described in section 4, enables the authority to recover the identity of any user who authenticates. This attack cannot be detected and the computational effort for the authority is linear in the number of registered users.

Even if those attacks may be fixed by modifications and additions to the protocol, we think that the technique used to issue certificates is conceptually flawed and that the choice of the parameters is of crucial importance. We propose in section 5 a way to repair the protocol using zero-knowledge proof techniques but we do not claim that the resulting protocol is secure.

2   Description of *Homage*

Throughout this paper, we use the following notations: for any integer n,

- we use $\mathbb{Z}_n$ to denote the set of integers modulo n,
- we use $\mathbb{Z}_n^*$ to denote the multiplicative group of invertible elements of $\mathbb{Z}_n$,
- we use $\varphi(n)$ to denote the Euler totient function, the cardinality of $\mathbb{Z}_n^*$.

The *Homage* group authentication protocol [11] consists of two main parts: registration and anonymous authentication. We recall the protocol with the characters Alice and Bob; Alice is a user, member of the group, and Bob is the authority who issues certificates in the first phase and authenticates users in the second one.

2.1   The Setup of the Scheme

During the *Homage* setup phase, the authority generates the following parameters:

- p a public prime integer,
- g a public generator of the multiplicative group $\mathbb{Z}_p^*$,
- $u \in \mathbb{Z}_{p-1}^*$ a public constant,
- z and w two private keys kept secret by the group authority (it is specified in [12] that $z \in \mathbb{Z}_{p-1}^*$ and $w \in [1, p-2]$),
- $v = u^w \bmod p - 1$ a public key of the authority.

In order to make the discrete logarithm problem intractable in $\mathbb{Z}_p^*$, it is required that $(p-1)/2$ should have few prime factors and that all of them should be large. It is specified that the size of p should be at least 2048 bits.

Furthermore, each user has got a private key $x \in \mathbb{Z}_{p-1}$ and the related public key $y = g^x \bmod p$. The public key y is associated with the identity of the user; it is used for group authentication but should also be used for other protocols such as personal identification (for example using the Schnorr scheme [19]), signature (DSA [14]) or encryption (El Gamal [8]). This surprising requirement is proposed as an efficient way to provide "strong dissuasion", i.e. to avoid that legitimate users of the system give their secret data to unauthorized people. We don't argue on such a problem that seems closely related to the anonymity the system wants to provide and consequently to the absence of an identity recovery mechanism.

2.2   Registration of a Member

Alice, identified by her public key y, first registers and obtains a group certificate issued by Bob. We assume that Bob is convinced that Alice is a legitimate member of the group and that her public key is y. He chooses a random number $a \in \mathbb{Z}_{p-1}^*$ and computes the two following values:

- $\alpha_1 = (gy^z)^a \bmod p$
- $\alpha_2 = a^w \bmod p - 1,$

that he sends to Alice as her certificate.

2.3   Anonymous Authentication

Alice, owning certificate (α_1, α_2), wants to convince Bob she is a member of the group without revealing her identity:

- she chooses two random numbers b and c,
- she computes
  - $\beta_1 = \alpha_1^{cu^b} \bmod p$
  - $\beta_2 = \alpha_2 v^b \bmod p - 1$
  - $\beta_3 = g^c \bmod p,$
- she sends β_1, β_2 and β_3 to Bob,
- Bob computes
  - $\gamma_1 = \beta_2^{\frac{1}{w}} \bmod p - 1$
  - $\gamma_2 = \beta_1^{\frac{1}{\gamma_1}} \bmod p$
  - $\gamma_3 = (\frac{\gamma_2}{\beta_3})^{\frac{1}{z}} \bmod p,$
- Alice finally proves to Bob that she knows the discrete logarithm x of γ_3 in basis β_3. The author of *Homage* proposes in [11] a zero-knowledge protocol to achieve this; notice that this protocol is exactly the Schnorr scheme [19] with challenges chosen in $\{0, 1\}$.

Completeness of the Authentication Protocol. If both parties are honest in their computations, i.e. follow the previously described protocol, we should have the following:

- $d = u^b \bmod p - 1$
  so $d^w = u^{wb} = v^b \bmod p - 1$
- $\beta_1 = \alpha_1^{cd} = (gy^z)^{acd} \bmod p$
- $\beta_2 = \alpha_2 v^b = \alpha_2 d^w = (ad)^w \bmod p - 1$
- $\beta_3 = g^c \bmod p$
- $\gamma_1 = \beta_2^{\frac{1}{w}} = ((ad)^w)^{\frac{1}{w}} = ad \bmod p - 1$
- $\gamma_2 = \beta_1^{\frac{1}{\gamma_1}} = ((gy^z)^{acd})^{\frac{1}{ad}} = (gy^z)^c \bmod p$
- $\gamma_3 = (\frac{\gamma_2}{\beta_3})^{\frac{1}{z}} = \left(\frac{(gy^z)^c}{g^c}\right)^{\frac{1}{z}} = (y^{zc})^{\frac{1}{z}} = y^c = g^{xc} = \beta_3^{x} \bmod p,$

and finally the discrete logarithm of γ_3 in basis β_3 must be the user's secret key x.

In other words, this means that the triplet $(\beta_1, \beta_2, \beta_3)$ must satisfy the equation:

$$\beta_1 = \left(\beta_3^{1+xz}\right)^{\beta_2^{\frac{1}{w}}} \bmod p$$

Consequently, the knowledge of four numbers β_1, β_2, β_3 and x satisfying the above equation enables their owner to be authenticated.

2.4   Soundness of a Certificate

As explained in [11], a dishonest group manager can break the anonymity of authentication if he issues bad certificates, i.e. certificates that are not computed using the formula $((gy^z)^a \bmod p, a^w \bmod p-1)$ or correctly computed but using bad secret keys w and z. As a consequence, when Alice receives her certificate (α_1, α_2), she has to make sure that Bob has not cheated. To do this, it is suggested in [11] that she goes through the verification protocol with Bob. The only difference is that, at the end, Bob sends Alice the number γ_3 he has computed and Alice verifies that $\gamma_3 = y^c \bmod p$ (see section 2.3).

Furthermore, this verification of the soundness of the certificate should be conducted in a way such that Bob has no way of guessing who Alice is. To achieve this, the author of *Homage* suggests the use of a third party acting as an anonymizer.

Note. Handley seems to have felt the danger of revealing γ_3 and replaced it by an hash value $H(\gamma_3)$ in the final paper [12]. Consequently, Alice's verification becomes $H(\gamma_3) = H(y^c \bmod p)$. The following attack is fixed by such a modification, even if the principle of looking for z^{th} roots modulo p remains the main way to forge certificates.

3   How to Forge Valid Proofs of Membership

3.1   Basic Idea

Assume we know a pair (n, m) such that $m = n^z \bmod p$ and that we want to construct a valid proof of membership. Remember that we know a pair (u, v) such that $v = u^w \bmod p$. We choose a random x and we compute the three values β_1, β_2 and β_3 that will be sent to Bob as follows:

- randomly choose $b \in \mathbb{Z}_{\varphi(p-1)}$ and $c \in \mathbb{Z}_{p-1}$,
- compute $\delta = n^c \times m^{xc} \bmod p$,
- compute $\beta_1 = \delta^{u^b} \bmod p$,
- compute $\beta_2 = v^b \bmod p - 1$,
- compute $\beta_3 = \frac{\delta}{m^{xd}} = n^c \bmod p$.

When Bob verifies the certificate, he obtains:

- $\gamma_1 = \beta_2^{\frac{1}{w}} = v^{\frac{b}{w}} = u^b \bmod p - 1$
- $\gamma_2 = \beta_1^{\frac{1}{\gamma_1}} = \left(\delta^{u^b}\right)^{\frac{1}{u^b}} = \delta \bmod p$
- $\gamma_3 = \left(\frac{\gamma_2}{\beta_3}\right)^{\frac{1}{z}} = \left(\frac{\delta}{\frac{\delta}{m^{xc}}}\right)^{\frac{1}{z}} = m^{\frac{xd}{z}} = n^{xc} \bmod p$

Finally, it is easy to prove to Bob that we possess the discrete logarithm x of $\gamma_3 = (n^c)^x$ in basis $\beta_3 = n^c$ since we have chosen such an x. Consequently, we can forge valid proof of membership for any secret key x provided we know a pair $(n, n^z \bmod p)$, i.e. a zth root modulo p.

3.2   Finding z^{th} Roots Modulo p

Preliminary Remark. Let us first remark that the pair $(1, 1)$ is a suitable couple (n, m) and that one of the pairs $(-1, -1)$ and $(-1, 1)$ is also suitable. However if these pairs are used to forge proof of membership Bob can observe that γ_3 and β_3 are equal to 1 or -1 and can consequently easily detect the forgery. Anyway, this has to be added in the protocol.

Verification of Soundness Leaks z^{th} Roots. In section 2.4, we have seen that, in the original protocol [11], when Alice receives her certificate, she goes with Bob through a verification protocol where, at the end, Bob sends her the γ_3 he has computed.

Suppose now that, instead of following the protocol, Alice proceeds as follows in order to make Bob compute and reveal a zth root of a randomly chosen integer $m \in \mathbb{Z}_p^*$. Firstly she randomly chooses $b \in \mathbb{Z}_{\varphi(p-1)}$ and $\delta \in \mathbb{Z}_p^*$. Then she sends β_1, β_2 and β_3 to Bob, where:

- $\beta_1 = \delta^{u^b} \bmod p$,
- $\beta_2 = v^b \bmod p - 1$,
- $\beta_3 = \frac{\delta}{m} \bmod p$.

Following the procedure described in section 2.3, Bob computes

- $\gamma_1 = \beta_2^{\frac{1}{w}} = v^{\frac{b}{w}} = u^b \bmod p - 1$,
- $\gamma_2 = \beta_1^{\frac{1}{\gamma_1}} = \left(\delta^{u^b}\right)^{\frac{1}{u^b}} = \delta \bmod p$,
- $\gamma_3 = \left(\frac{\gamma_2}{\beta_3}\right)^{\frac{1}{z}} = \left(\frac{\delta}{\frac{\delta}{m}}\right)^{\frac{1}{z}} = m^{\frac{1}{z}} \bmod p$.

and, as proposed in [11], he sends γ_3 to Alice so that she can verify he has not cheated. Consequently, Alice obtains a zth root of m and just tells Bob she is satisfied. Then, using the cheating strategy we have described above, she can be authenticated for any secret key x.

Note. Replacing γ_3 by $H(\gamma_3)$, as proposed in [12], is a simple fix to this way of finding z^{th} roots modulo p.

4   How to Break the Anonymity of Authentication

We now demonstrate how a dishonest authority can break the anonymity of authentication. We propose two attacks; the first one shows that the modulus p should be a safe prime and the second one shows how a dishonest authority can recover the identity of any authenticating user, even if p is a safe prime.

Attack 1. The basic idea of the first attack is to choose a modulus p such that $(p-1)/2$ has more than one prime factor: $p = 1 + 2 \times \prod_{i=1}^{\eta} q_i$. Then, the authority can distinguish 2^{η} different subgroups of users:

- first the authority associates to each subgroup a binary vector $v = (v_1, ...v_{\eta})$ of length η,
- when a user registers, the authority chooses a random number a' and computes $a = a' \times \prod_{i=1}^{\eta} q_i^{v_i} \bmod p-1$ according to the subgroup the user belongs to; then certificates are regularly computed,
- finally, when a user wants to be authenticated, the order of β_1 is a product of some of the q_is that reveals the vector v and consequently the subgroup of the user.

As an example, if p is 2048 bits long, the authority can choose $(p-1)/2$ with $\eta = 10$ prime factors and consequently distinguish more than 1000 different subgroups! However, such an attack can be easily avoided, just verifying that the second part α_2 of any certificate is relatively prime with $p-1$. Anyway, we think that using a safe prime as public modulus is a good precaution.

Attack 2. We now describe a much more serious attack; let us assume that the modulus p is a safe prime $p = 2q+1$ with q a prime integer and that $q = 2r_1r_2+1$ with r_1 and r_2 two large prime numbers. The set $\mathbb{Z}_{p-1}^*$ of invertible elements modulo $p-1$ has $\varphi(p-1) = \varphi(2q) = q-1 = 2r_1r_2$ elements. It is well known that the multiplicative order of each element is a divisor of $\varphi(p-1) = 2r_1r_2$ and that there are $\varphi(d)$ elements of order d. We obtain the following repartition for the elements of $\mathbb{Z}_{p-1}^*$:

multiplicative order ω	1	2	r_1	r_2	$2r_1$	$2r_2$	r_1r_2	$2r_1r_2$
number of elements of $\mathbb{Z}_{p-1}^*$ of order ω	1	1	r_1-1	r_2-1	r_1-1	r_2-1	$(r_1-1) \times (r_2-1)$	$(r_1-1) \times (r_2-1)$

Consequently, a randomly chosen element in $\mathbb{Z}_{p-1}^*$ has overwhelming probability $\left(1 - \frac{1}{r_1}\right) \times \left(1 - \frac{1}{r_2}\right) \approx 1 - \frac{4}{\sqrt{p}}$ to be of large order $q-1$ or $(q-1)/2$. Furthermore, if the factorization of $q-1$ is unknown, we do not know any efficient algorithm to compute the order of elements in $\mathbb{Z}_{p-1}^*$.

Let us consider an authority who chooses u of order r_1 in $\mathbb{Z}_{p-1}^*$; consequently, $v = u^w \bmod p - 1$ is also of order r_1 if $w \neq 0 \bmod r_1$, i.e. with overwhelming probability.

Then, following the protocol, the authority can recover the identity of any authenticating users. Just notice that $\beta_2 = \alpha_2 v^b \bmod p - 1$ is of order r_1r_2 or $2r_1r_2$ with very high probability but $\beta_2/\alpha_2 = v^b$ is of order r_1. Consequently, if the authority wants to test if β_2 comes from a user who received α_2' as second part of his certificate, he just checks if the order of β_2/α_2' is of "pathological" order r_1. Indeed, if α_2' corresponds to the good user, β_2/α_2' is equal to v^b that is of order r_1 whereas if α_2' belongs to another user, β_2/α_2' is of order r_1r_2 or $2r_1r_2$ with very high probability.

Consequently, the authority recovers the identity of the user in time complexity linear in the number of registered users: he just has to check the order of β_2/α_2' for all α_2' he has delivered.

Notice that if the authority can choose the modulus p and the parameter u as he wants, this attack cannot be detected. Furthermore, we have considered the case of a safe prime $p = 2q + 1$ such that $(q-1)/2$ has two large prime factors but the attack can of course be applied in many other situations where the description is more difficult but the attack always as efficient.

5   How to Repair the Protocol

The main flaw of the *Homage* protocol comes from the need of a certificate verification phase. A modification that avoids the extraction of zth roots described in section 3.2 simply consists of making Alice prove with a zero-knowledge protocol that she knows the discrete logarithm of γ_3 in basis β_3 before Bob reveals γ_3. Consequently, Bob is convinced that Alice already knows γ_3 and that he does not disclose any information when he gives it over to her.

However, a dishonest authority can use different secret keys z to compute certificates and then distinguish users during authentication. More precisely, the authority chooses various keys z_i for different subgroups of users and computes "correct" certificates with the formula $(\alpha_1, \alpha_2) = ((gy^{z_i})^a \bmod p, a^w \bmod p - 1)$.

Then, during authentication, he can check which z_i is used and consequently to which subgroup the user belongs. The repartee suggested in [11] is to use an anonymizer between users and the authority for the certificate verification phase. However, we believe that such a protection is not good since a user who wants to verify the correctness of his certificate, even using an anonymizer, is probably the user who last registered...! Consequently, we definitively think that the verification phase is the weak point of the protocol.

We are now going to propose a different approach based on classical zero-knowledge techniques and that seems to avoid many difficulties and that makes the first step in the direction of a provably secure variant of *Homage*.

How to Avoid Verification. The idea to avoid verification is to provide with each certificate (α_1, α_2) a proof that it has been correctly computed, i.e. that the authority knows an integer a such that $\alpha_1 = (gy^z)^a \bmod p$ and $\alpha_2 = a^w \bmod p - 1$, and that the correct secret keys w and z have been used. This is achieved with the following modifications:

- The prime modulus p is a safe prime $p = 2q + 1$ with $q = 2r + 1$ a safe prime as well,
- g is an element of $\mathbb{Z}_p^*$ of order q,
- u is an element of $\mathbb{Z}_q^*$ of order r,
- another basis h of order q is chosen such that the discrete logarithm of h in basis g is unknown to the authority,
- the secret key z is committed with a public key $Y = g^z h^{z'} \bmod p$ where $z' \in \mathbb{Z}_q$ is a randomly chosen value,
- a commitment scheme is selected and we note $\texttt{commit}(x)$ the commitment of data x; as an example of such a scheme, we can use Pedersen's protocol [16] using parameters g, h and p.

Then the authority proves the knowledge of secret values w, z, z' and a such that the following four relations are valid:

$$\alpha_1 = (gy^z)^{\mathbf{a}} \bmod p, \quad \alpha_2 = \mathbf{a}^{\mathbf{w}} \bmod p - 1,$$

$$v = u^{\mathbf{w}} \bmod p - 1 \text{ and } Y = g^{\mathbf{z}} h^{\mathbf{z'}} \bmod p$$

We can use well known proofs derived from the Schnorr scheme [19] such as the proof of equality of discrete logarithm of Chaum and Pedersen [5] and we obtain the following protocol:

- The prover (the authority), chooses a random value $t \in \mathbb{Z}_q$ and computes
  - $C_1 = \texttt{commit}(t)$
  - $C_2 = \texttt{commit}(t \times a \bmod q)$
  - $C_3 = (gy^z)^{ta} \bmod p$
  - $C_4 = (ta)^w \bmod q$,
- the prover sends C_1, C_2, C_3 and C_4 to the verifier (the registering user) who answers a challenge e randomly chosen in $\{0, 1\}$,
- if $\underline{e = 0}$, the prover opens the commitment C_1 and reveals τ; then he proves with subprotocol A (see fig.1) that $\log_\tau(C_4/\alpha_2) = \log_u(v)$; furthermore, the verifier checks that $C_3 = \alpha_1^\tau \bmod p$,

- if $e = 1$, the prover opens the commitment C_2 and reveals τ'; then he proves that $\log_{\tau'}(C_4) = \log_u(v)$ (with subprotocol A, fig.1) and that $\log_{y^{\tau'}}(C_3/g^{\tau'})$ is equal to the secret key z committed into $Y = g^z h^{z'}$ (with subprotocol B, fig.2).

The probability of success of a cheating prover is smaller than $1/2$ so this elementary round has to be repeated n times in order to make the cheating probability smaller than $1/2^n$.

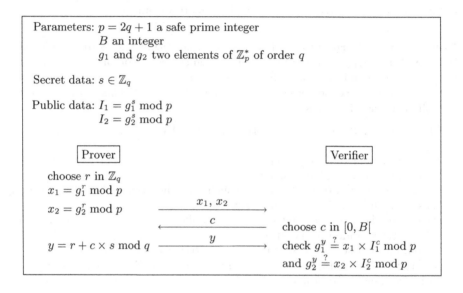

Fig. 1. Subprotocol A: Proof of equality of discrete logarithms

Security Analysis. Subprotocols A and B are complete and sound (see for example [10] and [9] for definitions); a prover who is accepted with probability larger than $1/B$ during the execution of subprotocol A can be used by an extractor which computes the common discrete logarithm s of I_1 and I_2 in basis g_1 and g_2 respectively. Similarly, s and s' can be computed using a prover accepted with probability $> 1/B$ in subprotocol B.

Those two protocols, like the Schnorr scheme, are not zero-knowledge when B is not polynomial because the communications cannot be simulated. Anyway, this does not lead to any known attack. Furthermore, if we want a zero-knowledge protocol, we can use a polynomial value for B and repeat the protocol ℓ times; the probability of success is smaller than $1/B^\ell$ and the simulation has polynomial complexity $O(\ell \times B)$. Another solution to obtain constant-round protocols is to have the verifier commit to his challenges by using, for instance, Pedersen's commitment scheme [16].

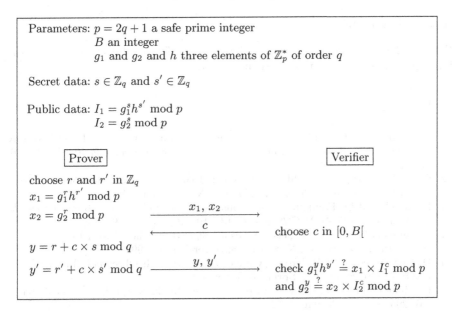

Fig. 2. Subprotocol B: Proof of equality of partial discrete logarithms

It is not difficult to prove that the protocol we propose is complete and zero-knowledge. The soundness is proved in the following way: if a prover is able to answer the two challenges $e = 0$ and $e = 1$ for the same commitments $C_1,...C_4$, we can extract w, z, z' and a such that $\alpha_1 = (gy^z)^a \bmod p$, $\alpha_2 = a^w \bmod p - 1$, $v = u^w \bmod p - 1$ and $Y = g^z h^{z'} \bmod p$. Consequently, if a prover is accepted with probability $> 1/2^n$, he can be used by an extractor to compute the four secret values.

Notes.

1. The basis h is used for the computation of public key Y in order to avoid revealing something like "$Y = g^z \bmod p$", i.e. a zth root.
2. A practical way to be sure that the authority as not chosen a second basis h of known discrete logarithm in basis g is to derive the basis from a publicly verifiable pseudo-random generation algorithm.
3. The modulus p is a safe prime $p = 2q+1$ so elements of $\mathbb{Z}_p^*$ have order 1 (the unity), 2 (the element -1), q or $2q$. A simple way to generate an element g of order q is to choose a random element $x \in [2, p-2]$; if x is a quadratic residue, let $g = x$ and otherwise let $g = x^2 \bmod p$. This avoids residual problems described in section 4 (attack 1).
4. The computation of a prime modulus p such that $q = (p-1)/2$ and $(q-1)/2$ are also prime integers can be done in reasonable time. Such modulus have already been used in protocols such as [20].

Acknowledgments

We would like to thank Giovanni Di Crescenzo for helpful comments on the bibliography related to group authentication.

References

1. G. Ateniese, J. Camenisch, M. Joye, and G. Tsudik. A Practical and Provably Secure Coalition-Resistant Group Signature Scheme. In *Crypto 2000*, LNCS 1880. Springer-Verlag, 2000.
2. G. Ateniese and G. Tsudik. Some Open Issues and New Directions in Group Signature. In *Financial Cryptography'99*, LNCS. Springer-Verlag, 1999.
3. D. Boneh and M. Franklin. Anonymous Authentication With Subset Queries. In *Proceedings of 6th ACM-CCS*, pages 113–119. ACM press, 1999.
4. J. Camenisch and M. Michels. A Group Signature Scheme with Improved Efficiency. In *Asiacrypt'98*, LNCS 1514. Springer-Verlag, 1998.
5. D. Chaum and T.P. Pedersen. Wallet Databases with Observers. In *Crypto'92*, LNCS 740, pages 89–105. Springer-Verlag, 1992.
6. D. Chaum and E. van Heyst. Group Signatures. In *Eurocrypt'91*, LNCS 547, pages 257–265. Springer-Verlag, 1992.
7. L. Chen and T.P. Pedersen. New Group Signature Schemes. In *Eurocrypt'94*, LNCS 950, pages 140–155. Springer-Verlag, 1995.
8. T. El Gamal. A Public Key Cryptosystem and a Signature Scheme Based on Discrete Logarithms. In *IEEE Transactions on Information Theory*, volume IT–31, no. 4, pages 469–472, july 1985.
9. U. Feige, A. Fiat, and A. Shamir. Zero-Knowledge Proofs of Identity. *Journal of Cryptology*, 1:77–95, 1988.
10. S. Goldwasser, S. Micali, and C. Rackoff. The Knowledge Complexity of Interactive Proof Systems. *SIAM Journal of Computing*, 18(1):186–208, february 1989.
11. B. Handley. Resource-Efficient Anonymous Group Identification. In *Prepoceedings of Financial Cryptography 2000*, 2000.
12. B. Handley. Resource-Efficient Anonymous Group Identification. In *Financial Cryptography 2000*, LNCS. Springer-Verlag, 2001. *(Personal communication from the author in January 2001)*.
13. J. Kilian and P. Petrank. Identity Escrow. In *Crypto'98*, LNCS 1462, pages 169–185. Springer-Verlag, 1998.
14. NIST. Digital Signature Standard (DSS). Federal Information Processing Standards PUBlication 186, november 1994.
15. T. Okamoto. A digital multisignature scheme using bijective public-key cryptosystems. *ACM transactions on computer systems*, 6(4):432–441, 1988.
16. T.P. Pedersen. Non-Interactive and Information-Theoretic secure Verifiable Secret Sharing. In *Crypto'91*, LNCS 576, pages 129–140. Springer-Verlag, 1992.
17. A. De Santis, L. di Crescenzo, and G. Persiano. Communication-Efficient Group Identification. In *Proceedings of the 5th ACM-CCS*. ACM press, 1998.
18. A. De Santis, L. di Crescenzo, G. Persiano, and M. Yung. On Monotone Formula Closure of SZK. In *Proceedings of the 35th FOCS*, pages 454–465. IEEE, 1994.
19. C.P. Schnorr. Efficient Identification and Signatures for Smart Cards. In *Crypto'89*, LNCS 435, pages 235–251. Springer-Verlag, 1990.
20. A. Young and M. Yung. Auto-Recoverable Auto-Certifiable Cryptosystems. In *Eurocrypt'98*, LNCS 1403, pages 17–31. Springer-Verlag, 1998.

Anonymity without 'Cryptography'
(Extended Abstract)

Dahlia Malkhi and Elan Pavlov

School of Computer Science and Engineering
The Hebrew University of Jerusalem, Israel
{dalia,elan}@cs.huji.ac.il

Abstract. This paper presents a technique for providing users with anonymity tools without using conventional cryptography. The method, Anonymous Multi Party Computation (AMPC), provides a generic building block for providing electronic anonymity in various applications, e.g., electronic voting and oblivious transfer. It uses a variation of Chaum's mix-nets that utilizes value-splitting to hide inputs, and hence requires no "conditionally-secure" operations of its users. This is achieved under the assumption that there are secure channels between good participants, and under a suitable resilience threshold assumption that, in our worst adversarial scenario, is a square-root of the system.

"The truth about a man lies first and foremost in what he hides" – Andre Malraux

1 Introduction

An important property for users of many electronic systems, such as E-commerce systems, electronic voting, and web browsing, is the ability to preserve their anonymity. This paper present an abstract building block for providing users with electronic anonymity in various applications. The building block, called *Anonymous multi-party computation* (AMPC), transforms a list of input values into a list of output values such that output values cannot be correlated via the computation to any input(s) (precise definition is given in the body of the paper). This generic paradigm is utilized for providing anonymity properties in several applications, e.g., electronig voting.

Generally, anonymity is the ability to hide a user or a value within a larger group of users or values. For example, in the context of anonymous communication, anonymity properties could relate to the sender, the receiver, or both [PW87], and various degrees of hiding could be achieved [RR98]. As another example, in digital cash, anonymity represents the ability to obtain n anonymous cash-notes. In this paper, the AMPC property is presented as an abstract anonymity property that does not derive from any particular application. Its applicability is then demonstrated within several applications.

P. Syverson (Ed.): FC 2001, LNCS 2339, pp. 117–135, 2002.

Unlike most existing methods for anonymity, where the user is required to use conventional cryptography, the AMPC method is realized without requiring users to employ conventional cryptography. The motivation to reduce the use of cryptography by users is a practical one. It allows users with fairly ubiquitous means, such as hand-held cards, palm devices, or cellular phones, to participate in our protocols. In particular, it alleviates the need to rely on a PC to guard cryptographic keys and perform conventional cryptographic protocols on behalf of users. It also alleviates the need to manage key distribution. Finally, the guarantee provided in this manner is information theoretic.

The implementation of AMPC is derived of Chaum's mix-nets [Cha81]. A mix-net is a tool for achieving anonymous communication. The underlying principle of a mix-net is a chain of mixing elements, through which values (messages) are sent encrypted and permuted in order to prevent linking the source of a value to its destination. The AMPC implementation proposed in this paper is essentially a variant of mix-net that is efficient to deploy, and that does not need to employ conventional cryptography. This is done by replacing each 'mix' by a group of mixes, and using secret splitting to hide input values. The primary price is that we tolerate a reduced threshold of colluding parties in the computation, compared with conventional mix-nets. In our worst adversarial scenario, this threshold is a square-root of the system size. With an eavesdropping adversary, the number of bad communication channels that can be tolerated is the total number of channels to the power of 2/3.

In order to hide by distribution, we need to assume that there exist communication channels that are secure against an eavesdropper between users and good participants (i.e., assume the *secure channels* model). On the practical side, it should be noted that the secure channels model is a reasonable one: First, reasonably secure channels can be established by sending One Time Pads at some initial stage using benign means such as telephones and regular mail. Second, even electronically, one may rely on existing infrastructure for secure communication channels (e.g., SSL communication), whereas adding cryptography at the application level is more difficult.

The AMPC network is constructed as follows. We build a graph of players, which is depicted in Figure 1. On the top level are m *input players* that receive lists of initial values at the start of the computation. The goal is to apply any chosen homomorphic output function on these input lists in order to produce permuted output values corresponding to these inputs, such that no correlation is revealed between the inputs and the outputs. This is achieved by employing m additional *auxiliary* levels. Between levels a permutation is applied to the list of inputs and partial values are calculated. At the final level all results are published.

As an example, consider a system with two players at the top level. These two players agree on a permutation and each of them permutes their list of inputs and sends it to a third player. The third player then calculates the output function, permutes the outputs using a second permutation, and publishes them. In this example, no single player can learn anything about the mapping between the inputs to outputs beyond that which results from knowledge it has of inputs and of the outputs.

The result is an efficient multi-party computation that can be used to anonymize input values from corresponding output values (for any homomorphic output function). The computation tolerates a threshold of $m - 1$ corrupt players (or $m^{2/3}$ in the eavesdropping adversarial model), that may be controlled by the adversary, out of $O(m^2)$. The scheme is easy to apply and understand and does not require the usage of higher mathematics.

In addition to obviously providing for an anonymous communication tool, we leverage from the efficiency and ease of the AMPC paradigm to achieve several additional important applications. The primary one is a full fledged electronic voting system, that requires participating voters only to add numbers in order to guarantee their privacy. Additionally, we provide an oblivious transfer protocol and a variant of signatures.

2   Related Work

Our work relates first and foremost to previous methods for achieving anonymity. One of the common methods used are mix-nets, which were first introduced by Chaum in 1981 [Cha81], and recently received considerable attention both on the theoretical and the practical levels. A mix net is a multi party protocol consisting of a set of mix-servers, that take a list of input messages and collectively produce as output a permuted list of messages, such that it is impossible to correlate between the input and output lists as long as a threshold of servers are honest. In order to achieve this the messages have to be encrypted. In classical mix nets the threshold is such that if at least one mix server is honest, then an adversary cannot correlate the input with the output. Mix-nets have been used as anonymizers, e.g. in [SGD97], in election schemes such as [FOO92] and in many other applications. Various enhancements were introduced to mix-nets, including enhanced configurations of mixes [RS91] and the protocol proposed in [J99], which requires only approximately 185 multiplications per server and input item. AMPC achieves in the secure channels model all of the functionality of a mix-net. Our techniques can be viewed as a mix-net in which cryptography on the level of individual mixes is replaced by splitting secrets among a group of players. Comparing with all of the above, AMPC is compute efficient, does not require conventional cryptography of the end user, and requires only a few arithmetic operations per server per input. The cost of the AMPC method is a reduced resilience to corruption of a square root of the system only.

Other methods for anonymous communication operate among peer groups only. The earliest of such works is the Dining Cryptographers (or DC-nets) by Chaum [Cha88], and its extension in [BB89]. In DC-nets, message transmission is hidden by XORing each message with several secret keys, each shared among some subset of the players. In this way, any collusion that does not control all of the subsets cannot reveal who–among the unknown subsets–is the sender of a message. Another peer method used for achieving anonymity is Crowds [RR98].

The Crowds system achieves anonymity for web browsing using a mechanism that resembles a mix-net but with significant differences. Similar to our adversarial model, Crowds assumes that the adversary is limited to controlling a threshold of the players, and does not require multiple encryptions at the originating point of a message. Unlike our scheme, the utilization of both Crowds and DC-nets is limited to peer-groups and to achieving anonymity in communication only, whereas AMPC is a scheme that can provide general permuted homomorphic function computation.

Our work also relates to the general problem of secure multi-party computation (SMPC); a good introduction to SMPC can be found in [Gol00]. Informally, in SMPC there are n players, each with a secret input $i_1, i_2, ..., i_n$. The goal is to devise a method that can compute any desired, recursive function $f(i_1, i_2, ..., i_n)$ on these inputs and reveal the result to all of the players without revealing any information on the inputs beyond that which the known inputs and output reveals. By its definition, SMPC can solve any multi-player problem that can be expressed as a function, including mix-nets and AMPC. However, the known methods for SMPC require laying out the output function f as a computation circuit at the level of individual primitive operations (e.g., XOR and AND), and hence, they are not very practical. In particular, expressing the function of AMPC at the individual operation level would require a very large circuit, due to the permutations.

While AMPC is less general than SMPC, it is sufficiently general to solve several multi-party problem models. One is *oblivious transfer*, which was first introduced in [R81], and some variations introduced in [BC86,NP99]. Another is *one-time receipt*, also investigated in [RB89,CR90]. For all of these, AMPC provides an unconditionally secure solution in the secure-channels model, which unlike existing SMPC methods, may be practical.

Finally, another example application of AMPC is *electronic voting*. A vast body of knowledge exists on electronic voting protocols. These range from centralized protocols to completely decentralized ones: The former include, e.g., [S91,NSS91,FOO92,CC97,HS98], that involve privacy schemes such as blind signatures [Cha85], All-or-Nothing-Disclosure of Secrets (ANDOS) [BC86], and anonymous communication channels [Cha81,RR98]. The latter include decentralized schemes that are based on homomorphic secret sharing [BY86,SK94,CFSY96,CGS97,Sch99], and a self-adjudicating scheme which requires public signatures only [DmLM82]. All of these protocols require the voter to seal and/or anonymize her ballot by employing fairly heavy cryptographic tools. We introduce a new voting scheme that relaxes this requirement.

3   Model

We assume a system of *players* that perform a multi-party computation. Players that follow their prescribed protocol are *good*. We assume a *secure channel* between every pair of good players, that maintains the secrecy of messages, is non-malleable and authenticated. That is, a good player receives a message from another good player if and only if the other good player sent the message. This is the standard *secure channels* model, e.g., as used in [BGW88,CCD88].

Some of the players may be *corrupt*, and consequently behave arbitrarily. This is known as Byzantine model, allowing an adversary full control of corrupt players. For the most part, the adversary we assume has unlimited computational power, is fully adaptive, and is limited only by restricting the number of players it can control to some designated threshold. In some of our applications, we will need to limit the computation power of the adversary, and will be explicit when we do so.

We further distinguish a group of m players as *input players*, and denote them by $P^1, ..., P^m$. These players receive initial values at the beginning of computation. The remaining players are called *auxiliary players*, and receive input only within our protocols. We use A^{index} to denote both kind of players.

Our model also naturally extends to include *users* that may provide the initial values to input players and/or receive the outputs of the multi-party computation. There is no restriction on the number of corrupt users.

Finally, all of the players agree on a prime p. Except where noted, all arithmetic calculations will be done in Z_p.

4   Anonymous Multi-party Computation

In this section we present the basic building block of our scheme, an AMPC. We exemplify the computation using as an output function the sum function, though it should be clear that it can be applies it to any homomorphic function. In the sequel, we assume that all output functions are homomorphic with respect to addition; the reader can easily adapt the techniques below for output functions that are homomorphic with respect to multiplication.

An AMPC of some multi-variate function f is a computation performed by multiple players. Each one of m input players receives an ordered list of initial values (pieces). The collection of input lists may be viewed as a list of tuples, each containing one piece from each player, ordered by the order that the players received the pieces. The computation yields as output a list of f-values that are computed on these input tuples. The property of an AMPC is: Players learn nothing about the relation between the inputs known to them to any specific output values, beyond the information provided by these values. More precisely, we use the following definitions. First, let G be a sub-group of players, and $\phi(I)$ be some function (possibly randomized) they compute together on input I (intuitively, ϕ will be an attempt to "guess" the placement of a particular part of the output). We denote by $\phi(I, AMPC^G)$ the computation of $\phi(I)$ using any internal values known to G during the AMPC (for any ϕ, $\phi(I)$ alone denotes the computation of ϕ without knowledge of any such internal values). We then define an *AMPC* as follows:

Definition 1. *Let the input consist of n tuples each consisting of m values from a domain D: $\{\langle X_j^1, X_j^2, ..., X_j^m \rangle\}_{1 \leq j \leq n} \subseteq D^m$. Let a function f be from domain D^m to some domain D'. Let $P^1, ..., P^m$ be a set of players. Suppose that* each P^i initially knows only $\{X^i_j\}_{1 \leq j \leq n}$. We say that a protocol is an AMPC of f on the inputs $\{X^i_j\}$ with robustness b if it calculates the set of values $\{f(X^1_j, X^2_j, \ldots, X^m_j)\}_{1 \leq j \leq n}$ such that for any set of players G, $|G| \leq b$, and any function ϕ, there exists a function ψ such that:

$$Pr[\phi(\{f(X^1_j, X^2_j, \ldots, X^m_j)\}_{j=1..n}, AMPC^G) = (X^1_j, X^2_j, \ldots, X^m_j)] \leq$$
$$Pr[\psi(\{f(X^1_j, X^2_j, \ldots, X^m_j)\}_{j=1..n}) = (X^1_j, X^2_j, \ldots, X^m_j)] .$$

Two things are worth noting about this definition. First, unlike the definition of SMPC, the above definition does not guarantee preserving secrecy of inputs. We could add this as requirement (see e.g. [Gol00], [BY86] for a formal definition of preserving secrecy of inputs), and in fact, using a variant of our method we could have achieved secrecy of all of the input values. As this is unnecessary for the applications we use we do not elaborate on this direction.

Second, the problem statement above assumes, similarly to SMPC, that the initial values that are held by the P^i's are originated by them. In later applications, we will explicitly add *users* which provide these inputs.

In the rest of this section we present a scheme for performing AMPC. We describe the scheme using as an example output the sum function. That is, we suppose that each player P^i, $i = 1..m$, has a set of values $\{X^i_j\}_{j=1..n}$ and we wish to calculate the sums $X_j = \sum_{i=1}^m X^i_j$ with AMPC.

We build a graph of players (see Figure 1). At the top level are m players that possess initial input values (which they may receive from an external source, e.g., the users, or generate themselves). This level is called the input level. At all other levels we have auxiliary players, with no intrinsic knowledge beyond what is given to them by the players in a higher level. Each level has one less player than the prior level. Messages pass on edges that connect two players on adjacent levels (the solid lines in the figure). Each player has two parents (except for the input level) and one or two children (except for the final (output) level/level 1). Messages also pass among players on the same level (dashed lines). The purpose of this communication is to decide on a permutation in each level.

Stage 1:

To bootstrap the protocol, the leftmost player P^1 players on the first level sends to $P^1, \ldots, P^m$ a randomly chosen permutation $\pi_m \in S_n$ on the input list.

Each player P^i applies π_m to its input list. It then splits each input X^i_j into an algebraic sum $a^i_j + b^i_j = X^i_j$. It then sends a^i_j to the left child, and b^i_j to the right child. The first and last players simply send to their only children X^i_j. This means that each auxiliary player $A^{m-1,i}$, $1 < i < m-1$, on level $m-1$, receives from its two parents $b^i_{\pi_m(j)}$, $a^{i+1}_{\pi_m(j)}$. The two extremal auxiliary players, $A^{m-1,1}$, $A^{m-1,m-1}$, receive the pairs $(X^1_{\pi_m(j)}, a^2_{\pi_m(j)})$, $(b^{m-1}_{\pi_m(j)}, X^m_{\pi_m(j)})$, respectively.

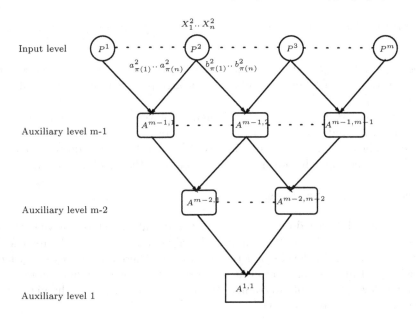

Fig. 1. The communication graph in a triangular AMPC

Stage 2:

Stage 2 is the same as stage 1 except that the inputs are not inputs that the players hold but inputs that the players received from the previous level.

For all levels k such that $m - 1 \geq k > 1$: Denote the pair of values received by any auxiliary player $A^{k,i}$ from its left and right parents by $L^i_{\pi(j)}$, $P^i_{\pi(j)}$, respectively. Since we describe each level separately, the level k should be clear from the context, and it should be understood that $\pi(j) = \pi_{(k+1)}(\pi_{(k+2)}(\ldots(\pi_m(j))\ldots))$. Note that as the j's are permuted, it is not possible (for any single player) to connect the L or R values to the original input order.

From here on we do exactly the same as the prior stage. To bootstrap the protocol, the auxiliary player $A^{k,1}$ sends a a randomly chosen permutation function $\pi_k \in S_n$ to auxiliary players $A^{k,1}, \ldots, A^{k,k}$. Each auxiliary authority $A^{k,i}$ combines its two inputs and applies π_k to the input list. That is, define $Z^i_{\pi(j)} = L^i_{\pi(j)} + P^i_{\pi(j)}$. Each player then randomly chooses new values $a^i_{\pi(j)}, b^i_{\pi(j)}$, such that $a^i_{\pi(j)} + b^i_{\pi(j)} = Z^i_{\pi(j)}$. It then sends $a^i_{\pi_k(\pi(j))}$ to the left child, and $b^i_{\pi_k(\pi(j))}$ to the right child. The two extremal players that have only one child send $Z^i_{\pi_k(\pi(j))}$.

Stage 3:

The last auxiliary player $A^{1,1}$ (the square one in Figure 1) chooses a random $\pi_1 \in S_n$. Denote by $\hat{\pi} = \pi_1 \circ \pi_2 \circ \ldots \circ \pi_m$. The player then combines its two inputs, permutes using π_1, and publishes the list $\{X_{\hat{\pi}(j)}\}_{j=1..n}$.

Theorem 1. *The above protocol is an AMPC of the sum function with resilience* $m - 1$.

Proof. We say that an adversary *dominates* a player if (i) the adversary controls this player, or (ii) if all of its inputs pass through players that are dominated by the adversary.

As the adversary can control less than m players it cannot dominate both an entire level and one player on each level above it. This stems from the fact that each player the adversary dominates requires at least one additional corrupt player. Furthermore, the adversary can't dominate the entire input level.

We now divide into two cases:

Case 1: The adversary dominates some level k but at some level above k, it does not dominate any player. We examine the highest level that it dominates. As mentioned above, this level is *not* the input level. Therefore the adversary lacks knowledge of at least one permutation, and at least one random summand at the input level, to be able to connect the value of the output to the pieces that are held only on the input level.

Case 2: The adversary does not control an entire level. In this case there is at least one value in the sum, as well as at least one permutation that it doesn't know. As all of the values are random numbers it cannot guess the sums given the information it has. Therefore all of the output numbers are unconnected to the numbers it knows (as we add at least one random number). This means that it cannot correlate the outputs to the information that it has.   □

Remark 1. In our protocol, we assume that any good player proposes a random permutation, but a corrupt player may choose any permutation and furthermore, might send different permutations to different players in the level. This is not a concern, as security only comes from permutations that dishonest players don't know, and therefore, if any player in a level is corrupt, the level does not add any security to the protocol irrespective of who proposes the permutation. Furthermore, a corrupt player can disrupt the computation anyway, e.g., by stopping it or by altering values. We will see below in Section 5 methods to robustify the AMPC so as to guarantee detection in these cases.

4.1   Secret Preserving AMPC

In many applications, the output of the mix-net needs to remain secret. We can preserve output secrecy using a variant of AMPC without resorting to conventional encryption. This is done by employing a square network, with m players at each one of m levels, as depicted in Figure 2. Computation proceeds similarly to the above, but side players split the values they pass to the next level just as middle players do. The bottom level produces the pieces of the desired output function, and sends the pieces over secure channels to the target recipient. By our assumption that the adversary can control at most $m-1$ of the bottom-level players, the output is thus secret and can be reconstructed only by its designated receiver.

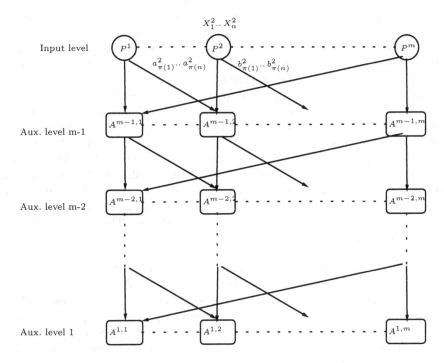

Fig. 2. The communication graph in a Secret Preserving AMPC

5   Robust AMPC

The AMPC method presented so far preserves input anonymity, but is not robust. Specifically, any player can undetectably modify any value and arbitrarily affect the output of the computation. Even if players are unable to identify any particular value to modify, they could corrupt the output undetectably, e.g., by adding a constant sum to all values or the like. Naturally, in most applications, it is desired to detect when such alterations have occurred. Below, we present a method that doesn't utilize cryptography for robustifying AMPC against alterations, that is suitable for Secret-Preserving AMPC. The method does not deal with alteration of initial values: Similarly to SMPC, any input player can undetectably change its initial value. However, we can and do detect when auxiliary players modify intermediate values.

In the full paper, we present a different method for robustifying AMPC that utilizes cryptography *by the servers*. Its main advantage is that this method is that it is suitable for the basic (triangular) AMPC architecture (as well as a Secret Preserving architecture), by using a homomorphic commitment scheme. Similar techniques can be applied to robustify it against *omission* and *duplication* of values; for brevity, we omit these from the discussion.

Our method for robustifying the Secret-Preserving AMPC works by introducing redundancy. Specifically, if the output function is homomorphic with respect to addition, then we replace each initial value $X_j = \langle X_j^1, ..., X_j^m \rangle$ with k transformations, for some security parameter k, such that each transformed value needs to be modified **differently** in order to consistently modify X_j. For example, we let initial input values contain a randomly shuffled list of the multiples $X_j, 2X_j, ..., kX_j$. From here on, we denote a randomly shuffled list of the k multiples of X_j by $\langle \rho(\ell)X_j \rangle_{1 \le \ell \le k}$. (In some settings, such multiples might leak information; other possibilities include sending $Y_j \pm X_j$, where Y_j and the operation to apply–addition or subtraction–are chosen at random, followed by the value Y_j itself, etc.). Correspondingly, the output value is a list that should contain k (shuffled) multiples of $f(X_j)$. To consistently modify all k outputs, a corrupt player would need to guess the correct value to add to each one of the relevant inputs, which has probability $1/(k!)$ of success. This is stated in the following lemma.

Lemma 1. *Let there be a Secret-Preserving AMPC computation for an output function f, as described above, such that f is homomorphic with respect to addition. Suppose that for each initial value X_j, the initial input to the AMPC network contains the randomly shuffled list of multiples $\langle \rho(\ell)X_j \rangle_{1 \le \ell \le k}$. Further assume that the output is accepted only it is contains for each value $f(X_j)$ a randomly shuffled list $\langle \rho(\ell)f(X_j) \rangle_{1 \le \ell \le k}$. Then the probability that any value $f(X_j)$ is undetectably altered is at most $1/(k!)$.*

Proof. In order to consistently change $\langle \rho(\ell)f(X_j) \rangle$, all k multiples should be appropriately modified. That is, to correctly change $f(X_j)$ to, say, $f(Y_j)$, players need to add $\ell(f(Y_j) - f(X_j))$ to the ℓ'th multiple. However, in a Secret Preserving AMPC, no player or collusion of up to $m - 1$ players has any information about the output values $f(X_j), 2f(X_j), ..., kf(X_j)$. Hence, players are able to perform such a modification only if they can identify the ℓ'th multiple of X_j as such, for all $1 \le \ell \le k$. By the properties of the Secret Preserving AMPC, this can be done with probability $1/(k!)$. Note that the adversary can't change all of the values on any level as there are m players on each level and the adversary controls at most $m - 1$ players. $\square$

6   An Eavesdropping Adversary

So far we have considered an adversary that controls players. In many applications the more appropriate adversary is one who can eavesdrop to communication channels. Additionally one might want to consider an adversary who controls a mixture of players and channels.

In this section we show that our model can be significantly more robust against such an adversary. We say that an adversary is an *eavesdropping adversary* if it can eavesdrop to a threshold of the communication lines. To work with this type of adversary, we work with yet another variant of the AMPC network (though similar analysis could be performed for the basic and the Secret Preserving AMPC that were introduced before). In the new variant, we build a *complete m-level graph*, i.e., there are m levels with m nodes in each level, and each node is connected to every node in the level below. In this case each node splits all outputs among all of the players on the next level. There are $O(m^3)$ edges in the graph.

Care should be taken when determining the permutation for each level. If the adversary knew all of the permutations as well as the output then it could correlate the outputs to inputs. Therefore, we wish to make the cost of knowing the permutation on each level as expensive as possible. In order to do this we have each player on level i choose a permutation, which we call a *simple permutation*, independently of all the other players. Each player then sends to all the other players on the level the simple permutation it chose. The simple permutations are composed by each player in the order of the players in the level to create a *composite permutation* for the level. Formally, each player $A^{i,j}$ chooses a permutation $\pi^{i,j}$ and sends it to each $A^{i,\ell}$. The permutation for the level is $\pi^i = \pi^{i,1} \circ \pi^{i,2} \circ \cdots \circ \pi^{i,m}$. Note that for the adversary to know the permutation it must eavesdrop to m edges. Therefore in order to know all the permutations it must eavesdrop to m^2 edges.

Definition 2. *We say that a node is* compromised *if an adversary knows all of its inputs.*

By the eavesdropping adversarial model, the top level of the graph is uncompromised by definition. We note that if every level has a node that is uncompromised then the secrecy is preserved, simply as there is a random summand that the adversary does not know.

Lemma 2. *Any node that has at least one input edge from a node that is not compromised that the adversary can't eavesdrop to is uncompromised.*

Proof. As the graph is a complete layered graph, for a node to be compromised each of the nodes on the prior level must either be compromised or the adversary must listen to the edge from the nodes. Otherwise, the adversary doesn't know the input from at least one uncompromised node in the prior level. □

Lemma 3. *If on level i there are k compromised nodes then in order for the adversary to compromise k' nodes on level $i-1$ it must be able to eavesdrop to $(m-k)k'$ edges.*

Proof. Follows from the previous lemma. □

Corollary 1. *In order for the adversary to compromise the graph it has to eavesdrop to $O(m^2)$ edges.*

Remark: The case in which the adversary controls some nodes and some edges follows similarly.

7 An Election Protocol

In this section, we describe in detail the use of the AMPC building block we have devised to construct a complete electronic voting protocol. We utilize the AMPC building block to build a voting system that requires the use of no conventional cryptography from the voter. The only requirement from the user is the ability to perform additions and to choose random numbers. In addition we require a threshold of secure channels between users and the top level of the AMPC network in the initialization of the protocol. As discussed before, this can be achieved with benign means.

In what follows we shall use the standard terminology of voting protocols. We therefore have a group of players that we call the *registrars*. We have another group of players that we call the *talliers*. There are m registrars, denoted $R^1, ..., R^m$ and m talliers, denoted $T^1, ..., T^m$, such that at least one tallier and one registrar are good. Our treatment will suppose that these groups are distinct from the AMPC network, although it is possible to identify them with the top level and bottom level, respectively. We note that in contrast to the previous discussion in the election protocol the registrars are not part of the AMPC network but rather provide input values into the network.

The voting protocol is as follows.

1. Each registrar R^i chooses for each voter v_j a random vector $\overline{VID_j^i}$ of length d, for some security parameter $d > 1$, unilaterally and without consulting other authorities. R^i sends to each voter v_j, $j = 1..n$, the vector $\overline{VID_j^i}$, over a secure channel.

2. Voting phase: Each voter v_j secretly chooses her ballot B_j, which is one of a finite set of valid possibilities. She calculates her VID vector $\overline{VID_j} = \sum_{i=1}^m \overline{VID_j^i}$ (where vector summation is done component-wise). The voter then chooses at random one of the coordinates $1..d$, and produces a vector $\overline{S_j}$ by adding B_j to that coordinate in $\overline{VID_j}$. Then, the voter prepares for each player in the top level of the robust Secret Preserving AMPC network A^i, $i = 1..m - 1$, a vector of random numbers (uniformly distributed) $\overline{X_j^i}$. To the last player A^m she prepares the vector $\overline{X_j^m} = \overline{S_j} - \sum_{i=1}^{m-1} \overline{X_j^i}$. Note that for all $1 \leq i \leq m$, these vectors are uniformly distributed, and that the sum of all such vectors is $\overline{S_j}$. To avoid modification by the AMPC players, the voter uses the robustifying method described above in Section 5, e.g., she sends $\langle \rho(\ell) \overline{X_j} \rangle$ for some security parameter k.

   At the end of this step, each player $A^{1,i}$ at the bottom level of the AMPC network sends its shares of the outputs $\overline{S_j}$'s to tallier T^i.

3. First Verification and tallying stage: Registrars send their VID vector shares to the top level of a robust Secret Preserving AMPC network, in order to compute the list of valid, anonymous VIDs. As in the previous step, the bottom level of the AMPC sends the shares of the outputs $\overline{VID_j}$'s to the talliers.
4. Commitment stage: Tallier T^i performs a commitment of the share vectors of $\overline{S_j}$ that it holds. Registrar R^i performs a commitment of the share vectors of $\overline{VID_j}$ that it holds. (The details of the commitment are irrelevant and left unspecified; see discussion below).
5. Second Verification and tallying stage: The talliers and registrars open their commitments, and all of the $\overline{S_j}, \overline{VID_j}$ vectors are computed. Valid votes corresponding to valid VID's are tallied.

We now elaborate in detail on the protocol outlined above. In a set-up stage (Registration) registration authorities issue voting credentials–VIDs–using a decentralized protocol such that no authority or collusion of up to $m - 1$ authorities knows the voting credentials. Each registrar R^i chooses for each voter v_j a random vector of length d. We denote the vector chosen by R^i for v_j by $(\overline{VID_j^i}) \in (Z_p)^d$. Registrar R_i sends to each voter v_j the vector $\overline{VID_j^i}$, over a secure channel. For any homomorphic function of the VID pieces that is strongly dependent on all of the shares, if at least one of the registrars is good then all of the VIDs, $\overline{VID_i} = f(\overline{VID_j^1}, \ldots, \overline{VID_j^m})$ are random vectors in $(Z_p)^d$. We can now choose any appropriate homomorphic function f. However, in order for the voters to be able to calculate any function over their input vector pieces (i.e., on her set of inputs) we choose to use as the output function f simply the *sum* function. This both allows the voter to calculate the value of her VID easily without knowledge of higher mathematics, and enables a randomization that is strongly dependent on each of the inputs. During the present stage no set of corrupt registrars of size less than m can calculate which VID's are valid. After ballots have been cast using these VIDs, in stage 3 above the authorities use AMPC to compute a list of anonymous VIDs, which is used to validate any ballot cast.

In the Voting phase, each voter v_j secretly chooses her ballot denoted B_j. She calculates her VID vector by summing the share vectors she received from the registrars. She then hides B_j (which could be only one of few possibilities) by adding it to one of the components (randomly designated) of $\overline{VID_j}$. We denote the resulting vector by $\overline{S_j}$. Each voter splits $\overline{S_j}$ and provides it as input to a robustified, Secret Preserving AMPC. As robust AMPC is used, then by Lemma 1 the adversary can't change any of the values without being detected (with high probability). The outputs of the bottom level of this AMPC are sent separately to the talliers.

For the first verification and tallying stage, registrars first provide their VID vector shares as input to the robustified, Secret Preserving AMPC, to compute a list of valid, anonymous VIDs. As in the previous step, the bottom level of the AMPC sends the shares of the output $\overline{VID_j}$'s to the talliers.

The use of the AMPC suffices to achieve anonymity of the voters. However, in the setting of a voting protocol we have an additional problem that we don't have in other settings, of ensuring that the registrars provide correct inputs to the players, and that the talliers do not change the values they receive from the players. In particular, the problem is to ensure that these authorities do not change values *dependent* on the values of the other players.

More specifically, in order to calculate the set of valid ballots we have to both calculate the valid VID's and to calculate the *ballot vectors* $\overline{S_j}$'s. Care should be taken here to avoid the following possible attack: For every voter v_j the ballot of the voter is related to $\overline{S_j}, \overline{VID_j}$: it is the *only* non zero component of the vector $\overline{S_j} - \overline{VID_j}$. Therefore if the adversary knows S_j, during this stage, it could modify $\overline{VID_j}$ to change the ballot. Therefore, we need to calculate the $\overline{S_j}, \overline{VID_j}$ pairs in the following manner:

1. Commit to all of the values $\overline{S_j}$ and $\overline{VID_j}$.
2. Open the commitment to calculate both values and publish them.

This is done in the next two steps of the voting protocol.

In the Commitment stage, talliers commit to the shares they receive from the AMPC, and registrars commit to their shares. This could be done in several ways. The first way, which is conceptually simple is for the i'th tallier to use a commitment scheme like that of Pederson [Ped92] to commit to values of $\overline{S_j^i}$ and likewise for the i'th registrar to commit to the VID share vectors $\overline{VID_j^i}$. Although this is conceptually simple and requires no cryptography on the side of the users it does require the use of conventional cryptography on the part of voting authorities.

The second way that we can commit, in the spirit of AMPC, is as follows: For a given security parameter d', each tallier chooses a set of random vectors $\langle \overline{c_j^{i,1}}, ..., \overline{c_j^{i,d'}} \rangle$ such that $\sum_{\ell=1}^{d'} \overline{c_j^{i,\ell}} = \overline{S_j^i}$. For each ℓ player i chooses a random permutation, permutes the vectors $\overline{c_j^{i,\ell}}$ and publishes the permuted list of vectors. The same is done by registrars with respect to VID share vectors. Note that it is computationally infeasible (depending on d') to discover the permutations used. In addition, when revealing the committed permutation, for a corrupt tallier (or registrar) i to choose different permutations than the ones committed to so as to coincidently produce legitimate entries is equivalent to a birthday attack on Z_p^d (the domain of VID vectors), which is also infeasible.

In the final stage, talliers calculate both $\overline{VID_j}$ and $\overline{S_j}$ and tally the valid votes.

7.1   Security Analysis

A good election protocol must provide certain security properties. In this section, we use the terminology of [CC97] to examine the characteristics of out voting scheme.

We first examine its Accuracy, i.e., the requirement that ballots cannot be omitted, changed, or added (stuffed).

– For a ballot to be changed, players (registrars or auxiliary authorities) need to modify their pieces of the ballot at some stage. With a robust AMPC, this can generally be done with probability no higher than $1/(k!)$, for the chosen security parameter k. In fact, this probability can only be reached in the worst case, namely, when authorities know what ballot value they change. As this information is not available to the authorities, they should randomly guess the difference $B' - B$ between their desired value B' and any (unknown) value B, which can be done with probability $\frac{1}{|B|}$ per ballot. Overall, the probability of undetectably changing x ballots is exponentially decreasing in x. Furthermore, if there are y *detected* changes, then with high probability (using Chernoff bounds) there is no more than $O(\frac{1}{k!}(\frac{1}{|B|} + \frac{1}{p})y)$ *undetected* modifications.
– For a ballot to be added, there must be a party with access to a VID_j by Stage 2. As the only party who has this at Stage 2 is the voter herself (unless *all* the registrars are corrupt), the probability of correctly guessing a valid VID is $\frac{1}{p^d}$.
– For a ballot to be omitted, all the players at some level need to drop it. As the adversary controls at most $m - 1$ players at each level of the Secret Preserving AMPC we employ, this cannot be done.

Next, we examine Democracy, i.e., that only eligible voters can vote, and can vote once only. That each eligible voter receives a valid VID pair depends on the reliability of the registration phase; presumably, there is sufficient time for the registration to ensure this. In order to be counted in the tally, a ballot must have a valid VID. Hence, only valid ballots corresponding to eligible voters are counted. Since no voter receives more than one usable pair of VIDs, each voter can vote once only. Note that not even the registrars know the VID's until *after* the voting is over.

For Verifiability, i.e. the ability of each voter to verify that her vote is correctly tallied, the protocol allows anyone to verify that published ballots are correctly tallied, i.e., it achieves universal verifiability in the sense of [BY86], and for each voter to separately verify that her ballot is included in the tally.

Finally, we consider Privacy. Since ballots are cast in pieces and combined using AMPC, and likewise the VIDs that validate them, no ballot can be linked to the voter who cast it.

An interesting property of the voting scheme above is that it provides *receipt freedom*. That is, once a voter has voted, it is impossible for the voter to prove how she voted. In other words, unless the voter sells her voting credential (VID) prior to voting, there is no way for others to learn what a particular voter has voted.

Finally, we note that while most of our techniques merely detect failures, they can further be employed to recover or prevent them. These will be discussed in the full paper.

8   Anonymous Communication

In this section we show how we can use the Secret Preserving AMPC to achieve anonymous communication. We ignore timing attacks, as they can be prevented by batching a large (possibly all) inputs together. If a player Alice wishes to communicate anonymously with a player Bob then Alice can send a pair (address,message) splitting up both address and message in the AMPC network. The network can then continue percolating the values as pairs until they reach the bottom level. At the bottom level the address is reconstituted while leaving the message split into shares. Each node on the bottom level then sends the message share that it holds to the designated recipient who can add all the values to receive the final value.

The network can also be used to return responses to the anonymous senders by forming a virtual circuit through the levels, in a manner similar to [Cha81,SGD97].

9   One Time Receipt

In this section we show how we can use AMPC to provide "one time receipts". In many applications where signatures are used the primary need is not for a long-term commitment but for the ability to ensure (even if only once) that the signature is indeed valid. For instance a signature on a cheque needs to be validated only at the time of deposit. The study of signatures that can be verified a finite number of times is not new, see for example [RB89,CR90]. Although such signatures are weaker than standard signatures inasmuch as they can be used only a constant number of times, they are interesting in that we can relax the requirements needed to achieve them.

At a high level, the protocol for achieving such one time receipts has the signer send to the verifier via an oblivious transfer with a "key escrow property" a set of random keys. The oblivious transfer primitive we need can be, in turn, implemented using AMPC. The verifier then chooses a message for the signer to commit to (in general as long as two separate entities choose the keys and the message the scheme will work). The signer then sends all of the keys along with the message added (or subtracted) to them. The verifier can immediately check that the keys that he holds are correctly calculated. A third party can check the signature upon receiving the keys that the verifier does not hold.

We proceed to describe the protocol in two stages: First, we use AMPC to achieve oblivious transfer with an additional property which we call a 'key escrow property'. We then show that any oblivious transfer with this property can be used to achieve such 'one time receipts'.

9.1   Oblivious Transfer with Key Escrow

We say that an oblivious transfer protocol has the *key escrow property* if there exists a set of players that can disclose all of the secrets of the protocol as well as which secret was actually transfered. We can utilize the Secret Preserving AMPC graph to achieve oblivious transfer as follows. The secrets are provided as input to a Secret-Preserving AMPC, but at the bottom level, instead of agreeing on a permutation the players agree simply on one index to output. All properties follow similarly to the presentation above. The width of the graph prevents more than one secret being passed on while the height of the graph prevents the sender from knowing which secret was actually given. This oblivious transfer trivially has the "key escrow property", as the players of the AMPC can reveal all of the keys, permutations, and the final index of the secret output.

9.2   One Time Receipts

A one time receipt is a protocol that has the following properties:

1. The party getting the receipt can verify its validity (at any time).
2. Other parties can verify it at the cost of revealing the key.

We can now define a method for signing using oblivious transfer with the key escrow property.

1. Alice does an oblivious transfer of k pairs of keys $\{(K_1^i, K_2^i)\}_{1 \leq i \leq k}$. For each pair, one of the keys is sent to Bob using oblivious transfer with key escrow. (This is the only stage that utilizes the properties of AMPC.)
2. Bob sends to Alice the value he wants her to sign. This could be a message where the last part is padded with a random value chosen by Bob.
3. For $1 \leq i \leq k$ Alice sends to Bob a pair of values $\langle K_1^i \; op_1 \; M, K_2^i \; op_2 \; M \rangle$, where op_1, op_2 are chosen at random from $\{+, -\}$.
4. Bob verifies that for $1 \leq i \leq k$, one of the pair of keys opens properly.
5. Bob can prove something simply by showing k' of the pairs of keys, for some chosen security parameter k', and asking that the commitment be opened on that pair, using the AMPC graph.

The following two lemmata state the correctness of the one-time receipt protocol.

Lemma 4. *If $m \neq 0$ then a signature on m is alterable to a signature on a message m' with probability at most $(\frac{1}{2} + \frac{1}{p})^k$.*

Proof. Let there be a signature on m. For each $1 \leq i \leq k$, if $m \neq 0$ then as one of each pair of keys is not known, the signature contains a random number with m either added or subtracted to it. Since it is not known which one–addition or subtraction–a forger can guess it with probability $1/2$. Any change will therefore succeed only if the operation is correctly guessed, or if the unknown values in the signature happen to form a valid signature on m'. This happens with probability $(\frac{1}{2} + \frac{1}{p})$. In order to forge the entire signature, the forger must correctly alter $k' \leq k$ keys, with probability of success at most $(\frac{1}{2} + \frac{1}{p})^{k'}$ □

Lemma 5. *If the message m is chosen randomly from a field of size p then the probability of successfully passing an invalid signature to Bob is* $(\frac{1}{2} + \frac{1}{p})^{(k-1)}$.

Proof. For each key pair if the signer doesn't know which one of the keys the recipient has he can only guess which key not to sign properly. His guess will succeed with probability $\frac{1}{2}$. If he does not succeed in guessing properly then he can succeed in cheating iff there exists an m' such that for every j, $K_1^j + m = K_1^j - m'$; this happens with probability $\frac{1}{p}$. As he must succeed in all of the pairs we get the desired probability.   □

Note that probabilities can be amplified by using k-tuples instead of pairs at the cost of larger communication.

Acknowledgments

We thank Michael Ben-Or, Yaacov Fernandess, Markus Jakobsson, Ofer Margoninski, Benny Pinkas, Mark Rabotnikov, and Ohad Rodeh for many helpful discussions. We thank Matthew Franklin and the anonymous referees for many comments that improved the readability of the paper.

References

BY86.   J. Benaloh and M. Yung. "Distributing the power of a government to enhance the privacy of voters". In *Proceedings of the 5th ACM Symposium on Principles of Distributed Computing (PODC)*, pp. 52–62, 1986.

BGW88.   M. Ben-Or, S. Goldwasser, and A. Wigderson. "Completeness theorems for fault-tolerant distributed computing". In *ACM Symposium Theory of Computing (STOC)*, pp. 1-10, 1988.

BB89.   J. Bos, B. den Boer. "Detection of disrupters in the DC protocol". LNCS 434, Advances in Cryptology – EUROCRYPT'97, pp. 320-327, 1990.

BC86.   G. Brassard and C. Crepeau. "All-or-nothing disclosure of secrets". LNCS 263, Advances in cryptology – CRYPTO'86, pp. 234-238, 1986.

Cha81.   D. Chaum. "Untraceable electronic mail, return addresses and digital pseudonyms". *Communications of the ACM* 24(2):84-88, 1981.

Cha85.   D. Chaum. "Security without identification: Transaction systems to make big brother obsolete". *Communication of the ACM* 28(1):1030-1044, 1985.

Cha88.   D. Chaum. "The dining cryptographers problem: Unconditional sender and recipient untraceability". *Journal of Cryptology* 1(1):65-75, 1988.

CCD88.   D. Chaum, C. Crepau, and I. Damgard. "Multiparty unconditionally secure protocols". In Proceedings of the 20th Annual ACM Symposium on the Theory of Computing (STOC), pp. 11–19, 1988.

CR90.   D. Chaum, S. Roijakkers. "Unconditionally secure digital signatures". LNCS 537, Advances in cryptology – CRYPTO'90, pp. 206-214, 1991.

CFSY96. R. Cramer, M. Franklin, B. Schoenmakers, and M. Yung. "Multi-authority secret-ballot elections with linear work". LNCS 1070, Advances in Cryptology – EUROCRYPT'96, pp. 72-83, 1996.

CGS97.   R. Cramer, R. Gennaro, and B. Schoenmakers. "A secure and optimally effi-
         cient multi-authority election scheme". LNCS 1233, Advances in Cryptology
         – EUROCRYPT'97, pp. 103–118, 1997.

CC97.   L. F. Cranor and R. K. Cytron. "Sensus: A security-conscious electronic
         polling system for the Internet". Proceedings of the Hawai'i International
         Conference on System Sciences, 1997, Wailea, Hawaii.

DmLM82. R. DeMillo, N. Lynch, and M. Merritt. "Cryptographic protocols". Pro-
         ceedings of the 14th Annual Symposium on the Theory of Computing, pp.
         383-400, 1982.

FOO92.   B. Fujioka, T. Okamoto, and K. Ohta. "A Practical Secret Voting
         Scheme for Large Scale Elections". LNCS 718, Advances in Cryptology –
         AUSCRYPT'92, pp. 244-251, 1992.

Gol00.   O. Goldreich. "Secure Multi-party Computation". Working draft. Available
         at http://www.wisdom.weizmann.ac.il/~oded/pp.html.

HS98.   Q. He and Z. Su. "A new practical secure e-voting scheme". IFIP/SEC'98
         14th International Information Security Conference, 1998.

J99.   M. Jakobsson. "Flash mixing". In Proceedings of the Eighteenth Annual
         ACM Symposium on Principles of Distributed Computing, pp. 83-89, 1999.

NP99.   M. Naor and B. Pinkas, "Oblivious transfer with adaptive queries". LNCS
         1666, Advances in Cryptology – CRYPTO'99, pp. 573-590, 1999.

NSS91.   H. Nurmi, A. Salomaa, and L. Santean. "Secret ballot elections in computer
         networks". Computers & Security, 36(10):553–560, 1991.

Ped92.   T. Pedersen. "Non-interactive and information secure verifiable secret shar-
         ing". LNCS 576, Advances in cryptology – CRYPTO'91, pp. 129-140, 1992.

PW87.   A. Pfitzmann and M. Waidner. Networks without user observability. Com-
         puters & Security 6(2):158–166, 1987.

R81.   M. Rabin. "How to exchange secrets by Oblivious transfer". TR-81 Aileen
         computation laboratory 1981.

RB89.   T. Rabin and M. Ben-Or. "Verifiable secret sharing and multiparty proto-
         cols with honest majority". In Proceedings of the 21st ACM Symposium on
         Theory of Computing (STOC), pp. 73–85, 1989.

RR98.   M. Reiter and A. Rubin. "Crowds: Anonymity for Web Transactions". ACM
         Transactions on Information and System Security, 1(1):66–92, November
         1998.

RS91.   D. Simon and C. Rackoff, "Non-interactive zero-knowledge proof of knowl-
         edge and chosen ciphertext attack". LNCS 576, Advances in Cryptology -
         CRYPTO'91, pp. 433–444, 1992.

SK94.   K. Sako and J. Killian. "Secure voting using partially compatible homomor-
         phisms". LNCS 839, Advances in Cryptology – CRYPTO'94, pp. 411-424,
         1994.

S91.   A. Salomaa. "Verifying and recasting secret ballots in computer networks".
         LNCS 555, New Results and New Trends in Computer Science, pp. 283-289,
         1991.

Sch99.   B. Schoenmakers. "A Simple publicly verifiable secret sharing scheme and
         its application to electronic voting". LNCS 1666, Advances in Cryptology –
         CRYPTO'99, pp. 148-164, 1999.

SGD97.   P. Syverson, D. Goldschlag, and M. Reed. "Anonymous connections and
         onion routing". In Proceeding of the IEEE Symposium on security and pri-
         vacy, 1997.

Fair Tracing without Trustees

Dennis Kügler and Holger Vogt

Department of Computer Science*
Darmstadt University of Technology
D-64283 Darmstadt, Germany
{kuegler,hvogt}@cdc.informatik.tu-darmstadt.de

Abstract. We present an electronic payment system offering a new kind of tracing mechanism. This mechanism is optimistic fair, as any misuse of the tracing mechanism is prevented by using an audit concept so that a violation of privacy can be detected and will be prosecuted. Thus, compared to previously proposed tracing methods our optimistic fair tracing approach offers more privacy for customers and does not need any trusted third parties, which simplifies the infrastructure of the payment system. Our payment system is able to defend against blackmailing, kidnapping, and bank robberies and can also be used to support investigations of money laundering and illegal purchases.

1 Introduction

Anonymous payment systems based on blind signatures [Cha83] have been proposed as a solution for privacy protecting payments over the internet. However, von Solms and Naccache [vSN92] have shown that *unconditional anonymity* may be misused for untraceable blackmailing of customers, which is also called "perfect crime". Furthermore, unconditional anonymity may ease money laundering, illegal purchases, and bank robberies [JY96]. Due to these anonymity related problems tracing of payments is a desired property for governments and banks, and thus payment systems with *revokable anonymity* [SPC95, CMS96, JY96, FTY96, DFTY97] have been invented, where one or more trusted third parties can link the withdrawal and the deposit of coins with two different tracing mechanisms:

Coin tracing: The withdrawn coins of a given customer are deanonymized so that the bank will recognize these coins at deposit.
Owner tracing: The coins deposited by a given merchant are deanonymized so that the identity of the withdrawer is revealed.

Compared to physical cash such tracing features of electronic cash are clearly superior, e.g. with physical cash owner tracing is not possible and coin tracing

---

* This work was supported by the Deutsche Forschungsgemeinschaft (DFG) as part of the PhD program (Graduiertenkolleg) "Enabling Technologies for Electronic Commerce" at Darmstadt University of Technology.

P. Syverson (Ed.): FC 2001, LNCS 2339, pp. 136–148, 2002.

is rather inefficient. In our opinion tracing capabilites of electronic payment systems should also be restricted to coin tracing, as owner tracing may offend the privacy of honest customers. For example, if a merchant sells legal and illegal goods and uncontrolled owner tracing is used to determine all his customers, then even innocent customers buying only legal goods will be suspected to be criminals, without being able to notice the investigations against them.

Furthermore, all currently known traceable electronic payment systems have one general problem, which we call the *fair-tracing-problem*: No one is able to control the *legal* usage of tracing, leading to the possibility of *illegal tracing*.

Legal tracing: Tracing is legal, if it has been permitted by a judge or by the withdrawer.

Illegal tracing: Tracing is illegal, if it is used without the permission of a judge or of the withdrawer.

Fair tracing: Fair tracing is achieved, if legal tracing is always possible, but illegal tracing is inhibited.

None of the previously proposed payment systems supports fair tracing, as it is hard to control the usage of tracing mechanisms: Even in the case that a quorum of trusted third parties have to agree to trace a given transaction, illegal tracing cannot always be prevented, as only a few number of parties have to conspire and even an honest trusted third party cannot detect illegal tracing performed by other trusted third parties. It is also impossible for a traced customer to detect afterwards that tracing has occurred, particularly in the case that tracing was illegal.

We introduce a new kind of tracing mechanism, which supports more privacy than all other known approaches, although our fair coin tracing can be carried out by the bank without any help of trusted third parties. We believe that fair coin tracing is the right balance between uncontrolled, undetectable trusted third party based tracing and no tracing at all. Our proposed tracing mechanism is *withdrawal based*, which means that the decision whether the coins should be traceable or not must be made at their withdrawal.

We call our approach *optimistic fair tracing* (according to the definition of optimistic fair exchange [ASW97]) as it doesn't strictly prevent illegal tracing. Instead tracing is always detectable afterwards by the traced person and if tracing turns out to be illegal this can be proven to a judge. We conclude that only legal tracing will be performed, as illegal tracing will be detected and prosecuted, which most likely discourages parties interested in illegal tracing.[1]

The remainder is structured as follows: We present our new approach for tracing in section 2 and show how to implement a payment system with this optimistic fair tracing in section 3. In section 4 we discuss how our payment system copes with blackmailing of customers and banks, and how it supports investigations of money laundering and illegal purchases. Finally, we compare our system to other approaches for tracing in section 5.

---

[1] A similar idea is used to prevent double spending in offline payment systems [CFN88], where the bank can only afterwards detect double spending and identify the cheating customer.

2   A New Approach for Tracing

We base our approach on the concept of marking which was invented by Kügler and Vogt [KV01] to prevent blackmailing of customers. In this section we will sketch this mechanism in short and show how to extend it to a new privacy protecting tracing mechanism.

2.1   The Marking Mechanism

Physical cash, particularly banknotes, have two important features, which can be used for tracing:

- The serial numbers of the banknotes can be annotated.
- The banknotes can be marked, e.g. with a special color.

The goal of both approaches is to support tracing of banknotes similar to coin tracing as they enable recognition of spent banknotes. An analogy to the marking of banknotes with a special invisible color was suggested in [KV01] for a new blackmailing resistant anonymous payment system. Due to the properties of electronic coins, the electronic marking mechanism is even stronger: In an online payment system the bank is involved in every payment and the usage of a marked coin will immediately be recognized by the bank, which leads to an effective tracing mechanism. However, an uncontrolled electronic marking mechanism may be misused by the bank to deanonymize payments of all customers, which obviously enables illegal tracing.

In the proposed payment system marking of coins is only possible with the admission of the customer, although marking is invisible for anybody but the bank. For every withdrawn coin the bank has to confirm that the coin is indeed unmarked (also called valid), unless the customer has requested marked coins. For this *confirmation protocol* a designated verifier proof [JSI96] is used, because only the legitimate customer shall be convinced of the validity of a coin. Every other party can falsely be convinced by the customer of the validity of a coin even if the coin is marked.

However, this marking mechanism cannot be used for withdrawal based coin tracing, because the customer always detects marked coins and thus knows that his payments will not be anonymous. Therefore, we extend the marking mechanism to support coin tracing.

2.2   Extending the Marking Mechanism

If all customers trust the bank not to do any illegal tracing, we may simply omit the confirmation protocol. However, not everyone is willing to trust a bank that way. Our solution is to make tracing auditable and illegal tracing provable: A customer can always verify his previously withdrawn coins later and may prove any attempt of illegal tracing to the public, especially to a judge or to the press. Thus a dishonest bank may be punished and denounced. In our opinion no bank can afford illegal tracing, because e.g. the bank may loose its license or its customers.

For auditable tracing the bank never proves to anybody that the withdrawn coins are unmarked. Instead a proof is given afterwards by publishing a single information which uncovers marked coins and enables every customer to check the validity of all his coins. If the bank traced a customer, this check will fail. In this case the bank must prove that this tracing was legal, by showing a judge's permission for tracing this customer.

2.3   Uncovering Marked Coins

Uncovering marked coins is strongly related to the life cycle of a coin generation, which is shown in figure 1. Those life cycles are necessary for security and storage reasons [Sch97]. For every new generation of coins new key pairs are generated, distributed, and activated. Then these key pairs are used during the *generate phase* to issue coins. The generate phase ends with the deactivation of the keys for withdrawal. Coins can be used for payments during the *accept phase*, which ends with the deactivation of the keys for payments.

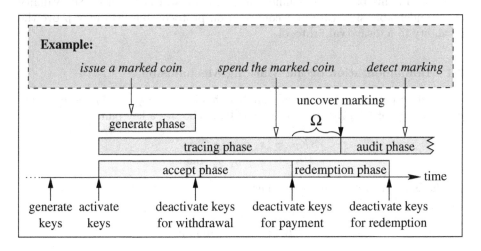

Fig. 1. Life-cycle of a coin generation with tracing extensions

Afterwards, during the *redemption phase* coins will only be accepted non-anonymously and the coins can only be deposited to the same account, from which they were withdrawn. Thus the bank need not check the coins for marking. As marks are ignored in the redemption phase, marking can safely be uncovered during this phase.

During the *tracing phase* marked coins are indistinguishable from unmarked coins, but only marked coins are traceable. Thus, tracing is undetectable and it is desired that the tracing phase is a certain time period Ω longer than the accept phase: If a coin is spent at the end of the accept phase, tracing is still guaranteed to be undetectable for at least the time period Ω. Finally, at the beginning of the *audit phase* marking is uncovered and the customers can check whether their coins have been marked or not.

From the customer's view the tracing phase should not be too long, as it is desired that illegal marking can be detected as soon as possible. However, the generate phase, the accept phase and Ω should not be chosen too short. For example these time periods can be chosen as follows: The tracing phase can be half a year, with an Ω of two months, which results in an accept phase of four months. Thus, the generate phase can be about two or three months.

3   Implementation of Auditable Marking

We base our implementation on the payment system of Kügler and Vogt [KV01]. Their marking mechanism was based on a variant of an Okamoto-Schnorr blind signature [Oka92] in combination with a Chaum-van Antwerpen undeniable signature [CvA89, Cha90]. The main idea of this construction is to use the blind signature to implement anonymity and the undeniable signature to implement marking. In this paper we assume that the bank will never prove the validity of an undeniable signature in a confirmation protocol, but still may prove the invalidity in a disavowal protocol.

3.1   Implementation of the Marking Mechanism

The system parameters are prime numbers p and q with $q|(p-1)$ and elements g_1, g_2 and g_3 of $(\mathbb{Z}/p\mathbb{Z})^*$ of order q. The bank chooses a key pair

$$SK_{\mathcal{B}} := (s_1, s_2) \in_R (\mathbb{Z}/q\mathbb{Z})^2$$
$$PK_{\mathcal{B}} := v = g_1^{s_1} g_2^{s_2} \bmod p$$

for the blind signature and a key pair

$$SK_{\mathcal{U}} := x \in_R \mathbb{Z}/q\mathbb{Z}$$
$$PK_{\mathcal{U}} := y = g_3^x \bmod p$$

for the undeniable signature scheme. Then it publishes the public keys $PK_{\mathcal{B}}$ and $PK_{\mathcal{U}}$.

The withdrawal protocol is shown in figure 2. For every withdrawal the bank creates a new random generator $\alpha = g_2^r \bmod p$, computes an undeniable signature $w = \alpha^x \bmod p$ as a certificate for α and sends these values to the customer. For every coin the bank and the customer interact in an Okamoto-Schnorr blind signature protocol, where the bank uses the generators g_1 and α. The customer transforms this signature to a signature based on the generators g_1 and $\alpha' = \alpha^\delta \bmod p$ using a randomly chosen $\delta \in_R (\mathbb{Z}/q\mathbb{Z})^*$ for every coin. This transformation is needed, because otherwise the bank could recognize coins at deposit on behalf of the generator α. Similarly, the certificate w has to be transformed to $w' = w^\delta = \alpha'^x \bmod p$ by the customer to circumvent recognition by the bank and to be a valid undeniable signature for α'. At the end of the withdrawal protocol the customer possesses coins of the form $(m, c', S_1', S_2', \alpha', w')$.

If the bank is instructed to issue marked coins, it simply chooses and stores a random undeniable signature key x_M, which is used instead of x to compute the certificate $w = \alpha^{x_M} \bmod p$. At deposit such a marking will be detected, as the key x will fail in the verification process. In this case the bank tests $w' \stackrel{?}{=} \alpha'^{x_M} \bmod p$ for all stored marking keys x_M. If this test succeeds for one of the marking keys, the coins can be associated with a certain withdrawal.

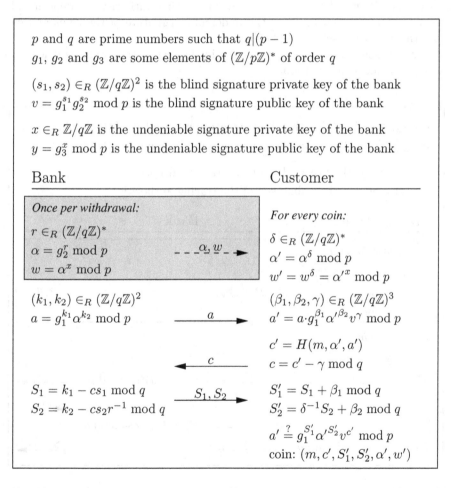

p and q are prime numbers such that $q | (p-1)$

g_1, g_2 and g_3 are some elements of $(\mathbb{Z}/p\mathbb{Z})^*$ of order q

$(s_1, s_2) \in_R (\mathbb{Z}/q\mathbb{Z})^2$ is the blind signature private key of the bank

$v = g_1^{s_1} g_2^{s_2} \bmod p$ is the blind signature public key of the bank

$x \in_R \mathbb{Z}/q\mathbb{Z}$ is the undeniable signature private key of the bank

$y = g_3^x \bmod p$ is the undeniable signature public key of the bank

Bank | **Customer**

Once per withdrawal:

For every coin:

$r \in_R (\mathbb{Z}/q\mathbb{Z})^*$

$\alpha = g_2^r \bmod p$

$w = \alpha^x \bmod p$

$\xrightarrow{\quad \alpha, w \quad}$

$\delta \in_R (\mathbb{Z}/q\mathbb{Z})^*$

$\alpha' = \alpha^\delta \bmod p$

$w' = w^\delta = \alpha'^x \bmod p$

$(k_1, k_2) \in_R (\mathbb{Z}/q\mathbb{Z})^2$

$a = g_1^{k_1} \alpha^{k_2} \bmod p$

$\xrightarrow{\quad a \quad}$

$(\beta_1, \beta_2, \gamma) \in_R (\mathbb{Z}/q\mathbb{Z})^3$

$a' = a \cdot g_1^{\beta_1} \alpha'^{\beta_2} v^\gamma \bmod p$

$c' = H(m, \alpha', a')$

$\xleftarrow{\quad c \quad}$

$c = c' - \gamma \bmod q$

$S_1 = k_1 - c s_1 \bmod q$

$S_2 = k_2 - c s_2 r^{-1} \bmod q$

$\xrightarrow{\quad S_1, S_2 \quad}$

$S_1' = S_1 + \beta_1 \bmod q$

$S_2' = \delta^{-1} S_2 + \beta_2 \bmod q$

$a' \stackrel{?}{=} g_1^{S_1'} \alpha'^{S_2'} v^{c'} \bmod p$

coin: $(m, c', S_1', S_2', \alpha', w')$

Fig. 2. Withdrawal of unmarked coins based on an Okamoto-Schnorr blind signature combined with a Chaum-van Antwerpen undeniable signature

3.2   Separating the Tracing Capabilities from the Bank

The capability of tracing can be removed from the bank and transfered to a separate tracing authority. The advantage of such a separation is that marking is invisible even for the bank. This clearly achieves a higher level of privacy protection, as the bank learns nothing about investigations against its customers. Again, the tracing authority need not be trusted, because illegal marking can always be detected and proven by the customer afterwards. It directly follows that the tracing authority is definitely not a trusted third party.

Figure 3 shows how the withdrawal is split into issuing coins by the bank and the possibility of marking coins by the tracing authority. At deposit only the tracing authority can check the undeniable signature of the coins and can trace the owner of each marked coin.

For simplicity we omit this extension in the rest of the paper as it leads in principle to the same solutions.

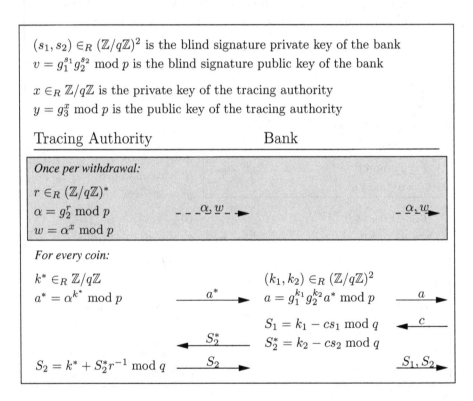

Fig. 3. The tracing authority takes the responsibility for marking, while the bank only issues coins

3.3   How to Uncover Marked Coins

We suggest the following mechanism to uncover marking: The private undeniable signature key x can be published at the beginning of the audit phase. Revealing this key has no impact on the security of the Okamoto-Schnorr signature, which is completely independent of the undeniable signature. Although anybody can use x to create valid undeniable signatures, this cannot be misused, as the undeniable signatures aren't checked anymore since the beginning of the redemption phase.

However, this enables the customer only to detect marking by testing whether $w \stackrel{?}{=} \alpha^x \bmod p$, but he needs additional information to prove this to other parties. Therefore, the bank has to issue an additional signature $S = \text{Sig}_{bank}(\alpha, w, customer\,ID, coin\,generation)$ at the beginning of every withdrawal. Then the customer is able to prove that the bank gave him marked coins of a specific coin generation.

3.4   Secure Redemption

Instead of spending the withdrawn coins, a customer can always redeem unspent coins to his own account. As marks can easily be removed after uncovering them in the audit phase, we do not check the mark w' of every coin during redemption. Anyway, marks are irrelevant in the redemption phase, as a coin can only be redeemed to the same account from which it has been withdrawn. We guarantee this property with the *secure redemption* method.

The idea for secure redemption of a coin $\mathcal{C} = (m, c', S'_1, S'_2, \alpha')$ is that the customer has to reveal the used blinding factors $\mathcal{B} = (\beta_1, \beta_2, \gamma, \delta)$ to the bank, which then takes advantage of the mapping between the bank's and the customer's view on a coin:

$$S'_1 = S_1 + \beta_1 \bmod q$$
$$S'_2 = \delta^{-1}S_2 + \beta_2 \bmod q$$
$$c' = c + \gamma \bmod q$$
$$\alpha' = \alpha^\delta \bmod p$$

With the given blinding factors the bank calculates the blinded values (c, S_1, S_2, α), looks them up in its database and checks that the customer has indeed withdrawn this coin. However, it is a property of blind signatures providing unconditional anonymity that for every other coin $\overline{\mathcal{C}} = (\overline{m}, \overline{c'}, \overline{S'_1}, \overline{S'_2}, \overline{\alpha})$ different blinding factors $\overline{\mathcal{B}}$ can be found that map this coin to the same blinded values (c, S_1, S_2, α).

In general the computation of blinding factors $\overline{\mathcal{B}}$ can be prevented, if one way functions are used for blinding, e.g. by choosing $\gamma = H(R) \bmod q$. In our case finding a blinding factor $\overline{\delta}$ already requires to calculate discrete logarithms. Therefore, to redeem a coin $\mathcal{C}$ it suffices to send $\mathcal{C}$ and the used blinding factor δ to the bank, which then calculates $\alpha = \alpha'^{\delta^{-1}} \bmod p$ and looks up α in its database to retrieve the identity of the withdrawer. If the signature of the coin $\mathcal{C}$ is valid, the coin is accepted for redemption and the amount is credited to the account of the ascertained withdrawer.

4   Properties of the Payment System

Based on the described marking mechanism, we will sketch how this mechanism may be applied to solve anonymity related problems.

4.1   Withdrawal Based Tracing

Withdrawal based tracing can be used in case a customer is suspected of money laundering or purchasing illegal goods. In such a case of legal tracing, marking has to be authorized by a judge, who issues a certificate for the marking key $y_M = g_3^{x_M} \bmod p$. This certificate must at least include y_M, an identification for the customer to be traced and the coin generation(s) for which marking of withdrawn coins is allowed (e.g. $C_{judge} = \text{Sig}_{judge}(y_M, customer\, ID, coin\, generation)$).

When a marked coin is deposited, the bank will recognize that the undeniable signature w' was not given with x and the bank will check whether the coin was generated with a stored marking key x_M. A traced coin is always accepted by the bank, which records this deanonymized transaction, as it can identify the traced customer on behalf of the used x_M.

In the audit phase the customer should be able to detect marking. Therefore, at the beginning of the audit phase the bank has to publish all marking keys x_M, which were used for tracing, together with an identifier of the judge, who is responsible for this tracing.

If the customer detects marking, he tests all the published marking keys to find out which judge issued the certificate for tracing. Then he can ask either the bank or the judge for the corresponding certificate C_{judge}, which proves that tracing was legal. Alternatively, the bank can directly give the used marking keys together with the corresponding C_{judge} to the traced customers. For privacy reasons this certificates should not be made available to persons other than the traced customers.

If none of the published marking keys was used for marking the customer's coins, the customer can prove the illegal marking by presenting S and $(\alpha, w, customer\, ID, coin\, generation)$ to a judge or to the press. If S is a valid signature on $(\alpha, w, customer\, ID, coin\, generation)$, but w was not generated with x or any of the published x_M, the fact of illegal marking may be made public and the bank can be punished.

4.2   Resistance against Blackmailing and Kidnapping

Withdrawal based tracing initiated by the customer can be used to fight blackmailing and kidnapping. The difference between blackmailing and kidnapping is that a kidnapper has physical control over his victim. Thus, the actions of the victim are observed by the kidnapper. In contrast to blackmailing, a kidnapper risks to be identified by his victim.

In both cases the customer should instruct the bank to issue marked coins, which will be detected at deposit. Depending on the choice of the customer the bank can accept or reject detected blackmailed marked coins at deposit. If the customer later instructs the bank to reject all his blackmailed coins, the bank will immediately refund all the unspent blackmailed coins to the customer. Then the bank can also prove with the disavowal protocol that the rejected coins have been blackmailed.

However, in the audit phase the bank must be able to prove that the issued marked coins are not illegally marked. Therefore, the bank needs a certificate from the customer, which proves that tracing was initiated by the customer. Then the bank will publish the corresponding marking key at the beginning of the audit phase together with a special flag, which indicates that the customer himself instructed the bank to trace his coins with this marking key.

In the case of kidnapping issuing such a certificate might be a problem, as the kidnapper observes the actions of the customer. This problem can be prevented, if the customer always has to issue a certificate $C_{customer} = \text{Sig}_{customer}(y_M, customer\,ID, coin\,generation)$ before a withdrawal. This certificate either authenticates the customer or it allows tracing depending on which of the following keys is used for the signature $C_{customer}$:

Authentication key: The customer uses this key for authentication towards the bank.

Emergency key: The customer uses this key for authentication in case of an emergency.

When the customer has set up his account, he certified both the authentication key and the emergency key with his signature key, for which a certificate is available from a PKI, and gave these certificates only to the bank.

As we assume that the kidnapper cannot distinguish between the usage of the authentication and the emergency key, the customer can inform the bank about a blackmailing or a kidnapping by using the emergency key for issuing the certificate $C_{customer}$ (a similar idea can be found in [DFTY97]).

Thus, for *every* withdrawal the bank chooses a new marking key x_M and calculates the challenge $(y_M, customer\,ID, coin\,generation)$ with $y_M = g_3^{x_M} \bmod p$. If the customer signs this challenge with the emergency key, the bank will issue coins marked by x_M and may prove that the customer instructed the bank to mark these coins by presenting a certificate $C_{customer}$ signed with the emergency key. As the emergency key itself is certified with the signature key, the customer cannot deny that he signed $C_{customer}$ with his emergency key.

4.3 Resistance against Bank Robberies

The ability to forge banknotes is a major threat for governments and banks, as a huge amount of forged banknotes will let the financial system of a country collapse. This situation is even worse with coin based anonymous electronic payment systems, as forged coins cannot be distinguished from regularly issued coins. This problem was first discovered by Jakobsson and Yung [JY96] who introduced the bank robbery attack, where the goal is to illegally obtain money from the bank: A robber can receive money either by gaining access to the bank's private signature keys, which are used to mint (unmarked) coins, or by blackmailing the bank to issue a number of coins in a non-regular withdrawal, so that tracing mechanisms will be circumvented by the blackmailer. The problem of bank robberies was already addressed in several papers (e.g. [JY96, PP97, JM98, Jak99]), however the previously proposed practical solutions rely on trust in a third party and thus offer only restricted privacy for the customers.

Our payment system cannot guarantee that the marking mechanism can also be used in the case of bank robberies, because the robber may gain the undeniable signature key x or force the bank to prove that the coins are unmarked (e.g. using a confirmation protocol for the undeniable signature).

A basic assumption of our approach to prevent bank robberies is that they do not occur often. After a bank robbery, the bank will immediately finish the accept phase of the affected coin generation to prevent spending of robbed coins. Then the customers have to redeem their coins with the secure redemption method and thus may exchange the legally withdrawn and unspent coins against new coins. The bank robber cannot redeem the robbed coins, as the bank always detects that these coins were not issued in a regular withdrawal, as their α will not be stored in the database of withdrawn coins and the secure redemption also prevents mapping of robbed coins to legally withdrawn and already spent coins (as explained in section 3.4).

We still have to prevent the bank from cheating by erasing withdrawal transcripts from its database so that those coins cannot be redeemed anymore. In this case the customer may present the signature $S = \mathrm{Sig}_{bank}(\alpha, w, customer\ ID, coin\ generation)$ given at the withdrawal (see section 3.3) to prove that the bank has indeed issued this coin. Note that a bank robber, who is able to forge this signature S and wants to accuse the bank of having erased his withdrawal transcripts, faces the problem that he has to identify himself to a judge and risks to be prosecuted for the bank robbery.

5   Comparison of Tracing Methods

The advantage of systems with revokable anonymity is the ability of tracing and even invalidating any withdrawn coin. Thus, blackmailing of customers and investigation of money laundering or illegal purchases can easily be solved. In our system tracing is only possible, if the customer or a judge has decided to make the coins of a certain withdrawal traceable. If it was not decided to make the coins traceable, this decision is unalterable afterwards.

An advantage of our scheme is it's strong privacy, because unmarked coins enjoy unconditional anonymity, while our payment system is very efficient in fighting anonymity related problems. Instead of using steamroller tactics to investigate blackmailing, money laundering, and illegal purchases our tracing method can only be applied for tracing suspicious persons by marking the withdrawn coins and tracing them to the depositing persons. Anyway, this tracing will be detected in the audit phase so that illegal tracing is inhibited.

Due to the unconditional anonymity, our payment scheme protects the privacy of payments until the end of time. In contrast, illegal tracing will be possible in payment systems offering only computational anonymity (e.g. [CMS96, DFTY97]) as soon as the used cryptosystem can be broken. Then even an honest trusted third party might not be able to inhibit illegal tracing.

The simple infrastructure of our system is clearly another advantage. In contrast to systems with revocable anonymity our approach doesn't rely on trusted third parties. In general a trusted third party causes additional costs, which the customer may not be willing to pay for. As a trusted third party manages sensitive personal data or even administrates security relevant data, it has to be protected carefully. However, the more secure the trusted third party is, the more expensive is the service of the trusted third party. Other arguments against the use of trusted third parties may be found in the discussion of key escrow [AAB+98].

6   Conclusion

We have presented a new payment system with a fair tracing mechanism, which is able to defend against blackmailing, kidnapping, and bank robberies and can also be used to support investigations of money laundering and illegal purchases.

Although our payment system allows tracing, it offers more privacy than any other system offering the same features: A traced customer will afterwards detect the fact of being legally or illegally traced. If the tracing turns out to be illegal, the customer can prove this violation of his privacy and the bank can be prosecuted. Nevertheless, our payment system requires only a simple and cheap infrastructure, as it does not rely on trusted third parties.

Finally we'd like to recall that our payment system is quite modular, as a separation of issuing and marking coins is possible. If desired, a tracing authority can mark and trace coins, which is even invisible to the bank. This tracing authority need not be trusted, as our tracing mechanism is auditable.

References

AAB+98. H. Abelson, R. Anderson, S. Bellovin, J. Benaloh, M. Blaze, W. Diffie, J. Gilmore, P. Neumann, R. Rivest, J. Schiller, and B. Schneier. The risks of key recovery, key escrow, and trusted third-party encryption. Online available at http://www.cdt.org/crypto/risks98, 1998. An earlier version appeared in World Wide Web Journal, v.2, n.3, 1997, pages 241–257.

ASW97. N. Asokan, M. Schunter, and M. Waidner. Optimistic protocols for fair exchange. In *4th ACM Conference on Computer and Communications Security – CCS'97*, pages 6–17, Zürich, Switzerland, 1997. ACM Press.

CFN88. D. Chaum, A. Fiat, and M. Naor. Untraceable electronic cash. In *Advances in Cryptology – CRYPTO'88*, volume 401 of *Lecture Notes in Computer Science*, pages 319–327. Springer-Verlag, 1988.

Cha83. D. Chaum. Blind signatures for untraceable payments. In *Advances in Cryptology – CRYPTO'82*, pages 199–203. Plenum, 1983.

Cha90.   D. Chaum. Zero-knowledge undeniable signatures. In *Advances in Cryptology – EUROCRYPT'90*, volume 473 of *Lecture Notes in Computer Science*, pages 458–464. Springer-Verlag, 1990.

CMS96.   J. Camenisch, U. Maurer, and M. Stadler. Digital payment systems with passive anonymity-revoking trustees. In *Computer Security – ESORICS'96*, volume 1146 of *Lecture Notes in Computer Science*, pages 31–43. Springer-Verlag, 1996.

CvA89.   D. Chaum and H. van Antwerpen. Undeniable signatures. In *Advances in Cryptology – CRYPTO'89*, volume 435 of *Lecture Notes in Computer Science*, pages 212–216. Springer-Verlag, 1989.

DFTY97.   G. Davida, Y. Frankel, Y. Tsiounis, and M. Yung. Anonymity control in e-cash systems. In *Financial Cryptography – FC'97*, volume 1318 of *Lecture Notes in Computer Science*, pages 1–16. Springer-Verlag, 1997.

FTY96.   Y. Frankel, Y. Tsiounis, and M. Yung. "Indirect discourse proofs": Achieving efficient fair off-line e-cash. In *Advances in Cryptology – ASIACRYPT'96*, volume 1163 of *Lecture Notes in Computer Science*, pages 286–300. Springer-Verlag, 1996.

Jak99.   M. Jakobsson. Mini-cash: A minimalistic approach to e-commerce. In *Public Key Cryptography – PKC'99*, volume 1560 of *Lecture Notes in Computer Science*, pages 122–135. Springer-Verlag, March 1999.

JM98.   M. Jakobsson and D. M'Raïhi. Mix-based electronic payments. In *Annual International Workshop on Selected Areas in Cryptography – SAC'98*, volume 1556 of *Lecture Notes in Computer Science*, pages 157–173. Springer-Verlag, 1998.

JSI96.   M. Jakobsson, K. Sako, and R. Impagliazzo. Designated verifier proofs and their applications. In *Advances in Cryptology – EUROCRYPT'96*, volume 1070 of *Lecture Notes in Computer Science*, pages 143–154. Springer-Verlag, 1996.

JY96.   M. Jakobsson and M. Yung. Revokable and versatile electronic money. In *3rd ACM Conference on Computer and Communications Security – CCS'96*, pages 76–87. ACM Press, 1996.

KV01.   D. Kügler and H. Vogt. Marking: A privacy protecting approach against blackmailing. In *Public Key Cryptography – PKC 2001*, volume 1992 of *Lecture Notes in Computer Science*, pages 137–152. Springer-Verlag, 2001.

Oka92.   T. Okamoto. Provably secure and practical identification schemes and corresponding signature schemes. In *Advances in Cryptology – CRYPTO'92*, volume 740 of *Lecture Notes in Computer Science*, pages 31–53. Springer-Verlag, 1992.

PP97.   H. Petersen and G. Poupard. Efficient scalable fair cash with off-line extortion prevention. In *International Conference on Information and Communications Security – ICICS'97*, volume 1334 of *Lecture Notes in Computer Science*, pages 463–477. Springer-Verlag, 1997.

Sch97.   B. Schoenmakers. Security aspects of the ecash payment system. In *COSIC'97 Course*, volume 1528 of *Lecture Notes in Computer Science*, pages 338–352. Springer-Verlag, 1997.

SPC95.   M. Stadler, J.-M. Piveteau, and J. Camenisch. Fair blind signatures. In *Advances in Cryptology – EUROCRYPT'95*, volume 921 of *Lecture Notes in Computer Science*, pages 209–219. Springer-Verlag, 1995.

vSN92.   B. von Solms and D. Naccache. On blind signatures and perfect crimes. *Computers and Security*, 11(6):581–583, 1992.

Why the War on Money Laundering Should Be Aborted

Richard W. Rahn

Chairman, Novecon Financial Ltd.
Senior Fellow, Discovery Institute
1020 16th Street, NW, Washington DC 20036

Financial cryptographers are heroes, because their efforts both increase the economic well being of most of the world's peoples, and more importantly, preserve their liberty. I shall explain.

Money laundering is a terrible crime—right? Government officials and their allies in the press seem on almost a monthly basis to demand new powers to deal with the terrible menace of money laundering. Exactly what is this crime?

If you hesitate while trying to come up with a definition, you have begun to understand part of the problem. Money laundering is hard to define because it is not a crime like murder, robbery, or rape, where the evil act is clear. It is a crime of motive rather than activity. In fact, two different people can engage in the exact same set of activities, and one can be guilty of money laundering while the other is not. In fact, money laundering has only been illegal in the US since 1986, and it is not illegal in all countries.

Government efforts to combat money laundering will directly or indirectly affect the institutions for which you work. Thus, it will be important to be aware of the rules and regulations against money laundering, and the detrimental effect that they have on economic growth and personal liberty.

To observe, let alone regulate, money laundering is the financial equivalent of the Heisenberg uncertainty principle in quantum mechanics, whereby the act of observing the activity changes its nature. There are close to an infinite number of ways to "launder" money, and sophisticated money launderers know what the government rules and regulations are, and what information financial institutions are supposed to monitor and report. Thus, the behavior of money launderers instantly changes as the rules, regulations, and monitoring systems change. It is a classic no-win situation for the regulators.

Money laundering is generally understood to be the practice of taking ill gotten gains and moving them through a sequence of bank accounts so they ultimately look like the profits from legitimate activity. Institutions, individuals, and even governments who are believed to be aiding and abetting the practice of money laundering can be indicted and convicted, even though they may be completely unaware that the money being transferred with their help was of criminal origin. This makes as much sense as convicting an automobile manufacturer or dealer because someone who has purchased a car uses it in a criminal act, or charging the telephone company with a crime when someone uses a telephone to facilitate a criminal act.

P. Syverson (Ed.): FC 2001, LNCS 2339, pp. 149–155, 2002.

Financial institutions are required to "know your customer," which means they are required to know that their customers are not doing anything wrong - an impossible task. This is a dangerous principle because it could obviously be extended to any business from which a good or service sold is used for illegal purposes.

We are told we must stop money laundering in order to combat terrorism, drug dealing, assorted criminality, and tax evasion. However, if you look at the results of this so-called war on money laundering, you find that it has failed to produce the advertised results and, in fact, has not been cost effective, has resulted in wholesale violations of individual civil liberties (including privacy rights), has violated the rights of sovereign governments and peoples, has created new opportunities for criminal activity, and has actually lessened our ability to reduce crime.

Anti-money laundering advocates claim that strong anti-money laundering legislation and regulations are needed to prevent terrorism. Without a doubt, terrorism is a real threat, and has the potential to destroy millions of lives and severely damage our economic and social infrastructure. Chemical, biological and even nuclear weapons probably have leaked into the hands of terrorists from the former Soviet Union and former communist Eastern European states. Simply stated, the threat is real and ought not to be treated lightly. However, that said, is there evidence that the anti-money laundering activities have stopped or are likely to stop terrorist activities? The answer is no, for the following reasons. Terrorists for the most part only need modest amounts of money to ply their trade, and such relatively small sums can easily be hidden in normal looking transactions. In fact, anti-terrorism experts report that terrorists frequently use innocent sounding NGO's to fund their activities. These same experts tell us that the only effective way to destroy terrorist organizations is to infiltrate them. In addition, the NSA and CIA have long had the legal authority they need to monitor the activities (including financial) of terrorist organizations. In sum, there is no evidence that the arsenal of anti-money laundering tools employed by governments has stopped any major terrorist activity, nor is it likely to have any impact on committed terrorists in the future. In fact, the claims made by some in the anti-money laundering war, that their activities reduce terrorism, may well be giving an erroneous and false sense of security, which only increases the risks.

The most common claim of the anti-money laundering advocates is that anti-money laundering tools, such as Currency Transaction Reports, Suspicious Activity Reports, and asset forfeitures are needed to stop illegal drug trafficking. Most objective observers of the "war on drugs" acknowledge that the war is not being won and, at best, is a stalemate. For instance, the Governor of New Mexico, Gary Johnson, recently wrote in the New York Times (Dec. 30, 2000):

> I'm neither soft on crime nor pro-drugs in any sense. Yet when I ask whether our costly, protracted war on drugs has made the world safer for our children, I must answer no. The federal anti-drug budget in 1980 was roughly $1 billion. By 2000, that number had climbed to nearly

$20 billion, with the states spending at least that much. Yet according to the federal government's own research, drugs are cheaper, purer and more readily available than ever before.

Governor Johnson's skepticism is shared by many knowledgeable and thoughtful people across the political spectrum, including former Secretary of State George Shultz and Nobel Prize winning economist Milton Friedman, who believe drugs should be decriminalized.

Those who call for decriminalization are not denying that drugs destroy the lives of many people and cause great harm to society. They are merely arguing that the war on drugs, including the war on money laundering, has many more negatives than positives.

The anti-money laundering laws certainly have made life more inconvenient for drug dealers, but not so inconvenient as to get them to change their ways. Part of the reason is that fewer than 1,000 people per year have been convicted of money laundering in the US since it became illegal. The amount of money confiscated is a tiny fraction of 1% of the total amount of money the government says is laundered each year. (It is worth noting that other governments, such as the UK, have been no more successful than the US in this endeavor.) In sum, the deterrent effect is almost nil. Laundering money is a far easier task than smuggling literally thousands of tons of marijuana plus vast quantities of other illegal drugs into the US each year.

The curse of the drug culture is not going to be stopped with sporadic attacks on drug supplies or increases in anti-money laundering activities. At times, after listening to those who advocate doing more of what clearly doesn't work, one cannot help but wonder what they might be smoking. The drug war is only going to be won by substantially reducing the demand for drugs, which is an educational task, not a police task.

Another common reason given in favor of anti-money laundering activities is to reduce various sorts of crimes such as kidnappings, smuggling and racketeering. However, the empirical evidence indicates that anti-money laundering (and anti-drug) laws have, in fact, stimulated kidnappings, smuggling and racketeering. Kidnappings are soaring in parts of Latin America, particularly Colombia, to many thousands per year, largely because of the drug war. Yet, at the same time, honest individuals are having increasing difficulties hiding their assets from potential kidnappers, corrupt governments, and other criminals because of the anti-money laundering laws and regulations. In fact, a whole new criminal industry has grown up because of these laws and regulations - the money laundering industry. We now know that much of what we call organized crime began during Prohibition, which gave rise to the bootlegging industry. Like Prohibition, what is happening is a classic case of the police creating an increased demand for their services by inventing new crimes which, in turn, creates a new criminal industry to evade the new laws.

Former Federal Reserve Governor Lawrence Lindsey (and now President George W. Bush's chief economic advisor) has been an outspoken critic of the current war on money laundering, primarily on the grounds that it has not been cost effective and has violated basic privacy rights. Lindsey has noted:

> Between 1987 and 1995, the government collected 77 million currency-transaction reports, something on the order of 62 tons of paper. Out of that, it was able to prosecute 3,000 money-laundering cases. That is roughly one case for every 25,000 forms filed. In other words, entire forests had to be felled in order to prosecute one case. But it gets worse: Of the 3,000 money-laundering cases prosecuted, the government managed to produce only 580 guilty verdicts. In other words, in excess of 100,000 reports were filed by innocent citizens in order to get one conviction. That ratio of 99,999 to one is something we normally would not tolerate as a reasonable balance between privacy and the collection of guilty verdicts.

It gets worse. Banks are required to supply the government with not only Currency Transaction Reports but also Suspicious Activity Reports. These reports impose huge regulatory costs on banks and require bank employees to operate as police officers. As a result, the total public and private sector costs greatly exceed $ 10,000,000 per conviction. This whole effort not only does not make any economic sense, but is clearly incompatible with a free society. The anti-money laundering laws allow almost complete prosecutorial discretion. For instance, any potential government official who did not pay the "nanny tax" could be subject to prosecution under the anti-money laundering statutes, because it was a crime involving money. Again, Governor Lindsey noted: "we have a literally unlimited application of that law to anyone engaging in any transaction who has ever committed a crime ? [no matter how minor]."

It is clear that former Vice President Al Gore and many of his staff could have been charged with violating the anti-money laundering statutes because of the Buddhist temple fundraising scam, if he did not have such a sympathetic prosecutor in Attorney General Janet Reno. Newspaper reports give the impression that there are many money laundering violations in political fundraising by all parties. However, virtually no one is prosecuted since such prosecutions would not be popular with the political class.

However, a corporate leader (particularly one who had not made large contributions to the appropriate politician) probably would have been subject to both civil and criminal liabilities for the same "studied ignorance" of activities performed by underlings that were ignored in Al Gore's case.

Thomas Jefferson said: "When the government fears the people, there is liberty. When the people fear the government, there is tyranny." The anti-money laundering statutes are a clear attempt to get the people to fear the government. For those of you who doubt that government officials use such statutes to routinely violate fundamental privacy rights and prosecutorial discretion, I suggest that you read an excellent new book by the very distinguished economist and former Assistant Secretary of the US Treasury, Dr. Paul Craig Roberts, entitled, *The Tyranny of Good Intentions*, as well as my own book, *The End of Money and the Struggle for Financial Privacy.* Former judge John Yoder, who was the first head of the Asset Forfeiture Office of the US Department of Justice, wrote:

> When I set up the Asset Forfeiture Office, I thought I could use my position to help protect citizens' rights, and tried to ensure that the US Department of Justice went after big drug dealers and other big time criminals, rather than minor offenders and innocent property owners. Today, overzealous government agents and prosecutors will not think twice about seizing a yacht or car if they find two marijuana cigarettes in it, regardless of where they came from. I am now ashamed of, and scared of, the monster I helped create.

There is a certain irony in the fact that many of those who are the biggest advocates of giving the government more power to control money laundering in the name of crime reduction are in fact impairing our ability to reduce crime. Perhaps the most common criminal act is for one person to try to steal another person's money. This is most often paper currency. There were approximately 18,000 murders in the US last year, and tens of millions of robberies and burglaries. Many of these crimes were, probably, in pursuit of paper currency. An easy way to reduce the amount of crime is to greatly reduce the amount of paper currency by going to various forms of electronic currency. The technology now exists - transfers from computer to computer, or to and from wireless devices and smart cards. A major barrier in the widespread adoption of such devices is the desire of the citizens to have the same degree of anonymity with such devices that they have with paper currency. Yet government officials have tried to restrict the use of the necessary encryption (those of you who are financial cryptographers well understand how absurd such restrictions are) and limit the amounts of money that can be transferred with such devices, unless there is an audit trail that enables government agents to spy on everyone's financial transactions. Those who advocate such restrictions have no understanding of costs and benefits and little appreciation of liberty and financial privacy.

The most dubious reason often given by the advocates of anti-money laundering laws and regulations is that of trying to stop tax evasion. First, such advocates seem to have problems differentiating between tax evasion and tax avoidance - which is not only legal but also a right. Second, such advocates seem to be unable to differentiate between evading reasonable taxes imposed by honest democratic governments and unreasonable taxes imposed by dishonest and corrupt governments.

Recently, the Organization for Economic Cooperation and Development (OECD), the club of 29 rich nations, has denounced and is threatening 35 mainly smaller and poorer nations for engaging in "unfair tax competition." What the leaders of the OECD are upset about is the fact that many of their citizens are moving financial assets to these non-OECD jurisdictions with less punitive tax laws. These smaller countries have found that it is good business to build financial sectors based on reasonable tax rates and financial privacy. Some arrogant bullies in the OECD are now trying to use international money laundering treaties, and more odious forms of coercion, to try to force these small countries to raise tax rates and abolish financial privacy. To do so would force many of these countries to go back to relying almost totally on tourism and sugar cane for economic sustenance. No nation has the right to tell another sovereign entity what its tax rates and financial privacy policies ought to be. To do so is nothing more than financial imperialism.

The facts are that most of the OECD countries now have at least some tax rates higher than the revenue maximizing rate and, to the extent these rates are on labor and capital, they diminish both economic growth and the social welfare of their citizens. Many of the taxes on capital are in essence expropriation. Such rates are both economically destructive and immoral. To remove one's capital from such mistreatment is rational and to be expected. Tax competition is very desirable because it forces governments to be both more cost effective and less coercive.

Given that not all the world's people can live in Switzerland, they at least ought to have the basic human right to opt out of financially repressive regimes. No one would argue that it was immoral for a citizen of Nazi Germany to avoid paying taxes that would be used to support the death camps and the war machine. There may not be regimes still left that are as criminal as Hitler's or Stalin's but, unfortunately, there are still many criminal and corrupt governments around the globe. Some of the shrillest voices in the anti-money laundering crowd are often very naïve about the nature of many of the criminal and corrupt governments that still inhabit our planet. The OECD nations quite simply have no moral right to prevent people from hiding taxes and other financial assets from such governments - and, in fact, the demands to end all bank secrecy and increase tax rates would do precisely that.

Those governments and politicians who are unhappy about "tax havens" might do well to look in the mirror and ask themselves why so many of their own citizens are moving assets and income elsewhere. Even in the relatively free democratic countries, it is hard to find governmental units where there is not considerable waste of the taxpayer monies. If a business delivered equally poor service for what many governments charge, it would either go out of business or its owners would be fined and perhaps sent to jail for misrepresentation. Given that governmental units are almost always monopolies and also control the police and justice functions, an abused taxpayer often only has the options of revolution or moving his or her assets. Capital flight is a peaceful signal to government authorities to "get your house in order." To cut off this alternative under the guise of fighting money laundering is likely to lead to far worse consequences.

As a result of easily usable and almost unbreakable public key encryption, the Internet, and rapidly developing digital money products, the ability of governments to detect and control the movement of money and other financial assets will be almost impossible without governments knowing everything about everyone's financial affairs. History teaches us that governments abuse the information they have about their citizens. Both the US Constitution and the UN Declaration of Human Rights recognize and guarantee basic privacy rights, including financial privacy.

The new technologies are developing so rapidly that government will not be able to keep up with the innovations. As Ronald Reagan once said, "The best minds are not in government. If any were, business would hire them right away." President Reagan's quip was not intended to disparage the many very hard-working, intelligent, and dedicated government employees, but only to illustrate that government is seldom on the cutting edge of new technologies. The serious money launderers will always be a couple of steps ahead of government. That does not mean that the money laundering police will not be able to catch a few people each year, but they will be primarily the slow, the careless, the small fish, and the politically targeted. The big, serious money launderers will be less likely to be caught in the future than they are now, which means it will be a relatively safe occupation.

We are always told by those who advocate giving government more information about us that it will be kept confidential and our trust and confidence will not be betrayed. Yet we are always betrayed. IRS and FBI files, again and again, are not kept secret. The government was even unable to keep our most sensitive nuclear weapons files secret, yet we are told to trust. Do you really think it was just a coincidence that many of the conservative public policy organizations that were critics of the Clinton Administration were audited, while none of liberal ones were?

Benjamin Franklin said it best: "They that can give up essential liberty to obtain a little temporary safety deserve neither safety nor liberty."

As I noted in the beginning of this talk, those of you in the financial cryptography business are heroes in that your work is critical in guaranteeing that people will still be able to enjoy a reasonable degree of liberty in the information age. Even those of you who are not motivated by belief, but by a desire for more wealth are nevertheless heroes, because as the great economist and philosopher Adam Smith noted 225 years ago, the invisible hand of your own self-interested efforts are benefiting all mankind. Keep it up!

I expect that most of those who advocate anti-money laundering laws and regulations are not mean-spirited, but decent folks who just have not thought through the consequences of what they are promoting and doing. I also realize that during the last two decades a sizable anti-money laundering industry has emerged with many billions of dollars to spend, and that those whose jobs depend on such an industry - law enforcement officials, equipment purveyors, and assorted bureaucrats, etc. - are not going to take kindly to my comments, even if they cannot refute my arguments.

But if you truly want less crime, more prosperity and opportunity, and more freedom, you will "just say no" to the anti-money laundering laws and regulations.

Provably Secure Implicit Certificate Schemes

Daniel R.L. Brown[1], Robert Gallant[1], and Scott A. Vanstone[1,2]

[1] Certicom Research, Canada
{dbrown,rgallant,svanstone}@certicom.com
[2] University of Waterloo, Canada

Abstract. Optimal mail certificates, introduced in [12], are efficient types of implicit certificates which offer many advantages over traditional (explicit) certificates. For example, an optimal mail certificate is small enough to fit on a two-dimensional digital postal mark together with a digital signature. This paper defines a general notion of security for implicit certificates, and proves that optimal mail certificates are secure under this definition.

Keywords: Implicit certificate, authentication, postal payment, elliptic curve cryptography, provable security.

1 Introduction

A certificate authority (CA) is a vital component of a secure public-key infrastructure. The primary role of the CA is to bind public keys to their legitimate owners by creating *certificates* for those users. Certificates are comprised of a data part which contains, at a minimum, a public key and a user identity, and the CA's signature on this data. If the CA's signature on the data part of a certificate is valid, then one has confidence that the data (and what the data implies) contained in the certificate is genuine.

Implicit certificates, introduced in the work of Günther [8] and Girault [7], are comprised of a user's identity I and some reconstruction public data P, which together with the CA's public key are used to reconstruct the user's public key. That is, the public key is not explicitly contained in the implicit certificate. The authenticity of a reconstructed public key is only established after it is subsequently used in a successful run of some protocol. In *identity-based* implicit certificate schemes, the user's private key is computed by the CA. In *self-certified* implicit certificate schemes, the user itself computes its private key and associated public key. For further details on this distinction, see [10]. This paper only considers self-certified implicit certificate schemes.

We consider the security aspects of the implicit certificate scheme introduced in [12], the *optimal mail certificate* scheme. This scheme has several desirable efficiency attributes, in particular, the bit length of an optimal mail certificate is short enough to fit in a two-dimensional digital postal mark together with an elliptic curve based digital signature with partial message recovery (a PVSSR signature [4,9]). The major contribution of this paper is the formulation of a

P. Syverson (Ed.): FC 2001, LNCS 2339, pp. 156–165, 2002.

general definition for the security of implicit certificate schemes, and a proof that the optimal mail certificate scheme of [12] is secure under this definition.

The remainder of this paper is organized as follows. Our notation and some security issues of implicit certificates are covered in §2. §3 reviews the optimal mail certificate scheme. The security model and proof and presented in §4. Finally, some conclusions are drawn in §5.

2 Background

2.1 Notation

Our notation for the elliptic curve[1] domain parameters specifying the group, its order and its generator are as follows. Let q denote the order of the underlying finite field $\mathbb{F}_q$, and let E be an elliptic curve defined over $\mathbb{F}_q$. Let G denote a point in $E(\mathbb{F}_q)$, the *generator point*, and let n denote the order of G. We assume that n is prime. Thus $nG = \mathcal{O}$ and $G \neq \mathcal{O}$. The group $\langle G \rangle$ of points generated by G will be used in the optimal mail certificate scheme. We assume that the discrete logarithm problem in $\langle G \rangle$ is intractable. More precisely, this means that there is no probabilistic polynomial-time algorithm (polynomial in the security parameter $l = \lfloor \log_2 n \rfloor$) which on input $C \in_R \langle G \rangle$, $C \neq \mathcal{O}$, can output $c \in [1, n-1]$ satisfying $C = cG$ with non-negligible probability.

Let $c \in [1, n-1]$ be the CA's private key, and $C = cG$ the CA's public key. Similarly, $b \in [1, n-1]$ is Bob's private key, and $B = bG$ is Bob's public key. Let P denote Bob's reconstruction public data, which is an elliptic curve point. We refer to the party that reconstructs Bob's public key as Alice.

Let I denote some information that is included in Bob's certificate. In the case of an implicit certificate, I should typically include data such as Bob's identifier, the CA's identifier, the validity period of the certificate, and possibly a serial number.

Let H denote a secure hash function, such as SHA-1. The selected hash function is an important part of the domain parameters of the system.

2.2 Implicit Certificates

Bob's implicit certificate is a pair (P, I) which, together with the CA's public key C, is used by Alice to reconstruct Bob's public key B. As in traditional, explicit certificates, Alice must trust the CA and the authenticity of C in order to arrive at the assurance that B is indeed Bob's public key. With explicit certificates, Alice verifies the signature with public key C, and thus is assured that B belongs Bob. However, such an explicit certificate alone is not sufficient for Bob to authenticate himself to Alice, because the explicit certificate is public information. To authenticate himself, Bob must demonstrate knowledge of his

---

[1] Although the implicit certificate scheme studied in this paper can be described using any cyclic group such as $\mathbb{Z}_p^*$, the efficiency of elliptic curve groups are better matched with the efficiency of the optimal mail certificate scheme.

private key b through some secure cryptographic protocol such as a key agreement scheme or a digital signature scheme. The same holds true for an implicit certificate: to authenticate himself to Alice, Bob must demonstrate knowledge of his private key b. Once Bob accomplishes this, Alice is assured that B belongs to Bob, and also that Bob has authenticated himself in the protocol used to prove his knowledge of b. In other words, one distinction between explicit and implicit certificates is that, for the latter, the authentication to Alice of B belonging to Bob and the authentication to Alice that she is communicating with Bob are not separable.

3   Optimal Mail Certificates

In [12], Pintsov and Vanstone proposed an implicit certificate scheme which has significant efficiency advantages. We review this scheme, also depicted in Figure 2. Suppose that Bob wishes to obtain an implicit certificate from a CA. Bob selects $r \in_R [1, n-1]$, computes $R = rG$, and sends R to the CA over an authentic channel. The CA checks Bob's credentials according to its policies, and establishes certificate information I for Bob's implicit certificate. The CA then selects $k \in_R [1, n-1]$, and computes Bob's reconstruction public data $P = kG + R$. The CA then computes $h = H(P, I)$ and $s = hk + c \bmod n.$[2] Finally, the CA sends (P, I, s) to Bob. Bob sets his private key to be $b = hr + s \bmod n$ where again $h = H(P, I)$. Bob's public key, $B = bG$, can be reconstructed by Alice from the implicit certificate (P, I) using the equation

$$B = H(P, I)P + C,$$

which holds because $B = bG = (hr + s)G = (hr + hk + c)G = h(k + r)G + cG = hP + C$, where $h = H(P, I)$. Thus Bob knows the logarithm of $B = H(P, I)P + C$ with respect to the generator point G. Alice can reconstruct B using only the point P, the certificate information I, and the CA's public key C.

Note that when Bob or any other party receives the response (P, I, s) to certificate request R, then it is possible to verify the authenticity of the response by checking the equation

$$H(P, I)R + sG = H(P, I)P + C.$$

Since this equation involves the CA's public key, an integer s, and a secure hash function, s would seem to depend on the private key of the CA in some way. Indeed this equation is similar to the equation used to verify digital signatures such as DSA and Schnorr signatures.

3.1   Applications

In environments where bandwidth is severely constrained, traditional X.509 certificates based on a digital signature algorithm such as RSA, DSA, or ECDSA,

---

[2] This signing equation is a variant of the Schnorr signing equation [16].

CA	Bob	Alice

$$r \in_R [1, n-1]$$
$$R = rG$$

$$\xleftarrow{\quad R \quad}$$
authentic

$$k \in_R [1, n-1]$$
$$P = R + kG$$
$$h = H(P, I)$$
$$s = kh + c \bmod n$$

$$\xrightarrow{\quad (P, I, s) \quad}$$

$$h = H(P, I)$$
$$b = rh + s \bmod n$$

$$\xrightarrow{\quad (P, I) \quad}$$

$$B = H(P, I)P + C$$

Figure 1. The optimal mail certificate scheme

may be too long to be transmitted in a public-key protocol. Instead, a shorter piece of information that identifies the certificate, such as the issuer and serial number or the eight bytes of the hash of the public key, is sent. However, this requires the recipient of the certificate to look up the certificate in some database, which would either be stored locally or remotely. Such a look-up may be costly, especially at remote locations or using limited resources. One method to alleviate this problem is random sampling, i.e., verifying only a small fraction of all certificates.

Optimal mail certificates are designed to be small enough to be sent completely, in order to avoid look-up and random sampling. Furthermore, their small size allows for larger local databases to be maintained, in case local look-up or random sampling is used.

The size of an optimal mail certificate (P, I) based on an elliptic curve over $\mathbb{F}_q$, where $q = 2^{163}$, is about 164 bits plus the length of the certificate information I. In comparison, the size of an explicit certificate containing a public key defined over the same elliptic curve and signed with ECDSA by a certificate authority with the public key on the same elliptic curve would be about 492 bits plus the length of the certification information. An explicit certificate based on RSA public keys and a digital signature using public keys of comparable security (namely, 1024 bits) would have length 2048 bits plus the length of the certificate information. For constrained environments, such as a two-dimensional bar code, even 492 bits may be too large for a reasonable density and size of bar code.

4   Security Model and Proof

In what follows we prove certain attributes of the optimal mail certificate scheme described in §3. Our proofs are in the random oracle model [3], in which the hash function is modeled by a perfectly random function. In reality, a hash function such as SHA-1 cannot be regarded as a random function. Nevertheless, a proof in the random oracle model suggests that if there is any attack against the scheme, then the attack must be specific to a particular hash function being used, or must process the description of the hash function itself. Intuitively, such attacks seem less feasible than generic attacks that simply invoke the hash function as a black-box. Indeed, almost all attacks in practice on such protocols are in fact generic attacks. For a more detailed discussion on the pros and cons of the random oracle model, see [2] and [6].

4.1   Security Model for Implicit Certificates

We formulate a notion of security for general implicit certificate schemes. The legitimate users in the system are denoted $Bob_1, Bob_2, \ldots$. The CAs in the system are denoted $CA_1, CA_2, \ldots$; CA_j's public key is C_j. We assume that all users have authentic copies of all CA public keys. User Bob_i's request for a certificate from CA_j is denoted (R_i, j). CA_j's response is denoted (P_i, I_i, s_i) which, together with C_j, is used by Bob_i to construct his public key B_i and associated private key b_i. Bob_i may make multiple requests for certificates from CA_j.

Definition 1. *A (τ, ϵ)-adversary A (of an implicit certificate scheme) is a probabilistic Turing machine which runs in time at most τ and interacts with the legitimate users and the CAs by performing each of the following operations any number of times:*

(i) *receive a request (R_i, j) from Bob_i for an implicit certificate from CA_j; and*
(ii) *send a request $(R'_{i'}, j')$ to $CA_{j'}$, and receive response $(P'_{i'}, I'_{i'}, s'_{i'})$ from $CA_{j'}$.*

With probability at least ϵ, A outputs a triple (P, I, b) such that b is the private key associated with the public key reconstructed from P, I and some C_k (that is, $bG = H(P, I)P + C_k$) such that either

(i) *(P, I) was never part of a response of CA_k; or*
(ii) *(P, I) was included in a response of CA_k to some request (R_i, j) originally from Bob_i.*

A (τ, ϵ)-adversary is successful if τ is polynomial in $l = \lfloor \log_2 n \rfloor$, and ϵ is a non-negligible function of l.

The security model if depicted in Figure 4.1. All requests (R_i, j) from user Bob_i are sent through the adversary A, who may pass on the request unchanged to CA_j, or may choose to modify the request point R_i, or the identity i of the requester, or the designated CA. In this model, the adversary A is deemed successful if it generates an implicit certificate that is a forgery in either one of the following two senses. In the first sense, A generates an implicit certificate and an associated private key that was not issued by a CA. This may be regarded as a successful attack by A against that CA. In the second sense, A generates an implicit certificate and a private key that was issued by a CA for a request of some user Bob_i. This may be regarded as a successful attack by A against Bob_i.

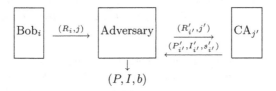

Figure 2. A security model for implicit certificates

Note that the security model is stronger in some regards that what may be required in practice. For example, Definition 1 does not insist that the string I output by A satisfy some formatting specification as might be the case in practice. Also, the model does not insist that communications from the requester to the CA be authentic.

Definition 2. *An implicit certificate scheme is* secure *if there does not exist a successful adversary of the kind described in Definition 1.*

A more concrete definition would be that an implicit certificate scheme is (τ, ϵ)-*secure* if there does not exist such an adversary A that runs in time at most τ and succeeds with probability at least ϵ. However, in this paper we will only consider the asymptotic form of security as given in Definition 2 above.

4.2   Security Proof

In order to prove the security of optimal mail certificates, we shall work in the random oracle model. Several signature schemes have been proved secure in the random oracle model. We shall use the following security result for Schnorr signature schemes.

Theorem 1 (Pointcheval and Stern [13]). *In the random oracle model, the Schnorr family of signature schemes over a group $\langle G \rangle$ is secure if the discrete logarithm problem in $\langle G \rangle$ is intractable.*

The proof of Theorem 1 follows easily from the proofs given in [13]. The proof involves the "forking lemma" and a reduction from a signature-forging algorithm to a discrete logarithm-solving algorithm. We shall use such a reduction in our proof. Theorem 1 is true for a variety of signing equations that can be used in the family of Schnorr signature schemes, and in particular it is true for the signing equation used in optimal mail certificates. That is, the following variant of the Schnorr signature is secure: For a message m and random oracle H, a signature (R, s) is generated by Bob with $R = kG$ for random nonzero k and $s = H(R, m)k + b \bmod n$ where b is Bob's private key. To verify the signature, one checks that $sG = H(R, m)R + B$, where B is Bob's public key.

Theorem 2. *In the random oracle model, the optimal mail certificate scheme is a secure implicit certificate scheme provided that the discrete logarithm problem in $\langle G \rangle$ is intractable.*

Proof. Assume that the optimal mail certificate scheme is not secure in the case where the hash function H is a random oracle. Then there exists a successful (τ, ϵ)-adversary A. We construct a polynomial-time algorithm S that uses A as a subroutine to compute logarithms in $\langle G \rangle$ with non-negligible probability.

The input to S consists of a discrete logarithm challenge $C \in_R \langle G \rangle$, $C \neq \mathcal{O}$, and the desired output of S is an integer $c \in [1, n-1]$ such that $C = cG$. We shall construct S in two stages. The first stage S_1 takes as input (C, m, H_1) where m is a random message, and H_1 is a random oracle independent of H. S_1 can use A as a subroutine. The desired output of S_1 is either (i) an integer $c \in [1, n-1]$ such that $C = cG$, or (ii) an ordered pair (P, b) such that $bG = H_1(P, m)P + C$ (i.e., (P, b) is a signature of message m with respect to the public key C). If case (i) occurs, then S outputs c and terminates. If case (ii) occurs, then Theorem 1 is used to reduce the signature forger S_1 to a discrete logarithm solver in order to extract c. If this stage is successful, then S outputs c and terminates.

To find c, algorithm S_1 runs algorithm A. Algorithm A expects there to be one or more CAs, each with a public key for which A is not given the private key, and zero or more requester Bob_i making one or more requests R_i for which A is not given the discrete logarithm r_i. Algorithm S_1 randomly selects one of the CA public keys or one of the requests to be the challenge point C which is the input of S. The other request points and CA public keys can be selected by S_1 according to the normal procedure of selecting a random secret integer and multiplying G by this value. Let t be the total number of CA public keys and requests. We shall see that there will be a ϵ/t probability that A can be used to obtain c or a forgery of a signature with public key C.

Since A can request a certificate from the CA with public key C (if S_1 has selected such a CA) and expect a legitimate response, S_1 must supply a response that seems legitimate at least from A's perspective. (Otherwise A is not guaranteed success, and S_1 may not find A useful to find c.) However, S_1 does not know the private key c associated with C. But since H is a random oracle, S_1 can simulate the role of the CA and answer A's certificate requests without knowing c by careful pre-selection of the random values of H. Algorithm S_1 simulates the role of the CA as follows: given a request R_i for a certificate with certificate information I_i, S_1 generates integers $s_i, h_i \in_R [0, n-1]$ and computes $P_i = R_i + h_i^{-1}(s_i G - C)$, where the inverse is computed modulo n. S_1 defines $H(P_i, I_i) = h_i$ and returns the triple (P_i, I_i, s_i) as the response to A's request. Since $H(P_i, I_i)R_i + s_i G = H(P_i, I_i)P_i + C$ holds, the response to the certificate request appears legitimate from A's perspective. Furthermore, the hash function will be random from A's perspective because the value h_i was initially chosen randomly.

The adversary A is of course allowed to query H directly. Given a hash query input, say, (P_A, I_A), which has not been previously queried or determined as above, S_1 outputs $H_1(P_A, m)$ where m is the message on which it is trying to forge a signature. Clearly, the distribution of the simulated hash values generated by S will be indistinguishable to A from the distribution of hash values generated by a random oracle.

Suppose that A is successful. Then A returns a triple (P, I, b) such that $bG = hP + C_k$ for some k, with $h = H(P, I)$, such that either:

(i) (P, I) is a certificate created by CA_k for a request from Bob_i; or
(ii) (P, I) is a certificate which was not issued by CA_k.

Assume we are in the first case. Then there is at least a $1/t$ probability that the request R_i of Bob_i was the challenge point C given as input to the algorithm S_1. The private key b of Bob_i discovered by A satisfies $b = rh + s \bmod n$. But $c = r$, and S_1 can observe s as CA_k's response. Thus S_1 can compute $c = h^{-1}(b - s) \bmod n$.

Assume we are in the second case. Then there is at least a $1/t$ probability that public key C_k of CA_k is the challenge point C given as input to the algorithm S_1. We can assume that (P, I) was an input query to the random oracle hash H, because otherwise the equation $H(P, I)P + C = bG$ will hold with negligible probability, contradicting the assumption that ϵ is non-negligible. Thus $H(P, I) = H_1(P, m)$ by definition of the simulation. But now (P, b) is a signature of the message m.

There is a minor problem that, if during execution of S_1 with A, the message (P, I) appears first as a direct query to H, and subsequently as a certificate constructed during the simulation of a CA. Since the values s_i and h_i are chosen randomly during simulation of the CA, the point P_i will be uniformly distributed, and thus, this event of $P = P_i$ will happen with negligible probability. Nevertheless, in this case S_1 can simply start over.

Clearly, if A runs in polynomial time and succeeds with non-negligible probability then so will S_1. By Theorem 1 and above, if A runs in polynomial time and succeeds with non-negligible probability then so will S. But by hypothesis, it was assumed that no such S for solving discrete logarithms in $\langle G \rangle$ existed. Therefore no adversary A exists in the random oracle model unless discrete logarithms in $\langle G \rangle$ can be efficiently solved. □

4.3   Secure Use of Optimal Mail Certificates

In §4.2 we argued that it is unlikely that an adversary can produce a "new" (P, I) pair such that the adversary knows the associated private key. Since public-key protocols are designed to be secure unless the adversary knows the private key associated with a user's public key, one might conclude that it is safe to now use optimal mail certificates instead of traditional certificates. However, it is possible that the use of optimal mail certificates in a given protocol could lead to insecurities. For example, if optimal certificates are used in conjunction with the Nyberg-Rueppel signature scheme [11], it would certainly be undesirable if an adversary could produce a (P, I) pair, and a triple (r, s, M) such that the pair (r, s) is a valid signature on the message M by the user with public key $H(P,I)P + C$. Nothing we have said thus far precludes this possibility. Although, in [5], the security of a implicit certificates used in conjunction with a signature scheme has been defined, and furthermore the instantiation with a certain version of optimal mail certificates and a certain signature scheme has been proved secure in the random oracle model. Similar questions could be posed concerning the use of optimal mail certificates in other public-key protocols such as key agreement and public-key encryption.

4.4   Denial-of-Service Attacks

One difference between traditional explicit certificates over implicit certificates is that when presented with a valid explicit certificate, we know that the certificate belongs to *someone*. Specifically, up to forgery of the signature scheme used to generate certificates, a valid certificate containing identifier I is proof that the CA signed this certificate for I, and so the party identified by I knows the private key associated with the public key included in the certificate. This guarantee does not hold with implicit certificates, such as the ones described in §3. In fact, an arbitrary pair (P,I) can be given to Alice to reconstruct a public key $B = H(P,I)P+C$. But, it should be infeasible to find such a pair (P,I) where the discrete logarithm b with respect to the generator point G of the reconstructed public key B is known. Since authentication of Bob is only completed once Bob has demonstrated knowledge of b in a subsequent protocol run, such arbitrary "faked" (P,I) will not deceive Alice.

The above discussion suggests a denial-of-service type attack, where Alice is flooded with protocol requests using "faked" implicit certificates. The fact that the logarithm of the faked public key is unknown is revealed only after Alice has performed most of the protocol. Of course, a similar attack can be launched in a system using regular certificates. In this case, though, the attacker floods Alice with various certificates belonging to other entities. Alice verifies the digital signature on each certificate received. The certificates are valid, but the attacker does not know the private keys of the associated public keys. In either case, Alice is forced to perform many cryptographic operations with no useful result, which may prevent her from doing something useful like authenticating a legitimate user.

5   Conclusions

Optimal mail certificates are more efficient in some respects than traditional explicit certificates and other types of implicit certificates. We have proposed a security definition for implicit certificate schemes, and proved that optimal mail certificates are secure under this definition. What remains to be proven is that the use of optimal mail certificates in conjunction with specific public-key protocols such as signature schemes does not in any way reduce the security of the protocols.

Acknowledgments

The authors would like to thank Alfred Menezes and Doug Stinson for their careful comments on earlier drafts of this paper. The authors would also like to thank the referees for their thoughtful comments.

References

1. B. Arazi, "An identity-based DL/EC key agreement technique", Presentation to IEEE P1363a, available from
   `http://grouper.ieee.org/groups/1363/addendum.html`
2. M. Bellare, " Practice-oriented provable-security", *Proceedings of First International Workshop on Information Security (ISW'97)*, 1998.
3. M. Bellare and P. Rogaway, "Random oracles are practical: a paradigm for designing efficient protocols", *1st ACM Conference on Computer and Communications Security*, 1993 pp. 62-73.
4. D. Brown and D. Johnson, "Formal security proofs for a signature scheme with partial message recovery", preprint, 2000.
5. D. Brown, "Implicitly Certifying Signatures Securely", preprint, 2000.
6. R. Canetti, O. Goldreich, and S. Halevi, "The Random Oracle Methodology, Revisited (Preliminary Version)", *Proceedings of the Thirtieth Annual ACM Symposium on the Theory of Computing*, 1998, pp. 209-218.
7. M. Girault, "Self-certified public keys", *Advances in Cryptology – Eurocrypt'91*, 1991, pp. 490-497.
8. C.G. Günther, "An identity-based key-exchange protocol", *Advances in Cryptology – Eurocrypt'89*, 1989, pp. 29-37.
9. IEEE P1363a, "Standard Specifications for Public-Key Cryptography: Additional Techniques", Working Draft, August 16, 2000.
10. A. Menezes, P. van Oorschot, and S. Vanstone, *Handbook of Applied Cryptography*, CRC Press, 1996.
11. K. Nyberg and R. Rueppel, "Message recovery for signature schemes based on the discrete logarithm problem", *Designs, Codes and Cryptography*, **7** (1996), pp. 61-81.
12. L. Pintsov and S. Vanstone, "Postal Revenue Collection in the Digital Age", *Proceedings of Financial Cryptography 2000*, to appear.
13. D. Pointcheval and J. Stern, "Security proofs for signature schemes", *Advances in Cryptology – Eurocrypt'96*, 1996, pp. 387-398.
14. D. Pointcheval, J. Stern, "Security arguments proofs for Digital Signatures and Blind Signatures", *Journal of Cryptology*, 2000, pp. 361-396.
15. M. Qu and S. Vanstone, "Implicit Certificate Schemes", preprint, 1997.
16. C. Schnorr, "Efficient signature generation by smart cards", *Journal of Cryptology*, **4** (1991), pp. 161-174.

Nonmonotonicity, User Interfaces, and Risk Assessment in Certificate Revocation
(Position Paper)

Ninghui Li[1] and Joan Feigenbaum[2]

[1] Department of Computer Science, Stanford University, Gates 4B
Stanford, CA 94305-9045, USA
ninghui.li@cs.stanford.edu
[2] Department of Computer Science, Yale University, PO Box 208285
New Haven, CT 06520-8285, USA
jf@cs.yale.edu

Abstract. We consider certificate revocation from three high-level perspectives: temporal nonmonotonicity, user interfaces, and risk management. We argue that flawed understanding of these three aspects of revocation schemes has caused these schemes to be unnecessarily costly, complex, and confusing. We also comment briefly on some previous works, including those of Rivest [16], Fox and LaMacchia [5], and McDaniel and Rubin [11].
Keywords: Certificates, Revocation, PKI, CRL.

1 Introduction

Public-Key Infrastructure (PKI) is an important enabling technology for e-commerce. However, the use of PKI can be limited by the cost, complexity, and sometimes confusion attributable to revocation. There has been a lot of debate over the meaning of certification and revocation [5,11,13,16], and different revocation mechanisms have been proposed [1,4,9,10,12,15,19,8,14]. In this paper, we argue that revocation is complex and confusing for the following reasons.

- Revocation makes certification nonmonotonic. More precisely, in a PKI that has revocation, the validity of a certificate is nonmonotonic with respect to time, *i.e.*, a certificate may go from valid to invalid as time passes.
- A PKI has a user interface and internal entities and mechanisms that implement this interface. In the literature, this distinction is not always drawn clearly, and thus discussions of user-interface issues and internal-mechanism issues are often intermingled.
- Traditionally, revocation schemes have been viewed as methods to provide "security" instead of methods to control risk. This view limits the ways in which revocation mechanisms are used and analyzed.

In this paper, we consider certification and revocation from the perspective of these three issues. We separate the user interface (UI) of a PKI from the internal

P. Syverson (Ed.): FC 2001, LNCS 2339, pp. 166–177, 2002.

mechanisms of a PKI and argue that the UI should be as simple as possible: It should provide only the information needed by the users and hide the rest. In particular, it is desirable for a PKI to have a monotonic user interface: Every piece of information shown through the interface should have a meaning that is monotonic with respect to time. In fact, the UI's of most existing PKI's can be made monotonic by making time an explicit element.

We also argue that revocation is a risk-management tool. Risk associated with a PKI cannot be completely removed, but it can be analyzed and controlled. With revocation, users control risk by, for example, setting recency requirements for certificate acceptance. Smaller recency requirements lead to lower risk but require higher communication and/or computation cost. Setting the right recency requirement requires risk analysis and balancing the risk and the cost. It is clear that different applications have different risk requirements and that different users have different preferences in the risk-cost balance. Therefore, a PKI aiming to support multiple applications should provide a revocation interface that is tunable. Users should be able to set different recency requirements based on their needs and resources.

The UI of a PKI should also be helpful in auditing, *e.g.*, it should be easy to obtain a proof that a certificate was valid at a particular time in the past. This is useful for detecting fraudulent transactions after they occur. It is also useful when a user's risk is assumed by a third-party insurer, and the insurer requires the user to provide a proof that she has followed the insurer's policy in a transaction.

2   Background

A *public-key certificate* (*certificate* for short) is a data record digitally signed by a private key; the entity that possesses the private key and signs the certificate is called the *issuer*, or the *certification authority (CA)*, of this certificate. Data in a certificate include a public key, which we call the *subject key* (of this certificate), and some information about the *subject-key holder* (*holder* for short), *i.e.*, the entity that holds the private key corresponding to the subject key. A certificate binds the subject key and the information together. For example, a certificate may bind the distinguished name (DN) of an entity and its public key. A certificate may also express implicitly some trust the issuer has in the holder. For example, a CA-to-CA certificate often implicitly suggests the trustworthiness of the holder, in addition to establishing a DN-to-public-key binding. In the following, we use *binding* to mean both the binding of the subject key to the other data in the certificate and the implicit trust semantics.

Normally, a certificate has a validity period that includes a beginning time and an ending time; the issuer only vouches for the binding during this period. However, even before the validity period of a certificate ends, things may happen to make the information in the certificate invalid, *e.g.*, the subject-key holder may report that the private key has been stolen or lost, the issuer may suspect that the private key has been stolen from the holder or has been given away by the holder, or the binding may be shown to be no longer accurate. The traditional approach to certificate revocation is certificate revocation lists (CRL's) [8]. A CRL, signed by a CA, contains an issuing time t and a list of entries, each of which contains the serial number of a certificate that was issued by this CA, has not expired,[1] and has been revoked at t.

An architectural model of PKI is given in [8,2]. In this model, a PKI has *end entities*, *PKI management entities*, and *repositories*. PKI management entities include CA's and, optionally, *registration authorities (RA's)*, to which CA's delegate certain management functions. Repositories are systems that store and distribute certificates and revocation data such as CRL's.

Here, we recommend a slightly different architecture. End entities are "users" of a PKI; thus the interface between end entities and the rest of a PKI is the user interface (UI) of the PKI. We further distinguish between two kinds of end entities: subject-key holders and entities that use certificates in making decisions, which we call *acceptors* or *verifiers*. In this paper, we focus on the acceptors's view of a UI, *i.e.*, the interface for providing information to help acceptors decide whether to accept a certificate, as opposed to the interface for requesting certificates.

As a general design principle for UI, we have the following.

Recommendation 1. *The UI of a PKI should be clear and simple. It should provide only the information needed by end users, and it should hide everything else.*

We also stress that, to be clear, a UI should precisely specify, for each piece of information it exposes to users, the meaning and the expected action.

We now review four kinds of user interfaces for PKI's, focusing on the data provided through the UI's.

- The first kind of UI's have certificates that cannot be revoked. This is the simplest kind. Certificates are valid for their life times, which are typically short.
- The second kind of UI's have certificates and CRLs. The standard X.509 PKI belongs to this kind. The characteristic of a CRL is that one piece of data (*i.e.*, the CRL) provides the current status of all the certificates issued by a CA. This is good for acceptors who process lots of certificates. However, the size of one typical CRL is quite large, and so the communication cost might be too high for acceptors who process only a small number of certificates.
- The third kind of UI's have certificates and validity proofs for individual certificates. Such proofs are much shorter than typical CRL's, but they can only prove the validity of one or several certificates. Examples of these kind include OCSP (Online Certificate Status Protocol) [14], CRS [12], *etc.* CRT (Certificate Revocation Tree) [9] and 23CRT [15] provide both short proofs for one certificate and CRL-like data at the same time.

---

[1] According to [8], a revoked certificate should appear in at least one CRL after it has expired.

– The fourth kind of UI's have certificates and revocation notices. See, *e.g.*, the work of Wright *et al.* [19]. In these UI's, acceptors who are interested in the status of a certificate register themselves with someone who distributes revocation notices for the certificate, *e.g.*, the CA. When a certificate is revoked, the CA broadcasts this information to all interested parties.

3 A Monotonic Interface for PKI

Revocation leads to nonmonotonicity. When more certificates are revoked, fewer are valid; the amount of validity information decreases when the amount of revocation information increases. Normally, revocation information increases over time, *i.e.*, as time passes, more certificates are revoked. Therefore, when a PKI allows revocation, the validity information is temporally nonmonotonic. More specifically, a certificate valid at time t_0 may become invalid at a later time t_1.

The nonmonotonicity introduced by revocation is similar to the notion of "negation-as-failure" in the logic-programming and nonmonotonic-reasoning literature. Negation-as-failure means that, to conclude "not r," one needs to try every way to prove r; if they all fail, then "not r" is concluded. In a PKI with revocation, one needs to prove "not revoked(cert)" at the time at which one decides whether to accept a certificate. To prove "not revoked(cert)," conceptually, one needs *complete* information about revoked(). Because the information about revoked() increases with time, one needs *current* information in order to conclude safely "not revoked(cert)." In a distributed system, distributing absolutely current information to all concerned parties is impossible. The best one can do is to deliver recent information. Even this is quite expensive in large-scale distributed systems. This is a major source of difficulty in revocation.

Recommendation 2. *The difficulty of revocation is caused by temporal nonmonotonicity, and thus a PKI should provide an interface that is monotonic.*

In fact, when viewed appropriately, existing PKI's have such an interface. In the following, we give a monotonic semantics of certificates and information provided by revocation mechanisms.

Without revocation, the meaning of a certificate is monotonic. A certificate means that the issuer vouches for the binding in the certificate for the validity period. Anyone who sees the certificate can check whether it has expired and decide whether to use it.

When revocation is possible, the meaning of a certificate becomes more complicated. In [16], Rivest discussed the following guarantee for standard certificates: "*This certificate is good until the expiration date. Unless, of course, you hear that it has been revoked.*" Rivest argued that this guarantee is not very useful, because the acceptor is always required to check whether a certificate has been revoked; he proposed a different general certificate guarantee: "*This certificate is definitely good from T_1 until T_2. The issuer also expects this certificate to be good until T_3, but a careful acceptor might wish to demand a more recent certificate. This certificate should never be considered valid after T_3.*"

The above guarantee is a combination of nonrevokable certificates and standard revokable certificates. It means that a certificate is nonrevokable from T_1 to T_2 and then is a standard certificate. We argue that this interpretation of certificate is still problematic. The meaning of this certificate is still nonmonotonic from T_2 and T_3.

A certificate states what its CA believed when the certificate was issued. This belief may change over time, and this change may be reflected by revocation. This is the cause of nonmonotonicity. However, the fact that the CA believed the content of the certificate at the time when it was issued doesn't change over time. Therefore, we can give a certificate a temporally monotonic meaning if we take the issuing time as part of the meaning of a certificate.

We now introduce a simple logic for representing meaning of certificates. A statement in this logic takes the following form:

- At time t_0, X believes b to be true in $[t_1, t_2]$, where $t_1 \leq t_2$.

We call t_0 the *fresh time* of this statement. This logic has the following two inferencing rules:

1. If, at t_0, X believes b to be true in $[t_1, t_2]$, then, at t_0, X believes b to be true in any $[t', t'']$ such that $t_1 \leq t' \leq t'' \leq t_2$.
2. If, at t_1, X believes b to be true in $[t_1, t_2]$, then, at any time t_0 such that $t_0 < t_1$, X believes b to be true in $[t_1, t_2]$.

Note that this logic doesn't interpret the belief b. In particular, it doesn't relate beliefs b and $\neg b$. Also note that one cannot express "disbeliefs" in this logic.

The first inferencing rule is straightforward and quite standard [18]. The second rule says that, if X believes something at time t_1, then X has been believing it at all times up to t_1. This is certainly false for general beliefs; however, it seems appropriate for our purpose, *i.e.*, monotonic reasoning about certificates and revocation. Next we show that certificates and revocation data such as CRL's can be represented by statements in this logic.

Recommendation 3. *We propose the following interpretation of certificates: At issuing time t_0, the issuer believes the information in this certificate to be true from t_1 to t_2.*

This reading is temporally monotonic; it is always true at any time after t_0. Note that our interpretation makes issuing time an explicit part (the fresh time) of the meaning of a certificate.

A certificate states the issuer's belief at the issuing time t_0, and one can view revocation schemes as mechanisms to reconfirm the issuer's belief at a later time. If one only has a certificate issued at t_0, the fresh time of the binding in the certificate is t_0. If one also obtains a proof that a certificate has not been revoked at a later time t_1, then one can update the fresh time to t_1.

Consider the case that, at time t_u, an acceptor wants to use a certificate that has validity period $[t_1, t_2]$, issuing time t_0, and fresh time t_f. The acceptor should check that, at a time in recent past, say, within a fresh requirement dt, the issuer of this certificate still believed the binding to be true at current time t_u. In other words, the verifier needs to check that at time $t_u - dt$, the issuer still believed the binding to be true in $[t_u, t_u]$. Following the inferencing rules, the verifier needs to check that $t_u \in [t_1, t_2]$ and that $t_f \geq t_u - dt$. The choice of dt is a policy that the acceptor needs to decide. If one doesn't want to check revocation, one can set dt to ∞, then $t_f \geq t_u - dt$ is always true.

Most existing certificate formats only have two time fields: *not-before* and *not-after*, and it is often assumed that the *not-before* time is the same as the issue time. If one is willing to make this assumption, one can interpret existing standard certificates as in Recommendation 3. However, we think that a certificate should have a separate issue time in order to allow post-dated certificates to be issued. A post-dated certificate can be revoked even before its validity period begins.

A CRL issued at t_1 is a claim that all certificates that are not listed should have a fresh time t_1 or later. Some argue that one can criticize CRL's because they make negative statements. We disagree. Although a notice that some certificates have been revoked is negative, a list of all revoked certificates provides positive information, because all those certificates that are not listed are still valid. In some cases, this is more efficient than listing all nonrevoked certificates. There is also the argument that a CRL doesn't provide positive information, because it doesn't prove the existence of a certificate. We disagree with this, too. The purpose of revocation is to complement certification, not to replace it. The purpose of a CRL is not to prove that a binding is valid but rather to update the fresh time of an existing proof (a certificate). One has to have a certificate first before caring about revocation.

Similarly, responses of the Online Certificate Status Protocol (OCSP) [14] and information from other revocation schemes can all be viewed as proofs that something is still believed at a later time.

In section 2, we reviewed four kinds of UI's for PKI. Among them, only the last kind, *i.e.*, the one that uses revocation notices, cannot be interpreted as in Recommendation 3. A revocation notice is a piece of negative information. If it fails to reach an acceptor, then the acceptor may accept a revoked certificate as valid.

We want to stress the point that the difficulty of revocation is caused by *temporal* nonmonotonicity. Because revocation information changes with time, one needs sufficiently recent information about revocation. Some previous work tries to make certification with revocation monotonic; however, this work does not address the time issue. In [6], Gunter and Jim argued that revocation information can and should be handled in the same way as certificates and that their system Query Certificate Manager (QCM) with revocation is monotonic. QCM has dual notions of positive sets and negative sets, *e.g.*, a CRL is a negative set. For a positive set, a QCM certificate states that an element is a member of the set. For a negative set, a QCM certificate states that an element is not a member of the set. An environment is a set of QCM certificates. In [6], the claim that QCM with revocation is monotonic means that a larger environment always leads to more conclusions. However, an environment itself is nonmonotonic with respect to time; more specifically, a QCM certificate for a negative set itself may go from true to false as time passes. For a user to decide whether to accept a certificate, she needs to forget an old environment and get a sufficiently recent one. This doesn't decrease the amount of information that needs to be transmitted.

4   The Semantics of Revoking a Certificate Is to Cancel It

A certificate may be revoked for several reasons. In [5], Fox and LaMacchia argued that revocation for different reasons should have different semantics. When a verifier knows that a certificate has been revoked, the verifier should remove the revoked certificate from any certificate chain (or graph) that she is using. In other words, revoking a certificate cancels it. A question that follows is whether revoking a certificate should do more than that. Consider an example given in [5].

Example 1. Let $C = c_0, c_1, \ldots, c_n$ be a chain of certificates, where c_n is the end-entity certificate of interest, c_0 is a self-signed, trusted-root certificate issued by K_0, and each c_i, for all $i = 1, \ldots, n$, is signed by the private key corresponding to K_{i-1}, the subject key of c_{i-1}. Let j be an integer in $[1..n-1]$, and let $C' = c'_0, c'_1, \ldots, c'_j$ be a second chain of certificates from K_0 to K_j. Suppose that the certificate c'_j is revoked and that all other certificates in the two chains are valid. If these are the only certificate chains that the user has that end in c_n, should the user accept the binding in c_n, or (equivalently in this acceptance decision) should c_j be treated as valid?

In [5], Fox and LaMacchia argued that whether c_j should be treated as valid depends on the reason for revoking c'_j. The certificate c'_j may be revoked in each of the following three cases:

(a) the key K_j has been compromised, in which case, c_j should be treated as revoked as well.

(b) the binding in c'_j is no longer valid, in which case, c_j should be treated as invalid if it contains the same binding as c'_j.

(c) the binding may still be valid, but the issuer doesn't want to vouch for it anymore, in which case, c_j should still be valid.

Although it is desirable to revoke all certificates concerning a compromised private key, we argue that this should be done internally, *i.e.*, on the other side of the PKI's UI from the external one that is exposed to users.

Interpreting revocation of c'_j as revoking c_j as well enlarges the domain over which an acceptor needs complete information. To use c_j, one not only needs to know that "not revoked(c_j)" but also needs to know "not revoked(c'_j)," for all c'_j's that are somehow related to c_j. This has the effect of changing the trust relationship. Under this interpretation, one certificate path is not enough. To use a certificate, one needs to have all the CA's agree that a private key has not been compromised or that a binding is valid; any CA can veto a binding by issuing a certificate and then revoking it for key-compromise reasons. This is not just expensive — it may also be undesirable.

We believe that revocation schemes shouldn't change the trust relationships of a PKI. If a CA wants to revoke a certificate whenever another CA revokes a related certificate, it should make this arrangement behind the user interface. If a user needs more than one source to confirm a binding, *e.g.*, a separate proof that the private key has not been compromised, then this should be clearly specified by the user's policy; it shouldn't be accomplished indirectly with revocation.

Recommendation 4. *Revocation of a certificate should cancel the certificate and do nothing else.*

5   Revocation Provides Risk Management for PKI

Traditionally, computer-security mechanisms try to ensure that insecure things do not happen. In [20], an alternative view is given. We summarize it as follows: Complex systems can be secured only up to a point. Insecurity always exists and cannot be destroyed. The question one should ask is not whether a system is secure, but how secure that system is relative to some perceived threat (page 119 of [20]).

That insecurity always exists is precisely the situation in a global-scale public-key infrastructure. Total security is unattainable, even under the unrealistic assumption that revocation information can be delivered to everyone instantaneously. A private key may be compromised long before the compromise is discovered and the certificates for the key revoked. This cannot be handled by revocation schemes, but it should be taken into consideration when analyzing the risk inherent in a PKI.

When we acknowledge that risk always exists, we can view revocation schemes as a way to control risk. Traditionally, it is often implicitly assumed that everyone should get the most recent CRL. One piece of evidence for this assumption is that each CRL has a next-update field; a CRL is assumed to be expired after that date, and a newer CRL is needed.

However, when taking the risk-management view of CRL's, it is clear that one doesn't always need the most current CRL. Instead, one should set recency requirements as a matter of policy. As long as a user has a CRL that is recent enough, it should be okay. More strict recency requirements have lower risk, but they have higher communication costs. Because risk is application-dependent, different applications and users have different recency requirements. Therefore, we have the following recommendation.

Recommendation 5. *A PKI that serves diverse applications should provide flexible revocation schemes that can be tuned to support different recency requirements.*

Whoever is exposed to the risk of wrongfully accepting a certificate should set recency requirements. However, which party has higher risk has been debated.

In [16], Rivest argued that recency requirements must be set by the acceptor of a certificate, not by the certificate issuer, because the acceptor is the one who is at risk if her decision is wrong. In [11], McDaniel and Rubin disagreed. They argued that, in business-to-consumer e-commerce scenarios, in which consumers (or their browsers) need to decide to whether to accept a merchant website's certificate as valid to establish a secure connection, consumers are usually transferring credit-card numbers through the connection and thus only have limited liability. Conversely, the merchant risks its reputation for unsafe operation; therefore, the risk is actually higher for merchants than for acceptors. In [5], Fox and LaMacchia said that "In theory, the certificate authority has the most to lose with continued circulation of a bad certificate."

In the above B2C credit-card transmission scenario, several parties are at risk in one fraudulent transaction. Both the merchant and the certification authorities risk some reputation damage, but their risk is limited and less tangible. Note that we are talking about the damage caused by *one* fraudulent transaction, *i.e.*, one in which a consumer accepts a certificate that she shouldn't and as a result sends her credit card number to an intruder, *not* the damage caused by revocation of a certificate. When a merchant's certificate is revoked because of key compromise, the merchant has *already* suffered great loss of reputation, even before a single fraudulent transaction occurs. This means that a merchant has high incentive to protect its private key, but it doesn't necessarily have higher risk than a customer in *one* fraudulent transaction. One can argue that more fraudulent transactions will do more damage to the merchant's reputation, but it is hard to quantify how much damage each additional fraudulent transaction does. More importantly, there is no way for merchants or CA's to enforce the requirements. They can make suggestions about the recency requirements suitable for particular kinds of transactions; CA's should also make revocation information available. However, if customers don't follow these suggestions, there isn't much that CA's or merchants can do. Thus, they are mostly free of reputation damage as long as they have made good suggestions.

The acceptor has the primary risk. In some cases, the acceptor is protected by insurance, and her risk is limited to a small deductible. In that case, the insurer has the highest risk. This is the case in the credit-card scenario. Note that credit-card numbers aren't the only kind of information transmitted through secure connections. In online banking or trading, a customer may be transmitting account numbers and PINs, which can be much more valuable than credit-card numbers.

When an acceptor is insured by someone, all or part of the acceptor's risk is transferred to the insurer. Then the insurer has a strong incentive to set and enforce recency requirements. However, at the point of decision, only the acceptor can enforce the recency standard, because it is she who actually decides whether to accept a certificate. Note that the granularity of the recency standard is limited by the revocation mechanisms available to the acceptor. If a PKI has CRL's as the only revocation interface, and CRL's are issued at time interval δt, then no one can operate with a recency requirement that is smaller than δt.

Although an insurer cannot enforce a recency requirement when the transaction occurs, the insurer can do so when something goes wrong and the acceptor makes a claim. The insurer can set a recency requirement and require the acceptor to provide proof that she has followed the requirement in the transaction.

Recommendation 6. *The UI of a PKI should support auditing.*

For example, a PKI that supports CRL's could maintain a CRL that keeps all the revoked certificates and the time at which they are revoked, whether they are expired or not. The insurer or some other parties can use this CRL to check whether a certificate is valid at a time in the past. Besides allowing a certificate to be revoked, PKIX also allows a certificate to be put on hold (temporarily disabled) and then activated again [8]. It is difficult for the above scheme to deal with such certificates, because the notion of "certificates-on-hold" significantly complicates revocation. When certificates can only be revoked, the revocation status of a certificate is temporally monotonic (although the validity status is not). Thus a certificate can only go from valid to revoked. Recording the time of this change or the fact that such a change has not occurred determines the status of the whole life of a certificate. When a certificate can be put on hold, the revocation status of a certificate is not temporally monotonic. To know the status history of a certificate, one needs to know all the changes that have occurred in the past. It is even harder to figure out whether a particular acceptor believes that a certificate is valid or not at a time in the past, especially when acceptors have different recency requirements. Therefore, we argue that it is better to disallow this notion of certificate-on-hold. As an alternative, the CA can revoke the certificate and later issue a new certificate with the same binding when needed.

Recommendation 7. *We recommend not allowing certificates to be put on hold, in order to simplify auditing and the semantics of revocation.*

In addition to being useful in scenarios that involve insurers, auditing can also be used for earlier detection of potentially fraudulent transactions. Consider an acceptor that has a CRL issued at time t_0 and is scheduled to obtain a new CRL at a later time t_1. Suppose that the CRL at time t_0 doesn't contain the certificate c. Then, at any time between t_0 and t_1, the acceptor would accept c as valid. However, if the certificate c is revoked during this time, then this is potentially problematic. It would be useful to detect this when the acceptor obtains a new CRL at t_1. To use CRL to support this kind of auditing and to support variable recency requirements at the same time, a CRL should keep an revoked certificate longer than required by [8]. In [8], a revoked certificate is required to appear in at least one CRL after it has expired. If the certificate c is revoked then expired after t_0, and several CRL's are issued after c expired and before t_1, then the acceptor won't know that the transaction involving c is potentially problematic. One solution to this is to have a CA set two parameters for issuing CRL, δt and Δt, where a new CRL is issued every δt and a revoked certificate will be kept on CRL for Δt after it has expired. Anyone who uses CRL's should set a recency requirement that is between δt and Δt.

Different revocation mechanisms have been proposed, and there has been extensive debate over which revocation mechanisms are the best and who should provide recency proofs. We think that the answers depend on the specific application and scenarios. No one scheme fits all scenarios. For example, CRL's work well when there are a small number of acceptors who have high communication capacity and who process lots of requests from a large number of certificate holders. This is often the case in an intranet setting, *e.g.*, an internal web server authenticating employees using certificates. In this case, it is more efficient for the web server to obtain and check a CRL than for certificate holders to be required to obtain and present proofs.

On the other hand, CRL's are not suitable in B2C e-commerce scenarios, in which customers' browsers are acceptors. There are a large number of acceptors, each of which processes only a small number of requests. Furthermore, acceptors often have limited network bandwidth. It is not efficient to have every browser deal with CRL's. It is better to have the server obtain a recency proof and reuse it with different browsers. In this case, revocation mechanisms that can generate short validity proofs for certificates are needed. The fact that existing PKI's lack the ability to provide short validity proofs is one reason that revocation is not used in B2C e-commerce scenarios.

6   Conclusions

In summary, a PKI should have a clear and simple user interface that is temporally monotonic and supports functionality needed for applications. Depending on the application, it may be necessary for a PKI to support tunable revocation services and auditing.

Acknowledgements

The first author is supported by DARPA contract N66001-00-C-8015. The second author is supported in part by DARPA grant AF F39502-99-1-0512.

References

1. Carlisle Adams and Robert Zuccherato, "A General, Flexible Approach to Certificate Revocation," June 1998.
   http://www.entrust.com/resourcecenter/pdf/certrev.pdf.
2. Carlisle Adams and Stephen Farrell, "Internet X.509 Public Key Infrastructure Certificate Management Protocols," IETF RFC 2510, March 1999.
   http://www.ietf.org/rfc/rfc2510.txt.
3. David A. Cooper, "A Closer Look at Revocation and Key Compromise in Public Key Infrastructures," in *Proceedings of the 21st National Information Systems Security Conference*, pp. 555–565, October 1998.
   http://csrc.nist.gov/nissc/1998/proceedings/paperG2.pdf.

4. David A. Cooper, "A More Efficient Use of Delta-CRLs," in *Proceedings of the 2000 IEEE Symposium on Security and Privacy*, pp. 190–202, May 2000. http://csrc.nist.gov/pki/documents/sliding_window.pdf.

5. Barbara Fox and Brian LaMacchia, "Certificate Revocation: Mechanics and Meaning," in FC'98 [7], pp. 158–164, 1998. http://www.farcaster.com/papers/fc98/fc98.ps.

6. Carl A. Gunter and Trevor Jim, "Generalized Certificate Revocation," in *Proceedings of the 27th ACM SIGPLAN-SIGACT Symposium on Principles of Programming Languages (POPL 2000)*, pp. 316–329, January 2000. http://www.cis.upenn.edu/~qcm/papers/popl00.pdf.

7. Rafael Hirschfeld (editor), *Financial Cryptography: Second International Conference (FC'98)*, Lecture Notes in Computer Science, vol. 1465, Springer, February 1998.

8. Russell Housley, Warwick Ford, Tim Polk, and David Solo, "Internet X.509 Public Key Infrastructure Certificate and CRL Profile," IETF RFC 2459, Janurary 1999. http://www.ietf.org/rfc/rfc2459.txt.

9. Paul Kocher, "On Certificate Revocation and Validation," in FC'98 [7], pp. 172–177, 1998.

10. Patrick McDaniel and Sugih Jamin, "Windowed Certificate Revocation," in *Proceedings of IEEE Infocom 2000*, pp. 1406–1414, March 2000. http://www.eecs.umich.edu/~pdmcdan/docs/info2000.pdf.

11. Patrick McDaniel and Aviel Rubin, "A Response to 'Can We Eliminate Certificate Revocation Lists?'," in *Proceedings of Financial Cryptography 2000*, February 2000. http://www.eecs.umich.edu/~pdmcdan/docs/finc00.pdf.

12. Silvio Micali, "Efficient Certificate Revocation," Technical Report TM-542b, MIT Laboratory for Computer Science, March, 1996. ftp://ftp.lcs.mit.edu/pub/lcs-pubs/tm.outbox/MIT-LCS-TM-542b.ps.gz.

13. Michael Myers, "Revocation: Options and Challenges," in FC'98 [7], pp. 165–171, 1998.

14. Michael Myers, Rich Ankney, Ambarish Malpani, Slava Galperin, and Carlisle Adams, "X.509 Internet Public Key Infrastructure Online Certificate Status Protocol – OCSP," IETF RFC 2560, June 1999. http://www.ietf.org/rfc/rfc2560.txt.

15. Moni Naor and Kobbi Nissim, "Certificate Revocation and Certificate Update," in *Proceedings of the 7th USENIX Security Symposium*, pp. 217–228, January 1998. http://www.wisdom.weizmann.ac.il/~kobbi/papers/revoke_usenix.ps.

16. Ronald L. Rivest, "Can We Eliminate Certificate Revocation Lists?" in FC'98 [7], pp. 178–183, 1998. http://theory.lcs.mit.edu/~rivest/revocation.ps.

17. Stuart G. Stubblebine, "Recent-Secure Authentication: Enforcing Revocation in Distributed Systems," in *Proceedings of the 1995 IEEE Symposium on Research in Security and Privacy*, pp. 224–234, May 1995. http://www.stubblebine.com/95oak.pdf.

18. Stuart G. Stubblebine and Rebbeca N. Wright, "An Authentication Logic Supporting Synchronization, Revocation, and Recency," in *Proceedings of the Third ACM Conference on Computer and Communications Security*, pp. 95–105, March 1996. http://www.stubblebine.com/96ccs.pdf.

19. Rebecca N. Wright, Patrick D. Lincoln, and Jonathan K. Millen, "Efficient Fault-Tolerant Certificate Revocation," in *Proceedings of the 7th ACM Conference on Computer and Communications Security (CCS 2000)*, November 2000. http://www.research.att.com/~rwright/ccs00.ps.

20. Committee on Information Systems Trustworthiness, National Research Council, *Trust in Cyberspace*, National Academy Press, 1999. http://www.nap.edu/html/trust/.

Mutual Authentication
for Low-Power Mobile Devices

Markus Jakobsson[1] and David Pointcheval[2]

[1] Information Sciences Research Center, Bell Labs
Murray Hill, New Jersey 07974
http://www.bell-labs.com/user/markusj
[2] Dépt d'Informatique, École Normale Supérieure
75230 Paris Cedex 05, France
http://www.di.ens.fr/users/pointche

Abstract. We propose methods for mutual authentication and key exchange. Our methods are well suited for applications with strict power consumption restrictions, such as wireless medical implants and contactless smart cards. We prove the security of our schemes based on the discrete log gap problem.

Keywords: Low power, medical informatics, mutual authentication, gap problem.

1 Introduction

Computers can be separated into *wired* and *wireless* devices, where no particular power restrictions are typically placed on the former, and the restrictions on wireless devices (typically cellular phones) relate mostly to the battery form factors. The use of wireless devices for medical applications – such as insulin meters and pacemakers – create a new category in terms of power restrictions, in which the power limitations are taken to their extreme. While traditional design of such devices have not relied on communication with nearby devices, there are great benefits associated with allowing this. Examples of such benefits include more accurate control of medical conditions, allowing doctors to constantly monitor health conditions; possibilities to detect inconsistent operation before it becomes a threat to the patient; and general collection of statistics for the improvement of the product.

At the same time, these are applications where errors and inconsistencies, whether due to interference or malice, may be fatal. In order to avoid security vulnerabilities, authentication methods and key exchange methods become crucial components in such systems. Authentication has traditionally been of an asymmetric nature, namely, an untrusted entity identifying itself to a trusted entity. With a trend towards decentralization, there is a greater need for symmetric or *mutual* authentication. The need for mutual authentication becomes particularly obvious in situations where users carry small wireless devices that monitor *and* control the operation of other wireless devices residing in the user's body.

P. Syverson (Ed.): FC 2001, LNCS 2339, pp. 178–195, 2002.

A situation with similar restrictions involves contact-free smart cards, whose advantages over standard smart cards range from the convenience they offer to their increased security – where the latter is due to the increased defense against power and timing attacks. Due to the absence of a local power source for such devices, electricity to perform computation is obtained by induction over a field moving in relation to the card. Only minute amounts of computation can be performed under such premises, severely restricting the choice of schemes that can be employed.

We propose two closely related schemes that allow for mutual authentication and key exchange, and which lower the computational requirements (and therefore the power consumption) by means of careful protocol design. One common technique we employ is that of precomputation, which allows for both the shifting of computation to another entity, and for a lower "peak performance" (and therefore a lower average power consumption). For applications in which devices are unable to perform such precomputation, and where the memory resources are limited, we show how trusted auxiliary devices can perform the computation and wirelessly upload this to the devices in question (after a successful mutual authentication, of course.) Our solutions have applications within a large set of seemingly unrelated fields, such as payment schemes, access control schemes, medical surveillance, and cellular billing schemes.

Outline: We begin by reviewing related work (section 2), followed by a discussion of our model (section 3). We then present two related schemes (section 4), both of which perform mutual authentication and key exchange. Not counting the amount of precomputation, we have that in the first scheme, the computational load for the client amounts to one modular multiplication and addition, while in the second scheme, we even avoid the modular reduction. Following this, we model the protocol and possible attacks on it (section 5), to prepare for the analysis of our solutions. We end by a careful security analysis of the two schemes, with further improvements (section 6 resp. section 7). We prove the schemes secure based on the *gap Diffie–Hellman* problem (which requires the standard Diffie–Hellman assumption.)

2   Related Work

2.1   Key Exchange and Mutual Authentication

Our paper hails back to the work on Diffie–Hellman key exchange [8], and the use of a shared key for purposes of authentication. While many methods can be employed in this later step – symmetric as well as asymmetric – we focus on asymmetric methods based on Schnorr signatures [17]. The reason is purely one of efficiency: Taking this approach, we can shift almost all the computational work to a preprocessing stage. One could use other methods for this second part, though, such as those proposed by Bellare and Rogaway [5].

Another direction for key exchange is that of Needham and Schroeder [11], later evolving into Kerberos (see [12] for a description.) There, a mutually trusted third party is involved in the key exchange. Under such a trust model, an alternative to our protocols is to use a trusted third party for key exchange or precomputation. In the latter case, one could use a simple table based method, in which the TTP distributes pairwise matching lists to the participants. One part of an entry could correspond to a request, the second to a response, and a third to the key to be used. However, and as noted, such a solution requires the TTP to be *mutually trusted* by the parties involved, and not only trusted by its client. Another important difference is that such a solution is not necessarily easy to distribute. The (unilaterally) trusted third party in our solution – if used at all – may perform all the exponentiation using quorum action, and send the portions of the result to the device, which then computes the corresponding database entry.

Coming back to the former type of model, we have that a key exchange scheme (without TTP) involves two participants, a *client* and a *server*, who want to share a secret session key in order to achieve confidentiality. They therefore communicate on a public channel and eventually compute a value that they both know but which nobody else knows. Many security models have been defined to cover this kind of schemes. Of these, the following two models have received the most consideration:

– The first model was proposed by Bellare and Rogaway [4,5], and refined in [2] (furthermore considering dictionary attacks). Here, the adversary can interact with all the participants, with an aim to learn some information about one session key. Therefore, one tries to prove the indistinguishability of the session key (from a random key) for the adversary.
– The second model was proposed by Bellare, Canetti, and Krawczyk [1], and is based on the multi-party simulatability technique. This means that one first defines an idealized version of a key exchange scheme. Then, to prove that the real-world scheme is secure, one shows that any adversary in the real world has to behave like an adversary in the ideal world.

Shoup [19] recently showed that the two models (with some refinements) are equivalent in preventing active adversaries to break forward secrecy: An adversary who can see all the public communication and has access to all the session keys *but one*, cannot obtain any information about *that last* session key, even if he later learns the long-term secrets of the parties.

When parties have established a common secret session key, most of the key exchange protocols, such as the Diffie–Hellman [8] key exchange scheme using public keys, *implicitly* ensure that any party is really partnered (sharing the session key) with the party he wanted, or with nobody. Indeed, if an adversary uses the public key of Alice, Bob will run the key exchange process, and at the end he thinks that the actual session key is shared with Alice. However, the adversary cannot extract the session key from the communication. Therefore, nobody but Alice can be partnered with Bob as a result of this process.

Thus, apart from performing the key agreement, one usually wants to verify the actual partner. This latter property for a key exchange scheme is called *mutual authentication*. However, as presented in [2], an implicitly authenticated key exchange protocol can be easily transformed into a scheme that provides mutual authentication, merely by adding one more flow, with a *key confirmation* step.

2.2 The Gap Problems

Very recently, Okamoto and Pointcheval [14] introduced a new class of problems to deal with the security of very efficient schemes. Informally, it considers the gap between a decision problem and its computational counterpart. More precisely, a gap-problem is a computational problem to solve given access to a decision oracle. Let us see what it means for the Diffie–Hellman family of problems, where all the elements belong in a group $\mathcal{G}$ of prime order q:

- *The Computational Diffie–Hellman Problem* (a.k.a. C-DH): given a triple (g, g^a, g^b), find the element $C = g^{ab}$.
- *The Decision Diffie–Hellman Problem* (a.k.a. D-DH): given a quadruple (g, g^a, g^b, g^c), decide whether $c = ab \bmod q$ or not.
- *The Gap Diffie–Hellman Problem* (a.k.a. G-DH): given a triple (g, g^a, g^b), find the element $C = g^{ab}$ with the help of a Decision Diffie–Hellman Oracle (which answers whether a given quadruple is a Diffie–Hellman quadruple or not).

Using the notation from the complexity theory, one could define the Gap Diffie–Hellman problem as the Computational Diffie–Hellman Problem with access to a Decision Diffie–Hellman oracle: G-DH = C-DH$^{\text{D-DH}}$. Thereafter, some relations between these problems become clear: first, if the C-DH problem is easy, so is G-DH; secondly, if the G-DH problem is easy, then C-DH = D-DH, which is very unlikely. This latter remark justifies the current assumption that the Gap Diffie–Hellman problem is hard to solve. The assumption of its hardness seems very similar to the Decision Diffie–Hellman assumption. Thus, the class of the gap-problems can be considered a dual to the class of the decision-problems.

This class of problems is already believed to be yield to many secure and efficient schemes. Indeed, it helped to prove the security of an undeniable signature scheme, the very old and well-known scheme proposed by Chaum [7,6,14], for which no security proof was previously known. It is also the basis of very efficient chosen-ciphertext secure cryptosystems [13].

3 Model

We have two primary types of participants, the *client* and the *server*. Although we strive to limiting the computational burden for both of these participants, it is the *client* that we assume have the strictest limitations. It is the purpose of our protocols to allow a client and a server to perform mutual authentication and to establish a shared key.

Our schemes can be used with a standard public key infrastructure. The use of certificates is straightforward; however, we must assume that these are verified beforehand to reduce the computational complexity. This only has to be assumed for the clients, given that the servers are assumed to have sufficient computational power to verify certificates. We note that this fits well into a model where many clients know of a few servers, but the servers do not know about any clients.

Furthermore, we may have *trusted devices*, who perform computation on behalf of clients and servers. A trusted device interacts with either a client or a server, but not both, as is only trusted by the entity it interacts with. The amount of trust that a device has to place in such a *trusted device* can be reduced by means of standard methods for distribution.

We assume that the entire communication network is managed by the adversary, who may schedule interactions arbitrarily, and who may inject and drop messages arbitrarily. We assume that all participants, and any adversary, can be modeled by poly-time Turing Machines.

Informally, we want our protocols to satisfy the following requirements.

- From a computational point of view, as said above, the on-line workload of the *client* must be minimal. Namely, we avoid the use of modular exponentiation, and avoid or reduce modular additions and multiplications.
- From the security point of view, we want to prevent active adversaries to learn any information about a session key. Forward-secrecy is also an important issue. However, under the above computational restriction, it seems impossible to achieve a forward-secrecy from both sides. We can assume a strong physical security level for the *server*, while the *client* may be a weak device. Therefore, the corruption of this device, and thus the leakage of the long-term secret key of the client, should not make public all the previous secret communication. Thus, the most important aspect is that all the session keys remain secret after the leakage of a *client* long-term key.

We will define the corresponding security requirements in more detail in the analysis section.

4   Solutions

We introduce two closely related protocols for mutual authentication and key exchange. While the protocols differ only on a few points in terms of their description, the security analysis differs substantially between the two. Still, the protocols are shown secure based on the same assumption: the intractability of the gap Diffie–Hellman problem.

Both protocols are based on the Diffie–Hellman key distribution scheme [8] together with the Schnorr's authentication scheme [17] (and the GPS scheme for the optimized version [9,16].) Thanks to the latter, much precomputation can be performed so that no on-line computation is required of the client. Therefore, the client can be any low-cost device.

The first scheme is presented in figure 1, the second differs on only a few points:

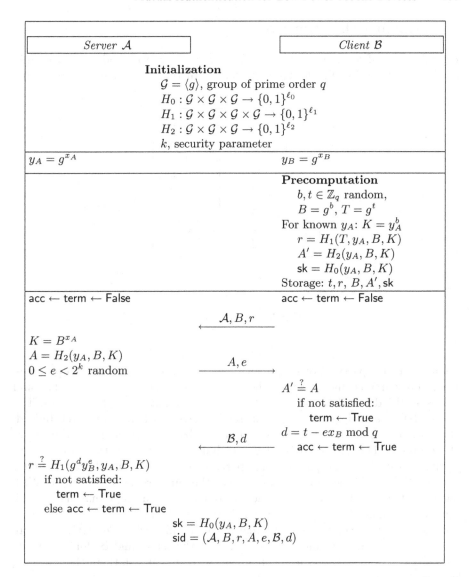

Fig. 1. Mutual Authentication

- It introduces a new security parameter, k'.
- Instead of selecting t uniformly at random from $\mathbb{Z}_q$, t is selected uniformly at random from $\mathbb{Z}_{q'}$, where $q' = q \, 2^{k+k'}$.
- Instead of computing d as $d = t - ex_B \bmod q$, it is computed as $d = t - ex_B$. (Note the absence of the modular reduction.)

5   Modeling the Protocol

For this proof of security, we use the Bellare and Rogaway model [4,5] revisited by Shoup [19] to handle the forward-secrecy. In this model (see figure 2), any

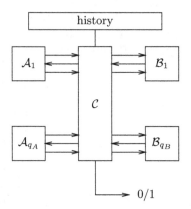

Fig. 2. Security Model

instance of each party, $\mathcal{A}$ or $\mathcal{B}$, is seen as an oracle. At the end of each protocol, when any party $\mathcal{U}_i$ has accepted, he gets a session key, denoted by sk_U^i, and a session ID, denoted by sid_U^i which is the concatenation of all the flows. The session ID's are made public, while the session keys clearly remain secret. Indeed, the session keys are the common secret shared by the two parties at the end of the protocol. The session ID's have a technical significance: they are used to define partnership. The partner of a party is an instance which has a similar session ID. Since the session ID's are public, the partnership is also public. With such a definition of partnership, one can remark that a party may have many partners, although we will show that it is very unlikely.

The adversary can interact, as a man-in-the-middle, with the parties, or more formally with many instances of them ($\mathcal{A}_i$ for the server and $\mathcal{B}_j$ for the client) as many times as he wants in a concurrent way. He can ask them the following queries

- Send ($\mathcal{U}$, i, *string*) – which means that the adversary sends the message *string* to the oracle $\mathcal{U}_i$ (either a server or a client). The oracle makes some computation according to the protocol and gives the answer back.
- Reveal ($\mathcal{U}$, i) – if the oracle $\mathcal{U}_i$ has accepted (the tag acc has been set to True), he returns the session key sk_U^i. It models the misuse of a session key by the parties after having established it.
- Test ($\mathcal{U}$, i) – if the oracle $\mathcal{U}_i$ has accepted, one tosses a coin b. If $b = 1$ then the session key sk_U^i is returned, else a random string is returned. The aim of the attack is then to guess this bit b. Therefore, there are trivial restrictions about this query:

- it can just be asked once;
- no Reveal-query has been asked to $\mathcal{U}_i$;
- no Reveal-query has been asked to $\mathcal{V}_j$, where $\mathcal{V}_j$ is partnered with $\mathcal{U}_i$.
- Corrupt $(\mathcal{U})$ – in order to deal with the forward-secrecy, one allows the adversary to corrupt the parties. Then, he obtains the secret key (the long-term secret key x_U) of the corrupted party $\mathcal{U}$. Therefore, the Test-query will have to be asked to a party which had accepted before any corruption.

The above game, with the Test-query, just deals with the key agreement property but not with authentication. We will say that the protocol provides mutual authentication if no instance accepts and not exactly one partner exists. Otherwise, it would mean that the adversary has impersonated a party. More precisely, if an instance $\mathcal{A}_i$ of the server accepts with no partner, it means that the adversary had impersonated the client, and therefore broken the client-to-server authentication.

In the other direction, if an instance $\mathcal{B}_j$ of the client accepts with no partner, it means that the adversary had impersonate the server, and therefore broken the server-to-client authentication.

A key exchange protocol guarantees mutual authentication if for any adversary, her probabilities in breaking the client-to-server authentication or the server-to-client authentication are both negligible. This is usually guaranteed by implicit authentication together with key confirmations from both parties [2].

6 Analysis of the First Scheme

6.1 Presentation

This section deals with the security of the scheme presented in figure 1. We prove that it achieves the security requirements:

- an adversary cannot learn any information about a session key which has not been revealed. This is proven by the fact that any adversary can just obtain a negligible advantage in guessing the bit b involved in the Test-query;
- an adversary cannot impersonate any of the parties, which guarantees the mutual authentication;
- forward-secrecy is ensured as long as the server is not corrupted.

As usual, some assumptions have to be made to provide the security result. The following proof just runs in the random oracle model [3] and assume the intractability of the gap Diffie–Hellman problem [14].

Indeed, we cannot hope to weaken the computational assumption, but can prove that it is sufficient.

6.2 The Gap Diffie–Hellman Problem: A Necessary Assumption

First, let us specify more formally the Diffie–Hellman problems we will use. In the protocol, $\mathcal{G}$ is any group of prime order q. For any pair (g, h) of $\mathcal{G}$-elements, we define the following Diffie–Hellman problems, which are particular instances of the general problems presented previously.

- $\mathsf{C\text{-}DH}_{g,h}$: given an element a, find the element $b = \mathsf{C\text{-}DH}(g,h,a)$.
- $\mathsf{D\text{-}DH}_{g,h}$: given a pair (a,b), decide whether $b = \mathsf{C\text{-}DH}(g,h,a)$, which is equivalent to decide whether $\mathsf{D\text{-}DH}(g,h,a,b)$ is true or not.
- $\mathsf{G\text{-}DH}_{g,h}$: given an element a, find the element $b = \mathsf{C\text{-}DH}(g,h,a)$ with the help of a $\mathsf{D\text{-}DH}_{g,h}$ oracle.

First, it is clear that if the discrete logarithm problem can be broken, then this authentication scheme is no longer secure. Furthermore, for the server, the computational Diffie–Hellman problem $\mathsf{C\text{-}DH}_{g,y_A}$ is enough to be broken so that the security of the overall scheme vanishes. However, one may also remark that the adversary has access to a kind of oracle $\mathsf{D\text{-}DH}_{g,y_A}$ that answers to any query $\mathsf{D\text{-}DH}_{g,y_A}(a,b)$, by saying whether $b = \mathsf{C\text{-}DH}(g,y_A,a)$ or not, for any pair (a,b) of her choice: indeed, the adversary chooses a random r and sends $\mathcal{A}, a, r$ to the server. This latter answers A, e. The adversary stops the game and simply checks whether $A = H_2(y_A, a, b)$, which answers the $\mathsf{D\text{-}DH}_{g,y_A}(a,b)$ query.

Therefore, if one can break the Gap Diffie–Hellman problem $\mathsf{G\text{-}DH}_{g,y_A}$, which is exactly to compute $\mathsf{C\text{-}DH}_{g,y_A}(B) = \mathsf{C\text{-}DH}(g,y_A,B)$ for a non-negligible part of B with non-negligible probability, with an access to a $\mathsf{D\text{-}DH}_{g,y_A}$ oracle, which answers whether $C = \mathsf{D\text{-}DH}(g,y_A,B)$ or not, for any pair (B,C), then one can use the server for simulating the $\mathsf{D\text{-}DH}_{g,y_A}$ oracle, as shown above.

Now, let us prove that this mathematical assumption is enough for the security of this scheme, which would prove the equivalence of the security and the Gap Diffie–Hellman problem [14]. Let us do it step by step. Whereas we want to prove the security of the key exchange protocol and of the mutual authentication, we do not proceed as usual. Indeed, we first study the client-to-server authentication, then the security of the key agreement (no leakage of information about any session key) and finally we complete the mutual authentication by proving the server-to-client authentication.

In all the following claims and proofs, we denote by

- q_A (resp. q_B), the number of instances of the server (resp. client) involved in the game;
- ℓ_0, ℓ_1 and ℓ_2, the output size of the oracles H_0, H_1 and H_2;
- q_0, q_1 and q_2, the number of queries asked to the oracles H_0, H_1 and H_2;
- q_H, the total number of queries asked to the oracles H_0, H_1 and H_2;
- k, the size of the challenge e.

6.3   Client-to-Server Authentication

Let us first deal with the authentication of the parties to each other. In this aim, we denote by Event^{c2s} the event that, at the end of the attack, there exists an instance $\mathcal{A}_i$ of the server which has accepted without exactly one partner. This event defines the violation of the client-to-server authentication. Respectively, we denote by Event^{s2c} the event that, at the end of the attack, there exists an instance $\mathcal{B}_j$ of the client which has accepted without exactly one partner. This latter event defines the violation of the server-to-client authentication.

The following lemma states that the protocol provides client-to-server authentication, relative to the discrete logarithm problem.

Lemma 1. *Let us assume that an adversary can violate the client-to-server authentication with probability ε within a time bound t. Then the discrete logarithm can be solved within an expected time*

$$t' \leq t \times \left(\frac{1}{\nu} + \left(\frac{\nu}{4q_A} - \frac{1}{2^k} \right)^{-1} \right), \quad \text{where } \nu = \varepsilon - \left(\frac{1}{2^{\ell_1}} \times \left(\frac{q_B^2}{q} + q_1^2 \right) + \frac{q_A q_1}{q} \right).$$

Proof. Let us assume that, for some ν,

$$\varepsilon = \Pr[\mathsf{Event}^{\mathsf{c2s}}] \geq \nu + \frac{1}{2^{\ell_1}} \times \left(\frac{q_B^2}{q} + q_1^2 \right) + \frac{q_A q_1}{q}.$$

First, one can easily simulate any client $\mathcal{B}$ instance without the secret key, thanks to the random oracle used to commit the first flow. On the other hand, there is no need to simulate the server instances, since we have the secret key. Let see the figure 3. On may remark that this simulation is perfectly indistinguishable from a real game, excepted in the case the definition $H_1(g^d y_B^e, y_A, B, K) \leftarrow r$ cannot be done in the Send $(\mathcal{B}, j, (A, e))$-query. Indeed, H_1 may have already been defined at that point before. But since d is randomly chosen in $\mathbb{Z}_q$, the simulation fails with probability less than $q_A q_1/q$.

Therefore, one can consider this simulation as the game to study, which is indistinguishable from a real game. Thus, one can remark that the probability for an $\mathcal{A}_i$ to have many partners is bounded by $q_B^2/q2^{\ell_1}$, since B and r are randomly chosen by the client instances. Furthermore, we condition, using $\Pr_H$, all the probabilities to the event $\neg\mathsf{Event}^{\mathsf{ColH}}$, where $\mathsf{Event}^{\mathsf{ColH}}$ denotes a collision for H_1. Therefore,

$$\nu + \frac{q_1^2}{2^{\ell_1}} \leq \varepsilon - \frac{q_A q_1}{q} - \frac{q_B^2}{q \cdot 2^{\ell_1}} \leq \Pr[\exists i \ \mathsf{Event}_i] \leq \Pr_H[\exists i \ \mathsf{Event}_i] + \Pr[\mathsf{Event}^{\mathsf{ColH}}]$$

$$\leq \Pr_H[\exists i \ \mathsf{Event}_i] + \frac{q_1^2}{2^{\ell_1}},$$

where Event_i denotes the event that, at the end of the attack in the simulated game, the instance $\mathcal{A}_i$ has accepted without any partner. Then $\Pr_H[\exists i \ \mathsf{Event}_i]$ is lower-bounded by ν. The end of the proof works exactly as the security proof of the signature schemes studied in [15], thanks to the *forking lemma*. Using this technique, we make a fork on the execution sid $= (\mathcal{A}, B, r, A, e, \mathcal{B}, d)$, on which occurred the violation of the client-to-server authentication, by changing e into e' at the right time. We then obtain a new violation on the execution sid$' = (\mathcal{A}, B, r, A', e', \mathcal{B}, d')$. This uses the same values for B and r: note that the correctness of B, and the knowledge of K, are both verified in the test $r = H_1(g^d y_B^e, y_A, B, K)$[1]. More precisely, let us group inside the set $\mathcal{I}$ all the

---

[1] We note that the absence of such a construction would allow a reuse of transcripts, which opens up to serious abuse. We refer to [20] for a description of how such vulnerabilities can be taken advantage of. Therein, a weakness of a previous version of our protocol is described and exploited.

Initialization	
Input	g and y
Keys	$x_A \in \mathbb{Z}_q$, $y_A = g^{x_A}$, $y_B \leftarrow y$

Hash functions H_0, H_1, H_2	
$H_0(\star)$, $H_1(\star)$, $H_2(\star)$	if the value is not determined at that point, one chooses a random value in the corresponding range and returns it.
	Any hash value used below is implicitly obtained with this simulation, unless something else is specified.

Instance $\mathcal{A}_i$ of $\mathcal{A}$	
Send $(\mathcal{A}, i, (\mathcal{A}, B, r))$	one computes $K = B^{x_A}$ and $A = H_2(y_A, B, K)$. Then one chooses a random challenge $0 \le e < 2^k$ and returns (A, e).
Send $(\mathcal{A}, i, (\mathcal{B}, d))$	one checks whether $r = H_1(g^d y_B^e, y_A, B, K)$. If satisfied, one accepts and terminates, else one just terminates, while still not accepting.

Instance $\mathcal{B}_j$ of $\mathcal{B}$	
Send $(\mathcal{B}, j, \text{"start"})$	one chooses random $b \in \mathbb{Z}_q$ and $r \in \{0,1\}^{\ell_1}$. Then, one computes $B = g^b$, $K = y_A^b$ and returns (B, r).
Send $(\mathcal{B}, j, (A, e))$	one checks whether $A = H_2(y_A, B, K)$. If satisfied, one chooses a random $0 \le d < q$, computes $T = g^d y_B^e$, defines $H_1(T, y_A, B, K) \leftarrow r$ and returns $(\mathcal{B}, d)$ while accepting and terminating, else one just terminates, while still not accepting.

Other queries	
Reveal $(\mathcal{U}, i)$	if the oracle $\mathcal{U}_i$ has accepted, one returns the corresponding $H_0(y_A, B, K)$.
Test $(\mathcal{U}, i)$	if $\mathcal{U}_i$ has accepted, one flips a coin and either returns the corresponding $H_0(y_A, B, K)$ or a random string.

Fig. 3. Game A: Client-to-server authentication

most likely indices i: $\mathcal{I} = \{i \mid \Pr_H[\text{Event}_i \mid \text{Event}^{c2s}] \ge 1/2q_A\}$. Then one can easily prove that we have $\Pr_H[\exists i \in \mathcal{I}, \text{Event}_i] \ge 1/2$.

Let us call $\text{Event}_i^{\text{Partial}}$ the event defined by the following property: when the instance $\mathcal{A}_i$ receives the Send $(\mathcal{A}, i, (\mathcal{A}, B, r))$ query,

$$\Pr_H[\text{Event}_i \mid \text{Event}_i^{\text{Partial}}] \ge \nu/4q_A.$$

Then, using the *splitting lemma* [15] one can claim that for any index $i \in \mathcal{I}$, $\Pr_H[\text{Event}_i^{\text{Partial}} \mid \text{Event}_i] \ge 1/2$. Indeed,

$$\Pr_H[\text{Event}_i] = \Pr_H[\text{Event}_i \wedge \text{Event}^{c2s}]$$

$$= \Pr_H[\text{Event}_i \mid \text{Event}^{c2s}] \times \Pr_H[\text{Event}^{c2s}] \ge \frac{1}{2q_A} \times \nu.$$

Therefore, if one runs the attack, until the event Event^{c2s} occurs, which requires an expected number of iterations bounded by $1/\nu$. In that case, with probability of $1/2$, we furthermore have Event_i with an instance $i \in \mathcal{I}$. That event means that the adversary (since it is not an instance of $\mathcal{B}$) has answered d which satisfies $r = H_1(g^d y_B^e, y_A, B, K)$. Therefore, with probability $1/2$, $\mathsf{Event}_i^{\mathsf{Partial}}$ occurs too. One rewinds the game up to the $\mathsf{Send}\ (\mathcal{A},\ i,\ (\mathcal{A}, B, r))$ query, answering with a random challenge e'. One resumes and rewinds with new challenges e' until another event $\mathsf{Event}^{\mathsf{c2s}}$ occurs, or at most $(\nu/4q_A - 1/2^k)^{-1}$ times. If $\mathsf{Event}_i^{\mathsf{Partial}}$ occurred, we obtain a second success Event_i with probability greater than $1/2$.

Globally, after at most $1/\nu + (\nu/4q_A - 1/2^k)^{-1}$ iterations of the game, we have obtained two answers d, d' to two distinct challenges $e \neq e'$ with probability greater than $1/8$, for the same $(\mathcal{A}, B, r, A)$.

Thanks to $e \neq e', d, d'$, since we have assumed that no collision has been found for H_1, we have the relation $g^e y_B^d = g^{e'} y_B^{d'}$, which leads to the discrete logarithm of y_B in basis g. □

Let us postpone the study of mutual authentication and study right now the security of the key agreement. Indeed, the proof relies on the previous result, and will be useful for the server-to-client authentication.

6.4   Key Agreement

Theorem 2. *Let us assume that an adversary can guess the bit involved in the* Test-*query with advantage ε within a time bound t. Then the computational Diffie–Hellman problem can be solved with probability $\varepsilon' \geq \varepsilon/2 - p_{c2s}$, within almost the same time, where p_{c2s} is the maximal probability for an adversary to violate the client-to-server authentication within a time bound t (cf. Lemma 1), with at most q_H queries to the decision Diffie–Hellman oracle. Thus the security relies on the gap Diffie–Hellman problem.*

Proof. Let us first remark that because of the randomness of the hash function, to gain any advantage in guessing correctly the coin involved in the Test-query, the adversary must ask the query (y_A, B, K) to H_0: $\Pr[\mathsf{AskK}] \geq \mathsf{Adv}/2$, where AskK denotes the event that the query (y_A, B, K) corresponding to the sid of the Test-query has been asked to H_0. Therefore, because of the constraints on the Test-query,

$$\Pr[\mathsf{AskK} \wedge \exists i\ \mathsf{Test}\ (\mathcal{A},\ i) \wedge \mathsf{Event}^{\mathsf{c2s}}] + \Pr[\mathsf{AskK} \wedge \exists i\ \mathsf{Test}\ (\mathcal{A},\ i) \wedge \neg\mathsf{Event}^{\mathsf{c2s}}]$$
$$+ \Pr[\mathsf{AskK} \wedge \exists j\ \mathsf{Test}\ (\mathcal{B},\ j)] \geq \mathsf{Adv}/2.$$

If one denotes by p_{c2s} the probability to break the client-to-server authenticity, one can claim that

$$\Pr[\mathsf{AskK} \wedge \exists i\ \mathsf{Test}\ (\mathcal{A},\ i) \wedge \neg\mathsf{Event}^{\mathsf{c2s}}] + \Pr[\mathsf{AskK} \wedge \exists j\ \mathsf{Test}\ (\mathcal{B},\ j)] \geq \mathsf{Adv}/2 - p_{c2s}.$$

Let us now consider the simulation of the parties, as described on figure 4. Thanks to the Decision Diffie–Hellman Oracle $\mathsf{D}\text{-}\mathsf{DH}_{g,\alpha}$, one can perfectly simulate all the parties and the random oracles. Indeed, the tables H_0^{DH}, H_1^{DH} and H_2^{DH} are managed using this decision Diffie–Hellman oracle, and record the answers of the oracles H_0, H_1 and H_2, when inputs are Diffie–Hellman triples.

The simulation may just fail, in the Test $(\mathcal{A}, i)$ query, since this latter simulation requires a client-partner, if the event Event^{c2s} occurs. Anyway, with this simulation, the event "$(\exists i)$ Test $(\mathcal{A}, i) \wedge \neg \mathsf{Event}^{c2s}$" implies event "$(\exists j)$ Test $(\mathcal{B}, j)$":

$$\Pr[\mathsf{AskK} \wedge (\exists j) \mathsf{Test}\,(\mathcal{B},\,j)] \geq \mathsf{Adv}/2 - p_{c2s}.$$

Because of the simulation of $\mathcal{B}_j$, we have

$$\mathsf{Adv}/2 - p_{c2s} \leq \Pr[\mathsf{AskK}\ \text{for}\ (y_A = \alpha, B = \beta^b, K = \mathsf{C\text{-}DH}(g, y_A, B))].$$

Therefore, the AskK event says that $K = \mathsf{C\text{-}DH}(g, \alpha, \beta^b)$ can be extracted from the queries asked to the H_0 oracle, while verifying the correctness thanks to the Decision Diffie–Hellman Oracle (the $\mathsf{D\text{-}DH}_{g,\alpha}$), with probability greater than $\mathsf{Adv}/2 - p_{c2s}$. Thus, $\mathsf{C\text{-}DH}(g, \alpha, \beta) = K^d$, where $d = b^{-1} \bmod q$.

To conclude the proof, one can just remark that if the Gap Diffie–Hellman problem $\mathsf{G\text{-}DH}_{g,y_A}$ is intractable, so do is the discrete logarithm problem too, which guarantees that p_{c2s} is small. $\qquad\square$

6.5   Mutual Authentication

Since we have already proven the client-to-server authentication, we just need to prove the server-to-client authentication to ensure mutual authentication.

Lemma 3. *Let us assume that an adversary can violate the server-to-client authentication (without any violation of the client-to-server authentication) of the protocol with probability π within a time bound t. Then the computational Diffie–Hellman problem can be solved with probability π' within almost the same time, where*

$$\pi' \geq \pi - \left(\frac{q_B}{2^{\ell_2}} + \frac{q_B^2}{q}\right).$$

Proof. As we have seen above, the simulation presented on figure 4 is perfect unless the event Event^{c2s} occurs. Therefore, let us study the event Event^{s2c}, knowing $\neg\mathsf{Event}^{c2s}$. It means that at some point, after having sent $(A, B = a^b, r)$ and received (A, e), a client accepts the proof whereas it has not been produced by a server:

– either the adversary guessed the value A (probability less than $q_B/2^{\ell_2}$)
– or the value B occurred in an other session (probability less than q_B^2/q, since it is randomly chosen by the client)
– or the adversary has asked for (y_A, B, K) to the oracle H_2

Then

$$\Pr[\mathsf{Event}^{s2c}\,|\,\neg\mathsf{Event}^{c2s}] \leq \Pr\left[\begin{array}{l}(y_A, B, K)\ \text{asked, with}\ y_A = \alpha, \\ B = \beta^b, K = \mathsf{C\text{-}DH}(g, y_A, B))\end{array}\right] + \frac{q_B}{2^{\ell_2}} + \frac{q_B^2}{q},$$

which completes the proof of the lemma. $\qquad\square$

Initialization	
Input	g, α and β
Keys	$y_A \leftarrow \alpha$, $x_B \in \mathbb{Z}_q$, $y_B \leftarrow g^{x_B}$

Hash functions H_0, H_1, H_2	
$H_0(a, b, c)$	two different situations may appear.
	– $a = \alpha$ and $c = \mathsf{C\text{-}DH}(g, a, b)$, checked by the $\mathsf{D\text{-}DH}_{g,\alpha}$ oracle: if $H_0^{\mathsf{DH}}(a, b)$ has been defined, to say d, (which occurs iff H_0 has been defined to d in the point (a, b, c), then returns d, else, (*i.e.* H_0 is undefined at the point (a, b, c)) then one chooses a random value $d \in \{0, 1\}^{\ell_0}$, defines $H_0^{\mathsf{DH}}(a, b) \leftarrow d$ and returns d.
	– otherwise: if H_0 is undefined at the point (a, b, c), then one chooses a random value in $\{0, 1\}^{\ell_0}$ and returns it.
$H_1(T, a, b, c)$	same as for H_0, but using ℓ_1 and $H_1^{\mathsf{DH}}(T, a, b)$.
$H_2(a, b, c)$	same as for H_0, but using ℓ_2 and $H_2^{\mathsf{DH}}(a, b)$.
$H_0^{\mathsf{DH}}(a, b)$	if the query (a, b) has not been asked to H_0^{DH} then one chooses a random value in $\{0, 1\}^{\ell_0}$ and returns it.
$H_1^{\mathsf{DH}}(T, a, b)$	same as for H_0^{DH}, but using ℓ_1, and queries of the form (T, a, b).
$H_2^{\mathsf{DH}}(a, b)$	same as for H_0^{DH}, but using ℓ_2.

Any hash value used below is implicitly obtained with this simulation, unless something else is specified. Furthermore, only the simulated parties have access to the H_0^{DH}, H_1^{DH} and H_2^{DH} oracles.

Instance $\mathcal{A}_i$ of $\mathcal{A}$	
Send $(\mathcal{A}, i, (A, B, r))$	one asks for $A = H_2^{\mathsf{DH}}(y_A, B)$, chooses a random challenge $0 \leq e < 2^k$ and returns (A, e).
Send $(\mathcal{A}, i, d)$	one checks whether $r = H_1^{\mathsf{DH}}(g^d y_B^e, y_A, B)$. If satisfied, one accepts and terminates, else one just terminates, while still not accepting.

Instance $\mathcal{B}_j$ of $\mathcal{B}$	
Send $(\mathcal{B}, j, \text{"start"})$	one chooses random $b, t \in \mathbb{Z}_q$ and computes $B = \beta^b$, $T = g^t$ as well as $r = H_1^{\mathsf{DH}}(T, y_A, B)$, and returns (B, r).
Send $(\mathcal{B}, j, (A, e))$	if $A = H_2^{\mathsf{DH}}(y_A, B)$ then one computes $d = t - e x_B \bmod q$ and returns d while accepting and terminating, else one just terminates, while still not accepting.

Other queries	
Reveal $(\mathcal{U}, i)$	if $\mathcal{U}_i$ has accepted, one returns the corresponding $H_0^{\mathsf{DH}}(y_A, B)$.
Test $(\mathcal{B}, j)$	if $\mathcal{U}_i$ has accepted, one flips a coin and either returns the corresponding $H_0^{\mathsf{DH}}(y_A, B)$ or a random string.
Test $(\mathcal{A}, i)$	let us denote by $\mathcal{B}_j$ the partner of $\mathcal{A}_i$ (abort if not uniquely defined), and run Test $(\mathcal{B}, j)$.
Corrupt $(\mathcal{B})$	one returns x_B.

Fig. 4. Game B: Key agreement protocol

Thanks to both lemma 1 and lemma 3, one can easily claim the following theorem.

Theorem 4. *Let us assume that an adversary can violate the mutual authentication of the protocol with probability ε within a time bound t. Then the computational Diffie–Hellman problem can be solved within an expected time bound*

$$t' \leq t \times \left(\frac{1}{\nu} + \left(\frac{\nu}{4q_A} - \frac{1}{2^k} \right)^{-1} + \left(\frac{\varepsilon}{2} - \frac{q_B}{2^{\ell_2}} - \frac{q_B^2}{q} \right)^{-1} \right),$$

where

$$\nu = \frac{\varepsilon}{2} - \left(\frac{1}{2^{\ell_1}} \times \left(\frac{q_B^2}{q} + q_1^2 \right) + \frac{q_A q_1}{q} \right).$$

Proof. Simply adding results of both Lemmas 1 and 3, one gets the expected result, since $\varepsilon \leq \Pr[\mathsf{Event}^{\mathsf{ma}}] = \Pr[\mathsf{Event}^{\mathsf{c2s}}] + \Pr[\mathsf{Event}^{\mathsf{s2c}} \mid \neg\mathsf{Event}^{\mathsf{c2s}}]$, and therefore either $\Pr[\mathsf{Event}^{\mathsf{c2s}}] \geq \varepsilon/2$ or $\Pr[\mathsf{Event}^{\mathsf{s2c}} \mid \neg\mathsf{Event}^{\mathsf{c2s}}] \geq \varepsilon/2$. □

6.6   Forward Secrecy

This protocol furthermore provides partial forward-secrecy. Indeed, it is clear that if the server is corrupted, then all the session keys can be recovered from the transcript. However, the corruption of the client may not help to recover the session keys: the forward-secrecy just deals with the key agreement property which can be perfectly simulated by the game presented on figure 4. This simulation provides the Corrupt-query, since the client secret key is known. Then the theorem 2 still holds, since the Test-query has to be asked for a session which occurs before the corruption.

7   Improvements

7.1   Analysis of the Second Scheme

Without the q-modular reduction, the simulation of the client-to-server authentication, while choosing $0 \leq d < q \cdot 2^{k+k'}$, is not perfect [16]. However the distance of the distribution of the transcripts is less than $1/2^{k'}$ (statistical indistinguishability). Therefore, all the security results still remain, under the condition that $1/2^{k'}$ is negligible.

7.2   Hash Functions

Using the proof technique proposed by Girault and Stern [10], one can still prove the client-to-server authentication even with a short hash function H_1, just considering the multi-collision resistance. Indeed, if one can avoid ℓ-collisions for H_1, with probability greater than p_ℓ, then the lemma 1 is slightly modified, as follows.

Lemma 5. *Let us assume that an adversary can violate the client-to-server authentication with probability ε within a time bound t, then the discrete logarithm can be solved within an expected time*

$$t' \leq t \times \left(\frac{1}{\nu} + (\ell - 1) \times \left(\frac{\nu}{4q_A} - \frac{1}{2^k} \right)^{-1} \right), \quad \text{where } \nu = \varepsilon - \left(\frac{q_B^2}{2^{\ell_1}q} + \frac{q_A q_1}{q} + p_\ell \right).$$

The main modification appears in the time complexity, since in the forking lemma, one has to rewind many times to obtain ℓ values, so that at least 2 are distinct.

7.3 Size of the Parameters

One can use the following sizes for achieving a good security level, assuming that the adversary cannot ask more than $q_A, q_B \leq 2^{30}$ queries to the instance-oracles and $q_0, q_1, q_2 \leq 2^{64}$ queries to the random oracles:

- a 160-bit order q for the group $\mathcal{G}$ prevents baby-step/giant-step attacks [18] or any other generic attack. Then a convenient group as to be chosen to avoid any other kind of attack (*e.g.* $\mathcal{G} = \langle g \rangle \subset \mathbb{Z}_p^\star$, or an elliptic curve). The integer n will denote the bit-size of the encoding of the elements in $\mathcal{G}$;
- $k = k' = 64$ make the simulation indistinguishable but with a very small distance (less than 2^{-64});
- $\ell_1 = 80$, for providing a 5-collision resistant hash function; $\ell_2 = 64$ or 128; and ℓ_0, whatever needed for a session key, say 64.

7.4 Storage and Computation

With these parameters, the client can precompute anything required during the protocol:

- two exponentiations before knowing the server;
- one exponentiation and three hashings when he knows the server;

Then, he has to store

- B, a group element (of size n);
- t and r, where t is a $|q| + k + k' = 288$-bit long integer and r a 80-bit hash value;
- A' and sk, two 64-bit hash values.

The total memory required for one authenticated key agreement is $n + 496$ bits. Using an elliptic curve group, this is less than 82 bytes.

Thereafter, the client will just have to perform on-line,

- one test of equality between two 64-bit elements;
- one multiplication between a 64-bit and a 160-bit integers;
- one addition between a 224-bit and a 288-bit integers.

One can even decrease the storage-memory by choosing and storing $0 \leq t < q$, but computing $d = t + \rho \cdot q + e \cdot x_B$, where ρ is a random 128-bit element.

Then the storage-memory required for one authenticated key agreement is $n + 368$ bits. Using an elliptic curve group, this is less than 66 bytes. But one multiplication and one addition more have to be performed on-line.

8   Conclusion

In this paper, we have proposed a key exchange scheme which achieves mutual authentication and forward-secrecy (but just for the leakage of the client long-term key). The main interest of this scheme is the computational efficiency. Indeed, it requires the client to perform only a few additions and multiplications of short integers, and a few comparisons between 64-bit strings. The storage requirements are less than 70 bytes per process, which allows more than 15 pre-computed tuples per kilobyte.

Acknowledgments

We are grateful to Wong and Chan [20] for detecting a vulnerability in the presented version. Our paper, as it appears here, takes their findings into consideration by ensuring that transcripts are not inappropriately reused. We refer to their publication for a detailed description of the importance of protecting against such attacks.

References

1. M. Bellare, R. Canetti, and H. Krawczyk. A Modular Approach to the Design and Analysis of Authentication and Key Exchange Protocols. In *Proc. of the 30th STOC*. ACM Press, New York, 1998.
2. M. Bellare, D. Pointcheval, and P. Rogaway. Authenticated Key Exchange Secure Against Dictionary Attacks. In *Eurocrypt 2000*, LNCS 1807, pages 139–155. Springer-Verlag, Berlin, 2000.
3. M. Bellare and P. Rogaway. Random Oracles Are Practical: A Paradigm for Designing Efficient Protocols. In *Proc. of the 1st CCS*, pages 62–73. ACM Press, New York, 1993.
4. M. Bellare and P. Rogaway. Entity Authentication and Key Distribution. In *Crypto'93*, LNCS 773, pages 232–249. Springer-Verlag, Berlin, 1994.
5. M. Bellare and P. Rogaway. Provably Secure Session Key Distribution: The Three Party Case. In *Proc. of the 27th STOC*. ACM Press, New York, 1995.
6. D. Chaum. Zero-Knowledge Undeniable Signatures. In *Eurocrypt'90*, LNCS 473, pages 458–464. Springer-Verlag, Berlin, 1991.
7. D. Chaum and H. van Antwerpen. Undeniable Signatures. In *Crypto'89*, LNCS 435, pages 212–216. Springer-Verlag, Berlin, 1990.
8. W. Diffie and M.E. Hellman. New Directions in Cryptography. *IEEE Transactions on Information Theory*, IT–22(6):644–654, November 1976.
9. M. Girault. Self-Certified Public Keys. In *Eurocrypt'91*, LNCS 547, pages 490–497. Springer-Verlag, Berlin, 1992.

10. M. Girault and J. Stern. On the Length of Cryptographic Hash-Values used in Identification Schemes. In *Crypto'94*, LNCS 839, pages 202–215. Springer-Verlag, Berlin, 1994.

11. R.M. Needham and M.D. Schroeder. Using Encryption for Authentication in Large Networks of Computers. *Communications of the ACM*, 21:993–999, 1978.

12. B.C. Neuman and T. Ts'o. Kerberos: An Authentication Service for Computer Networks. *IEEE Communications Magazine*, 32(9):33–28, September 1994.

13. T. Okamoto and D. Pointcheval. REACT: Rapid Enhanced-security Asymmetric Cryptosystem Transform. In *RSA 2001*, LNCS 2020, pages 159–175. Springer-Verlag, Berlin, 2001.

14. T. Okamoto and D. Pointcheval. The Gap-Problems: A New Class of Problems for the Security of Cryptographic Schemes. In *PKC 2001*, LNCS 1992, pages 104–118. Springer-Verlag, Berlin, 2001.

15. D. Pointcheval and J. Stern. Security Arguments for Digital Signatures and Blind Signatures. *Journal of Cryptology*, 13(3):361–396, 2000.

16. G. Poupard and J. Stern. Security Analysis of a Practical "on the fly" Authentication and Signature Generation. In *Eurocrypt'98*, LNCS 1403, pages 422–436. Springer-Verlag, Berlin, 1998.

17. C.P. Schnorr. Efficient Identification and Signatures for Smart Cards. In *Crypto'89*, LNCS 435, pages 235–251. Springer-Verlag, Berlin, 1990.

18. D. Shanks. Class Number, a Theory of Factorization, and Genera. In *Proceedings of the Symposium on Pure Mathematics*, volume 20, pages 415–440. AMS, 1971.

19. V. Shoup. On Formal Models for Secure Key Exchange. Technical Report RZ 3120, IBM Research, April 1999.

20. D.S. Wong and A.H. Chan. Efficient and Mutually Authenticated Key Exchange for Low-Power Computing Devices In *Asiacrypt 2001*, LNCS. Springer-Verlag, Berlin, 2001. To appear.

Off-Line Generation of Limited-Use Credit Card Numbers

Aviel D. Rubin and Rebecca N. Wright

AT&T Labs – Research
180 Park Avenue,Florham Park, NJ, 07932 USA
{rubin,rwright}@research.att.com

Abstract. Recently, some credit card companies have introduced limited-use credit card numbers—for example, American Express's single-use card numbers and Visa's gift cards. Such limited-use credit cards limit the exposure of a traditional long-term credit card number, particularly in Internet transactions. These offerings employ an *on-line* solution, in that a credit card holder must interact with the credit card issuer in order to derive a limited-use token. In this paper, we describe a method for cryptographic *off-line* generation of limited-use credit card numbers. This has several advantages over the on-line schemes, and it has applications to calling cards as well. We show that there are several trade-offs between security and maintaining the current infrastructure.

1 Introduction

The proliferation of e-commerce on the Internet has not resulted in a wide diversity of on-line payment mechanisms. While novel schemes such as PayPal [7] have gained in popularity, most business to customer transactions still utilize standard credit card numbers over a Secure Socket Layer (SSL) connection [5]. SSL provides encryption so that data is not revealed in transit, and server authentication so that the merchant identity is confirmed to the customer. (While SSL provides for mutual authentication, most consumers do not have the necessary public key certificates for it and virtually all consumer-oriented Web merchants implement only server authentication.)

Unfortunately, despite the use of SSL, there is no guarantee that the user is not being fooled by a malicious merchant (c.f. [6]) or, at least in earlier versions of SSL, that an outside attacker might not be able to break the encryption [3]. There are several ways SSL can break down even if the encryption mechanism is not broken. Most users do not actually verify the certificate on a secure site. That is, most users simply look for the browser's indication that a page has been encrypted, such as Netscape's blue padlock, rather than actually looking at the certificate itself to verify that the merchant name in the certificate matches their expectations. Many users do not do check even for this encryption indicator. Furthermore, even if users do check certificates, it is relatively easy for just about anyone to obtain one. There are over 50 root certificate authorities' public keys in a typical Netscape browser, and many more in Internet Explorer. In addition,

P. Syverson (Ed.): FC 2001, LNCS 2339, pp. 196–209, 2002.

there are other ways that users can be fooled into thinking they are visiting an intended site when in fact they are at an attacker's site [4].

Besides the risk of exposure of card numbers during transit, there is also the risk of exposure of card numbers while stored at a merchant's site. There have recently been several high profile cases in the news where merchants' sites were broken into and stored credit card numbers were stolen (c.f. [10]). Even in the physical world, credit cards are exposed simply by being used. Fraudulent merchants or employees may sell or use their customers' credit card numbers, and attackers can look for discarded credit card receipts in trash bins.

By having a single credit card number that is reusably and indefinitely used as an authorization token, the traditional credit card system creates substantial risk for the credit card companies, who lose millions or billions of dollars a year due to fraud.[1] The big companies—Visa, Mastercard, and American Express— insulate their customers from risk by shouldering any loss above $50 themselves; in many cases, even the $50 charge to the customer is waived. Thus, there is great incentive for credit card companies to implement schemes that make it more difficult for credit card numbers to be compromised. Fraud reduction is also advantageous to customers and merchants because the cost of fraud results in higher transaction costs charged by credit card companies to merchants, which must in turn either be absorbed by the merchant or passed to customers. Additionally, customers whose cards are compromised must deal with the inconvenience of replacing their cards and the potentially devastating and difficult-to-correct effects on their credit ratings.

The Secure Electronic Transactions (SET) protocol was designed to protect credit card numbers from malicious parties, and even from merchants. Unfortunately, SET never took off. There was too much overhead required, and buy-in was needed from too many different parties. Credit cards over SSL, on the other hand, require no additional infrastructure, and are easy for users to understand. It is not surprising that this is currently the standard for business to consumer commerce.

1.1   Related Work

Realizing the security problem in indefinitely reusable credit card numbers, credit card issuers have recently started to introduce limited-use credit card number solutions that can be layered over the existing infrastructure. American Express offers single-use credit cards and Visa offers limited-value gift credit cards. The design and architecture of another solution is presented by Shamir [9]. The main idea is to enable users to shop at existing Web merchant sites without exposing long-term credit card numbers, and without requiring changes to the Web pages. All of the existing solutions require users to have an on-line secure interaction with the credit card issuer during or shortly before a purchase, in

---

[1] Although part of the authorization token eventually changes due to the expiration date, this is only infrequently (typically, once every one to three years) and furthermore it is easy to guess the subsequent expiration date from the current one.

which a new single-use or limited-use credit card number, which we call a *token*, is obtained. The token is linked to the user's existing account, in that charges made with the token will be charged to the original account. Such tokens provide more security than standard reusable credit cards because even if they are learned by an attacker, they are either of no further use or of limited further use.

In the on-line setting used by these solutions, a card holder who wishes to make a purchase visits the Web site of the card issuer to obtain limited-use tokens. There, the card holder has the option to enter his name and account number, or perhaps a stronger method of authentication is performed, and then the card holder obtains a token to use for his purchase. The card issuer stores the token with the account, along with any restrictions on its use such as dollar amount or merchant name. When the token user shops at a merchant site, the token is entered into a Web form as if it were a traditional credit card number. From the merchant's point of view, the credit card is like any other. The merchant clears the credit card number with the issuing bank. The issuing bank then looks up the account and checks that the token has been stored with the account and is therefore valid.

There are several problems with the on-line setting. When the card holder obtains the token, the connection to the card issuer needs to be secured, typically by SSL, because the traditional long-term credit card number will be communicated over this connection. SSL places a performance burden on the server. Many simultaneous SSL connections could bring a server to its knees, and any solution involving a central SSL server does not scale well. Furthermore, a spoofed credit card company site could collect legitimate credit card numbers from unsuspecting users. In general, it is not a good idea for a site to exist with the sole purpose of collecting credit card numbers from people. It promotes bad habits and creates desirable targets. A simple attack against DNS and a certificate from any root CA is all an attacker needs to run a credit card collection site in this model.

1.2   Our Work

In our work, we consider an off-line model, where limited-use tokens (including tokens limited to a single use) can be implemented from traditional credit cards without requiring that a user interact with the credit card issuer as part of every transaction. Like the on-line solutions, our solution is designed so that it can be layered on top of the existing e-commerce infrastructure without any change to the merchant's systems or the user's browser. Off-line protocols have the advantage that the card holder need not interact with the credit card issuer to create limited-use tokens, and in particular, no secure channel to the credit card issuer is required at the time of token generation. This is useful because it removes the reliance on authentication with SSL. In our solution, expenses are billed to the original card without exposure of the card number; token generation is off-line for the credit card holder. Off-line schemes have the advantage that they can be used even for purchases where there may not be user access to a computer network, such as purchases made over the telephone.

Limited-use tokens can be useful for features other than limiting risk. In our work, a token can have various restrictions associated with it: we can limit the number of uses of a token, its validity period, the set of recipients, the amount of money, and even the category of product for which it can be used. For example, a token might only be good for $100 worth of books from either Amazon or Barnes & Nobles during the first week of classes. Tokens might be used to enforce or keep track of a personal budget. A user could create a token with a particular monetary limit that can only be used in restaurants, and thus enforce a limit on how much she spends eating out; different token with a different monetary limits could be created for additional expense categories. A parent could create a token with special restrictions to give to a child in college. There are all sorts of creative gift possibilities with credit card tokens, such as a token good for three days of restaurant and entertainment expenses up to $1000.

In Section 2, we present design requirements for token-based solutions. We present a proposed solution in Section 3, including an intuitive and easy-to-use user interface for the token-derivation application, and we discuss some security issues in Section 4. In Section 5, we discuss the use of limited-use tokens for telephone calling cards. We conclude in Section 6.

2   Requirements

In order to be successfully deployed, a system for generating and using limited-use tokens must satisfy several requirements.

Ease of use. The system should not place unreasonable burden on the users. This point cannot be overstated. If a system is bulky or requires users to learn new techniques and to adopt new ways of shopping, then it is likely to fail. For instance, users should only be required to type fairly short strings that consist of alphanumeric characters and are not case-sensitive. The use of more general strings might be viable if they need only be cut and pasted, but even then the strings should not be too long, since strings that "wrap" from one line to the next are not always handled correctly by cutting and pasting.

Interoperability. The system should be layerable on top of existing infrastructure. We should be able to deploy it without requiring merchants to change their Web sites. In particular, this means the tokens should preferably be 16 characters long, so that users can enter them into the existing credit card number field on Web forms; they may even be required to be strictly numeric due to type-checking on existing merchant Web forms.

Limited transparency. It should be clear to the card holders that they are not sending long-term credit card numbers to the merchant, if that is not the case. For example, if one wishes to design a system that intercepts merchant Web forms and automatically replaces traditional credit card numbers by limited-use tokens, care must be taken to ensure it is done in such as way that the user understands that the card number is not being transmitted over the network to the merchant.

Security. A limited-use token should not be usable beyond its intended uses, whether by the user, the merchants, or an attacker. Similarly, it should not be possible for an attacker to successfully generate and use tokens whose expenses are charged to someone else's credit card.

We use these requirements to guide our design process. Each requirement represents an objective that is difficult to quantify, but the more we adhere to the spirit of the requirements, the more likely it is our system will be adopted.

In the off-line model, card holders generate tokens on their own. Since it is not generally reasonable to assume personal computers are safe from hacking by outsiders, we assume that the credit card holder has an auxiliary tamper-resistant computing device that can protect secrets and has a reliable clock. For example, this device might be a PDA, such as a Palm Pilot or Windows CE device, or a PC equipped with a smart card reader or other tamper-resistant hardware. We assume that the owner can control access to the data on it by physical or cryptographic means.

Throughout the rest of this paper, we refer to the entity with whom people have credit card accounts as a *card issuer*.[2] We refer to a traditional credit card number held by a person as their *account number*, and we refer to the person as a *card holder*. The intended user of a limited-use token (who may be either the card holder or another person such as a gift recipient) is referred to as the *token user* or simply the *user*. We refer to the PDA or computer that is used for the off-line computation of tokens as the *device*.

3   Off-Line Token Generation

In this section, we present our proposed system, which consists of two parts. The first part, discussed in Section 3.1, is the token generation application. The second part, discussed in Section 3.2, is the protocol for using generated tokens.

3.1   Token Generation

We have already discussed several applications of limited-use tokens. In order to support as many of these applications as possible, our goal is to represent as many restrictions as possible while still meeting our ease-of-use and security requirements. To this end, we propose the following design.

Restrictions. In our system, there is a set of possible restrictions that is universal. For example, the monetary restrictions can be $20, $50, $75, $100, $150, $200, $300, $500, $1000, $5000. The categories of expense can be food, books,

---

[2] For simplicity, we do not in this paper separate out other entities that may be involved in transaction processing such as a merchant acquirer, but rather assume that the merchant talks directly to the card issuer. In order to implement this in the real system, intermediaries would be required to forward the appropriate messages.

travel, entertainment, luxury, clothing, electronics, etc. The validity periods can be one hour, four hours, twelve hours, one day, three days, a week, a month. It might also be desirable to include the identity of a merchant in the restrictions. Since we want to limit the size of the description, we suggest allowing the user only to specify the first few characters of the merchant name.

In the token generation application, all of the possible values are enumerated. Then, the values are laid out in a table, and the plaintext of the token consists of an index into the table. For readability, selected restrictions can be represented as an enumeration of the various restrictions. This is analogous to the way cryptographic algorithms and parameters are listed in SSL ciphersuites. For example, a setting of restrictions on a credit card might be:

one-hundred-dollars–books–one-week–same-store–two-uses

As discussed in Section 3.2, tokens are formed by encrypting the selected restrictions. If we want tokens to look like traditional credit card numbers, tokens must be 16 characters long, possibly restricted to 16 digits since non-numeric characters may break some Web sites that check credit card numbers to make sure they are digits. The symmetric cipher may require that the plaintext token be padded, and we also add a value for timestamping and uniqueness (as discussed in Section 3.2 below). Further, in traditional credit card numbers, the first four digits are typically used to represent a bank code, and the last digit is usually a checksum. Hence, if we wish to stick with 16 character tokens, then we can only use 11 characters to represent the restrictions. This means we can represent somewhere between 10^{11} and 36^{16} combinations of restrictions. While it seems that 10^{11} is more than enough combinations of restrictions for most interesting applications, there are also security issues based on the size of the space of possible tokens. We discuss security issues further in Section 4.

User Interface. User interface is crucial in any system that involves many users, especially if their level of experience with computers varies widely. We envision a set of pull-down menus or other graphical interface, independent of the particular device, for selecting from a predetermined set of restrictions. The user's device must contain the table of possible restrictions. Every time the user generates a token, the application can present the user with a list of choices, say via a pull-down menu for the restrictions.

In order to allow the largest possible number of interesting settings of restrictions and to reduce visual clutter for the user, some less interesting combinations of restrictions will be disallowed. That is, certain choices early on will restrict the set of choices for other restrictions. For example, if the user selects the number of uses of the token to be one, the system may not allow for any transaction over $500. It is up to the credit card companies to define the set of possible restrictions. The user chooses which restrictions from the set of possible restrictions to utilize for a particular token when creating the token.

Once the user picks all of the restrictions, the device should display the properties of the token in a manner that the user can confirm that this is what is desired. The user can then approve it, in which case the encryption takes place and the token is displayed, the user can modify it, or the user can discard it.

3.2   The Protocol

The main idea behind our protocol is a simple one: the card holder and the credit card issuer already have a relationship. In order to start using limited-use credit card numbers, the card holder must obtain a long-term secret key K from the card issuer. The key K must be stored in the user's device and remembered by the card issuer. Note that the card holder and the card issuer already share the semi-secret traditional credit card number, but we prefer to use a different key because it allows us to make K longer than a traditional credit card number, and because it is reasonable to expect that even if a limited-use system is adopted, it will be gradual and incomplete. That is, card holders will still use their traditional credit cards for some purchases. Given that, it is not wise to use the same card number as the secret shared by a card holder and the card issuer.

To generate a token, the card holder starts by choosing the desired restrictions. Once the restrictions are chosen, the device encrypts using K using an authenticated encryption scheme (discussed more in Section 4.2). Assuming the scheme used is secure, an attacker will not be able to learn the key K and use it to forge new tokens. However, it does introduce a new way that an attacker might be able to make charges to an account number—namely, by guessing a valid limited-use token. This is discussed further in Section 4.3.

We also must address the issue of "replay" attacks. In order to ensure that a limited-use token cannot be replayed for additional uses once its specified restrictions have been met, the card issuer maintains a database of "used up" tokens and checks before verifying a token that it has not already been used up. In order to avoid a database whose entries must be stored and looked at forever, we follow the standard technique of using expiration dates. That is, before encryption, the device adds a timestamp to the restrictions indicating the time of generation. In order to be valid, the token must first be used within a specified time—say, one month. Tokens first received after the one month expiration of their timestamps are rejected as invalid. Thus, the card issuer can remove used up tokens from the database once their expiration period has elapsed. Once seen by the card issuer, a single-use token has to be stored until a month from the timestamp in the token, and can then be removed from the database. A multiple-use token is stored when it is first used, and must then be stored for the larger of one month or the time limit in the token. (For example, a multiple-use token good for a year would need to be stored for the full year so that it would still be recognized as valid on subsequent uses even after one month.)

Our protocol has three parts, which occur sequentially, but need not be in quick sequence. The first part is a transformation (via encryption) from the restrictions and the long-term key K to the token. The second part is the communication of the token and the identifying information via the merchant to the credit card issuer. The third part is the verification of the token by the credit card issuer. Figure 1 shows the execution of the protocol. The card holder interacts with a token-generation application on the device locally, probably first authenticating to the application with the account number or another human-enterable password. Using this application, the user picks from a set of restrictions to specify the type of limited usage desired as described in Section 3.1. Once selected, the restrictions, along with the timestamp for avoiding replays, are encrypted with the long-term key K to form a token. Note that the timestamp also ensures that different tokens generated with the same restrictions are different, provided that sufficient time granularity is used, which ensures that different instances of the same restrictions with the same account number are distinguishable.

Later, when the token is to be used, it is communicated to the merchant along with identifying information such as the card holder's name and billing address. Such identifying information is already typically requested by merchants for Web and telephone purchases. In the case that the restrictions are not very restrictive (for example, if the merchant is not specified), it may still be desirable to send the limited-use token over an encrypted channel (SSL) to the merchant so eavesdroppers cannot overhear the token and use it before the user. However, note that even if the token itself is overheard, the eavesdropper won't know a priori which purchases are compatible with the restrictions in the token, since the restrictions are encrypted. Even if SSL must be used, a limited-use token provides additional security over a general-use one if the merchant is not known to be trustworthy or if there is concern about whether its databases are properly secured.

Once the merchant receives the token, it need not communicate further with the token user. The merchant must then get verification from the card issuer before fulfilling the user's order. To do this, the merchant passes the token and identifying information to the credit card issuer. The card issuer then attempts to verify that the token is a valid token and has not yet been used to the limits specified. If the merchant need not immediately respond to the user (for example, if the user is purchasing physical goods that will be shipped by mail), the merchant can wait to complete this step, perhaps batching several transactions together.

Once the card issuer receives the token and identifying information, it uses the identifying information to look up the long term key. The card issuer then uses the key to decrypt the token. If the decrypted token is not of the proper form, the card issuer notifies the merchant that the transaction is denied. If it is of the proper form, the issuer checks that the restrictions are met and that the token is not already in the "used-up" database. If the restrictions are not met or if the token is in the used-up database, the transaction is denied. If the restrictions are met and the token is not in the used-up database, the transaction is approved. If approved, the issuer approves the transaction to the merchant, who then fulfills the user's order.

Finally, the card issuer updates its databases: first, if the token is now used up (and not yet expired), whether due to monetary limits or transaction number

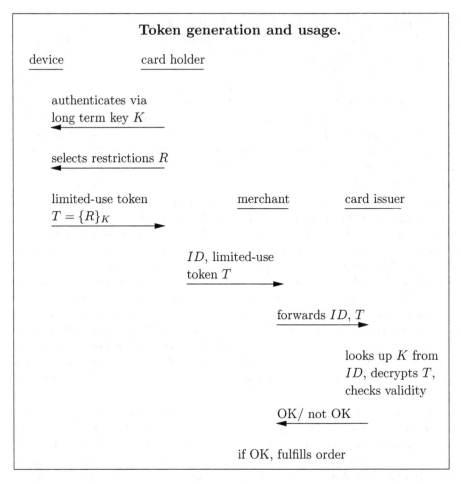

Fig. 1. The card holder authenticates to the device and selects the set R of restrictions. The device uses a key derived from the credit card number to encrypt R and produce a token T. The card holder then transmits T to the merchant, along with some identifying information ID. The merchant forwards these to the card issuer, who uses ID to look up the account, retrieve the card holder's long term key K, and decrypts the token. If the restrictions are met, the transaction is processed; otherwise, it is denied

limits, it is added to the used-up database. Additionally, if the token is a multiple-use token, the issuer looks for it in a database of current multiple-use tokens, adds it if it is not already there (because this is the first use), and accounts for the current use (e.g. subtracting the monetary amount and decrementing the transaction count). When the remaining amount or the transaction count reaches zero, or the token expires, the token is removed from the current multiple-use database.

4   Discussion

In this section, we discuss some security aspects of our proposed system.

4.1   Token Length

It would be desirable for security reasons to have tokens be longer than traditional credit card numbers. For example, 128-bit tokens (38 digits) would allow the use of AES, together with a MAC, as the encryption function. However, our interoperability and ease-of-use requirements suggest that our tokens must be at most 16 digits, or as little as 11 digits if part of the credit card number must be fixed.

There are several problems that arise if we restrict our tokens to be a specific small number of digits, which we address in the following subsections. Most encryption functions have a fixed, longer, block size, and it is not immediately clear how to apply them in this case. Additionally, a small token makes the tokens more susceptible to guessing attacks and causes collisions between tokens created by different users with different restrictions.

One possibility for increasing the size of the token space without requiring changes to merchants' Web sites is to divide a longer token into several parts that can be used in various parts of the name and address fields. While we think this solution violates our ease-of-use requirement and possibly our interoperability requirement, it may be necessary to maintain security.

4.2   Encryption of the Tokens

In our protocol, it is important that the tokens are authenticated so that the credit card company knows that they were generated by a valid card holder and that they have not been modified. The resulting token is used both to protect the authenticity of the token and to convey the information in the token privately to the card issuer, in as little space as possible. Authenticated encryption schemes provide encryption and some authentication properties. Decryption returns either the plaintext or an indication that the ciphertext is not a valid ciphertext for the key that was used. Several methods involving encryption and MACs have been proposed; many are analyzed by Bellare and Namprempre [1].

In our protocol, the output of the encryption is limited to the token space. The credit card company server must be able to decrypt the token, so truncating the encrypted token does not work. Furthermore, the token size will not typically fall on the block boundary of most symmetric ciphers. Fortunately, Black and Rogaway [2] describe several ciphers for arbitrary finite domains. In fact, their motivating example is generation of unpredictable credit card numbers, closely related to our application.

4.3   Guessing Attacks

A potential problem with our proposal is that an attacker might be able to guess a valid token and use it to make purchases. Since we include identifying information in a transaction (i.e. the user's name and billing address), the attacker must guess a token that works both for a particular name and address (ID) and for the purchase the attacker is making. That is, the attacker must find an ID and token such that the token is the encryption under that card holder's long-term key of a set restrictions compatible with the current purchase. Note that it is possible that two different settings of restrictions for different users with different account numbers may encrypt to the same token. These potential collisions can make an attacker's job easier because a given token will have more valid uses.

Using the most limited set of possible restrictions will make guessing harder, as there will be fewer tokens compatible with a given purchase. For example, one might implement the system to always require tokens to contain the merchant name, to have relatively short expiration dates, and to have only a small number of uses. In addition to making guessing attacks harder, this also reduces the usefulness of overheard tokens that an attacker might learn and try to reuse.

Even if there were exactly one valid token for a particular purchase, a token space of size 10^{11} appears dangerously small, in that it takes only a few days on a current computer to search the entire space, and an expected time of half that to find a valid token. Note that the use of traditional long-term credit cards results in a search space of size at most 10^{16} (less if some parts of the number are fixed), and once a card number is guessed, it can be reused for additional purchases until it is detected and revoked. Simply allowing non-case-sensitive alphanumeric credit-card length tokens gives us a search space of $36^{11} \approx 10^{17}$— already a small improvement over current credit cards in the time required to find a token valid for a particular purchase. Furthermore, in our case, subsequent purchases will usually require a different token, so a new guessing attack will be required.

More importantly, note that it is not sufficient for an attacker to simply guess a token by enumerating it. In order to learn whether or not the token is valid (without either already knowing the long term key or breaking the encryption another way), the attacker must actually attempt to use the token. This exposes the attacker to possible detection, as well as increasing the amount of resources an attacker must use to perform the attack. If the attacker fixes a specific user ID and attempts different tokens with it, the corresponding user's account will be suspended after a fairly small number of attempts, at least temporarily, and the attack will be very unlikely to succeed. While this is an inconvenience to the user, it is preferable to the alternative of allowing the attacker to succeed. If the attacker instead tries different IDs, he is less likely to succeed because now he also has to either guess valid IDs or find them through other means. Also, whether using the same or different IDs, if the attacker tries his attempts with the same (possibly collaborating) merchant, the issuer can temporarily suspend the merchant, and also can ask for the merchant's cooperation in tracing the attacker through information such as IP addresses from the merchant's Web logs. If the attacker tries to subvert detection by using multiple merchants, he must spend more effort setting up his purchases (and finding desirable purchases will be harder). Although multiple-merchant attacks are harder to isolate from legitimate purchase attempts than single-merchant attacks, they still may be preventable and even traceable with the cooperation of Internet Service Providers using various infrastructure-level tools that respond to denial-of-service attacks (c.f. [8]). If most attacks will be detected before they succeed, and particularly if the attacker will sometimes be identified and punished, attackers will be less likely to even mount these attacks.

One might expect that if the use of limited-use tokens becomes common, merchants might gradually change their Web forms to allow for non-numeric and/or longer credit card numbers, which would allow the use of a larger token space, providing more security against guessing attacks. Note that on-line solutions have the advantage that a token can be validated only for a very short period of time, so guessing attacks are less likely to succeed there, and they may be the best solution unless, or until, the infrastructure changes. But with even minor infrastructural changes such as allowing non-numeric or longer strings in the credit card number field, the off-line setting offers sufficient security, and provides other advantages for the user.

4.4 Collisions

A collision occurs when two different settings of restrictions encrypt to the same token, either with the same key or with different keys. Clearly, collisions are more likely to occur with a smaller token space. Provided the number of possible settings of restrictions is smaller than the token space and the encryption function is truly a permutation, there will not be collisions of tokens for the same user (i.e. with the same key). Since timestamps are also used as part of the input to the encryption function to create the token, it will be necessary for users to change keys from time to time.

If desired, collisions between different users could be avoided entirely by using sufficiently large tokens, divided into part that is fixed and unique to each user and part generated by encryption as we have described. However, it should not be necessary to avoid such collisions, since the card issuer always looks up the appropriate long-term key from the ID, and so will not be confused by them.

4.5 Anonymity

As presented, our system is not anonymous, since the user's name and address is sent with every transaction. While we think anonymity is an important and worthwhile goal, it is orthogonal to protection of the credit card number. We chose to focus only on protection of the credit card number, rather than to cloud the issue by also designing our system to be an anonymous payment system. If desired, our system could easily be modified to provide anonymity to the user from the merchant, for example by encrypting the identifying information for the card issuer using a card issuer's public key stored in the user's device. Note that this would require merchant forms to be able to accept the resulting encryptions in the user name and address fields or elsewhere. Further note that in the case of physical purchases, some valid shipping address is required, so full anonymity may be compromised in any case.

5   Calling Cards

The off-line protocol presented here can be modified for use with telephone calling cards as well. It is often a problem that "shoulder surfers" see people entering a calling card number into a public phone; the surfers then use the calling card numbers themselves, or worse, sell them to a number of people with instructions to make a single (usually lengthy and international) call with it in a specified time window. The security of a calling card account lies exclusively in the knowledge of the calling card number. If someone sees this number, that person can, until detected, make virtually unlimited calls that are charged to the account holder. This can go undetected until the end of the billing cycle. Since many people now pay their phone bills automatically each month, rather than in response to an itemized bill, they may not notice unusual activity in their accounts until it reaches drastic proportions.

Limited-use tokens are also useful in this situation. In this case, restrictions involve time of day, area code called, number of minutes, number of calls, which numbers can be called, and so forth. For example, a parent might provide a child with a calling card number (token) that only allows calls to home. To create a limited-use token, the user enters the calling card number into the device, and then picks a set of restrictions. The device then outputs the new limited-use calling card number which is an encrypted token containing those restrictions. The encryption key is derived from the calling card number. When a user places a call with a token, the system asks for some identifying information, such as the user's home phone number and zip code, in addition to the calling card number. This can be accomplished by having a different toll-free access phone number for calls using limited-use tokens. When a user enters the token, the system uses the identifying information to look up the user's account number, derive a key, and then decrypt the token to check the restrictions.

As with credit cards, the use of temporary limited-use tokens in calling cards allows a user greater flexibility to manage risk and set parameters on a single long-term account than is achieved by always reusing the traditional account number.

6   Conclusions

We have presented a protocol for generating and using restricted credit card or calling card numbers. At some cost in security, these numbers can be of the same format as the traditional ones, allowing for easy layering of the protocol on the existing e-commerce infrastructure. In our system, users can generate limited-use tokens in an off-line manner, without requiring any interaction with the credit card company. We discussed the advantages of this scheme over currently deployed ones, and also discussed the security issues that may limit the deployment of such schemes without some infrastructural changes.

While the protocol that we present in this paper is not ideal from a security standpoint, it provides greater security than standard reusable credit cards and represents a practical solution that can be accomplished under a strict yet realistic set of assumptions about the current Web commerce infrastructure.

Acknowledgments

We thank Yoshi Kohno, Rick Johnson, and Barbara Fox for helpful comments. We also thank the anonymous and non-anonymous reviewers for their helpful comments.

References

1. Mihir Bellare and Chanathip Namprempre. Authenticated encryption: Relations among notations and analysis of the generic composition paradigm. In *Advances in Cryptology – Asiacrypt 2000, LNCS vol. 1976*. Springer-Verlag, 2000.
2. John Black and Phillip Rogaway, Ciphers with Arbitrary Finite Domains. In *Proceedings of RSA Security 2002 Cryptographer's Track*, Springer-Verlag 2002.
3. Daniel Bleichenbacher. Chosen ciphertext attacks against protocols based on RSA encryption standard PKCS #1. In *Advances in Cryptology – CRYPTO'98, LNCS vol. 1462*, pages 1–12. Springer-Verlag, 1998.
4. Edward W. Felten, Dirk Balfanz, Drew Dean, and Dan S. Wallach. Web spoofing: An Internet con game. In *Proc. 20th National Information Systems Security Conference*, 1997.
5. Kipp E.B. Hickman and Taher Elgamal. The SSL protocol. *Internet draft draft-hickman-netscape-ssl-01.txt*, 1995.
6. D. Kormann and A. Rubin. Risks of the Passport single signon protocol. *In Proceedings of 9th International World Wide Web Conference*, May 2000.
7. PayPal. http://www.paypal.com, 2000.
8. Stefan Savage, David Wetherall, Anna Karlin, and Tom Anderson. Practical network support for ip traceback. In *Proceedings of the 2000 ACM SIGCOMM Conference*, pages 295–306, 2000.
9. Adi Shamir. SecureClick: A Web payment system with disposable credit card numbers. In *these proceedings*, 2001.
10. Bob Tedeschi. Technology: Real-time challenges, in Cyberspace and on the ground. *The New York Times on the Web*, January 1, 2001.

A Security Framework for Card-Based Systems

Yiannis Tsiounis

InternetCash Corp., New York, NY
yiannis@internetcash.com

Abstract. The legal framework provided by the Electronic Signature Act, enacted to law as of October 1, 2000, has fueled the interest for digital signature-based payment transactions over the Internet. The bulk of formalization and security analysis to date on such secure payments has focused on creating new secure *channels* for existing credit or debit card systems (iKP and SET). But there has been no formal modeling, or an attempt to strengthen of the security of, the card systems themselves.

In this paper we present a simple but formal communication and security model for all card-based payments, encompassing credit, debit and pre-paid cards, and proceed to propose *CardSec*, a new family of card-based systems which can be proven secure under this model. In the process we also analyze the security of existing credit, debit and pre-paid card systems, both for Internet and for brick and mortar payments. We then present an efficient implementation of *CardSec* in the form of the InternetCash^{TM} card system and analyze its security in detail. We take the opportunity to describe the InternetCash Payment Protocol *(ICPP)* which can be used for creating a secure channel between Transaction Processor and Customer for all Internet-bound transactions, thus acting as an alternative to iKP and SET, and offering more security than systems utilizing limited-use credit card numbers. We conclude with a discussion on pre-authorization, refunds and customer service issues.

1 Introduction

Card-based payments are the dominant method for Internet and phone transactions and rival cash transactions for volume on the brick and mortar world. This highlights the importance of a formal model for such payment systems, and a security definition to aid as a roadmap for how the design of such systems can be judged. In this paper we propose a model for all card-based payment systems. This model is designed to be as generic as possible and encompasses credit, debit and pre-paid cards regardless of whether they are distributed in physical or electronic form, whether they are eponymous[1] or anonymous, or even whether they utilize smart-cards or other security methods. The same model also covers other types of card-based systems such as phone cards, metro cards, gift certificates or physical access cards.

We take the opportunity to present an analysis of the most common card-based payment systems, in particular credit cards, debit cards and anonymous

---

[1] Eponymous: (GR) "With a name". Anonymous: (GR) "Without a Name".

P. Syverson (Ed.): FC 2001, LNCS 2339, pp. 210–231, 2002.

pre-paid cards, based on the proposed model. The analysis extends to both brick and mortar as well as electronic and other "card-non-present" transactions with such cards. We conclude that the current systems do not satisfy the desired security requirements, especially in card-non-present transactions.

We then proceed to present a family of systems, called *"CardSec"* for which we can prove security based on the proposed model. CardSec is an easily understood and straightforward family of systems, based on two cryptographic primitives: pseudorandom function families [GGM86] and existentially unforgeable digital signatures [GMY83]. CardSec allows for either symmetric-key digital signatures (message authentication functions) or public-key digital signatures to be used at payment time, and it is defined independently of whether the end system is credit based, debit based, or pre-paid. An analysis of CardSec's security is included. A concrete efficient implementation of CardSec is then presented, in the form of InternetCash's anonymous pre-paid cards. We proceed to present the InternetCash Payment Protocol *(ICPP)* which is the way InternetCash establishes a secure connection over the Internet and can be used as an alternative to iKP and SET. We take the opportunity to discuss ICPP versus iKP, SET and limited-use credit card numbers. A discussion on preauthorizations, refunds and customer-service issues is included. Last, we analyze the security of Internet-Cash based on the assumption that HMAC [BCK96] is a pseudorandom function.

Organization: A formal model for card-based systems is presented in section 2. We overview credit, debit and pre-paid cards in section 3 and discuss their security based on the proposed model. We proceed to propose *CardSec* in section 4. Section 5 describes a sample implementation of *CardSec* in the form of the InternetCash card, including details about the actual implementation of the InternetCash Payment Protocol (ICPP) and comparison with iKP, SET and limited-use credit card numbers in section 5.1. Pre-authorization, refunds and customer service issues are discussed in section 5.2, and an extensive security analysis based on the actual security parameters used by InternetCash is presented in section 5.3. The paper is concluded in section 6 with a discussion of applications and open problems.

2   Modeling of Card-Based Systems

We lay the foundation for discussing the security of card-based systems by defining a concrete communication and security model.

A card-based system consists of three parties, a bank (also called "Issuer") $\mathcal{B}_1$, users (cardholders) $\mathcal{U}$ and merchants $\mathcal{M}_1$, and three main procedures: issuing, payment and clearing. A user $\mathcal{U}$ obtains a "card number" [2] by engaging

---

[2] The "card number" is not necessarily a number; it includes all the information identifying a card. In the case of credit cards for example it includes the cardholder's name, issuer's name, expiration date and in some cases the cardholder's address

in the *issuing protocol* with the bank. $\mathcal{U}$ makes a purchase by participating in a *payment protocol* with a merchant $\mathcal{M}_1$. $\mathcal{M}_1$ then performs a *clearing protocol* with the bank $\mathcal{B}_1$, to clear the transaction; as part of the clearing protocol the bank debits the user's card and credits the merchant's account. The system is *on-line* if a purchase is guaranteed only after the clearing protocol is performed; i.e., if the bank has to be on-line at all times, so that the merchant can clear each payment transaction before sending the goods to the user.

Remark: Note that the definition makes no reference to credit, debit, or pre-paid cards; in fact it encompasses all such concepts as these are handled at the time of "funding" of the user's card. Such funding can be part of the issuing protocol (pre-paid cards), part of the clearing protocol (debit cards), or be performed in a batch form at the end of every month (credit cards).

We must also stress that the model originates from the standard electronic cash model [Fra93] and concentrates on the payment protocol itself. In order to keep the model simple, we chose to keep procedures such as the shipping of goods, customer service, but also refunds and pre-authorizations outside the scope of this model, although any practical system must be designed to address these as well. However, in section 5.2, we do show how the model is easily extended to cover pre-authorizations, refunds and customer service related issues.

We now proceed to define security for card-based systems.

Definition 1. (Security) *An on-line card-based payment system with security parameter k is secure if it satisfies the following conditions with overwhelming probability in k:*

1. **Unforgeability:** *For any positive number N, no probabilistic polynomial time Turing Machine (p.p.t. TM) can, from the views of merchants of N distinct payment and clearing protocols, perform an additional $(N+1)$, distinct from the first N, successful payment or clearing protocol.*

2. **Unexpandability:** *No probabilistic polynomial time Turing Machine (p.p.t. TM) can, from the views of users and merchants of arbitrarily many issuing, payment and clearing protocols, perform a successful payment or clearing protocol for which none of the cards that are included in the users' and merchants' views is debited.*

The use of a p.p.t. TM in the definition is used to model user collaboration as views to the TM. Thus, in establishing security, we prove that a collaboration of users and/or merchants still cannot break the scheme. Informally, a p.p.t. TM is a machine that can make random choices ("flip coins") and it is used to model randomized algorithms. All current computing devices (excluding exotic and as of this writing impossible to construct devices, such as quantum computers) can be modeled under the p.p.t. TM model.

(referred to as "billing address"). The terminology "card number" is used for ease of reference.

The security parameter is controlling the security of the system; typically it equates to the size of the secret keys used in the system.

Note that unforgeability guarantees that payment transactions cannot be forged or altered by the merchants or any other third parties - since these third parties would have no more information than the merchants do. Unexpandability, on the other hand, guarantees that card numbers cannot be forged or guessed by cardholders, even in collaboration with merchants or other third parties.

3   Background and Current Systems

In this section we describe the most common card-based systems and their security. We first discuss credit cards, debit cards, and anonymous pre-paid cards which use the existing credit-card numbering scheme. Then we discuss some existing proposals aimed at enhancing the security of such systems, namely iKP and S.E.T.

3.1   Credit Cards

Credit cards conform to the banking standards which dictate that the card number consists of 12 to 19 decimal digits. All credit cards (Visa, MasterCard, American Express, Discover, Diners, JCB, etc) consist of 19 digits, of which either 15 (American Express) or 16 (all others) are clearly displayed on the front and the back of the card. Of those 15 or 16 digits the first 6, called the Banking Identification Number (B.I.N.) signify the issuing bank, while the last is a "check digit" whose purpose is to identify typing mistakes and to form a first (weak) authorization of the card number. The remaining 4 (for American Express) or 3 (for all others) digits, called the CVV2 or CVC, are usually a cryptographic authentication (typically a 3-digit portion out of a DES [ANS] output) of the first 15 or 16 resp. digits and are printed either on the front or the back of the card, but are usually not required for a purchase.

Credit cards have barely adequate levels of security for Brick and Mortar ("card present") purchases, mainly due to the requirement for hand-written signatures for each purchase. The card number itself offers minimal security, since it is visible at every payment and therefore can be copied and reused. At payment time, the presentation and verification of a hand-written signature against the signature on the back of the card and, if available, the cardholder's photograph on the card, guarantee unforgeability of the payment protocol. In practice, however, it is all too easy to conduct a payment transaction with a forged hand-written signature since few merchants closely verify that the signature is the same as the one appearing on the credit card itself. Additionally, the clearing protocol cannot be considered complete until the user's signature has been presented and cleared by the issuing bank. In practice this verification takes place usually only after a dispute over a particular transaction. Unexpandability on the other hand is achieved mostly by physical means, i.e., via the presence of a hologram in the card facia and other standard physical features. Unexpandability is slightly aided by the fact that valid transactions require a valid credit card number and expiration date – although this data is all too easy to steal.

In practice "card present" credit card transactions experience some amount of fraud, allegedly less than 1% of transactions, mainly due to inadequate signature verification at payment time and because some transactions are not on-line but are verified in batch mode – thus leaving a window of opportunity for presentation of a canceled or otherwise invalid card (e.g., a card whose purchase limit has been reached).

Credit cards on the other hand have, both in theory and in practice, inadequate security levels for electronic or over-the-phone purchases, collectively called "card non-present" transactions by the credit card associations. On the average, Internet credit card fraud seems to be at about the 4% mark [Int00,Com00], although reliable data are usually hard to obtain, since information about fraud is usually regarded by corporations as confidential. It is relatively easy to see why *"card non-present" credit card transactions are forgeable:*

Transactions are cleared based on the card number, expiration date, cardholder's name and billing address (billing address check (AVS) is only available in the U.S.) and potentially other data, such as CVV2/CVC, etc. However, the data required for each purchase are the same, and there is no binding of amount, merchant information, or other information to that data. Therefore it is straightforward for a merchant or any other entity that possesses the card data (such as a Brick and Mortar merchant) to forge or alter the data in a purchase. Thus unforgeability is not guaranteed, and in fact there are everyday examples of fraudulent (forged) credit card transactions over the Internet or over the telephone. Theft of credit card purchase information also impacts unforgeability, exactly because the data available to the merchant at payment is sufficient to create new purchase information. Several instances of such theft have recently been reported [San00,Lem00].

Furthermore, it is impossible to distinguish, solely from the payment data, whether the forging was performed by a user or by a merchant; therefore the bank cannot determine the fraudulent party since all it has to work with is the payment information. By default, credit card associations assume (in the U.S.) that the fraudulent party is the merchant,[3] unless the merchant can prove otherwise; the merchant however has no way of providing such proof! The immediate and significant implication is that a legitimate merchant cannot guarantee that s/he will not experience fraudulent transactions, and there have been examples of merchants who have experienced very high costs of fraud [Per00,Ber00]. For example, sites such as Register.com report a 2% reserve on total sales to cover expected chargebacks [Ang00], whereas studies indicate that fraud costs the average Internet merchant about 4% [Int00,Com00].

---

[3] In countries other than U.S. the consumer is by default assumed to be the fraudulent party. The security implications are the same, with the only difference being on who shoulders the fraud.

On the other hand, for U.S. transactions, unexpandability is less of an issue, since most card issuers provide, as a service to U.S. merchants, the ability to check the cardholder's name and billing address together with the card number (Address Verification Service, or commonly referred to as "AVS check"; however, AVS is only available within the U.S.). Therefore an adversary needs to guess a valid card number and the corresponding valid cardholder's name and address.

3.2   Debit Cards

By debit cards we refer to "on-line" debit cards, i.e., those that *do not* include the Visa^{TM} or MasterCard^{TM} logo. Transactions with such debit cards are cleared directly by the issuing bank, whereas transactions with "off-line" (Visa/MasterCard based) debit cards *whenever a PIN is not used* are cleared by Visa or MasterCard and are transferred to the issuing bank in batch form. In terms of transaction clearing, and therefore as far as we are concerned in this paper, off-line debit cards are equivalent to credit cards, *unless they are used in combination with a PIN* in which case they are equivalent to debit cards. On the other hand, credit cards are sometimes also assigned a PIN; PIN-based credit card transactions are, again for transaction clearing purposes and for the duration of this paper, equivalent to debit-based transactions.

Debit cards conform to the same standards as credit cards; although debit card numbers are anywhere from 12 to 19 digits in length. The main differences from credit cards however are that (1) debit cards can only be used in combination with a Personal Identification Number (P.I.N.) and (2) banking standards currently require that the PIN is encrypted in hardware at the point of sale (POS),[4] thus prohibiting "card non-present" transactions (over the Internet or over the telephone) without some type of tamper-resistant hardware at the client side.

The presence of a PIN which is encrypted at the POS and the requirement of a handwritten signature offer adequate unforgeability protection for "card-present" debit card transactions. Unexpandability also benefits from the presence of the PIN, since this is an additional variable which needs to be guessed by the adversary.

It is important to note, however, that unforgeability requires a signature; otherwise the merchant can substitute the purchase data and thus forge the amount of the purchase or even the entity that gets paid. This is usually not a problem off-line, where the retailer would have to go to great efforts to intercept and alter the card information, since its infrastructure is typically provided by a third party and requires no servicing. In addition a fraudulent Brick & Mortar merchant is easy to track and prosecute. But in card-non-present transactions, such as debit-based Internet transactions, the e-merchant typically owns its infrastructure and records all information transmitted through its website. The merchant can also be physically located outside a local jurisdiction, and in fact

---

[4] The regulations state that the P.I.N. can never be in the clear, i.e., it has to be encrypted at the point of entry with a hardware device.

its locale may prove extremely difficult to trace. Therefore for such transactions to be secure two requirements must be met: (1) PIN security, and (2) digital signing of each transaction, verified at clearing time.

The current debit regulations reflect requirement (1) only, but they state that the PIN must be encrypted in hardware, which means that hardware encrypting devices (e.g., smart-cards or tamper-resistant Pin-pads) must reside *at every consumer desktop*; a costly proposition. The approach we take in this paper and CardSec is to enforce both requirements, but without requiring hardware encryption – although if hardware encryption is available the added security level is of course welcome.

3.3   Anonymous Pre-paid Cards

In this section we discuss anonymous pre-paid cards whose numbering scheme follows the credit-card standards, as these are described in section 3.1. Eponymous pre-paid cards, also called "pre-paid credit cards", that require authentication for their issuance and are bound to a cardholder's name are, for purposes of security and transaction processing, equivalent to credit cards, and therefore we refer to section 3.1 for their analysis.

Anonymous pre-paid cards that have recently appeared by American Express^{TM} [Amea] utilize the same structure as credit cards. Therefore, intuitively, they are at least as insecure as credit cards. A short analysis, however, shows that *they are less secure than credit cards*, both in card present and in card non-present transactions. In fact, *anonymous credit-card based pre-paid cards are almost as insecure in card-present transactions as in card non-present transactions:*

- *No unforgeability.* Since the cards are anonymous, there is no hand-written signature to which they can be bound and which can serve to provide non-repudiation for each card-present transaction. Thus forgeability on brick and mortar transactions requires nothing more than copying of the card number on the card's magnetic stripe. We note that this can be done without having to manufacture a new card – but by simply swiping an existing card through a mag-stripe encoder. Such encoders sell for less than USD $2,000 making card copying cost-effective for a fraudulent merchant after less than 100 copies, considering that the average card value for such cards is $50 and a copier can take advantage of the remaining amount of each copied card. For card-non-present transactions no digital signatures are utilized either. Therefore, in both card present and card non-present transactions, any party in possession of the card number (such as any merchant that has accepted the card for purchases, for example) can forge transactions. Worse, the cardholder cannot prove such fraud and the fact that s/he is anonymous makes repudiation by calling the issuing bank much more difficult [Amec, item 2].
- *Minimal unexpandability.* We will show how an adversary can emulate a payment with a card that she does not possess:
  Since the cards are not bound to a person's name and address, the only thing that an adversary has to do is guess a card number. But as we saw the real

entropy of a credit card, if one subtracts the 6 digit B.I.N. and the check digit, is 9 decimal digits (8 in the case of American Express), or less than 30 bits (less than 26 bits in the case of American Express). In the best case, i.e., where the issuer creates card numbers using a collision intractable hash function (CIHF) [Dam88], the adversary has to produce $1,000,000,000 /N$ card numbers before guessing a valid card number, where N is the number of valid issued cards. For 1,000,000 valid card numbers in circulation (again, in the case of American Express, for 100,000 cards in circulation) this means that after 1,000 trials the adversary will guess a valid card number. These trials can be check balances or payment transactions, or a combination of these. At an assumed speed of 10 transactions per second (tps), which most transaction processors need to satisfy to handle potential volume, it would take 100 seconds to guess a valid card number. In fact this is only an upper limit, because if the card numbers are created with a CIHF a collision is expected after approx. 31,600 cards ($1,000,000,000^{1/2}$) have been created; i.e., after the 31,600-th card, there exists a p.p.t. TM that finds a card number better than random guessing. Again, this number is 10,000 cards in the case of American Express. In the case of mass generation of card numbers an intelligent adversary can use this advantage and perform an attack much better than random guessing.

It is important here to note that this attack is quite feasible and *cannot* be easily stopped by simply monitoring the number of failed purchases. This is because (a) the attacker can appear identical as multiple customers, by using an IP anonymizer (proxy server); (b) the adversary attempts purchases or check balances on different cards, so the attack looks the same as 1,000 customers typing an incorrect number; distributing the attack over time, e.g., one day, can mask it relatively simply; and (c) one would think that one counter-measure would be to limit the *total* number of failed transaction requests over some time, in order to put an upper limit on the amount of fraud (e.g., only one card number leaked per 1,000 faulty requests); however, an attacker only needs to know whether a request succeeded or failed; if the bank does not respond to incorrect transaction requests but responds to true requests, then the attacker can still guess card numbers. Thus the bank needs to completely shut down its service to prevent guessing of card numbers. Otherwise an attacker would bombard the site with fraudulent requests coming from distributed IPs; the bank would not know whether the requests are legitimate or not; the bank can either reply and risk fraudulent card generation or turn its transaction service off! We assume that limiting such fraud potential is the reason why the "Check Balance" information on American Express' pre-paid card is currently disabled [Ameb].

It is obvious that once a card has been forged on-line, the only barrier preventing its usage off-line (in a Brick and Mortar merchant) are the physical properties of the card – which are neither extremely difficult to reproduce, nor are meticulously verified by every merchant. In addition, as we mentioned in the unforgeability discussion above, it is financially feasible for an adversary to imprint new card numbers on existing cards.

4   CardSec: A Secure Card-Based System

After analyzing the shortcomings of existing card-based payment systems we now define a card system for which we can prove security based on definition 1. This card-based system can be used in a credit, debit, or pre-paid mode.[5]

Definition 2. (CardSec) *CardSec is a card-based system with a security parameter k and the following properties:*

1. *Every card number contains* **a Public Identifier**, *used to uniquely identify the card. The public identifier may be revealed to third parties without security implications.*[6]
2. *Every card number contains* **a Card Key** *of length k provided by the issuer. The Card Key is derived from the Public Identifier with a pseudorandom function family indexed by a secret key of the Issuer. Optionally, the Issuer's public-key digital signature of the Card Key is included.*
3. **Signing of each payment transaction by the user**, *using the card key as the key itself or, if the signing key must have a specific structure, as the random seed for the key's creation. This signature is performed with an existentially unforgeable secret key digital signature (message authentication) [GMY83] or a public key digital signature algorithm [GMY83,GMR88].*

The protocols of CardSec are defined as follows:

- The issuing protocol *is nothing more than distribution of the Public Identifier and the Card Key from the issuer to the user over an encrypted channel on which the issuer is authenticated.*[7] *Optionally, if a public-key digital signature of the Card Key is included, the user may verify that signature.*
- The payment protocol *is the creation of a digital signature of the payment data, including amount and identifying information for the merchant and the particular transaction, based on the card key. This signature is sent to the merchant together with the public identifier of the card used. In the case of a public key signature the user's certificate may optionally be included, allowing the merchant to verify the signature. This certificate is provided by the issuer at issuing time.*
- At the clearing protocol *the merchant sends a transcript of the payment protocol to the issuer over a mutually authenticated channel; the issuer verifies the signature, clears the transaction and notifies the merchant.*

Before we proceed with the proof, let us make a few **remarks:**
The structure above, although not the only one that can provide a secure card-based system, is meant to imitate to a large degree the way credit and debit

---

[5] Patent Pending.

[6] The size of the public identifier has no security implications; it simply limits the number of cards that can be issued, in the same way that, e.g., the size of a primary key limits the size of a database table.

[7] See section 5 for examples.

cards operate right now. This results in a familiar construction that is simple for the end consumers to use. A credit card, for example, contains a Public Identifier (the 15 or 16 digit card number), and a Card Key (the CVV2 or CVC) - although the key does not have enough entropy (length), is not adequately protected (it is visible at card-present transactions and whenever used for Internet transactions) and is not used to create a digital signature. A handwritten signature is used for card-present transactions instead. A debit card uses the user's selected PIN as the card key, although again this is not used for signing but merely to verify that the card is being used by its card-holder (who is the only entity, besides the issuer and potentially a trusted transaction processor, who knows the PIN).

CardSec makes one implicit assumption about the issuer that allows for greater efficiency by making public-key digital signatures optional rather than mandatory at issuing time. This assumption is that the users trust the issuer to not defraud them, i.e., to provide them with a valid card number (public identifier and card key) and to not impersonate their transactions. This alleviates the necessity for a public-key based digital signature of the card key by the bank. In theory this deprives users proof that a fraudulent issuer did not provide them with valid card numbers or did not impersonate their purchases. In practice, however, issuers have been giving out credit and debit card numbers either through physical cards or over the Internet with no such signatures and no case of fraud or user impersonation by the issuer has ever been reported. This is easily justifiable: an issuer has no incentive to fraud its own customers or else it will soon go out of business; furthermore, an issuer who has fraudulently given out card numbers is easy to identify and incriminate whether it is signing its own fraudulent transactions or not.

4.1 Sketch of Security Proof

We sketch the proof of security based on the security definition 1. We assume that the digital signatures used at issuing and payment are secret-key based. Obviously the proof carries along for public-key digital signatures as well.

- **Unforgeability**. Every payment transaction is signed with an existentially unforgeable symmetric digital signature (message authentication), and a clearing protocol requires verification of this signature. Thus, constructing a $(N + 1)$-th successful payment or clearing protocol requires forging a signature by looking at N previous signatures or obtaining a new public identifier/signing key pair. The first attack contradicts the definition of existential unforgeability of digital signatures; while the second contradicts the properties of the pseudorandom family used by the issuer.
- **Unexpandability**. For a collaboration of users and merchants to obtain an additional card, they need to obtain a public identifier/card key pair which they do not currently hold. But note that, by definition, the card key is (i) a secure message authentication of the Public Identifier based on the issuer's secret key (a pseudorandom function family results in secure message authentication [GMY83]), and (ii) computationally indistinguishable from a

string of the same length chosen uniformly at random (the output's computational indistinguishability from a string chosen uniformly at random is also a property of a pseudorandom function family). The attack therefore contradicts the properties of the pseudorandom function family used by the issuer.

5   A Sample Implementation: InternetCash^{TM}

Now that we have presented a general framework for a secure card-based payment system, we proceed with a concrete implementation that exemplifies the feasibility of the concept. A slight variation of the system described here is used by InternetCash Corp. for its anonymous pre-paid Internet cards, thus we refer to this system as the *"InternetCash^{TM} card system"* or simply InternetCash.

InternetCash^{TM} cards are comprised of the following three components, conforming to definition 2:

- **The Card ID *(CID)***, also called the Card Index, which is the public part of the card number, i.e., the Public Identifier for each card. The CID of current InternetCash cards is 9 alphanumeric (base 32) digits.
- **The Card Secret Code *(CSC)***, which is the key used for card transactions. Currently the CSC is 11 alphanumeric (base 32) digits. The CSC is an HMAC [BCK96] based on SHA-1 [SHA93] of the CID truncated to the necessary length, where the HMAC is keyed by an InternetCash secret key:
  $CSC = [HMAC - SHA1_{ICKey}(CID)]_{\{bits\ 1-55\}}$
- **A secret Personal Identification Code *(PIN)***, which is not modeled under CardSec, but is used for additional security in case the CID and CSC are compromised.

The concatenation of CID and CSC is called the "InternetCash card number" and it is 20 alphanumeric digits long.

Base 32 uses the alphabet $\{0, 1, 2, 3, 4, 5, 6, 7, 8, 9, A, B, C, D, E, F, G, H, J, \}$ $\{K, L, M, N, P, R, S, T, U, V, W, X, Y\}$ $(0-9$ and $A-Z$ except $I, O, Q, Z)$ and of course it means that every character can be represented with 5 bits $(32 = 2^5)$.

The system's protocols are as follows:

- **The Issuing Protocol** consists of the following two steps:
  1. The user is given an InternetCash number over an encrypted channel with only the InternetCash server being authenticated (i.e., the user can remain anonymous). This can happen either online, e.g., through SSL or TLS, or via physical means, i.e., by purchasing a physical card at an authorized InternetCash retailer.
  2. The user selects a PIN for the given InternetCash number, again over an encrypted channel with only the InternetCash server being authenticated. In practice this takes place over SSL or TLS.

- **The Payment Protocol** consists of a secret-key digital signature (message authentication) of the payment information, based on the CSC and the user's PIN. The generated signature is called the *Payment Authentication Number (PAN)*. Again, HMAC-SHA1 is used as the pseudorandom function family to perform the digital signature. Multiple cards can be used for a single payment; here we show a PAN created when i cards are used for payment:

$$PAN = HMAC - SHA1_{CSC_i||f(PIN_i)}(HMAC_{CSC_{i-1}||f(PIN_{i-1})}(\cdots$$
$$(HMAC_{CSC_1||f(PIN_1)}(\text{Amount, Date/Time, Merchant ID,}$$
$$\text{Transaction ID, Payment Info}))\ldots)\,,$$

  where f can be a one-way function (such as SHA-1). If a one-way function is used, only a hashed version of the user's PIN need be stored, for additional security.

  The user's CIDs and the PAN are sent to the merchant. Notice that the use of a secure channel is *not* necessary for payment security, although encryption may be used to prevent third parties from viewing the payment information and creating profiles for the user and merchant.
- During **the Clearing Protocol** the merchant simply forwards the payment data (amount, date/time, etc), the CIDs and the PAN to InternetCash over a secure and authenticated channel. InternetCash recreates the PAN (it is easy to see that all the information can be recreated given InternetCash's secret key) based on the payment data and CIDs provided, and compares it with the received PAN; if they match the transaction is cleared, the user's card(s) are debited and the merchant's account is credited.

5.1   The InternetCash Payment Protocol (ICPP)

Before proceeding with the security analysis of InternetCash, we describe the actual implementation of the InternetCash Payment Protocol (ICPP). This implementation is important for a number of reasons:

- The payment protocol as described above requires computation at the client (customer) side. Here we describe a way to lift that requirement with no security implications.
- Details of the implementation can make the difference between a secure or an insecure end system. E.g., in some payment-system implementations it is possible for an adversary to change the price of an item, thus bypassing any theoretic advantage offered by the more secure cryptographic protocols.

  Here we describe how the implementation of the InternetCash Payment Protocol prevents such attacks and thus maintains the security offered by the underlying algorithms.
- The ICPP is important in its own right, since it establishes a secure channel directly between the customer and InternetCash and *can facilitate the secure processing of additional payment types, such as credit cards or debit cards –*

where InternetCash acts as the trusted third party that receives the customer's sensitive information. Unfortunately, space limitations do not allow us to elaborate on the details of such processing.

To prevent the use of client software, InternetCash takes a server-based approach. At payment time, the customer is redirected by the merchant to an InternetCash-serviced SSL or TLS secure web site which performs the payment computation (1) on behalf of the customer. Note that InternetCash already knows all the information that the customer uses to create the signature (PAN), namely the Card Secret Code (CSC) of the card and a function of the customer's PIN, $f(PIN)$. In fact as part of the clearing protocol InternetCash *has* to be able to recreate that signature. Therefore, creating the PAN on behalf of the customer at payment time does not reduce the security of the protocol. Instead, it adds more convenience for the customer, because it allows InternetCash to check the balance and status of a particular card in real time before creating the PAN, so that the customer is notified of typos or other issues (such as no balance left on the card) at the beginning rather than at the end of the payment process.

The only entity which needs to add software for InternetCash processing is therefore the Internet merchant. This software is provided pre-compiled by InternetCash for any requested merchant platform.

The payment process therefore proceeds as follows:

1. The customer visits an InternetCash enabled website. After selecting the goods to buy, consumer selects InternetCash as payment method.
2. Merchant redirects customer to an "InternetCash payment window" served over 128 bit SSL or TLS by InternetCash. All the required payment information is sent to InternetCash at this time (merchant ID, Transaction ID, description of goods, etc.)
3. Customer enters payment information (InternetCash card number and PIN) and authorizes payment.
4. InternetCash verifies the selected cards have enough funds and creates the Payment Authentication Number (PAN).
5. PAN is forwarded to on-line merchant.
6. Merchant verifies that the payment information (amount, transaction ID, description, etc.) have not been altered, signs the payment information (including the PAN) and submits a payment request to InternetCash. The merchant signature is using HMAC-SHA1 with a 160 bit key. The communication to InternetCash is (optionally) SSL encrypted.
7. InternetCash transfers funds from the card to the merchant account *in an atomic transaction* and sends a signed response back to the merchant. This signature is again using HMAC-SHA1 with a 160 bit key. If InternetCash sees the same PAN twice, it sends a positive response to the merchant but does *not* transfer funds again.
8. Customer informed of successful payment.

Observe the following properties of ICPP:

- **Security against parallel attacks.** If a customer tries to use the full amount of a card on two different web sites at the same time (i.e., double-spend) only one transaction will succeed, based on the atomicity of step 7 above.
- **Guarding against adversarial changes of payment information.** An adversary cannot alter the payment information because the merchant will capture the changes and abort the transaction at step 6 above.
- **Immunity against replays.** The payment request from Merchant to InternetCash in step 6 above can be replayed either legitimately (say, if the communication failed the first time) or by an adversary without resulting in duplicate charges, since if the PAN is seen twice no payment action is taken in step 7 above.
- **Creation of secure channel between InternetCash and customer.** This secure channel, created by the redirection of the customer to an InternetCash served secure web site in step 2 above, can be used to facilitate additional payment methods over the same secure channel, such as credit card or debit card payments.

iKP and SET. Unfortunately we do not have the space to present a formal security analysis of ICPP, but we briefly compare it with iKP and SET as its scope is similar to those systems.

Recognizing the shortcomings of the existing credit card infrastructure for Internet processing, a group of IBM researchers proposed iKP [BGH+95], a family of systems intended to provide secure credit card processing over the Internet. iKP is defined in three different stages, each providing additional security, with the minimum requirement being customer-generated encryption of the payment information, to prevent exposure of the credit card number. iKP is intended to keep the same card numbering structure that credit cards already have, and add a layer of security for Internet use. Without going into details we note that iKP is more relevant to ICPP (see section 5.1) than to CardSec (section 4) or InternetCash (section 5). ICPP provides security similar to iKP v.3 (most secure iteration), under the assumption that InternetCash is a trusted third party (TTP) for the customer and merchant, since the signatures used by all parties are symmetric instead of asymmetric.

SET [SET] is a proposal for secure credit card payments that evolved from merging the SEPP proposal from MasterCard and the STT proposal from Visa. In turn, SEPP roots to iKP. SET is very similar to iKP v.3 in terms of security and scope, and therefore it is more relevant to ICPP than to InternetCash or CardSec. The security of SET is, as with iKP v.3, similar to ICPP under the assumption that InternetCash is a trusted third party (TTP). However, the actual implementation and certification for SET is quite complex. An important characteristic of SET is that all parties involved in a transaction, namely customer, merchant, transaction processor and banking institution, must change their infrastructure or install specific SET software. We believe that this is directly related to the slow rate of adoption of SET for Internet transactions.

Disposable Credit Card Numbers. Recently several banks have released client-based solutions aimed at enhancing payment privacy and convenience, by substituting an interim credit-card number valid only for one purchase, and by potentially automatically filling the billing information on behalf of the customer. Examples of these systems are American Express' "Private Payments^{SM}, MBNA's Shop Safe^{SM}, and others. For details on the architecture of such systems refer to [RW01,Sha01]. Although ICPP is slightly different in scope than such systems, we briefly compare its security with these systems.

In the current commercial disposable credit card number systems the interim credit card numbers are either generated by the consumer on the bank's web site, or are generated for the user automatically by a client-side software that the user has previously installed into his/her computer. These disposable credit card number systems are similar to the generation of a digital signature at the time of purchase, with the following crucial differences (for security purposes):

- The full payment data such as amount, merchant name, transaction ID, may not be available at the time of generation of the credit card number, therefore this number does not constitute a signature of the transaction.
- The credit card number offers limited entropy, in which it is difficult to incorporate a true digital signature. In fact, card numbers are reused over time.
- The generated card numbers are valid only for a short period of time.

Given that the payment information is not truly signed, even with enough available entropy, the scope of such systems is more towards user privacy than security. In other words, a few very simple attacks are for the merchant to substitute a different amount and over-charge the user; or change the transaction ID and send different products; or change the merchant ID/Name and forward the transaction to a different merchant (man-in-the-middle attack). Nevertheless, these systems do offer higher security than conventional credit-card purchasing, due mainly to the time limitation of the generated numbers - since the actual credit card number is too small to provide adequate security. However, they do not provide the same security level and non-repudiation as a digital signature, and are therefore inferior to ICPP in this respect, since ICPP guarantees both user and merchant security and non-repudiation.

An issue is also the way refunds are processed. Since clearing and refunds/pre-authorizations happen through the existing credit card systems they are referenced by credit card numbers. These numbers are reused over time, however, therefore there is the possibility of referencing the wrong transaction for refund. ICPP resolves these issues by issuing refunds based on the PAN (see section 5.2 below), which is unique for every transaction.

Last but not least, such systems may be incompatible with certain heuristic or knowledge-based systems for credit card fraud control such as eFalcon or

CyberSource. These fraud control systems may assign a high score to these one-time credit card numbers and cause rejections of valid transactions. This incompatibility may end up in the merchant having to tune their system to treat these one-time credit card numbers differently, thus introducing a merchant component into the system architecture.

5.2   Pre-authorization, Refunds, and Other Extensions

We briefly discuss how InternetCash deals with pre-authorizations, refunds and customer service issues. We chose to not include these functions in the formal model in order to keep the presentation simple. Security arguments for each additional functionality are included here but are kept brief due to space limitations.

An important attribute that facilitates all functions related to a transaction is that the PAN is guaranteed to be known by all parties, i.e., InternetCash, merchant and customer: the customer is both emailed the PAN at purchase time and can access it using her/his card number in a "transaction history" web page, while the merchant and InternetCash save the number in their database and associate it with the payment information.

InternetCash pre-authorization includes three message types: pre-authorization request, release and cancellation. The pre-authorization request is similar to a payment transaction, with the addition of defining a default cancellation time for the pre-authorization. Funds are subtracted from the user's card(s) and are kept in escrow until the pre-authorization is cancelled or released. A pre-authorization is automatically canceled at the specified time and the funds transferred back to the consumer's card(s), unless explicitly released by the merchant. A pre-authorization release or cancellation refers to a specific PAN, can be applied on the full or only part of the order, and is comprised of a signed message exchange between the merchant and InternetCash, in effect using mostly the same protocols as steps 6 and 7 of ICPP. A refund is similar to a pre-authorization cancellation, except that it does not need to be preceded by a pre-authorization request. All messages here are mutually signed and therefore are non-repudiable assuming that InternetCash is a TTP; asymmetric signatures, such as certificate-based SSL, can be added modularly to alleviate the TTP requirement.

For customer service inquiries InternetCash asks the user for the first 12 (twelve) digits of their card. This includes the 9 digit CID and 3 digits of the CSC. No customer care agent is authorized to ask for the user's PIN. The security in this case is the first 3 digits of the CSC, or 15 bits. An attack on this part would require $2^{15}/2 = 16,384$ attempts on the average, after an adversary has guessed or obtained a CID. But 16,000 customer service requests will raise a flag even in the largest of International organizations, so this security is deemed adequate. An InternetCash customer care agent on the other hand, which is treated as a semi-trusted party, has an advantage of 15 bits over in breaking a card which, by looking at the analysis in section 5.3 below, is still sufficient, especially in view of the fact that only a limited number of customers will have revealed the first 12 digits of their cards, therefore it is easier to trace an attack of this type to the fraudulent customer care agent.

5.3 Security of InternetCash

It is straightforward to see that, if HMAC is a pseudorandom function family, then the InternetCash card system is secure with security parameter K for card generation (unexpandability), where $K = min\{$Size of HMAC output, Size of InternetCash's secret key, Size of Card Key$\} =$
$min\{160,$ Size of InternetCash's secret key, $55\} = 55$; and secure with security parameter
$k = min\{$Size of HMAC output, Size of Card Key plus PIN$\} = min\{160, 55 + n\} = 55 + n$, where n is the randomness provided by the user's PIN, for unforgeability. This is because a pseudorandom function is a secure message authentication function [GMY83], and therefore both conditions (2) and (3) of definition 2 are satisfied. The purpose of the PIN is to (1) add security to the CSC, and (2) provide some level of security in case the CSC is compromised, e.g., if the card number is lost or revealed to a third party during a physical transaction. In this case the security parameter for unforgeability is equal to n.

We now proceed to discuss the adequacy of the security parameters. In this discussion we also take into account the actual implementation of InternetCash's system, by looking at ways the attacker can, e.g., "split" the attack against the CSC and PIN into two separate attacks, first attacking the CSC, then the PIN.

First we observe that 55 bits are more than enough for unexpandability because the adversary's attack cannot be off-line as in the case of unforgeability, but has to be against InternetCash as an attempt to activate a card – therefore it would take 2^{55} web hits to guess a single card key. A web hit for card activation requires at least one database access, an operation which is difficult to scale to more than a few hundred per second. We skip further formulation since this is clearly an infeasible attack: it would take more than a year at 115 *million* web hits *per second*. In addition, InternetCash cards are not valid until a PIN is selected and they are invalid until bought – therefore the window of opportunity for the adversary for guessing a Card Key is between the time a card is sold and the time it is "PIN-activated".

In terms of unforgeability, the InternetCash anonymous cards offer security of $55 + n$ bits for the consumer, where n is the entropy of the user's PIN. We need to discuss here why this level of security is adequate. As in all systems, the goal of the designer is to make the attacker's effort disproportionate to the gains obtained by breaking the system. Or, put in fudiciary terms, to make the cost of breaking the system higher than the potential gains of breaking it, with some margin for future unanticipated attacks. Under the assumption that HMAC is a pseudorandom function, the only way to "break" InternetCash, i.e., to forge a single payment or clearing transaction or to obtain a user's card number, is via a brute force attack at guessing a correct HMAC signature. Thus, what we need to show is that:

Cost of Brute Force attack on HMAC signed PAN $>$ Value of an IC card   (1)

The "brute force attack" here occurs by the adversary obtaining a payment signature (PAN) and then performing (off-line) 2^k HMAC operations where every time s/he is guessing the secret key, which is comprised of the CSC and the user's PIN.

We need to mention here that, in theory, an attacker can break the attack in two separate attacks: one requiring 2^{55} web hits to the "activation" page for guessing the CSC, and an off-line attack to guess the user's PIN using a PAN. However, as we saw this is clearly infeasible. Also, an attacker could theoretically first guess the PIN from InternetCash's site and then guess the CSC off-line. However, InternetCash does not verify the PIN before verifying the CSC first, i.e., it uses the hardware-performed CSC computation as a "security layer" to protect its Database – so this attack is again not feasible. Since neither of these two attacks is feasible, we thus discuss the possibility of success of an off-line attacker which tries to guess the CSC and PIN given a PAN.[8]

In our calculations we make the following assumptions for the parameters that influence the financial feasibility of an attack:

1. *Value of InternetCash cards, V.* For our results we assume that an *average* InternetCash card holds $10,000 USD, even though the average value of an InternetCash pre-paid card today is well below $100.

    Our motivation for this difference is to show that InternetCash card numbers can be used as-is to provide security for credit cards or other situations that result in larger amounts, such as reloading of cards. We note that reloading of InternetCash cards is allowed today over the Internet: users can transfer funds from one or more InternetCash cards to another card.

2. *Entropy of User's PIN, n, in bits.* We assume for concreteness that the entropy is at least 20 bits, i.e., 4 characters base 32 (alphanumeric, case insensitive). Simple techniques for enforcing good PINs, such as selecting both a number and a character, can be used to help users create PINs with sufficient entropy. A base 32 PIN can be used as-is in physical Debit card readers in the US, all of which contain, by regulation, a keypad that can accept entries in both letters and numbers.

    We note that InternetCash PINs are between 4 and 8 characters in length and they are not base 32, but base 128: they include all printable characters and are case-sensitive.

    Thus InternetCash allows much higher entropy for the security-conscious user.

3. *Computational Cost of the Attacker, P.* This variable is expressed in USD per HMAC operation.

4. *Years of Security Required, Y.* Here we assume that the Moore's law governs the computational power of the attacker (i.e., its power doubles every 18 months) to help us compute for how many years will the level of security be sufficient. Again, for concreteness, we define $Y = 20$.

---

[8] Possession of multiple PANs gives the adversary no advantage, based on our security model, i.e., on the assumption that HMAC is a pseudorandom function family.

5. *Average Lifetime of Hardware (Depreciation factor), D.* We assume that $D = 5$, i.e., that an average lifetime for the adversary's hardware equipment is 5 years; this assumption compares favorably to Moore's law, since the latter implicitly assumes that the adversary must change or update hardware every 18 months. This assumption also implies that the adversary will break-even on her/his original investment after 5 years of constant machine operation.
6. *Cost of an HMAC calculator.* We assume that a machine that computes ("cracks") HMAC is at least as costly as a machine that computes DES [ANS]. We justify this assumption as follows: although HMAC-SHA1 is much faster in software than DES, the fastest computations will happen in hardware; since DES was designed to be fast in hardware there are several specialized hardware chips performing up to millions of DES operations per second, thus evaporating HMAC's theoretical speed advantage.

We now calculate P based on our assumptions, i.e., the required maximum computational cost in USD per HMAC operation to make it financially feasible for an adversary to break the system:

$$P \leq \text{Avg \$ on IC card} * \text{Power of H/W in Y years}/\text{\# of codes to crack}$$
$$\leq V * 2^{(Y*12/18)}/2^{(55+n)}$$
$$= 2^{Y*2/3-55-n} * V$$

For $n = 20$, $V = \$10,000$, $Y = 20$ we have:

$$P \leq 2^{20*2/3-55-20} * 10,000$$
$$\leq 2^{13.34-75} * 10,000$$
$$\leq 2^{13.34-75} * 2^{13.3}$$
$$= 2^{-48.3}(\text{USD})$$

Now we discuss whether this value of P is realistic. We perform two separate analyses.

The first uses as guideline the specialized EFF DES cracker machine [EFF] which took 3 days to crack a 56 bit DES key and cost \$250,000 in 1998. With this attack we model an adversary who is willing to put a large initial investment into the attack. We do not use the latest attack which took 23 hours because (a) this was a distributed attack and we assume that only collaborative research attempts, vs. attempts to steal cash, will achieve such wide academic collaboration; and (b) because the second attack only searched 1/4 of the key space, thus taking half of the expected time to execute. What we do, however, is adjust 1998's attack with Moore's law. Under the assumption that an HMAC cracker can be constructed at a cost similar to the EFF DES cracker, we calculate P to be:

$$P = \text{EFF cost}/[\text{ \# operations to break DES} * \text{\# days in 5 years}$$
$$*\text{adjust EFF speed}/\text{\# days it took to break DES }] =$$
$$= \$250,000/[\, 2^{56} * 5 * 365 * 2^{2*12/18}/3 \,] \approx 2^{-48.65}$$

where $2^{2*12/18}/3$ is used to calculate the effect of Moore's law after 2 years (1998 to 2000) on the 3 days that it originally took to break DES, and 5 is our assumption on the number of years the cracking machine would be operational (again, even though we assume a doubling of computational power every 18 months and we factor no maintenance or upgrade costs for the course of 5 years).

This analysis shows that by investing \$250,000 the adversary barely breaks-even in 5 years, by cracking 25 InternetCash cards worth \$10,000 (each) on the *average*. Again, note that the average value of an InternetCash card today is well below \$100.

Our second analysis is based on third party performance results of HMAC-SHA1 in optimized software [Rog00]. Our goal here is to model an attacker with less initial capital, to give a concrete description of a cracking machine, and to explore the feasibility of attacking the problem solely in software.

The fastest machine analyzed in [Rog00] is a Pentium III at 700 MHz.

The speed of HMAC-SHA1 in [Rog00] is expressed in terms of machine cycles per byte. Reportedly, it takes 50.3 machine cycles per byte to process one HMAC-SHA1 computation, when the input is 43 bytes, or $50.3 * 43 = 2,162.9$ cycles for a complete HMAC-SHA1 computation. We will adjust this value favourably, based on the following observations: first, the natural input of SHA-1 is in 20 byte blocks, hence an input of 43 bytes may result in an unfavourable speed; second, the input that the adversary has to feed into HMAC-SHA1 can be, based on equation (1), less than 40 bytes (but never as small as 20 bytes) in the best scenario, i.e., when the description field is small and only one InternetCash card is used for the purchase. We will perform our computation using the best terms for the adversary, namely:

- The input value for the PAN computation (1) is less than 40 bytes,
- The speed of HMAC-SHA1 increases linearly with the number of input blocks, i.e., an HMAC-SHA1 computation with a 21-40 byte input takes two-thirds (it is 50% faster) than a 41-60 byte input, and
- An HMAC-SHA1 computation at a Pentium 4 at 1.4 GHz, representing today's state of the art, takes one-third (it is 200% or three times faster) than the same computation in a Pentium III at 700 MHz.

Based on those assumptions, a candidate PAN computation would take $(2/3 * 2,162.9) * 1/3 = 481$ machine cycles. Therefore a 1.4 GHz Pentium 4 can perform $1,000,000,000/481 = 2,081,165$ PAN computations per second. Assuming a cost of \$1,000 for a Pentium 4 with minimal peripherals, we can now compute the cost of a single PAN computation:

$$P = \text{P4 cost}/[\# \text{ days in 5 years} * \text{PAN computations per day}] =$$
$$= \$1,000/[5 * 365 * 2,081,165 * 3,600 * 24] \approx 2^{-38.22}\text{USD}$$

Since the value of P that we are seeking is $2^{-48.3}$ USD, this attack is therefore completely uneconomical, by a factor of $2^{10} = 1,000$.

In conclusion we have shown that, assuming an HMAC cracking machine is of similar complexity to a DES cracking machine, the security parameters used for today's InternetCash cash cards are secure for the next 20 years, even if the *average* amount of each card is USD $10,000.

6   Conclusion

We have presented a formal communication model for all card-based systems, encompassing current credit, debit and pre-paid cards. We have also presented a concrete definition of security for such systems, and a family of systems which satisfies that definition. An efficient implementation from that family, the InternetCash pre-paid card system, was presented and its security analysed based on the assumption of HMAC [BCK96] being a pseudorandom function family. The InternetCash Payment Protocol (ICPP) was overviewed and its relevance to iKP and SET was briefly discussed. Pre-authorizations, refunds and customer service issues were also discussed.

Although the current model can be applied to both physical (brick and mortar) and electronic transactions and our discussion includes security of the PIN, an interesting direction for further research would be to extend the *model* to clearly distinguish between these two types of transactions and include common assumptions such as the exposure of the card number at physical locations and the security of the user's PIN. A more formal treatment of refunds and pre-authorizations would also be an interesting additional direction; we do not formalize them here in an attempt to keep the model simpler.

Acknowledgments

The author wishes to thank the InternetCash team for making InternetCash a reality, and in particular Cameron Gregory for his insight and contribution to the ICPP. Additional thanks to Moti Yung for his advice towards the final version of the paper, as well as the anonymous referees for their helpful comments and suggestions.

References

Amea.   7 Eleven-American Express Internet Shopping Card.
         http://www.7-eleven.com/products.html.
Ameb.   7 Eleven-American Express Internet Shopping Card Balance Check.
         http://www.7-eleven.com/products/card_bal.html.
Amec.   7 Eleven-American Express Internet Shopping Card F.A.Q.
         http://www.7-eleven.com/products/AMEX_12_13.html.
Ang00.   Julia Angwin. Credit-card fraud has become a nightmare for e-merchants,
         September 19 2000. Wall Street Journal Archives.
ANS.   ANSI X3. 92-1981, Data Encryption Algorithm, *American National Standards Institute*, New York, December 31, 1980.

BCK96.   M. Bellare, R. Canetti, and H. Krawzcyk. Keying hash functions for message authentication. In N. Koblitz, editor, *Advances in Cryptology — Crypto'96, Proceedings (Lecture Notes in Computer Science 1109)*, pages 1–15, Santa Barbara, California, U.S.A., August 1996. Springer-Verlag.

Ber00.   Matt Berger. Fraud part of life for online retailers, September 28 2000. http://www.upside.com/texis/mvm/ebiz/story?id=39c689cb0.

BGH+95. M. Bellare, J.A. Garay, R. Hauser, A. Herzberg, H. Krawczyk, M. Steiner, G. Tsudik, and M. Waidner. iKP – A family of secure electronic payment protocols, 1995. The most recent version is available at http://www.zurich.ibm.com/Technology/Security/extern/ecommerce/.

Com00.   Jupiter Communications. The real cost of credit card processing, 2000.

Dam88.   I.B. Damgård. Collision free hash functions and public key signature schemes. In D. Chaum and W.L. Price, editors, *Advances in Cryptology — Eurocrypt'87 (Lecture Notes in Computer Science 304)*. Springer-Verlag, Berlin, 1988. Amsterdam, The Netherlands, April 13–15, 1987.

EFF.   EFF. Electronic Frontier Foundation DES cracker. http://www.eff.org/descracker/.

Fra93.   M.K. Franklin. *Complexity and security of distributed protocols*. PhD thesis, Columbia University, New York, 1993.

GGM86.   O. Goldreich, S. Goldwasser, and S. Micali. How to construct random functions. *Journal of ACM*, 33(4):792–807, October 1986.

GMR88.   S. Goldwasser, S. Micali, and R. Rivest. A digital signature scheme secure against adaptive chosen-message attacks. *Siam J. Comput.*, 17(2):281–308, April 1988.

GMY83.   S. Goldwasser, S. Micali, and A. Yao. Strong signature schemes. In *Proc. 15th. Annual Symp. on the Theory of Computing*, pages 431–439, Boston, April 1983.

Int00.   Cybersource fraud 2000 survey, 2000. http://www.cybersource.com/fraud_survey/.

Lem00.   Robert Lemos. Top 10 security stories of 2000, December 24 2000. http://www.zdnet.com/zdnn/stories/news/0,4586,2668051-2,00.html No. 6.

Per00.   Lewis Perdue. E-tailers squeezed by credit card cheats, December 3 2000. http://www.zdnet.com/zdnn/stories/news/0,4586,2660192,00.html.

Rog00.   P. Rogaway. UMAC Performance, August 29 2000. http://www.cs.ucdavis.edu/~rogaway/umac/perf00.html.

RW01.   A. Rubin and R. Wright. Off-line generation of limited-use credit card numbers. In *Financial Cryptography 2001*. LLNCS, Feruary 19–February 22, 2001. Cayman Islands, AI. These proceedings.

San00.   Greg Sandoval. Extortionist targers creditcards.com, December 12 2000. http://www.zdnet.com/zdnn/stories/news/0,4586,2664008,00.html.

SET.   Secure Electronic Transactions Specification. http://www.setco.org.

SHA93.   FIPS 180, Secure Hash Standard, Federal Information Processing Standards Publication 180, May 11 1993.

Sha01.   A. Shamir. SecureClick: A web payment system with disposable credit card numbers. In *Financial Cryptography 2001*. LLNCS, Feruary 19–February 22, 2001. Cayman Islands, AI. These proceedings.

SecureClick: A Web Payment System with Disposable Credit Card Numbers

Adi Shamir

Dept. of Applied Math, The Weizmann Institute of Science
Rehovot 76100, Israel
shamir@wisdom.weizmann.ac.il

Abstract. This paper describes the design philosophy and overall architecture of a new web payment system which uses disposable credit card numbers to solve the major security issues associated with card based e-commerce.
Keywords: e-commerce, payment system, disposable credit card numbers.

1 Introduction

The problem of developing a secure payment system for the internet had attracted an enormous amount of interest in recent years, both in academia and among companies. Hundreds of possible solutions had been proposed, but most of them failed in the marketplace, or remained untested (an excellent compilation of about 130 proposals with descriptions and links can be found at [P]). In fact, almost all the web shopping conducted on the internet today is done with old fashioned credit card payment systems. These systems were not designed to handle web payments, but they are widely deployed and have a lot of inertia due to the billions of dollars which were spent on their infrastructure.

The problem of web shopping security has both a real and a psychological element. There are frequent press reports about hackers stealing credit card numbers and customers suffering from devastating identity thefts, and as a result most surfers do not shop on the internet. In one survey conducted in April 2000 (see [C]), 64% of internet users said that they are "very concerned" about the security of their credit card transactions online, 79% said that they would be "much more likely" (37%) or "somewhat more likely" (42%) to shop online if they were convinced that their credit card information was secure, and 65% say they would spend "much more" (19%) or "somewhat more" (46%) money online if they didn't have to give out their credit card information when making a purchase. While it is true that most shoppers do not encounter any difficulties, the web tends to be a more dangerous environment, and fraud rates in online transactions are more than ten times higher than fraud rates in normal transactions.

Over the last few months, several companies have announced new web payment systems based on the intuitively appealing concept of *disposable credit*

P. Syverson (Ed.): FC 2001, LNCS 2339, pp. 232–242, 2002.

card numbers (in the sense that they can only be used to pay once a particular amount to a particular web merchant). A major seal of approval for this approach was provided by American Express, which announced in September 2000 that they will offer a similar Private Payment system to their customers within a few months (see [AMEX]). This approach uses the existing credit card verification and clearance infrastructure, but solves the "stickiness" problem of regular credit card transactions, since any other use of these numbers (if they are later stolen from the merchant's web server) will be rejected by the issuer. It is interesting to note that this disposability idea had been very successfully used to solve the related stickiness problem of passwords, by changing the password required to login into a remote computer system every few seconds in a pseudo-random way (e.g., with the widely used SecureID token). I believe that payment systems based on disposable credit card numbers have major advantages over existing and other proposed systems, and that over the next few years they will become a popular alternative to regular credit card payments on the web.

In this paper I'll describe the design philosophy and general architecture of one of these proposals, SecureClick from Cyota.com, with which I was involved as a security consultant. The company started developing this system in 1999, and publicly introduced it in May 2000. Further information can be found at the company's web site [C].

2   Design Criteria

The goal of the project was to develop a truly practical system which is easy to deploy on a small scale in a matter of months, and easy to scale up into a universal web payment system. It should address real rather than hypothetical security concerns in today's systems, in a way which is easy to explain to non-technical surfers in order to overcome their psychological reluctance to shop on the web. In addition, it should be easy to use, without burdening the parties with unreasonable costs or intolerable complexity (as happened in the case of the SET protocol, for example).

The first decision one has to make is whether to use a classical or novel payment paradigm. People are very conservative about using new types of payment systems, and it can take 10-20 years before a new concept (such as a debit card or an ATM machine) becomes popular. A standard payment paradigm is one which is already widely deployed, such as a coin, a banknote, a check, or a credit card. These are known entities to most users, and thus they do not require a lengthy and expensive educational process. Novel paradigms such as beenz and probabilistic payments may be very appealing theoretically, but they are not intuitive and thus cannot become a widely deployed solution in the short term.

When we try to migrate a standard payment paradigm to the web, we should try to keep its "look and feel" by using either the same paradigm (e.g., in the case of a credit card payment) or by modifying only its hidden technical elements (e.g., in the case of an electronic coin). This can make the new system easier to explain and to understand, and thus speed up and smooth the transition period.

If the real version and web version of the payment paradigm are sufficiently similar, we can even use the same infrastructure for handling both types of payments. Electronic coins are so different from physical coins that we cannot use the same vending machine or payphone mechanisms, but web-based credit card payments can easily use the enormous networks built at great expense over a long period of time to authorize and clear physical credit card payments.

The main disadvantage of using a classical payment paradigm is that we are bound by all kinds of annoying constraints imposed by the legacy systems, which are either irrelevant or counterproductive in the web environment. In the case of credit cards, one of these restrictions is that a customer is associated with a single semi-secret number which is valid for many years. This makes sense in an environment in which a new plastic card has to be issued and securely delivered to the customer whenever he needs a new number, but not in a web environment in which the customer/number association can be made much more dynamic.

Another design consideration is whether we would like to have a limited or universal system. A limited system in which "funny money" can be exchanged only among members of a small group, or in which micropayments can be used only in order to buy low-value items is worth studying, but is not our goal here.

One of the hardest problems in deploying a new universal system is how to handle the transition period, due to the chicken and egg problem: until sufficiently many people start using the system, banks and merchants will be reluctant to adopt it, and vice versa. This is the main reason that smart cards had not been adopted in the US so far, in spite of their obvious security advantages. To break this vicious cycle, one party can try to subsidize the initial deployment of the system until it becomes self sustaining. This was tried in several local electronic wallet experiments (e.g., in the Mondex pilot program in Swindon, UK), but it proved to be both expensive and unattractive. One way to spread the expense and associated risk is to convince many parties to support a single new standard. However, it takes a lot of time and effort to go through standards committees, get governmental approval, and win against competing proposals and entrenched interests. A classical example of a standard setting effort was the SET protocol, which was severely handicapped in the process and ended up as a bloated compromise which is seldomly used nowadays.

The ideal web payment system is thus a universal system which has the same "look and feel" as some widely deployed payment system, and can share with it the same infrastructure. A single party (such as a bank or a credit card issuer) should be able to launch it quickly without waiting for the approval of other parties, and the system should be attractive at any size and thus scale up without subsidies. It should be designed primarily for payments in the range of $1 to $1,000, which represent the vast majority of current web payments. Finally, it should offer higher security (both real and perceived) compared to today's payment mechanisms, even though it is unrealistic to expect it to be perfectly risk-free.

All these considerations indicate that the best short term universal solution should be based on the credit card paradigm, but adapted to the unique requirements and capabilities of the web. This is the philosophy behind the SecureClick system, which is described in the next section.

3   The SecureClick System

The credit card was originally developed in order to enable guaranteed payments in real world transactions. Many of its security mechanisms were based on the assumption that a human sales clerk will be able to check the correct physical appearance of the card, look at its hologram, compare its recorded signature to the actual handwritten signature, and verify the name against a second form of identification. All these mechanisms are absent in the web shopping context, and the only security elements which survived the transition are the semi-secret 16 digit credit card number itself (which is kept unchanged for many years) and the 4 digit expiration date (which changes in a predictable way every two years) [1]. If someone had proposed this as a new web-based payment system today, it would have been considered totally inadequate, but this is what we have today due to the huge inertia of existing payment systems.

Since web payments are considered as higher risk "card not present" transactions, they are almost always checked in real time with the card issuer before the transaction is completed. The issuer can check that the card had not been canceled or stolen, that its credit bound had not been exceeded, and that the transaction does not look suspicious (based on its previous pattern of use).

This authorization approach has many security risks. If a card is physically stolen, it can take several hours before it is reported missing. If a card number is copied by a sales clerk or downloaded from a web server, the owner is completely unaware of this fact. An illegally obtained card number which is used in a prudent way will not raise an alarm, and the false transactions will only be discovered when the card owner gets his bill a month later.

In the context of web shopping, the problem of outside hackers grabbing IP packets containing credit card numbers is almost non-existent, since the shopping forms are almost always protected in transition by strong SSL encryption, and it is not cost effective to work very hard in order to gain access to a single card number. The real problem is that these numbers are "sticky", and may be kept in insecure databases in the merchant's web server long after the transaction is completed. There are many reported cases of hackers stealing and then distributing thousands of card numbers from such servers. The problem is particularly serious among small or new merchants, who do not install elaborate security mechanisms and do not keep them up-to-date with security patches, but even in a well protected site an insider with valid access to the database can be bribed to sell its contents to outsiders, and in case of bankruptcy the database can fall into the wrong hands. In a sense, once a credit card number

---

[1] New cards also contain a 3 digit cryptographic checksum of the card number which is called CVC (card verification checksum). It is printed on the back of the card but completely ignored in most web transactions.

is sent to the web merchant, the customer has no control over how it will be handled and who will see it months or years later.

The result of all these published security incidents is that most surfers feel uneasy about web shopping with their credit cards. The risk is not just the actual threat of losing money (which is limited to $50 in the US), but the psychological aggravation involved in canceling cards, fighting charges, and clearing credit records. The problem is particularly acute at web sites without established reputations, since most surfers feel that saving a few dollars by shopping with a small and unknown merchant is simply not worth the risk. This greatly limits the potential of the web as a global marketplace which provides instant access to a huge number of merchants. The right way to fight this fear is not to say "trust me, its secure", but to visibly add to the shopping experience simple and intuitive security mechanisms which would convince the customer that he is not at risk if he fills this shopping form from that unknown web site.

Each credit card transaction involves three parties: a customer, a merchant, and a card issuer. The most substantial relationship is between the customer and issuer, since the issuer knows the customer, his credit history, and his buying habits, and the relationship typically lasts many years. The merchant/issuer relationship is weaker since the issuer may not know the merchant, but there are fewer merchants than customers, and they tend to be larger entities which satisfy stricter criteria. The weakest link is between the customer and the merchant, since neither one of them typically knows or trusts the other, and they may have a single transient interaction.

All three parties must be made aware of each transaction. The way it is done today on the web is to use two 2-party protocols based on the customer/merchant and merchant/issuer links, which are the two weakest relations. This is again a legacy decision, since in the real world it is cumbersome to ask a customer to contact the card issuer in real time to complete each transaction. However, on the web all the parties can communicate with equal ease, and thus it would make more sense to include the potentially strongest customer/issuer link in a tighter 3-party approval process.

The recommended sequence of events is thus the following: When the customer is ready to complete a web transaction, he should first inform the issuer about the identity of the merchant and the (approximate) value of the transaction, and then send the shopping form to the merchant. Upon receiving the order, the merchant should contact the issuer in the usual way, but the issuer will only approve transactions about which he had already been directly notified by the customer. Note that the additional customer/issuer interaction does not create major new communication bottlenecks in web shopping, since such transactions already require real-time customer/merchant and merchant/issuer communication, and thus they add only a small additional overhead.

The customer/issuer interaction is new, and requires new software at both ends, accompanied by a strong form of authentication. The customer/merchant and merchant/issuer parts of the protocol can be either new or traditional. There are several alternative mechanisms:

1. The customer can send his regular credit card number to the merchant. The purpose of the customer/issuer interaction in this case is to ask the issuer in effect to activate his card number for a short period of time. This is insecure if the same card number can also be used in other transactions which do not require real time approval, or if a hacker can sneak additional transactions into the card activation period. To reduce this vulnerability, the activation period should be made very short, but this can be problematic for merchants who request real-time transaction approvals, and then settle their daily transactions as a single batch. In addition, it makes it more complicated to handle communication difficulties, customer queries, split shipments, recurring purchases, or chargeback situations.

2. Instead of sending his credit card number, the customer can send to the merchant a unique transaction number (known in the cryptographic literature as a nonce) which is generated during the customer/issuer interaction. However, most merchants would reject an empty or invalid value in the credit card field in the shopping forms. This situation may change if this approach becomes universally accepted, but it will make it impossible to roll out an attractive system by a single issuer, since initially its customers will be able to shop at very few web sites.

3. The best approach is to use a nonce which has the same "look and feel" as a standard credit card number, and thus can be placed in the card number field of the merchant's form without causing any legacy problems. The issuer can easily recognize these incoming authorization requests if their numbers come from a batch of credit card numbers which are used only for this purpose. However, the merchant is unaware that the credit card number he is given is just a transaction number, and can use his standard customer/merchant and merchant/issuer protocols to complete the transaction.

The SecureClick solution is thus based on the following three simple principles:

1. Each web transaction requires an additional real-time preapproval protocol, and thus follows the path customer $\longrightarrow$ issuer $\longrightarrow$ customer $\longrightarrow$ merchant $\longrightarrow$ issuer.
2. Each web transaction is characterized by a nonce which is generated during the customer/issuer preapproval protocol.
3. Each nonce has the form and functionality of a regular credit card number, and thus the existing customer/merchant and merchant/issuer protocols can remain unchanged.

In this solution the credit card payment paradigm, the existing protocols, and the installed infrastructure elements remain unchanged. The system can be adopted by a single issuer, and its customers can shop anywhere on the web. They can intuitively understand that they are not risking long term consequences by sending a disposable credit card number to a party they do not know or trust, provided that their preapproval communication with the card issuer (whom they usually trust) was secure.

An interesting benefit of the SecureClick approach is that card issuers can get an almost instantaneous warning when hackers break into merchants' databases and start using the stolen card numbers. Such a database is likely to contain both regular and disposable credit card numbers, and most hackers will not be able to distinguish which is which. Misuse of a regular credit card number is usually detected only when the customer contests a transaction weeks later, and it is not easy to identify the source of the problem. However, any attempt to reuse a stolen disposable credit card number at another merchant will immediately raise an alarm, pinpoint the compromised database, and make it easy to stop the misuse of other numbers (even regular ones!) which were stored in the same database.

It is important to note that the SecureClick system is not anonymous with respect to the issuer, since he learns about the transaction from both the customer and the merchant, and links the disposable credit card number to the customer's real credit card account. It can be made more anonymous than standard credit card transactions with respect to the merchant if the issuer allows the customer to fill incorrect details (such as name and address) in the shopping form, but this can conflict with the AVS security mechanism which allows physical shipments only to the registered address of the credit card owner. Shoppers who would like to use the credit card paradigm but keep the transaction anonymous from both the issuer and the merchant can use an alternative payment system in which customers buy at a supermarket (with cash!) a secret credit card number that contains a fixed prepaid value. Consecutive transactions with such a card are linkable, but the owner of the card can remain anonymous, as in the case of prepaid payphone and GSM cards. This is ok for small or particularly sensitive transactions, but such a system cannot be used as a general replacement for regular credit cards on the web since considerable amounts of money have to be prepaid, unspent money may be difficult to retrieve, a lost or stolen card is equivalent to losing cash, and a card number grabbed by hackers in one transaction can be used to quickly max out the card.

The Private Payment system developed by American Express seems to follow a strict policy in which each disposable card number is associated with a single transaction during its lifetime. However, our analysis of actual payment patterns indicate that such a policy is too rigid, and one should consider additional trade-off points between a system based on a single long term number and a system based on one disposable number per transaction. For example, some web merchants use a registration process for first time customers, and automatically reuse the same memorized card number in later transactions. The only way to change this number is to go through a reregistration process, which is very inconvenient. A reasonable compromise in this case is to allow disposable card numbers to be reused, but only when they involve the same customer and merchant, and follow a specific customer/issuer preapproval process for each transaction. Another example involves a split shipment, in which the customer buys two books and authorizes a single payment. If one of the books can be sent immediately while the other has to be reordered from the publisher, the merchant often splits both the shipment and the credit card payment. A reasonable compromise in this case is to allow the merchant to report several transactions with the same disposable number, provided that they involve the same merchant and customer and their total value does not exceed the amount declared in the original preapproval process. Another common example involves recurring payments, in which the merchant splits a single transaction into several monthly payments, and automatically uses the same card number in all of them. A rigid system such as the AMEX solution will not function well in these common situations, whereas Cyota's SecureClick system uses a flexible approach called Intelligent Card Technology, which allows some disposable card numbers to be reused under carefully controlled circumstances. I believe that such flexibility will be necessary in any practical system, and will have a major impact on its commercial success.

4   Some Technical Details

The SecureClick approach is conceptually simple, but its secure implementation and seamless integration with existing issuer and customer systems requires a lot of care and hard work.

One of the most important security issues is the way customers authenticate themselves to issuers during the preapproval protocol. Due to the close relationship between these parties it is possible to handle this problem by a variety of known methods such as a time-dependent password, a digital signature, a biometric device, or any other method which is agreed between the parties when the customer joins the system. Note that there is no need to standardize the same authentication technique across the whole system, and each issuer can choose the point on the cost/security tradeoff curve which best fits his needs.

The recommended implementation of the SecureClick approach is based on a small browser plugin, which is provided (along with the authentication information or device) by the card issuer to the customer when he first joins the system. It is automatically invoked whenever the customer clicks on the "pay" button in a web shopping form. Most of the details in this form are filled in the usual way, but the credit card fields are left empty. The plugin intercepts this form before it is sent to the merchant, and initiates the customer/issuer protocol in which the parties are authenticated, the details of the proposed transaction are sent to the issuer, and a disposable credit card number and expiration date are generated. The customer can then copy these numbers to the relevant fields in the shopping form, and then the plugin forwards the form to its original destination.

Perhaps the most interesting technical issue is how to choose the disposable credit card numbers. Visa and Mastercard numbers have 16 decimal digits, but the first digit is used to identify the card type and the last digit is used for error detection purposes, and thus there are only 14 usable digits which represent one hundred million million possible cards numbers. Clearly, there is no shortage of regular card numbers, but if we want to issue disposable and unpredictable numbers for each transaction we have to consider the possibility of reusing previously issued numbers.

Issuers obtain exclusive rights to batches of consecutive credit card numbers, which are called bins. There are bins of various sizes: The smallest bins contain 100,000 numbers which start with a particular value at the 10 most significant digits, and the largest bins contain 100,000,000 numbers which start with a particular value at the 6 most significant digits. Issuers can buy additional bins (for several thousand dollars) as their business grows.

The SecureClick approach makes it possible to consider the expiration date as an extension of the nonce, but due to the existence of legacy systems this 4-digit number must look like a valid date in the next three years, so at most 36 out of the 10,000 possible values can be used. In addition, some merchants do not properly report this number to the issuer, even though it is defined as a mandatory field. It is thus both risky and of marginal value to use the expiration date as an extension of the actual card number.

Each transaction number should be kept unique for several months in order to enable the parties to refer to the transaction, answer queries about it, and perform a chargeback if necessary. After this period the issuer can reuse the card number, unless it is flagged as an unresolved case, which is extremely rare. If a medium size issuer has 1,000,000 customers, each one of them makes 5 web transactions per day, and the numbers should be kept unique for 200 days, the total number of credit card numbers required is 1,000,000,000. This number is large but feasible, since it represents only 1/100,000 of the space of numbers allocated to either Visa or Mastercard.

The simplest way to reissue the bounded set of available numbers is to use the cyclically increasing order $0, 1, 2, 3, \ldots, 0, 1, 2, 3, \ldots$ However, this makes consecutive transaction numbers highly predictable to hackers, which is undesirable. The issuer can randomize the order of the issued numbers, but if they are repeated with the same permuted order $3, 1, 2, 0, \ldots, 3, 1, 2, 0, \ldots$ a hacker can watch the numbers issued in one round and then infer the numbers which will be issued in the next round.

A different approach is to issue all the available numbers in some pseudorandom order, and then to reissue them in the next round in a new pseudorandom order. This makes the numbers highly unpredictable, except towards the end of each round where fewer and fewer numbers remain available. To solve this problem, we can stop each round prematurely after distributing only 90% of the available numbers. A more serious problem with this approach is that with high probability, some numbers will be used twice within a short period of time (towards the end of one round, and again near the beginning of the next round). This violates the assumption that each transaction number is uniquely associated with one customer throughout its active lifetime, and lead to procedural complications and possible errors.

The problem can be mathematically stated in the following way: Let m be the number of available card numbers, let $n >> m$ be the number of transactions, and let $r \leq m$ be the smallest distance we can tolerate between two consecutive occurrences of the same transaction number. Our goal is to find an efficient algorithm for generating random *large distance sequences* $x_1, x_2, \ldots, x_n$ where each x_i is an integer in $0 \leq x_i < m$, such that whenever $x_i = x_j$ and $i \neq j$, $|(i - j)| \geq r$.

When $r = m$, the only sequences of this type start with an arbitrary permutation of $\{0, 1, \ldots, m - 1\}$, followed by repeated occurrences of the same permutation. When $r = m - 1$, consecutive blocks of length $m - 1$ are almost identical, except that arbitrary nonoverlapping blocks in it can be cyclically left-shifted by a single step, and one number missing from the previous block can be reintroduced at an arbitrary position. This slow evolution of the permutations represented by the various blocks can lead to first and last blocks which are completely different.

We can extend this structural analysis to any smaller value of the distance r. The basic observation is that for any $i > r$, x_i can be chosen as any value which does not occur among the $r - 1$ previous sequence elements $x_{i-r+1}, x_{i-r+2}, \ldots, x_{i-1}$. Since these values must be distinct, there are exactly $m - r + 1$ possible values for each x_i with $r < i \leq n$. The first r values can be chosen as any ordered sequence of distinct values from $\{0, 1, \ldots, m-1\}$, and thus the total number of large distance sequences with parameters m, n, r is exactly $(m - r + 1)^{(n-r)} m!/(m - r)!$.

This characterization makes it possible to sample the space of large distance sequences with perfectly uniform probability distribution. However, this generation algorithm is inherently sequential, and thus it is difficult to map i to x_i and x_i to i (in a particular round) without generating all the previous sequence elements by repeatedly searching large databases which contain all the transaction numbers issued in the last few months. What we really want in practice is an algorithm which relates i to x_i by applying a small number of pseudorandom functions, and generates (for $r \approx m$) sequences whose numbers are reasonably hard to predict by hackers who know only a relatively small number of previously issued numbers.

A simple solution to this practical problem is to pseudorandomly partition the m available values into c disjoint groups $S_1, \ldots, S_c$ of size m/c. The output sequence consists of an arbitrary pseudorandom permutation of the values in S_1, followed by an arbitrary pseudorandom permutation of the values in S_2, and so on in cyclic order over the c groups. The internal permutation in each S_i is different in each one of its occurrences. The closest possible distance between two consecutive occurrences of the same value is $r = ((c-1)/c)m$, which can be made arbitrarily close to m.

A more sophisticated solution uses dynamic set partitions in which we merge and then resplit consecutive pairs of sets after each round. In other words, we choose disjoint pairs of sets S_i, S_{i+1}, and then pseudorandomly split each union $S_i \bigcup S_{i+1}$ into a new pair of equal sized sets S_i', S_{i+1}' for the next round . This reduces the shortest possible distance to $r = ((c-3)/c)m$. By choosing $c \approx 20$, we can make sure that transaction numbers start repeating only in the last 15% of each cycle, without overly restricting the number of possible sequences. While it is possible to use more complicated strategies to create large distance sequences whose elements can be pseudorandomly generated, it is not clear that we need this extra margin of security.

Payment systems based on disposable credit card numbers (like anything else) are not perfectly secure. In particular, a successful attack on the issuer's computing system can be catastrophic, but this is true even for regular credit card payments, and as a result these systems tend to be exceptionally well protected. Similarly, a Trojan horse planted at the customer's computer can compromise the security of his transactions, but this is again true for any PC-based web payment system. In the long term, customers can overcome this vulnerability by using dedicated computing devices such as smart cards, or by getting at least part of the disposable number from the issuer through an alternative path such as an SMS message to the customer's cellular telephone.

5   Conclusion

In this paper I described the overall design of the SecureClick web payment system. Similar systems were simultaneously and independently developed by several other companies, including American Express. This practical approach addresses real problems, is easy to explain, easy to use, and easy to launch on a small scale. I believe that it will play an important role in the development of e-commerce in the next few years.

Acknowledgments

The ideas described in this overview paper were jointly developed by many people. In particular, I would like to thank the founders of Cyota.com for proposing this project, and the employees of Cyota.com for identifying and overcoming many technical difficulties.

References

AMEX. http://www.wirednews.com/news/business/0,1367,38648,00.html.
C.   http://www.cyota.com.
P.   *Payment Mechanisms Designed for the Internet*,
        http://ntrg.cs.tcd.ie/mepeirce/Project/oninternet.html.

The Business of Electronic Voting

Ed Gerck[1], C. Andrew Neff[2], Ronald L. Rivest[3],
Aviel D. Rubin[4], and Moti Yung[5]

[1] Safevote.com, egerck@safevote.com
[2] VoteHere.net, aneff@votehere.net
[3] Laboratory for Computer Science
Massachusetts Institute of Technology, Cambridge, MA 02139
rivest@mit.edu
[4] AT&T Laboratories – Research
180 Park Avenue, Florham Park, NJ 07932
rubin@research.att.com
[5] CertCo Inc., New York, NY
moti@cs.columbia.edu, moti@certco.com

Abstract. This work reports on a Financial Cryptography 2001 panel where we concentrated on the emerging business of electronic voting.

1 Preliminaries

The problems associated with traditional voting machines in a national election, their unreliability, inaccuracy and other potential hazards, were put in the public limelight, after the last USA presidential election (especially in the state of Florida). At the same time, but less conspicuously, an industry centered around electronic voting (national, boardroom, company wide, and otherwise) has started to emerge, offering various solutions. Therefore, it seems to be an emerging area where cryptography is crucial to industrial progress, which, in turn, makes it a proper subject within the area of "financial cryptography."

Indeed, for about 20 years, the cryptographic research community has dealt with issues related to security and robustness of e-voting as a fundamental protocol problem. Numerous election protocols with many provable properties have been designed and some have been prototyped as well. This research developed insight, and some of its results will surely influence future systems. However, here we concentrate on issues regarding to "real life" aspects of actual implementations of voting systems.

Obviously, the e-voting problem possesses some of the integrity and secrecy issues that underly many protocol problems in the area of financial transactions. Yet, the problem has certain requirements and characteristics which are unique and perhaps harder to achieve.

The discussion in this report includes the panelists' views of basic requirements and problem specifications, their views of major challenges in the field, their opinions regarding technical and social feasibility and their approaches to

P. Syverson (Ed.): FC 2001, LNCS 2339, pp. 243–268, 2002.

possible solutions. Then the notion of building "businesses" around electronic election is discussed as well. The basic issues are centered around technology, yet legal, social, financial, market and policy issues play important roles in investigating the reality of electronic voting business. The report consists of this preliminary section and a summary section by the moderator (M. Yung) and sections contributed by each of the panelists.

The original issues and problems which the panelists were directed to were: (1) reliability, (2) fairness, (3) scalability (does one solution fit all situations), (4) how much security is actually required? (5) is e-voting for real? (6) how far are we from "real" voting? (namely, is the technology ready?) (7) is the Internet the arena for voting? (8) is there interaction between the technology and its quality and the business success? (9) is it a business at all (namely, is there money to be made and how?) (10) what are e-voting's social and legal implications?

The rest of the paper includes the panelists' sections. Each panelist is fully responsible for his own contribution and each contribution has its own personal characteristics and its own level of optimism. The contributions reflect faithfully the positions expressed in the panel discussion. In section 2 Ron Rivest presents perspectives on electronic voting where he reviews some of the history of voting machines, some of the basic problems with systems and his personal views of the subject. In section 3 Andy Neff presents the difference between general e-voting and Internet-voting, he then presents basic requirements and practical considerations and challenges. In section 4 Avi Rubin considers the feasibility of remote voting, especially when taking into account the current state of the art of platform and Internet security (or, more accurately, insecurity). In section 5 Ed Gerck presents a general background related to the notion of trust and to secure and trustworthy election systems; he then reviews basic requirements for e-voting scheme. The summary then tries to report some of the discussion which followed the presentations by the panelists.

2   Ronald L. Rivest:
Perspective on Electronic Voting

2.1   Introduction

Over the years, with varying degrees of success, inventors have repeatedly tried to adapt the latest technology to the cause of improved voting.

For example, on June 1, 1869 Thomas A. Edison received U.S. Patent 90,646 for an "Electric Vote-Recorder" intended for use in Congress. It was never adopted because it was allegedly "too fast" for the members of Congress.

Yet it is clear that we have not reached perfection in voting technology, as evidenced by Florida's "butterfly ballots" and "dimpled chads."

Stimulated by Florida's election problems, the California Institute of Technology and MIT have begun a joint study of voting technologies [CTM00], with the dual objectives of analyzing technologies currently in use and suggesting improvements. This study, funded by the Carnegie Foundation, complements the Carter/Ford commission [FER01], which is focusing on political rather than technological issues. Electronic voting will be studied.

Among people considering electronic voting systems for the first time, the following two questions seem to be the most common:

Could I get a receipt telling me how I voted?

Could the U.S. Presidential elections be held on the Internet?

The first question is perhaps most easily answered (in the negative), by pointing out that receipts would enable vote-buying and voter coercion: party X would pay $20 to every voter that could show a receipt of having voted for party X's candidate. Designated-verifier receipts, however, where the voter is the only designated verifier—that is, the only one who can authenticate the receipt as valid—would provide an interesting alternative approach to receipts that avoids the vote-buying and coercion problem. See [JSI96] for a discussion of this idea.

The second question—can we vote remotely over the Internet– is more problematic.

We start by noting that "electronic voting" includes a wide range of possible implementations. The California Internet Voting Task Force [Ca00] distinguished between (a) voting at a supervised poll-site using electronic equipment, (b) voting at an unsupervised electronic kiosk (say, in a shopping mall), and (c) "remote voting"— voting from home or business using the voter's equipment.

Before proceeding to comment on the security of electronic voting systems, we should at least pause to consider the desirability of such systems. Is remote electronic voting over the Internet desirable? Why bother?

"Because we can" and "for increased voter convenience" are arguably insufficient justifications for electronic voting. "For increased confidence in the result" might be acceptable, if a convincing case could be made. Political scientists claim that the best justification is "to increase voter turnout."

In the remainder of this note, I discuss the "secure platform problem" as a key impediment to remote voting, and then provide a list of personal opinions regarding the security of electronic voting systems.

2.2   The "Secure Platform Problem"

There is a fundamental problem we must face when trying to design remote electronic voting systems: the "secure platform problem."

Cryptography is not the problem. Indeed, many wonderful cryptographic voting protocols have been proposed; see [Gr00] for a sample bibliography.

The problem is interfacing the voter to the cryptography.

Almost all proposed cryptographic voting protocols *assume* that a voter (e.g. Alice) has a secure computing platform that will faithfully execute her portion of the protocol. The platform (e.g. a PC) will correctly display to Alice her intended vote, and cryptographically submit her vote during the protocol. The platform acts as Alice's "trusted agent" during the voting protocol.

In essence, the platform is Alice as far as the voting protocol is concerned.

In reality, the current generation of personal computers running Windows or Unix are not sufficiently secure to act as trusted voting agents. These operating systems and their applications are far too vulnerable to viruses and Trojan horses. A hacker could easily write a virus that would cause Alice's computer to display her voting for one candidate while actually voting for another. If thousands of PC's are similarly infected, an election could be rigged. This is an unacceptable risk.

Other studies and reports have reached similar conclusions that current technology is not secure enough to support electronic voting from home. In particular, I note the report of the California Task Force on Electronic Voting [Ca00], Avi Rubin's note [R00], and the Internet Policy Institute Report on Internet Voting[IPI00].

Of course, the secure platform problem is not the only significant security problem that needs to be addressed regarding the possibility of electronic voting from home over the Internet. The Internet itself, while remarkably useful and reasonably robust, is all too vulnerable to flooding and denial of service attacks. The possibility that a foreign power could bring down the Internet on U.S. election day is all too real. For this reason alone, remote electronic voting from home over the Internet would be at best an available alternative, and it would be reasonable to expect existing poll-site voting systems to be prepared to handle everyone should the Internet be taken down.

2.3   Some Personal Opinions

E-Voting Is not Like E-Commerce. Electronic voting is unlike electronic commerce in several important ways, so it is insufficient to argue that secure electronic voting is merely a corollary to secure electronic commerce and that the same security mechanisms should apply.

For example, in electronic commerce there is always time to dispute a transaction if something hasn't worked correctly. With voting, there is a deadline that must be met.

Also, in an electronic commerce transaction, the buyer typically gets a receipt that can be used later to resolve disputes. In contrast, it is important, as noted earlier, that voters do *not* get receipts showing how they voted, since this may enable the voter to sell his vote.

In electronic commerce, transaction records identify the parties involved. In electronic voting, the ballots cast should *not* identify the voters who cast them, as this might violate the voter's privacy and subject them to coercion. (For example, if election officials could see how each voter voted, then the lead election official could see how his employees voted.)

It is more important that no one "has their thumb on the scale" than having a scale that is easy to use or even very accurate. The primary purpose of a voting system is to correctly determine the will of the voters. Given human nature, the likelihood of getting an incorrect result is much higher if there are significant security vulnerabilities than if the vote-counting is a bit inaccurate. Fraud can be a problem in any election; counting errors affect only close elections. Ease of use is relevant only inasmuch as it affects voter turnout or introduces systematic biases.

Electronic voting from home runs the risk of allowing an adversary to put a "big thumb" on the scale, since the adversary may be able to automate his attack. For example, he could bring down the Internet in Democratic neighborhoods, or create a virus that affects computers with certain characteristics (e.g. those with ".edu" suffix). Such risks threaten the primary purpose of the voting system, and suggest exceptional caution in moving forward with such systems.

The voting system must be simple to understand and operate. Electronic voting systems are often complex. Voting systems must be certified before they are used. Election officials must have confidence that the voting system will prevent fraud and perform reliably.

Complexity is the enemy of security. Complex systems are difficult to understand and debug. Asking an election official to certify that thousands of lines of code provide a secure and trust-worthy election system is an entirely different matter than asking him to certify a set of procedures for managing a collection of paper ballots. Electronic voting systems place a substantial burden on the election officials who must certify the systems, and may weaken the credibility of the entire process in the voters' minds.

Even with poll-site electronic voting, the complexity of electronic voting systems may also challenge the election officials (who are often volunteers) who must install and operate the election equipment. The failure to educate both election officials and voters to use new equipment properly is a major source of election problems.

Physical ballots can provide better audit trails than purely electronic systems. The integrity and trust-worthiness of a voting system is greatly enhanced by having an audit trail recording each ballot cast. Many states require voting systems to have such audit trails.

Audit trails with very high integrity can be obtained when the audit trail is created directly by the voter, as with a paper ballot. Electronic voting systems are *indirect*—they interpose a layer of mechanism between the voter and the audit trail, risking the possibility that the mechanism is not faithfully capturing the voter's preferences.

Nonetheless, paper ballots are not perfect either, and Shamos [Sh93] gives interesting arguments in favor of electronic audit trails. Saltman's classic work [Sa88] discusses in some detail audit-trail requirements for electronic voting systems.

County-level decisions on voting technology has benefits. There are clear and probably compelling advantages to specifying and purchasing voting systems on a state-wide basis rather than county by county, as is currently the case in the U.S. But we should not lose sight of two arguments to the contrary.

First, just as a woodland's diverse variety of plants can provide better resistance to pathogens than the farmer's single crop, so too can a variety of voting technologies provide resistance to an adversary's attack, as there is no common point of vulnerability for the whole system.

Second, we need ways to gain experience with new voting systems. One good way is to allow individual counties to experiment with techniques that are different than the state-wide norms.

The ability to handle disabled voters will become increasingly important. Existing voting systems tend to be poor at accommodating the needs of disabled voters. For example, blind voters have had to trust election officials to read the ballots and enter their votes. Electronic voting systems are capable of supporting a diversity of interfaces to the voter.

Our largest security problem is likely to be *absentee ballots*. Absentee voting has increased dramatically over the past decade. Indeed, some states, such as Oregon, vote entirely by mail. Remote electronic voting can be viewed as a version of absentee voting.

In my opinion, however, by allowing such an increase in absentee voting we have sacrificed too much security for the sake of voter convenience. While voters should certainly be allowed to vote by absentee ballot in cases of need, allowing voting by absentee ballot merely for convenience seems wrong-headed. I would prefer seeing "Voting Day" instituted as a national holiday to seeing the widespread adoption of unsupervised absentee or remote electronic voting.

2.4   Summary

Some paper-based voting technologies, such as optical scanning, offer reasonable balances of security, ease of use, cost, simplicity, and reliability. (Other paper-based technologies, such as punch cards, should definitely be phased out.)

Electronic voting systems promise benefits in terms of ease of use, especially for disabled voters. Because of the software-based and indirect character of electronic voting systems, these benefits come at the cost of increased complexity and at the risk of decreased security.

While electronic voting from home should perhaps forever remain too risky a fantasy, electronic poll-site voting may provide, even in the near term, worthwhile improvements to paper-based voting technologies. Cryptographic techniques will certainly be essential in any electronic voting technology, as will better methods for addressing the "secure platform problem."

References

Ca00.   California Internet Voting Task Force. Final report. Available at
         http://www.ss.ca.gov/executive/ivote/.

Gr00.   Rachel Greenstadt. Electronic voting bibliography, January 2000. Available
         at http://theory.lcs.mit.edu/~cis/voting/
         greenstadt-voting-bibliography.html.

IPI00.   Internet Policy Institute. Internet voting. Available at
         http://www.internetpolicy.org.

JSI96.   M. Jakobsson, K. Sako, and R. Impagliazzo. Designated verifier proofs and
         their applications. In Ueli Maurer, editor, *Advances in Cryptology - Euro-
         Crypt'96*, pages 143–154, Berlin, 1996. Springer-Verlag. Lecture Notes in
         Computer Science Volume 1070.

CTM00.   California Institute of Technology and Massachusetts Institute of Technology.
         Voting technology project. http://www.vote.caltech.edu/.

FER01.   National Commission on Federal Election Reform.   Available at
         http://www.reformelections.org.

R00.   Avi Rubin. Security considerations for remote electronic voting over the
         internet, 2000. Available at http://avirubin.com/e-voting.security.pdf.

Sa88.   Roy G. Saltman.   Accuracy, integrity, and security in computer-
         ized vote-tallying.   Technical report, Computer Science and Tech-
         nology, National Bureau of Standards, Gaithersburg, MD 20899,
         August 1988.   NBS Special Publication 500-158. Available at
         http://www.itl.nist.gov/lab/specpubs/500-158.htm.

Sh93.   Michael Shamos. Electronic voting—evaluating the threat. Presented at
         CFP'93. Available at
         http://www.cpsr.org/conferences/cfp93/shamos.html.

3   C. Andrew Neff:
E-Voting: Proceed with Caution

3.1   Introduction

Election 2000 has shown the need for a well-defined audit process that can be independently verified – at very least by multiple parties with disparate interests in the outcome of the election; better yet, by anyone who cares about the results. There is a growing groundswell of opinion that computers could be used to make elections more accurate and efficient, but they bring with them their own pitfalls. Since electronic data is so easily altered, simple-minded electronic voting systems cannot produce an audit trail that is as strong as a paper audit trail. Further, limitations on the reliability of the supporting electronic hardware and software are also an important concern. However, it would be both naive and unscientific to conclude that it is *impossible* to implement an electronic voting system which meets or exceeds the integrity standards of our best conventional systems. If designed properly, an electronic voting system can actually produce an audit trail that is even stronger than conventional ones – including paper based systems. This is exactly what was needed in the 2000 U.S. Presidential

Election to avoid the costly and time consuming dispute process that ensued; a system that is automated and indisputable, while preserving ballot secrecy.

3.2   Fundamentals – E-Voting vs. I-Voting

In any discussion of "high-tech" voting solutions, it is important to make a distinction, from the start, between systems which use digital data to *capture the original voter selections* and/or act as *official record* thereof – *"e-voting"* systems – and systems which use the remote connectivity of the Internet, or other public network to cast, collect and tabulate ballots – *"i-voting"* systems. Clearly the class of e-voting systems includes all i-voting systems, but there are e-voting systems *already in use* today – so called DRE equipment – which are obviously not i-voting systems. Unless one is careful, it is easy to lose track of this distinction in the arguments for and against either one of them.

Assuming that all systems must meet certain standards for integrity and dependability, i-voting clearly presents a much greater set of problems than e-voting alone. However, the problems associated simply with e-voting are already challenging ones. To be sure, electronic computers can manage election data far more easily and efficiently than physical methods, the trouble is that computers are inherently only as trustworthy as the people who administer them. They are also completely opaque, unlike the physical paper ballot box that can be watched at all times; and electronic data is far more easily altered or destroyed than physical ballots – especially in large quantities.

The key to building systems that do not suffer these problems is to leverage the strengths of digital data, rather than trying to employ the same procedures that are used to protect conventional systems. Attention must be focused on ways to guarantee integrity of the election data itself, rather than on the custody of machines that are handling it. If a complete record, or *transcript*, of all election data – from who has voted to the specific computation steps used to arrive at the final tally – can be collected and represented in such a way that not one bit of it can be altered without creating intrinsic inconsistency, then the goal of an indisputable electronic election can be achieved. This is really the only way an e-voting recount makes any sense at all. Running a count over and over on the same machine, or set of machines, proves nothing about the true election results. It only proves that the software that is running can display the same numbers repeatedly. Of course, the transcript must also not compromise voter privacy.

An election transcript provides a tool for better election audit than ever. Without the power of modern electronic systems, a central audit of this scope was out of reach. With conventional systems, each election participant – voters and candidates – have to trust parts of the audit that are only enforced by local procedural requirements. There is no way to verify after the fact that these procedures have been sufficiently implemented, or if they have been subverted.

3.3   Requirements Must Be Scientific and Unbiased

As new election systems are proposed, it is important to keep the debate from sinking to unscientific levels. New systems should not be shoehorned to fit old ones simply because we are used to the old ones. A good example of this is the debate over media. Paper ballots have many desirable qualities, but the requirements for new systems should be phrased in terms of the *fundamental qualities* that should be maintained, rather than artificially insisting that they continue to use paper for ballot recording. For example, a reasonable storage requirement might be that the storage media have "99.99% chance of surviving a 8.0 Richter scale earthquake". An example of an unreasonable, biased requirement is "the system should be capable of printing *paper ballots* for hand recount."

Once a suitable set of fundamental system requirements is agreed upon, the unsettling vulnerabilities of our conventional election systems become apparent. In this light, the benefits of moving to new election system technology may begin to outweigh the risks. Typically, the definition of specific requirements are the responsibility of legislative, or administrative bodies. However, VoteHere's experience with technology and its capabilities can be a source of useful information to legislators. To that end, we suggest an outline for the general requirements decisions that must be made at the highest level.

1. **Fairness**. Only votes from *distinct, eligible* voters should be counted in the final tally.
2. **Accessibility**. No eligible voter should be prevented, or "deterred" from casting his/her vote, either by malicious or accidental forces.
   - The difference between "deterred" and "inconvenienced" will be difficult to pinpoint. Many voters already feel that the voting process is an inconvenience.
3. **Accuracy**. The final published election results should be, mathematically, an exact "count" (i.e. sum, or in general, aggregation when using more complex tabulation rules) of the collection of *intended choices* made by all the participating voters. This requirement breaks into two pieces:
   3.1. The results should be an exact "count" of the ballots recorded in the "ballot box", or on the "ballot media".
   3.2. Each vote in the "ballot box" should be an accurate representation of the voter's intended choice.
      - As with accessibility, a requirement of this type can only be specified with "reasonable precision". No system is capable of preventing *all* types of voter errors.
4. **Privacy**. The contents of each ballot should be known only to the voter who cast it. This is simple, but there are subtleties that can only be addressed with a complete threat model. For example
   4.1. No system can protect a voters ballot secrecy from a collusion of all the other voters.

4.2. Current "mail in" absentee voting does not protect privacy against all threats. In fact, privacy can be broken by a collusion of two at the time that envelopes are opened. Given this, is cryptographically protected privacy sufficient, especially if only the voter has the corresponding key? There are many ways to spy on voter choices that are easier and less expensive than breaking RSA, for example.

5. **Receipt Freeness.** To discourage both vote buying and coercion, it is important that a voter not be able to *prove* how he/she voted.
   – Cooperative vote selling will never be prevented by legislation or by any election system. The best that can be done is to significantly limit the attractiveness of such activity, a goal that is accomplished when a prospective buyer, or coercer, can not be sure of the success of his/her efforts. (It should be noted, however, that current "mail in" absentee voting does nothing to address this problem.)

Specific requirements imposed on election systems should be chosen so as to most effectively *implement* the general considerations above. They should not be imposed as a means of *a priori design or engineering*.

3.4 Practical Considerations

In addition to the general considerations of the previous section, there are practical issues that any new voting technology must take into consideration.

Integration with other systems. It would be unreasonable to expect that conventional voting systems will disappear overnight, even in isolated precincts. It will take time for voters to gain comfort with new systems, and for counties to migrate to them. As a result, new voting systems must be able to fit as part of an aggregate system – the way that, in many jurisdictions, "mail in" voting fits together with poll site voting. This, then, requires some care to be sure that overall election integrity remains in tact – voters shouldn't be able to vote once with each system, for example.

Lack of PKI. For i-voting especially, it is crucial to be able to associate eligible voters – *people* – with digital credentials. For now, an infrastructure to support this which is both widely used, and robust is missing. This may change in the near future, but for now, election systems will need to build custom solutions. This means some integration with voter registration systems.

Mechanism of verification. Election systems in the theoretical literature generally fall into two categories – those that are *universally verifiable* and those that are *voter verifiable*. The former produce election transcripts that allow complete verification of election integrity by any independent entity, while the latter require that voters check the validity of their vote in the ballot box to be sure that data has not been changed. The integrity of a voter verifiable system is based on the premise that "enough" voters *will* verify their ballots. In practice, these systems are undesirable for two reasons

1. Some voters will be mischievous, or forgetful. There is then no good mechanism for deciding whether the system has been compromised, or if just some group of voters wishes to make the system appear compromised.
2. It is hard to get a large fraction of voters to vote in the first place. It will be much harder still to get them to verify their ballots.

Redundant infrastructures not viable. A brute force attempt at assuring election integrity is through redundancy. The idea is that each voter submits multiple copies of her ballot to multiple, *independent* tabulation authorities. Results are then determined by way of "majority rule", or some variant. In practice, such solutions are seriously flawed.

1. From a business perspective, how will the authorities be maintained in a truly independent manner? It is not cost effective, competitive, or interesting to each of the replicated authorities. We could propose that the government subsidize them all, but isn't this even worse?
2. Dispute resolution is complicated and potentially costly.
3. Voters now have a new mode of malicious behavior – submit conflicting votes to the various authorities.
4. Network reliability problems go up exponentially with the number of authorities.

In this respect, the right model for e-voting comes from the conventional poll site model itself: *One poll site, lot's of observers*, leads to *One tabulation center, lot's of crypto keys*.

Client trust. Theoretical voting protocols presume that the voter does "her own" computation. In fact, the computation is done by a computing device, which may itself not be trusted. Supervised e-voting systems may be able to prevent this threat through careful procedure, but it is much more difficult to address in the situation of i-voting.

Network weaknesses. Even if all election data can be protected from compromise, there is still the practical problem of getting it from one place to another. The Internet is vulnerable to *Denial of Service* attacks, and these must be taken seriously. However, the criteria put on e-voting systems for reliability should be reasonable. All systems are subject to some risk of DoS. Conventional poll sites can be forced closed for several reasons, such as earthquake, fire, or bomb threat. Voters can be prevented from getting to them by something as common as a traffic jam. As long as voters using an e-voting system as "first choice" can use other systems as a fall back, the standards for reliability should not be absurdly high.

3.5   VoteHere Philosophy

The philosophy at VoteHere, Inc., is to build systems completely transparent to public review and scrutiny. Our *ambition* is to achieve this by way of published and accepted protocol, thereby eliminating the need for trusted, audited or otherwise independently inspected software and hardware. Where components cannot clearly meet this goal, they must be "sun lighted" by careful, independent certification. This combination of open cryptographic protocol and component review creates the requisite level of trust and dependability vital to any public election system.

4   Avi Rubin:
The Feasibility Of Remote E-Voting

The feasibility of remote electronic voting in public elections is currently being studied by the National Science Foundation by request of the former President of the United States (see `http://www.netvoting.org/`). Remote electronic voting refers to an election process whereby people can cast their votes over the Internet, most likely through a web browser, from the comfort of their home, or possibly any other location where they can get Internet access. There are many aspects of elections besides security that bring this type of voting into question. The primary ones are:

coercibility. the danger that outside of a public polling place, a voter could be coerced into voting for a particular candidate.
vote selling. the opportunity for voters to sell their vote.
vote solicitation. the danger that outside of a public polling place, it is much more difficult to control vote solicitation by political parties at the time of voting.
registration. the issue of whether or not to allow online registration, and if so, how to control the level of fraud.

The possibility of widely distributed locations where votes can be cast changes many aspects of our carefully controlled elections as we know them. The relevant issues are of great importance, and could very well influence whether or not such election processes are desirable. However, in this paper, we focus solely on the security considerations as they relate to conducting online public elections. In particular, we look at remote online voting, as opposed to online voter registration, which is a separate, but important and difficult problem. We also focus solely on public elections, as opposed to private elections, where the threats are not as great, and the environment can be more controlled.

4.1   The Platform

On the platforms currently in the most widespread use, once a malicious payload reaches a host, there is virtually no limit to the damage it can cause. With today's hardware and software architectures, a malicious payload on a voting client can actually change the voter's vote, without the voter or anyone else noticing, regardless of the kind of encryption or voter authentication in place. This is because the malicious code can do its damage before the encryption and authentication is applied to the data. The malicious module can then erase itself after doing its damage so that there is no evidence to correct, or even detect the fraud. To illustrate, let's look at a program that exemplifies the level of vulnerability faced by hosts.

The program we describe, Backorifice 2000 (BO2K) is packaged and distributed as a legitimate network administration toolkit. In fact, it is very useful as a tool for enhancing security. It is freely available, fully open source, extensible, and stealth (defined below). The package is available at http://www.bo2k.com/. BO2K contains a remote control server that when installed on a machine, enables a remote administrator (or attacker) to view and control every aspect of that machine, as though the person were actually sitting at the console. This is similar in functionality to a commercial product called PCAnywhere. The main differences are that BO2K is available in full source code form and it runs in stealth mode.

The open source nature of BO2K means that an attacker can modify the code and recompile such that the program can evade detection by security defense software (virus and intrusion detection) that look for known signatures of programs. A signature is a pattern that identifies a particular known malicious program. The current state of the art in widely deployed systems for detecting malicious code does not go much beyond comparing a program against a list of attack signatures. In fact, most personal computers in peoples' houses have no detection software on them. BO2K is said to run in stealth mode because it was carefully designed to be very difficult to detect. The program does not appear in the Task Menu of running processes, and it was designed so that even an experienced administrator would have a difficult time discovering that it was on a computer. The program is difficult to detect even while it is running.

There can be no expectation that an average Internet user participating in an online election from home could have any hope of detecting the existence of BO2K on his computer. At the same time, this program enables an attacker to watch every aspect of the voting procedure, intercept any action of the user with the potential of modifying it without the user's knowledge, and to further install any other program of the attackers desire, even ones written by the attacker, on the voting user's machine. The package also monitors every keystroke typed on the machine and has an option to remotely lock the keyboard and mouse. It is difficult, and most likely impossible, to conceive of a web application (or any other) that could prevent an attacker who installs BO2K on a user's machine from being able to view and/or change a user's vote.

4.2   The Communication Infrastructure

A network connection consists of two endpoints and the communication between them. The endpoints here are a user's host and an elections server. While it is in no way trivial, the technology exists to provide reasonable protection on the servers. This section deals with the communication between the two endpoints.

Cryptography can be used to protect the communication between the user's browser and the elections server. This technology is mature and can be relied upon to ensure the integrity and confidentiality of the network traffic. This section does not deal with the classic security properties of the communications infrastructure; rather, we look at the availability of the Internet service, as required by remote electronic voting over the Internet.

Most people are aware of the massive distributed denial of service (DDOS) attack that brought down many of the main portals on the Internet in February, 2000. While these attacks brought the vulnerability of the Internet to denial of service attacks to the mainstream public consciousness, the security community has long been aware of this, and in fact, this attack was nothing compared to what a dedicated and determined adversary could do. The February attack consisted of the installation and execution of publicly available attack scripts. Very little skill was required to launch the attack, and minimal skill was required to install the attack.

The way DDOS works is that a program called a daemon is installed on many machines. Any of the delivery mechanisms described above can be used. One other program is installed somewhere called the master. These programs are placed anywhere on the Internet, so that there are many, unwitting accomplices to the attack, and the real attacker cannot be traced. The system lies dormant until the attacker decides that it is time to strike. At that point, the attacker sends a signal to the master, using a publicly available tool, indicating a target to attack. The master conveys this information to all of the daemons, who simultaneously flood the target with more Internet traffic than it can handle. The effect is that the target machine is completely disabled.

We experimented in the lab with one of the well known DDOS programs called Tribe Flood Network (TFN), and discovered that the attack is so potent, that even one daemon attacking a Unix workstation disabled it to the point where it had to be rebooted. The target computer was so overwhelmed that we could not even move the cursor with the mouse.

There are tools that can be easily found by anyone with access to the web that automate the process of installing daemons, masters, and the attack signal. People who attack systems with such tools are known as script kiddies, and represent a growing number of people. In an election, the adversary is more likely to be someone at least as knowledgeable as the writers of the script kiddy tools, and possibly with the resources of a foreign government.

There are many other ways to target a machine and make it unusable, and it is not too difficult to target a particular set of users, given domain name information that can easily be obtained from the online registries such as Register.com and Network Solutions, or directly from the WHOIS database. The list of examples of attacks goes on and on. A simple one is the ping of death, in which a packet can be constructed and split into two fragments. When the target computer assembles the fragments, the result is a message that is too big for the operating system to handle, and the machine crashes. This has been demonstrated in the lab and in the wild, and script kiddy tools exist to launch it.

The danger to Internet voting is that it is possible that during an election, communication on the Internet will stop because attackers cause routers to crash, election servers to get flooded by DDOS, or a large set of hosts, possibly targeted demographicly, to cease to function. In some close campaigns, even an untargeted attack that changes the vote by one percentage point could sway the election.

4.3   Conclusions

A certain amount of fraud exists in the current offline election system. It is tolerated because there is no alternative. The system is localized so that it is very unlikely that a successful fraud could propagate beyond a particular district. Public perception is that the system works, although there may be a few kinks in it here and there. There is no doubt that the introduction of something like remote electronic voting will, and should, come under careful scrutiny, and in fact, the system may be held up to a higher standard. Given the current state of widely deployed computers in peoples' homes and the vulnerability of the Internet to denial of service attacks, we believe that the technology does not yet exist to enable remote electronic voting in public elections.

A full paper on this topic is available at
http://avirubin.com/e-voting.security.html.

5   Ed Gerck:
Voting System Requirements

This section presents a set of voting system requirements that are consistent, technologically neutral, can be applied to paper, electronic and network (Internet) voting, and exceed the current requirements for paper-based ballots and electronic voting DRE (Direct Recording Electronic) machines. The requirements are based on the principles of "Information Theory" and of "trust as qualified reliance on information." The principles favoring multiple, independent channels of information over one purportedly "strong" channel. However, adding multiple channels can also decrease reliance if the design principles laid out in these requirements are not followed.

5.1   Background

As defined by Alan Turing some fifty years ago, a mathematical method is effective if, loosely speaking, it can be set out as a list of instructions which a human clerk who works obediently with paper and pencil can follow, for as long as is necessary, but without insight or ingenuity. Together with Alonzo Church, Turing, in fact, argued that every effective mathematical method can be carried out by a sufficiently powerful computer (represented by the universal Turing machine).

The above mentioned Voting System Requirements were born out of the desire to create products that would allow modern computer-based technology to automate and truly emulate the secure desirable properties motivated by what has been collected throughout centuries of public voting. Put differently, we ask: *can we use a perfect clerk in elections—one who works obediently with paper and pencil, for as long as is necessary, but without insight or ingenuity?*

Indeed, if perfect clerks were to conduct an election using paper-ballots, this would provide the best model we have for a public election. Such an election would be, for example: anonymous (avoiding collusion, coercion), secret (all cast votes are unknown until the election ends) and yet correct (all votes are counted) and honest (no one can vote twice or change the vote of another participant), oftentimes also complete (all voters must either vote or justify absence). In such an election system, if we know the voter (e.g., in voter registration) we cannot know the vote and if we know the vote (e.g., in tallying) we cannot know the voter. After an election, all votes and all voters are publicly known—but their connection is both unprovable and unknown.

But: real-life clerks are not perfect! Neither are computer systems! Thus, we need to introduce the concept of qualified reliance on information in terms of providing proofs (e.g., proof of voting, proof of correctness) that can be objectively evaluated and not just subjectively accepted or taken at face value.

To discover and rate such proofs, the requirements employ the idea that one should favor multiple, independent communication channels over one "strong" channel. Such an idea was successfully used by the Moguls in India some 500 years ago in the context of combating corruption [1], and was mathematically described by Claude Shannon some 50 years ago in the context of combating noise when he introduced his Information Theory [2], a well-known general theory of communication processes.

Thus, for example, how can a voting system prove that the vote received at the ballot box is the same vote seen and cast by a voter? This question is not easier to answer if the voter is close to the ballot box then if he is far away. Distance plays no role, contrary to what one might think at first. The *fundamental problem of voting* is that the voter cannot see his tallied vote, hence the voter has no way of knowing if information sent through the communication channel (which may be very short) equal that which was received and tallied. This problem is oftentimes called the "vote-gap problem" by the author.

To solve this question in electronic voting, some advocate printing a paper copy of the ballot, which the voter can see and verify that it is identical to the ballot she intended to cast, and then sending the paper copy to ballot box A while an electronic copy of that same ballot is sent to ballot box B. The idea is that ballot box B can be tallied quickly while ballot box A will be used as a physical proof for a manual recount. Such a suggestion is oftentimes advanced as the sine qua non solution to voting reliability in electronic voting.

But what makes the introduction of a paper ballot special is not the fact that it is paper instead of bits. It is the fact that the voter is actually casting his vote twice. We now have two independent channels of information for the ballot, one from the terminal as source B, the other one from the printer as source A. We denote the multiplicity of such channels N (In our case N = 2).

In other words, this design provides for two outputs: ballot A and ballot B. However, in the event of a discrepancy between the two, no resolution is possible inside the system. The situation can thus be summarized:

- N = 1: If the system is always similar to a perfect clerk then N = 1 (one channel) suffices, whether paper or electronic. But if we use a system with N = 1, we cannot define any level of reliance on the final result except that which was assigned a priori.
- N = 2: If we add one independent channel (e.g., the paper ballot) to a system that already provides one channel (e.g., electronic ballot), this creates a system with N = 2. However, this additional channel makes the system indeterminate and still incapable of, by itself, defining any level of reliance on the final result except that which was assigned a priori (e.g., paper is more trustworthy).

Clearly, before considering other well-meant suggestions (which might be similarly ill-fated), what is necessary is to seek a logically provable solution to reliability problems caused by imperfect communication systems.

Such a solution needs to consider not only machine-machine communication channels but also human-machine communication channels because the voter can act as a source and as verifier in more than one part of the system. Further, human-human communication channels must be considered because we do not want machines to have the potential to "run amok", unchecked.

Information Theory [2] can be used to describe such communication channels and, as previously noted, the concept of qualified reliance on information can be introduced as a formal definition of trust [3] in order to rate such channels in terms of providers of proofs.

As a result, the only provable solution to increased reliability in communications (e.g., the communication between the voter as a sender and the ballot box as a receiver) turns out to be increasing the number/capacity of independent channels until the probability of error is as close to zero as desired (direct application of Shannon's Tenth Theorem in Information Theory [2]). To be complete, the solution should consider not only machine-machine communication channels but also human-machine and human-human ones. Thus, if an electronic system is able to provide N proofs (human and machine based), these N proofs for some value of N larger than two will become more reliable than one so-called "physical proof"—even if this one proof is engraved in gold or printed on paper.

An undefined system also presents opportunities for fraud (e.g., someone can change and/or delete some paper ballots after the election in order to cast doubt on the integrity of the entire election). It is also open to attacks (e.g., a group of voters might agree beforehand to call out a "discrepancy" after they vote and thereby disrupt an election, which is similar to a "denial of service" attack).

Thus, we need a real-world voting system—not one that is based on perfect parts (N = 1) or one that produces an undefined result in the case of a single error (N = 2). In order to provide for qualified

reliance on information, such a voting system needs to have multiple independent channels.

In plain English, the greater the number of independent channels for the verification of a result, the greater trustworthy the result is.

However, suppose the terminal where the voter enters his choices changes them to something else and then sends this information over N different channels, what difference does it make if it is N = 1, 2 or 500?

None! In such a case N would still be 1 for the ballot channel. The 2 or 500 channels are not independent for the ballot because they all originate as copies of that single stored potentially corrupted ballot. So, it does not make a difference in terms of ballot reliance. This would, however, make a difference in terms of communication reliance, in which there are now different transmission channels, 2 or 500 channels for which each channel could behave as a correction channel for the others. Namely, in this case the ballot box would more probably receive the right ballot (even though it may have been corrupted before transmission) and more so for N = 500 than for N = 1.

What is needed is therefore a requirement to include several truly independent ballot, transmission and audit channels—whether or not electronic transactions are used. These channels should be employed in rating the reliance on each node of an end-to-end balloting system, even during the election and in real time. There should be several ways to implement this requirement and channels could be added also in time and context, not just in space. Channels can also transport information by reference, not just information by value.

What is also needed is a way to allow the voter to verify results, for example the presence/absence of her ballot at the ballot box and whether her ballot at the ballot box is a valid one. This is useful because sufficient indirect verification does produce trust. "Trust but verify" is a mode typically preferred by our collective wisdom and it is definitely applicable here. It is important to note that even if just a fraction of the voters (e.g., 5%) do verify the results, the capability of verification is already a deterrence to fraud because a cheater has no way of knowing who will verify, or not.

Another characteristic of a good voting system is that the only person whom you prove the vote to is the voter. If the proof can be shown to someone else, then the vote can be coerced or sold. Therefore, when using multiple channels of information, they either have to be deniable by the voter or else temporary so that the voter cannot be threatened or hurt as a result of the vote.

Regarding the use of paper, it is important to note that the reason to distrust a paper/electronic voting system with N = 2 is not based on distrust in paper. Paper is just another communication channel. The reason is that adding paper does not solve the problem and, in fact, makes the problem indeterminate. This is so, since we need N larger than 2. Certainly, paper can be one of the channels, if desired, because the channel make-up is irrelevant. But a cost-benefit analysis might result in the use of non-paper channels.

Next, another question that must be addressed is the possibility of all-electronic voting systems. Should we trust them and why?

Nowadays, all-electronic systems and computers are used in flying commercial and military jets. And yet, no one in the public is afraid that a terrorist will introduce a virus in the system and will down all commercial jets worldwide, or all U.S. military jets. Why? Because there is a designed redundancy at many levels in the system. For example, there are three independent laser inertial navigation sensors and any decision on the plane's position depends on the agreement of at least two of them, which decision is further verified by a GPS system, as well as flight time and speed calculations.

Thus, voting systems—like any other type of systems—derive their trustworthiness from the fact that they work consistently, both conceptually and perceptually. However, in the absence of an easy conceptual understanding of the system (e.g., a laser inertial navigation sensor) that the average user is able to grasp, a sufficiently coherent perceptual understanding (e.g., observing that the system works) is enough to eventually build trust in the system.

Trust may also be denied by the design itself, because disasters may occur at any time if the principles of communication reliance (i.e., trust itself) are not taken into account. To visualize this, imagine a plane that would be flown with just two navigation sensors, one compass-based and the other electronic—we would then have an idea of the disastrous consequences of using a paper/electronic voting system with N = 2, even though a physical channel is used (compass, paper).

Thus, we can conclude that the deciding factor in trusting a system is not whether it includes one or even two sources of information that can be touched or seen in physical form (e.g., a paper in your hands, a paper behind a screen, a compass needle behind a screen).

A factor that mitigates against an all-electronic voting system is the fact that although paper and electronic records are both vulnerable to subversion, it is a lot easier to change what is in an electronic record than it is to change what is on paper.

Thus, electronic records need to be bound to other references in a manner that is demonstrably inaccessible to an attacker, both through physical access controls and through cryptographic protocols.

Moreover, there really needs to be a step-by-step description of the voting process, so that when someone asks, "What if the intruder succeeds in breaking into the system to change X?" this can be clearly answered, for example, by:

(i) to change X would cause a subsequent binding failure, thus it would be detectable except with parallel access to Y and Z, which are independently inaccessible, or

(ii) knowledge of an alternate (and attacker-desirable) value for X is insurmountably difficult to achieve, and the effort could not be leveraged to any other X.

Put most plainly, people know that ordinary voting systems can be subverted by someone who can bribe enough individuals to collude, but the physical fact of several tons of paper ballots still represents somewhat of an obstacle to an "easy subversion" in the eyes of many.

In contrast, people are well aware that electronically one can modify a million records with as little as a few keystrokes. This is the "fear" that needs to be addressed in an all-electronic system. Further, such a subversion can be massive and rapid, executed from the safety of a remote laptop, etc. so that it would be unavoidable.

Of course, one alternative to reduce fear would be education. To educate voters regarding the very nature of distributed cryptographic assurances and at a level where the concepts are not hidden behind excessive abstractions.

But cryptography is not, by itself, the critical issue, nor is it the silver bullet. Further, no amount of education will stop attackers, on the contrary, it may aid them.

Instead, *voting systems can use the concept of multiple independent communication channels to make it as impossible as desired to tamper with the electronic ballot both before and after it is cast.*

Here, the question is not how many copies of paper or bits one has, but how many independent channels the attacker needs to subvert versus how many independent correction channels one has available during such an attack. Of course, if the attacker is able to subvert the correction channels while attacking the other channels, then they will not be independent.

Therefore, the same mechanism that protects the casting of a ballot must also be used to protect presenting the ballot. And this needs to be given as a set of requirements which work together in an end-to-end design.

These requirements are therefore general principles, valid for any physical implementation of a "ballot"—whether as print marks on paper, pits on a CD-ROM surface, electrons hitting a video screen (electronic ballot), modulated electromagnetic waves, bits in a network protocol or any other form of information transfer to and from the voter. They also apply to any form of voting, including majority voting and single transferable votes. The requirements may be applied in their entirety or merely a subset may be used.

To achieve these goals, the requirements should be able to handle voting rules of any type and should apply to voting systems anywhere in the world. However, the main objective here is for the requirements to be as complete and as independent from one another as possible, without sacrificing consistency. It is understood that "completeness" is an elusive goal that might never be reached when we consider the diversity of election needs [4], while "consistency" is a necessary feature for the requirements to work together in a particular election. In short, this was the reason to stop after 16 requirements. Increasing the number of requirements can risk decreasing their consistency, in general [4]. Of course, other requirements may be added, or deleted, as needed.

Some of the words used in the requirements may have different (and equally valid) meanings in other contexts (e.g., "voter privacy"). Therefore, the requirements also include the operational definitions of the main words used. Three words are, however, used without a definition even though they could also be misunderstood. These words are "trust" [3], "manifold" and "meshwork" [5], as defined in the references.

5.2   Summary of Requirements

A voting system of any type and media needs to satisfy various requirements which are summarized in the following 16 points.

1. Fail-safe voter privacy. Definition: "Voter privacy is the inability to link a voter to a vote." Voter privacy MUST be fail-safe—i.e., it MUST be assured even if everything fails, everyone colludes and there is a court order to reveal all election data. Voter privacy MUST be preserved even after the election ends, for a time long enough to preserve backward and forward election integrity (e.g., to prevent future coercion due to a past vote, which possibility might be used to influence a vote before it is cast).

2. Collusion-free vote secrecy. Definition: "Vote secrecy is the inability to know what the vote is." Vote secrecy MUST be assured even if all ballots and decryption keys are made known by collusion, attacks or faults (i.e., vote secrecy MUST NOT depend only on communication protocol and cryptographic assumptions, or on a threshold of collusion for the keyholders).

3. Verifiable election integrity. Definition: "Election integrity is the inability of any number of parties to influence the outcome of an election except by properly voting." The system MUST provide for verifiability of election integrity for all votes cast. For any voter the system MUST also provide for direct verifiability that there is one and only one valid ballot cast by the voter at the ballot box.

4. Fail-safe privacy in verification. If all encrypted ballots are verified, even with court order and/or with very large computational resources, the voter's name for each ballot MUST NOT be revealed.

5. Physical recounting and auditing. We MUST provide for reliability in auditing and vote recounting, with an error rate as low as desired or, less strictly, with an error rate comparable or better than conventional voting systems [8]. The auditing and vote proofs MUST be capable of being physically stored, recalled and compared off-line and in real-time during the election, without compromising election integrity or voter privacy, and allowing effective human verification as defined by election rules.

6. 100% accuracy. Every vote or absence of vote (blank vote) MUST be correctly counted, with zero error [8].

7. Represent blank votes. We MUST allow voters to change choices from 'vote' to 'blank vote' and vice-versa, at will, for any race and number of times, before casting the ballot.

8. Prevent overvotes. As defined by election rules. We MUST provide automatic "radio button" action for single-vote races. If overvoting is detected in multiple-vote races, we MUST warn the voter that a vote has to be cleared if changing choices is desired. This warning MUST be made known only to the voter, without public disclosure.

9. Provide for null ballots. As defined by election rules, we MAY allow voters to null races or even the entire ballot as an option (e.g., to counter coercion; to protest against lack of voting options). Overvoting, otherwise prevented by requirement #8, MAY be used as a mechanism to provide for null ballots.

10. Allow undervotes. As defined by election rules, the voter MAY receive a warning of undervoting. However, such a warning MUST NOT be public and MUST NOT prevent undervoting.

11. Authenticated ballot styles. The ballot style and ballot rotation (changes between individual ballot representations) to be used by each voter MUST be authenticated and MUST be provided without any other control structure but that which is given by the voter authentication process itself.

12. Manifold of links. We MUST use a manifold [5] of redundant links and keys to securely define, authenticate and control ballots. We MUST avoid single points of failure—even if improbable. If networks are used, we MUST forestall Denial-of-Service (DoS) and other attacks with an error rate comparable or better than conventional voting systems [8].

13. Off-line secure control structure. We MUST provide for an off-line secure end-to-end control structure for ballots. We MAY use digital certificates under a single authority. Ballot control MUST be data-independent, representation-independent and language-independent.

14. Technology independent. We MUST allow ballots and their control to be used off-line and/or in dial-up and/or in networks such as the Internet, with standard PCs or hand-held devices used to implement their components in hardware or in software, alone or in combination for each part.

15. Authenticated user-defined presentation. We MUST enable the ballots to dynamically support multiple languages, font sizes and layouts, so that voters can choose the language and display format they are most comfortable with when voting as allowed by law and required by voters with disabilities, without any compromise or change to the overall system, from an authenticated list of choices defined by the election rules.

16. Open review, open code. We should allow all source code to be publicly known and verified (open source code, open peer review). The availability and security of the system must not rely on keeping its code or rules secret (which cannot be guaranteed), or in limiting access to only a few people (who may collude or commit a confidence breach voluntarily or involuntarily), or in preventing an attacker from observing any number of ballots and protocol messages (which cannot be guaranteed). The system SHOULD have zero-knowledge properties (i.e., observation of system messages do not reveal any information about the system). In fact, only keys MUST be considered secret.

5.3 Comments

Implementations and examples [9] are discussed in the full paper, available in [10].

These requirements include comments and references from Tony Bartoletti, Thomas Blood, Netiva Caftori, Gordon Cook, Hal Dasinger, Hugh Denton, Rosario Gennaro, Jason Kitcat, Brook Lakew, Elaine Maurer, Don Mitchel, Erik Nilsson, Michael Norden, Marcelo Pettengill, Roy Saltman, Bernard Soriano, Gene Spafford, Einar Stefferud, Arnold Urken, Eva Waskell, Thom Wysong, the IVTA tech WG (http://www.mail-archive.com/tech@ivta.org/), the CPSR-activists list, several cryptography lists, contributions from comments collected at Safevote's website, and from articles published in The Bell (http://www.thebell.net).

5.4 References

[1] *"... one of the earliest references to the security design I mentioned can be found some five hundred years ago in the Hindu governments of the Mogul period, who are known to have used at least three parallel reporting channels to survey their provinces with some degree of reliability, notwithstanding the additional efforts."* Ed Gerck, in an interview by Eva Waskell, "California Internet Voting." The Bell, Vol. 1, No. 6, ISSN 1530-048X, October 2000. Available online at http://www.thebell.net.

[2] Shannon, C., "A Mathematical Theory of Communication." Bell Syst. Tech. J., vol. 27, pp. 379-423, July 1948. Available online at http://cm.bell-labs.com/cm/ms/what/shannonday/paper.html. Shannon begins this pioneering paper on information theory by observing that

"the fundamental problem of communication is that of reproducing at one point either exactly or approximately a message selected at another point." He then proceeds to thoroughly establish the foundations of information theory, so that his framework and terminology have remained standard practice. In 1949, Shannon published an innovative approach to cryptography, based on his previous Information Theory paper, entitled Communication Theory of Secrecy Systems. This work is now generally credited with transforming cryptography from an art to a science. Shannon's Tenth Theorem states (cf. Krippendorf and other current wording): *"With the addition of a correction channel equal to or exceeding in capacity the amount of noise in the original channel, it is possible to so encode the correction data sent over this channel that all but an arbitrarily small fraction of the errors contributing to the noise are corrected. This is not possible if the capacity of the correction channel is less than the noise."*

[3] *"When we want to understand what trust is, in terms of a communication process, we understand that trust has nothing to do with feelings or emotions. Trust is that which is essential to communication, but cannot be transferred in the same channel. We always need a parallel channel. So the question is having redundancy. When we look at the trust issue in voting, it is thus simply not possible to rely on one thing, or two things even if that thing is paper. We need to rely on more than two so we can decide which one is correct. In this sense, the whole question of whether the Internet is trusted or not is simply not defined. The Internet is a communication medium and whatever we do in terms of trust, it is something that must run on parallel channels."* Ed Gerck, testimony before the California Assembly Elections & Reapportionment Committee on January 17, 2001, in Sacramento. Assemblyman John Longville (D), Chair. For an application of this model of trust to digital certificates, see "Trust Points" from http://www.mcg.org.br/trustdef.txt excerpted in "Digital Certificates: Applied Internet Security' by J. Feghhi, J. Feghhi, and P. Williams, Addison-Wesley, ISBN 0-20-130980-7, p. 194-195, 1998.

[4] This is similar to the situation found in Goedel's incompleteness theorem. The requirements form a logical system of some complexity and thus we do not expect such a system to be both complete and consistent.

[5] "Manifold" means a whole that unites or consists of many diverse elements and connections, without requiring these elements and connections to depend upon one another in any way. "Meshwork" is used to denote a manifold in the context of the Multi-Party protocol designed by Safevote to implement the requirements. A meshwork builds a meta-space in relationship to a space—a meshwork describes relationships about a space, not the space itself.

[6] *"We say that information-theoretic privacy is achieved when the ballots are indistinguishable independent of any cryptographic assumption; otherwise we will say that computational privacy is achieved."* In Ronald Cramer, Rosario Gennaro, Berry Schoenmakers, "A Secure and Optimally Efficient Multi-Authority

Election Scheme," Proc. of Eurocrypt'97. (available online at
`http://www.research.ibm.com/security/election.ps`).

[7] E. Gerck, "Fail-Safe Voter Privacy", The Bell, Vol.1, No.8, p. 6, 2000. ISSN
1530-048X. Available online at
`http://www.thebell.net/archives/thebell1.8.pdf`.

[8] *Accuracy* and *Reliability* are used here in the sense of standard engineering
terminology, even though these different concepts are usually confused in non-
technical circles. Lack of accuracy and/or reliability introduces different types
of errors:

> (i) Reliability affects a number of events in time and/or space, for exam-
> ple, errors in transfers between memory registers. We know from Shan-
> non's Tenth Theorem [2] that reliability can be increased so that the
> probability of such an error is reduced to a value as close to zero as de-
> sired. This is a capability assertion. It does not tell us how to do it, just
> that it is possible. This is the realm of requirements #12 and also #5,
> where one can specify an error rate as low as desired or, less strictly, an
> error rate "comparable or better than conventional voting systems".
>
> (ii) Accuracy affects the spread of one event, for example whether a vote
> exists. Here, requirement #6 calls for 100% accuracy. The requirement is
> that no "voter-intent" or "chad" or "scanning" issue should exist—which
> is feasible if, for example, each voting action is immediately converted to
> a standard digital form that the voter verifies for that event. Accuracy
> error can be set to zero because 100% accuracy is attainable in prop-
> erly designed digital systems that (e.g., by including the voter) have no
> digitization error.

For an illustration of the above definitions of accuracy and reliability, see the
four diagrams in `http://www.safevote.com/caltech2001.ppt`.

[9] "Contra Costa Final Report" by Safevote, Inc. Available upon request. Summary available at `http://www.safevote.com`.

[10] "Voting System Requirements", The Bell newsletter, ISSN 1530-048X,
February 2001, archived at
`http://www.thebell.net/archives/thebell2.2.pdf`.

6   Summary

Given the presentations above and the relative popularity of the subject, a large
numbers of questions and remarks were raised by the conference participants. We
thank the participants for their active role and contributions to the usefulness
of our panel. Since many opinions were expressed it is hard to report on all of
them (and surely important comments are omitted herein).

Many shared the caution expressed by some of the panelists. The paraphrased
comment "I am not sure what the next election technology is going to be, but

the next to next such technology will definitely be a paper technology" (by Matt Blaze) perhaps best represents this healthy skepticism. Specific concerns about the Internet reliability and immunity to attacks were raised by many participants. A doubt was raised (by Stefan Brands), claiming that the current theoretical work does not provide a sufficient level of privacy. The specific concern was that votes can be revealed if administrating machines collaborate, even in the most advanced protocols.

Social concerns regarding the suitability of modern technology to running democracy were discussed. The fear that aggressive modernization may generate a "voting divide" between those who use computers and those who do not, was expressed. The idea that politicians may not like the technology and will oppose its introduction, was raised as another potential hurdle to technological progress in political processes like voting.

Some more optimistic views were also expressed. They pointed out the problems of current systems on the one hand, and on the other hand they reminded us that electronic voting was somewhat successful in trials in the USA and in actual votings in countries like Brazil. Also noted is the fact that the current technology cannot remain forever the technology of choice for election, since this technology, even though it has been evolving very slowly, has been nevertheless evolving.

Overall, the panel represented the current state of the art of the business of electronic voting. We covered the commercial possibilities of supplying modern technology with sufficient levels of privacy, security, reliability and flexibility. We covered the basic requirements and the challenging issues that we need to cope with before the adoption of the new technology. We heard various opinions and interesting remarks regarding the diversified aspect of electronic voting. Naturally, e-voting industry researchers were more optimistic than their colleagues. The mix of opinions and variety of perspectives were instrumental in understanding the basic issues and problems regarding the reality of nation-wide e-voting, especially through the Internet. In fact, due to its popularity, the discussion centered around national (political) voting, and ignored other potential applications of the technology: e.g., inter-organizational small scale voting.

It is obvious that since there is quite uneasiness with the current election technology, the opportunity for using more modern technology exists. The actual adoption of electronic voting within electronic government and electronic democracy is going to stay a "hot issue" in the coming years. What technology is going to be adopted, and what level of cryptographic support will be used for the election itself and in securing election platforms, are open issues. Regardless of the differences of opinions and the various points of view, during the panel we learned about new angles to look at voting problems. We realized what are the burning issues in the area; issues of all kinds (social, business, systems, technology, policy and politics, etc.). Our hope is that we have stimulated further thinking, research and technological development which will motivate further studies of new subjects in all the relevant research areas.

Privacy for the Stock Market[*]

Giovanni Di Crescenzo

Telcordia Technologies Inc.
445 South Street, Morristown, NJ, 07960
giovanni@research.telcordia.com

Abstract. We investigate the problem of performing Stock Market operations, such as buying or selling shares of a certain stock, in a *private* way, which had recently been left open.

We present a formal definition for a private stock purchase protocol, addressing several privacy and security concerns on usual on-line stock market operations. According to our definition, a client would not reveal how many shares she is buying or selling (not even which of these two cases is happening), and what price she is offering for those. We then present an efficient protocol meeting this definition, based on the hardness of the decisional Diffie–Hellman problem. Our protocol requires no interaction between the clients, can be executed in a constant number of rounds between the clients and the server, and requires several technical contributions, such as a new and efficient zero-knowledge protocol for proving sum-related statements about encrypted values, which is of independent interest.

1 Introduction

The overwhelming expansion of the internet is today being accompanied with a large increase of financial activities and transactions that are conducted online. A few minutes navigation on the internet allows to realize the existence of electronic cash systems, payment protocols, auctions, lotteries, digital casinos and gambing systems. The sometimes crucial importance and often large interest around such transactions raises several concerns about the security and the privacy of the information that users and organizations are willing to use on a network.

In this paper we consider a important financial transaction: buying and selling shares of a particular stock on the Stock Market. Such transactions seem to have received not enough attention from the security and privacy literature, and, in fact, an assessment of the privacy problems deriving from these transactions and the construction of a protocol which addresses them had been left as an open problem. We present a formal definition for what it means for a stock purchase protocol to be secure and private, and present an efficient protocol which allows to privately purchase and sell shares of a certain stock.

---

[*] Copyright 2001, Telcordia Technologies, Inc. All Rights Reserved.

P. Syverson (Ed.): FC 2001, LNCS 2339, pp. 269–288, 2002.
© Springer-Verlag Berlin Heidelberg 2002

Our Model and Definition. We consider a model composed of several clients who intend to purchase or sell shares of a particular stock, and a server, taking care of such operations and of the current share price and current share amount. While the server is assumed to behave honestly (or, more precisely, as a honest-but-curious party), the clients may behave in a malicious way. Therefore, we ask that clients are allowed to perform their operations without revealing to all other clients private information such as how many shares they are buying or selling, which prize they offer for those, and not even whether they are buying or selling. In fact, even the server cannot derive any information about these operations other than what he needs to update the current share amount (namely, the sum of all shares bought/sold) and the current share price (namely, some prespecified function of external information and all private inputs of the clients). Still, at the end, each client who behaves honestly should obtain from the server a certificate for that particular transaction, despite the behavior of all dishonest clients.

Our Results. We present a protocol that satisfies all the mentioned properties and can be implemented in a constant number of rounds. In the important case in which the function that updates the share price is linear in the private amounts of the clients, our protocol has an efficient implementation based on the hardness of the Decisional Diffie Hellman problem. We also present a general solution for arbitrary functions, which uses any 2-party secure function evaluation protocol for computing the same function. Even in this case our solution can be implemented in a constant number of rounds; moreover, a variant of our solution also keeps the function private from the client. Some technical contributions include novel and efficient zero-knowledge protocols for proving sum-related statements about encrypted values, that may find applications somewhere else. In particular, we show a protocol for proving in zero-knowledge that given three ciphertexts, encrypted according to the El-Gamal cryptosystem, the first plaintext is the modular sum of the remaining two. Although we only present an efficient implementation of it, we note that our protocol can be implemented by only assuming the existence of any oblivious transfer protocol.

Related Results . Our model of a honest-but-curious server and several clients who do not need to interact has been already used in several investigations on the topic of auctions [9,4,23,24,16] (other related investigations on auctions which do not use a trusted party have been done in [26]). In particular, the paper [16] posed the open question of investigating privacy in stock market operations. The problem of anonymity in stock market operations has been investigated in [18]. More generally, our model and solution can be considered as belonging to the area of designing efficient protocols for specific multi-party private computation problems (as, for instance, for threshold cryptography [7]).

Organization of the Paper. In Section 2 we present some background on number theory and various cryptographic primitives. In Section 3 we present a detailed definition of the requirements that a private stock purchase protocol has to satisfy, and a high-level description of our solution. The description of the main two subcomponents of our private stock purchase protocol, is divided into two sections: in Section 4 we present the capital update (sub)protocol and in Section 5 we present the price update (sub)protocol.

2 Preliminaries

In this section we review some background notions and protocols as: oblivious transfer (OT), zero-knowledge proofs, the El-Gamal encryption scheme and an OT protocol based on it.

The El Gamal Public-Key Encryption Scheme [12]. Let p be a prime such that $p-1$ has a large prime factor q, and let g be a generator of a subgroup G of Z_p of order q. The key generation algorithm of the El Gamal public-key encryption scheme consists in uniformly choosing $s \in Z_p$ and computing $h = g^s \bmod p$, publishing (p, q, g, h) as a public key and keeping s as a secret key. The encryption algorithm consists of uniformly choosing $r \in Z_p$ and returning (u, v), where $u = g^r \bmod p$ and $v = h^r m \bmod p$, and m is the message. The decryption algorithm consists of outputting m, computed as $m = v/u^r \bmod p$. The semantic security of this proof system is equivalent to the difficulty of deciding the Diffie–Hellman problem.

Oblivious Transfer. The notion of Oblivious Transfer (OT) protocol was introduced by Rabin [21]. Informally, an OT protocol can be described as a game between two polynomial time parties Alice and Bob, where Alice wants to send a message to Bob in such a way that with probability $1/2$ Bob will receive the same message Alice wanted to send, and with probability $1/2$ Bob will receive nothing. Moreover, Alice does not know which of the two events really happened. There are other equivalent formulations of Oblivious Transfer (see, e.g., [5]), such as 1-out-of-2 OT, in which Alice has two messages m_0, m_1, Bob has one bit c and at the end Bob will receive m_c, without receiving any information about m_{1-c} and without Alice guessing c. This primitive has found numerous implementations and applications in the cryptographic literature. For our constructions, we can use any oblivious transfer protocol based on the difficulty of deciding the Diffie–Hellman problem (a two-round protocol for this task appears in [19]).

Conditional Oblivious Transfer. The notion of conditional oblivious transfer was introduced in [10], where applications were given to the problem of timed-release encryption, or 'sending information to the future'. Informally, a conditional oblivious transfer protocol is the following generalization of ordinary (1-out-of-2) oblivious transfer: Alice and Bob also have a private input (call those x_A and x_B, respectively), and a public predicate ρ such that if $\rho(x_A, x_B) = 1$ (resp., $\rho(x_A, x_B) = 0$) then Bob receives m_0 (resp., m_1), without learning any additional information about the message he has not received. In [10] a conditional oblivious transfer was given for the predicate 'greater than or equal to', based on the intractability of deciding quadratic residuosity. We remark that the same techniques used in [10] for this protocol can be used to construct an implementation based on the difficulty of deciding the Diffie–Hellman problem.

Zero-Knowledge Proof Systems. Informally, zero-knowledge proof systems [15] are interactive protocols allowing a possibly infinitely powerful prover to convince a polynomial time verifier that a statement (e.g., the membership of a string x to a language L) holds without revealing any additional information that the verifier could not compute alone before running the protocol. Now we expand on the definition of such protocols. First of all, an *interactive proof system* for a language L is an interactive protocol satisfying the two requirements of *completeness* and *soundness*. The completeness requirement says that if the prover and the verifier follow the protocol, then the verifier has to accept with probability very close to 1. The soundness requirement says that if the verifier follow the protocol, then no matter which arbitrarily powerful strategy is used by the prover, the verifier accepts with probability very close to 0. Then, a *zero-knowledge proof system* for a language L is an interactive proof system for L satisfying the additional requirement of *zero-knowledge*. This requirement states that for any probabilistic polynomial time strategy used by the verifier, there exists an efficient algorithm S, called the simulator, such that for all $x \in L$, the following two distributions are "indistinguishable": 1) the output of S on input x, and 2) the messages seen by the verifier when interacting with the prover on input x (including the verifier's random tape). According to the specific formalization of indistinguishability, we obtain different variants of the zero-knowledge requirement, called *computational, statistical* and *perfect*. A zero-knowledge *argument* [3] is a zero-knowledge proof system for which the soundness is only required to hold under polynomial-time adversaries.

3   Private Stock Purchase Protocol: Definition and Solution Sketch

In this section we present a definition and a high-level view of our solution for the main protocol of interest in this paper: a private stock purchase protocol.

3.1   A Formal Definition

We start by presenting the players, the phases and the (sub)protocols involved in an execution of such protocol, and then describe the requirements that a private stock purchase protocol has to satisfy.

Players. The players involved in a private stock purchase protocol are the *clients*, denoted as $C_1, C_2, \ldots, C_n$ and a *server*, denoted as S. A client C_i is any individual that intends to buy stock shares. The server S is the machine (or the individual) that takes care of handling the stock shares; including, for instance, selling the shares, updating the number of shares, updating the share price.

Connectivity. Although potentially all clients are connected among them and to the server through some communication link, for practical purposes, we are especially interested in protocols where each client only interacts with the server, and not necessarily at the same time.

Phases. Generally speaking, the lifetime of a stock purchase payment protocol is divided into a large number of time intervals of fixed and known length. In each of these intervals, a set of clients registers with the servers, requests a number of stock shares at a certain offered price, the share price is consequently updated, the number of available shares is properly updated as well, and clients are eventually given the requested number of shares. Since the execution of the protocol is conceptually the same in each interval, from now on we concentrate our study on a single, generic, time interval, and, for simplicity, refer to the protocol executed in this interval as the private stock purchase protocol. In this protocol we distinguish four phases. A first phase, called the *registration phase*, consists of each individual registering herself as a client by committing to the number of stock shares that she is willing to buy or sell and to a price they she is willing to pay for each of them, which we will call the 'offered price'. A second phase, called the *price update phase*, contains an interactive protocol in which each client interacts with the server; at the end the price of the stock shares is updated as a known and polynomial-time computable function of the amounts of shares and the offered prices that clients committed to in the first phase. A third phase, called the *capital update phase*, contains an interactive protocol in which each client interacts with the server; at the end the number of stock shares is eventually updated by subtracting the number of shares bought and by adding the number of shares sold; we call the resulting number the 'new price'; note that the shares for which the offered price was lower (higher) than the new price are not sold to (bought by) the client. In the fourth phase, called the *certification phase*, each client finally obtains from the server some certification of the transaction, namely, a certificate that a certain number of shares (if any) have been bought or sold by that client.

Protocols. Each phase contains an interactive protocol, where the interaction is between all clients and the server only (i.e., there is no interaction between the clients). Specifically, the *registration protocol* is executed between each client and the server, and at the end returns some keys and parameters that will be used in the rest of the payment protocol. The *price update protocol* is executed between all registered clients and the server, and at the end the server knows the output of the price updating function over the clients' private inputs (namely, the number of shares they want to buy and the intended prices) without learning any new information about such inputs; such output will be the new share price of the stock in the new time interval. The *capital update protocol* is executed between all registered clients and the server, and at the end the server knows a partial sum of all clients' private inputs. Here, a private input contributes a positive (resp., negative) amount if the client wants to buy (resp., sell) that amount of shares at an offered price larger (resp., smaller) than the new price; note that clients intending to buy (resp., sell) shares at an offered price smaller (resp., larger) than the new price will contribute no value to this sum. The *certification phase* is executed by the server who sends a single message to each client who successfully executed the previous phases, containing a certification of the client's acquisition or deposition of shares (if any) for the amount committed to during the registration phase, and the current share price, to later allow verification that the purchase was valid.

Requirements. Let us denote by (b_i, x_i, op_i), for $b_i \in \{0,1\}$ and $x_i \in \{0,1\}^t$, the private input of client C_i, for $i = 1, \ldots, n$, where $b_i = 0$ (respectively, $b_i = 1$) means that the i-th client wants to buy (respectively, sell) x_i stock shares at an offered price op_i. Also, let us denote by cp the current stock price per share, by f the price updating function, by np the new stock price per share at the end of the protocol and by k a security parameter. Finally, let us denote by $cert_i$ the time-stamped certificate eventually issued by S to client C_i at the end of the protocol. A *private stock purchase protocol* for function f and for n clients has to satisfy the following four requirements:

Correctness. If S and all clients $C_1, \ldots, C_n$ follow their protocol then with probability 1 at the end of the private stock purchase protocol the following holds: (1) $np = f((b_1, x_1, op_1), \ldots, (b_n, x_n, op_n))$, and (2) each client receives a certificate $cert_i$ containing its private input (b_i, x_i, op_i) and the new price np, which is verifiable to be valid by S.

Security against Clients. If S follows its protocol, then for all i and for all probabilistic polynomial time algorithms $C'_1, \ldots, C'_{i-1}, C'_{i+1}, \ldots, C'_n$, the probability that at the end of the private stock purchase protocol the client C_i does not output $cert_i$, a valid certificate associated with input (b_i, x_i, op_i) and new price np, is exponentially small (in k). Moreover, for any coalition of clients running in probabilistic polynomial time, the probability that at the end of the private stock purchase protocol, they are able to convince S to have a valid certificate $cert$ associated with an input different from all $(b_i, x_i, op_i), np$, for $i = 1, \ldots, n$, is negligible (in k).

Privacy against Clients. Let $i_1, \ldots, i_j \in \{1, \ldots, n\}$; if S follows its protocol, then for any probabilistic polynomial-time algorithms $C'_{i_1}, \ldots, C'_{i_j}$, the distribution of the view of such clients during an execution of the entire protocol is independent from the value of (b_i, x_i, op_i), for each $i \in \{1, \ldots, n\} \setminus \{i_1, \ldots, i_j\}$.

Privacy against the Server. Assume S follows its protocol; for any polynomial time strategy s_1 used by S at the end of the protocol, there exists a polynomial time strategy s_2 that can be used by S before the protocol starts, such that the probability that s_1 allows S to obtain some information about $(b_1, x_1, op_1), \ldots, (b_n, x_n, op_n)$ differs by the probability that s_2 allows S to do the same before the protocol only by a negligible (in k) amount, where both probabilities are conditioned by the fact that $np = f((b_1, x_1, op_1), \ldots, (b_n, x_n, op_n))$.

Remarks. We note that typically the first and the fourth phase of a private stock purchase protocol would require standard registration, certification and verification protocols to be executed, also varying according to non-cryptographic issues deriving from the specific application setting; instead, the second and third phases are supposed to contain the main cryptographic novelties of the protocol. We also note that private stock purchase protocols are very much related to private multi-party computation [27,14], for which no agreement on the 'right notions' of security or privacy has been reached yet, after several research efforts. Finding the 'right notions' of privacy and security for private stock purchase protocols is therefore beyond the scope of this work. Still, we believe that the above definition (following most principles in the current best definitions of private multi-party computation) describes a satisfactory notion of security and privacy for the application of interest in this paper and that the protocol that we present would essentially satisfy alternative notions, eventually claimed to be the 'right notion'. Let us point out however two main differences between the setting considered here and private multi-party computation. In terms of connectivity among the participants, here we only consider solutions in which the clients only talk to the server, and do not need to talk to each other. In terms of adversarial setting, here the server is assumed to be honest-but-curious (rather than being possibly malicious); moreover, we require and achieve security against arbitrary coalitions of up to all-but-one malicious clients (rather than only bounded-size coalitions). These differences are motivated by practical considerations and significantly differentiate our investigation from those in private multi-party computation. In particular, as a consequence, protocols given in the literature within the area of private multi-party computation do not solve the problems considered in this paper (and vice versa).

3.2   A High-Level View of Our Solution

As done for the definition, we describe our solution as divided into four phases: a registration phase, a price update phase, a capital update phase and a certification phase. Recall that we are describing a generic interval of the lifetime of the stock purchase protocol; therefore, we can assume that permanent information such as the current share price and the capital (or the number of available shares) are publicly available. Moreover, here and in the rest of the paper, for simplicity, we will assume that the parties are connected through private channels (that can be implemented, for instance, using a non-malleable encryption scheme).

Registration Phase. First of all the server publishes two public keys: one for an encryption scheme, and one for a signature scheme. Now, a client that wants to take part in the stock purchase protocol makes a commitment to its private input (representing the amount of shares to be bought or sold and the offered price for those) and sends this commitment to the server. Then the server signs such a commitment and sends the resulting signature to the client. Now, the client publishes his commitment, the signature received from the server, a public-key of an encryption scheme, and standard information such as his identity.

Implementation of this Phase. We require that the commitment by the client is implemented as an El-Gamal encryption of the input to be committed to (this choice is for efficiency and compatibility with the remaining protocols in the paper). No particular implementation is required for the signature scheme.

Price Update Phase. In this phase the server and all clients who successfully completed the previous phase run a protocol, called UPDATE, and described in Section 5, which has the following properties. At the end, the server obtains the value output by an evaluation of a known function over all private inputs of clients, (such value being the new share price) but no other information about all private inputs of the clients. Even for this protocol each client only interacts with the server and is also guaranteed that no coalition of malicious clients can receive any information about her private input. At the end of this phase, the server publishes the new share price.
Implementation of this Phase. We note that the efficiency of the implementation of this protocol may depend on how complicated the function for updating the share price is. In the particular case in which the function is linear (which is really an important case since it captures typical functions such as the average), we can use a simple extension of the protocol SUM also used in the following phase; the resulting implementation would therefore be efficient and constant-round. In order to cover the more general case of an arbitrary (and therefore, non-linear) function, in Section 5, we present an implementation for protocol UPDATE, by reducing the private computation of a function in this model to the private computation of a function in the two-party model (which is of independent interest). We note two attractive properties of our solution: it can be run in a constant number of rounds, and it reveals no information about function f to the clients (although we did not explicitly require this property in the definition of previous section, we believe it may still be an interesting property to achieve). The protocol UPDATE can be implemented under the assumption of the hardness of deciding the Diffie–Hellman problem (or, more generally, of the existence of any oblivious transfer).

Capital Update Phase. In this phase the server and all clients who successfully completed the previous two phases run a protocol, called PSUM, and described in Section 4, which has the following properties. At the end, the server obtains a partial sum of the private inputs of clients. Specifically, clients who intended to buy (resp., sell) shares contribute a positive (resp., negative) amount if their offered price was larger (resp., smaller) than the new price. In this protocol, each client only interacts with the server and is guaranteed that no additional information about her private input is revealed to the server or to any coalition of malicious clients (precisely, the server only obtains the partial sum of the share amounts and the other clients obtain no information at all). At the end of this phase, the server publishes the new capital (or amount of available shares).

Implementation of this Phase. In Section 4 we present an efficient and constant-round implementation for protocol PSUM, under the assumption of the hardness of deciding the Diffie–Hellman problem.

Certification Phase. In this phase the server only interacts with all clients who successfully completed the previous three phases and sends to each of them another signature of her commitment, of the new price, and of a special message indicating that she has completed her transaction.

Implementation of this Phase. No specific implementation for the signature scheme is required.

Properties of Our Protocol. Given the simplicity of the registration and certification phase, and the stated properties of subprotocols PSUM and UPDATE, it is not hard to verify that the protocol described in this section satisfies the definition of Section 3.

4   A Private Stock Purchase Protocol: Capital Update Phase

In this section we present the protocol that will be executed by the participants in the capital update phase. At the beginning of this phase each client C_i has already committed to her desired amount of shares to be sold and bought and to the offered price for each of those shares. Then the goal of this phase is to update the capital of stock shares, by transferring to the server S a partial sum of these committed amounts of shares. Specifically, each client who intended to buy (resp., sell) some amount of shares will contribute a positive (resp., negative) amount to the final sum if her offered price op_i was larger (resp., smaller) than the new price. The new capital is then obtained by the server by subtracting the final sum from the current capital.

More precisely, the protocol we would like to construct, called PSUM, is run by a server S and n clients $C_1, \ldots, C_n$, where each client C_i has, as private input, an integer x_i, that may be positive or negative (let $b_i = 1$ denote a negative sign for x_i and $b_i = 0$ denote a positive one) and an integer op_i. We require that at the end of the protocol S obtains a partial sum of the clients' committed amount of shares (i.e., the value $z = \sum_{i \in T}(-1)^{b_i} x_i$, where $T = \{i : ((b_i = 0) \land (op_i \geq np)) \lor ((b_i = 1) \land (op_i < np))\} \subseteq \{1, \ldots, n\}$). We also require that the server's view is independent on the values of the x_i's, given the value z of the final sum, and that each coalition of clients, no matter how it behaves, receives a view that is independent on the other clients' private inputs.

The description of this construction is divided as follows. First, in Section 4.1 we describe a zero-knowledge protocol for proving a sum-related statement on El-Gamal encryptions. Then, in Section 4.2 we show how to use this protocol in order to obtain protocols for proving more elaborated statements. In Section 4.3 a protocol for privately computing the sum of several El-Gamal encryption, thus solving a slightly simpler version of our problem. Finally, in Section 4.4 we extend the protocol of previous section to privately computing a partial sum, as defined above.

4.1   A Novel Zero-Knowledge Protocol

In this section we present a zero-knowledge protocol for the language EG-SUM, defined as follows. Given (p, q, g, h) such that $p = 2q + 1$, p, q are primes, g generates a subgroup of order q, and h is a member of this subgroup, the language EG-SUM is the set of tuples $((u_1, v_2), (u_2, v_2), (u, v))$ for which there exist r_1, r_2, r, m_1, m_2, m such that

1. $u_1 = g^{r_1} \bmod p$, $v_1 = h^{r_1} m_1 \bmod p$;
2. $u_2 = g^{r_2} \bmod p$, $v_2 = h^{r_2} m_2 \bmod p$;
3. $u = g^r \bmod p$, $v = h^r m \bmod p$, $m_1 + m_2 = m \bmod p$.

We now describe an efficient perfect zero-knowledge argument (A,B) for language EG-SUM, where the soundness property holds under the assumption that computing discrete logarithms is hard. The proof system is efficient in two ways: first, it does not require reductions of the statement to be proven to an NP-complete statement; second, the prover A, given values r_1, r_2, r, m_1, m_2, m, can run in probabilistic polynomial time.

An Informal Description. The zero-knowledge protocol we propose uses the cut-and-choose technique of [15,11]. A first idea in constructing our protocol is that of combining the linearity of the equation to be proved (namely, that $m_1 + m_2 = m \bmod p$) with the fact that the encryption function of the El-Gamal cryptosystem satisfies some (weak) sum-homomorphism property (specifically, if encryptions (u_1, v_1) of m_1 and (u_1, q_2) of d_1 are computed using the same randomness, then the pair $(u_1, v_1 + q_2 \bmod p)$ is an encryption of $(d_1 + m_1) \bmod p$). Using this idea alone, a (still incorrect) protocol could consist of showing that either the equality $d_1 + d_2 = d \bmod p$ holds, or the equality $(m_1 + d_1) + (m_2 + d_2) = (m + d) \bmod p$ holds, for random values d_1, d_2. This protocol reveals the randomness used to encrypt d_1, which is the same as that used to encrypt m_1, and therefore is not zero-knowledge. To solve this problem, we use the fact that the encryption function of the El-Gamal cryptosystem is product-homomorphic with respect to componentwise product modulo p, (specifically, given encryptions (u_1, v_1) of m_1 and (c, e) of a, then the pair $(cu_1 \bmod p, ev_1 \bmod p)$ is an encryption of $am_1 \bmod p$). Using this property, we can modify the protocol so that it consists of showing that either the equality $am_1 + am_2 = am \bmod p$ holds, or the equality $(am_1 + d_1) + (am_2 + d_2) = (am + d) \bmod p$ holds, where the encryptions of d_1, d_2, d have to be computed using the same randomness as the encryption of am_1, am_2, am, respectively. This modified protocol still does not work since all these encryptions, when sent by the prover to the verifier, would not be simultaneously secure. To solve this last problem, we hide the encryptions by committing to them using a non-interactive commitment protocol that is also sum-homomorphic (namely, given commitments com_1 of m_1 and com_2 of m_2, it is possible to efficiently compute a commitment com of m). An example of a commitment scheme that satisfies this property is the one in [20]; this scheme, in the honest-receiver version, can be implemented in one round of communication, is perfectly-secure (namely, not even a computationally-unbounded receiver can obtain any information about the committed value), and is computationally-binding (namely, assuming that computing discrete logarithms is hard, the committer can reveal the committed value in a unique way). Moreover, given commitments com_1 of m_1, com_2 of m_2, the value $com = com_1 \cdot com_2 \bmod p$ is a commitment to $m_1 + m_2 \bmod p$. In the description of our proof system, we will refer to this scheme as Pedersen's commitment scheme.

A More Formal Description. We proceed by first describing an atomic protocol (A,B), having soundness error 3/4.

1. A uniformly chooses $r'_1, r'_2, r', a, d_1, d_2, d \in Z_p$ such that $d_1 + d_2 = d \bmod p$;
   A computes the following El-Gamal-encryptions:
   > an encryption (u'_1, v'_1) of am_1 using $r'_1 + r_1$ as randomness;
   > an encryption (u'_2, v'_2) of am_2 using $r'_2 + r_2$ as randomness;
   > an encryption (u', v') of am using $r' + r$ as randomness;
   > an encryption (p_1, q_1) of d_1 using $r'_1 + r_1$ as randomness;
   > an encryption (p_2, q_2) of d_2 using $r'_2 + r_2$ as randomness;
   > an encryption (p, q) of d using $r' + r$ as randomness;

   A computes two commitments using Pedersen's commitment scheme: com_1 of $(u'_1, v'_1, u'_2, v'_2, u', v')$ and com_2 of $(p_1, q_1, p_2, q_2, p, q)$;
   A sends com_1, com_2 to B
2. B uniformly chooses $b \in \{1, 2, 3\}$ and sends it to A
3. If $b = 1$ then
   > A decommits com_1 as $(u'_1, v'_1, u'_2, v'_2, u', v')$ and sends r'_1, r'_2, r', a to B;
   > using the above, B checks that $(u'_1/u_1, v'_1/v_1), (u'_2/u_2, v'_2/v_2), (u'/u, v'/v)$ are all encryptions of a;

   if $b = 2$ then
   > A decommits com_2 as $(p_1, q_1, p_2, q_2, p, q)$ and sends $r_1 + r'_1, r_2 + r'_2, r + r'$;
   > using the above, B checks that com_2 is correctly decommitted, decrypts (p_1, q_1) as d_1, (p_2, q_2) as d_2, and (p, q) as d, and checks that $d_1 + d_2 = d \bmod p$;

   if $b = 3$ then
   > using com_1, com_2, A computes commitment com to $(u'_1 + p_1, v'_1 + q_1, u'_2 + p_2, v'_2 + q_2, u' + p, v' + q)$;
   > A decommits com as $(u'_1 + p_1, v'_1 + q_1, u'_2 + p_2, v'_2 + q_2, u' + p, v' + q)$;
   > A computes $z_1 = am_1 + b_1, z_2 = am_2 + b_2, z = am + b$ and sends $(z_1, z_2, z, 1 + r'_1, r_2 + r'_2, r + r')$ to B
   > B checks that com is correctly computed from com_1, com_2, that com is correctly decommitted, that $u'_1 + p_1$ is an encryption of z_1, $u'_2 + p_2$ is an encryption of z_2, $u' + p$ is an encryption of z, and that $z_1 + z_2 = z \bmod p$.
   > if at least one verification is not satisfied then B returns: REJECT else B returns: ACCEPT.

We now show that the above protocol satisfies the three properties of completeness, soundness and perfect zero-knowledge.

Completeness. Assume that the input is in the language; then, A, who is given r_1, r_2, r, m_1, m_2, m, can meet B's verifications with probability 1.

Soundness. Note that any tuple $((u_1, v_1), (u_2, v_2), (u, v))$ can be written as a triple of El-Gamal encryptions for some m_1, m_2, m. Therefore, if the input is not in the language it must happen that $m_1 + m_2 \neq m \bmod p$. Thus, let us assume that the latter inequality holds. As a consequence either (a) the inequality $(am_1 + d_1) + (am_2 + d_2) \neq (am + d) \bmod p$ holds, or (b) the inequality $d_1 + d_2 \neq d \bmod p$ holds, for any $a, d_1, d_2, d \in Z_p$. By the binding property of the Pedersen commitment scheme, we have that: in case (b), A cannot meet the question $b = 2$, and, in case (a), A cannot meet at least one of the questions $b = 1$ and $b = 3$. Therefore the probability that A can cheat is at most $2/3$ plus the probability that he can cheat in any of the decommitment, which is negligible (assuming the hardness of computing discrete logarithms); therefore, the overall probability that A can cheat is at most, say, $3/4$.

Perfect Zero-Knowledge. We construct a simulator S that, using a potentially dishonest verifier B', generates a transcript having distribution computationally indistinguishable from that of a transcript generated after a real execution of the protocol between A and B'. The algorithm S uses the usual trial-and-error strategy, with rewinding. Specifically, S randomly chooses $b' \in \{1, 2, 3\}$ and computed a simulated transcript assuming that the challenge b sent by B' is equal to b'; if yes, S outputs the computed transcript; if not, S rewinds B' and tries again. The computation of a simulated transcript for each value of b is done as follows. In the case $b = 1$ it is easy to efficiently simulate the second message from A and the commitment com_1; the commitment com_2 is simulated as a commitment to a random value of the same length. The case $b = 2$ is analogue to the case $b = 1$. In the case $b = 3$ it is easy to efficiently simulate the second message from A and the commitment com; the commitment com_1 is simulated as a commitment to a random value of the same length, and the commitment com_2 is computed as com/com_1. By using the perfect security property of Pedersen's commitment scheme we can show that the simulation is perfect.

Remark. We remark that the soundness error of the above protocol can be decreased to exponentially small by running several parallel repetitions of it, and then having the verifier commit to his random bits by using a discrete-log based information-theoretically secure commitment scheme (see, e.g., [2]) and give a 3-round witness-indistinguishable proof of knowledge of the discrete log of the message sent during the execution of Pedersen's commitment scheme. The resulting protocol is a perfect zero-knowledge argument for language EG-SUM that has exponentially small soundness error and can be implemented in a constant number of rounds.

4.2   More Zero-Knowledge Protocols

We show how to use the protocol in previous section to obtain zero-knowledge protocols for more elaborated statements, that will be used later, in the construction of our capital update protocol.

Linear Equalities over El-Gamal-Encrypted Values. We note that in the protocol in previous section, for simplicity, we have considered the case of the equality between a value and two addends. However, the same technique naturally extends to the case of n addends, for any n. More generally, the same technique can be used to give an efficient and constant-round perfect zero-knowledge argument for the language n-EG-LIN1, defined as follows. Given (p, q, g, h) such that $p = 2q + 1$, p, q are primes, g generates a subgroup of order q, and h is a member of this subgroup, the language n-EG-LIN1 is the set of tuples $((\alpha_1, u_1, v_1), \ldots, (\alpha_n, u_n, v_n), (\alpha, u, v))$ for which there exist $r_1, \ldots, r_n, r$ and $m_1, \ldots, m_n, m$ such that

1. $u_i = g^{r_i} \bmod p$, $v_i = h^{r_i} m_i \bmod p$, for $i = 1, \ldots, n$;
2. $u = g^r \bmod p$, $v = h^r m \bmod p$, $\alpha_1 m_1 + \ldots + \alpha_n m_n = \alpha m \bmod p$.

We also note that by combining this protocol with techniques in [8], we obtain a protocol for proving any monotone formula over membership statements to language n-EG-LIN1.

Linear Equalities with Unencrypted Known Term. In our main construction we will need a zero-knowledge protocol for a language similar to language n-EG-LIN1, the only difference being in that the known term of the linear equality is in clear (rather than encrypted). By simply encrypting the known term and revealing the randomness used to compute this encryption, one can use the same protocol, thus obtaining an efficient and constant-round perfect zero-knowledge argument for the language n-EG-LIN2, defined as follows. Given (p, q, g, h) such that $p = 2q + 1$, p, q are primes, g generates a subgroup of order q, and h is a member of this subgroup, the language n-EG-LIN2 is the set of tuples $((\alpha_1, u_1, v_1), \ldots, (\alpha_n, u_n, v_n), \alpha, m)$ for which there exist $r_1, \ldots, r_n, m_1, \ldots, m_n$ such that

1. $u_i = g^{r_i} \bmod p$, $v_i = h^{r_i} m_i \bmod p$, for $i = 1, \ldots, n$;
2. $\alpha_1 m_1 + \ldots + \alpha_n m_n = \alpha m \bmod p$.

Linear Equalities with Encryptions under Different Public Keys. Another variation over language n-EG-LIN1 that we will need in our main construction is that in which the addends in the linear equality are decryptions of El-Gamal ciphertexts computed according to different public keys (but using the same parameters; namely, the same prime p and generator g). A protocol for this variation can be obtained by using multiple applications of the protocol in Section 4.1, as follows. For each ciphertext c_i computed according to a different public key, the prover computes a ciphertext c_i' computed according to a single, fixed, public key, and sends c_i' to the verifier. Then the prover proves that the plaintext associated with c_i' and the plaintext associated with c_i are the same, for each i (note that this can be proved by using a simplified version of the protocol in Section 4.1). Finally, the prover proves that the linear equality holds by using all ciphertexts c_i' that are computed according to the same public key, and therefore she can use the protocol for language n-EG-LIN2. This gives an efficient and constant-round zero-knowledge protocol for language n-EG-LIN3, defined as the set of tuples $((\alpha_1, u_1, v_1, h_1), \ldots, (\alpha_n, u_n, v_n, h_n), (\alpha, u, v, h))$ for which there exist $r_1, \ldots, r_n, r, m_1, \ldots, m_n, m$ such that

1. $u_i = g^{r_i} \bmod p$, $v_i = h_i^{r_i} m_i \bmod p$, for $i = 1, \ldots, n$;
2. $u = g^r \bmod p$, $v = h^r m \bmod p$, $\alpha_1 m_1 + \ldots + \alpha_n m_n = \alpha m \bmod p$.

4.3 Privately Computing the Sum of Encrypted Values

In this section we describe a protocol for privately computing the sum of *all* share amounts committed by clients, regardless of whether their offered price was larger or smaller than the new stock price. We call this protocol SUM.

Description of Protocol SUM. Let p be a prime given by S to each of the clients, that is much larger than any of the x_i's (e.g., $|p| > 2n|x_i|$ for any i would suffice). Assume that at the beginning of the protocol each client C_i has published a public key pk_i generated using algorithm KG and an encryption c_i of private input (b_i, x_i, op_i), and let $y_i = (-1)^{b_i} x_i \bmod p$. Then protocol SUM goes as follows:

1. Each client C_i writes his input as $y_i = s_{i,1} + \cdots + s_{i,n} \bmod p$ for $s_{i,j}$'s chosen randomly in Z_p and such that the equality holds;
2. each client C_i encrypts each $s_{i,j}$ according to algorithm E and using the j-th client's public key, thus obtaining encryptions $c_{i,j}$, for $j = 1, \ldots, n$;
3. each client C_i sends all $c_{i,j}$ to S together with a zero-knowledge proof that the encryptions $c_{i,1}, \ldots, c_{i,n}$ have been correctly computed; that is, proving that $y_i = s_{i,1} + \cdots + s_{i,n} \bmod p$ (using the zero-knowledge protocol from Section 4.2 for language n-EG-LIN3);
4. for $i = 1, \ldots, n$, server S verifies the proof from client C_i; if this proof is rejected, client C_i is discarded and the computation continues with the remaining clients; if this proof is accepted, S sends all encryptions $c_{1,j}, \ldots, c_{n,j}$ to client C_j, for $j = 1, \ldots, n$;
5. for $j = 1, \ldots, n$, client C_j decrypts all encryptions $c_{1,j}, \ldots, c_{n,j}$ as $s_{1,j}, \ldots, s_{n,j}$ and sends $t_j = s_{1,j} + \cdots + s_{n,j} \bmod p$ to S along with a zero-knowledge proof that t_j has been correctly computed; that is, proving that $t_j = s_{1,j} + \cdots + s_{n,j} \bmod p$ (using the zero-knowledge protocol from Section 4.2 for language n-EG-LIN2);
6. for $j = 1, \ldots, n$, server S verifies the proof from client C_j; if this proof is rejected, client C_j is discarded and the computation continues with the remaining clients;
7. S computes *sum* as the sum modulo p of all t_j's corresponding to clients C_j which have not been discarded from the protocol. If $|sum| \leq |x_1|$ then S returns $(0, sum)$ else S returns $(1, p - sum)$.

Properties of Protocol SUM. We show that protocol SUM satisfies several properties, such as correctness, security against clients, privacy against clients and privacy against server (although we have not exactly defined such properties in this context, their semantic meaning is along the lines of the definition of private stock purchase protocols and will be made clearer in the following discussion). We also show that SUM can be implemented in a constant number of rounds.

Correctness. First of all we note that it is possible to implement protocol SUM, as described above, since it is possible to implement the zero-knowledge protocols in steps 3 and 5 because of the protocols proposed in Section 4.2. Moreover, we note that if all parties follow their protocol then the output of server S is exactly equal to the sum of the clients' private inputs.

Security against Clients. Here we consider the case of clients who may deviate from the protocol and try to compromise the server's final computation. We see from the construction of protocol SUM that clients always have to provide proofs of correctness of their computations to the server (specifically, in both step 3 and step 5), or they are discarded from the execution. Therefore, at the end of protocol SUM, the server is always able to compute the sum of the private inputs of the clients who have not been discarded.

Privacy against Clients. Here we consider the case of clients who may deviate from the protocol and try to obtain information from the other clients' private inputs. We see from the construction of protocol SUM that each private input of a client is shared among all the clients using an n-out-of-n secret sharing (implemented using sum modulo p of the n values) and therefore even a coalition of $n - 1$ values does not obtain any information at all (namely, even if clients are not computationally limited) from the values sent by the server in step 4.

Privacy against Server. Here we consider the question of whether the view of the server reveals any information at all about the client's private inputs (other than their sum). We see that in step 3 of protocol SUM the server only obtains encryptions of shares of the clients' private inputs, along with zero-knowledge proofs of correctness of the computation of such shares, and therefore, since the encryption scheme used is assumed to be semantically secure, no information is revealed to the server in this step. Then we note that in step 5 of protocol SUM the server only obtains values $t_1, \ldots, t_n$, along with a zero-knowledge proof of correctness of their computation, and we can see that the distribution of such values is that of n random values in Z_p such that their sum modulo p is equal to the sum of all the y_i's.

Round-Complexity. The number of rounds of protocol SUM is constant provided the zero-knowledge proofs in step 3 and 5 can both be executed in a constant number of rounds. This fact has been established already in Section 4.1.

4.4   Privately Computing the Partial Sum of Encrypted Values

In this section we show how to extend the protocol of previous section for privately computing a sum of values into computing a 'partial' sum of values. The resulting protocol can be directly used as a capital update protocol in our private stock purchase protocol.

More specifically, recall that we denote by (b_i, x_i, op_i) the private input to client C_i, where $b_i \in \{0, 1\}$ is the sign denoting whether C_i wants to buy or sell the share amount x_i and op_i is the offered price for each of these shares. Moreover, by np we denote the new share price computed at the end of the price updating phase. We note that the protocol SUM can be used by the server to privately compute the value $\sum_{i=1}^{n}(-1)^{b_i}x_i$; however, this value does not take into account the offered prices committed by the clients. In other words, in our capital update protocol, we would like the server to retrieve the sum of the x_i's only for those clients whose offered prices are valid (i.e., larger than the new price np if they are buying shares or smaller otherwise). Therefore, we need to modify the protocol SUM into a protocol for computing a partial sum; namely, a sum over all clients satisfying the above property (i.e., S will be able to compute $sum = \sum_{i \in T}(-1)^{b_i}x_i$, where $T = \{i : ((b_i = 0) \wedge (op_i \geq np)) \vee ((b_i = 1) \wedge (op_i < np))\} \subseteq \{1, \ldots, n\})$.

Our protocol PSUM uses as a tool a 'conditional oblivious transfer' [10]. More formally, this is a protocol used by S to transfer to client C_i one of two strings s_0, s_1 such that client C_i will obtain s_0 if $op_i \geq np$ or s_1 otherwise, without S learning any information about the value of op_i, including whether C_i received s_0 or s_1.

Description of Protocol PSUM. This protocol is executed between each client C_i and the server S. The basic idea of this protocol is that client C_i will create two ciphertexts, one with plaintext equal to 0 and one with plaintext equal to $-x_i$. Server S will help C_i select one of the two based on the inequality $op_i \geq np$ and on the value of b_i without obtaining any information about these, so that later C_i can contribute to the final sum ciphertexts with associated plaintexts $x_i, 0$ if his offered price if valid (namely, if $op_i \geq np$ and $b_i = 0$ or $op_i < np$ and $b_i = 1$) or ciphertexts with associated plaintexts $x_i, -x_i$ otherwise. Note that effectively client C_i is contributing to the final sum her share amount if her offered price is valid or zero otherwise. The actual protocol we describe below has some additional technical complication for two reasons: first, an El-Gamal encryption of 0 is not secure (therefore, we split it into two encryptions of values which sum up to 0); second, we need to protect the server from possible malicious behavior from the client.

We can assume that in the following description all encryptions and decryptions will be computed according to the El-Gamal public-key cryptosystems. Then the protocol PSUM goes as follows:

1. Client C_i uniformly chooses r_1, computes $z = -x_i - r_1 \bmod p$ and an encryption c_1 of z, and sends c_1, r_1 to S;

2. S uniformly chooses r_2, s_1, s_2, computes $r_3 = r_1 - r_2 \bmod p$, $s_3 = -s_1 - s_2 \bmod p$, encryptions d_j of s_j, for $j = 1, 2, 3$, and encryptions c_l of r_l, for $l = 2, 3$;

3. S transfers to C_i strings $a_0 = (c_1, c_2, c_3)$ and $a_1 = (d_1, d_2, d_3)$ using a conditional oblivious transfer based on the condition ($op_i \geq np$ AND $b_i = 0$) OR ($op_i < np$ AND $b_i = 1$).

4. let a_b, for some $b \in \{0, 1\}$, be the string obtained by C_i at the end of the execution of the conditional oblivious transfer subprotocol;

5. C_i decrypts the 3 ciphertexts in a_b, encrypts the obtained plaintexts using independently chosen random strings, thus obtaining triple $v = (e_1, e_2, e_3)$ and sends it to S;

6. S sends a_0, a_1 to C_i;

7. C_i sends to S a zero-knowledge proof that the plaintexts associated with v are either the same as the plaintexts associated with a_0 or the same as those associated with a_1;

8. all clients and S run the protocol SUM, where client C_i contributes to the final sum with the plaintexts associated with ciphertexts x_i, e_1, e_2, e_3.

5   A Private Stock Purchase Protocol: Price Update Phase

In this section we present the protocol that will be executed by the participants in the price update phase. We consider the sufficiently general case in which the next share price can be a function of the previous share price and of the private inputs of the clients in the most recent time interval.

Specifically, the protocol we would like to construct, called UPDATE, is run by a server S and n clients $C_1, \ldots, C_n$, where each client C_i has, as private input, an integer x_i, that may be positive or negative (let $b_i = 1$ denote a negative sign for x_i and $b_i = 0$ denote a positive one). Both S and the clients have the description of a circuit computing function f as a common input. We require that at the end of the protocol S obtains the output of an application of function f over the clients' private inputs (i.e., the value $z = f((b_1, x_1), \ldots, (b_n, x_n)))$; that the server's view is independent on the values of the clients' inputs, given that z is the output of function f over those, and that each coalition of clients, no matter how it behaves, receives a view that is independent on the other clients' private inputs. We note that if f is a linear function of the x_i's, then protocol UPDATE can be constructed by performing minor modifications to the protocol PSUM in Section 4. This would give a very efficient construction for the entire private stock purchase protocol. In the rest of this section, we deal with the case f is an arbitrary (and thus possibly non-linear) function. In achieving generality, our construction loses the attractive efficiency properties of protocol PSUM; in particular, our protocol builds over a general protocol for 2-party secure computation [27].

The description of this construction is divided as follows. First, in Section 5.1 we recall a protocol for 2-party secure computation [27,6] and then in Section 5.2 we show how to adapt this scheme to our model.

5.1   A 2-Party Secure Computation Protocol

The problem of 2-party secure computation, first considered by Yao in the influential paper [27], asks whether two parties Alice and Bob, having private inputs x and y, respectively, can compute a value $z = f(x, y)$, for some public function f, without revealing any additional information about their private input. Recently, other protocols have been proposed (e.g., [25,6]); here we recall an abstracted version of the protocol in [6], which makes our construction easier to describe.

The 2-Party Secure Protocol in [6]. We describe the case in which both Alice and Bob are honest since the case in which both can be malicious is dealt with using well-known techniques from [14] (i.e., by compiling the honest case with each party proving in zero-knowledge that the messages she is sending have been correctly computed according to the protocol's instructions). The honest version of this protocol combines Yao's construction [27] with oblivious transfer. Yao's construction consists of three procedures: an algorithm C that Bob uses to construct an encrypted circuit, an interactive protocol T between Alice and Bob, and an algorithm E that Bob uses to evaluate $f(x, y)$. More precisely, algorithm C outputs an encrypted version of function $f(\cdot, y)$, including a pair of k-bit strings for each input bit x_i. In order to compute $f(x, y)$, one of these two k-bit string is necessary for each bit x_i of x (which one of the two strings it depends on the value of x_i). In [6] oblivious transfer is used by Bob to transfer to Alice the appropriate k-bit string according to the value of x_i, without Bob revealing to Alice any information on the other string and without Alice revealing to Bob any information on the value of x_i. The rest of the computation proceeds as in Yao's protocol and will stay unchanged in our protocol as well. The oblivious transfer protocol used by Bob to Alice could be the one given in Section 2, or even an abstraction of it, as we now describe. We can consider an oblivious transfer as the following protocol between a sender and a receiver. The receiver publishes two channels such that he can read messages received over only one of them, but the sender cannot tell which one; then the sender sends each of the two messages through each of the channels.

5.2   The Adaptation to Our Setting

We now consider the possibility of adapting the protocol in [6,27] to our setting. Recall that from a communication standpoint, in our setting we would like clients not to talk to each other and that the server is assumed to behave honestly. Moreover, clients want their inputs to be private not only against the server but also against any coalition of other possibly malicious clients.

Description. We now describe the intuitions behind our adaptation. If we could consider all clients together as a single participant Alice and the server as participant Bob, then any 2-party secure protocol would be enough since Bob does not obtain any information about Alice's private input, and in the end Bob obtains the output of the function of Alice's input. However, the setting at hand is more complicated since Alice's input is in fact distributed among the various clients, who should not communicate. One fix to the lack of communication is to ask help from the server; indeed, since the server is honest, he might as well help the clients share their private inputs somehow. Even sharing the private inputs has to be done carefully, since the privacy requirements that our protocol has to satisfy ask that each client keeps her input private even if all other clients behave maliciously. In our solution we have each client send to all other clients, through the server, some information which is enough to allow other clients to play as Alice but still does not reveal any information about all other client's inputs. Specifically, using the oblivious transfer abstraction at the end of Section 5.1, they will send a channel that is readable (without sending the other, unreadable channel); therefore, the other client will not be able to understand which private bit this channel is associated with, but she will still be able to use it to run the oblivious transfer protocol. Finally, an execution of the 2-party protocol has to be executed for each client, and at the end the server checks that all outputs received by these executions are the same. We note that each of these executions can be run in parallel and therefore the resulting protocol can still be executed in a constant number of rounds. The correctness, security and privacy properties follow from the related properties of the 2-party protocol.

Acknowledgments

Remarks from Bob Hettinga and Ronald Rivest helped in further generalizing the real-life setting captured by our solution.

References

1. M. Bellare and S. Micali, *A Non-Interactive Oblivious Transfer Protocol and its Applications*, in Proceedings of "Advances in Cryptology – CRYPTO'88", Lecture Notes in Computer Science, Springer Verlag.
2. M. Bellare, S. Micali, and R. Ostrovsky, *Perfect Zero-Knowledge in Constant Rounds*, in Proceedings of 22th Annual ACM Symposium on Theory of Computing (STOC'90).
3. G. Brassard, C. Crépeau, and D. Chaum, *Minimum Disclosure Proofs of Knowledge*, Journal of Computer and System Sciences, vol. 37, no. 2, 1988, pp. 156–189.
4. C. Cauchin, *Efficient Private Bidding and Auctions with an Oblivious Third Party*, in Proc. of ACM Conference on Computers, Communications and Security, 1999, Springer Verlag.
5. C. Crépeau, *Equivalence between Two Flavors of Oblivious Transfer*, in Proceedings of "Advances in Cryptology – CRYPTO'87", Lecture Notes in Computer Science, Springer Verlag.
6. C. Cachin, J. Camenish, J. Kilian, and J. Muller, *One-Round Secure Computation and Secure Autonomous Agents*, in Proceedings of ICALP 2000, Springer Verlag.
7. A. De Santis, Y. Desmedt, Y. Frankel, and M. Yung, *How to Share a Function Securely,* in Proceedings of 26th Annual ACM Symposium on Theory of Computing (STOC'87).

8. A. De Santis, G. Di Crescenzo, G. Persiano, and M. Yung, *On Monotone Formula Closure of SZK*, in Proceedings of 35th Annual IEEE Symposium on Foundations of Computer Science (FOCS'94).

9. G. Di Crescenzo, *Private Selective Payment Protocols*, in Proceedings of Financial Cryptography 2000, Springer Verlag.

10. G. Di Crescenzo, R. Ostrovsky, and S. Rajagopalan, *Conditional Oblivious Transfer and Timed-Release Encryption*, in Proceedings of "Advances in Cryptology – EUROCRYPT'99", Lecture Notes in Computer Science, Springer Verlag.

11. U. Feige, A. Fiat, and A. Shamir, *Zero-Knowledge Proofs of Identity*, in Journal of Cryptology, vol. 1, n. 2, pp. 77–94, 1988.

12. T. El Gamal, *A Public key Cryptosystem abd a Signature scheme based on Discrete Logarythms*, in Proceedings of "Advances in Cryptology – CRYPTO'84", Lecture Notes in Computer Science, Springer Verlag.

13. M. Franklin and M. Reiter, *The Desing and Implementation of a Secure Auction Service*, in IEEE Transactions on Software Engineering, vol. 22, n. 5, pp. 302–312, 1996.

14. O. Goldreich, S. Micali, and A. Wigderson, *How to Play any Mental Game*, in Proceedings of 19th Annual ACM Symposium on Theory of Computing (STOC'87).

15. S. Goldwasser, S. Micali, and C. Rackoff, *The Knowledge Complexity of Interactive Proof-Systems*, in SIAM Journal on Computing, vol. 18, n. 1, 1989.

16. M. Harkavy, D. Tygar and H. Kikuchi, *Electronic Auctions with Private Bids*, in Proceedings of 3rd USENIX Workshop on Electronic Commerce, 1998.

17. M. Jakobsson and A. Juels, *Addition of El-Gamal Plaintexts*, in Proceedings of "Advances in Cryptology – ASIACRYPT 2000", Lecture Notes in Computer Science, Springer Verlag.

18. P. MacKenzie and J. Sorensen, *Anonymous Investing: Hiding the Identities of Stockholders*, in Proceedings of Financial Cryptography 1999, Springer Verlag.

19. M. Naor and B. Pinkas, *Efficient Oblivious Transfer Protocols*, in Proceedings of the 12th ACM-SIAM Symposium on Discrete Algorithms (SODA 2001).

20. T. Pedersen, *Non-Interactive and Information-Theoretic Secure Verifiable Secret Sharing*, in Proceedings of "Advances in Cryptology – CRYPTO'91", Lecture Notes in Computer Science, Springer Verlag.

21. M. Rabin, *How to Exchange Secrets by Oblivious Transfer*, TR-81 Aiken Computation Laboratory, Harvard, 1981.

22. A. Shamir, *How to Share a Secret*, in Communications of the ACM, vol. 22, pp. 612–613, 1979.

23. K. Sako, *An Auction Protocol Which Hides Bids of Losers*, in Proceedings of Public-Key Cryptography 2000, Springer Verlag.

24. K. Sakurai and S. Miyazaki, *A Bulletin-Board based Digital Auction Scheme with Bidding Down Strategy*, in Proceedings of 1999 International Workshop on Cryptographic Techniques and E-Commerce.

25. T. Sander, A. Young, and M. Yung, *Cryptocomputing in NC^1*, in Proceedings of 40th Annual IEEE Symposium on Foundations of Computer Science (FOCS'99).

26. S. Stubblebine and P. Syverson, *Fair on-line Auctions without Special Trusted Parties*, in Proceedings of Financial Cryptography 1999, Springer Verlag.

27. A.C. Yao, *Protocols for Secure Computations*, in Proceedings of 23th Annual IEEE Symposium on Foundations of Computer Science (FOCS'82).

Secure Distributed Computing
in a Commercial Environment

Philippe Golle[1]* and Stuart Stubblebine[2]

[1] Department of Computer Science, Stanford University
Stanford, CA 94305, USA
pgolle@cs.stanford.edu
[2] CertCo, 55 Broad St. - Suite 22
New York, NY 10004, USA
stuart@stubblebine.com

Abstract. The recent successes of a number of nonprofit computing projects distributed over the Internet has generated intense interest in the potential commercial applications of distributed computing. In a commercial setting, where participants might be paid for their contributions, it is crucial to define a security framework to address the threat of cheating and offer guarantees that the computation has been correctly executed. This paper defines and analyzes such a security framework predicated on the assumption that participants are motivated by financial gain. We propose a scheme which deters participants from claiming credit for work they have not done, and puts a high cost on attempts to disrupt the computation. We achieve these two goals by integrating an algorithm to assign computations to participants, an algorithm to verify their work, and an algorithm to pay participants.
Keywords: Distributed computing.

1 Introduction

The Internet has created the possibility of cooperative computing on an unprecedented scale. Connected computers everywhere may join forces to execute in parallel tasks so computationally expensive that they were once reserved for supercomputers.

Several projects have demonstrated with success the spectacular power of distributing computations over the Internet. For example, the Search for Extra-Terrestrial Intelligence project (SETI@home) [SETI], which distributes to thousands of users the task of analyzing radio transmissions from space, has achieved a collective performance of tens of teraflops. Another Internet computation, the GIMPS project directed by Entropia.com, has discovered world-record prime numbers.

Participation in these computations has so far been limited to volunteers who support a particular project. But with the rapid growth of distributed computing applications, there is intense commercial interest in recruiting a lot more

---

* Supported by Stanford Graduate Fellowship.

P. Syverson (Ed.): FC 2001, LNCS 2339, pp. 289–304, 2002.

Internet users. Harnessed and marketed, the idle computer time of 25 million AOL users, for example, has the potential to generate tremendous profit. There are already a dozen companies [DC00] which have begun recruiting participants for the next generation of distributed applications. A sample of these applications includes those to accelerate anti-HIV drug design research, simulate protein folding, design and manufacture robotic lifeforms, produce digital entertainment, and simulate economic models.

Nevertheless, a major obstacle to the widespread growth of commercial distributed computing is the absence of a security framework to verify the correctness of the computation. Today, the results of computations are mostly taken on faith. Bob Metcalfe, the inventor of ethernet said, "...people with serious computations are not likely to trust results coming from unreliable machines owned by total strangers" [R00].

This paper begins to address the difficult issues of security and reliability in a commercial distributed environment. We define two security goals: preventing participants motivated by financial gain from claiming credit for work they have not done, and raising the cost of attempts by malicious participants to disrupt the computation. We propose a high-level infrastructure for administering distributed computations in a way that deters and detects cheating. Our approach is based on integrating an algorithm for assigning tasks to participants, an algorithm for checking their work, and a payment scheme.

The building block of our security schemes is the ability to verify the result of a computation. Much work has been devoted to that goal in a variety of contexts, with an emphasis on making the verification process general and efficient. While our security schemes build on these results, our focus is different. Rather than considering verification at the level of individual computations, we propose a high-level infrastructure for administering distributed computations. We assume the existence of an algorithm for double-checking computations, and study how best to integrate verification into the general organization of a distributed computation.

In the rest of this section, we start by reviewing related work. Section 2 presents our security framework. In section 3, we introduce our basic scheme for running secure distributed computations. In section 4 and 5, we discuss variants of our scheme. The first variant addresses the issue of accommodating participants with varying computational resources. The second variant improves on the computational overhead of the basic scheme. We conclude in section 6.

1.1 Related Work

We start with a brief survey of results on verifying computations. We will then review proposals on how to integrate the verification primitives into distributed computations.

A general method to detect faulty execution is to incorporate a checksum in the program, and execute the computation redundantly. If independent executions fail to produce the same checksum, a majority vote determines the correct result. Ideally, checksums capture the whole execution of the computation and detect any accidental error with high probability. See [MWR99] for an example of secure checksums for general Java programs.

For specific applications, it is possible to design checksums with a shortcut for verification. Once produced, such checksums can be verified much more efficiently than by doing the computation all over again. Program checkers [BW97,BK89], proofs of work [GM00,JJ99] or uncheatable benchmarks [CLSY93] propose efficient checksums for specific arithmetic applications, such as factoring or repeated modular squarings. It is not known how to design efficient checksums for general computations.

To guard against malicious errors, checksums may be combined with cryptographic tools. Digital signatures guarantee the integrity of checksums, assuming it is impossible to analyze the code of the computation to recover the secret signing key. Thus, security against a malicious computing environment relies on the impossibility to reverse-engineer the computation code to find the key.

Computation on encrypted functions provides one way of hiding the code from the participant. Yao proved in [Y82] that any function may be computed with an encrypted circuit, which leaks no information about what is being computed, but encrypted circuits are too large for practical use. For restricted classes of functions [F85], computing on encrypted data has been shown to be practical. Code obfuscation is another approach to protect code from prying eyes. It is an assortment of ad-hoc techniques to produce garbled assembly code. Given the existence of efficient decompilation techniques, it provides short-lived security at best. Hohl proposes in [H97] the use of dynamic code obfuscation in conjunction with time restrictions.

We turn now to the problem of integrating the verification primitive into a distributed computation scheme to make it secure. An idea common to many schemes is to spot-check computations at random (see for example [GM00]). A very complete framework for spot-checking arbitrary computation in the Java environment is described in [MWR99]. [MRS93] proposes a scheme based on replication and voting to achieve fault-tolerance in the setting of mobile agents. The use of quorum systems has been proposed for the related problem of improving the efficiency and availability of data access while still protecting the integrity of replicated data.

Like these schemes, our approach is based on spot-checking work at random, but our focus is specifically to tie the verification algorithm with the algorithm for assigning tasks and the payment scheme.

2   Basic Framework

The supervisor of a distributed effort maintains a pool of registered participants, who are willing to run computations for the supervisor. Participants may range from large companies offering idle computer time at night to individual users with a single machine. The supervisor advertises the computational power under her control, and bids for large computations. Computations are divided into smaller tasks, each of which is assigned to one or possibly several participants. Participants execute the tasks independently and return the results to the supervisor. The supervisor compares the results for consistency, distributes payment where it is due and announces the result of the whole computation when it becomes available. Formally, we define a scheme for organizing distributed computations as follows.

Definition 1. *A scheme for organizing distributed computations consists of:*

- *A protocol to register new participants.*
- *A probabilistic algorithm S for assigning tasks to participants. Given a task T, the algorithm S specifies the set $S(T)$ of (one or more) participants to whom T should be assigned.*
- *A payment scheme to reward participants. It is defined by a payment function H which specifies how much a participant should be paid for executing a task.*
- *A protocol to take leave of participants who do not wish to be considered for future computations.*

In the registration step, participants signal their willingness to contribute to distributed computations. In keeping with the state of things on the Internet, we assume that participants do not necessarily reveal their physical identity to the supervisor. An entity may register an arbitrary number of distinct participants with the supervisor, and the supervisor can not track participants to the real world. Consequently, the supervisor's leverage over participants is limited to withholding payment. It is impossible for example to take legal action against a participant who failed to do the work, or who returned an incorrect result.

We assume that all the tasks distributed by the supervisor take approximately the same time to execute (say, one day) and are verifiable. A task T is verifiable if there exists a task T' such that the output of T' indicates with high probability whether T was executed correctly or not. We have presented in the section on related work various techniques for verifying tasks. See for example [MWR99] for a very general technique. From here onwards, we will ignore this issue and make the assumption that $T = T'$. In effect, we assume that if a task produces the same output in two independent runs, it was executed both times correctly. Observe that if randomized tasks are to be included in this model, participants must agree on a random-number generator and use the same seeds.

We also assume for simplicity that all participants are equally capable of handling any task, and of returning the result to the supervisor within the same time bounds (say, every day). This is not to say that all participants have the same computational resources. Faster participants will process more tasks within one period, but all participants will return their results by the end of the period. This model reflects reality: processor speeds are roughly comparable across computers, but some participants have many more computers at their disposal than others.

A participant may choose to take a temporary leave from the computation, for example during the week-end or a vacation. But while executing a task for the supervisor, the common rate of computation must be met and results returned by the deadline, under penalty of expulsion from the computation.

The computation proceeds as follows. Let us write $T_t(J)$ for the ordered set of tasks assigned to participant J at time t. A participant J unqueues one or more tasks from $T_t(J)$ at time t, executes them, and returns the result at time $t + 1$. For the purposes of this discussion we assume it is safe for participants to observe and execute problem instances they are assigned.

Meanwhile, as new tasks are received, the supervisor assigns them to participants according to the algorithm S. A new task T is queued to the sets $T_t(J)$ for all $J \in S(T)$. The set $S(T)$ is only known to the supervisor, so that participants do not know whether the tasks they are assigned have also been assigned to someone else. The supervisor keeps track of who performs what computations. If a participant is caught cheating, the past computations of that participant, as well as dependent computations, can be rerun.

After returning a result, a participant may start executing a new task or take a leave. If participant J takes a leave at time t, all the tasks in $T_t(J)$ are redistributed among active participants as if they were new tasks, taking care however never to re-assign a task to a participant to whom it has already been assigned.

2.1   Security Framework

We study the interaction between the supervisor and the participants in game-theoretical terms. The supervisor assigns each task to one or several participants according to the probabilistic algorithm S. We assume that the algorithm S is public and known to all participants. The supervisor is trusted not to collude with participants and to distribute payment where it is due.

A participant can either cooperate with the supervisor and execute the computation correctly, or defect and return an incorrect result. In this paper, we assume that all errors are malicious and do not consider the possibility of errors for which the participant may not be responsible (hardware or software failures). A simple variant of our results would allow participants to return occasional incorrect results.

An adversary may control a potentially large number of distinct participants without the supervisor's knowledge, but me make the important assumption that such alliances can only be created before a task is assigned. Once a task is assigned, we assume that is is impossible for an adversary to find and corrupt the other participants to whom the same task was assigned. We justify this assumption as follows. In the limited time available, a low-scale effort to find the participants to whom a particular task has been assigned is bound to fail, while a large-scale effort would not go unnoticed and could be punished.

The following variables define the utility function of a participant:

- **Payment received per task:** $H(J)$. This is the amount paid by the supervisor to participant J for a task not known to have been incorrectly executed. Observe that the function H is independent of the task executed, since we assume that all tasks require the same computational effort.

- **Utility of (successfully) defecting: E.** The variable E is the utility of corrupting a computation. For example, E might be the reward paid by an adversary to disrupt the computation of a competitor.
- **Cost of getting caught defecting: L.** This is the loss incurred by a participant when the defection is detected by the supervisor. The cost L reflects the resulting punishment, in terms of payment being withheld by the supervisor for example.

With these variables, we can compute the expected utility of cooperating and the expected utility of defecting for a participant. Let us write P for the probability that cheating is *undetected* by the supervisor.

$$E[\text{Cooperating}] = H$$
$$E[\text{Defecting}] = (H + E) \cdot P - L \cdot (1 - P)$$

In accordance with standard economic theory, we assume that all participants are rational and either risk-averse or risk-neutral, but not risk-seeking. Let us recall that for a non-risk-seeking agent, the utility function of money is concave. Consequently, given two options with the same expected outcome, a non-risk-seeking participant will always choose the option with the smallest standard deviation.

Definition 2. Secure Computations. *A computation is perfectly secure if no rational risk-neutral or risk-averse participant ever cheats.*

Proposition 1. *A computation is perfectly secure if for every participant involved $E[\text{Defecting}] \leq 0$.*

Proof. Recall the important assumption that participants are given the freedom to take a leave from the computation at any time. The optimal strategy for a non-risk-seeking participant is to execute the highest-paying task for which $E[\text{Cooperating}] \geq E[\text{Defecting}]$, defect for all tasks for which $E[\text{defecting}] \geq 0$, and not take part in any other computation. Therefore to ensure that no rational participant ever defects, it is enough to guarantee that $E[\text{Defecting}] \leq 0$.   □

3   Probabilistic Redundant Execution

We describe in this section our basic scheme with perfect security. New participants are required to execute a few tasks for free before being allowed to register. These tasks serve both as a barrier against frivolous registrations and as a "computational" deposit with the supervisor. This deposit will be forfeited in the event that cheating is detected. A participant who signals his intention to leave the computation is paid some amount to compensate for the tasks executed for free prior to registration.

Our approach to deterring cheating is to double-check some tasks with some probability and to ban from all future computations any participant who is caught returning an incorrect result. Being banned is a loss for a participant, regardless of whether that participant intended to take part in future computations. Indeed, a participant who wanted to take part in more computations would have to go through the registration phase again. As for participants who did not wish to be considered for future computations, they have forfeited the amount that the supervisor would have returned to them had they left the computation honestly.

Let us now describe our scheme in detail. For simplicity, we start here with the assumption that all participants have the same computational resources. We will discuss in the next section how to adapt our scheme to participants of varying computational resources. The supervisor organizes the distributed computation as follows:

- **Registration.** In the registration step, a participant is asked to run $d+1 \geq 2$ unpaid tasks. The results of these tasks is known to the supervisor. The participant is allowed to register only if all $d+1$ tasks were executed correctly.
- **Probability distribution of assignments Q:** A task T is distributed to n distinct participants where the number n is chosen at random according to the probability distribution Q. The probability distribution Q is central to our scheme. We will compare in the next two sections several possible choices for the function Q.
- **Payment function:** The payment function is a constant amount α per task. Participants are free to withdraw the money they have earned at any time.
- **Severance.** A participant who notifies the supervisor of his desire to leave the computation is paid an amount $d\alpha$.

Definition 3. Probabilistic Redundant Execution.

Given a task T to execute, the supervisor draws a random number n from the probability distribution Q. The supervisor chooses n distinct participants uniformly at random from among the pool and assigns each to the task T. At the end of the computation, the supervisor collects the results and compares them for validity. A participant who fails to return a result by the deadline is banned from future computations.

If all the results agree, they determine the correct output of the task. (If the task T was assigned to a single participant, it is assumed to have been executed correctly.) Each participant is paid an amount α.

In the event that not all the results agree, or that some results were not returned by the deadline, the supervisor re-assigns the task to n' new participants where n' is drawn at random from the probability distribution Q. Should this second round also fail to produce an agreement, the task is assigned again until an agreement emerges. At that time, all participants who produced the correct result are paid, while all the others are banned from future computations.

According to Proposition 1, this scheme is perfectly secure if:

$$E[\text{Defecting}] = (H + E) \cdot P - L \cdot (1 - P) \leq 0$$

where P is the probability that cheating is *undetected*, $H = \alpha$ is the amount that a participant gets paid for running the task correctly, and $L > 0$ is the loss incurred if cheating is detected. For participants who intend to be considered for future computations, L is the cost of re-registering: $L = (d+1)\alpha$. For participants who do not intend to be considered for future computations, L is the amount forfeited by being ejected from the computation: $L = d\alpha$. Thus in either case, $L \geq d\alpha$. Let us define the ration $e = E/\alpha$. We can rewrite the condition for perfect security as:

$$P \leq \frac{d}{1+e+d}$$

The choice of P involves a trade-off between security and computational overhead. The more participants a task is assigned to, the smaller the probability P that cheating goes undetected, but also the higher the computational overhead. To get the lowest possible computational overhead, the supervisor should choose the largest value P for which the security condition above holds. In the following two sections, we study how P is affected by the choice of the probability distribution Q.

3.1   Exponentially Decreasing Q

Recall that the function Q is the probability distribution according to which the supervisor chooses the number of participants to whom a task is assigned. We study in this section the properties of our scheme when $Q = Q_c$ for one of the probability distributions Q_c defined as follows:

$$Q_c[n = i] = (1 - c) \cdot c^{i-1} \text{ for all } i \geq 1$$

This is an exponentially decreasing probability distribution of coefficient $0 < c < 1$. The factor $(1-c)$ is a normalization term to ensure that the probabilities sum to 1.

Proposition 2. *Let us write p for the maximum fraction of all participants under the control of a single adversary. We have $0 < p < 1$. The scheme is perfectly secure as long as $(1 - c(1 - p))^2 \leq (1 - p)\frac{d}{1+e+d}$.*

Proposition 3. *When the scheme is perfectly secure, its average computational cost is $\frac{1}{1-c}$, and thus the average computational overhead is $\frac{c}{1-c}$.*

Proof. If the scheme is perfectly secure and all the participants are rational, cheating never occurs. Thus, there is never a need to redistribute a task. Given the probability distribution $Q_c[n = i] = (1 - c) \cdot c^{i-1}$ for $i \geq 1$, it follows that the computational cost is $\sum_{i=1}^{\infty} i(1-c)c^{i-1} = (1 - c)\sum_{j=1}^{\infty}\sum_{i=j}^{\infty} c^{i-1} = \frac{1}{1-c}$ $\square$

Corollary 1. *Asymptotically, the computational overhead of this scheme grows like $\sqrt{1 + e/d}$, for small enough values of p.*

The corollary follows directly from Proposition 2 and 3. Before proving proposition 2, let us consider a few numerical examples. The table below summarizes the characteristics of our scheme for different values of the parameters. Observe that our scheme remains very efficient as the maximum coalition size p increases. As expected, the computational overhead grows with the square root of the ratio e/d. The computational overhead becomes quite significant for large values of e/d. This comes as no surprise: the only way to defend against an adversary willing to pay much more to disrupt the computation than the supervisor is paying for correct execution, is to distribute the tasks to a large number of participants. Only the near certainty that cheating will be detected can redress the imbalance between what participants are offered to defect and what they are offered to cooperate.

Computational Overhead (c)	Max coalition size (p)	Ratio e/d
10%	1%	0.1
17%	10%	0.1
46%	1%	1
243%	1%	10

Proof. (Proposition 2)
Consider an adversary who controls a fraction $0 < p < 1$ of the total number of active participants, and has been assigned the same computation k times through various of these participants. We denote this event E.

Let us now compute P. Let P' denote the probability that cheating is not detected during a particular round (recall that the task may be distributed multiple times if the results returned after the first round do not all agree). Then

$$P \le \frac{P'}{1 - p(1 - P')}$$

Let us compute P'. Recall that n denotes the total number of times that the task has been assigned.

$$P' = \Pr[n = k|E]$$
$$= \frac{\Pr[E|n = k] \Pr[n = k]}{\Pr[E]}$$

Now $\Pr[E|n = k] = p^k$ and

$$\Pr[E] = \sum_{i=k}^{\infty} p^k (1 - p)^{i-k} \binom{i}{k} \Pr[n = i]$$

Since $\Pr[n = i] = (1 - c)c^{i-1}$, we get after simplification:

$$P = \frac{c^k (1 - p)^k}{\sum_{i=k}^{\infty} c^i (1 - p)^i \binom{i}{k}}$$

Let us define the function

$$I_k = \sum_{i=k}^{\infty} c^i (1-p)^i \binom{i}{k}$$

It follows easily from the equality $\binom{i}{k} + \binom{i}{k+1} = \binom{i+1}{k+1}$ that

$$I_k = I_{k+1}\left(\frac{1}{c(1-p)} - 1\right)$$

And $I_0 = 1/(1 - c(1-p))$. It follows that

$$P' = (1 - c(1-p))^{k+1}$$

And thus $P \le \frac{(1-c(1-p))^2}{1-p}$ for all $k \ge 1$. It follows that the scheme is perfectly secure as long as $(1 - c(1-p))^2 \le (1-p)\frac{d}{1+e+d}$. □

3.2   Another Definition of Q

We study here another family of distributions Q for the number of participants to whom a task is assigned. We wish to increase the minimal number of participants to whom a task may be assigned. As before, the functions Q are exponentially decreasing with parameter c, but we now also require Q to assign each task to at least s distinct participants. The new family of probability distributions is defined as follows:

$$Q_{c,s}[n = i] = (1-c) \cdot c^{i-s} \text{ for all } i \ge s$$
$$Q_{c,s}[n = i] = 0 \text{ for } i < s$$

Proposition 4. *Using the probability distribution $Q_{c,s}$, the scheme of section 3 (Probabilistic Redundant Execution) is perfectly secure as long as:*
$(1 - c(1-p))^{s+1} \le (1-p)\frac{d}{1+e+d}$.

Proposition 5. *When this scheme is perfectly secure, its average computational overhead is $s - 2 + \sqrt[s+1]{1 + e/d}$.*

The proofs of propositions 4 and 5 are omitted, as they are similar to the proofs of propositions 2 and 3 respectively. The family of functions $Q_{c,s}$ results in lower computational overhead for large values of the ratio e/d. Since each task is assigned to a minimum of s distinct participants, we have to pay upfront a computational overhead of s, but asymptotically the computational overhead grows like the $s + 1$ root of e/d.

Observe that the definitions of Q analyzed in this section and the previous one are by no means the only possible. We could investigate yet other distributions. However, as we will see in section 5, the most computationally efficient schemes come from another approach: defining the function Q dynamically.

4   Participants with Varying Computational Resources

We have assumed in the previous section that all participants have the same resources to contribute to the distributed computation. This assumption is not only unrealistic, but also introduces the following threat. Consider an adversary with little computational power, who is bent on disrupting one particular computation (for example, that of a competitor). That adversary might register a very large number of inactive participants, which she would activate just before the target computation is distributed. In effect, it is possible for our adversary to briefly control a number of participants which is out of proportions with her real computational power, and inflict damage on targeted computations at little cost.

We address this issue in this section. We introduce the activity, a measure of the relative throughput of each participant compared to others. Based on this measure, we modify the assignment algorithm to enable faster participants to process more tasks than slower ones. We also counter the threat we have just described by allowing only gradual increases in activity.

The activity A_t is a probability distribution over the pool of participants, which evolves dynamically over time. Whereas before participants were drawn uniformly at random from the pool, they are now drawn at time t according to the activity A_t. This leads to the following variant of our basic scheme:

Definition 4. Scheme with Activity. *The assignment algorithm S, the payment function H and the probability distribution Q are defined as in the previous section, and the scheme is run as described in Definition 3 (probabilistic redundant execution). The only difference is that participants needed at time t are drawn at random according to the distribution A_t instead of uniformly at random.*

Initially, A_0 is the uniform probability distribution over all registered participants. At the end of each time period, the activity A_t is updated, to reflect the throughput of each participant on the one hand, and on the other hand to account for the arrival or departure of participants.

Recall that we write $T_t(J)$ for the ordered set of tasks yet to be processed by participant J at time t. Let $n_t(J) = |T_t(J)|$ be the number of these tasks. We write $\tilde{n}_t$ for the average over all participants of the $n_t(J)$. We define A_{t+1} as a function of A_t as follows:

$$A_{t+1}(J) = A_t(J)\Big(1 + e \cdot (\tilde{n}_t - n_t(J))\Big)$$

for all active participants J. In this formula, the coefficient $e \geq 0$ is the elasticity of the activity. At the end of the time period t, a participant who has fewer tasks left to execute than average will see her activity increase. On the other hand, a participant who can not keep pace with the tasks assigned to him will see his activity decrease ($\tilde{n}_t - n_t(J) < 0$).

The choice of the value e involves a trade-off. A higher value of e will respond faster to changes in a participant's activity, and result in fewer computational resources being left at times untapped. On the other hand, a lower value of e will more effectively prevent adversaries from creating spikes of activity. Experience will tell what elasticity is best suited to a particular set of participants.

Observe that the way we have defined the evolution of activity so far,

$$\sum_J A_{t+1}(J) = \sum_J A_t(J) = 1$$

and thus A_{t+1} is again a probability distribution over the set of all participants. But we still need to account for the arrival of new participants and the voluntary departure or expulsion of participants:

- $A_{t+1}(J) = 0$ for all participants J who leave the computation at time t (either voluntarily or as a result of submitting an incorrect result.)
- $A_{t+1}(J_i) = 1/(n.m)$ for the m new participants J_i who wish to join the computation at time t. Here n is the total number of participants, and m is the number of new participants. Observe that all new participants share equally one n^{th} of the total activity.
- Finally A_{t+1} is normalized so that the sum of the values adds up to 1.

Proposition 6. *This scheme is perfectly secure under the same condition as that given in Proposition 2.*

Proof. The proof is exactly similar to that of Proposition 2. Indeed, the new probability distribution does not affect the strategy of cheaters motivated by financial gain. □

The activity is an indirect measure of the current throughput of each participant, relative to other participants. Observe that an absolute measure of activity, while apparently simpler, can not cope with situations where the total computational power of all participants exceeds the work available. Indeed in such situations, participants who are lucky enough to be assigned some work see their absolute activity increase, as a result of which they get assigned even more work in the next time period. Short of creating bogus tasks to keep all participants busy, such a scheme would become unstable and unfair.

4.1   Security Implications

Our goal is to prevent an adversary from rapidly creating a large number of participants, who collectively represent a significant fraction of the distribution A, just ahead of the computation that is targeted for sabotage. If the process of amassing a significant share of activity takes a long time, an adversary will be forced to contribute much computational power for a long time before having a chance to disrupt a particular computation. We study the evolution of activity in two distinct situations.

Suppose first that work is scarce, i.e. the combined computational resources of all participants exceeds the work available. In that situation, the set of tasks

$T_t(J)$ yet to be processed by a participant J is either empty, or contains very few tasks, and for all J, $\tilde{n}_t \approx n_t(J)$. Consequently $A_{t+1}(J) \approx A_t(J)$. Regardless of the resources available to participants, they always keep more or less the activity that they started with. In that setting, it takes at least k time periods to accumulate a share k/n of the activity, where n is the total number of participants. In effect, it is practically impossible for an adversary to control a significant fraction of the activity.

Let us now consider the opposite situation in which the amount of potential work available exceeds the combined computational power of all participants. Recall the formula used to update A:

$$A_{t+1}(J) = A_t(J)\Big(1 + e \cdot (\tilde{n}_t - n_t(J))\Big)$$

To slow down the potential increase of activity, we can set the elasticity e to a small value. This has the drawback of making the distribution of tasks more rigid for everyone. A better solution might be to place an upper bound e_0 on the increase of activity. For example, we could define:

$$A_{t+1}(J) = A_t(J)\Big[1 + \min\big(e_0, e \cdot (\tilde{n}_t - n_t(J))\big)\Big]$$

5   Dynamic Probability Distribution

Let us return to the scheme of section 3, probabilistic redundant execution. We propose in this section a more computationally efficient variant of this scheme, based on a dynamic definition of the probability of re-assignment Q. Recall that in our original scheme, the function Q is defined statically, in the sense that the number of participants to whom a task is assigned is chosen independently of who these participants are. It makes sense however to adjust the number of participants involved according to how trustworthy they are. For example, we might have the same degree of confidence in a result returned independently by two trustworthy participants as we have in a result returned independently by four less trusted participants.

In our model, the trustworthiness of a participant is measured by the amount L that the participant stands to lose if cheating is detected. The registration step of our scheme ensures that $L \geq d\alpha$ for all participants. Using this value for L, we proved in section 3 that our scheme is secure as long as the probability P that cheating is undetected satisfies:

$$P \leq \frac{d}{1 + e + d}$$

The variant we propose here is based on estimating the value L more precisely for each participant. Consider a participant who has already earned an amount $d'\alpha$ for running computations, but has not yet withdrawn that amount. Since that amount would be forfeited alongside the deposit of $d\alpha$ should cheating be discovered, the total potential loss for this participant amounts to:

$$L = d\alpha + d'\alpha$$

Accordingly, the security condition for our scheme becomes:

$$P \le \frac{d + d'}{1 + e + d + d'}$$

where as before P is the probability that cheating is undetected.

The following scheme takes advantage of this weaker condition:

Definition 5. Dynamic Scheme. *Given a task T to execute, the supervisor chooses distinct participants iteratively at random from among the pool and assigns each to the task T. The choice of participants proceeds as follows. The supervisor chooses a first participant A_1 uniformly at random. With probability $1 - Q(A_1)$, the task is assigned to no other participant and this completes the assignment protocol (the discussion on how to choose the function Q follows the definition of the scheme). With probability $Q(A_1)$, the supervisor assigns T to another participant A_2 chosen uniformly at random from the set of all participants minus A_1. Conditionally on having chosen a second participant, the protocol selects a third participant A_3 with probability $Q(A_1, A_2)$, and selects no other participant with probability $1 - Q(A_1, A_2)$. In the general case, conditionally on having chosen an ith participant, the protocol selects and $(i+1)^{th}$ participant with probability $Q(A_1, \ldots, A_i)$ and selects no more participant with probability $1 - Q(A_1, \ldots, A_i)$.*

At the end of the computation, the supervisor collects the results and compares them for validity. If they are not all the same, the task is re-assigned to a new group of participants selected according to the same protocol (if the task T was assigned to a single participant, it is assumed to have been executed correctly). Should this second round also fail to produce an agreement, the task is re-assigned until a unanimous result emerges. At that time, all participants A_i who executed the task correctly are paid α, whereas the participants who returned an incorrect result are banned from future computations.

With the notations of section 3, we define the probability of re-assignment Q as follows:

$$Q(A_1, \ldots, A_i) = \frac{i + e}{i + e + \sum_{k=1}^{i}(d_k + d'_k)}$$

where d_k and d'_k are the deposits of participant A_k.

Proposition 7. *With the assumption that the maximum coalition size is a negligible fraction of the total number of active participants, the dynamic scheme is perfectly secure.*

Proof. Let us consider an adversary who has been assigned i times the same task T through various of the participants that he controls. Since we assume that the adversary controls only a negligible fraction of the total number of participants, he can not learn anything about the total number of participants to whom T has been assigned. The only information available to the adversary is that the probability of re-assignment of a task already distributed to his i participants is $Q(A_1, \ldots, A_i)$. The probability that cheating is undetected is

$$P = 1 - Q(A_1, \ldots, A_i) = \frac{\sum_{k=1}^{i}(d_k + d'_k)}{i + e + \sum_{k=1}^{i}(d_k + d'_k)}$$

This is exactly the condition required for perfect security.   □

The computational overhead of the dynamic scheme is hard to estimate, since it depends on the behavior of the participants. The more participants are inclined to leave with the supervisor the money they have earned, the more efficient the scheme. The faster participants withdraw their earnings, the less efficient the scheme.

6   Conclusion and Further Work

We give a security framework for distributed computing, based on the assumption that participants are motivated by financial gain. We present a secure scheme and its analysis, as well as two variants. The first variant addresses the issue of participants with varying computational resources. The second variant offers improved computational efficiency.

We are currently working on an implementation of the schemes proposed in this paper. It is hoped that this implementation will help us determine the optimal practical value of the elasticity for the activity (section 4), and the computational overhead of the dynamic scheme (section 5) depending on the population of participants.

Acknowledgments

The first author would like to thank Bo Loevschall and Ilya Mironov for helpful discussions and comments on the subject of this paper.

References

BK89.   M. Blum and S. Kannan. Programs that Check their Work. In *Proceedings of the Twenty First Annual ACM Symposium on Theory of Computing*, 1989.

BW97.   M. Blum and H. Wasserman. Software reliability via run-time result-checking. In *Journal of the ACM*, vol. 44, no. 6, pp. 826-849, November 1997.

CLSY93.   J. Cai, R. Lipton, R. Sedgewick, and A. Yao. Towards uncheatable benchmarks. In *Proceedings of the 8th Annual Structure in Complexity Theory Conference*, pp. 2–11, 1993.

DC00.   CNET News.com. Buddy, can you spare some processing time? CNET Networks, Inc. 150 Chestnut Street San Francisco, CA 94111. http://news.cnet.com/news/0-1003-200-2671550.html.

F85.   Joan Feigenbaum. Encrypting problem instances: Or..., Can you take
          advantage of someone without having to trust him? In *Proceedings of
          CRYPTO'85*, pages 477-488. Lecture Notes in Computer Science, No. 218.
GM00.   P. Golle and I. Mironov. Uncheatable Distributed Computations. To appear
          in *Proceedings of the RSA Conference 2001, Cryptographers' Track.*
H97.   Fritz Hohl. An Approach to Solve the Problem of Malicious Hosts. Technical
          Report TR-1997-03, Universitat Stuttgart, Fakultat Informatik, Germany,
          March 1997.
JJ99.   M. Jakobson and A. Juels. Proofs of work and bread pudding protocols. In
          *Proceedings of the 1999 Communications and Multimedia Security Confer-
          ence.*
MRS93.   Y. Minsky, R. van Renesse, F. Schneider, and S. Stoller. Cryptographic
          Support for Fault-Tolerant Distributed Computing. In *Proceedings of the
          First ACM Conference on Computer and Communications Security, Nov.
          1993.*
MWR99.   F. Monrose, P. Wyckoff, and A. Rubin. Distributed Execution with Remote
          Audit. In *Proceedings of the 1999 ISOC Network and Distributed System
          Security Symposium, pages 103-113, 1999.*
R00.   H. Rheingold. You got the power. In *Wired magazine*, August, 2000.
SETI.   The Search for Extraterrestrial Intelligence project. University of Califor-
          nia, Berkeley. `http://setiathome.berkeley.edu`.
V97.   G. Vigna. Protecting Mobile Agents through Tracing. In *Proceedings of the
          3rd Workshop on Mobile Object Systems,* June 1997.
Y82.   A. Yao. Protocols for Secure Computations. In *Proceedings of the 23rd
          Annual IEEE Symposium on Foundations of Computer Science,* 1982, pages
          160-164.

Monotone Signatures

David Naccache[1], David Pointcheval[2], and Christophe Tymen[1]

[1] Gemplus Card International – 34, rue Guynemer
F-92447 Issy-les-Moulineaux cedex, France
{david.naccache,christophe.tymen}@gemplus.com
http://www.gemplus.com/smart
[2] Ecole Normale Supérieure
45 rue d'Ulm, F-75230 Paris cedex 5, France
david.pointcheval@ens.fr
http://www.di.ens.fr/users/pointche

Abstract. In many real-life situations, massive quantities of signatures have to be issued on cheap passive supports (*e.g.* paper-based) such as bank-notes, badges, ID cards, driving licenses or passports (hereafter IDs); while large-scale ID replacements are costly and prohibitive, one may reasonably assume that the updating of verification equipment (*e.g.* off-line border checkpoints or mobile patrol units) is exceptionally acceptable.

In such a context, an attacker using coercive means (*e.g.* kidnapping) can force the system authorities to reveal the infrastructure's secret signature keys and start issuing signatures that are indistinguishable from those issued by the authority.

The solution presented in this paper withstands such attacks up to a certain point: after the theft, the authority restricts the verification criteria (by an exceptional verification equipment update) in such a way that the genuine signatures issued before the attack become easily distinguishable from the fresher signatures issued by the attacker.

Needless to say, we assume that at any point in time the verification algorithm is entirely known to the attacker.

Keywords: Digital Signatures, Coercion, Bank Notes, ID Cards.

1 Introduction

In settings where passive (paper-based) bank notes, passports or ID cards are massively delivered to users, document security specialists (*e.g.* [22]) distinguish between two different threats:

- *Duplication*, which consists in copying information from a genuine document into a new physical support (the copy). By analogy to the *double-spending problem* met in e-cash schemes and software copyright protection, it seems impossible to prevent duplication without relying on specific physical assumptions, simply because symbols are inherently copyable. This difficulty explains why duplication is mainly fought by optical means such as holograms, iridescent printing (different colors being displayed at different angles of observation), luminescent effects (the emission of radiation by an atom in

P. Syverson (Ed.): FC 2001, LNCS 2339, pp. 305–318, 2002.

the course of a transition from a higher to a lower state of energy, which is typically achieved by submitting the ID to ultraviolet excitation) or standard document security features such as planchettes, fibers and thread.

In the last decade, chip-based IDs appeared (e.g. Venezuela's driving license). Again, these are based on the assumption that appropriately designed microchips can reasonably withstand malicious cloning attempts.

— Forgery, which assumes that attackers have successfully passed the physical barrier and are now able to reproduce documents using exactly the same materials and production techniques used to create the original. Note that although forgers may copy any existing ID, they can still fail in creating new contents ex nihilo if the ID happens to rely on logical protections such as MACs or signatures.

It seems very hard to quantify or compare the security of physical anti-duplication technologies; partially because the effectiveness of such solutions frequently relies on their secrecy, let alone the wide diversity of physical technologies mixed in one specific protection. By opposition, the protection of digital assets against alteration is much better understood and can be easily used to fight forgery.

As is obvious, if the authority's signature or MAC keys are compromised (e.g. by theft, cryptanalysis or coercion) forgery becomes possible, and the whole system collapses. Theft can be easily prevented by physically protecting the production facility or better more, by having data signed in protected remote locations and by exchanging information and signatures through a properly protected logical channel.

This is however not sufficient to resist coercion, a scenario in which the attacker uses a threat (e.g. a kidnapping) to force the authorities to publish the signature keys (e.g. in a newspaper [21]). The attacker can then check in vitro the correctness of the revealed keys, stop coercing and start issuing fake IDs that are indistinguishable from the genuine ones. The attack can also be motivated by the sole intention to cause losses (global ID replacement).

Large scale ID replacement is, of course, a radical solution but it may both entail prohibitive costs and require a transition period during which intruders can still sneak through the borders. A second solution consists in performing systematic on-line verifications to make sure that all controlled IDs are actually listed somewhere, but this might be cumbersome in decentralized or poorly networked infrastructures.

As mentioned in the abstract, the problem is, of course, not limited to IDs. Bank notes, public-key directories and any other passive supports carrying signatures or MACs are all equally concerned.

Several authors formalized similar concerns [9] and solutions based on pro-active key updates [8] which, although very efficient in on-line contexts (e.g. Internet), do not suit our passive (non-intelligent) IDs; others share the key between n individuals amongst which a quorum of k is necessary to sign [10,19]. This does not seem to solve the fundamental coercion problem either, since the forger can force the authority to instruct k of the share-holders to reveal their secrets, or coerce k share-holders directly.

2   The Idea and a Few Definitions

The proposed solution targets the attacker's ability to ascertain the correctness of the stolen keys; this is achieved by updating the verification algorithm $\mathcal{V}$ so as to distinguish the fake (new) signatures from the genuine (old) ones. We denote by $\{\mathcal{V}_1, \ldots, \mathcal{V}_n\}$ the successive updates of $\mathcal{V}$ in a system designed to withstand at most n coercions.

In our system, the authority's (genuine) signatures are designed to:

- remain *forward compatible i.e.* be valid for all the verification algorithms $\mathcal{V}_i$ to come.
- remain *computationally indistinguishable* from the signatures generated by the i-th attacker until the disclosure of $\mathcal{V}_{i+1}$.

The technique is thus analogous to the strategy of national banks who implement several (secret) security features in their bank notes. As forgeries appear, the banks examine the fakes and publicize some of the secret features to stop the circulation of forgeries.

Our construction relies on the following definitions:

Definition 1 (Monotone Predicates). *Let* $\mathcal{V}_1(x), \ldots, \mathcal{V}_n(x)$ *be* n *predicates. The set* $\{\mathcal{V}_i(x)\}$ *is* monotone *if*

$$\forall i < n, \quad \mathcal{V}_{i+1}(x) \Rightarrow \mathcal{V}_i(x)$$

Example 2. The set of predicates:

$$\mathcal{V}_1(x) \stackrel{\text{def}}{=} x \in \mathbb{R}$$
$$\mathcal{V}_2(x) \stackrel{\text{def}}{=} x \in \mathbb{N}$$
$$\mathcal{V}_3(x) \stackrel{\text{def}}{=} x \text{ is prime}$$
$$\mathcal{V}_4(x) \stackrel{\text{def}}{=} x \text{ is a strong prime}$$

is monotone since
$$\mathcal{V}_4(x) \Rightarrow \mathcal{V}_3(x) \Rightarrow \mathcal{V}_2(x) \Rightarrow \mathcal{V}_1(x).$$

Definition 3 (Signature Schemes). *A* signature scheme *is a collection of three sub-algorithms* $\{\mathcal{G}, \mathcal{S}, \mathcal{V}\}$,

- *a probabilistic key-generation algorithm* $\mathcal{G}$, *which produces a pair of related public and secret keys, on input a security parameter* k: $\{v, s\} = \mathcal{G}(1^k)$, *where* v *and* s *respectively denote the public and secret keys used by* $\mathcal{V}$ *and* $\mathcal{S}$, *the verification and the signature algorithms (see below).*
- *a possibly probabilistic signature algorithm* $\mathcal{S}$, *which produces a signature, given a secret key and a message:* $\sigma = \mathcal{S}(s; m)$.
- *a verification algorithm, which checks whether the given signature is correct relatively to the message and the public key:* $\mathcal{V}(v; m, \sigma) \in \{\text{true}, \text{false}\}$. *It must satisfy*

$$(\sigma = \mathcal{S}(s; m)) \Rightarrow (\mathcal{V}(v; m, \sigma) = \text{true}).$$

Definition 4 (Monotone Signature Schemes). *A monotone signature scheme (MSS) is the following generalization of definition 3,*

- *a probabilistic key-generation algorithm $\mathcal{G}$, which produces a list of public and secret keys, on input two security parameters k and n:*

$$\{v_1, \ldots, v_n, s_1, \ldots, s_n\} = \mathcal{G}(1^k, 1^n),$$

where $\{v_i\}$ and $\{s_i\}$ respectively denote the public and secret keys used by the $\mathcal{V}_j$ and $\mathcal{S}$.
- *a possibly probabilistic signature algorithm $\mathcal{S}$, which produces a signature, given the list of the n secret keys and a message: $\sigma = \mathcal{S}(s_1, \ldots, s_n; m)$.*
- *a list of monotone verification algorithms $\mathcal{V}_j$ which check whether the given signature is correct, relatively to the message and the list of public keys:*

$$\mathcal{V}_j(v_1, \ldots, v_j; m, \sigma) \in \{\text{true}, \text{false}\}.$$

In other words, we require the three following properties.

1. *Completeness*:

$$\sigma = \mathcal{S}(s_1, \ldots, s_n; m) \Rightarrow \forall j \leq n, \ \mathcal{V}_j(v_1, \ldots, v_j; m, \sigma) = \text{true}.$$

2. *Soundness*: for any adversary $\mathcal{A}$ which does not know s_{j+1}, the probability, over his internal random coins, to produce an accepted message-signature pair $\{m, \sigma\}$ is negligible

$$\Pr[\mathcal{V}_{j+1}(v_1, \ldots, v_{j+1}; m, \sigma) = \text{true} \mid (m, \sigma) = \mathcal{A}] \text{ is negligible}.$$

3. *Indistinguishability*: for any index $j \leq n$, there exists a simulator $\mathcal{S}_j$ such that the distributions of $\mathcal{S}(s_1, \ldots, s_n; x)$ and $\mathcal{S}_j(s_1, \ldots, s_j; x)$, for the internal random coins of the algorithms, are indistinguishable by opponents who do not possess $\{s_{j+1}, \ldots, s_n\}$.

We now categorize the opponents that MSSs will withstand. In essence we consider two types of attackers: *immediate* and *delayed*. Both are going to coerce the signer, get some of his secrets, check their validity (as much as possible, *i.e.* with respect to the currently enforced public-key $\{v_1, \ldots, v_j\}$) and start forging.

Definition 5 (Immediate Attackers). Immediate attackers *forge signatures using the obtained secret keys $\{s_1, \ldots, s_j\}$, but stop their activity as soon as the new verification algorithm $\mathcal{V}_{j+1}(v_1, \ldots, v_{j+1}; \cdot, \cdot)$ is published.*

The next section will be devoted to the study of the long-term validity of such forgeries, produced before $\mathcal{V}_{j+1}(v_1, \ldots, v_{j+1}; \cdot, \cdot)$ is known.

Definition 6 (Delayed Attackers). Delayed attackers *wait until a new verification algorithm $\mathcal{V}_{j+1}(v_1, \ldots, v_{j+1}; \cdot, \cdot)$ is published and use both the obtained secret keys $\{s_1, \cdots, s_j\}$ and the new verification rules to compute their forgeries.*

The global picture is presented on figure 1.

- key generation: the authority gets $\{v_1, \ldots, v_n, s_1, \ldots, s_n\} = \mathcal{G}(1^k, 1^n)$
- keys: the authority keeps $\{s_1, \ldots, s_n\}$ secret
  and publishes $\{v_1, \ldots, v_j\}$ for some $j < n$
- signature generation: the authority runs $\mathcal{S}(s_1, \ldots, s_n; m)$ to sign m
- coercion
  - start
  - the authority reveals, to the attackers, the signature algorithm,
    together with the secret keys $\{s_1, \cdots, s_j\}$
  - stop
- *immediate attackers* try to issue signatures using only $\{s_1, \cdots, s_j\}$ and $\mathcal{V}_j$
- authority updates $\mathcal{V}_j$ to $\mathcal{V}_{j+1}$ and informs the verifiers
- *delayed attackers* try to issue signatures using $\{s_1, \cdots, s_j\}$, $\mathcal{V}_j$ and $\mathcal{V}_{j+1}$

Fig. 1. Coercion Model

3 Immediate Attacks and Symmetric Monotone Signatures

As one may suspect, immediate attackers are the easiest to deal with. In theory, the situation does not even call for the use of asymmetric primitives. It suffices to add secret information to m or σ (*e.g.* using a subliminal channel as suggested by [20]) but unless secret keys are shared with the verifiers, which is not the case in our setting, the information rate is very low (narrow-band subliminal channel).

Better results are obtained by adding to σ some hidden randomness. In other words, the actually signed message will be $\mu(m, r)$ where μ is a padding function and r a randomly-looking (pseudo-random) bit string. The expression *randomly-looking* translates the fact that r embeds information which is meaningful to who knows how to interpret it :

$$\text{let} \quad r = <r_1 \ldots r_n > \in \{0,1\}^n$$

$$\text{and} \quad \begin{cases} r_i = f_{k_i}(\{r_\lambda\}_{\lambda \in E'}) \text{ for all } i \in E \subseteq \{1, \ldots, n\}, \\ r_i \in_R \{0,1\} \text{ for all } i \notin E, \end{cases}$$

where E and E' are two disjoint subsets of $\{1, \ldots, n\}$; $\{f_i\}$ is a family of pseudo-random functions returning one bit; and the values $\{k_i\}$, for $i \in E$, are auxiliary secret keys. More concretely, the set E' contains the indices of the bits used for generating redundancy, and the set E contains the indices of the redundancy bits.

The signer knows s as well as the complete collection of auxiliary secrets $\{k_i\}$. To issue an ID containing m, he generates a randomly looking r (which satisfies the required secret redundancy) and a signature σ of $\mu(m, r)$. The ID contains $\{m, r, \sigma\}$.

The verifier knows v and the values of some k_i, for $i \in F \subseteq E$. Upon presentation of the ID, he verifies the redundancy of r with respect to the k_i values that *he* knows. If this succeeds, he proceeds and verifies σ.

After coercion, the attacker obtains s and the k_i for $i \in G$ with, at least, $F \subseteq G$ (recall that the attacker verifies the validity of the produced signatures before stopping coercion). As long as $G \neq E$, the verification algorithm can be fixed and the system saved.

After revealing H (strictly bigger than G) and the k_i, for $i \in H$, signatures are considered valid if and only if all the r_i for $i \in H$ are correct. Given the unpredictable nature of the $\{r_i\}$ for $i \in H \backslash G$ (and well-chosen functions $\{f_i\}$), the forged signatures are accepted with probability smaller then $\epsilon = 2^{-c}$ where $c = \#(H \backslash G)$. If c is sufficiently large, ϵ is negligible and the forgeries are almost certainly spotted.

Figure 2 describes this protocol that we call *symmetric MSS*, since it relies on auxiliary *secrets*, eventually revealed to the verifiers. More formally, the ver-

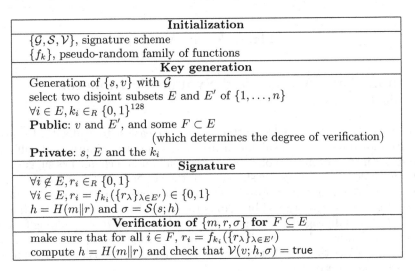

Fig. 2. Symmetric Monotone Signature Scheme

ification algorithm $\mathcal{V}_F$ checks the validity of the signature σ, but furthermore checks the redundancy of all the bits indexed by F. We can state the following theorem.

Theorem 7. *Let $\{\mathcal{G}, \mathcal{S}, \mathcal{V}\}$ be a signature scheme transformed into a symmetric MSS as suggested in figure 2.*

- *The signatures issued by the authority leak no information on the subset E;*
- *Assume that an attacker manages to obtain s, and then the k_i for $i \in G \supseteq F$. Let $H \subseteq E$ be such that G is strictly included in H. Let us denote by c the cardinality of $H \backslash G$. The signatures issued by an attacker knowing G will be accepted with respect to H with probability smaller than 2^{-c}.*

Proof. First assume that $f_k(.) = f(k, .)$, where f is, in the first part of the proof, modeled by a random oracle which outputs one bit to each query:

- The r_i are all random for $i \notin E$, by construction, as well as for $i \in E$ because of the randomness of f. Therefore, the signatures do not reveal any information on E (other than the fact that $F \subseteq E$).
- By virtue of this indistinguishability property for E in $\{1, \ldots, n\}$, the attacker can not know if G is the entire set E. Assume that this is not the case and G is strictly included in E. Define H as an intermediate subset, $G \subset H \subseteq E$, and let c denote the cardinality of $H \backslash G$. Since f is a random oracle, without knowing the k_j for $j \in H \backslash G$, the attacker can not produce the valid r_j bits without a bias. Therefore the probability to produce a valid forgery is smaller than 2^{-c}.

Now, if by replacing f (secret random oracle [13]) by the family f_k, the attacker manages to produce valid signatures with probability larger than $2^{-c} + \alpha$, then the attacker can be used as distinguisher between the family of functions $\{f_k\}$ and a perfectly random function with an advantage α, which contradicts the assumption that $\{f_k\}$ is a family of pseudo-random functions.   □

Given the symmetric nature of the auxiliary secrets (except the unique asymmetric private key revealed immediately after an attack), it is clear that this process can not withstand *delayed* attacks. Actually, the information owned by the verifier after the update is sufficient for producing valid forgeries. We therefore focus the coming section on asymmetric MSS that can thwart delayed attacks.

4   Delayed Attacks and Asymmetric Monotone Signatures

4.1   Simple Concatenation

A trivial example of asymmetric MSS can be obtained by concatenating signatures:

- Let $\{\mathcal{G}, \mathcal{S}, \mathcal{V}\}$ be a signature scheme and denote by ℓ the size of each signature;
- The concatenated signature of m over the set $E \subseteq \{1, \ldots, n\}$, is the tuple:

$$\mathcal{S}'\left(\{s_i\}_{i \in E}; m\right) = \sigma = \{\sigma_1, \ldots, \sigma_n\}$$
$$\text{where } \sigma_i = \begin{cases} \mathcal{S}(s_i; m) & \text{if } i \in E, \text{ using the secret key } s_i \\ \rho_i \in_R \{0,1\}^\ell & \text{if } i \notin E \end{cases}$$

- Verification consists in evaluating the predicate:

$$\mathcal{V}'_F(\{v_i\}_{i \in F}; m, \sigma) = \wedge_{i \in F} \mathcal{V}(v_i; m, \sigma_i),$$

where the set $F \subseteq E$ determines the degree of verification.

However, for E not to be detectable, the two following distributions must be indistinguishable, for any pair $\{s, m\}$ of secret key and message:

$$\delta_0 = \{\rho \in_R \{0,1\}^\ell\}$$
$$\delta_1(s, m) = \{\mathcal{S}(s, m)\}$$

This latter distribution is over the internal random coins used in the probabilistic signature process. Thus, not all signature algorithms lead themselves to such a construction. For instance, the concatenation of RSA [17] signatures does not yield an asymmetric MSS, because of the deterministic nature of σ as a function of m (unless one uses a probabilistic padding scheme such as PSS [3] or PKCS#1 v 2.0, the distribution $\delta_1(s, m)$ contains only one point, by opposition to the uniform distribution δ_0.)

On the other hand, if the distribution of signatures is indistinguishable from the uniform distribution, a mix between random numbers and signatures of m will resist coercion up to a certain point. We formalize this in the following theorem.

Theorem 8. *Let $\{\mathcal{G}, \mathcal{S}, \mathcal{V}\}$ be a signature scheme for which the distribution $\delta_1(s, m)$ is indistinguishable (for any pair $\{s, m\}$) from the uniform distribution. Let $\{\mathcal{G}', \mathcal{S}', \mathcal{V}'\}$ be the concatenated version of $\{\mathcal{G}, \mathcal{S}, \mathcal{V}\}$.*

- *The signatures produced by the authority do not reveal any information on the subset E;*
- *Consider an attacker $\mathcal{A}$ who got hold of the s_i for $i \in G \supseteq F$. Let $H \subseteq E$ be such that G is strictly included in H, whose associated verification keys have been published. If $\mathcal{A}$ can produce a forgery for $\{\mathcal{G}', \mathcal{S}', \mathcal{V}'\}$ with respect to H then he is able to produce a forgery for $\{\mathcal{G}, \mathcal{S}, \mathcal{V}\}$.*

A second disadvantage of RSA is the size of σ (recall that we actually talk about n such signatures). A more compact alternative is Schnorr's signature. The next paragraph describes a concatenated signature based on this scheme.

4.2   Concatenation of Schnorr's Signatures

We recall the description of the Schnorr's scheme [18]:

- An authority generates a (k_1 bit) prime p such that $p - 1$ has a large prime factor q of k_2 bits. The authority also generates an element g of $\mathbb{Z}_p^*$ of order q and publishes a hash function H which outputs are in $\mathbb{Z}_q$;
- $\mathcal{G}(p, q, g)$ returns $x \in_R \mathbb{Z}_q^*$ and $y = g^x \bmod p$;
- $\mathcal{S}(x; m) = \{e, s\}$ where $t \in_R \mathbb{Z}_q^*$, $r = g^t \bmod p$, $e = H(m, r)$ and $s = t - ex \bmod q$;
- $\mathcal{V}(y; m, e, s) = (H(m, g^s y^e \bmod p) \overset{?}{=} e)$.

This scheme is provably secure in the random oracle model [16]. More precisely, it withstands existential forgeries even against adaptive chosen-message attacks [7]. Moreover, $\delta_1(x, m) = \{\mathcal{S}(x, m)\} = \{\{e, s\} \in_R \mathbb{Z}_q \times \mathbb{Z}_q\}$ is indistinguishable from a uniform distribution, when y is unknown.

Remark 9. We insist on the format of the Schnorr's signature. Indeed, sometimes one outputs $\{r, s\}$ as the signature, instead of $\{e, s\}$. We use this latter for two reasons:

- Because of the shorter size of the resulting signature. Note that in elliptic curve settings, this is irrelevant, since both representations are as short.

- For the randomly-looking property of the pair $\{e, s\}$. Indeed, to distinguish a list of actual signatures $\{\{e_i, s_i\}\}$, for a given pair of keys $\{x, y\}$, from a list of truly random pairs, one has to find this common y, which can not be found without the r_i (hidden in the query asked to H). But with the r_i, one could easily compute $e_i = H(m, r_i)$ and $(r_i/g^{s_i})^{1/e_i}$. This latter value would be a constant: y.

By virtue of theorem 8, we can construct a concatenated variant that is as secure as the initial scheme, that is, existentially unforgeable against adaptive chosen-message attacks. Figure 3 describes such a variant.

Initialization
p, q, g and H as in Schnorr's scheme
Key generation
Select a subset E of $\{1, \ldots, n\}$
$\forall i \in E$, let $x_i \in \mathbb{Z}_q^*$ and $y_i = g^{x_i} \bmod p$
Private: E and the x_i for $i \in E$
Public: some $F \subset E$, and y_i for $i \in F$
Signature
$\forall i \in E, \sigma_i = \{e_i, s_i\} = \mathcal{S}(x_i; m)$
$\forall i \notin E, \sigma_i = \{e_i, s_i\} \in_R \mathbb{Z}_q \times \mathbb{Z}_q^*$
let $\sigma = \{\sigma_1, \ldots, \sigma_n\}$
Verification of $\{m, \sigma\}$ for $F \subseteq E$
$\forall i \in F, H(m, g^{s_i} y_i^{e_i} \bmod p) \overset{?}{=} e_i$

Fig. 3. Concatenated Schnorr's Signatures

The resulting MSS outputs $2nk_2$ bit signatures, and since usually $k_2 \cong 160$, this would amount to $320n$ bits in practice. Note that efficient batch algorithms for generating and verifying multiple Schnorr's signatures may considerably improve the parties' workloads [12,1,11].

4.3   Introducing Degrees of Freedom

Instead of concatenating signatures and random values, the asymmetric MSS described in this section relies on hidden relations between the different parts of the signature that give additional degrees of freedom to the signer. It's main advantage over concatenation is a substantial improvement in signature size (50%).

The Okamoto-Schnorr Signature. The new scheme is based on the Okamoto's variant of Schnorr's scheme [15]. The mechanism relies on the representation problem [4], and is recalled in figure 4.

Initialization
p, q and H as in Schnorr's scheme
$g_1, \ldots, g_n \in \mathbb{Z}_p^*$ of order q
Key generation
Private: $x_1, \ldots, x_n \in \mathbb{Z}_q^*$
Public: $y = g_1^{x_1} \times \ldots \times g_n^{x_n} \bmod p$
Signature
$t_1, \ldots, t_n \in \mathbb{Z}_q^*$ and $r = g_1^{t_1} \times \ldots \times g_n^{t_n} \bmod p$
$e = H(m, r)$ then for $i = 1, \ldots, n$, $s_i = t_i - e x_i \bmod q$
$S(x_1, \ldots, x_n; m) = (e, s_1, \ldots, s_n)$
Verification
$H(m, g_1^{s_1} \times \ldots \times g_n^{s_n} \times y^e \bmod p) \overset{?}{=} e$

Fig. 4. Okamoto–Schnorr Signatures

General Outline. The main idea is to impose and keep secret relations between the g_i. For simplicity, suppose that $n = 2$. Instead of choosing g_1 and g_2 at random, we choose g_2 as before, but set $g_1 = g_2^a \bmod p$ and $y = g_2^x \bmod p$, where a is a secret element of $\mathbb{Z}_q^*$, and thus $x = ax_1 + x_2 \bmod q$ (with the notations of the figure 4). Then we keep the verification condition

$$H(m, g_1^{s_1} g_2^{s_2} y^e) \overset{?}{=} e \tag{1}$$

But now, we can choose s_1 as we want (e.g. at random), as well as a random t, compute $r = g_2^t \bmod p$, $e = H(m, r)$ and then we want

$$g_2^{s_2} = r y^{-e} g_1^{-s_1} = g_2^t g_2^{-ex} g_2^{-as_1} = g_2^{t - ex - as_1} \bmod p.$$

Therefore, $s_2 = t - ex - as_1 \bmod q$ provides a valid signature. As the signer can choose s_1 arbitrarily (even after having chosen t), we say that he gets an additional *degree of freedom*. This signature will still satisfy the verification formula (1), and will be indistinguishable from a classical Okamoto-Schnorr signature. Furthermore, instead of choosing s_1 at random, we may choose it to be randomly-looking. Explicitly, we may set $s_1 = f_k(m\|r)$ where f_k is a pseudo-random function and k an auxiliary secret. When coerced, the signer reveals x_1 and x_2, but keeps a and k secret. The attacker is thus capable of forging signatures satisfying formula (1). Then, the signer publishes an additional verification condition, namely $s_1 \overset{?}{=} f_k(m\|r)$. ¿From that moment, in order to forge valid signatures, the attacker must compute a from g_2^a, or equivalently, find a discrete logarithm in $\mathbb{Z}_p^*$.

This idea can be generalized to any arbitrary n. We set an i in $\{2, \cdots, n-1\}$, and for $j = 1, \cdots, i-1$, we impose $g_j = g_i^{a_i} \bmod p$, where the a_i are kept secret, and therefore $y = g_i^{x_i} \times \ldots \times g_n^{x_n} \bmod p$ for some tuple $\{x_i, \ldots, x_n\}$. To produce a signature, we proceed as follows: set $r = g_i^{t_i} \cdots g_n^{t_n} \bmod p$, for random t_j. The signer has $i-1$ *degrees of freedom*, that is, he can set, for all $j < i$, $s_j = f_{k_j}(m\|r)$. In addition, to be compatible with the verification condition

$$H(m, g_1^{s_1} \times \ldots \times g_n^{s_n} \times y^e \bmod p) \overset{?}{=} e, \tag{2}$$

we set $s_i = t_i - ex_i - a_1 s_1 - \cdots - a_{i-1} s_{i-1} \bmod q$, and $s_k = t_k - ex_k \bmod q$ for $k > i$. Trivially, the verification formula (2) still works for this signature generation:

$$g_1^{s_1} \times \ldots \times g_n^{s_n} \times y^e = g_i^{a_1 s_1} \times \ldots \times g_i^{a_{i-1} s_{i-1}} \times g_i^{s_i} \times \prod_{k=i+1}^{k=n} g_k^{s_k} \times y^e$$

$$= g_i^{a_1 s_1 + \cdots + a_{i-1} s_{i-1}} \times g_i^{t_i - ex_i - a_1 s_1 - \cdots - a_{i-1} s_{i-1}} \times \prod_{k=i+1}^{k=n} g_k^{t_k - ex_k} \times y^e$$

$$= g_i^{t_i - ex_i} \times \prod_{k=i+1}^{k=n} g_k^{t_k - ex_k} \times y^e = \prod_{k=i}^{k=n} g_k^{t_k - ex_k} \times \prod_{k=i}^{k=n} g_k^{ex_k} = \prod_{k=i}^{k=n} g_k^{t_k} = r \bmod p.$$

But now, we can disclose some partial secrets k_i and a_i to an attacker, and then add new verification conditions as shown in the case $n = 2$.

As a last generalization, we suppress the special role played by the first i indices in the previous construction, and hide the indices of the generators for which one knows some relations. That means that we can apply a secret permutation P to the indices, imposing that $g_{P(j)} = g_{P(i)}^{a_{P(j)}}$ for $1 \leq j \leq i-1$. The signature generation remains the same, except that the sets $\{1, \cdots, i-1\}, \{i\}$ and $\{i+1, \cdots, n\}$ are replaced respectively by $P\langle\{1, \cdots, i-1\}\rangle$, $\{P(i)\}$ and $P\langle\{i+1, \cdots, n\}\rangle$.

Formal Description of the Scheme. The complete protocol is described in figure 5. The validity of this new scheme comes from the fact the

$$g_1^{s_1} \times \ldots \times g_n^{s_n} \times y^e = g_{P(1)}^{s_{P(1)}} \times \ldots \times g_{P(n)}^{s_{P(n)}} \times y^e \bmod p.$$

After the first coercion, the signer reveals $x_1, \cdots, x_n$, for some randomly chosen $x_1, \ldots, x_{i-1}$ thanks to the a_j's. He also reveals a set G, which necessarily satisfies $F \subseteq G \subseteq E$, and the values a_j and k_j for $j \in G$. The point is that G strictly includes the indices possibly known from previous attacks (and thus included in the current public key). If such a G, strictly included in E, exists, the signer can withstand the attack. When the choice of such a G is impossible, the system finally collapses. Note that for the first attack, it is possible to choose $F = \emptyset$.

After the attack, the signer publishes an additional verification condition,

$$s_\kappa \overset{?}{=} f_{k_\kappa}(m\|r),$$

where $\kappa \in E\backslash G$. The forgery of valid signatures will require knowing a_κ. For an attacker, this implies determining a_κ from $g_{P(i)}^{a_\kappa}$, and the difficulty of this problem is equivalent to the security of the initial scheme.

Initialization
p, q and H as in Schnorr's scheme.
$f_k(.) = H(k,.)$, a family of random functions
Key generation
Choose a permutation P of $\{1, 2, \ldots, n\}$
Choose $i < n$, the degree of freedom
Set $E = P(\{1, \cdots, i-1\})$
Choose $F \subset E$
Choose $x_i, \ldots, x_n \in_R \mathbb{Z}_q^\star$
Choose $a_{P(1)}, \ldots, a_{P(i-1)} \in_R \mathbb{Z}_q^\star$
Choose $k_{P(1)}, \ldots, k_{P(i-1)}$ random keys
Choose $g_{P(i+1)}, \ldots, g_{P(n)} \in_R \mathbb{Z}_p^\star$ of order q
Set $g_{P(j)} = g_{P(i)}^{a_{P(j)}} \bmod p$ for $j = 1, \ldots, i-1$
Set $y = g_{P(i)}^{x_i} \times \ldots \times g_{P(n)}^{x_n} \bmod p$
Private: P, $\{a_j, k_j\}_{j \in E}$ and $x_i, \ldots, x_n$
Public: y, g_j for $j = 1, \ldots, n$,
$\quad\quad F$ and k_j for $j \in F$
Signature generation
Pick $t_i, \ldots, t_n \in_R \mathbb{Z}_q^\star$
Set $r = g_{P(i)}^{t_i} \times \ldots \times g_{P(n)}^{t_n} \bmod p$
$e = H(m, r)$
Set, for $j = 1, \ldots, i-1$, $s_{P(j)} = f_{k_{P(j)}}(m\|r)$
Set $s_{P(i)} = t_i - ex_i - a_{P(1)}s_{P(1)} - \ldots - a_{P(i-1)}s_{P(i-1)} \bmod q$
Set, for $j = i+1, \ldots, n$, $s_{P(j)} = t_j - ex_j \bmod q$
$\sigma = (e, s_1, \ldots, s_n)$
Verification of (m, σ) for $F \subseteq E$
$H(m, g_1^{s_1} \times \ldots \times g_n^{s_n} \times y^e \bmod p) \stackrel{?}{=} e.$
$\forall j \in F$, $s_j \stackrel{?}{=} f_{k_j}(m\|r)$

Fig. 5. Okamoto–Schnorr Signatures with $i-1$ degrees of freedom

Security. We can claim the following security result.

Theorem 10. *Consider the Okamoto-Schnorr signature scheme with $i-1$ degrees of freedom of figure 5, in the random oracle model.*

- *The signatures produced by the authority do not reveal any information on the subset E;*
- *Consider an attacker $\mathcal{A}$ knowing a representation of y, $k < i$ relations between the g_j and k secret keys k_j. If, after revealing one more k_i, $\mathcal{A}$ can still produce a signature accepted by the new verification algorithm, then $\mathcal{A}$ can compute discrete logarithms.*

Proof. We assume H to behave like a random oracle. For the first part of the theorem, using classical simulation techniques ([6,16]), we can prove that there exists a simulator that does not know any secret value, but which is able to generate signatures that are indistinguishable from the true signatures, thanks to the random oracles simulation (for H but also the f_k's). This simulator proceeds as follows: it chooses e, then the s_j's, and computes the correct value of r. Finally, it sets $H(m, r) = e$, and when a k_κ is revealed, it sets $f_{k_\kappa}(m\|r) = s_\kappa$.

Consequently, no information on E or the a_i's leaks from the signatures produced by the scheme.

For the second part, assume that an attacker knows a representation of y in the base g_j. Assume also that he knows k values $P(j)$, the associated $a_{P(j)}$, and $k + 1$ elements k_j. Let i_0 be the index of the last verification condition disclosed by the signer. Producing valid signatures is now equivalent to finding an α such that $g_{i_0} = g^\alpha_{P(i)}$, and if $\mathcal{A}$ succeeds in doing so with a non-negligible probability, then it can be used as an oracle to solve the discrete logarithm problem.   □

Efficiency. This technique offers several advantages compared to concatenation:

- Signature generation requires $n - i + 1$ exponentiations, this parameter depends on the number of coercions that the system has to withstand.
- Verification requires the same number of exponentiations as the concatenated Schnorr variant.
- The size of a signature is $(n + 1)160$ bits, instead of $320n$ bits

Roughly speaking, most characteristics are improved by a factor of two, which represents a significant improvement.

5   Conclusion

We proposed new signature mechanisms that tolerate, up to a certain point, secret disclosure under constraint. More precisely, we introduced symmetric and asymmetric monotone signatures to thwart different types of attacks. The asymmetric monotone scheme offers the broadest protection for the signer. We gave a practical example of such a scheme, based on the Okamoto-Schnorr signature. The new scheme, called Okamoto-Schnorr with i degrees of freedom, is provably secure against adaptive chosen-message attacks. We believe that the proposed solution can be practically deployed at the scale of a country.

References

1. M. Bellare, J.A. Garay, T. Rabin, *Fast Batch verification for modular exponentiation and digital signatures*, Advances in Cryptology EUROCRYPT'98, Springer-Verlag, LNCS 1403, pp. 236–250, 1998.
2. M. Bellare, P. Rogaway, *Random oracles are practical: A paradigm for designing efficient protocols*, Proceedings of the 1-st ACM conference on computer and communications security, pp. 62–73, 1993.
3. M. Bellare, P. Rogaway, *The exact security of digital signatures - How to sign with RSA and Rabin*, Advances in Cryptology EUROCRYPT'96, Springer-Verlag, LNCS 1070, pp. 399–416, 1996.
4. S. Brands, *An efficient off-line electronic cash system based on the representation problem*, Technical report, CWI (Centrum voor Wiskunde en Informatica), 1993. Also available on-line: http://www.cwi.nl/cwi/publications CS-R9323.

5. T. El Gamal, *A public key cryptosystem and a signature scheme based on discrete logarithms*, IEEE Transactions on Information Theory, vol. IT–31, no. 4, pp. 469–472, 1985.
6. U. Feige, A. Fiat, A. Shamir, *Zero-knowledge proofs of identity*, Journal of Cryptology, vol. 1, no. 2, pp. 77-95, 1988.
7. S. Goldwasser, S. Micali, R. Rivest, *A Digital signature scheme secure against adaptative chosen-message attacks*, SIAM journal of computing, vol. 17, pp. 281–308, 1988.
8. A. Herzberg, S. Jarecki, H. Krawczyk, M. Yung, *Proactive secret sharing, or: how to cope with perpetual leakage*, Advances in Cryptology CRYPTO'95, Springer-Verlag, LNCS 963, pp. 339–352, 1995.
9. M. Jakobsson, M. Yung, *Revokable and versatile electronic money*, Proceedings of the 3-rd ACM conference on computer and communications security, pp. 76–87, 1996.
10. C. Li, T. Hwang, M. Lee, (t, n)-*threshold signature schemes based on discrete logarithm*. Advances in Cryptology EUROCRYPT'94, Springer-Verlag, LNCS 950, pp. 191–200, 1995.
11. D. M'raïhi, D. Naccache, S. Vaudenay, D. Raphaeli, *Can D. S. A. be improved ? Complexity trade-offs with the digital signature standard*, Advances in Cryptology EUROCRYPT'94, Springer-Verlag, LNCS 950, pp. 77–85, 1995.
12. D. M'raïhi, D. Naccache, *Batch exponentiation - A fast DLP-based signature generation strategy*, 3-rd ACM conference on communications and computer security, pp. 58–61, 1996.
13. D. M'raïhi, D. Naccache, D. Pointcheval, S. Vaudenay, *Computational alternatives to random number generators*, Proceedings of the fifth annual workshop on selected areas in cryptography, LNCS 1556, pp. 72–80, 1998. Springer-Verlag.
14. NIST, *Digital Signature Standard (DSS)*, Federal Information Processing Standards Publication 186, 1994.
15. T. Okamoto, *Provably secure and practical identification schemes and corresponding signature schemes*, Advances in Cryptology CRYPTO'92, Springer-Verlag, LNCS 740, pp. 31–53, 1992.
16. D. Pointcheval, J. Stern, *Security arguments for digital signatures and blind signatures*, Journal of Cryptology, vol. 13, no. 3, pp. 361–396, 2000.
17. R. Rivest, A. Shamir, L. Adleman, *Method for obtaining digital signatures and public key cryptosystems*, Communications of the ACM, vol. 21, pp. 120–126, 1978.
18. C. Schnorr, *Efficient signature generation by smart cards*, Journal of Cryptology, vol. 4, no. 3, pp. 161-174, 1991.
19. V. Shoup, *Practical threshold signatures*, Technical report, IBM Research, June 1999. Report RZ 3121.
20. G. Simmons, *The subliminal channel and digital signatures*, Advances in Cryptology EUROCRYPT'84, Springer-Verlag, LNCS 209, pp. 364–378, 1985.
21. S. von Solms, D. Naccache, *On blind signatures and perfect crimes*, Computers & Security, vol.11, pp. 581–583,1992
22. R.L. Van Renesse, *Optical document security*, Artech House Optoelectronics Library, 2-nd edition, 1998.

The Power of RSA Inversion Oracles and the Security of Chaum's RSA-Based Blind Signature Scheme

Mihir Bellare[1], Chanathip Namprempre[1],
David Pointcheval[2], and Michael Semanko[1]

[1] Dept. of Computer Science and Engineering
University of California, San Diego
9500 Gilman Drive, La Jolla, CA 92093, USA
{mihir,cnamprem,msemanko}@cs.ucsd.edu
http://www-cse.ucsd.edu/users/{mihir,cnamprem,msemanko}
[2] Dépt. d'Informatique-CNRS, École Normale Supérieure
45 rue d'Ulm, 75230 Paris, Cedex 05, France
David.Pointcheval@ens.fr
http://www.dmi.ens.fr/users/pointche/

Abstract. Blind signatures are the central cryptographic component of digital cash schemes. In this paper, we investigate the security of the first such scheme proposed, namely Chaum's RSA-based blind signature scheme, in the random-oracle model. This leads us to formulate and investigate a new class of RSA-related computational problems which we call the "one-more-RSA-inversion" problems. Our main result is that two problems in this class which we call the chosen-target and known-target inversion problems, have polynomially-equivalent computational complexity. This leads to a proof of security for Chaum's scheme in the random oracle model based on the assumed hardness of either of these problems.

Keywords: Blind digital signature schemes, digital cash, RSA.

1 Introduction

Blind signatures are the central cryptographic component of digital cash schemes. Withdrawer and Bank run the blind signature protocol to enable the former to obtain the latter's signature on some token without revealing this token to the bank, thereby creating a valid but anonymous ecoin. In this paper, we investigate the security of the first such scheme proposed, namely Chaum's RSA-based blind signature scheme [7]. This leads us to formulate and investigate a new class of RSA-related computational problems which we call the "one-more-RSA-inversion" problems. We begin with a high-level description of our approach and its motivation.

THE GAP BETWEEN PROOFS AND PRACTICE. Chaum's RSA-based blind signature scheme [7] is simple and practical, and (assuming the underlying hash

P. Syverson (Ed.): FC 2001, LNCS 2339, pp. 319–338, 2002.

function is properly chosen) has so far resisted attacks. Yet there seems little hope of proving its security (even in a random oracle model [3]) based on the "standard" one-wayness assumption about the RSA function: it seems that the security of the scheme relies on different, and perhaps stronger, properties of RSA.

This is a common situation. It exhibits a gap created by what assumptions we prefer to make and what schemes we want to validate. The reliance on unproven computational properties of RSA for security naturally inclines us to be conservative and to stick to standard assumptions, of which the favorite is that RSA is one-way. Designers who have worked with RSA know, however, that it seems to have many additional strengths. These are typically exploited, implicitly rather than explicitly, in their designs. The resulting schemes might well resist attack but are dubbed "heuristic" because no proof of security based on the standard assumption seems likely. This leads designers to seek alternative schemes that can be proven under the standard assumptions. If the alternatives have cost comparable to that of the original scheme then they are indeed attractive replacements for the latter. But often they are more expensive. Meanwhile, the use of the original practical scheme is being discouraged even though it might very well be secure.

We take a different approach. Rather than going "forward" from assumptions to schemes —meaning, trying to find a scheme provable under some given standard assumption— we try to go "backwards" from schemes to assumptions — meaning to distill properties of RSA that are sufficient to guarantee the security of the *given* scheme.

We suggest that practical RSA-based schemes that have resisted attack (in this case, Chaum's RSA-based blind signature scheme) are manifestations of strengths of the RSA function that have not so far been properly abstracted or formalized. We suggest that one should build on the intuition of designers and formulate explicit computational problems that capture the above-mentioned strengths and suffice to prove the security of the scheme. These problems can then be studied to see how they relate to other problems and to what extent we can believe in them as assumptions. Doing so will lead to a better understanding of the security of the schemes. It will also highlight computational problems that might then be recognized as being at the core of other schemes, and enlarge the set of assumptions we might be willing to make, leading to benefits in the design or analysis of other schemes.

In this paper, we formalize a class of computational problems which we call *one-more-RSA-inversion* problems. They are natural extensions of the RSA-inversion problem underlying the notion of one-wayness to a setting where the adversary has access to a decryption oracle, and we show that the assumed hardness of one problem in this class —namely the *chosen-target inversion problem*— suffices to prove the security of Chaum's RSA-based blind signature scheme in the random oracle model. We then study this assumption, taking the standard approach in a domain of conjectures: we try to gain confidence in the assumption by relating it to other assumptions. Below, we first discuss the new computational problems and their properties and then tie this in with the blind signature scheme.

THE RSA SYSTEM. Associated with a modulus N and an encryption exponent e are the RSA function and its RSA-inverse defined by

$$\mathsf{RSA}_{N,e}(x) = x^e \bmod N \text{ and } \mathsf{RSA}_{N,e}^{-1}(y) = y^d \bmod N$$

where $x, y \in Z_N^*$ and d is the decryption exponent. To *invert* RSA at a point $y \in Z_N^*$ means to compute $x = \mathsf{RSA}_{N,e}^{-1}(y)$. The commonly made and believed assumption is that the RSA function is one-way. In other words, the following problem is hard:

RSA single-target inversion problem: RSA-STI

Input: N, e and a random target point $y \in Z_N^*$
Find: $y^d \bmod N$

Hardness (i.e. computational intractability) is measured via the usual convention: the success probability of an adversary, whose time-complexity is polynomial in the length k of the modulus, is negligible, the probability being over the choice of keys N, e, d as well as over any random choices explicitly indicated in the problem, in this case y. A problem is easy if it is not hard.

THE ONE-MORE-RSA-INVERSION PROBLEMS. We are interested in settings where the protocol is such that the legitimate user —and hence the adversary— has access to an oracle $\mathsf{RSA}_{N,e}^{-1}(\cdot)$ for the inverse RSA function. (The adversary can provide a value $y \in Z_N^*$ to its oracle and get back $x = \mathsf{RSA}_{N,e}^{-1}(y) = y^d \bmod N$, but it is not directly given d. We will see later how the RSA-blind signature scheme fits this setting.) A security property apparently possessed by RSA is that an adversary can only make "trivial" use of this oracle. We capture this in the following way. The adversary is given some random *target points* $y_1, \ldots, y_n \in Z_N^*$, and we say it wins if the number of these points whose RSA-inverse it manages to compute exceeds the number of calls it makes to its oracle. That is, it computes "one more RSA-inverse." Within this framework we consider two specific problems. They are parameterized by polynomially-bounded functions $n, m: \mathsf{N} \to \mathsf{N}$ of the security parameter k satisfying $n(\cdot) > m(\cdot)$–

RSA known-target inversion problem: RSA-KTI[m]

Input: N, e and random target points $y_1, \ldots, y_{m(k)+1} \in Z_N^*$
Oracle: RSA-inversion oracle computing $\mathsf{RSA}_{N,e}^{-1}(\cdot) = (\cdot)^d \bmod N$
         but only $m(k)$ calls allowed
Find: $y_1^d, \ldots, y_{m(k)+1}^d \bmod N$

RSA chosen-target inversion problem: RSA-CTI[n, m]

Input: N, e and random points $y_1, \ldots, y_{n(k)+1} \in Z_N^*$
Oracle: RSA-inversion oracle computing $\mathsf{RSA}_{N,e}^{-1}(\cdot) = (\cdot)^d \bmod N$
         but only $m(k)$ calls allowed
Find: Indices $1 \le i_1 < \cdots < i_{m(k)+1} < n(k)$ and $y_{i_1}^d, \ldots, y_{i_{m(k)+1}}^d \bmod N$

In the first problem, the number of oracle calls allowed to the adversary is just one fewer than the number of target points, so that to win it must compute the RSA-inverse of all target points. In the second version of the problem, the adversary does not have to compute the RSA-inverses of all target points but instead can choose some $m(k) + 1$ points out of $n(k)$ given points and wins if it can find their RSA-inverses using only $m(k)$ oracle calls.

The RSA-KTI[0] problem is identical to the standard RSA-STI problem. (When $m(\cdot) = 0$ the adversary's task is to find the RSA-inverse of one given random point y_1 without making any oracle queries.) In this sense, we consider security against known-target inversion to be a natural extension of one-wayness to a setting where the adversary has access to an RSA-inversion oracle.

We note in Remark 2 that if factoring reduces in polynomial time to RSA inversion then both the above problems are easy. Accordingly, these problems can be hard only if factoring does not reduce to RSA inversion. Some evidence that the latter is true is provided by Boneh and Venkatesan [6].

RELATIONS AMONG ONE-MORE-RSA-INVERSION PROBLEMS. We note in Remark 1 that if problem RSA-CTI$[n, m]$ is hard then so is problem RSA-KTI$[m]$. (If you can solve the latter then you can solve the former by RSA-inverting the first $m(k) + 1$ target points.) However, it is conceivable that the ability to choose the target points might help the adversary considerably. Our main result is that this is not so. We show in Theorem 1 that if problem RSA-KTI$[m]$ is hard then so is problem RSA-CTI$[n, m]$, for any polynomially-bounded $n(\cdot)$ and $m(\cdot)$. (This result assumes that the encryption exponent e is prime.) We prove the theorem by showing how given any polynomial-time adversary B that solves RSA-KTI$[m]$ we can design a polynomial-time adversary A that solves RSA-CTI$[n, m]$ with about the same probability. The reduction exploits linear algebraic techniques which in this setting are complicated by the fact that the order $\phi(N)$ of the group over which we must work is not known to the adversary.

THE RSA-BASED BLIND SIGNATURE SCHEME. The signer's public key is N, e, and its secret key is N, d where these quantities are as in the RSA system. The signature of a message M is

$$x = \mathsf{RSA}_{N,e}^{-1}(H(M)) = H(M)^d \bmod N \tag{1}$$

where $H: \{0,1\}^* \to Z_N^*$ is a public hash function. A message-tag pair (M, x) is said to be *valid* if x is as in Equation (1). The blind signature protocol enables a user to obtain the signature of a message M without revealing M to the signer, as follows. The user picks r at random in Z_N^*, computes $\overline{M} = r^e \cdot H(M) \bmod N$, and sends $\overline{M}$ to the signer. The latter computes $\overline{x} = \mathsf{RSA}_{N,e}^{-1}(\overline{M}) = \overline{M}^d \bmod N$ and returns $\overline{x}$ to the user, who extracts the signature $x = \overline{x} \cdot r^{-1} \bmod N$ of M from it. Two properties are desired, *blindness* and *unforgeability*. Blindness means the signer does not learn anything about M from the protocol that it did not know before, and it is easy to show that this is unconditionally true [7]. Unforgeability in this context is captured via the notion of one-more-forgery of Pointcheval and Stern [18,19]. (The standard notion of [13] does not apply to blind signatures.) The forger can engage in interactions with the signer in which it might not follow the prescribed protocol for the user. (As discussed further in Section 3 there are, in general, a variety of attack models for these interactions [18,19,14,16], but in the case of the RSA blind signature protocol, all are equivalent.) Nothing prevents it from coming up with one valid message-tag pair per protocol execution (to do this, it just has to follow the user protocol) but we want it to be hard to come up with more. We ask that the number of valid message-tag pairs that a forger can produce cannot exceed the number of executions of the blind-signature protocol in which it engages with the signer.

It is the unforgeability property that has been the open question about the RSA-based blind signature scheme. Michels, Stadler and Sun [15] show that one can successfully obtain one-more forgery if the hash function is poorly implemented. Here, we will assume that the hash function is a random oracle. (The forger and signer both get an oracle for H.) In that case, the signature scheme is the FDH scheme of [4]. This scheme is proven to meet the standard security notion for digital signatures of [13] in the random oracle model assuming that RSA is one-way [4,8], but this result won't help us here. To date, no attacks against the one-more-forgery goal are known on the blind FDH-RSA signature scheme. We would like to support this evidence of security with proofs.

When the forger interacts with a signer in Chaum's blind signature protocol detailed above, the former effectively has access to an RSA-inversion oracle: it can provide the signer any $\overline{M} \in Z_N^*$ and get back $\overline{M}^d$ mod N. It is the presence of this oracle that makes it unlikely that the one-wayness of RSA alone suffices to guarantee unforgeability. However, the one-more-RSA-decryption problems were defined precisely to capture settings where the adversary has an RSA-inversion oracle, and we will be able to base the security of the signature scheme on hardness assumptions about them.

UNFORGEABILITY OF THE FDH-RSA BLIND SIGNATURE SCHEME. In Lemma 4, we provide a reduction of the security against one-more-forgery of the FDH-RSA blind signature scheme, in the random oracle model, to the security of the RSA chosen-target inversion problem. Appealing to Theorem 1 we then get a proof of unforgeability for the blind FDH-RSA scheme, in the random oracle model, under the assumption that the RSA known-target inversion problem is hard. (Again, this is for prime encryption exponents.) These results simplify the security considerations of the blind FDH-RSA scheme by eliminating the hash function and signature issues from the picture, leaving us natural problems about RSA to study.

PERSPECTIVE. An obvious criticism of the above result is that the proof of security of the blind FDH-RSA signature scheme is under a novel and extremely strong RSA assumption which is not only hard to validate but crafted to have the properties necessary to prove the security of the signature scheme. This is true, and we warn that the assumptions should be treated with caution. But we suggest that our approach and results have pragmatic value. Certainly, one could leave the blind RSA signature scheme unanalyzed until someone proves security based on the one-wayness of RSA, but this is likely to be a long wait.

Meanwhile, we would like to use the scheme and the practical thing to do is to understand the basis of its security as best we can. Our results isolate clear and simply stated properties of the RSA function that underlie the security of the blind signature scheme and make the task of the security analyst easier by freeing him or her from consideration of properties of signatures and hash functions. It is better to know exactly what we are assuming, even if this is very strong, than to know nothing at all.

EXTENSIONS. The analogues of the one-more-RSA-inversion problems can be formulated for any family of one-way functions. We can prove that the known-target inversion and chosen-target inversion problems have polynomially-equivalent computational complexity also for the discrete logarithm function in groups of prime order. (That proof is actually a little easier than the one for RSA in this paper because in the discrete log case the order of the group is public information.)

RELATED WORK. Other non-standard RSA related computational problems whose study has been fruitful include strong-RSA [11,2,12,9] and dependent-RSA [17]. For more information about RSA properties and attacks see [5].

2   Complexity of the One-More-RSA-Inversion Problems

Throughout this paper, $k \in \mathsf{N}$ denotes the security parameter. We let KeyGen be the *RSA key generation algorithm* which takes k as input and returns the values N, e and d where N is a k-bit RSA modulus (product of two $k/2$ bit random primes p_1, p_2) and $e, d \in \mathsf{Z}^*_{\phi(N)}$ with $ed \equiv 1 \bmod \phi(N)$ where $\phi(N) = (p_1 - 1)(p_2 - 1)$. (The public key is N, e and the secret key is N, d.) *The results in this paper will assume that e is prime.*

Below, we provide the formal definitions corresponding to the computational problems discussed in Section 1. In each case, we associate to any given adversary an *advantage* function which on input the security parameter k returns the probability that an associated *experiment* returns 1. The problem is *hard* if the advantage of any adversary of time-complexity poly(k) is negligible, and we say that a problem is *easy* if it is not hard. Furthermore, we adopt the convention that the time-complexity of the adversary refers to the function which on input k returns the execution time of the full associated experiment including the time taken to compute answers to oracle calls, plus the size of the code of the adversary, in some fixed model of computation. This convention will simplify concrete security considerations.

ONE-WAYNESS OF RSA. We recall the standard notion, couching it in a way more suitable for comparison with the new notions.

Definition 1. (Single-Target Inversion Problem: *RSA-STI) Let $k \in \mathsf{N}$ be the security parameter. Let A be an adversary. Consider the following experiment:*

Experiment $\mathbf{Exp}_A^{\text{rsa-sti}}(k)$

   $(N, e, d) \stackrel{R}{\leftarrow} \text{KeyGen}(k)$
   $y \stackrel{R}{\leftarrow} Z_N^* \; ; \; x \leftarrow A(N, e, k, y)$
   If $x^e \equiv y \pmod{N}$ *then return 1 else return 0*

We define the advantage of A via

$$\mathbf{Adv}_A^{\text{rsa-sti}}(k) = \Pr[\,\mathbf{Exp}_A^{\text{rsa-sti}}(k) = 1\,] \,.$$

The RSA-STI problem is said to be hard —in more standard terminology, RSA is said to be one-way— if the function $\mathbf{Adv}_{A,m}^{\text{rsa-kti}}(\cdot)$ is negligible for any adversary A whose time-complexity is polynomial in the security parameter k. ∎

THE KNOWN-TARGET INVERSION PROBLEM. We denote by $(\cdot)^d \bmod N$ the oracle that takes input $y \in Z_N^*$ and returns its RSA-inverse y^d. An adversary solving the known-target inversion problem is given oracle access to $(\cdot)^d \bmod N$ and is given $m(k) + 1$ targets where $m : \mathsf{N} \to \mathsf{N}$. Its task is to compute the RSA-inverses of *all* the targets while submitting at most $m(k)$ queries to the oracle.

Definition 2. (Known-Target Inversion Problem: *RSA-KTI[m]) Let $k \in \mathsf{N}$ be the security parameter, and let $m : \mathsf{N} \to \mathsf{N}$ be a function of k. Let A be an adversary with access to an RSA-inversion oracle $(\cdot)^d \bmod N$. Consider the following experiment:*

Experiment $\mathbf{Exp}_{A,m}^{\text{rsa-kti}}(k)$

   $(N, e, d) \stackrel{R}{\leftarrow} \text{KeyGen}(k)$
   For $i = 1$ *to* $m(k) + 1$ *do* $y_i \stackrel{R}{\leftarrow} Z_N^*$
   $(x_1, \dots, x_{m(k)+1}) \leftarrow A^{(\cdot)^d \bmod N}(N, e, k, y_1, \dots, y_{m(k)+1})$
   If the following are both true then return 1 else return 0
   $\quad$ – $\quad \forall i \in \{1, \dots, m(k) + 1\} : x_i^e \equiv y_i \pmod{N}$
   $\quad$ – $\quad$ *A made at most $m(k)$ oracle queries*

We define the advantage of A via

$$\mathbf{Adv}_{A,m}^{\text{rsa-kti}}(k) = \Pr[\,\mathbf{Exp}_{A,m}^{\text{rsa-kti}}(k) = 1\,] \,.$$

The RSA-KTI[m] problem is said to be hard if the function $\mathbf{Adv}_{A,m}^{\text{rsa-kti}}(\cdot)$ is negligible for any adversary A whose time-complexity is polynomial in the security parameter k. The known-target inversion problem is said to be hard if RSA-KTI[m] is hard for all polynomially-bounded $m(\cdot)$. ∎

Notice that RSA-KTI[0] is the same as RSA-STI. That is, the standard assumption that RSA is one-way is exactly the same as saying that RSA-KTI[0] is hard.

THE CHOSEN-TARGET INVERSION PROBLEM. An adversary solving the chosen-target inversion problem is given access to an RSA-inversion oracle as above, and

$n(k)$ targets where $n : \mathsf{N} \to \mathsf{N}$. Its task is to compute $m(k) + 1$ RSA-inversions of the given targets, where $m : \mathsf{N} \to \mathsf{N}$ and $m(k) < n(k)$, while submitting at most $m(k)$ queries to the oracle. The choice of which targets to compute the RSA-inversion is up to the adversary. This choice is indicated by the range of the injective map π. (Notationally, this is different from the definition provided in Section 1. There, indices for elements chosen by the adversary are explicitly indicated. These indices constitute the range of the map π used here.)

Definition 3. (Chosen-Target Inversion Problem: *RSA-CTI[n, m]*) *Let $k \in \mathsf{N}$ be the security parameter, and let $m, n : \mathsf{N} \to \mathsf{N}$ be functions of k such that $m(\cdot) < n(\cdot)$. Let B be an adversary with access to an RSA-inversion oracle $(\cdot)^d \bmod N$. Consider the following experiment:*

Experiment $\mathbf{Exp}^{\text{rsa-cti}}_{B,n,m}(k)$

> $(N, e, d) \xleftarrow{R} \text{KeyGen}(k)$
> *For $i = 1$ to $n(k)$ do* $\overline{y}_i \xleftarrow{R} \mathsf{Z}^*_N$
> $(\pi, \overline{x}_1, \ldots, \overline{x}_{m(k)+1}) \leftarrow B^{(\cdot)^d \bmod N}(N, e, k, \overline{y}_1, \ldots, \overline{y}_{n(k)})$
> *If the following are all true then return 1 else return 0*
> - $\pi : \{1, \ldots, m(k) + 1\} \to \{1, \ldots, n(k)\}$ *is injective*
> - $\forall i \in \{1, \ldots, m(k) + 1\} : \overline{x}^e_i \equiv \overline{y}_{\pi(i)} \pmod{N}$
> - *A made at most $m(k)$ oracle queries*

We define the advantage of A via

$$\mathbf{Adv}^{\text{rsa-cti}}_{B,n,m}(k) = \Pr[\,\mathbf{Exp}^{\text{rsa-cti}}_{B,n,m}(k) = 1\,].$$

The RSA-CTI[n, m] problem is said to be hard if the function $\mathbf{Adv}^{\text{rsa-cti}}_{B,n,m}(\cdot)$ is negligible for any adversary A whose time complexity is polynomial in the security parameter k. The chosen-target inversion problem is said to be hard if RSA-CTI[n, m] is hard for all polynomially-bounded $n(\cdot)$ and $m(\cdot)$. ∎

RELATIONS AMONGST THE PROBLEMS. We note a few simple relations before going to the main result.

Remark 1. Let $n, m : \mathsf{N} \to \mathsf{N}$ be polynomially-bounded functions of the security parameter k. If the RSA-CTI[n, m] problem is hard then so is the RSA-KTI[m] problem. This is justified as follows: given an adversary A for RSA-KTI[m], we let B be the adversary for RSA-CTI[n, m] that runs A on input the first $m(k) + 1$ of B's target points and returns the values returned by A. Then B's advantage is the same as A's.

Remark 2. If factoring reduces to RSA inversion then there exists a polynomially-bounded function $m : \mathsf{N} \to \mathsf{N}$ such that RSA-KTI[m] is easy. (So the assumption that either the known-target or chosen-target inversion problems is hard is at least as strong as the assumption that factoring does not reduce to RSA inversion.) Let us briefly justify this. Assume that factoring reduces to RSA inversion. This means there is a polynomial-time algorithm R such that the probability that the following experiment returns 1 is non-negligible:

$(N, e, d) \overset{R}{\leftarrow} \text{KeyGen}(k)$

$(p_1, p_2) \leftarrow R^{(\cdot)^d \bmod N}(N, e, k)$

If p_1, p_2 are prime and $p_1 p_2 = N$ then return 1 else return 0.

Let m be the number of oracle queries made by R. We define adversary A as follows:

Adversary $A^{(\cdot)^d \bmod N}(N, e, k, y_1, \ldots, y_{m(k)+1})$

$\quad (p_1, p_2) \leftarrow R^{(\cdot)^d \bmod N}(N, e, k)$

$\quad$ Compute d from p_1, p_2

$\quad$ Compute and return $y_1^d, \ldots, y_{m(k)+1}^d \bmod N$

The adversary A runs the algorithm R, answering to its inversion queries with the answers from its own oracle. It uses the fact that possession of the prime factors of N enables computation of the decryption exponent d, and having computed d, it can of course compute the RSA-inversions of as many points as it pleases.

Our main result is a converse to the claim of Remark 1.

Theorem 1. *Let* $n, m \colon \mathsf{N} \to \mathsf{N}$ *be polynomially-bounded functions of the security parameter* k. *If the RSA-KTI[m] problem is hard then so is the RSA-CTI[n, m] problem. Concretely, for any adversary* B, *there exists an adversary* A *so that*

$$\mathbf{Adv}^{\text{rsa-cti}}_{B,n,m}(k) \leq \frac{9}{5} \cdot \mathbf{Adv}^{\text{rsa-kti}}_{A,m}(k) \qquad (2)$$

and A *has time-complexity*

$$T_A(k) = T_B(k) + O\left(k^3 n(k)m(k) + k^4 m(k) + k^2 m(k)^5 + k m(k)^6\right) \qquad (3)$$

where $T_B(\cdot)$ *is the time-complexity of* B.

We will now present some technical lemmas, and then proceed to the proof of Theorem 1. The reader might prefer to begin with Section 2.2 and refer to Section 2.1 as needed.

2.1 Technical Lemmas

Before proving our main result we state and prove some relevant technical lemmas.

Lemma 1. *Let* $s \geq 1$ *be an integer, let* I_s *be the* s *by* s *identity matrix, and let*

$$C = \begin{bmatrix} c_{1,1} & \cdots & c_{1,s} \\ \vdots & & \vdots \\ c_{s,1} & \cdots & c_{s,s} \end{bmatrix} \quad \text{and} \quad D = \begin{bmatrix} d_{1,1} & \cdots & d_{1,s} \\ \vdots & & \vdots \\ d_{s,1} & \cdots & d_{s,s} \end{bmatrix}$$

be integer matrices such that $C \cdot D = \det(C) \cdot I_s$. *Suppose* N, e *is an RSA public key and* N, d *is the corresponding secret key. Suppose* $y_i, \overline{y}_i, v_i \in \mathsf{Z}_N^*$ *for*

$i = 1, \ldots, s$ *are related via*

$$\bar{y}_i \equiv v_i^{-e} \cdot \prod_{j=1}^{s} y_j^{c_{j,i}} \pmod{N}. \tag{4}$$

Let $\bar{x}_i = \bar{y}_i^d \bmod N$ *for* $i = 1, \ldots, s$. *Then, for* $j = 1, \ldots, s$, *we have*

$$(y_j^d)^{\det(C)} \equiv \prod_{i=1}^{s} (v_i \cdot \bar{x}_i)^{d_{i,j}} \pmod{N}. \tag{5}$$

Proof (Lemma 1). Let $\delta_{l,j} = 1$ if $l = j$ and 0 otherwise. Since $C \cdot D = \det(C) \cdot I_s$ we know that

$$\sum_{i=1}^{s} c_{l,i} d_{i,j} = \det(C) \cdot \delta_{l,j} \tag{6}$$

for all $l, j = 1, \ldots, s$. We now verify Equation (5). Suppose $1 \le j \le s$. In the following, computations are all mod N. From Equation (4), we have

$$\prod_{i=1}^{s}(v_i \cdot \bar{x}_i)^{d_{i,j}} = \prod_{i=1}^{s}\left[v_i \cdot \left(v_i^{-e} \cdot \prod_{l=1}^{s} y_l^{c_{l,i}}\right)^d\right]^{d_{i,j}} = \prod_{i=1}^{s}\left[v_i \cdot v_i^{-1} \cdot \prod_{l=1}^{s}(y_l^d)^{c_{l,i}}\right]^{d_{i,j}}.$$

Simplifying the last expression, we obtain

$$\prod_{i=1}^{s}\prod_{l=1}^{s}(y_l^d)^{c_{l,i}d_{i,j}} = \prod_{l=1}^{s}\prod_{i=1}^{s}(y_l^d)^{c_{l,i}d_{i,j}} = \prod_{l=1}^{s}(y_l^d)^{\sum_{i=1}^{s} c_{l,i}d_{i,j}} = \prod_{l=1}^{s}(y_l^d)^{\det(C)\cdot\delta_{l,j}}$$

where the last equality is by Equation (6). Finally, we use the fact that $\delta_{l,j} = 1$ if $l = j$ and 0 otherwise. This tells us that the above is $(y_j^d)^{\det(C)}$ as desired. ∎

Lemma 2. *Let* N, e *be an RSA public key and* N, d *the corresponding secret key. Let* $\alpha \in \mathbb{N}$ *and* $y, z \in \mathbb{Z}_N^*$. *If* $\gcd(\alpha, e) = 1$ *and* $(y^d)^\alpha \equiv z \pmod{N}$ *then* $(z^a y^b)^e \equiv y \pmod{N}$ *where* a, b *are the unique integers such that* $a\alpha + be = 1$.

Proof (Lemma 2). This is a standard calculation:

$$(z^a y^b)^e = (y^{d\alpha})^{ae} y^{be} = y^{\alpha a + be} = y^1 = y$$

where the computations are all mod N. ∎

Next, we consider a question in probabilistic linear algebra.

Definition 4. *Let* $q \ge 2$ *be a prime, and let* $s \ge 1$ *be an integer. We define* $\text{SProb}(q, s)$ *to be the probability that* $\det(M) \equiv 0 \pmod{q}$ *when* M *is an* s *by* s *matrix formed by choosing all entries uniformly and independently from* $\mathbb{Z}_q$. ∎

It is tempting to think that the determinant of a random matrix is a random value and hence that $\text{SProb}(q, s) = 1/q$. This, however, is not true. For example, a simple computation shows that $\mathrm{SProb}(q,2) = 1/q + 1/q^2 - 1/q^3$. There is actually a standard formula (whose proof we will recall later) for this quantity–

$$\mathrm{SProb}(q,s) = 1 - \prod_{i=1}^{s}\left(1 - \frac{q^{i-1}}{q^s}\right). \tag{7}$$

This formula, however, does not lend itself well to estimates. We would like a simple upper bound on $\mathrm{SProb}(q,s)$. We prove the following. (We don't use the lower bound in this paper but include it for completeness.)

Lemma 3. *Let $q \geq 2$ be a prime, and let $s \geq 1$ be an integer. Then*

$$\frac{1}{q} \leq \mathrm{SProb}(q,s) \leq \frac{1}{q} + \frac{1}{q^2}. \tag{8}$$

Proof (Lemma 3). View the matrix M as formed by successively choosing random row vectors from Z_q^s. Let M_i denote the vector which is the i-th row of M, and let LI_i denote the event that the vectors $M_1, \ldots, M_i$ are linearly independent over Z_q, for $i = 1, \ldots, s$. It is convenient to let LI_0 be the event having probability one. Let $\mathrm{SProb}(q,s,i) = \Pr[\neg\mathrm{LI}_i]$ for $i = 0, \ldots, s$ and note that $\mathrm{SProb}(q,s) = \mathrm{SProb}(q,s,s)$.

We briefly recall the justification for Equation (7) and use it to derive the lower bound. (The upper bound is derived by a separate inductive argument.) We have

$$1 - \mathrm{SProb}(q,s) = \prod_{i=1}^{s}\Pr[\,\mathrm{LI}_i \mid \mathrm{LI}_{i-1}\,] = \prod_{i=1}^{s}\frac{q^s - q^{i-1}}{q^s} = \prod_{i=1}^{s}\left(1 - \frac{q^{i-1}}{q^s}\right)$$

which is Equation (7). We derive the lower bound by upper bounding the product term of Equation (7) by the biggest term of the product:

$$\mathrm{SProb}(q,s) \geq 1 - \left(1 - \frac{1}{q}\right) = \frac{1}{q}.$$

For the upper bound, we first claim that the following recurrence is true for $i = 0, \ldots, s$:

$$\mathrm{SProb}(q,s,i) = \begin{cases} 0 & \text{if } i = 0 \\ \dfrac{q^{i-1}}{q^s} + \left(1 - \dfrac{q^{i-1}}{q^s}\right) \cdot \mathrm{SProb}(q,s,i-1) & \text{if } i \geq 1 \end{cases} \tag{9}$$

The initial condition is simply by the convention we adopted that $\Pr[\mathrm{LI}_0] = 1$. The recurrence is justified as follows for $i \geq 1$:

$\mathrm{SProb}(q,s,i)$
$= \Pr[\neg\mathrm{LI}_i]$
$= \Pr[\,\neg\mathrm{LI}_i \mid \mathrm{LI}_{i-1}\,] \cdot \Pr[\mathrm{LI}_{i-1}] + \Pr[\,\neg\mathrm{LI}_i \mid \neg\mathrm{LI}_{i-1}\,] \cdot \Pr[\neg\mathrm{LI}_{i-1}]$
$= \Pr[\,\neg\mathrm{LI}_i \mid \mathrm{LI}_{i-1}\,] \cdot (1 - \mathrm{SProb}(q,s,i-1)) + 1 \cdot \mathrm{SProb}(q,s,i-1)$
$= \Pr[\,\neg\mathrm{LI}_i \mid \mathrm{LI}_{i-1}\,] + (1 - \Pr[\,\neg\mathrm{LI}_i \mid \mathrm{LI}_{i-1}\,]) \cdot \mathrm{SProb}(q,s,i-1)$
$= \dfrac{q^{i-1}}{q^s} + \left(1 - \dfrac{q^{i-1}}{q^s}\right) \cdot \mathrm{SProb}(q,s,i-1).$

We claim that

$$\mathrm{SProb}(q,s,i) \le \frac{q^i}{q^s} \cdot \frac{1}{q-1} \qquad \text{for } i = 0, \ldots, s. \qquad (10)$$

This will be justified below. It already gives us an upper bound on $\mathrm{SProb}(q,s) = \mathrm{SProb}(q,s,s)$, namely $1/(q-1)$, but this is a little worse than our claimed upper bound. To get the latter, we use the recurrence for $i = s$ and use Equation (10) with $i = s - 1$. This give us

$$\mathrm{SProb}(q,s) = \mathrm{SProb}(q,s,s) = \frac{q^{s-1}}{q^s} + \left(1 - \frac{q^{s-1}}{q^s}\right) \cdot \mathrm{SProb}(q,s,s-1)$$

$$\le \frac{q^{s-1}}{q^s} + \left(1 - \frac{q^{s-1}}{q^s}\right) \cdot \frac{q^{s-1}}{q^s} \frac{1}{q-1}$$

Simplifying this further, we get

$$\mathrm{SProb}(q,s) \le \frac{1}{q} + \left(1 - \frac{1}{q}\right) \cdot \frac{1}{q} \frac{1}{q-1} = \frac{1}{q} + \frac{1}{q-1}\left(\frac{1}{q} - \frac{1}{q^2}\right) = \frac{1}{q} + \frac{1}{q^2}.$$

This is the claimed upper bound. It remains to justify Equation (10) which we do by induction on i. When $i = 0$, Equation (10) puts a positive upper bound on $\mathrm{SProb}(q,s,0)$, and hence, is certainly true. So assume $i \ge 1$. Substituting into the recurrence of Equation (9), we get

$$\mathrm{SProb}(q,s,i) = \frac{q^{i-1}}{q^s} + \left(1 - \frac{q^{i-1}}{q^s}\right) \cdot \mathrm{SProb}(q,s,i-1)$$

$$\le \frac{q^{i-1}}{q^s} + \mathrm{SProb}(q,s,i-1).$$

Using the inductive hypothesis and simplifying, we have

$$\mathrm{SProb}(q,s,i) \le \frac{q^{i-1}}{q^s} + \frac{q^{i-1}}{q^s} \frac{1}{q-1} = \frac{q^{i-1}}{q^s}\left(1 + \frac{1}{q-1}\right) = \frac{q^i}{q^s} \frac{1}{q-1}$$

as desired. ∎

2.2   Proof of Theorem 1

OVERVIEW. The adversary A is depicted in Figure 1. Its input is $(N, e, k$ and) $s = m(k) + 1$ target points $y_1, \ldots, y_s$. Its goal is to compute $y_1^d, \ldots, y_s^d \bmod N$.

Adversary A will begin by computing $n(k)$ points $\overline{y}_1, \ldots, \overline{y}_{n(k)}$ as a (randomized) function of the given points $y_1, \ldots, y_s$. The property we want these to have is that, given the RSA-inverses of any s of the points $\overline{y}_1, \ldots, \overline{y}_{n(k)}$, it is possible to extract in polynomial time the RSA-inverses of the original target points, at least with high probability. If such a "reversible embedding" can be implemented then A's work is complete since invoking B on the points $\overline{y}_1, \ldots, \overline{y}_{n(k)}$ will cause the RSA-inverses of some s of these points to be returned. The question is, thus, how to compute and later reverse this "reversible embedding."

Algorithm $A^{(\cdot)^d \bmod N}(N, e, k, y_1, \ldots, y_{m(k)+1})$

1    $q \leftarrow e$; $s \leftarrow m(k) + 1$
2   For $i = 1$ to $n(k)$ do
3      $v[i] \stackrel{R}{\leftarrow} Z_N^*$
4   For $j = 1$ to s do $c[j, i] \stackrel{R}{\leftarrow} Z_q$
5      $\overline{y}_i \leftarrow v[i]^{-e} \prod_{j=1}^{s} y_j^{c[j,i]} \bmod N$
6    $(\pi, \overline{x}_1, \ldots, \overline{x}_s) \leftarrow B^{(\cdot)^d \bmod N}(N, e, k, \overline{y}_1, \ldots, \overline{y}_{n(k)})$
7   For $j = 1, \ldots, s$ do
        $v_j \leftarrow v[\pi(j)]$
        For $l = 1, \ldots, s$ do $c_{j,l} \leftarrow c[j, \pi(l)]$

8    $C \leftarrow \begin{bmatrix} c_{1,1} \cdots c_{1,s} \\ \vdots \qquad \vdots \\ c_{s,1} \cdots c_{s,s} \end{bmatrix}$

9    $\alpha \leftarrow \det(C)$
10   If $\alpha = 0$ then abort
11   Compute a matrix

     $D = \begin{bmatrix} d_{1,1} \cdots d_{1,s} \\ \vdots \qquad \vdots \\ d_{s,1} \cdots d_{s,s} \end{bmatrix}$

     with integer entries such that $C \cdot D = \det(C) \cdot I_s$
12   For $j = 1$ to s do
13     $z_j \leftarrow \prod_{i=1}^{s} (v_i \cdot \overline{x}_i)^{d_{i,j}} \bmod N$
14   If $\gcd(\alpha, e) \neq 1$ then abort
15   Compute $a, b \in Z$ such that $a\alpha + be = 1$ via extended Euclid algorithm
16   For $j = 1$ to s do
17     $x_j \leftarrow z_j^a \cdot y_j^b \bmod N$
18   Return $x_1, \ldots, x_s$

Fig. 1. Adversary A of the proof of Theorem 1

Lines 2–5 of Figure 1 show how to compute it. For each j, the point $\overline{y}_j$ is created by first raising each of $y_1, \ldots, y_s$ to a random power and then multiplying the obtained quantities. (This product is then multiplied by a random group element of which A knows the RSA-inverse in order to make sure that $\overline{y}_1, \ldots, \overline{y}_{n(k)}$ are uniformly and independently distributed and thus are appropriate to feed to B.) A detail worth remarking here is the choice of the range from which the exponents $c[j, i]$ are chosen. This is Z_q where we have set q equal to the encryption exponent e. We will see the reasons for this choice later.

Once the points $\overline{y}_1, \ldots, \overline{y}_{n(k)}$ have been defined, B is invoked. In executing B, adversary A will invoke its own oracle to answer RSA-inversion oracle queries of B. Notice that this means that the number of oracle queries made by A is exactly equal to the number made by B which is $s - 1 = m(k)$. Assuming that

B succeeds, A is in possession of $\overline{x}_j \equiv \overline{y}_{\pi(j)}^d \pmod{N}$ for $j = 1, \ldots, s$ where $\pi(j)$ are indices of B's choice that A could not have predicted beforehand. The final step is to recover the RSA-inverses of the original target points.

To this end, A creates the matrix C shown in line 8 of the code. If this matrix has zero determinant then A will not be able to reverse its embedding and aborts. Assuming a non-zero determinant, A would like to invert matrix C. Since the entries are exponents, A would like to work modulo $\phi(N)$ but A does not know this value. Instead, it works over the integers. A can compute a "partial" RSA-inverse, namely an integer matrix D such that $C \cdot D$ is a known integer multiple of the s by s identity matrix I_s. The integer multiple in question is the determinant of C, and thus the matrix D is the adjoint of C. (We will discuss the computation of D more later.) Lines 12–18 show how A then computes $x_1, \ldots, x_s$ which we claim equal $y_1^d, \ldots, y_s^d$. We now proceed to the detailed analysis.

ANALYSIS. Let NS be the event that $\det(C) \not\equiv 0 \pmod{q}$. (If this is true then not only is $\det(C) \neq 0$, meaning C is non-singular, but also $\gcd(\det(C), e) = 1$ because $q = e$ is prime.) Let "A succeeds" denote the event that $x_i = y_i^d$ for all $i = 1, \ldots, s$. Let "B succeeds" denote the event that $\overline{x}_j = \overline{y}_{\pi(j)}^d$ for all $j = 1, \ldots, s$. Then,

$$\Pr[\,A \text{ succeeds}\,]$$
$$\geq \Pr[\,A \text{ succeeds} \wedge B \text{ succeeds} \wedge \text{NS}\,]$$
$$= \Pr[\,A \text{ succeeds} \mid B \text{ succeeds} \wedge \text{NS}\,] \cdot \Pr[\,B \text{ succeeds} \wedge \text{NS}\,] . \quad (11)$$

We claim that

$$\Pr[\,A \text{ succeeds} \mid B \text{ succeeds} \wedge \text{NS}\,] = 1 \quad (12)$$

$$\Pr[\,B \text{ succeeds} \wedge \text{NS}\,] \geq \frac{5}{9} \cdot \mathbf{Adv}_{B,n,m}^{\text{rsa-cti}}(k) . \quad (13)$$

Equations (11), (12), and (13) imply Equation (2). So it remains to verify Equations (12), (13) and the time-complexity claimed in Equation (3). We begin with Equation (12). Lemma 1 tells us that, assuming B succeeds and $\det(C) \neq 0$, after line 13 of Figure 1, we have

$$(y_j^d)^{\det(C)} \equiv z_j \pmod{N} \quad (14)$$

for $j = 1, \ldots, s$. Assume $\gcd(\alpha, e) = 1$. Then Equation (14) and Lemma 2 imply that at line 17 we have $x_j^e = y_j$ for all $j = 1, \ldots, s$, in other words, A succeeds. Now note that event NS implies that $\det(C) \neq 0$ and that $\gcd(\det(C), e) = 1$ because $q = e$ and e is prime. This completes the proof of Equation (12).

We now move on to the proof of Equation (13). Due to the random choice of $v[1], \ldots, v[n(k)]$, the points $\overline{y}_1, \ldots, \overline{y}_{n(k)}$ computed at line 5 and then fed to B are uniformly and independently distributed over $\mathbb{Z}_N^*$ regardless of the choices of $c[j, i]$. This means that the events "B succeeds" and NS are independent and also that the probability of the former is the advantage of B. Thus, we have

$$\Pr[\,B \text{ succeeds} \wedge \text{NS}\,] = \Pr[\text{NS}] \cdot \Pr[\,B \text{ succeeds}\,] = \Pr[\text{NS}] \cdot \mathbf{Adv}_{B,n,m}^{\text{rsa-cti}}(k) .$$

Code	Cost
"For" loop at line 2	$O(k^3) \cdot n(k) \cdot s$
$\det(C)$	$O(s^4 k + s^3 k^2)$
Matrix D	$s^2 \cdot O(s^4 k + s^3 k^2)$
"For" loop at line 12	$O(k^2 s) \cdot O(sk)$
Lines 14, 15	$O(sk) \cdot O(k)$
Line 17	$O(k^2) \cdot O(k^2 s)$
Total	$O(k^3 n(k)s + k^4 s + k^2 s^5 + k s^6)$

Fig. 2. Costs of computations of the algorithm of Figure 1. Recall that $s = m(k) + 1$

So to complete the proof of Equation (13), it suffices to show that

$$\Pr[\,\mathrm{NS}\,] \geq \frac{5}{9} \, . \tag{15}$$

Recall that our adversary A sets $q = e$ (line 1 in Figure 1) and that $e \geq 3$ for RSA. We now apply Lemma 3 to get

$$\Pr[\,\mathrm{NS}\,] = 1 - \mathrm{SProb}(q, s) \geq 1 - \left(\frac{1}{q} + \frac{1}{q^2}\right) = 1 - \frac{1}{e} - \frac{1}{e^2} \geq 1 - \frac{1}{3} - \frac{1}{3^2} = \frac{5}{9} \, .$$

This proves Equation (15) and, hence, completes the proof of Equation (13). To complete the proof of Theorem 1, it remains to justify the claim of Equation (3) about the time complexity. The costs of various steps of the algorithm of the adversary A are summarized in Figure 2. We now briefly explain them.

As in the code, we let $s = m(k) + 1$. The "For" loop beginning at line 2 involves $n(k) \cdot s$ exponentiations of k-bit exponents which has the cost shown. Computation of determinants is done using the algorithm of [1]. This takes $O(r^4(\log(r) + k) + r^3 k^2)$ time to compute the determinant of an r by r integer matrix each of whose entries is at most k-bits long. (Although somewhat faster algorithms are known [10], they are randomized, and for simplicity, we use a deterministic algorithm.) We use this algorithm in Step 9. In the worst case, e (and hence q) is k-bits long. So the entries of C are at most k-bits long, and the cost of computing $\det(C)$ is $O(s^4(\log(s) + k) + s^3 k^2)$, which is $O(s^4 k + s^3 k^2)$ since $\log(s) = O(k)$. The matrix D is the adjoint matrix of C, namely the transpose of the co-factor matrix of C. We compute it by computing the co-factors using determinants. This involves computing s^2 determinants of submatrices of C so the cost is at most s^2 times the cost of computing the determinant of C. Line 13 involves computing exponentiations modulo N with exponents of the size of entries in D. The Hadamard bound tells us that the entries of D are bounded in size by $O(s(\log(s) + k))$, which simplifies to $O(sk)$, so the cost is this many k-bit multiplications. Euclid's algorithm used for lines 14, 15 runs in time the product of the lengths of α and e. Finally, the lengths of a, b cannot exceed this time, and they are the exponents in line 17.

3   The RSA Blind Signature Scheme

The RSA blind signature scheme [7] consists of three components: the key generation algorithm KeyGen described in Section 2; the *signing protocol* depicted in Figure 3; and the *verification algorithm*. The signer has public key N, e and secret key N, d. Here H: $\{0, 1\}^* \to Z_N^*$ is a public hash function which in our security analysis will be modeled as a random oracle [3]. In that case, the signature schemes is the FDH-RSA scheme of [4]. A message-tag pair (M, x) is said to be valid if $x^e \bmod N$ is equal to $H(M)$. The verification algorithm is the same as that of FDH-RSA: to verify the message-tag pair (M, x) using a public key (N, e), one simply checks if the message-tag pair is valid.

UNFORGEABILITY. In the standard formalization of security of a digital signature scheme —-namely unforgeability under adaptive chosen-message attack [13]— the adversary gets to submit messages of its choice to the signer and obtain their signature, and is then considered successful if it can forge the signature of a new message. This formalization does not apply for blind signatures because here nobody submits any messages to the signer to sign, and in fact the user is supposed to use the signer to compute a signature on a message which the signer does not know. Instead, we use the notion of security against one-more-forgery introduced in [18,19]. The adversary (referred to as a *forger* in this context) is allowed to play the role of the user in the blind signature protocol. After some number of such interactions, it outputs a sequence of message-tag pairs. It wins if the number of these that are valid exceeds the number of protocol instances in which it engaged.

There are numerous possiblities with regard to the manner in which the adversary is allowed to interact with the signer, giving rise to different attack models. Some that have been considered are the sequential [18,19] (where the adversary must complete one interaction before beginning another), the parallel [18,19] or adaptive-interleaved [14] (where the adversary can engage the signer in several concurrent interactions), and a restricted version of the latter called synchronized-parallel [16]. However, in the blind signature protocol for FDH-RSA, the signer has only one move, and in this case the power of all these different types of attacks is the same.

Notice that in its single move the signer simply inverts the RSA function on the value supplied to it by the user in the previous move. Thus, the signer is simply an RSA inversion oracle. With this simplification we can make the following definition for security against one-more forgery which will cover all types of attacks.

Below, we let $[\{0, 1\}^* \to Z_N^*]$ denote the set of all maps from $\{0, 1\}^*$ to Z_N^*. It is convenient to let the notation $H \xleftarrow{R} [\{0, 1\}^* \to Z_N^*]$ mean that we select a hash function H at random from this set. The discussion following the definition

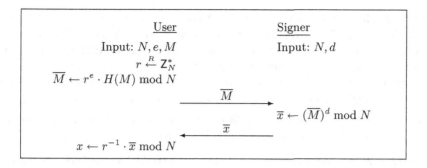

Fig. 3. Blind signing protocol for FDH-RSA

clarifies how we implement this selection of an object at random from an infinite space.

Definition 5. [Unforgeability of the Blind FDH-RSA Signature Scheme] *Let $k \in \mathbb{N}$ be the security parameter, and let $m, h : \mathbb{N} \to \mathbb{N}$ be functions of k. Let F be a forger with access to an RSA-inversion oracle and a hash oracle, denoted $(\cdot)^d \bmod N$ and $H(\cdot)$, respectively. Consider the following experiment:*

Experiment $\mathbf{Exp}_{F,h,m}^{\text{rsa-omf}}(k)$

$\quad H \overset{R}{\leftarrow} [\{0,1\}^* \to \mathbb{Z}_N^*]$

$\quad (N, e, d) \overset{R}{\leftarrow} \text{KeyGen}(k)$

$\quad ((M_1, x_1), \ldots, (M_{m(k)+1}, x_{m(k)+1})) \leftarrow F^{(\cdot)^d \bmod N, H(\cdot)}(N, e, k)$

$\quad$ *If the following are all true, then return 1 else return 0:*

$\quad\quad$ 1. $\forall i \in \{1, \ldots, m(k)+1\} : H(M_i) \equiv x_i^e \bmod N$

$\quad\quad$ 2. *Messages $M_1, \ldots, M_{m(k)+1}$ are all distinct*

$\quad\quad$ 3. *F made at most $m(k)$ queries to its RSA-inversion oracle*

$\quad\quad$ 4. *The number of hash-oracle queries made in this experiment is at most $h(k)$*

We define the advantage of the forger F via

$$\mathbf{Adv}_{F,h,m}^{\text{rsa-omf}}(k) = \Pr[\, \mathbf{Exp}_{F,h,m}^{\text{rsa-omf}}(k) = 1 \,] \, .$$

The FDH-RSA blind signature scheme is said to be polynomially-secure against one-more forgery if the function $\mathbf{Adv}_{F,h,m}^{\text{rsa-omf}}(\cdot)$ is negligible for any forger F whose time-complexity is polynomial in the security parameter k. ∎

Several conventions used here need to be detailed. The count of hash-oracle queries refers to the entire experiment, not just those made directly by the adversary, meaning those made in verifying the signatures in Step 3 are included in the count. We also need a convention regarding choosing the function H since it is an infinite object. The convention is that we do not actually view it as being chosen all at once, but rather view it as being built dynamically and stored in a table. Each time a query of M to the hash oracle is made, we charge the cost of the following: check whether a table entry $H(M)$ exists and if so return it; otherwise, pick an element y of Z_N^* at random, make a table entry $H(M) = y$, and return y. Recall that the time-complexity refers to the entire experiment as per conventions already stated in Section 2. In this regard, the cost of maintaining this table-based implementation of the hash function is included.

SECURITY. We show that the FDH-RSA blind signature scheme is secure as long as the RSA known-target inversion problem is hard.

Theorem 2 (Unforgeability of the FDH-RSA Blind Signature Scheme). *If the RSA known-target inversion problem is hard, then the FDH-RSA blind signature scheme is polynomially-secure against one-more forgery. Concretely, for any functions $m, h : \mathsf{N} \to \mathsf{N}$ and forger F, there exists an adversary A so that*

$$\mathbf{Adv}_{F,h,m}^{\mathrm{rsa\text{-}omf}}(k) \ \leq \ \frac{9}{5} \cdot \mathbf{Adv}_{A,m}^{\mathrm{rsa\text{-}kti}}(k)$$

and the time-complexity of A is

$$T_A(k) \ = \ T_F(k) + O(k^3 n(k)m(k) + k^4 m(k) + k^2 m(k)^5 + km(k)^6)$$

where $T_F(k)$ is the time-complexity of the forger F.

Theorem 2 follows directly from Theorem 1 and the following lemma saying that the FDH-RSA blind signature scheme is secure if the RSA *chosen*-target inversion problem is hard.

Lemma 4. *If the RSA chosen-target inversion problem is hard, then the FDH-RSA blind signature scheme is polynomially-secure against one-more forgery. Concretely, for any functions $m, h : \mathsf{N} \to \mathsf{N}$ and any forger F, there exists an adversary B so that*

$$\mathbf{Adv}_{F,h,m}^{\mathrm{rsa\text{-}omf}}(k) \ \leq \ \mathbf{Adv}_{B,h,m}^{\mathrm{rsa\text{-}cti}}(k)$$

and the time-complexity of B is

$$T_B(k) \ = \ T_F(k)$$

where $T_F(k)$ is the time-complexity of the forger F.

Proof (Lemma 4). Adversary B uses the forger F to achieve its goal by running F and providing answers to F's oracle queries. In response to hash-oracle queries, B simply returns its own targets to F. RSA-Inversion oracle queries of F are forwarded by B to its own RSA-inversion oracle and the results returned to F.

A detailed description of B is in Figure 4. It uses a subroutine $Find$ that looks for a given value in a given array. Specifically, it takes as its inputs an array of values A and a target value a assumed to be in the array, and returns the least index i such that $a = A[i]$.

The simulation is a largely straightforward use of random oracle techniques [3,4] so we confine the analysis to a few remarks. Note that B simulates hash-oracle queries corresponding to the messages in the message-tag pairs output by

Algorithm $B^{(\cdot)^d \bmod N}(N, e, k, y_1, \ldots, y_{n(k)})$

1    $count \leftarrow 0$; $s \leftarrow m(k) + 1$
2   Initialize associative arrays $Hash$ and Ind to empty
3   Initialize arrays Msg, X to empty
4   Run F on input N, e, k replying to its oracle queries as follows:
5   When F submits a hash query M do
6   If $Hash[M]$ is undefined then
7                $count \leftarrow count + 1$; $Hash[M] \leftarrow y_{count}$; $Msg[count] \leftarrow M$
8   Return $Hash[M]$
9   When F submits an RSA-inversion query y do
10   Submit y to the RSA-inversion oracle $(\cdot)^d \bmod N$ and
                return its response.
11    $((M_1, x_1), \ldots, (M_s, x_s)) \leftarrow F$
12   For $j = 1$ to s, do
13   If $Hash[M_j]$ is undefined then
14            $count \leftarrow count + 1$; $Hash[M_j] \leftarrow y_{count}$; $Msg[count] \leftarrow M_j$
15        $Ind[j] \leftarrow Find(Msg, M_j)$; $X[Ind[j]] \leftarrow x_j$
16   Return $(Ind, X[Ind[1]], \ldots, X[Ind[s]])$

Fig. 4. Adversary B for the proof of Lemma 4

F in case these are not already made. This ensures that the advantages of the two algorithms are identical. The time spent by B to maintain the hash-oracle table is the same as that spent in $\mathbf{Exp}_{F,h,m}^{\text{rsa-omf}}(k)$ as per the conventions discussed following Definition 5. We omit the details. ∎

References

1. J. Abbott, M. Bronstein, and T. Mulders. Fast deterministic computation of determinants of dense matrices. In *Proceedings of ACM International Symposium on Symbolic and Algebraic Computation*, pages 197–204. ACM Press, 1999.
2. N. Barić and B. Pfitzmann. Collision-free accumulators and fail-stop signature schemes without trees. In W. Fumy, editor, *Advances in Cryptology – EURO-CRYPT'97*, volume 1233 of *Lecture Notes in Computer Science*, pages 480–494. Springer-Verlag, Berlin Germany, May 1997.
3. M. Bellare and P. Rogaway. Random oracles are practical: A paradigm for designing efficient protocols. In V. Ashby, editor, *1st ACM Conference on Computer and Communications Security*. ACM Press, Nov. 1993.
4. M. Bellare and P. Rogaway. The exact security of digital signatures—how to sign with RSA and Rabin. In U. Maurer, editor, *Advances in Cryptology – EURO-CRYPT'96*, volume 1070 of *Lecture Notes in Computer Science*, pages 399–416. Springer-Verlag, Berlin Germany, 12–16 May 1996.
5. D. Boneh. Twenty years of attacks on the RSA cryptosystem. *Notices of the American Mathematical Society*, 46(2):203–213, Feb. 1999.
6. D. Boneh and R. Venkatesan. Breaking RSA may not be equivalent to factoring. In K. Nyberg, editor, *Advances in Cryptology – EUROCRYPT'98*, volume 1233 of

Lecture Notes in Computer Science, pages 59–71. Springer-Verlag, Berlin Germany, 1998.

7. D. Chaum. Blind signatures for untraceable payments. In D. Chaum, R. Rivest, and A. Sherman, editors, *Advances in Cryptology – CRYPTO'82*, Lecture Notes in Computer Science, pages 199–203. Plenum Press, New York and London, 1983, Aug. 1982.

8. J. Coron. On the exact security of full domain hash. In M. Bellare, editor, *Advances in Cryptology – CRYPTO 2000*, volume 1880 of *Lecture Notes in Computer Science*, pages 229–235. Springer-Verlag, Berlin Germany, Aug. 2000.

9. R. Cramer and V. Shoup. Signature schemes based on the strong RSA assumption. In *5th ACM Conference on Computer and Communications Security*, pages 46–51. ACM Press, Nov. 1999.

10. W. Eberly, M. Giesbrecht, and G. Villard. Computing the determinant and Smith form of an integer matrix. In *Proceedings of the 41st Symposium on Foundations of Computer Science*. IEEE, 2000.

11. E. Fujisaki and T. Okamoto. Statistical zero knowledge protocols to prove modular polynomial relations. In B. Kaliski Jr., editor, *Advances in Cryptology – CRYPTO'97*, volume 1294 of *Lecture Notes in Computer Science*, pages 16–30. Springer-Verlag, Berlin Germany, 17–21 Aug. 1997.

12. R. Gennaro, S. Halevi, and T. Rabin. Secure hash-and-sign signatures without the random oracle. In J. Stern, editor, *Advances in Cryptology – EUROCRYPT'99*, volume 1592 of *Lecture Notes in Computer Science*, pages 123–139. Springer-Verlag, Berlin Germany, May 1999.

13. S. Goldwasser, S. Micali, and R. Rivest. A digital signature scheme secure against adaptive chosen-message attacks. *SIAM Journal on Computing*, 17(2):281–308, Apr. 1988. Special issue on cryptography.

14. A. Juels, M. Luby, and R. Ostrovsky. Security of blind digital signatures. In B. Kaliski Jr., editor, *Advances in Cryptology – CRYPTO'97*, volume 1294 of *Lecture Notes in Computer Science*, pages 150–164. Springer-Verlag, Berlin Germany, 17–21 Aug. 1997.

15. M. Michels, M. Stadler, and H. Sun. The security of some variants of the RSA signature scheme. In Y. Deswarte, editor, *Computer Security – ESORICS'98*, volume 1485 of *Lecture Notes in Computer Science*, pages 85–96. Springer-Verlag, Berlin Germany, 1998.

16. D. Pointcheval. Strengthened security for blind signatures. In K. Nyberg, editor, *Advances in Cryptology – EUROCRYPT'98*, volume 1403, pages 391–405. Springer-Verlag, Berlin Germany, 31–4 June 1998.

17. D. Pointcheval. New public key cryptosystems based on the dependent-RSA problems. In J. Stern, editor, *Advances in Cryptology – EUROCRYPT'99*, volume 1592, pages 239–255. Springer-Verlag, Berlin Germany, 1999.

18. D. Pointcheval and J. Stern. Provably secure blind signature schemes. In K. Kim and T. Matsumoto, editors, *Advances in Cryptology – ASIACRYPT'96*, Lecture Notes in Computer Science, pages 252–265. Springer-Verlag, Berlin Germany, 1996.

19. D. Pointcheval and J. Stern. Security arguments for digital signatures and blind signatures. *Journal of Cryptology*, 13(3):361–396, 2000.

Optimistic Fair Exchange with Transparent Signature Recovery

Olivier Markowitch and Shahrokh Saeednia

Université Libre de Bruxelles
Département d'Informatique,CP 212, Boulevard du Triomphe
1050 Bruxelles, Belgium
{omarkow,saeednia}@ulb.ac.be

Abstract. We propose a new protocol allowing the exchange of an item against a signature while assuring fairness. The proposed protocol, based on the Girault-Poupard-Stern signature scheme (a variation of the Schnorr scheme), assumes the existence of a trusted third party that, except in the setup phase, is involved in the protocol only when one of the parties does not follow the designated protocol or some technical problem occurs during the execution of the protocol. The interesting feature of the protocol is the low communication and computational charges required by the parties. Moreover, in case of problems during the main protocol, the trusted third party can derive the same digital signature as the one transmitted in a faultless case, rather than an affidavit or an official certificate.

Keywords: Fair exchange, electronic commerce, digital signature.

1 Introduction

With the phenomenal growth of open networks in general and the Internet in particular, many security related problems have been identified and a lot of solutions have been proposed. Applications in which the fair exchange of items between users is required are becoming more frequent. Payment systems, electronic commerce, certified mail and contract signing are classical examples in which the fairness property is of crucial importance in the overall security of the related protocol. As defined originally, fairness must ensure that during the exchange of the items, no party involved in the protocol can gain a significant advantage over the other party, even if the protocol is halted for any reason. This paper addresses the problem of the fair exchange of an electronic item against a digital signature (which could be considered as an acknowledgment of receipt of the item).

The previous major works about fair exchange assume the existence of a trusted third party (TTP) in the protocol[1]. Independently of how the TTP is involved in the protocol, its role is mainly to resolve the problems that may occur between parties. Some proposals [22,13,11] use the TTP to store the details of the

---

[1] Though some fair exchange protocols without a TTP have already been proposed [7,19,20,21] (implying often some communication and computation overheads).

P. Syverson (Ed.): FC 2001, LNCS 2339, pp. 339–350, 2002.

transaction in order to complete the exchange if one of the parties does not follow the predetermined protocol. As the TTP is actively involved in the protocol, this approach considerably reduces the efficiency of the exchange. To remedy this shortcoming, independently Micali and Asokan et al. [1,4,18] proposed a solution that avoids the presence of the TTP between the parties. They proposed not to use the TTP during the transaction when the parties behave correctly and the network works, but to invoke the TTP to complete the protocol in case of problems with one of the parties or the network. Such protocols are said to be *optimistic*.

The idea in that approach is as follows: one of the parties (that we call the *client*) sends a signature to the other party (that we call the *provider*) in exchange of a requested item. The provider should be convinced that the client's request and all other information he received from the client before sending him the item are sufficient to convince the TTP that the client actually asked that item. If so, in case of problem, the TTP can either make the client's signature available or give its own signature as an affidavit that has the same legal value than the client's signature. Methods based on this approach have firstly been proposed in [23,22,2,3]. In these protocols, the TTP can complete the protocol by producing its own signature rather than the client's signature.

Recently Liqn Chen [10] proposed a protocol using discrete logarithm based signatures, in which the client commits his signature in a verifiable way for the provider. If the client does not send his final signature after having received the item, the TTP transmits information which has the same properties as a client's final signature when combined with the earlier committed signature. This recovered signature is not the same signature expected in a faultless case but is also a client's signature.

The use of an invisible TTP was first proposed by Micali [14] in the framework of certified mails. Asokan et al. [5] and Bao et al. [6], proposed fair exchange protocols allowing to recover, in case of problem, the original client's signature committed earlier in the protocol rather than affidavits produced and signed by the TTP. This kind of signatures is said to be *transparent*. Bao et al. proposed two protocols, from which the first one is inefficient, while the second one, though more efficient, has recently been broken by Boyd and Foo [8]. In the same paper, Boyd and Foo [8] proposed a fair exchange protocol for electronic payment. Their method allows to recover the original client's signature from the committed one, using designated convertible signatures [9]. They also proposed a concrete protocol based on the RSA signature scheme.

In this paper, we propose a new protocol that allow the exchange of an item against a signature while assuring fairness. The protocol, based on the Girault-Poupard-Stern (GPS) signature scheme [12,16] (a variation of the Schnorr signature scheme [17]), uses an offline TTP, acting only in case of problem, which produces the same digital signature that the client and the provider would produce in a normal case.

We assume that the communication channel between the provider and the client is unreliable (the transmitted data may be lost or modified), and the communication channels between the provider and the TTP, and also between the client and the TTP are resilient[2] (the transmitted data is delivered after a finite, but unknown amount of time; the data may be delayed, but will eventually arrive).

The last point we wish to make before describing our protocol is the following. In [8], Boyd and Foo denoted that the client's committed signature must be in such a way that only the provider can verify its correctness. For this purpose, they propose to use an interactive protocol between the client and the provider during which the latter is convinced that, in case of problem, the TTP can convert the committed signature into a normal one that anyone could verify. In our protocol we do not follow this point of view. In fact, we believe that the use of an interactive verification just increases uselessly the amount of communication and provides nothing useful in exchange. All we want is that the security from the client's and the provider's point of view be respected. If the final signature (that is accepted as a valid signature by anyone) is different from the committed signature and if the latter cannot be forged, nor converted into a valid final signature by someone else than the TTP and the client, this partial signature gives sufficient credence about the "non-transferability" of information exchanged during the protocol. We believe that this is sufficient for the purpose of fair exchange and this is what we implement in our protocol.

2 Generic Fair Exchange Protocol

As it is also the case in recently proposed fair exchange protocols with offline TTP, in our protocol the provider and the client can verify the validity of a committed signature without being able to extract the final signature from it. More precisely, the provider and the client, after having received a committed signature, can make sure that it contains enough information for the TTP to open it and produce the final signature, if problems occur during the transaction.

Hereafter, we give an outline of our protocol, inspired by the Asokan et al. fair exchange protocol [4], that may be used to provide fair exchange with various signature schemes. We will see an instantiation in the following section.

Main Protocol.

1. The provider sends to the client the item ciphered with a session key together with the session key ciphered with the TTP's public key, those ciphered information signed by the provider and a committed signature on the item's description.

2. If the provider's committed signature may be opened by the TTP to provide the final signature and if the provider's signature on the ciphered information is valid, the client transmits to the provider his committed signature on the description of the requested item.

---

[2] This kind of channel is also said asynchronous [15].

3. Upon receiving the committed signature from the client, the provider verifies its correctness and checks if it may be opened by the TTP to provide the client's final signature. If so, the provider answers by sending the item and his final signature to the client[3].

4. After having checked the validity of the received item, the client sends to the provider his final signature on the requested item.

Provider's Recovery Protocol. If, during the main protocol, the provider does not receive the client's final signature or if the one received is not valid, he initiates a recovery protocol with the TTP.

1. The provider sends to the TTP the item, his final signature on the item's description and the client's committed signature of the item's description.

2. If the protocol has already been recovered or aborted, the TTP stops the recovery protocol. Otherwise, it verifies if the item corresponds to the item's description, checks the validity of the provider's signature, the client's committed signature and whether the signature is actually addressed to the provider and is on the item's description. If all the checks are correct, the TTP extracts the client's final signature from the committed one and forwards it to the provider and transmits to the client the item and the final provider's signature. Otherwise, the TTP sends an abort token to the provider and the client.

Client's Recovery Protocol. If, during the main protocol, the client does not receive the session key from the provider or if the one received is not valid, he initiates a recovery protocol with the TTP.

1. The client sends to the TTP the ciphered item, the ciphered session key, the provider's signature on those ciphered information, his committed signature on the item's description[4] and the provider's committed signature on the item's description.

2. If the protocol has already been recovered or aborted, the TTP stops the recovery protocol. Otherwise, it verifies if the item (obtained by deciphering) corresponds to the item's description, checks the validity of the client's final signature and the provider's committed signature and whether the signature is actually addressed to the client. If the received signatures are invalid the TTP stops the protocol. If the other checks are incorrect, it sends an abort

---

[3] The provider may just send the session key, rather than the item, in order to decrease the amount of communications.

[4] If the client sends directly his final signature when realizing a recovery, just after the provider has aborted the protocol (see the abort protocol hereafter), then the provider can obtain the client's final signature by observing the communication channel between the client and the TTP, while the client does not obtain the requested item, as the protocol has been aborted.

token to the provider and to the client. Otherwise, if all the checks are correct, the TTP extracts the provider's final signature from the committed one, transmits it to the client along with the item. The TTP extracts the client's final signature from the committed one and forwards it to the provider.

Abort Protocol. If, during the main protocol, the provider does not receive the committed signature from the client or if the one received is not valid, he initiates an abort protocol with the TTP.

1. The provider sends to the TTP an abort request.

2. If the protocol has not already been recovered or aborted, the TTP sends an abort confirmation to the client and to the provider.

As mentioned in the introduction, in [8] the sending of a committed signature is followed by an interactive proof of correctness of this committed signature. In our protocol, described in the next section, when receiving a committed signature, its correctness may be checked non-interactively and efficiently, without being able to take any advantage from it.

Remarks:

− At the beginning of the main protocol, the provider sends the item ciphered with a session key. The client cannot check if the ciphered item corresponds to the item that he asked, however if the provider does not give the expected item at the third step of the main protocol, when, thanks to the ciphered item, the client runs a recovery protocol, the TTP will detect that the provider has cheated, and so sends an abort token to both parties, ending this protocol run.
− The provider must send his signature on the ciphered information in step 1 of the main protocol, in order to prevent the client to take advantage from the protocol. In fact, the client can stop the main protocol after having received the requested item and the provider's final signature (in the step 3) and launch a recovery protocol with the TTP. Without the provider's signature on the ciphered information, the client can hand an incorrect ciphered session key, which leads to an incorrect item deciphered by the TTP, forcing the latter to send an abort token to the provider. This prevent the provider to obtain the client's final signature afterward by launching a recovery protocol.
− The provider's committed signature cannot relate to the ciphered item and to the ciphered session key because it must be converted into a final signature that should only be related to the item's description.

Fairness. After a successful execution of the main protocol, the final signature is exchanged against the item. If the client stops the main protocol after receiving the first message of the main protocol, the provider can realize the abort protocol. If the provider does not send the session key or if the client stops the main protocol after receiving the item, they can initiate independently their recovery protocol and the TTP will either send the final client's signature to the provider and the requested item to the client or an abort token if the information are inconsistent; the protocol is remaining fair, due to the resilient channels between the TTP and respectively the provider and the client. If the client does not receive the first message of the main protocol, he stops the main protocol and the protocol remains fair as no target information (neither the item nor the final client's signature) has been transmitted.

3   A Fair Exchange Protocol Based on the GPS Signature Scheme

Before describing our protocol, let us introduce some definitions and notations:

- *item* is an item to be transmitted to the client.
- *descr* is a string containing the client's request, the description of the requested item and some other information allowing the provider, the TTP and any other external party to recognize the item.
- C, P, TTP identify respectively the following entities: the client, the provider and the trusted third party.
- $A \rightarrow B : X$ denotes that the entity A sends a message X to the entity B.
- $h(X)$ is the output of a one-way hash function h applied to the message X.
- $S_P(X)$ is a "classical" provider's digital signature (and not recoverable) of the message X.
- $E_k(X)$ is a symmetric encryption of the message X with the session key k.
- $E_{TTP}(X)$ is an asymmetric encryption of the message X with the TTP's public key.
- $f_{com,msg,ack,rec,abort,aborted}$ are flags indicating the purpose of a message sent (respectively "committed signature", "expected message", "final signature", "ask for recovery", "ask for abort" and "confirmation of abort").
- l is a label identifying, with the identities P and C, the protocol run.

The protocol is based on the GPS signature [12,16]. The signature of a message m is realized on one hand by choosing a random value r and computing $t = \alpha^r \bmod n$ where n is a composite modulus and α is a basis of maximum order, $\lambda(n)$, and on the other hand by computing $z = r + xh(t, m)$ where x is a secret value associated to $y \equiv \alpha^{-x} \bmod n$ the corresponding public value. The verification is achieved by comparing t and $\alpha^z y^{h(t,m)} \bmod n$.

Initialization. Our protocol assumes the existence of a TTP that knows some secret information. In this phase of the protocol, the TTP chooses an integer $n = pq$, where p and q are large random primes of almost the same size such that $p = 2p' + 1$ and $q = 2q' + 1$ for some primes p' and q'. The TTP chooses also a base α of order $s = p'q'$ and a very small integer c such that $\gcd(s, c) = 1$. We recommend $c = 3$ for some reasons that we discuss further is this section.

The TTP now computes d such that $cd \equiv 1 \pmod{s}$ and $\beta = \alpha^c \bmod n$. Finally, the TTP makes n, β, c, h and α public, keeps d secret and discards p and q.

Key Generation. In order to prepare a pair of public and secret keys, each user u chooses respectively a random integer x_u as secret key and computes the relative public key $y_u = \alpha^{x_u} \bmod n$.

Note that, here, for the purpose of simplicity we do not consider the authenticity of the public keys. However, it is easy to see that public keys may be converted to self-certified keys as explained in [12] and be used in a straightforward way in the following protocol.

Main Protocol. When a client wishes to receive an item from a provider against a valid signature, they follow this protocol:

1. The provider chooses a random r_P and computes:

$$t_P = \beta^{r_P} \bmod n \qquad \text{and} \qquad z_P = c \cdot r_P + h(t_P, m_P) \cdot x_P$$

   where $m_P = (f_{msg}, P, C, l, descr)$. He also selects a random session key k and forms $E_k\,(item)$ and $E_{TTP}\,(k)$. The pair (t_P, z_P) (being the provider's committed signature) is sent to the client together with $E_k\,(item)$, $E_{TTP}\,(k)$ and the provider's signature on those ciphered information.

$$P \rightarrow C : f_{com_1}, P, C, l, descr, E_k\,(item), E_{TTP}\,(k), sigP, t_P, z_P$$

   where $sigP = S_P\,(f_{com_1}, P, C, l, E_k\,(item), E_{TTP}\,(k))$.

2. The client forms m_P and checks whether $sigP$ is valid and whether

$$\alpha^{z_P} \equiv t_P \cdot y_P^{h(t_P, m_P)} \pmod{n}$$

   If so, the client chooses a random r_C and computes

$$t_C = \beta^{r_C} \bmod n \qquad \text{and} \qquad z_C = c \cdot r_C + h(t_C, m_C) \cdot x_C$$

   where $m_C = (f_{ack}, C, P, l, descr)$. The pair (t_C, z_C), being the client's committed signature, is sent to the provider.

$$C \rightarrow P : f_{com_2}, C, P, l, t_C, z_C$$

3. The provider forms m_C and checks whether

$$\alpha^{z_C} \equiv t_C \cdot y_C^{h(t_C, m_C)} \pmod{n}$$

   If so, the provider computes

$$t'_P = \alpha^{r_P} \bmod n$$

   and sends the item and t'_P to the client. The pair (t'_P, z_P) being the final signature.

$$P \rightarrow C : f_{msg}, P, C, l, item, t'_P$$

4. The client verifies that

$$\alpha^{z_P} \equiv t'_P{}^c \cdot y_P{}^{h(t'_P{}^c \bmod n, m_P)} \pmod{n}$$

If so, after having checked the validity of the received item, the client computes

$$t'_C = \alpha^{r_C} \bmod n$$

and sends t'_C to the provider. The pair (t'_C, z_C) being the final signature.

$$C \rightarrow P : f_{ack}, C, P, l, t'_C$$

5. The provider verifies that

$$\alpha^z \equiv t'_C{}^c \cdot y_C{}^{h(t'_C{}^c \bmod n, m_C)} \pmod{n}$$

If so, the provider accepts the signature, since it will also be accepted by any external party.

Remarks:

- The occurrence of f_{ack} and f_{msg} (rather than f_{com_2} and f_{com_1}) in m_P and m_C are just because m_P and m_C are used in z_P and z_C and they constitute a part of the final signature.
- The use of the identities (P and C) in m_P and m_C is of particular importance, because this guarantees that a committed signature is addressed to a given recipient. In fact, without P in m' (for example), any provider (providing the requested item) can capture the committed signature and use it afterward to obtain a client's final signature by launching a recovery protocol with the TTP. So, it is essential that the TTP verifies the provider's identity in the recovery protocol and checks the correctness of a committed signature with respect to it (see below).
- In steps 4 and 5, it is actually sufficient to check whether $t'_P{}^c \equiv t_P \bmod n$ and $t'_C{}^c \equiv t_C \bmod n$. The full equations are described above in order to highlight how to check the the final signature.

Provider's Recovery Protocol. If the client does not send his final signature or if the last signature is not valid, the provider runs the following protocol with the TTP, in order to recover the client's final signature.

1. The provider sends the item, *descr*, the pair (t_C, z_C) and his final signature to the TTP.

$$P \rightarrow TTP : f_{rec_P}, P, C, l, descr, item, t_C, z_C, t_P, t'_P, z_P$$

2. If the protocol was not already recovered or aborted, the TTP makes sure that the item corresponds actually to *descr* and if so it forms m_C and m_P

and verifies the validity of (t_C, z_C) and (t_P, t'_P, z_P). If all the checks are successful, the TTP sends

$$t'_C = t_C{}^d \bmod n$$

to the provider and the item to the client. Otherwise, it sends an abort token to both parties.

$$TTP \rightarrow P : f_{ack}, C, P, l, t'_C$$

$$TTP \rightarrow C : f_{msg}, P, C, l, item, t'_P$$

Client's Recovery Protocol. If the provider does not realize the third sending of the main protocol or if this message is not valid, the client runs the following protocol with the TTP.

1. The client sends the received ciphered information, *descr*, the provider's signature on them, the pair (t_p, z_p) (the provider's committed signature) and his final signature to the TTP.

$$C \rightarrow TTP : f_{rec_C}, C, P, l, descr, \mathrm{E}_k\,(item), \mathrm{E}_{TTP}\,(k), sigP, t_P, z_P, t_C, z_C$$

where $sigP = \mathrm{S}_P\,(f_{com_l}, P, C, l, \mathrm{E}_k\,(item), \mathrm{E}_{TTP}\,(k))$.

2. If the protocol was not already recovered or aborted, the TTP first makes sure that the received item (obtained after deciphering) corresponds actually to *descr* and that the provider's signature *sigP* is valid, if so it forms m_C and m_P and verifies the validity of (t_P, z_P) and (t_C, z_C). If the signatures are invalid the TTP stops the recovery protocol. If the other checks are not successful the TTP sends an abort token to the provider and to the client, as in the abort protocol. Otherwise, if the checks are successful, the TTP sends $t'_P = t_P{}^d \bmod n$ and the item to the client and $t'_C = t_C{}^d \bmod n$ to the provider.

$$TTP \rightarrow C : f_{msg}, P, C, l, item, t'_P$$

$$TTP \rightarrow P : f_{ack}, C, P, l, t'_C$$

Abort Protocol. If the client does not send the second message of the main protocol, the provider runs the following protocol with the TTP, in order to abort the protocol.

1. The provider sends an abort request to the TTP.

$$P \rightarrow TTP : f_{abort}, C, P, l, \mathrm{S}_P\,(f_{abort}, C, P, l)$$

2. If the protocol was not already recovered or aborted, the TTP sends an abort confirmation to the provider and to the client.

$$TTP \rightarrow P : f_{aborted}, P, C, l, S_{TTP}\left(f_{aborted}, P, C, l\right)$$

$$TTP \rightarrow C : f_{aborted}, P, C, l, S_{TTP}\left(f_{aborted}, P, C, l\right)$$

Security. The security of the protocol may be discussed around two questions:

1. Is it possible to create false signatures linked to a given client?
2. Is it possible to convert a committed signature to a final one without knowing r or d?

First, let us see why we recommend to choose $c = 3$. When a committed signature is given, we have $z = cr + h(t, m)x$, where c and h are known. Since there is no modular reduction (unlike the Schnorr scheme), we can immediately compute $x \bmod c$. Hence, with $c = 3$ we minimize the amount of information that anybody can learn about the secret key.

To answer the first question, let us notice that the committed signature is essentially the same as the Schnorr scheme with composite modulus. Since r is random, cr in z may be seen as a random r' (even though the knowledge of c gives a "bit" of information about x), while t may be considered as $\alpha^{r'} \bmod n$. So, the pair (t, z) actually constitutes a GPS signature on m'. The security of this scheme is already discussed in [16] by Poupard and Stern.

On the other hand, creating a final signature just from the public key and known signatures (but without having the corresponding committed signature) is at least as hard as forging a committed signature. In fact, if it is possible to create such a signature, i.e., producing a pair (t', z) for a message m', then it is also possible to create $(t = t'^c \bmod n, z)$, as a committed signature, or more generally a GPS signature on m'.

To answer the second question, it is straightforward to see that, in order to compute t', one should either know r (to do as the real client does) or d (to do like the TTP). Otherwise, it would be possible for a cheater to use a committed signature (t, z) to create a correct final signature $(\hat{t}', \hat{z})$ such that $\hat{z} \neq z$ (that implies that $\hat{t}'^c \neq t$) or $\hat{z} = z$ but $\hat{t}'^c \neq t$. We believe that in either cases, establishing a final signature using t and z is equivalent to forging a GPS signature. In fact, this precisely means that it is possible to create a GPS signature $(\hat{t} = \hat{t}'^c, \hat{z})$ on m' from a signature (t, z) on the same message. However, creating a new signature from an existing signature on the same message is equivalent to forging a signature for a message m from known signatures of messages $m_1, m_2, \ldots$. This can clearly be shown by the same techniques used in theorem 10 in [16].

4   Conclusion

We have considered a new protocol, based on the GPS signature scheme (a variation of the Schnorr signature schemes), allowing the exchange of an item against a signature while assuring fairness. Our protocol assumes the existence of a trusted third party whose role is to guarantee fairness and that, expect in the setup phase, is involved in the protocol only when one of the parties does not follow the protocol correctly. We proposed to use a committed signatures that gives sufficient assurance about the TTP's ability of recovering the final signature from the committed signature, in case of problem. The interesting feature of the protocol is the low communication and computational charges required by the parties during the transactions.

It seems to us that our protocol is not an isolated instance based on the framework introduced in section 2. We are currently working on protocols based on Guillou-Quisquater and Fiat-Shamir signature schemes.

The possibility of using DSA and ElGamal schemes for designing fair exchange protocols based on our model is not clear to us and remains as an open problem.

Acknowledgment

We are grateful to Michael Waidner for his criticism of the earlier version of our protocol and for many helpful discussions. We also wish to thank Guillaume Poupard and David Pointcheval for their invaluable remarks. We would like to express our gratitude to anonymous referees for their interesting suggestions.

References

1. N. Asokan. *Fairness in Electronic Commerce*. PhD thesis, University of Waterloo, May 1998.
2. N. Asokan, M. Schunter, and M. Waidner. Optimistic protocols for fair exchange. Research Report RZ 2858 (#90806), IBM Research, Sept. 1996.
3. N. Asokan, M. Schunter, and M. Waidner. Optimistic protocols for fair exchange. In T. Matsumoto, editor, *Proceedings of the fourh ACM Conference on Computer and Communications Security*, pages 6, 8–17, Zurich, Switzerland, Apr. 1997. ACM Press.
4. N. Asokan, V. Shoup, and M. Waidner. Asynchronous protocols for optimistic fair exchange. In *Proceedings of the IEEE Symposium on Research in Security and Privacy*, pages 86–99, May 1998.
5. N. Asokan, V. Shoup, and M. Waidner. Optimistic fair exchange of digital signatures. In *Advances in Cryptology: Proceedings of Eurocrypt'98*, volume 1403 of *Lecture Notes in Computer Science*, pages 591–606. Springer-Verlag, 1998.
6. F. Bao, R.H. Deng, and W. Mao. Efficient and practical fair exchange protocols with off-line TTP. In *IEEE Symposium on Security and Privacy*, May 1998.
7. D. Boneh and M. Naor. Timed commitments. In *Advances in Cryptology: Proceedings of Crypto 2000*, volume 1880 of *Lecture Notes in Computer Science*, pages 236–254. Springer-Verlag, 2000.

8. C. Boyd and E. Foo. Off-line fair payment protocols using convertible signatures. *Lecture Notes in Computer Science*, 1514:271–285, 1998.

9. D. Chaum. Designated confirmer signatures. In A. D. Santis, editor, *Advances in Cryptology: Proceedings of Eurocrypt'94*, volume 950 of *Lecture Notes in Computer Science*, pages 86–91. Springer-Verlag, 1995, 9–12 May 1994.

10. L. Chen. Efficient fair exchange with verifiable confirmation of signatures. *Lecture Notes in Computer Science*, 1514:286–299, 1998.

11. T. Coffey and P. Saidha. Non-repudiation with mandatory proof of receipt. *ACM-CCR: Computer Communication Review*, 26, 1996.

12. M. Girault. Self-certified public keys. In *Advances in Cryptology: Proceedings of EuroCrypt'91*, volume 547 of *Lecture Notes in Computer Science*, pages 490–497. Springer-Verlag, 1991.

13. Y. Han. Investigation of non-repudiation protocols. In *ACISP: Information Security and Privacy: Australasian Conference*, volume 1172 of *Lecture Notes in Computer Science*, pages 38–47. Springer-Verlag, 1996.

14. S. Micali. Certified E-mail with invisible post offices. Available from author; an invited presentation at the RSA'97 conference, 1997.

15. B. Pfitzmann, M. Schunter, and M. Waidner. Optimal efficiency of optimistic contract signing. In *PODC: 17th ACM SIGACT-SIGOPS Symposium on Principles of Distributed Computing*, pages 113–122, 1998.

16. G. Poupard and J. Stern. Security analysis of a practical "on the fly" authentication and signature generation. In *Advances in Cryptology: Proceedings of Eurocrypt'98*, volume 1403 of *Lecture Notes in Computer Science*, pages 422–436. Springer-Verlag, 1998.

17. C.P. Schnorr. Efficient identification and signatures for smart cards. In *Advances in Cryptology: Proceedings of Crypto'89*, pages 239–252, Berlin, Aug. 1990. Springer.

18. M. Schunter. *Optimistic Fair Exchange*. PhD thesis, Technische Fakultät der Universität des Saarlandes, Saarbrücken, Oct. 2000.

19. P. Syverson. Weakly secret bit commitment: Applications to lotteries and fair exchange. In *Proceedings of the 1998 IEEE Computer Security Foundations Workshop (CSFW11)*, pages 2–13, june 1998.

20. T. Tedrick. How to exchange half a bit. In D. Chaum, editor, *Advances in Cryptology: Proceedings of Crypto'83*, pages 147–151, New York, 1984. Plenum Press.

21. T. Tedrick. Fair exchange of secrets. In G. R. Blakley and D. C. Chaum, editors, *Advances in Cryptology: Proceedings of Crypto'84*, volume 196 of *Lecture Notes in Computer Science*, pages 434–438. Springer-Verlag, 1985.

22. J. Zhou and D. Gollmann. A fair non-repudiation protocol. In *IEEE Symposium on Security and Privacy*, Research in Security and Privacy, pages 55–61, Oakland, CA, May 1996. IEEE Computer Society,Technical Committee on Security and Privacy, IEEE Computer Security Press.

23. J. Zhou and D. Gollmann. An efficient non-repudiation protocol. In *Proceedings of The 10th Computer Security Foundations Workshop*, pages 126–132. IEEE Computer Society Press, June 1997.

$(M + 1)$st-Price Auction Protocol

Hiroaki Kikuchi

Dept. of Electrical Engineering, Tokai University
1117 Kitakaname, Hiratsuka, Kanagawa 259-1292, Japan
kikn@ep.u-tokai.ac.jp

Abstract. This paper presents a new protocol for $M + 1$st-price auction, a style of auction in which the highest M bidders win and pay a uniform price, determined by the $(M + 1)$st price. A set of distributed servers collaborates to resolve the $(M + 1)$st price without revealing any information in terms of bids including the winners' bids. A new trick to jointly and securely compute the highest value as a degree of distributed polynomials is introduced. The building block requires just one round for bidders to cast bids and one round for auctioneers to determine the winners.

1   Introduction

The Internet is a prime vehicle for supporting electronic auction, a primitive pricing mechanism for setting prices. The most common auction style is the open-bid English auction, in which bidders incrementally raise the prices bid for goods until as many winners are left as the number of units of goods. Bidders are required to be watching the current prices, and it usually takes a long time to close the auction. As an alternative to this classical style of auction, an automatic agent system called "proxy bidding" [1] is becoming popular. First, a bidder B specifies the maximum amount he/she wants to bid, which is kept secret in the agent system. If someone else has the highest current bid, the system immediately raises B's bid, and so on until someone exceeds B's maximum bid, or B wins the auction.

This works, but what if all bidders choose proxy bidding? The result would be equivalent to that of a sealed-bid auction. In this paper, therefore, we consider a secure protocol for sealed-bid $(M + 1)$st-price auction:

$(M+1)$**st-price Auction.** Multiple units of a single item are auctioned. The M highest bidders win and pay a uniform price, the $(M+1)$st highest bid.

By letting M be 1, the definition includes as a special case the second-price auction, or so called Vickrey auction[7]. Wurman et al. proved that the $(M+1)$st-price auction satisfies a useful property, *incentive compatibility*, i.e., the dominant strategy is for a bidder to bid to his/her true valuation[20], as is well known for the widely advocated Vickrey auction. Since a winner's payment will be determined by the $(M + 1)$st highest bid, which is the highest of all losing bids,

P. Syverson (Ed.): FC 2001, LNCS 2339, pp. 351–363, 2002.

every bidder who agrees to bid the maximum price he/she is willing to pay for a given item maximizes his/her chance to win without being worried that he/she might bid too much. Furthermore, the sealed-bid auction is fast. All that bidders have to do is to cast their sealed bids just once. No interaction between auctioneers and bidders is required.

In this paper, we present a solution for $(M+1)$st price sealed-bid auction protocol. First, we show the first price version using secret multiparty computation, and then use it to extend $(M+1)$st price auction in later section.

2 $(M+1)$st-Price Auction

2.1   Assumptions and Model

Given M units of a single good, n bidders are going to buy goods at a uniform price, which is determined in a meaningful procedure. Let $W = \{w_1, \ldots, w_k\}$ be a set of k possible discrete bidding prices. The i-th bidder has his/her true evaluation $e_i \in W$. The objective of the auction game is to find the $(M+1)$st highest price w^* of all bids without revealing any bids, even those higher than w^*, and to find all winners who have bids higher than w^*.

We assume that bidder has independent private evaluation for goods. The evaluation, e_i, is not affected by the evaluations other bidders place on the good. This assumption is widely accepted and makes theoretical analysis possible. In the theory of economics, it is known that a social surplus is maximized when bidders whose bid is higher than w^* win the auction game and pay the uniform winning price which is independent of their evaluation. The Vickery auction, in which the winner who has the highest bid pays the second highest bid, is a special case with $M = 1$.

The m auctioneers corroborate to resolve the winning price in such a way that no c auctioneers can be faulty. Auctioneers are m independent servers. Bidders do not trust each of the auctioneers, but trust an agreement of more than c auctioneers. Auctioneers do not trust bidders, who might violate the specified protocol in order to disrupt the auction.

We assume confidentiality of every session, entity authentication, and integrity of messages based on appropriate cryptographical tools including PKI. Hence, eavesdropping links give no information about bids or bidders.

2.2   Requirements

Privacy of bid. No bid is revealed to anyone except the $(M+1)$st highest bid. For the sake of the incentive compatibility, we want to make leakage of information as small as possible. Thus, even the bids higher than the winning bid must be secret even after the auction closes. No statistics can be used to identify the distribution of bids even after the auction closes.

Proof of winner. The winner must publicly prove that his/her bid is higher than the winning bid without revealing how high the bid is.

Non-repudiation. No bidder can repudiate his bid. If bidders are allowed to cancel their bids, a collusion of malicious bidders can control the winning price as they like (this attack was mentioned first in [3].)

Accountability of bidder. Any auctioneer can verify that bidders follow a protocol to cast their bids. No malicious bidder can disrupt the auction with an unmannered bid without being detected.

Accountability of auctioneer. Any bidder can verify that auctioneers correctly follow a protocol to resolve the winning bid. No malicious auctioneer can alter the result of auction without being detected.

Round efficiency. The protocol is efficient in terms of rounds involved in resolving the winner. We say a protocol is efficient if up to $O(\log n)$ rounds are involved.

Communication efficiency. The protocol is efficient in terms of bandwidth consumption between bidders and auctioneers. The communication among servers must be minimized.

2.3   Related Work

Franklin and Reiter present a sealed-bid auction protocol in [5]. The protocol uses a verifiable signature sharing in order to prevent malicious bidder from canceling their bids. Bids are kept secret until the opening phrase, and then all bids are opened and compared to determine the highest one. Kikuchi, Hakavy, and Tygar [8] improve the privacy of bids among distributed auctioneers even after the opening phrase comes using a secure function computation of summation. The protocols runs in linear time to the number of possible bidding prices and cannot deal with tie breaking.

Any Dutch-style auction naturally satisfies the property that privacy of losing bids is preserved after auction closes. In [11,12], Sako implements a Dutch-style auction using a group signature which bidders use as container of their bids. Similarly, Miyazaki, and Sakurai use an undeniable signature [14], and Kobayashi and Morita use a one-way hash chain [16]. Recently, several works have been made in [17,18,19,21,13,15].

Auctions in the electronic commerce are more complicated. Multiple buyers and sellers are involved and multiple unit of goods are auctioned in several environments. Wurman, Walsh and Wellman examined a several auction designs and analyzed in terms of the incentive compatibility in [20]. They showed that the $(M+1)$st-price sealed-bid auction is incentive compatible for single-unit buyers. The secure second-price ($M = 1$) auction protocol is presented by Hakavy et al. in [9]. They use the secure multiparty protocol of multiplication, presented in [4] in order to resolve the second highest bid in $O(\log(k))$ rounds. Recently, Miyamoto et al. implement this protocol but due to the communication cost among auction servers, $O(n)$, an enormous amount of time is required to decide the winning price. Kikuchi presents a more general protocol for $(M+1)$st-price auction in [24]. The protocol, however, is definitely inefficient because it takes a cost of n-choose-k and has a serious security flaw.

3   Protocol Description

3.1   Overview

Our proposed protocol is based on the secure multiparty computation protocol of [4], which allows distributed computation of the sum and product of every pair of secrets encoded as free variables of random polynomials, namely, $f(0) + g(0)$, and $f(0) \cdot g(0)$.

We present a new trick to jointly and securely compute the $(M+1)$st highest value for n bids without revealing any statistics of bids, such as their distribution or the highest value. The well-known technique due to [4], in which arbitrary functions are computed bit-by-bit, would take an enormous number of rounds. Instead, our underlying idea involves only a constant number of rounds between bidders and auctioneers.

The basic idea is to encode secret information (bid) in the degree of a random polynomial and secretly compute a function of polynomials in order to give the intended computation of bids. For example, if we sum some shares of polynomials generated by each bidder, then the result gives the share of a new polynomial whose degree is the maximum of bids. Introducing a fair and secure order-resolution protocol, we learn whether or not the degree is greater than a given value (M). In the proposed protocol, instead of summation, the auctioneers collaborate to compute the product of bidders' polynomials, which in turn gives the number of bidders willing to bid at a given price. Polling several prices, a set of auctioneers finally identifies the maximum price at which there are just M bidders who are willing to buy.

There is some possibility that a malicious bidder could disrupt an auction just by casting an unmannered bid. On the other hand, malicious auctioneers would alter the result of computation they have to show. Hence, we present a verifiable protocol of bidding so that auctioneers are able to verify if a bidder follows the protocol or not. The verifiable secret sharing is not sufficient for our purpose because the degree can be resolved by any entity from commitment values. Thus, we use the information-theoretic secure verifiable secret sharing proposed by Pedersen in [6].

3.2   Preliminary

Let p and q be large primes such that q divides $p - 1$. All arithmetic operations are done in modular p unless otherwise stated. Let $\alpha_1, \ldots, \alpha_m$ be some m distinct non-zero points in field Z_p^* and be published to mean common m points, assigned to m auctioneers. Let $g \in Z_p^*$ of order q.

3.3   Properties of Polynomial Degree

Definition 1. Let f be a polynomial of degree t of the form $f(x) = a + a_1 x + \cdots + a_t x^t$. The s-th interpolation of f, denoted by $f^{(s)}(0)$, is defined as (Lagrange)

$$f^{(s)}(0) = \sum_{j=1}^{s} \prod_{i \neq j \in A_s} \frac{\alpha_i}{\alpha_i - \alpha_j}$$

where $A_s = \{\alpha_1, \ldots, \alpha_s\} \subset Z_p^*$.

Note that t-th interpolation always satisfies that $f^{(t)}(0) = f(0)$, while the contrary holds with very high (but not 1) probability. Assuming random picking from Z_p^* gives 0 with probability of $1/p$, we have the probability that the degree resolution succeeds, which can be negligible with p increasing.

Remark 1. Probability of $t \leq s$ given $f^{(s)}(0) = f(0)$ is $1 - 1/p$.

Given $g^{f(\alpha_1)}, \ldots, g^{f(\alpha_t)}$, we can learn the degree as the least s that satisfies

$$g^{f(0)} = \prod_{j=1}^{s} (g^{f(\alpha_j)})^{\gamma_j}$$

where

$$\gamma_j = \prod_{i \neq j \in A_s} \frac{\alpha_i}{\alpha_i - \alpha_j} \quad (\text{mod } q).$$

Arithmetic operation of polynomials yields operation of degrees as follows.

Remark 2. Let t and s be degrees of polynomials f and h, respectively. The $f + h$ is a polynomial of degree $\max(t, s)$ with probability of $1 - 1/p$. The $f \cdot h$ is of degree $t + s$ with probability of 1.

3.4 First-Price Auction

We begin with the first-price auction, which will be used to construct more secure protocol as building block. Let us assume that $m > k$. To find the highest price from n bids without revealing any of bids, we have the following protocol.

PROTOCOL MAX
Step 1: Let $b_i \in \{1, \ldots, k\}$ be a bid of bidder i such that $w_{b_i} = e_i$. Bidder i randomly picks a polynomial

$$f_i(x) = \sum_{j=1}^{t_i} a_j x^j$$

of degree $t_i = b_i + c$, where c is a number of faulty auctioneers. Note that $a_0 = 0$, which will play a role of flag in resolving degree.
Bidder i sends share $f_i(\alpha_j)$ to auctioneer j for $j = 1, \ldots, m$.
Step 2: Auctioneer j adds n shares, $f_1(\alpha_j), \ldots, f_n(\alpha_j)$, sent from bidders, to have

$$F(\alpha_j) = \sum_{i=1}^{n} f_i(\alpha_j)$$

and publishes $F(\alpha_j)$ in a fair manner using an appropriate commitment protocol.

Step 3: With $F(\alpha_1), \ldots, F(\alpha_n)$, any entity (bidders or auctioneers) can find the smallest s such that $F^{(s)}(0) = 0$, which gives the maximum bid as $b^* = s - c = \max(t_1, \ldots, t_n) - c$.

Any set of more than $t^* + 1$ shares is enough to recover the whole polynomial F, but reveals no secret information. Even if up to c faulty auctioneers try to collude or to disrupt the auction, they can be excluded by choosing an alternate group of $t^* + 1$. (Detection of faulty auctioneers will be discussed later.) The protocol is quite effective because the communication cost of a bidder is $O(m)$ and just one round is involved between bidders and auctioneers.

Running time to determine s is linear to the number of price candidates, k, which is bounded by m, thus $O(m)$, but computations can be done locally once all necessary information $F(\alpha_1), \ldots, F(\alpha_m)$ are published by broadcasting or through a bulletin board.

The functions provided by the Protocol MAX are very limited because entities are assumed to be honest. To make this more realistic, we need deal with

- case when multiple bidders are tied with the same price,
- malicious bidders who cast bogus shares in order to disrupt the auction,
- malicious auctioneers who forge $F(\alpha_j)$ to alter the winning price,
- malicious winner who tries to figure out how high the second highest bid is by subtracting his share $f_i(\alpha_j)$ from $F(\alpha_j)$, resulting polynomial of the second highest degree.

3.5   Verification Protocol

With information-theoretic verifiable secret sharing in [6], we show the revised protocol prevents both malicious bidders and auctioneers from misbehaving. Let g_1 and g_2 be distinct elements of multiplicative group Z_p^* of order q.

PROTOCOL VMAX

Step 1: Bidder i chooses random polynomials $f_i(x) = a_1 x + a_2 x^2 + \cdots + a_{t_i} x^{t_i}$ of degree $t_i = b_i + c$ and $h_i(x) = b_1 x + b_2 x^2 + \cdots + b_s x^s$, where $s = k + c$ and $s > t_i$. He secretly sends $f_i(\alpha_j)$ and $h_i(\alpha_j)$ to auctioneer j for $j = 1, \ldots, m$. As commitments of polynomials, he publishes

$$E_{i,1} = g_1^{a_1} g_2^{b_1}, \ldots, E_{i,t_i} = g_1^{a_{t_i}} g_2^{b_{t_i}},$$
$$E_{i,t_i+1} = g_2^{b_{t_i+1}}, \ldots, E_{i,s} = g_2^{b_s}.$$

Step 2: Auctioneer j verifies that the share sent from bidder i is consistent with the commitments as,

$$g_1^{f_i(\alpha_j)} g_2^{h_i(\alpha_j)} = X_{i,j} = \prod_{l=1}^{s} (E_{i,j})^{\alpha_j^l}.$$

If the identity holds, she is convinced that $f_i(x)$ has no constant ($a_0 = 0$) and is of degree of at most s, and then publishes

$$Y_j = g_1^{F(\alpha_j)} \text{ and } Z_j = g_2^{H(\alpha_j)}$$

where $F(\alpha_j) = f_1(\alpha_j) + \cdots + f_n(\alpha_j)$ and $H(\alpha_j) = h_1(\alpha_j) + \cdots + h_n(\alpha_j)$.

Step 3: Any entity now can verify that Y_j and Z_j are computed correctly by testing

$$Y_j Z_j = \prod_{i=1}^{n} X_{i,j} = g_1^{F(\alpha_j)} g_2^{H(\alpha_j)}.$$

If this holds then the highest price is given by $b^* = t^* - c$ where t^* is the least element in $\{1, \ldots, k\}$ such that

$$\prod_{j=1}^{t^*} Y_j^{\gamma_j} = g_1^{F^{(t^*)}(0)} = 1,$$

where $\gamma_j = \prod_{i \neq j \in A_{t^*}} \alpha_i/(\alpha_i - \alpha_j) \pmod{q}$.

The protocol ensures that neither of bidder or auctioneer can cast bogus values without being detected. In [6], for any $a \in Z_q^*$ and for randomly chosen $b \in Z_q^*$, $E_{i,j} = g_1^a g_2^b$ is uniformly distributed in subgroup of Z_p^* of order q. Note that the weakness of the protocol is that it is still vulnerable to the winner attack, which will be mentioned in later section.

3.6   Identifying Winners

After the winning price is determined, the winner must prove the fact that he actually has sent the winning bid. On the other hand, the winner should be able to be publicly determined without his help; otherwise a malicious bidder can repudiate to collaborate just in order to cancel the overestimation. Hence, bidders pick three random polynomials $f_i(x)$, $G_i(x)$ and $h_i(x)$, which will be used for determining winning price, winner's identities and for randomizing commitment value, respectively. The degree of product of $f_i(x)$ and $G_i(x)$ is equal to degree of $h_i(x)$.

PROTOCOL WINNER
Step 1: Bidder i chooses random polynomials

$$f_i(x) = a_1 x + a_2 x^2 + \cdots + a_{t_i} x^{t_i},$$
$$G_i(x) = b_1 x + b_2 x^2 + \cdots + b_{s-t_i} x^{s-t_i},$$
$$h_i(x) = c_1 x + c_2 x^2 + \cdots + c_s x^s,$$

and sends $f_i(\alpha_j), G_i(\alpha_j)$ and $h_i(\alpha_j)$ to auctioneer j for $j = 1, \ldots, m$. He publishes $E_{i,l} = g_1^{a_l b_l} g_2^{c_l}$ for $l = 1, \ldots, s$.
Step 2: Auctioneer j verifies that

$$g_1^{f_i(\alpha_j)G_i(\alpha_j)} g_2^{h_i(\alpha_j)} = X_{i,j} = \prod_{l=1}^{s} (E_{i,j})^{\alpha_j^l}$$

and then publishes

$$Y_j = g_1^{F(\alpha_j)} \text{ and } Z_j = g_2^{H(\alpha_j)}$$

where $F(\alpha_j) = f_1(\alpha_j) + \cdots + f_n(\alpha_j)$ and $H(\alpha_j) = h_1(\alpha_j) + \cdots + h_n(\alpha_j)$. Note that, unlike to Protocol VMAX, shares $G_1(\alpha_j), \ldots, G_n(\alpha_j)$ are kept secret locally at this point.

Step 3: The first-price b^* is determined in the same manner as Protocol VMAX. Then, a subset of auctioneer whose size is $u = s - t^*$ collaborate to re-solve winners by revealing a sequence of shares, $G_1(\alpha_j), \ldots, G_n(\alpha_j)$ for $j = 1, \ldots, u$. There must be (at least one) bidder i^* such that

$$G_{i^*}^{(u)}(0) = 0,$$

which proves his bid is the highest.

Even if multiple bidders are tied with t^*, the third step detects all of the winner candidates, and thus the final auction will be held among them. One drawback of this protocol is the lost of verification process of auctioneers, which is with protocol VMAX.

3.7   Simple $(M+1)$st-Price Auction

To extend the first-price auction to $(M+1)$st-price, the simplest way is to iterate Protocol WINNER excluding the winner i^* from the set of bidders as

$$Y_j^{(l)} = \frac{Y_j^{(l-1)}}{g_1^{f_{i^*}(\alpha_j)}},$$

for $l = 1, \ldots, M$ and $j = 1, \ldots, m$. Let $Y_j^{(0)} = Y_j$ at Step 3 in Protocol WINNER or VMAX. After $M+1$ winners are determined, the set of auctioneer use Protocol VMAX to identify the $(M+1)$st price, say t^*, with keeping the $(M+1)$st highest bidder anonymous.

Remark 3. Protocol WINNER determines a set of winners without revealing loosers' bids.

Unless more than t^* auctioneers collude and leak the corresponding $G_i(\alpha)$, the privacy of $(M + 1)$st highest bidder is preserved. The protocol, however, reveals all winners' private bids, which are not required because the winners pay the uniform price, $t^* - c$, and thus should be secret in the protocol in the next section.

3.8   Majority Protocol

Suppose bidder i has one-bit secret, $b_i \in \{0, 1\}$, meaning *Yes* and *No*, and wants to know if there are more than S entities with *Yes* for n entities. (This can be used in a vote of confidence.)

The technique known as the secure multiparty protocol for addition[4] might be used, but it finally reveals the number of *Yeses*, which must be secret for our requirements.

PROTOCOL MAJORITY

Step 1: For $i = 1, \ldots, n$, bidder i picks a random polynomial $f_i(x)$ of the form

$$f_i(x) = 1 + a_1 x + \cdots + a_{c+1} x^{c+1}$$

where

$$a_{c+1} = \begin{cases} r & \text{if } b_i = 0, \\ 0 & \text{if } b_i = 1. \end{cases}$$

The degree of $f_i(x)$ is $c + 1$ only if $b_i = 1$. Entity i ($i = 1, \ldots, n$) sends to server j $f_i(\alpha_j)$, for $j = 1, \ldots, m$.

Step 2: Auctioneer j computes

$$H(\alpha_j) = \prod_i^n f_i(\alpha_j),$$

which yields a share of unknown function of degree $T = cn + B$, where $B = \sum_i^n b_i$. Given the shares, auctioneers wish to see whether T is greater than a threshold value S without revealing B.

Step 3: A trusted dealer D privately picking a random polynomial of degree S, say $R(x) = r_1 x + \cdots r_S x^S$, uses secret sharing scheme to distribute $R(x)$ into m auctioneers. Each auctioneer computes and publishes

$$\overline{H}(\alpha_j) = H(\alpha_j) + R(\alpha_j),$$

in which true degree T of H is masked by $R(x)$ if $T \leq S$. Any verifier applies the Lagrange interpolation to reconstruct $\overline{H}^{(S)}(0)$, which would be 1 if $T \leq S$; otherwise it fails to recover the secret polynominal.

When $T > S$, the degree is too high to reconstruct the polynomial $\overline{H}$ and just bogus value appears as the result of S-th interpolation. No information about B is revealed. When $T \leq S$, the Lagrange interpolation converges at the common constant, 1. Note the secret B is kept under the trust of dealer D. Obviously, the trusted party D can be eliminated by using an extra multiparty protocol that generates a random polynomial of common degree. With $S = 1/n$, the protocol gives if the yes players are majority or not, which is what the election scheme requires.

Multiplication of polynomials involves increasing degree up to n times. Thus, degree reduction technique presented in [4] must be applied here.

3.9   Binary Search of M+1st Highest Price

The majority protocol allows us to determine if there are more than M bidders who are willing to buy an item at the given price. A naive implementation of $(M+1)$st-price resolution takes a time of $O(k)$. We use a well-known binary search scheme to reduce the round complexity for winning price resolution. After the $M+1$st price is determined through the protocol, auctioneers use Protocol WINNER to identify bidders whose bid is higher than the $M+1$st price.

PROTOCOL MPLUS1

Step 0: Let $W = \{w_1, \ldots, w_k\}$ be a set of bidding prices and $w_* = w_1$, $w^* = w_k$ and $w = w_i \in W$ where $i = \lceil k/2 \rceil$.

Step 1: A representative auctioneer publishes w to bidders, who then cast their willingness to buy at the current call w using Protocol MAJORITY.

Step 2: In Protocol MAJORITY, the auctioneers can test if more than $M+1$ bidders are willing to buy at w. According to the result, they update $w^* = w$ if there are more than $M+1$ bidders willing to buy, otherwise they set $w_* = w$. A new polling price is determined by an index $i = \lceil (w^* - w_*)/2 \rceil$ as $w = w_i$. They iterate Step 1 and 2 until $w_* = w^*$ holds. The $(M+1)$st highest price is given by $w^* = w_* = w_{i^*}$.

To show the soundness of the protocol, we need to examine three cases; i) there is just one bidder whose bid is the $(M+1)$st highest; ii) multiple bidders are tied for the $(M+1)$st highest; and iii) there are several possible prices between M-th and $(M+1)$st highest price. In Case i), the iteration completed at the $(M+1)$st-highest price (of loser) and we successfully identify all M winner at w_{i^*+1} (the following bidding price). In Case ii), the protocol outputs the least price at which less than or equal to $M+1$ bidders want to buy. Hence, less than M winners cannot be elected. Even if the auctioneers reveal one extra share, then more than M winners happen. Accordingly, the winner candidates might have to replay to resolve the tiebreak. Finally, in Case iii), the following bidding price w_{i^*+1} might be too low to exclude the $(M+1)$st bidder (loser) from the winner set since the output w^* is likely to be the least element in the interval between $(M+1)$st and M-th highest bids. The chance to unfortunately reveal the $M+1$st loser can be small as making the breadth larger than 1.

Obviously, Protocol MPLUS1 runs in $O(\log k)$ round complexity, although it requires all bidders to participate the protocol to determine the winning price. Alternatively, we can make it non-interactive by having bidders send a batch of shares for each of all k possible prices in W. In this non-interactive version, bidders are involved just one time in the expense of communication cost.

The privacy of winners' bids is preserved based on the assumption of no more than c auctioneers being faulty.

4 Analysis

4.1 Performance

The proposed Protocol MPLUS1 requires a number of rounds proportional to $\log k$ when a bidder sends a bid. The communication cost from bidder to m auctioneers is of the order of $O(m)$, which can be considered reasonable because the

Table 1. Communication costs in Auction Protocols

style	protocol	bidder		auctioneers		
		rounds	bandwidth	number	rounds	bandwidth
First price	[8]	1	$O(km)$	m	1	$O(k)$
	[11,12]	1	$O(1)$	m	$O(k)$	$O(n)$
	[14]	$O(k)$	$O(1)$	1	$O(k)$	$O(1)$
	[19]	1	$O(m \log k)$	2	$O(n)$	$O(\log k)$
	proposed	1	$O(m)$	m	1	$O(n)$
Second price	[9]	1	$O(m \log k)$	m	$O(\log k)$	$O(n)$
$M+1$st price	proposed	$O(\log k)$	$O(m)$	m	$O(\log k)$	$O(n)$

population of auctioneers is much smaller than that of bidders. The computation cost at auctioneers is independent of the number of bidders, n, and some related with M, which is a negligibly small constant. In the Protocol MPLUS1, a quite small bandwidth of size p is required while $O(\log k)$ iterations are expected to happen to determine the winning price. On the other hand, just one round is involved in identifying winners at Protocol WINNER though $O(n)$ bandwidth is required. Thus, we can say that the protocol for $(M+1)$st-price auction runs in $O(\log k)$ rounds and consumes $O(n)$ bandwidth in communication. The cost for the Lagrange interpolation is not considerable large.

Table 1 shows the comparison of auction protocols in terms of communication complexity. The column labeled as 'rounds' indicates (average) number of rounds to proceed the protocol at each entity. In the comparison, we estimate the cost of the proposed first-price auction protocol since no other $M+1$st-highest-price auction protocol presented so far. The round complexity of the first-price protocol is just one for both of bidders and auctioneers, thus can be said as the optimal in multi-parity approach.

5   Conclusion

We presented an efficient protocol for the first-price auction which identifies the first price only without revealing any bids and the winner. The proposed protocol does not need a single trusted third parity and allows any entity to detect misbehavior of bidders and auctioneers. The privacy of bids is protected under assumption of no more than c auctioneers being faulty. Note that the requirement of non-repudiation is satisfied because the winner can be determined without help of bidders. The communication complexity is optimal in the sense the bandwidth spent by every entity is constant and does not depend the number of possible prices, k.

We showed a solution to the problem of $(M+1)$st-price auction in which no information about bids is revealed. Using the binary-search tree, the protocol takes a $O(\log k)$ rounds to identify the $(M+1)$st-highest price. The efficient tie-breaking protocol is the future study.

It should be noted that in the current protocol, any auctioneer can learn which bidder wins the auction. The requirement of anonymity, which has been achieved through some assumptions such as an anonymous channel or bulletin board in some protocols, will be studied in future work.

References

1. eBay, http://www.ebay.com
2. Imamura, Matsumoto, and Imai, Anonymous auction protocol, The 1994 Symposium on Cryptography and Information Security, 1994, pp.11B
3. Nakanishi, Watanabe, and Fujiwara, Anonymous auction protocol using undeniable signature, The 1995 Symposium on Cryptography and Information Security, 1995, pp.B1.4
4. M. Ben-Or, S. Goldwasser, and A. Wigderson, Completeness theorems for non-cryptographic fault-tolerant distributed computation, STOC88, 1988, pp.1-10
5. M.K. Franklin, and M.K. Reiter, The design and implementation of a secure auction service, *IEEE Trans. on Software Engineering*, 22(5), 1996, pp. 302-312.
6. T.P. Pederson, Non-Interactive and Information-Theoretic Secure Verifiable Secret Sharing, in Proc. of CRYPTO'91, pp.129-140, 1992.
7. P. Milgrom, Auctions and bidding: a primer, *Journal of Economic Perspectives*, 3(3), 1989, pp.3-22
8. H. Kikuchi, M. Harkavy, and J.D. Tygar, Multi-round anonymous auction, IEICE Trans. Inf.& Syst., E82-D(4), 1999, pp.769-777
9. M. Harkavy, J.D. Tygar, and H. Kikuchi, Electronic auction with private bids, In Third USENIX Workshop on Electronic Commerce Proceedings, August 1998, pp.61-74
10. C.-S. Peng, J.M. Pulido, K.J. Lin, and D.M. Blough, The design of an Internet-based real time auction system, In *Proc. of the First IEEE Workshop on Dependable and Real-Time E-Commerce Systems*, 1998, pp.70-78.
11. K. Sako, Universal verifiable auction protocol which hides losing bids, In Proc. of SCIS'99, 1999, pp.35-39
12. K. Sako, An auction protocol which hides bids of losers, In *Proc. of PKC 2000*, pp.422-432, 2000.
13. Secure electronic sealed-bid auction protocol with public key cryptography, *IEICE Trans. Fundamentals*, E81-A(1), pp.20-26, 1998.
14. S. Miyazaki and K. Sakurai, A bulletin board-based auction system with protecting the bidder's strategy, in *Trans. of IPSJ*, 40 (8), 1999, pp.3229-3336.
15. Y. Watanabe and H. Imai, Optimistic Sealed-Bid Auction Protocol, in *Proc. of SCIS 2000*, B09, pp.1-8, 2000.
16. K. Kobayashi and H. Morita, Efficient sealed-bid auction with quantitative competition using one-way functions, In Technical Report of IEICE, ISEC99-30, 1999, pp.31-37
17. M. Naor, B. Pinkas, and R. Sumner, Privacy preserving auctions and mechanism design, ACM Workshop on E-Commerce, 1999
18. F. Stajano and R. Anderson, The cocaine auction protocol: on the power of anonymous broadcast, Proc. of Information Hiding Workshop 1999 (LNCS), 1999
19. C. Cachin, Efficient private bidding and auctions with an oblivious third party, ACM Conference on Computer and Communications Security, 1999, pp.120-127
20. P.R. Wurman, W.E. Walsh, and M.P. Wellman, Flexible Double Auctions for Electronic Commerce: Theory and Implementation, *Decision Support Systems*, 24, pp.17-27, 1998.

21. S.G. Stubblebine and P.F. Syverson, Fair On-Line Auctions without Special Trusted Parties, in *Proc. of Financial Cryptography 1999*, LNCS 1648, pp.230-240, 1999.
22. Y. Sakurai, M. Yokoo, and S. Matsubara, A limitation of the generalized Vickrey auction in electronic commerce: robustness against false-name bids, in *Proc. of AAAI annual conference*, 1999.
23. M. Miyamoto, H. Kikuchi, and K. Ogino, Dispersive auction server to calculate only the second win-price keeping the bids secret, in *Proc. of DICOMO 2000 Symposium*, IPSJ Symposium Series 2000 (7), 2000, pp.547-552, (in Japanese).
24. H. Kikuchi, Power auction protocol without revealing bidding prices, in Proc. of SCIS 2000, 2000, pp.B10, (in Japanese).

Non-interactive Private Auctions

Olivier Baudron and Jacques Stern

École Normale Supérieure, LIENS
45, rue d'Ulm, F-75230 Paris Cedex 05, France
{Olivier.Baudron,Jacques.Stern}@ens.fr

Abstract. We describe a new auction protocol that enjoys the following properties: the biddings are submitted non-interactively and no information beyond the result is disclosed. The protocol is efficient for a logarithmic number of players. Our solution uses a semi-trusted third party T who learns no information provided that he does not collude with any participant. The robustness against active cheating players is achieved through an extra mechanism for fair encryption of a bit which is of independent interest. The scheme is based on homomorphic encryption but differs from general techniques of secure circuit evaluation by taking into account the level of each gate and allowing efficient computation of unbounded logical gates. In a scenario with a small numbers of players, we believe that our work may be of practical significance, especially for electronic transactions.

Keywords: Auctions, bidding, homomorphic encryption, secure circuit evaluation.

1 Introduction

In web electronic commerce, the question of auctions has become a major issue. They offer a very flexible way to exchange goods while minimizing negotiation costs, and as expected, a variety of software architecture have been discussed [1,15]. Additionally, it is desirable to ensure privacy of each customer through cryptographic mechanisms. Ideally, at the end of the protocol, no information on the submitted bids should be disclosed. Depending on the auction settings, only the winner and the highest (or 2nd highest) bid should be revealed. So far, several approaches have been considered. Based on multi-party computation [2,6] and secret sharing [22], Harkavy, Tygar and Kikuchi [14] have described a distributed protocol, that ensures privacy but needs several rounds of interaction between the auctioneers. In a novel direction, Cachin has proposed a non-interactive protocol [3] based on the so-called Φ-hiding assumption that allows to secretly compare two numbers. However bidders have to interact in a direct manner and, furthermore, for a number of users greater than 2, it is necessary to consider two non-colluding third parties and partial order of bids is leaked to one of them. Finally, a more promising and efficient technique using two third parties has been introduced by Naor, Pinkas and Sumner [19]; it uses pseudo-randomness and oblivious transfer to securely compute arbitrary circuits.

P. Syverson (Ed.): FC 2001, LNCS 2339, pp. 364–377, 2002.

Our solution uses a different approach which is built on a new one round secure circuit evaluation [23,10,9,11] tailored for our specific problem. Although, it is more efficient than general techniques, it is limited to a logarithmic number of players. In practice, 5 or 6 participants keep the amount of network traffic at a reasonable level. We also require a semi-trusted third party T (the server), who learns no information provided that he does not collude with any participant. To achieve robustness against active cheating players, the hardness of deciding composite residuosity classes is assumed. We point out that no interaction between the bidders is required, which is a main achievement of our work. A high level description of the protocol is as follows.

1. *Registration.* Bidders who wish to participate publish their public encryption key.
2. *Submission.* Each bidder encrypts the figure of his choice under all participant's public keys and sends the result to the server using a secure communication channel.
3. *Results.* The server publishes, in a encrypted way, whether each participant is the winner.
4. The winner reveals himself by proving to the server that he has actually won.
5. The server sends to each subscriber (or to the winner only) an encryption of the highest (or 2nd highest) bid.

The core of the problem is to decide whether a given participant has submitted the highest bid. This is accomplished in the next section. In section 3, we extend the submission scheme to withstand cheating players. In section 4, we propose some solutions to deal with a larger number of players. The conclusion comes in section 5.

2   Computing over Encrypted Bids

2.1   Preliminaries

We consider a protocol with p participants, who submit ℓ-bit numbers representing their bids. A probabilistic encryption scheme E satisfying the following properties is fixed:

- The set of plaintext messages $\mathcal{M}$ is a group of order N such that $1/N$ is a negligible function of the security parameter k. In the sequel we will use an additive notation.
- E is self-randomizable: there exists a probabilistic polynomial time function $\mathcal{R}$ such that for any $m \in \mathcal{M}$, $\mathcal{R}(E(m))$ is uniformly distributed over the sets of encryptions of m.
- E is homomorphic: for any $m_1, m_2 \in \mathcal{M}$, $E(m_1 + m_2) = E(m_1).E(m_2)$.
- E is semantically secure against a chosen plaintext attack: no probabilistic polynomial time adversary can distinguish, with a non-negligible success, between encryptions of two plaintexts of its choice [12].

- There exists a full decryption algorithm D: for any pair of public key and secret key (pk, sk), for any encryption c of m under pk, $D_{sk}(c)$ outputs (m, r) such that $E_{pk}(m, r) = c$.

Known efficient schemes meeting these requirements are: Naccache-Stern [16], Okamoto-Uchiyama [17] and Paillier [18]. The latter will be used for the robust version of our protocol together with proofs of membership, so it should be given more attention.

Each participant encrypts p times each bit of his bid using the p candidates' public key (including his own one). The output, of length $\ell \times p$ times the length of an encryption, is sent to the server through a private channel. The ultimate goal of this section is for the server, to compute, for each integer i in $\{1, ..., n\}$ the predicate: $(P_i) : a_i \overset{?}{\geq} max(a_1, ..., a_p)$ where the $a_j = (a_j^{\ell-1} a_j^{\ell-2} \cdots a_j^0)_2$ are the binary representations of the biddings. To perform the comparison of two numbers using logical bit operations, we observe that $a_i > a_j$ if and only if there exists an index s in $\{0, ..., \ell - 1\}$ such that the following predicate is satisfied

$$(Q_{i,s}) : \bigwedge_{m=\ell-s}^{\ell-1} \left(a_i^m \Leftrightarrow a_j^m \right) \bigwedge a_i^{\ell-s-1} \bigwedge \left(\neg a_j^{\ell-s-1} \right) \tag{1}$$

Namely, the first s bits of a_i match the first s bits of a_j and the $(s+1)^{th}$ bit of a_i is greater than the $(s+1)^{th}$ bit of a_j. Observe that the predicate deciding the equality of a_i and a_j is given by $(Q_{i,\ell}) : \bigwedge_{m=0}^{\ell-1} \left(a_i^m \Leftrightarrow a_j^m \right)$. In the next stage, the existential quantifier is evaluated by OR-ing over the various boolean formulae. Finally, to decide whether a number a_i is the maximum of a set of p numbers $(a_1, ..., a_p)$, it remains to compute a logical AND of the $p-1$ subexpressions comparing a_i with all others a_j. Consequently, the circuits representing the predicates (P_i), using unbounded AND nd OR gates, are given by

$$(P_i) : \bigwedge_{\substack{j=1 \\ j \neq i}}^{p} \bigvee_{s=0}^{\ell} Q_{i,s} \tag{2}$$

Considerable efforts have been made to provide general protocols that enable a third party to blindly compute each logical gate of a circuit with the help of the secret inputs' owners. However, efficient protocols require a number of interaction rounds linear in the depth of the circuit. As told in the introduction, it is essential from a practical viewpoint to perform the whole circuit evaluation non-interactively. Recently, Sander, Young and Yung showed how to compute in a single round any NC^1 circuit over encrypted data [21]. They recursively define structures allowing the computation of logical gates. However, it must be pointed out that an OR-gate inflates the length of the input datas by a factor of 8, and the same holds for AND-gates. Thus, considering our initial circuit of the max function, the algorithm would produce a string of length $\Theta(8^{2 \log \ell + \log(p-1)}) = \Theta(\ell^6 (p-1)^3)$ encryptions.

Our solution differs from Sander et al. by applying different rules to a given gate according to its level in the circuit. Also, the use of a message space of order N enables us to build an efficient method for computing unbounded gates directly, rather than considering the equivalent binary sub-circuit. Against a curious but honest server, the privacy of the submitted inputs is ensured throughout the semantic security of the encryption scheme E. Similarly, privacy towards curious participants is guaranteed provided the encryption of the result is independent of the posted data. This is achieved throughout the self-randomization of E.

2.2   Efficient Computation of the max Function

We now precisely describe our specific solution to compute the various predicates P_i. The security parameter k is fixed. We denote by $\mathcal{C}$ the space of ciphertexts: $\mathcal{C} = \mathcal{E}(\mathcal{M})$. We define $(Enc_t^0)_{t \in \mathbb{N} \setminus \{0\}}$ and $(Enc_t^1)_{t \in \mathbb{N} \setminus \{0\}}$ two family of sets representing encryptions of bit 0 and bit 1 respectively. For each $t \in \mathbb{N} \setminus \{0\}$, Enc_t^0 is the set of t-coordinates vectors in $\mathcal{C}^t$ such that the decryption of any coordinate is non zero, and Enc_t^1 is the set of t-coordinates vectors in $\mathcal{C}^t$ such that there exists exactly one coordinate which encrypts zero. We also define Enc_t to be the set $Enc_t^0 \cup Enc_t^1$. In symbols:

$$Enc_t^0 = \{(c_1, \ldots, c_t) \in \mathcal{C}^t \mid \forall i \in \{1, \ldots, t\} \; D(c_i) \neq 0\}$$
$$Enc_t^1 = \{(c_1, \ldots, c_t) \in \mathcal{C}^t \mid \exists! i \in \{1, \ldots, t\} \; D(c_i) = 0\}$$

Each logical gate G takes as input elements from $Enc_{f(G)}$ and outputs an element in $Enc_{g(G)}$, where f and g are positive integer functions which only depend on the type and the level of the given gate G. Namely, $f(G)$ is the length of the inputs of G and $g(G)$ is the length of its output, both in number of encryptions. The server propagates the cipher bits in the circuit by the following algorithm:

– Inputs: cipher bits are elements of the sets:

$$In^0 = \{c \in \mathcal{C} \mid D(c) = 1\} \subsetneq Enc_1^0$$
$$\text{and} \quad In^1 = \{c \in \mathcal{C} \mid D(c) = 0\} = Enc_1^1$$

We note $In = In^0 \cup In^1$.

– Level 1, $\neg$ gates: $f = 1, g = 1$
  $NOT_1 : In \longrightarrow Enc_1$
  $\quad E(x) \longmapsto \mathcal{R}([E(x)/E(1)]^r) = \mathcal{R}(E(r(x-1)))$
  $\quad$ where r is uniformly drawn in $\mathbb{Z}_N \setminus \{0\}$.

– Level 1, $\Leftrightarrow$ gates: $f = 1, g = 1$
  $EQUIV_1 : In \times In \longrightarrow Enc_1$
  $\quad (E(x), E(y)) \longmapsto \mathcal{R}([E(x)/E(y)]^r) = \mathcal{R}(E(r(x-y)))$
  $\quad$ where r is uniformly drawn in $\mathbb{Z}_N \setminus \{0\}$.

- Level 2, $\wedge$ gates: $f = 1$, $g = 1$
  $AND_2 : (Enc_1)^s \longrightarrow Enc_1$
  $$(E(x_1), \ldots, E(x_s)) \longmapsto \mathcal{R}([\Pi_{i=1}^s E(x_i)]^r) = \mathcal{R}(E(r \sum_{i=1}^s x_i))$$
  where r is uniformly drawn in $\mathbb{Z}_N \setminus \{0\}$.

- Level 3, $\vee$ gates: $f = 1$, $g = \ell$
  $OR_3 : (Enc_1)^\ell \longrightarrow Enc_\ell$
  $$(c_1, \ldots, c_\ell) \longmapsto (c_{\sigma(1)}, \ldots, c_{\sigma(\ell)})$$
  where σ is a random permutation of ℓ elements.

- Level 4, $\wedge$ gate: $f = \ell$, $g = \ell^{p-1}$
  $AND_4 : (Enc_\ell)^{p-1} \longrightarrow Enc_{\ell^{p-1}}$
  $$(E(x_1^i), \ldots, E(x_\ell^i))_{1 \leq i \leq p-1} \longmapsto \left(\mathcal{R}(\Pi_{i=1}^{p-1} E(x_{j_i}^i)) \right)_{(j_1,..,j_i) \in [1,p-1]^i}$$
  coordinates of the final vector are randomly permuted.

The final result is a string of $\Theta(\ell^{p-1})$ encryptions. Although it is asymptotically exponential in the number of participants, it is better than what can be achieved by general techniques for a limited number of players. For example, considering 32-bit precision of bids and 4 participants, our scheme leads to strings of length 2^{15} whereas [21] would produce strings of length $2^{34.8}$. Now, we prove that our computation is correct and leaks no information on the inputs. First the following lemma results from the particular structure of the boolean circuit.

Lemma 1. *For any s and s' such that $s \neq s'$, the predicates $Q_{i,s}$ and $Q_{i,s'}$ are mutually exclusive.*

Proof. Without loss of generality, assume that $s < s'$. We focus on the particular bit position $r = \ell - s - 1$ in the integers a_i and a_j. As $s \leq \ell$, it follows that $Q_{i,s}$ is a conjunction of terms including $a_i^r \wedge \neg a_j^r$. Similarly, $Q_{i,s'}$ is a conjunction of terms including $a_i^m \Leftrightarrow a_j^m$, for each m in $\{\ell - s', \ell - 1\}$. Since r lies in this interval, the conjunction includes $a_i^r \Leftrightarrow a_j^r$. Consequently, either $a_i^r = a_j^r$ and $Q_{i,s}$ is false, either $a_i^r \neq a_j^r$ and $Q_{i,s'}$ is false.

Then, we prove correctness of the crypto computing algorithm.

Theorem 1. *For any bit precision ℓ, for any number of participants p, for any integer $i \in \{1, ..., p\}$ the proposed algorithm correctly outputs with probability $1 - \mathcal{O}(\ell^{p-1}/N)$ a random element uniformly distributed in $Enc_{\ell^{p-1}}^1$ (resp. $Enc_{\ell^{p-1}}^0$) iff the predicate P_i is true (resp. false).*

Proof. We will prove that the probabilistic computation is correct at each level of the circuit. For the input encrypted data, and the first level, the verification is obvious and true with probability 1. For the AND gates at the second level: if some bits are 0 then $r \sum_{i=1}^s x_i \neq 0$ holds with probability $(N-1)/N$ and if all the bits are 1 then $\sum_{i=1}^s x_i = 0$ with probability 1. Since this layer includes $\ell(p-1)$ such AND gates, the set of its output is correctly computed with probability $((N-1)/N)^{\ell(p-1)}$. We now consider the OR gates at the third level. If each of the input bits is 0, then the sequence of such bits is also 0. Otherwise, from the previous Lemma, it follows that exactly one input is 1, so the output sequence lies in the correct space. In both cases, it is easily verified that the output is uniformly distributed in Enc_ℓ. Furthermore, assuming correct inputs, the whole computation of this ℓ-gate layer is correct with probability 1. Finally, the AND gate at the fourth level outputs a sequence of encryptions that performs the product of each $(p-1)$-tuples of Enc_ℓ. Thus, if each input is 1, each input includes one encryption of zero, and this combination leads to exactly one zero. If there exists a zero input, then, assuming inputs are correct, it is encryptions of only non zero terms, and thus each sum is non-zero with probability $(N-1)/N$. The conditional probability of correctness of this whole layer is then $((N-1)/N)^{\ell^{p-1}}$. The uniformity is easily seen. In conclusion, it results that the success of the computation holds with probability $(1 - 1/N)^{\ell(p-1)+\ell^{p-1}}$ which is greater than $1 - (\ell(p-1) + \ell^{p-1})/N$. □

Having performed these computations, the server publishes a bulletin board containing the results of the predicates P_i encrypted under the public key of the ith player. The amount of data is $\Theta(p\ell^{p-1})$ which is reasonably small for 4 to 5 players. Then each player decrypts its sequence of encrypted data, which either leads to a set of non-zero values, in case he has lost the auction, or to exactly one zero in case he is the winner. To prove his status, the winner sends the full decryption of the encrypted value of zero to the server. This transaction may occur publicly, or through a secure channel. If several players have submitted the same maximum bid, then they may all prove they did and an additional round can take place. It should be noticed that the initial input bits are only a small subset of the plaintext space. Therefore, dishonest bidders could encrypt values that are not real bits (ie: not 0 nor 1). Then the whole protocol would collapse, since circuit evaluation would produce only false value, for example if the leading bit is "2". The next section proposes an enhanced version of our scheme where each participant proves that he has only encrypted fair bits. Before doing so, we turn to the last part of the protocol.

2.3   End of the Protocol

In the standard case, it is assumed that the winner makes himself known. Otherwise, if he remains silent, one may consider various solutions, e.g. asking other users to prove that they really lose the auction by decrypting each of the messages announcing the results. We underline that such a hiding player does not compromise privacy. Next, it remains to set the price. First, we consider a scenario where the transaction is done at the highest price (sealed-bid auctions). Since the server has no information on the initial plaintexts, the winner has to reveal the full decryptions of his bid and the zero message proving that he has won. Remind that a full decryption provides the cleartext message and the random coins that enables to check the validity of a given encryption. Using the homomorphism of E, this phase is very efficient: from the initial data $E(x_i)$ he has sent, the winner computes the encrypted message

$$E\left(\sum_{i=0}^{\ell-1} x_i.2^i\right) = \prod_{i=0}^{\ell-1} E(x_i)^{2^i} \tag{3}$$

and sends its full decryption to the server. Then this one checks the validity of the computation. In a second scenario, where we consider that the value of the transaction is set at the 2nd highest price (as is well known, this scheme is equivalent to a public "English" auction) further computation and an additional round of interaction are needed. Basically, once the winner has revealed himself by decrypting a zero from the bulletin board, the server withdraws this encrypted bid and computes the maximum predicates over the remaining bids. Then, it sends a random permutation of the predicates to the winner and asks him to provide the full decryption of the zero value it contains, together with the underlying ℓ-bit bid. Then the server checks the decryption values he has received, and publicly announce the price of the transaction as in the previous case.

3   A Robust Protocol against Cheating Players

We now turn to a scenario where some dishonest players may send arbitrary data, possibly not encrypting fair bits or encrypting different bids under the different public keys. We have already observed that this could compromise the auction: if the jth player submits the encryption of an ℓ-bit integer a_j with an unfair leading "bit" then for each predicate (P_i), the evaluations of $(\neg a_j^{\ell-1})$ and $(a_i^{\ell-1} \Leftrightarrow a_j^{\ell-1})$ would both leads to false. The same holds for the predicate (P_j) considering $a_j^{\ell-1}$ and $(a_j^{\ell-1} \Leftrightarrow a_i^{\ell-1})$. As a result, none of the participant could be declared the winner. It may be asked to each player to decrypt his own data, but contrary to the situation where we considered a fair but silent player, this would compromise privacy and is not acceptable here. Therefore, in order to achieve robustness, each participant adds a short proof of fairness to his encrypted bid. We will consider the specific homomorphic encryption scheme proposed by Paillier [18] at Eurocrypt'99 whose overview is given below. Using this system, we will design a proof of fair encryption of bits.

3.1   Overview of Paillier's Encryption Scheme

Key Generation. Let N be a RSA modulus of $k + 1$ bits, where k is a security parameter. Let g be an element of $Z_{N^2}^*$ whose order is a large multiple of N. The public parameters are N and g whilst the factorization of N, or equivalently $\lambda(N)$, remains secret. Recall that in this case the Carmichael function λ is $\lambda(N) = \text{lcm}(p - 1, q - 1)$.

Encryption. The space of plaintext messages $\mathcal{M}$ is $\mathbb{Z}_N$. The encryption of a message $m \in \mathcal{M}$ is $E(m) = g^m r^N \mod N^2$ where r is randomly chosen in $\mathbb{Z}_N^*$. m

is called the Nth residuosity class of c with respect to g.

Decryption. Let L be the function $L(u) = (u-1)/N$ defined over the subgroup $\mathcal{S}_N = \{u < N^2 \mid u = 1 \mod N\}$. For any ciphertext $c = g^m r^N \mod N^2$, using the trapdoor $\lambda(N)$, it holds that $m = \dfrac{L(c^{\lambda(N)} \mod N^2)}{L(g^{\lambda(N)} \mod N^2)}$. Full decryption is achieved by extracting the Nth root mod N of $(cg^{-m} \mod N)$.

Assuming the hardness of deciding composite residuosity classes, this encryption scheme is proven to be semantically secure against a chosen plaintext attack. Using appropriate optimizations, the workload for encryption and decryption is of the same order of magnitude as RSA. The required properties for our auction protocol are efficient and easily verified: self-randomization is achieved through a single modular exponentiation and the additive homomorphic property is obvious. Furthermore, the scheme enjoys the advantage of encrypting 0 in a Nth residue. Therefore, using the additive homomorphic property, c encrypts a fair bit if and only if either c or $c/E(1)$ is a N-residue. This leads to an efficient proof of fair encryption described below.

3.2   Zero-Knowledge Proof of Fair Encryption of a Bit

To prove that one correctly encrypted a plaintext in $\{0,1\}$, we combine a Guillou-Quisquater proof of knowledge of a Nth root [13] with a proof of knowledge of one discrete log out of two [7,8,4]. Firstly, we propose a 3-round interactive protocol between a prover P and a verifier V, then we turn it into an non interactive protocol using hash functions, as usual.

Settings: $k \in \mathbb{N}$ and A are security parameters. N is a RSA modulus of k bits. P owns a secret value $b \in \{0,1\}$ and publishes $c = g^b r^N \mod N^2$ where r is a random secret value in $\mathbb{Z}_N^*$. We note $c_0 = c$ and $c_1 = c/g$. The following 3 rounds of interaction is iterated t times.

1st round : $P \rightarrow V$
P picks at random two values ρ_0 and ρ_1 in $\mathbb{Z}_N^*$. He has to commit to u_0 and u_1, as if he was trying to prove in parallel that both c_0 and c_1 are N-residues. To this end, since only c_b is an actual residue, further messages indexed by b are fairly computed, whereas messages indexed by $1 - b$ take advantage of the malleability of the challenge. So, the prover chooses half of the challenge in advance, by picking at random $e_{1-b} \in \mathbb{Z}_A$. This knowledge enables him to choose at random the corresponding final answer v_{1-b} in $\mathbb{Z}_{N^2}^*$. Then he computes a fake commitment u_{1-b} satisfying the verifier's equality and a fair commitment u_b such that

$$\begin{cases} u_b & = \rho_b^N & \mod N^2 \\ u_{1-b} = v_{1-b}^N / c_{1-b}^{e_{1-b}} & \mod N^2 \end{cases}$$

Finally he sends u_0 and u_1 to the prover.

2nd round : $V \to P$

V picks a random a challenge e in $\mathbb{Z}_A$ and sends it to P.

3rd round : $P \to V$

P computes the regular challenge e_b such that $e = e_0 + e_1 \mod A$. It also computes $v_b = \rho_b r^{e_b}$. Then he sends v_0, v_1, e_0, e_1 to V.

$$V \text{ verifies that } \begin{cases} v_0^N = u_0 c_0^{e_0} & \mod N^2 \\ v_1^N = u_1 c_1^{e_1} & \mod N^2 \\ e = e_0 + e_1 \mod A \end{cases}$$

Remark 1. In the last round of interaction, the prover may be asked not to send e_1 since it is deducible from e and e_0. Also, the last test performed by the verifier may be discarded by using $e - e_0$ instead of e_1. This presentation is for convenience only. The figure shows the actual protocol.

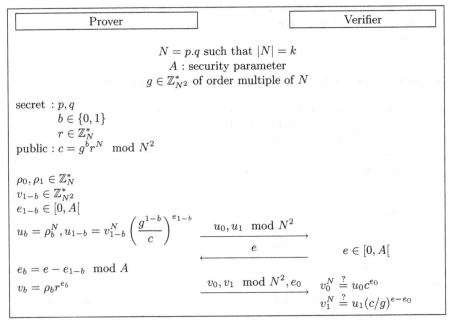

Fig. 1. Zero-knowledge proof of fair encryption of a bit

Theorem 2. *For any positive constants α and β, for any non-zero parameters A and t such that $A = \mathcal{O}(k^\alpha)$ and $t = \Omega(\log^{1+\beta} k)$, it holds that t iterations of the previous protocol is a perfect zero-knowledge proof of membership that c is a fair encryption of a bit.*

Proof. We note L the language of fair encrypted bits:

$$L = \{g^b r^N \mod N^2 \mid b \in \{0,1\}, r \in \mathbb{Z}_N^*\}$$

Completeness. Assume $c \in L$. Then either c or c/g is a Nth residue. For this residue, the prover may answer to any challenge e_b. Thanks to the degree of freedom, he has the ability to fix in advance the challenge e_{1-b} and forge the appropriate answer v_{1-b}. Therefore the prover is accepted with probability 1.

Soundness. Assume $c \notin L$. Suppose that a cheating prover P^* successfully completes an iteration of the protocol. From the final verifying equations and the expression of c we have

$$\begin{cases} v_0^N = u_0 \, g^{be_0} r^{e_0 N} & \mod N^2 \\ v_1^N = u_1 \, g^{(b-1)e_1} r^{e_1 N} & \mod N^2 \end{cases}$$

Taking the logarithms of each expression, it follows

$$\begin{cases} \log u_0 + be_0 & = 0 \mod N \\ \log u_1 + (b-1)e_1 = 0 \mod N \end{cases}$$

So we have the system of 3 equations in the variables e_0 and e_1

$$\begin{cases} be_0 & = -\log u_0 \mod N \\ (b-1)e_1 = -\log u_1 \mod N \\ e_0 + & e_1 = e \mod A \end{cases}$$

If b is different from 0 and 1, it follows that e_0 and e_1 are functions of b and the original commitment $\{u_0, u_1\}$. Therefore, the third equation holds with probability at most $1/A$. If the protocol is iterated t times, then standard arguments show that the probability that P^* passes the protocol cannot significantly exceed $1/A^t$. Since A is a positive integer and $t = \Omega(\log^{1+\beta} k)$ the probability of success is $\mathcal{O}(k^{-\log A \log^\beta k})$ which is a negligible function of k.

Simulation. Fix any verifier V^*. First guess the challenge: pick e' randomly in $[0, A[$. Then choose e_0 and e_1 such that $e' = e_0 + e_1$. Next compute $u_0 = v_0^N/c^{e_0}$ and $u_1 = v_1^N/(c/g)^{e_1}$ and send u_0 and u_1 ($\mod N^2$) to V^*. If V^* answers e such that $e = e'$ then this iteration is successfully completed by sending v_0, v_1, e_0 and e_1. Otherwise, rewind the simulation to the beginning of the iteration. It results that the whole protocol is perfectly simulated in expected time $\mathcal{O}(A.t)$. $\square$

From a practical point of view, it may be desirable to perform a single iteration of the 3-round protocol. Then, since a large A is require to ensure soundness of the protocol, the resulting scheme is not zero-knowledge anymore. However, no strategy is known to increase the probability of accepting a dishonest prover.

3.3 Equalities of Bids under Multiple Encryptions

To achieve robustness of the submission protocol, it is also required that each bidder proves that he has encrypted the same bits under the different public keys. As shown in equation (3), the server learns an encryption of the ℓ-bit integer submission. Therefore it remains to prove equality of p discrete logs lying in a given interval [5]. Following the previous section, we first propose an interactive zero-knowledge proof between a prover P and a verifier V.

Settings: k, k' and A are security parameters such that $2^\ell A < 2^{k+k'}$. The set $\{N_i\}_{1 \le i \le p}$ are RSA moduli of $k+1$ bits. P owns a secret value $x \in [0, 2^\ell[$ and publishes $\{c_i = g_i^x r_i^{N_i} \bmod N_i^2\}_{1 \le i \le p}$ where the r_i are p random secret values in $\mathbb{Z}_{N_i}^*$.

1st round : $P \to V$
P picks at random $\rho \in [0, 2^k[$, and $s_i \in \mathbb{Z}_{N_i}^*$ for each $i = 1, ..., p$. Then he commits to $\{u_i = g_i^\rho s_i^{N_i} \bmod N_i^2\}_{1 \le i \le p}$.

2nd round : $V \to P$
P picks at random a challenge $e \in [0, A[$ and sends it to P.

3rd round : $P \to V$
P computes $z = \rho + xe$, and $\{v_i = s_i r_i^e \bmod N_i^2\}_{1 \le i \le p}$ and sends them to V. Then V verifies that $z < 2^k$ and $g_i^z v_i^{N_i} = u_i c_i^e \bmod N_i^2$ for each $i = 1, ..., p$.

Theorem 3. *For any positive constants α, β and γ, for any non-zero parameters A, t and ℓ such that $A = \mathcal{O}(k^\alpha)$, $t = \Omega(\log^{1+\beta} k)$ and $\ell = k - \Omega(\log^{1+\gamma} k)$, it holds that t iterations of the previous protocol provides a statistical zero-knowledge proof of membership that elements $\{c_1, ..., c_p\}$ encrypt the same ℓ-bit message.*

Proof.
Completeness. For any $i \in \{1, ..., p\}$, it holds that $g_i^z v_i^{N_i} = g_i^{\rho + xe} s_i^{N_i} r_i^{eN_i} = u_i c_i^e \bmod N_i^2$, with probability 1. Furthermore, since $z = \rho + xe$, the inequality $z < 2^k$ holds with probability at least $1 - 2^\ell A / 2^k$. Thus, a honest prover successfully completes t iterations of the protocol with probability at least $1 - 2^{\ell-k} At$. Since t and A are upper-bounded by polynomials and $2^{\ell-k} = \mathcal{O}(k^{-\log^\gamma k})$, this probability is overwhelming.

Soundness. Assume there exists i_1 and i_2 in $\{1, ..., p\}$ such that c_{i_1} encrypts x_1 and c_{i_2} encrypts x_2 with $x_1 \ne x_2$. Then, from the equalities verified by V

$$\begin{cases} g_{i_1}^z v_{i_1}^{N_{i_1}} = u_{i_1} g_{i_1}^{x_1 e} u_{i_1}^{eN_{i_1}} & \bmod N_{i_1}^2 \\ g_{i_2}^z v_{i_2}^{N_{i_2}} = u_{i_2} g_{i_2}^{x_2 e} u_{i_2}^{eN_{i_2}} & \bmod N_{i_2}^2 \end{cases}$$

Taking the logarithms it follows

$$\begin{cases} z = \log u_{i_1} + ex_1 & \bmod N_{i_1} \\ z = \log u_{i_2} + ex_2 & \bmod N_{i_2} \end{cases}$$

Since $z < 2^k$ then $z - e < N_{i_1}, N_{i_2}$ and both equalities hold without the moduli. It results that $\log u_{i_1} + ex_1 = \log u_{i_2} + ex_2$ in the integers. So, if $x_1 \ne x_2$, $e = (\log u_{i_1} - \log u_{i_2})/(x_2 - x_1)$, which occurs with probability at most A.

Simulation. Following the previous proof, the same resettable simulation works. However, since the simulator uniformly picks z in $[0, 2^k[$ and not in $[xe, 2^k + xe[$, only a statistical indistinguishability can be achieved (see [20] for a complete proof).

We are now ready to design a robust auction protocol. The main operation is to replace the verifiers by a secure hash function such as SHA-1. This leads to non-interactive proofs that has to be stuck to the bit encryptions. To reduce the amount of data, the following trick may be used. The ℓp proofs of fair encryption consist of their last two rounds $\{e; v_0, v_1, e_0\}$ and a hash of the parallel commitments. To check the proof, these commitments are first computed from the last predicates of equality, then the whole verifications are performed. As a result the total length of these ℓp proofs is no more than $3\ell p$ encryptions. In the same way, the proof of equality of logs consists of the last $p + 2$ messages from rounds 2 and 3. Thus its length is about $p + 2$ encryptions. One can also ask that the proofs are given only in the case that the server is unable to provide any winner. This makes an additional round of interaction, but still preserves the privacy of each bidder.

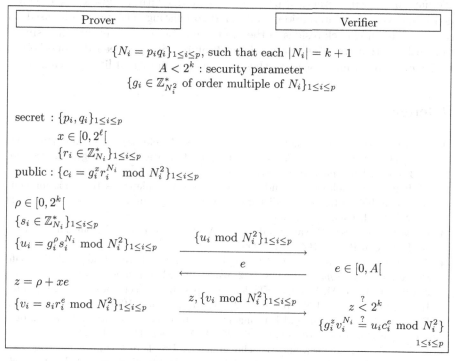

Fig. 2. Zero-knowledge proof of equality of logs

4 Dealing with Many Participants

To cope with real-life Internet business application, it is obvious that the number of total participants should be increased. Under the hypothesis that we accept a partial leak of information and reasonable interaction, we can substantially gain efficiency and deal with a polynomial number of players. A possible approach is to form small groups of users and perform the protocol to decide who owns the maximum bid inside of them. Assume that we allow q participants in each group, then we can build a q-ary tree and achieve the whole protocol of bid submission in a number of rounds proportional to $\log_q(p)$. Next, if we have to find the second highest bid, we consider the following algorithm: form the path of the progression of the winner in the q-ary tree and select all the participants that are present in one of the winner's subgroup along this path. This list contains at most $q \log_q p$ players where it remains to extract the highest bid.

5   Conclusion

We have proposed a practical protocol of auctions with a high degree of confidence and very few interaction. Compared to existing schemes, we focused on security. The drawback resides in the limited number of players that may simultaneously participate in a scenario where absolute privacy is needed. Nonetheless, we believe that in many scenarii these parameters meet real life applications.

References

1. C. Beam and A. Segev. Auctions on the internet: A field study. Working Paper 98-WP-103, Fisher Center for Management and Information Technology, Haas School of Business, University of California, Berkeley, 1998.
2. M. Ben-Or, S. Goldwasser, and A. Widgerson. Completeness theorems for non-cryptographic fault-tolerant distributed computing. In *Proceedings of the 20th STOC*, ACM, pages 1–10, 1988.
3. C. Cachin. Efficient Private Bidding and Auctions with an Oblivious Third Party. IBM research Report RZ 3131, 1999.
4. J. Camenisch and M. Michels. Proving that a Number Is the Product of Two Safe Primes. In *Eurocrypt'99*, LNCS 1592, pages 107–122. Springer-Verlag, 1999.
5. J. Camenish and M. Stadler. Efficient group signature schemes for large groups. In *Crypto'97*, LNCS 1294, pages 17–21. Springer-Verlag, 1997.
6. D. Chaum, C. Crepeau, and I. Damgaard. Multiparty unconditionally secure protocols. In *Proceedings of the 20th STOC*, ACM, pages 11–19, 1988.
7. R. Cramer, I. Damgård, and B. Schoenmakers. Proofs of Partial Knowledge and Simplified Design of Witness Hiding Protocols. Technical report, CWI, 1994. CS-R9413.
8. A. de Santis, L. di Crescenzo, G. Persiano, and M. Yung. On Monotone Formula Closure of SZK. In *Proc. of the 35th FOCS*, pages 454–465. IEEE, 1994.
9. Z. Galil, S. Haber, and M. Yung. Secure Fault-tolerant Protocols and the Public-Key Model. In *Crypto'87*. Springer-Verlag, 1987.
10. O. Goldreich, S. Micali, and A. Widgerson. How to play any mental game. In *Proceedings of the 19th STOC*, ACM, pages 218–229, 1987.
11. O. Goldreich and R. Vainish. How to Solve any Protocol Problem - An efficiency Improvement. In *Crypto'87*. Springer-Verlag, 1987.

12. S. Goldwasser and S. Micali. Probabilistic Encryption. *Journal of Computer and System Sciences*, 28:270–299, 1984.

13. L. C. Guillou and J.-J. Quisquater. A Practical Zero-Knowledge Protocol Fitted to Security Microprocessor Minimizing Both Transmission and Memory. In *Eurocrypt'88*, LNCS 330, pages 123–128. Springer-Verlag, 1988.

14. L. Harkavy, D. Tygar, and H. Kikuchi. Electronic Auctions with private bids. In *Proc. 3rd USENIX Workshop on Electronic Commerce (Boston)*, 1998.

15. M. Kumar and S.I. Feldman. Internet Auctions. In *Proc. 3rd USENIX Workshop on Electronic Commerce (Boston)*, 1998.

16. D. Naccache and J. Stern. A New Public-Key Cryptosystem. In *Eurocrypt'97*, LNCS 1233, pages 27–36. Springer-Verlag, 1997.

17. T. Okamoto and S. Uchiyama. A New Public Key Cryptosystem as Secure as Factoring. In *Eurocrypt'98*, LNCS 1403, pages 308–318. Springer-Verlag, 1998.

18. P. Paillier. Public-Key Cryptosystems Based on Discrete Logarithms Residues. In *Eurocrypt'99*, LNCS. Springer-Verlag, 1999.

19. B. Pinkas, M. Naor, and R. Sumner. Pricacy Preserving Auctions Mechanism Design. In *Proceedings of the 1st conf. on Electronic Commerce*, ACM, November 1999.

20. G. Poupard and J. Stern. Security Analysis of a Practical "on the fly" Authentication and Signature Generation. In *Eurocrypt'98*, LNCS 1403, pages 422–436. Springer-Verlag, 1998.

21. T. Sander, A. Young, and M. Yung. Non-Interactive CryptoComputing for NC^1. In *Proceedings of the 31st STOC*, ACM, 1999.

22. A. Shamir. How to Share a Secret. *Communications of the ACM*, 22:612–613, November 1979.

23. A. Yao. How to generate and exchange secrets. In *Proc. of the 27th FOCS*, pages 162–167. IEEE, 1986.

Author Index

Lecture Notes in Computer Science

For information about Vols. 1–2338
please contact your bookseller or Springer-Verlag